To Bowdoin College Library

Lawrence Sargent Hall

A GRAMMAR OF LITERARY CRITICISM

Essays in Definition of
Vocabulary, Concepts, and Aims

Lawrence Sargent Hall

BOWDOIN COLLEGE

A Grammar of

Literary Criticism

Essays
In Definition of
Vocabulary, Concepts,
and Aims

THE MACMILLAN COMPANY
NEW YORK

FOREWORD

This book is diagnostic.

If you organize the subject matter of literary criticism in the traditional way—that is, historically—you invite confusion among various theories, since critical thinking from century to century and culture to culture did not develop systematically. If you organize it theoretically—maybe we should say dialectically—you risk other vexations. Either you have something too coherent to be realistic or liberal, because it turns out to be your own canon or that of some particular critical school, or you have something so abstract that, while creating the illusion of organization in the table of contents, it leaves your readers to make connections which are less tenuous or to abandon the struggle for connections altogether.

And from any of these positions, what will you offer the reader who is looking for some working matrix through which he can collect his own critical faculties for specific, direct, and practical acts of criticism?

All literary analyses and judgments are primarily and fundamentally problems in definition.

Whether or not it is the primary purpose for which they were written, the primary function of all essays within this collection is to define the terms of critical thinking. The synopsis introducing each essay is designed as a preliminary glance at its central statement and as a guide to its place within the context of the other essays—that is, as a convenience for general reference and for indicating coherence and continuity. Just as it is not the intent of this book to represent the errant history of criticism, so is it not its intent to represent the positions or systems of various critics. The principles and language of criticism at large are the objects of focus here.

Any study of criticism may most functionally begin with defining criticism's instruments and methods, its ordering concepts and vocabulary, as they have developed through theory and the application of theory. The final step will then be to test these definitions, and the discipline of the critical intelligence, by bringing to bear on various writers the three critical acts: discovering what a work of art is, how and how well it becomes what it is, and how worthwhile is what it is.

LAWRENCE SARGENT HALL
Bowdoin College

ACKNOWLEDGEMENTS

Acknowledgement is appreciatively made to the Beinecke Foundation for a grant in aid of rethinking the purposes and strategy of teaching literary criticism; to the several classes of English Twenty-nine at Bowdoin for their collaboration on that project during the last ten years; to Professor Thomas Arp of the University of California for his close editorial discrimination; to Mrs. Meredith Klaus for research assistance; to Mrs. Mae Chatterjee for the logistics of permissions; and to Professors Nathan Dane, Gerald Kamber, and James Hodge, of Bowdoin College, for translations.

CONTENTS

PART I

Modes

ix

PART II
Perspectives and Techniques

PART III
Form

PART IV
Critical Approaches and Methods

PART V

Value

PART I

MODES

MODERN critics have found suspect the strict division of literary works into genres; recent critical thinking has made clear that overlapping of such categories may and does take place. Consequently, the heroic, tragic, comic, and lyric are considered here as being modes of literary expression. Although the old terms may no longer designate generic species of this expression, they are still viable as labels of specific attributes. While there may be no such thing, for example, as The Lyric, we may and do use the word *lyric*, and we mean by it very definite qualities or elements that appear not only in a certain kind of poetry but as components of plays and novels as well. We make similar use of *heroic, tragic,* and *comic*. In this way Fielding speaks of *Tom Jones* as a prose epic, and, below, Sean O'Faolain discusses the heroic, and Richard Sewall the tragic, in connection with fiction.

CHAPTER 1

Heroic Mode

FROM SOME CHARACTERISTICS OF LITERARY EPIC
C. M. Bowra[*]

Bowra traces the change in the concept of the hero that occurred as civilization became more complex. He claims that Virgil created the archetype of the literary epic, followed in the Renaissance and Reformation by Tasso, Camões, and Milton. These four poets best represent the spirit of their times, each attempting to capture through the heroic mode the particular glory of an age for the edification of future generations.

...The difference in the methods of epic composition coincides on the whole with another difference which is social and even spiritual. For most oral epics display what is commonly and rightly called a heroic spirit and come from societies which hold heroic standards of conduct, while literary epics, though they have their "heroes," have a different conception of heroism and of human greatness and come from societies which cannot really be called heroic. The heroic world holds nothing so important as the prowess and fame of the individual hero. The single man, Achilles or Beowulf or Roland, surpasses others in strength and courage. His chief, almost his only, aim is to win honour and renown through his achievements and to be remembered for them after his death. He is ruthless to any who frustrate or deride him. In his more than human strength he seems to be cut off from the intercourse of common men and consorts with a few companions only less noble than himself. He lacks allegiance, except in a modified sense, to suzerain or cause. What matters is his prowess. Even morality hardly concerns him; for he lives in a world where what counts is not morality but honour.

* The selection is reprinted from Chapter I of *From Virgil to Milton,* by C. M. Bowra, by permission of Macmillan & Company, Ltd., and St. Martin's Press, Inc. Copyright 1948 by Macmillan & Company, Ltd.

3

Historically, this ideal seems to have grown in societies which have burst through the stiff forms of primitive life. It is the reflection of men's desire to be in the last degree themselves, to satisfy their ambitions in lives of abundant adventure, to be greater than other men in their superior gifts, and to be bound by no obligation except to do their uttermost in valour and endurance. If they succeeded, such men were thought to be comparable almost to gods. This ideal, outmoded though it has long been in most parts of the world and intolerable as it is in civilised society, had its uses when peoples were on the move, as the Greeks were in the dawn of their history or the Angles and Saxons were when they came to England from their continental homes. In such times the hero, the superman, is the leader who inspires and commands others in the work of war which precedes the establishment of a new order.

The claim of this heroic ideal is that after all it is an ideal and that its adherents are ready to make any sacrifice for it. Even though Achilles lives mainly to win glory and assumes that it is his right, his life is darkened by suffering and at the end he dies for his belief in his heroic manhood. His aim is not ease but glory, and glory makes exacting demands. A man who is willing to give his life for it wins the respect of his fellows, and when he makes his last sacrifice, they honour him. Even Roland, who ostensibly fights for Charlemagne and for Christendom, comes to his heroic end simply because his honour has been wounded and he feels that he must make amends by facing incalculable odds. In fact, what counts in the high estimate in which such men are held is not so much their power to destroy as their readiness to die. Their heroism is the greater because they sacrifice pre-eminent gifts of strength or beauty or eloquence or counsel. The doom of a short and glorious life which hangs over Achilles is tragic in its menace that he, the noblest and most gifted of men, is soon to go down to the dust and be made equal to the humblest servant. The memory of Roland haunted the Middle Ages because he, the greatest of soldiers, was willing to give his life for something that he valued above everything else,—his honour. It is because they are ready to make this last annihilating sacrifice that heroes are honoured. Compared with this even their courage and prowess are of secondary importance.

The truly heroic ideal and standards of conduct did not exist for the writers of literary epic. Though Virgil was a devoted student of Homer and owed much to him, he had quite a different conception of human worth and lived in a society from which Homer's heroes were remote and alien. When he took the traditional epic form, he had to adapt it to the changed conditions of his own day. Between him and his heroic models lay a vast tract of history. He looked to the past for inspiration, but his work was inevitably shaped by the present. His epic has rightly been called "secondary"; for it was an attempt to use again in new circumstances what had already been a complete and satisfactory form of poetry. Virgil differs from Homer in at least two essential points. First, his method of composition, as we have seen, is meant for readers, and in consequence the whole texture of his poetry is different. Secondly, his conception of heroism is equally different. He has one, but it is not Homer's, or indeed that of any heroic age. The whole temper of the *Aeneid* is far from that of the *Iliad*. Virgil created a poetry which was epic in its scope and nobility and sense of human worth but was unlike any other epic before it. So great was his success that other poets have followed his example, and their performance is such that we can mark a whole class of literary epic, discern its special characteristics and consider it as a whole.

It may seem artificial to class the work of such men as Camões, Tasso and Milton with that of Virgil,—for the good reason that not only did they write after him but they knew his work well and consciously imitated it in many ways. Indeed the whole theory of epic in the Renaissance was built upon Virgil's practice. When the "immortal" Vida wrote his *Ars Poetica,* he laid down rules for epic of an exact and exacting kind, and insisted that any modern epic must closely follow a Virgilian model. To these rules the epic poets of the Renaissance were in their different ways obedient. Epic had become almost a standard form, and the poets competed in the new turns which they gave to a traditional theme or device. It might therefore be claimed that these poets model themselves on Virgil and are his successors and imitators but not his peers in the same kind of poetry. This might well be true, but the facts suggest a different conclusion. The epic poets of the Renaissance were indeed Virgilians both in their desire to rival him and in their dependence on him, but they were also his peers because they did in their own way what he had done in his and because the conditions in which they worked were often like his and led to independent results which are comparable to his. Literary epic is the work of a real class of poets who resemble each other in aim and outlook, and it is widely separated from heroic epic both ancient and modern.

The fundamental difference between literary and oral epic is in the circumstances of origin. The writers of literary epic lived in highly organised societies where unfettered individualism had no place. Neither Virgil under the all-pervading influence of Augustus Caesar, nor Camões under the Catholic monarchy of Portugal, nor Tasso under the Counter-Reformation, nor Milton under Cromwell and the Puritans, was likely to praise the virtues of a noble barbarian. Even their lords and patrons did not claim to be heroes in the old sense. Augustus liked to be thought the first citizen of Rome, bound by all the decencies of conventional morality; the potentates and prelates of the Renaissance, Reformation and Counter-Reformation were Christian rulers who believed that they were at least subordinate to God. Man had changed his place in the universe. His life was no longer a short span of light in the encompassing darkness, his duty no longer towards himself. From the eminence of his own glory he had been reduced to a subordinate position where he was much inferior to the state or the church to which he belonged. Cosmogonies and theologies had arisen which displayed his insignificance before the vast abyss of time, the claims of empire, or the will of God. The very qualities for which the old heroes had been honoured were themselves suspect or barely understood. That Achilles or Roland should harm their sovereign lieges from motives of injured pride was not a notion to appeal to the potentates of imperial Rome or Renaissance Europe. Nor in such times could individual prowess have the significance that it had for Homer. The great prince was not the warrior who defeated his enemies in hand-to-hand encounter but the organiser of victory and the administrator who imposed his will upon other men. It was impossible for the epic poet to treat his subject in the old heroic spirit. If he wished to present a heroic theme, he must create a new type of hero and a new ideal of heroism.

It is certainly paradoxical that civilised societies and their poets should claim for those whom they admire names and titles which belong to ages very unlike their own, and that the conception of heroic man should appeal as it did to the Augustan age and the Renaissance. In such a quest different forces were at work. Both at Rome and in the Renaissance the epic was thought to be the grandest and noblest form of poetry and the right means to celebrate great achievements. No doubt its scale was felt to be appropriate to such subjects. Its mere size appealed to a love of grandeur and magnificence. But more important was the spirit of the epic, its attempt to find significance in the achievements of man and to show him in his essential nobility. The writers of literary epic held new and different conceptions of human greatness, but such was their concern for it that epic alone could suffice to portray it. Moreover they were particularly impressed by the special form which the old heroic outlook took. The great hero, Achilles or Roland, appeals to two deep impulses of the human heart, the desire for glory and the respect for sacrifice. Through the second the first is satisfied; the hero sacrifices his life and wins thereby an immortal glory. When this happens, the human state gains in dignity, and the value of its efforts is triumphantly affirmed. It must have been for this reason more than for any other that Virgil and his successors believed that only through epic could they say all that they wished. It was the right means for them to assert their belief in human greatness and to show the special form of it which they honoured.

Virgil revealed a new field both for glory and for sacrifice. The cause which deserves the one and inspires the other was for him not an ideal of individual prowess but of service to Rome. It is Rome to whom in the last resort the glory of her sons belongs, and it is for her that they make their sacrifices not merely of life but of happiness and personal ambitions and all that the old heroic type took for granted as its right. Virgil abandons the scheme of life by which the hero lives and dies for his own glory, and replaces a personal by a social ideal. The old concept of a man's honour is merged in a scheme of morality where duties are laid down with precision and must be fulfilled if the gods' will is to be done. Virgil revealed an entirely new use for epic to an age for which the old heroic outlook was too anarchic and anti-social. With him the epic became national, and though later it was to extend its scope beyond the boundaries of nations and of continents, his was the first step in a new direction. Moreover, because he had a new outlook on human greatness, he brought into the epic much that earlier poets denied or neglected. Above all he made it contain almost a philosophy of life and death, a view of the universe which answered many desires in the heart of man and provided an impressive background to the new ideal. Virgil's epic is still epic because it treats of what is greatest and noblest in man; it is of a new kind because this greatness and this nobility are themselves new....

In Virgil the poets of the Renaissance found a poet after their own hearts, and their admiration for him explains why the literary epic took its most notable form. The poets wished to rival him by his own means and in his own way, they were his fellows in a special kind of poetry. For not only did they do in their way what he had done in his, but their situations resembled his and called for a poetry like his. Neither he nor they could do again what Homer had done.

The epic was faced with a new task, and Virgil defined its character. Because he wished to write a poem about something much larger than the destinies of individual heroes, he created a type of epic in which the characters represent something outside themselves, and the events displayed have other interests than their immediate excitement in the context. He sought to provide a poem on the Roman character by linking his fabulous hero Aeneas to his living patron Augustus, to bracket past and present in a single whole, and to give a metaphysical unity to Rome by displaying the abilities which had made it great in his own day and had existed in it from the beginning. His first aim is to praise the present, but the present is too actual, too complex and too familiar to provide the material of his poem. So he joins it to the past and exalts it as the fulfilment of a long, divinely ordained process. Augustus gains in glory by being associated with Aeneas, Rome by being traced back to its humble origins. The plan was bold, but there were no limits to its possibilities....

From this an important result followed. The literary epics, unlike those of Homer, are not content to present individuals as such. They present something that is more like a symbol or even an ideal, a person who represents something else. As Aeneas stands for Rome, so Gama stands for Portugal, Goffredo for Christian chivalry, and Adam for all mankind. This means that enormous issues, not immediately relevant to the story, are sooner or later introduced, and the poet attempts to convey almost the whole duty and the whole circumstances of man. In consequence his work is instructive as Homer's never is. Homer may have wished to present one noble type in Achilles and another in Hector; he may have felt a strong predilection for his astute Odysseus. But these heroes are

not set out as ideals to be followed, and they convey no direct or immediate lessons. But the writers of literary epic are almost forced to point a moral. Their heroes are examples of what men ought to be or types of human destiny whose very mistakes must be marked and remembered. In themselves they may be misty and even characterless, but they are not meant to be characters so much as examples. The writers of literary epic would all agree with Dryden's account of a heroic poem: "The design of it is to form the mind to heroic virtue by example; 'tis conveyed in verse that it may delight, while it instructs." This didactic intention is never far away, though it need not have an immediate or contemporary reference. While Camões and Tasso wished Europe to prosecute a crusade against Islam, Virgil wished to explain the destiny of Rome and Milton the workings of Eternal Providence. Nor need this didactic purpose be explicit. A poet can teach by indirect means, by appealing to the hearts and imaginations and consciences of his readers. But if he is anxious that they should really believe what he says, he can hardly avoid being to some degree didactic. So these poets wished to inspire, to elevate, to instruct. They did not share the common belief that poetry merely beguiles hours of leisure or stimulates to a refined enjoyment. They believed that their calling was extremely serious and that its object was to make men better....

In their different ways these poets wrote because their times stressed an ideal to them and stirred them to spend their great powers on presenting it. The ideal seems always to have reached or to have passed its prime and to have lost its hold on the mass of mankind. Only so could it be seen in its fullness and displayed in its true worth. So, because they were to some degree fighting against the flow of history, the poets had to face hostile elements in their circumstances or in themselves. But from this some of their finest effects arise. The struggle not only makes their work more human and more imaginative but it widens their scope and enriches their subject. In Homer there is no such discord. He has no purpose like Virgil's, no doubts and no mission. But once we begin to grasp the various elements which make the complex art of literary epic, we are on the way to appreciate poetry of a special kind, which, though it claims to deal with a single subject, attacks it from different angles and at different levels. The mere story is less important than what it represents in the poet's vision of life. It is for this that we go to him, in this that we find his special contribution to our experience. The writers of literary epic set themselves a task of uncommon difficulty when they tried to adapt the heroic ideal to unheroic times and to proclaim in poetry a new conception of man's grandeur and nobility. Each had his own approach, his own solution, and his own doubts and reservations, but because all were concerned with ultimately the same issues and used the same kind of poetical form, their labours belong to a single chapter in the history of the human spirit.

FROM DISCOURSES ON THE HEROIC POEM
Tasso[*]

From the point of view of the sixteenth century, Tasso considers what is appropriate to the epic. He discusses the proper subject, characters, and style, pointing out that only the most noble and heroic actions, the greatest men, and the most magnificent style—exceeding both the tragic and lyric in the "splendor of its wonderful majesty"—are suitable to the epic poem.

Book I
[Truth and the Marvelous]

... [14] But now let us go on with our inquiry into how what is true to life can be joined with the marvelous, without relying on the grace and the charm of verses, which are as it were enticements to persuade the ear. The natures of these two things, the marvelous and the life-like, are very different, and different in such a way that they are like contraries, yet both of them are necessary in a poem, though the art of an excellent poet is required to couple them. The fact has, however, been performed by many, though, so far as I know, no one has taught how it is to be done. Some men of great learning, seeing the mutual repugnance of these two kinds of things, have judged that the lifelike parts of poems cannot be marvelous, and the marvelous cannot be lifelike; but since both are necessary, one should give at-

* The selection is reprinted from *Literary Criticism, Plato to Dryden*, edited by Allan H. Gilbert, by permission of the editor and the Wayne State University Press. Copyright 1961 by the Wayne State University Press.

tention part of the time to what is true to fact, part of the time to the marvelous, in such a manner that one will not yield to the other, but the one may be tempered by the other. But I do not approve this opinion, nor do I think there should be any part of the poem that does not represent the truth. The reason that moves me to this belief is as follows: Poetry is nothing else than imitation; this cannot be called in question; imitation cannot be separated from verisimilitude, for imitation is nothing else than giving a resemblance; no part, then, of poetry can be other than true to fact. In short, truth is not one of the conditions demanded from poetry for its greater beauty and ornament, but it is intrinsic to its very essence and in every part is necessary above anything else. But though I hold the epic poet to a perpetual obligation to keep to the truth, I do not therefore exclude the other quality, that is, the marvelous; rather I hold that the same action can be both marvelous and true. I believe there are many modes of joining these discordant qualities; so . . . we shall speak here of what is most important for this matter. Some actions which greatly exceed the power of men the poet attributes to God, to his angels, to devils, or to those to whom God or the devils have conceded this power, such as the saints, magicians, and fairies. These actions, if they are considered of themselves, appear marvelous; in fact, they are called miracles in ordinary speech. If one regards the virtue and power of the doer, these same things will be judged true to life, because the men of the present age drank in this opinion with their milk when they were in their swaddling clothes and were confirmed in it by the teachers of our holy faith, namely that God and his ministers, and by his permission the demons and the magicians, are able to do wondrous

things exceeding the force of nature; by reading and observation they seem every day to get new instances; therefore not merely what they believe is possible but what they think has often happened and can happen many times again will not seem beyond the limits of verisimilitude, just as the ancients who lived in the error of their vain religion saw no improbability in the miracles that not the poets alone but the historians as well fabled of their gods. But if learned men give us little credit, the opinion of the multitude is enough for the poet in this as in many other things, and leaving the exact truth, he does and should attend to it. The same action, then, can be both marvelous and according to verisimilitude, marvelous when thought of for itself and circumscribed within the limits of nature, true to life when considered apart from those limits and with respect to its cause, which is a force, supernatural, powerful, and accustomed to bring about similar marvels. . . .

[Good Examples]

[15] And in addition if anyone wishes to form the idea of a perfect knight, I do not see that we can by any means deny him the right to praise piety and religion; for this purpose I should greatly prefer the person of Charles or Arthur to that of Theseus or Jason. Finally, since the poet should be much concerned for the profit of his readers, he can much better set on fire the souls of our knights with the example of Christians than of infidels, since the authority of those like ourselves is always more influential than that of those unlike us, and that of those we know than of strangers. . . . The subject of a heroic poem should then be derived from true history and from religion that is not false. But histories and writings are sacred or not sacred, and of the sacred some have greater authority,

if it is permitted to say so, for all spiritual things are sacred, as it appears to Saint Thomas, but not all sacred things are spiritual; the others without doubt have less authority. The poet hardly dares put his hand to histories of the first quality; but they can be left in pure and simple truth, for there is no labor in obtaining the subject, and it appears that feigning is hardly to be allowed in this matter; and he who may not feign and may not imitate, since he is tied down to the exact particulars that are contained there, would not be a poet but rather a historian. In these same histories another distinction can be made, namely, that they contain events of our days or of very remote times or else things neither very new or very old. In some ways the history of an age or a nation very distant from us appears a subject well-suited for a heroic poem, because, since those things are so buried in antiquity that there scarcely remains a weak and obscure memory of them, the poet is able to change them and change them again and tell of them as he pleases. . . .

[Tragedy and Epic]

[17] If the epic and the tragic actions were of the same nature, they would produce the same effects, for from the same causes the same effects are derived, but since they produce diverse passions it follows that they are diverse in nature. Tragic actions excite horror and compassion, and if the piteous and the horrifying are lacking the tragic no longer remains. But epics do not generally in the same way produce a feeling of sadness nor is it a necessity of their nature that they should. Aristotle says that the taking of pleasure in the suffering of the wicked, though pleasing to the spectators, is not of the essence of the tragic plot, but in the heroic poem it is certainly praiseworthy. If sometimes in heroic poems there is seen something horrible or worthy of pity, horror or compassion is not sought for in all the weaving of the plot, in which we take pleasure in the victory of friends and the overthrow of enemies, but for enemies, since they are barbarians or infidels, we should not have the same pity. Nor do the actions of the tragedy and the epic present high matters in the same fashion; for their concern with great affairs is diverse in nature and form. In tragedy it appears in an unexpected and sudden change of fortune, and in the greatness of the happenings that produce pity and terror, but the splendid action of the heroic poem is founded on lofty military virtue and on a magnanimous resolution to die, on piety, on religion, and on actions in which these virtues are resplendent, which are in harmony with the nature of the epic and not fitting in a tragedy. Thence it comes about that the persons introduced in the two types of poem are not of the same nature, though both types deal with kings and great princes. Tragedy demands persons neither good nor wicked, but of a middle sort; such as Orestes, Electra, Jocasta, Eteocles, and Oedipus, who were judged by Aristotle very suitable for a tragic plot. The epic poet, on the contrary, requires the highest degree of virtue; therefore the persons are heroic, as their virtue is. In Aeneas is found the excellence of piety, in Achilles that of military courage, in Ulysses that of prudence. And if sometimes the tragic and the epic poet both take the same person as their subject, he is considered diversely by them and from different points of view. The epic writer considers in Hercules, Theseus, Agamemnon, Ajax, and Pyrrhus their valor and ability in arms; the tragedian is concerned with them in so far as they have fallen into infelicity through some error. Epic poets, however, run much less risk than tragedians do in

taking as their subject not only the highest attainment of virtue in the persons described by them but the utmost of vice as well. Such are Mezentius, Busiris, Procrustes, Diomede, Thersites, and others of the sort; of the same kind, or not much different, are the Cyclops and the Laestrygonians, in which savagery stands in the place of vice, though it is much more terrible than vice and more horrifying. . . .

[Love As a Poetic Subject]

[18] Some are of the opinion that love is not suitable material for the heroic or the tragic poet and say that in his two poems, the *Iliad* and the *Odyssey*, Homer scarcely speaks of love. . . . They assign love rather to comedy. But I have ever been of the contrary opinion, since it seems to me that the most beautiful things are well adapted to heroic poetry, and love is very beautiful, as Phaedrus thought, according to Plato. But if it is neither beautiful nor ugly, as on the other hand Diotima thought, it is not therefore fitting to comedies, which delight their audiences with ugly things and those that move to laughter. For this reason the old comedy ought perchance to be more praised, as Maggi believed,[1] for the new comedy has many times presented to us love as so beautiful that it could hardly be described with more colors in heroic poetry. But it cannot be denied that love is a passion suitable to heroes. . . . If love is not merely a passion and a movement of the sensitive appetite but also a noble habit of the will, as Saint Thomas thought, love will be praiseworthy in heroes and consequently in the heroic poem. The ancients did not know this love, or did not wish to describe it in heroes. But if they did not

honor love as a human virtue, they adored it as divine; therefore they should have esteemed no other virtue more fitting to heroes. Hence those actions resulting from love, in addition to the others, could appear to them heroic. But modern poets, if they do not wish to describe the divinity of love in those who exposed their lives for Christ, are yet able in creating a knight to describe love as a constant habit of the will. . . . In short, love and friendship form a most fitting subject for a heroic poem, and if we wish to give the name of friendship to the attachment of Achilles and Patroclus, no other theme can give matter for writing in a more heroic strain. But the opinion of Dante should not be neglected, for his authority in this tongue, which is not small, can be used as the foundation of our opinion. He says in his book *On the Vulgar Tongue* that there are three things that should be sung in the most elevated style: salvation, love, and virtue, salvation because it is profitable, love because it is delightful, virtue because it is noble. But if the highest style is the tragic in so far as it is the same as the epic or in so far as it includes it, there is no doubt that love should be sung in the heroic poem. But such a poem considers love delightful, and love can also be considered as noble, or as a knightly virtue, that is, as a habit of the will. Let it be admitted, then, that a heroic poem can be formed with an amorous subject, such as the love of Leander and Hero, of which Musaeus,[2] a very ancient Greek poet, wrote, and that of Jason and Medea, of which Apollonius wrote among the Greeks and Valerius Flaccus among the Latins,[3] . . . and the loves of Theagenes and Chariclea, and of Leucippe and Clitophon,

[1] Author, with Lombardi, of a commentary on the *Poetics* of Aristotle (1550).

[2] Musaeus (sixth century B.C.), *Hero and Leander*.

[3] Apollonius Rhodius, *Argonautica*, Bks. III and IV. Valerius Flaccus, *Argonautica*, Bks. V–VIII.

which were written of in the same language by Heliodorus[4] and Achilles Tatius;[5] or the others of Arcite and Palamon, and of Florio and Biancofiore, of whom Boccaccio wrote poems in our language;[6] or the adventures of Pyramus and Thisbe, who gave matter for a little poem by Tasso my father;[7] or the madness of Narcissus, from which Alamanni took a subject.[8]

[The Noble Action]

[19] But in this idea of the perfect poem that we now go searching for, it is needful for us to consider nobility and excellence more than everything else. Therefore we should select actions in which there is the greatest possible amount of nobility, as in the undertaking of the Argonauts who went for the golden fleece, of which first Orpheus[9] and then Apollonius[10] wrote their poems. This requirement is equally satisfied by the Trojan war and the wanderings of Ulysses sung by Homer, the siege of Thebes and the youth of Achilles written by Statius,[11] the *Civil War* put in verse by Lucan, and the second African

war versified by Silius Italicus[12] and Petrarch, who in the loves of Massinissa surpassed the first by a great distance.[13] But an action noble beyond all the others is the coming of Aeneas into Italy, because the subject is in itself great and splendid, and yet more great and splendid because the Roman Empire took origin from it, as in the beginning of the *Aeneid* the divine poet writes:

> So great a labor was it to lay the
> foundations of the Roman people.

Such was the liberation of Italy from the Goths, which furnished material for the poem of Trissino;[14] such are those enterprises for the confirmation of the Christian faith or for the exaltation of the Church and the Empire that were fortunately and gloriously accomplished.[15] These actions in themselves win over the souls of the readers and produce expectation and marvelous pleasure, and when the art of an able poet is added there is nothing they cannot accomplish in our souls.

[The Perfect Subject]

[20] The poet should then avoid feigned subjects, especially if it is feigned that something has come about in a land near at hand and well known and among a friendly people, for among distant peoples and in unknown countries we can easily feign many things without taking away authority from the story. Therefore from the land of the Goths and from Norway and Sweden and Iceland or from the East Indies or the

[4] The *Aethiopica* of Heliodorus, the most famous of Greek romances, tells of the loves of Theagenes and Chariclea. A Latin translation appeared in 1552....

[5] Achilles Tatius, *Leucippe and Clitophon*, a Greek romance of the fifth or sixth century. A Latin translation appeared in 1554.

[6] Boccaccio (1313–75) in the *Teseide*, or poem on Theseus, presents Palamon and Arcite. Chaucer retold their story in "The Knight's Tale." The *Filocolo* gives the story of Florio and Biancofiore.

[7] Bernardo Tasso, *The Story of Pyramus and Thisbe*.

[8] Alamanni, *The Fable of Narcissus*, published in 1532.

[9] To him was attributed an epic poem, called *Argonautica*, on his own exploits during the voyage of the Argonauts.

[10] Apollonius Rhodius, *Argonautica*, a Greek epic composed in the third century B.C.

[11] Statius, *The Thebaid*, the story of the strife at Thebes between the children of Oedipus; *The Achilleid*.

[12] Lucan (first century A.D.), *The Pharsalia*. Silius Italicus (died in 102 A.D.), *Punica*.

[13] Petrarch (1304–74) left unfinished the *Africa*, an epic poem in Latin on the second Punic war.

[14] The *Italy Liberated from the Goths*....

[15] Apparently a reference to the Crusades, the first of which Tasso dealt with in his epic of *Jerusalem Delivered*.

countries recently discovered in the vast ocean beyond the pillars of Hercules, the subjects of such poems should be taken.[16] The poet should not touch those subjects that cannot be treated poetically and in which there is no place for fiction and artistry, and he should reject subjects too rude, to which he cannot add splendor, and should remember that precept of Horace:

Abandon a subject if you fear you cannot make it splendid by your treatment.[17]

He should reject what is badly arranged as though it were a stick of timber too crooked to be good for building; he should refuse materials too dry and arid, which do not give much scope to the ability and art of the poet, and above all those that are unpleasant and annoying, and those that end unhappily, as the death of the Paladins and the defeat at Roncesvalles.[18] ... The poet should not become fascinated with material too subtle, and fitted for the schools of the theologians and the philosophers rather than the palaces of princes and the theaters, and he should not show himself ambitious in the questions of nature and theology, and should not forget what Horace says in praise of Homer, putting him higher than many philosophers who have written of virtue and nobility, as may be read in the second epistle to Lollius:

While you, Lollius Maximus, declaim at Rome, I have been reading afresh at Praeneste the writer of the Trojan War; who tells us what is fair, what is foul, what is helpful, what is not, more plainly and better than Chrysippus or Crantor (ll. 1–4).

Nor should the poet show himself too curious in the knowledge of antiquity that is obscure and as it were forgotten, when the obscurity is not that of things that are very great and worthy of knowledge; he should despise trifles rather than not; in the witty he should be magnificent, in the hidden he should be clear, and in all he should excite wonder; he should not be too lengthy in describing sacred or secular ceremonies; in games he should be ornate, and vigorous, and put events before our eyes, and not describe all that is done, but the more famous and splendid, and those that are imitations of war or warlike exercises, as Homer and Vergil did, one in the obsequies of Patroclus, the other in the burial of Anchises. But now the place of games has been taken by tournaments and jousts, which have been splendidly described by our poets, as by Ariosto that of Damascus and by Tasso that of Cornwall with more propriety,[19] for in England they were accustomed to conduct them but it was not the custom of the Turks and Saracens to joust; hence Gemma, the brother of Bajazet II, when he was a prisoner in Rome was in the habit of saying that there was too much play and too little reality. The poet should also have in mind the glory of the nation, the origin of cities, famous families, and princes of kingdoms and empires, as did

[16] The *Lusiad* of Camoens, the national epic of Portugal, deals with the East Indies, and *La Araucana*, by Alonso de Ercilla, with South America. Both authors were contemporaries of Tasso. The curate in *Don Quixote* pronounced the *Araucana* one of the three best heroic poems in Spanish, able to compete with the most famous of Italy (*Don Quixote* I, 6).

[17] Modified from Horace, *Art of Poetry*, 149–50.

[18] The defeat of part of Charlemagne's army on its retirement from Spain is the subject of *The Song of Roland*. Tasso looked on it as an overthrow of Christians by pagans.

[19] For Damascus, see Ariosto, *Orlando Furioso*, XVIII, 132. But these jousts are not fully described; we are merely told that they were held and that Sansonetto won the prize. Bernardo Tasso tells of jousts in Cornwall in *Amadigi*.

Vergil beyond all the others. But he should not be too free in feigning things that are impossible, monstrous, supernatural, and unfitting, as did the man who wished to imitate the fable of Tiresias, who struck the serpents twice and was first transformed from a man to a woman and then from a woman to a man, for it was not a happy thought to transform Rinaldo into a woman. The author should consider the power of the magic art and of nature itself, as though inclosed within certain limits and confined by certain laws, and ancient and forgotten prodigies, and the occasions of marvels and miracles and monstrous events, and the diversity of religions, and the dignity of the persons, and should seek as much as he can to increase faith in the marvel without diminishing the pleasure. . . .

Book III

[Qualities of Heroic Poetry]

[33] The heroic style is not remote from the gravity of tragic style nor from the beauty of lyric style, but it exceeds both the one and the other in the splendor of its wonderful majesty. Yet it is not inappropriate to the epic poet that issuing sometimes from the limits of his splendid magnificence, he should cause his style to approach the gravity of the tragic writer, as he often does; at other times, though more rarely, he can cause it to approach the flowery ornament of lyric style. But the style of a tragedy, though it describes glorious events and royal personages, for two reasons should be less sublime than the heroic. The first is that it normally deals with matter of a more passionate sort, and passion demands purity and simplicity, for it is likely that in that manner a person would speak who is full of anxiety, fear, pity, or some similar disturbance. The other cause is that in a tragedy the poet never speaks, but only those who carry on the action of the play, to whom should be assigned a manner of speaking less strange and less unlike that of ordinary life than epic diction. But the chorus perhaps should speak more loftily, for, as Aristotle says in the *Problems*,[20] it is a sort of guardian that is additional and separate, and for the same reason the poet speaks more loftily in his own person and discourses as though with another tongue, like one who feigns to be rapt out of himself by divine inspiration. . . .

[20] The chorus "takes no active part" (*Problems*, trans. by E. S. Forster [Oxford, 1927], XIX, 48, 922b26). But in 922b20, Aristotle says that a quiet musical mode is suited to the chorus.

FROM THE EPIC SPIRIT
E. M. W. Tillyard[*]

Tillyard's requirements for the epic begin with a demand for
excellence and high seriousness, combined with amplitude,
breadth, and inclusiveness. An epic, he says, must always show
control and conscious will; it must exhibit contemporaneity and
group consciousness, which are the essence of the heroic spirit
and one of the characteristics that distinguish it from the tragic
mode.

Whether or not the reader likes the ensuing account of the epic, he will have to admit that it squares with a modern practice of going outside the bare form or the bare fact and seeking the essential spirit. A. W. Schlegel used the words *classical* and *romantic* in a very simple sense. *Classical* meant ancient Greek and Roman; *romantic* the Gothic that came after. About a hundred years later Middleton Murry declared that "Romanticism and Classicism are perennial modes of the human spirit."[1] The tragic has now for a long time been allowed to exist outside the limits of strict tragedy; it has been found in *Beowulf, Lycidas,* the *Ancient Mariner,* and *Madame Bovary*: the comic exists in many places outside the comic drama. By such analogy there is warrant enough for refusing to identify epic with the heroic poem and for seeking its *differentia* in matters other than nominal and formal.

To have any value the definition of a literary term must rest on induction; and anyone who has tried to make his own

definition and not merely taken one ready made will find that he has been drawing his generalisation from certain (and for the most part unconsciously selected) examples. Experiments with the word *Metaphysical* (in its poetic sense) convinced me that to define it was to generalise on the data of some of Donne's poems. By such a generalisation other metaphysicising poems, whether by Donne or someone else, had been unconsciously measured. Aristotle defined tragedy through the data supplied by a very small number of plays, and in so doing succeeded well enough to invite imitation. The works that first led me to reflect on the spirit of the epic were the *Iliad,* the *Odyssey,* the *Aeneid,* the *Divine Comedy,* the *Lusiad,* and *Paradise Lost.* It was through the conviction of Dante's being as true an epic writer as Virgil that I abandoned any notion of using the heroic subject as a criterion. Finding the *Aeneid* closer in essentials to the *Divine Comedy* than to the *Argonautica* or *Gondibert,* I had to seek a definition of the epic other than the old heroic one. Of course, one must not conceive of the inductive process too simply. It is not a case of drawing conclusions from a limited set of data

* The selection is from *The English Epic and Its Background* by E. M. W. Tillyard. Copyright 1954 by E. M. W. Tillyard. Reprinted by permission of Oxford University Press, Inc.
[1] *To the Unknown God* (London 1924) 136.

uninterrupted to the end and then applying those conclusions to works not yet
considered. Rather it is a case of passing
to and fro between the works you know
you will include and those you think
doubtful, and allowing each class to influence the other. Thus I soon inclined
to include certain novels among the
epics. And such inclusion may have affected my general notions. Sometimes
the lack of a quality in a work that could
not be included might indicate the
presence of it (and hence its general
desirability) in a work included beyond
doubt though not on precisely realised
grounds. I did not include the *Book of
Job* among the fully authenticated epics
because it does not contain enough; nor
Don Quixote, not because it is in prose
but because its construction does not
show the human will stretched and sustained to the utmost. And such negative
conclusions may have reinforced or even
prompted my criteria of wide inclusiveness and sustained will-power. It has
therefore been by finding out what works
I admit and what reject, and why, that
I have gained my conception of the epic.

The first epic requirement is the simple
one of high quality and of high seriousness. It is just conceivable, though superlatively improbable, that the other
conditions required to give the epic effect
could be fulfilled by mediocre means.
Hence the need to insist that the writer
of epic must use words in a very distinguished way. So to insist excludes from
the epic category, as now being char-
acterised, the *King Arthurs* and the
Leonidas's and all the other inferiorities
cast in the traditional form of the heroic
poem.

The second epic requirement can be
roughed out by vague words like amplitude, breadth, inclusiveness, and so on.
Aristotle indicates it with considerable
emphasis through his flagrant failure to

perceive it in his infamous last chapter
of the *Poetics*. Among his reasons for
classing the tragic above the epic form
is the reason that tragic imitation gains
its end in narrower space—τὸ ἐν ἐλάττονι
μήκει τὸ τέλος τῆς μιμήσεως εἶναι—and that
the concentrated is more pleasurable
than the diluted effect. And he asks us
to imagine the *Oedipus* of Sophocles
expanded to the length of the *Iliad*. Further, he asserts that genuine unity is impossible in an epic, which provides the
material for several tragic unities. Taking
tragedy, a highly concentrated form, to
be the measure of excellence, Aristotle
begs the question by calling epic diluted,
but, through the very unfairness of so
calling it, directs us to that greater amplitude in the epic, that ability to deal with
more sides of life, which differentiates it
from the tragic drama....

There are different kinds of variety,
and not every kind belongs to the epic.
An essay by Aldous Huxley, *Tragedy and
the Whole Truth*,[2] will help to make the
proper distinction. Huxley begins from
the passage in the *Odyssey*, Book Twelve,
where Odysseus describes how Scylla
snatched six of his men from his ship
and devoured them at the threshold of
her cave as they cried out in terrible
struggle,

αὐτοῦ δ᾽ εἰνὶ θύρῃσι κατήσθιε κεκλήγοντας,
χεῖρας ἐμοὶ ὀρέγοντας ἐν αἰνῇ δηιοτῆτι.

[and there at the entrance to her lair she
gulped them down, as they screamed
stretching forth their hands to me in their
dire slaughter.]

Later Odysseus and his men landed in
Sicily, ate their supper, and then be-
wailed their lost fellows. Huxley observes
that the intense limited world of tragedy
could never have admitted the cool truth

2 In *Music at Night* (London 1931) 3–18.

to life of the men lamenting only after they satisfied their appetite. Tragedy can exist only through sacrificing what Huxley calls the "Whole Truth." And works that admit the Whole Truth are alien to tragedy.

Tragedy is an arbitrarily isolated eddy on the surface of a vast river that flows on majestically, irresistibly, around, beneath, and to either side of it. Wholly-Truthful art contrives to imply the existence of the entire river as well as of the eddy.... In Wholly-Truthful art the agonies may be just as real, love and the unconquerable mind just as admirable, just as important, as in tragedy.... But the agonies and the indomitabilities are placed by the Wholly-Truthful writer in another, wider context, with the result that they cease to be the same as the intrinsically identical agonies and indomitabilities of tragedy.[3]

At first Huxley might seem to be thinking of epic in opposition to tragedy; but he ends his essay by finding his "Whole Truth" principally in modern literature, which has become

more and more acutely conscious ... of the great oceans of irrelevant things, events and thoughts stretching endlessly away in every direction from whatever island point (a character, a story) the author may choose to contemplate.[4]

And he goes on to cite Proust, D. H. Lawrence, Gide, Kafka, and Hemingway as authors all concerned with the whole truth; thus ending in very different places from his point of departure in the *Odyssey*.

Huxley is quite right in implying that the epic can contain the tragic. Even in the *Odyssey*, usually considered as an epic touching comedy, two at least of the characters who most have our sympathy

[3] *Ib.* 14–15.
[4] *Ib.* 16.

are subjected to suffering sufficiently acute to rouse their deep passions and to force them like the tragic sufferer to consider their own predicaments in the total world they inhabit. But in another matter Huxley is wrong; and here he can serve us, as Aristotle did, and through his very error point to the truth. His error is to introduce the *Odyssey*, an epic, into his particular modern context, for the epic is alien to the wandering and fortuitous concatenations that Huxley considers typical of recent literature. It will not tolerate amplitude for its own sake; it is not content with an undifferentiated and unorganised display of life's many phenomena. Like tragedy, although its material is ampler, epic must select, arrange, and organise.

But to dwell on this necessity is to leave the present topic for my next; and it is more to the point to consider the five authors Huxley cites as exemplifying his idea of the whole truth as he believes it to be expressed in recent literature. All five—Proust, D. H. Lawrence, Gide, Kafka, Hemingway—are exceptionally introverted, even at times the victims of morbid sensibilities. Anyhow, none of them is near achieving the psychological strength and the healthy balance of mental parts which must mark the writer of epic. (It is in this matter, among others, that tragedy differs from epic. Being narrower and requiring among its first qualities intensity, it is less liable than the epic to be destroyed by the pathological. Swift and Kafka might reasonably ask to be considered tragic writers, but epic writers never.) While at home in large areas of life, the epic writer must be centred in the normal, he must measure the crooked by the straight, he must exemplify that sanity which has been claimed for true genius. No pronounced homosexual, for instance, could succeed in the epic, not so much for being one as for what his being one cuts him off from. Granted the fundamental sanity, the wider the epic poet's mental span, the better. And ideally he should be able to range from the simple sensualities to a susceptibility to the numinous.

The third epic requirement has been hinted already through what I said about fortuitous concatenations. Exuberance, however varied, is not enough in itself; there must be a control commensurate with the amount included. Once again, the clearest illustrations may be from things that fail in the given requirement. The works of Rabelais include a great deal, they may be ample enough. It is their lack of organisation that keeps them remote from the epic. *Don Quixote*, because less remote, illustrates even better. Here at any rate is the true epic range and a superb quality of prose style. And there are passages (and conspicuously the first quarter of the second part) of such weight and density as to bear comparison with those poems I am using unconsciously as criteria. Cervantes must have exerted his will powerfully to have achieved the sustained excellence of these parts. But the work as a whole is not epic because it is governed by no powerful predetermination. Cervantes gathers weight as he writes. Beginning with a pleasant little buccaneering expedition, he insensibly picks up reinforcements on the way until he realises he has collected an army. And he puts that army to fluctuating use. But this is a very different matter from the author's having his strategy settled beforehand and keeping the whole suspended in his mind until composition is complete.

That indeed is the structural ideal: that the whole, however long, should remain fluid and unset till the last word has been written, that the writer should have everything simultaneously in mind and keep it open to modification throughout the process of composition. This must remain an ideal, for no man has possessed the powers of memory and control necessary to fulfil it. Even Dante was inconsistent. And one should not exclude from all possibilities of epic success a work that settles its parts as it goes along, provided it makes one part truly evolve out of the others, provided it retains a general recollection of what has gone before. Such, I conjecture, was the structural method of the *Faerie Queene*.

This insistence on rigorous control and predetermination as necessary in a certain type of poetry is alien to two powerful trends in recent thought. The first is a hostility to the long poem in general: a hostility due partly to theory and partly to the prevalent taste. The theory is that of Poe,[5] which seeks to prove that a long poem is by nature impossible, poetic inspiration being always evanescent and no verse counting as poetry unless written under inspiration. Any so-called long poem, of however high quality, can do no more than consist of a number of short poems connected by verse that is not poetry at all. Poe's theory suited both the French Symbolist poets and those who, like A. E. Housman, had narrowly inspirational theories of poetry. (Housman, in an unpublished paper on Burns, stated that there were six[6] and no more than six lines of poetry in all Burns's works.) And the influence of the theory has extended well into the twentieth century. As to the matter of taste, how

[5] In his essay, *The Poetic Principle*. Some art criticism shows the same trend. For instance that which cries up Claude's drawings and cries down his elaborate classical landscapes. Of course the drawings are spontaneous in a way the oil-paintings are not; but to make such spontaneity the only test is critical bigotry.

[6] I cannot vouch for the exact figure, having to rely on my memory of hearing the paper read.

should an age which multiplies and abbreviates, which favours many short items in its radio programmes, less time devoted to more subjects in schools, readers' digests, and miniature sermons, take to its heart a long poem calling for sustained concentration?

The other trend is psychological, that towards valuing the spontaneous, unconscious element in art or in life and towards distrusting the exercise of the conscious will. Aldous Huxley's assertion just quoted, that modern literature is concerned with "the great oceans of irrelevant things, events and thoughts stretching endlessly away in every direction," is a good enough illustration.

It is obvious that in writing a long poem or a long highly organised work in prose, the composition of which is perforce extended over years, an author cannot sustain a spontaneous vein of creation. At intervals he will be tempted to break the unity of the original conception and stray after new emotional interests. Spontaneity will not suffice, and the author will have to summon his will to help him abide by the plans he has resolved on. The writing of any poem (except one dictated in dream or trance) needs some effort of the will to control and shape it. But the effort is different in a lyric, a short story, and a play, while only in the most intensely written long works is the will taxed to the utmost. Such sustained writing corresponds to certain phases of the active life. Just as the will may force a man's conduct at a particular time (for instance on an expedition of exploration) to conform to a previously adopted set of resolves, against his present inclinations, so a poet may use his will to suppress new interests and preserve a unity previously resolved on.

Further, in the making of a long poem the will is more than an external driving force; the fact of its exercise and the belief in it become a highly important part of the total experience. Milton speaks of how the Dorian mood of flutes and soft recorders raised

To highth of noblest temper Hero's old
Arming to Battel, and in stead of rage
Deliberate valour breath'd.

But even if Milton had never used the phrase, "deliberate valour" (which describes my meaning so concisely), his belief in the quality of considered courage, aware of issues, which implies the application of the will, would be apparent from the whole trend of his rhetoric. Moreover, in *Paradise Lost*, as in other genuine epics, the very passages which the will has forced into harmony with the more spontaneously composed ones are significant as declaring the value of the quality to which they owe a large part of their being.

This exercise of the will and the belief in it, which are a corollary of our third epic requirement, help to associate epic poetry with the largest human movements and solidest human institutions. In creating what we call civilisation the sheer human will has had a major part.

Although, for my own purposes, I have dissociated epic from the heroic poem, that is the verse narrative of heroic deeds in the heroic age, I want to insist that the true epic creates a "heroic impression." And that impression has to do with, is a by-product of, the present topic: the control of a large material and the exercise of the conscious will. Heroic poetry often concerns actions in which men know exactly what they are doing and rise through deliberate valour to a great height of resolution. And it is natural enough to attribute the heroic impression to a poem's heroic subject matter. But in fact that impression depends also, indeed ultimately, on the temper of treatment. A heroic theme may encourage a writer to treat it in a sustained, "heroic" way, to exercise his will to the utmost; but this does not prevent the treatment's being the decisive element. If this is the case with heroic poetry, it follows that literature lacking a heroic subject is not debarred from making the heroic impression. Here Dante is especially apt. His subject is not at all the old heroic one, though certain of his characters, Farinata and Ulysses for instance, may be of the antique heroic cast. But it is not they that make the heroic impression; it is rather the vast exercise of the will which went to the shaping of the whole poem. The *Faerie Queene* fails of the full heroic impression in spite of its chivalrous setting. And it does so because its organisation is rather loose....

The fourth requirement can be called choric. The epic writer must express the feelings of a large group of people living in or near his own time. The notion that the epic is primarily patriotic is an unduly narrowed version of this requirement. Should a country command at some time an exceptionally clear ethical temper, that temper may serve an author well enough. Spenser, for instance, does express the Elizabethan temper successfully in the *Faerie Queene*. But the group-feeling need not be national. Dante is medieval rather than Italian. And it is wise not to bring in nationalism at all. Better, with Lascelles Abercrombie,[7] to look on the epic poet as

accepting, and with his genius transfiguring, the general circumstance of his time ... symbolizing, in some appropriate form, whatever sense of the significance of life he feels acting as the accepted unconscious metaphysic of the time.

[7] *The Epic* (London, not dated) 39.

We can simplify even further and say no more than that the epic must communicate the feeling of what it was like to be alive at the time. But that feeling must include the condition that behind the epic author is a big multitude of men of whose most serious convictions and dear habits he is the mouthpiece.

It is in this matter that epic most differs from tragedy. Tragedy cannot lack some imprint of its age, but its nature is to be timeless. It deals with the recurrent human passions and it presents them (having no space to do more) in their bare elements with the least local circumstantiation. It teaches not what it is like to be alive at a certain time but what it is like to be a human being. But though the choric element is necessary to epic and at best adventitious in tragedy, it does not exclude from epic the presentation of those timeless feelings which it is tragedy's privilege to isolate and clarify. Indeed, the greatness of epic will partly depend on the inclusion of such feelings. It is when the tragic intensity coexists with the group-consciousness of an age, when the narrowly timeless is combined in a unit with the variegatedly temporal, that epic attains its full growth.

Lascelles Abercrombie postulates that the epic not only should express the "accepted unconscious metaphysic" of its age but do so through a clear and authentic story, a story known and already part of the mythology of the audience. I disagree with this further demand. Certainly, the material of the epic should be largely public, but not necessarily in the form of a narrative where the concatenation of sequent events holds a large proportion of the reader's interest. The "accepted unconscious metaphysic" is the essential starting-point, but the method of conveying it must vary from age to age. When an age holds one kind of opinion on the nature of man, the heroic story may best represent the current metaphysic. But other forms may suit other ages. The Middle Ages regarded man differently and they could not make the heroic story the most serious literary form. Allegory better answered their requirement. In the age of Elizabeth, when the Middle Ages and the new classicism of the Renaissance met, heroic action and allegory combined to express the most serious concerns. In the eighteenth century, prose fiction began potentially to be the best epic medium invading what had been mainly the province of verse. In sum the choric nature of the epic does not dictate any rigidly answering form.

Finally, not every "accepted unconscious metaphysic" can prompt an epic. If for instance it is predominantly elegiac or nostalgic, it cannot serve. Nietzsche believed tragedy to be possible only in an age of optimism. Epic, in similar fashion, must have faith in the system of beliefs or way of life it bears witness to. The reason for this belongs to other qualities of the epic than the choric. Only when people have faith in their own age can they include the maximum of life in their vision and exert their will-power to its utmost capacity.

FROM THE VANISHING HERO
Sean O'Faolain*

This essay traces the development of the hero in the novel, beginning with the eighteenth century, where the hero is allied with society, through the French novel of the nineteenth century, where the hero begins to feel himself at odds with his society, to the twentieth-century English and American novel, where the concept of heroism has almost vanished—to be replaced by what O'Faolain describes as the "anti-hero."

...As I see the matter, the Hero, as we commonly try to use the word and the idea, is a purely social creation. He represents, that is to say, a socially approved norm, for representing which to the satisfaction of society he is decorated with a title. The traditional novel—the term "traditional" will have to be considered and qualified later on—had always moved about this socially acceptable character, so that even when he was not visibly or obtrusively present, as in *Les Liaisons Dangereuses* or *Manon Lescaut*, a form of lip service was given to his hovering spirit by at least a final, formal admission that "crime does not pay." The Hero was on the side of the long arm of the law, the *Sûreté*, the church, the kirk, the headmaster and the head of the family. He was on the side of Squire Allworthy, Mr. John Knightley, Père Goriot, Mrs. Proudie and Sherlock Holmes, or at least he was after he had been permitted a certain license to roam in order to entertain us, and had duly returned to the bosom of conventional

* The selection is reprinted from *The Vanishing Hero*, by Sean O'Faolain, by permission of Little, Brown and Co.–Atlantic Monthly Press. Copyright, ©, 1956, 1957, by Sean O'Faolain.

behavior, as, for example, young Chuzzlewit returned, after "Eden" had reformed him, to the bosom of Mary Graham. Naturally some of the best novelists always kicked against this social convention, much to the satisfaction of the reading public and to the annoyance of the social critics; as happened to Scott when he wrote *Rob Roy* about a freebooter and Fielding when he wrote *Tom Jones* about a rascal. "A hero," cried Thackeray, of Tom Jones, somewhat hypocritically, one fears, "with a flawed reputation, a hero sponging for a guinea, a hero who cannot pay his landlady, and is obliged to let his honour out to hire, is absurd, and the claim of Tom Jones to heroic rank is quite untenable." The reference to the landlady is the revealing item in the list. No man could be a hero if he was so antisocial as not to pay his debts.

The Hero, and his opposite number, the Villain, represented in the traditional novel conflicts which they more or less clearly defined. That was in those good old days when novelists were prepared to accept the fact that certain current ideas expressed firmly and clearly what the majority of people meant by a good or wholesome life. The novelist might not subscribe fully to these ideas or ideals himself; he might feel critical about them, poke fun at them, even reject them in his heart; but he could not deny that they formed the basis of the society in which he lived and which he described, and that anybody who rebelled against them, whether in real life or in fiction, must find himself not only in conflict with his community but in conflict with his origins and probably with his own nature. In admitting so much he admitted the social concept of Heroism. If the novelist were a Stevenson, a Thackeray or a Dickens his readers knew where they were, and where the

author stood, immediately they had identified the Hero. But the identification was not always so easy, especially with the French novelists. Many readers of the Abbé Prévost's entertaining account of the career of Manon Lescaut must have closed the book in a somewhat puzzled frame of mind as to the Abbé's convictions, in spite of his effort to clarify his position in the last few pages by bringing disaster on the head of his heroine. Even here, however, one thing at least was clear: Manon, like all other such strays from the narrow path, was agin the government, and she was therefore in a very proper danger of life and happiness. This would have soothed the Abbé's readers and increased their ambivalent pleasure in reading of her adventures. On the other hand, the first readers of de Laclos's *Les Liaisons Dangereuses* (1782) can have been in no doubt that his was a thoroughly subversive book in so far as it denied all social and moral values. It is, perhaps, the first European novel without a social Hero. Its rank as a masterpiece forces us to note that the term "traditional novel" does not exclude rivals, exceptional in more senses than one, whose increasing effect from the seventeenth century on was to put the social concept of the Hero more and more on the defensive until it was finally overthrown completely.

II

The struggle, though it was not immediately apparent, began early. Even in the seventeenth century we are sensible of the insidious intrusion of other and less moral values; which is, no doubt, no more than one would expect of a period governed overtly by rigid laws and conventions but secretly as licentious as any other. After all, the central seventeenth-century classical ideas of *amour-*

vertu—the idea, or the hope, that once man beheld the Good he must naturally love it—not only did not exclude the basic fact of natural desire but by definition emphasized it. For *amour-vertu*, seen as that force which builds the soul's perfection (*cette puissance d'ajouter à la perfection de nos âmes*), not only implies imperfection but implies also that imperfection is a highly attractive thing against which the soul has to struggle long and painfully. (There could be no drama at all otherwise.) This in turn implies something even more important to our immediate interest—that both the writer and the public were enormously interested in the emotional tug-of-war between the "soul" and "imperfection." So, for instance, although in the great novel of the century before de Laclos, Madame de Lafayette's *La Princesse de Clèves*, virtue triumphs over weakness, the contemporary reader may or not have been vicariously relieved, but he could not have meantime been much interested if his sympathies had not been engaged and the struggle long in doubt. A certain ambivalence, one perceives, thereby enters into the novel, dividing admiration and sympathy, virtue and pleasure.

Sympathy thus opened the first assault on the social code, and on the Hero who represented it. If one's sympathy for human unhappiness begins to dominate one's moral sense, the senses, the stern moralist will maintain, must end by dominating both. "Man," says Cousin, in his *Philosophie du xviii Siècle*, "is a creature who naturally finds the unhappiness of others hard to bear; to blot out the sight of unhappiness he is, so to speak, obliged to collaborate with the unhappy." The result is that virtue and happiness soon become coterminous and "the words goodness and beauty agree to define whatever qualities add to our pleasure in anything..."; in the end, "anything that soothes the passions ends by being called 'good.'" On this basis the sensibilities began, little by little, to impose a new set of values on the old.

Yet it only happened little by little, ambiguously and inexplicitly, and nothing was overtly admitted or acknowledged. Readers of, say, the sentimental novels of Crebillon might, when the heroine yields to passion, water her burning heart with their tears, dare to feel that love is the only true criterion of joy, even go so far as to hold that *l'amour doit détruire tous les préjugés* (should override all prejudices); but they still had to admit—because it was so—that the whole tragedy and tension of illicit love lay in the fact that the dictates of established society (*les préjugés*) were opposed to these lawless dictates of the heart and would inevitably condemn and destroy those who dared yield to them. The reader, to put it in a vulgar way, got his fun out of the Hero's sense of tension; rather in the manner of a spectator at a bullfight who gets his "fun" out of the matador's tensions. The interest to us here is that, imperceptibly, the Hero and the Villain are changing sides, though nobody will yet admit it. The spectator ought to be on the side of the bull—symbol of society, tradition, the good earth, the herd, the life-giver, the head of the family; he gets his pleasure instead, or some of his pleasure, in watching the bull-baiter. But, then, being himself a bull, a head of a family, a one-of-the-herd, a social man, he must, at the end, when the bull-baiter is gored by the bull, lean back, close the book, and say aloud for the benefit of his attendant family: "Well, of course, yes! One should not bait bulls." In other words, the readers' and the novelists' ambivalence increases. Society is cruel. Society is even to be criticized. Society

. . . But nobody will go quite so far as to reverse traditional roles and say that society is the villain of the piece.

L'Abbé Prévost certainly did not dare say so, though he did by playing on the sensibilities of his readers tempt them to think so. Indeed, he is more than evasive about it all, as when, washing his hands over his *L'Homme de Qualité*, he says, surely not without some hypocrisy: "*Les coeurs sensibles, les esprits raisonnables, tous ceux, en un mot, qui—sans suivre une philosophie trop sévère—ont du goût pour la vertu, la sagesse, et la vérité, pourront trouver quelque plaisir dans la lecture de cet ouvrage.*" (Every sensitive heart, every rational spirit, in a word, everybody who—*without yielding to too severe a philosophy of life*—has a feeling for virtue, wisdom and truth, will find some pleasure in the perusal of this work.) Not that the public was not occasionally more frank, as witness this kind of remark from a review of Prévost's *Manon Lescaut* (1733): "Manon is an interesting creation. She may deceive her lover twenty times; it does not matter. She is unfaithful, yet never perfidious. She continues to love her adoring knight. Because of that love we forgive her everything."[1]

Rousseau is quite another pair of sleeves. The Abbé Prévost made no attempt to teach, or point a moral, or state a social problem. He neither had time for it in these novels of adventure, nor—here in full keeping with the traditions of the novel of feeling—were such matters his main interest. His main interest was in the personages whose fates attracted him. *La Nouvelle Héloïse* (1761), on the other hand, has been well described by Lanson as "*un rêve de*

[1] *L'Année littéraire*, 1784, p. 107 seq. Quoted in *Le Genre Romanesque en France depuis l'apparition de la* Nouvelle Héloïse *jusqu'aux approches de la Révolution*. Gervais Étienne. Paris, 1922.

volupté redressé en instruction morale" —a dream of happiness devoted to the purposes of moral teaching. Unfortunately, most readers of Rousseau's novel remember only the first part, in which Julie becomes the lover of Saint Preux, and forget, or never even read, the second part, in which she is presented as the faithful wife of Wolmar, whom she does not love. Perhaps they forget, too, that the whole point of the novel is that it is a fictional representation of the essential burthen of the Social Contract —which is that while nature made men happy and society makes them unhappy *la nature humaine ne rétrograde pas* (human nature cannot go back). Social living has its own charms and triumphs, and all that men in society can now do is to recover certain attributes of primitive life, such as innocence and liberty. So, while Julie and Saint Preux do not sin against nature, they do sin against society; but society, by insisting rigidly on moral behavior, in turn presses Julie so hard that it also sins by making it well-nigh impossible for her not to transgress. Her dilemma thus poses, once more, and for the first time intelligently, that antagonism between the person and the social group which earlier novels were content to evoke by the appeal to feelings of pity.

De Laclos (his novel appeared twenty-one years later: 1782) is uncompromising. Mme. de Merteuil and Valmont, enemies of society and of each other, would have found in Julie's faithfulness to Wolmar nothing but another delightful incentive towards inflicting a new defeat on society by corrupting her—another blow, that is, for the social idea that love makes demands on honor, and that honor respects the social structure erected on the basis of faithful love. The Age of Reason has not only arrived but gone too far in *Les Liaisons Dangereuses*, or rather in the behavior of its two active ingredients—whom one cannot well call its Hero and Heroine since they are, at bottom, opposed to everything still inherent in those two words. This is well put by Martin Turnell: "The eighteenth century *philosophes* had no difficulty in continuing the work of the seventeenth century and in completing the destruction of moral sanctions on the rational plane.... The Man of Honour and the Man of Passion had had their day and disappeared from the scene. Laclos' theme is the tragedy of the Rational Man, the man who was carefully conditioned through the removal of all moral scruples and the sense of guilt, but inevitably condemned to action in a very limited field. The novel is a masterpiece because it gives final expression to this phase of human experience."

Still, it could only be a phase. De Merteuil and Valmont are indeed, by being enemies of society, limited in their scope and possible ambitions. Their lives as corrupters of virtue are lived on the periphery of normalcy. They have the freedom only of gangsters, brigands, cutthroats or pickpockets. As Turnell says so vividly, these people are always *whispering*. Yet they foreshadow in their limited and corrupt way something immensely important: the fact that, since sniping at the world is hardly a full-time occupation, any man of real ambition must either decide to be part of the world of accepted values and rise to power within its framework, or else decide to conquer it. We are on the threshold of the age of Napoleon, the age of the man of ambition, of energy, of dreams all his very own. The novelists who, like Prévost, had concentrated on the interest of individual emotions will now concentrate on the individual in action—and probably in active revolt. The social Hero is about to discover that his opposite number is not the Villain but himself imbued by new and disturbing forms of discontent.

The first real flag of revolt was the romantic's angry and agonized cry of distress at the cruelty of society in Benjamin Constant's *Adolphe* (1816). It is lucid and unillusioned. It paints not the ecstasies of irregular love but its inevitable and continuing misery. From start to finish Adolphe and Ellénore are torn by unhappiness, and the great merit of this little masterpiece of doomed passion is in its clear realization that things could not have gone otherwise. In the Epilogue the author is explicit. All ambivalence is dissipated:

The story of Ellénore's tragedy shows that the most passionate feeling cannot prevail against the established order. The power of society is strong and takes too many shapes. It pours bitterness and gall into the sort of love whose existence it refuses to admit. It encourages inconstancy and ennui, twin maladies which take the soul unawares in the very heart and center of love. In the name of morality the poor-in-spirit sow discord, and in their zeal for virtue they sow evil. It is as if because they themselves are incapable of love they hate the sight of it and under any possible pretext revel in attacking it and destroying it.... Society arms itself with everything that is mean and evil in the human heart to destroy whatever is good in it.

The only words of condemnation are those which insist that Adophe's virtues were not founded on principles but on emotions, so that all he is left with in the end are the memories of his unkindness to Ellénore.

With Balzac the novel frees itself from the limited scope of fated passion and the subjective obsession with affairs of the heart. The Napoleonic inspiration is here at its fullest voltage. The mark of it throughout his work is his enormous admiration for pure energy. For example, this kind of excited outburst: "*Il n'y a plus énergie à Paris. Un poignard est une curiosité qu'on suspend à un clou doré.*" (But there is no energy any more in Paris. Here a dagger is simply a curio that we hang on the wall on a gilded nail.) And so on: "Now, in Italy everything is much more clear-cut! There the women are ravening animals, dangerous sirens, following no other logic, responding to no other reasons than their appetites and their hungers. You have to be as careful with them as you would with tigresses." (Though this may be also an echo of the contemporary admiration for *Robinson Crusoe*, the modern myth of man's conquest of wild nature.) For Balzac, man *must* conquer something. That has been in the air of France ever since the Corsican made all Frenchmen feel that man is a free creature with no limits to his ambition but those of his own audacity. Accordingly, to Balzac the man of ruthless and amoral ambition is the proper man to take center stage and his novels are full of such men. True, something of the usual ambiguity and ambivalence still creeps in to confuse the issue a little—such as pious platitudes about the need to preserve church and state; sentiments more or less sincerely felt according as Balzac's own efforts to make a place for himself in the *haute monde* succeed or flag—but the general effect is unmistakably that of a struggle between ruthless individual ambition and what is sometimes nowadays called in Britain the "Establishment."

One could cull from his novels many observations to enforce this impression, along the lines of this sentence from the *Médecin de Campagne*: "*Le contrat social sera toujours un pacte perpetuel entre ceux qui possèdent contre ceux qui ne possèdent pas.*" (The Social Contract will always be a pact between those who have against those who have not.) Where, here, one asks, is the Hero? On which side is he in this? Victim or accomplice? Which is Rastignac, the ambitious young gallant of *Père Goriot*? Social Hero? Or rebellious brigand? What are we to think when we are told that the experience of any young man, such as Rastignac, coming to Paris to make his way in the world must be to see vice successful and virtue mocked (*la vertu persiflé*)? Are we to anticipate that the Balzacian hero will take the side of virtue? We are told in fact that "the young man begins to totter, his will and his conscience become divorced, and"—here is a typical piece of ambivalence, a moral observation from a novelist who is scarcely *preaching* morality—"the infernal work of demoralization is soon complete." But the moral observation does not succeed in impressing us. Every novelist reveals his sympathies by his obsessions. He cannot, by throwing in a moral observation, imagine he has then made a fair counterbalance of justice. Balzac, thinking of his own struggles, ambitions and failures, and projecting them in men like Rastignac, is constantly evoking sympathy for ambitious men by the very passion of his intensity in depicting them.

The views he makes them express, though not necessarily his views, vibrate with a force which is his force. So, at the beginning of the *Maison Nucingen* —which begins where *Père Goriot* left off—the narrator (Balzac) overhears a group of dandies discussing Rastignac's rise to fortune. Their comments, which are Balzac's invention, are not necessarily his opinions, but he does nothing to contradict them and he does much to make them plausible or at least palatable to the reader. The burthen of the story is put into Bixion's mouth: "Rastignac, from the moment of his debut in Paris, looked at society with a skeptical eye. From 1820 onward he thought, just like the baron, that honest men are so only in appearance and he therefore saw the world as a blend of every kind of corruption and deceit. He admitted that there were individual exceptions, but he condemned the majority of men. He denied the existence of virtue, though he admitted that in certain circumstances men do display it. This decision was arrived at in a single moment. He acquired his knowledge of the world on the hilltop of Père Lachaise the day he buried there that poor, honest man who had been the father of his Delphine, who died, abandoned by his daughters and his sons-in-law, the dupe of society and of his own sincere feelings. He decided there and then to play the world's game, to assume the mantle of virtue, of honesty, of fine sentiments, while in fact clothing himself from head to foot in the armor of his own egoism. . . ."

The implication is that Rastignac did well because he did successfully. This becomes clear when we cast our minds back from this summary to the last dramatic and poignant scene of *Père Goriot* where the old man is being buried in Père Lachaise, and recall his sacrifices for his daughters, and Rastignac's earlier naïvetés and sufferings, and the rude contrast with Vautrin's ruthless schemings. We must see then how sardonically the Grand Design of the *Comédie Humaine* underlines the word *comedy*, if only by pointing out that the heroes whom society acclaims are not all as admirable either as society pretends or imagines them to be. Rastignac in the cemetery had not had, we remember, a coin with which to pay the gravediggers. "As he looked down at the grave he dropped into it the last tear of his youth." Then he moved up to the higher part of the

cemetery and looked down at the glittering lights of Paris, darted glance after glance over its humming hive, and said: "Now for our turn! Hers and mine!" Then—"as a first challenge to society, he went to dine with Madame de Nucingen." It is the final line of the novel.

It may evoke another rebel of a very different metal and another ambition, also proposing to conquer in Paris—young Stephen Daedalus. But the differences are immense. Rastignac seeks to conquer the world; Daedalus abandons all hope of it to conquer himself; the ambition of the one is material, of the other metaphysical; the one is a rebel, the other is a martyr; and where Byron would have admired both, Shelley would have admired Daedalus the more; as for Rastignac as man of energy and action—he would have considered Daedalus either a fool, or one of the world's few exceptions to the almost universal rule that the only thing that makes men toil is self-interest, and that their only reward is its satisfaction.

With Stendhal the destruction of the Social Hero is completed. Stendhal's concept of the spur and the reward of toil is the refinement of Balzac in proportion as he deals in finer spirits, has a more lyrical view of life, a more lucid though less robust intelligence and is, in sum, the superior writer of the two. After all, while Julien Sorel realizes that he must either conquer the world or be conquered by it, become a Napoleon or—as he does—end on the gallows, his aim is not just success, pleasure or power but, ultimately, to satisfy his own ego and to prove an idea: that life is to those who dare to live it. This intrusion of a subjective note marks Stendhal as the true father of the modern anti-Hero, who is almost always subjective, and one might dare say *therefore* always a failure. For life is not to those who dare to live it if, in effect, they live it as much within their minds as Julien, and apparently as Stendhal did before and after him. That famous scene in *Le Rouge et le Noir* (1831), where Julien decides to prove himself to himself by taking the hand of the mayoress at a certain moment by the clock, reveals the flaw in the theory: for Julien does take her hand, and from that moment he does believe in his own audacity—but what has happened to the hand of the mayoress? If a man loves not for love's sake but for an idea's sake where has "living" gone to? In effect Julien, like Madame de Merteuil before him in *Les Liaisons Dangereuses,* tends to kill every emotional experience by subserving it to ends other than itself.

But this is one of the main differences between the art of Balzac (and of all who went before him and carried on his tradition after him) and the art of Stendhal and of all those who are of *his* tradition: that Balzac aims to re-create the objective world in terms of its own actual, tangible, verifiable truth—admittedly, inevitably as the writer sees it or interprets it—whereas Stendhal aims to express his own personal, subjective truth in terms of the objective world. The heroes of Balzac are men of the world; the heroes of Stendhal are men who want to be men of the world. Neither type of hero really accepts the world in which he moves or towards which he is drawn; but because of his gift of irony Stendhal is much more lucid about it all than Balzac, whose heroes are forever weltering in the thick of the battle.

One might say that, of the two, Stendhal is the greater anarchist, simply because he is so devastatingly lucid. When Count Mosca in *La Chartreuse de Parme* (1839) tells young Fabrizio that it is silly to complain about the rules and conventions of the world, of society or of politics, considering that one does not complain about the rules of the game of whist, could moral subversion go farther? If one "plays the game" in this sense of the term, nothing, it is evident, is left of social morality but whatever natural, innate decency there may be in the individual sufficiently endowed to be able to play the game with skill and grace. The Hero then becomes, it is surely obvious, not society's Hero but society's secret exploiter. If he succeeds, he becomes his own private Hero, applauded by nobody else, possibly even visible as such to nobody else. At that point the old terms Hero and Heroine, though they may go on being used through idle habit, no longer have any general validity or clear meaning as far as fiction is concerned; while as for what is called "real life," they will continue to be applicable publicly only for so long as large masses of people are ready to believe that any man who acts bravely in their cause is a heroic character, whereas men acting as bravely for some contrary cause are not. Such a usage equally ignores the fact that the word *heroic,* or *heroism,* can therefore have so little moral content that the public "hero" may be a private "villain." (There are, of course, many other examples of life outmoding language in this way: for instance the continuing use of the now almost meaningless title Liberal.) It would be difficult to show this process at work in the English novel at any period; impossible over the same period. The whole English idea of society was that it was a system to be accepted; it was a game played so instinctively that nobody realized that it was a game. Nobody stood outside the thing and observed it analytically, so that English literature lacks the French cutting-edge until we come to Wilde and Shaw; and Shaw, we note, is a critic of social problems rather than individual crises. There are one or two swallows: one could build something on Becky Sharp as a likable *corsaire*; on the victim-heroines of the Brontës; on Trollope's angry reactions to the spites and compressions of small-town society—but there is, as one might say, no party line within the English novel to suggest that other concepts of the Hero are burrowing underneath it. We are almost on the threshold of the twentieth century before we observe English novelists begin to take on something of the individualistic spirit of the French; and the same naturally applies to the novel in America. . . .

CHAPTER 2

Tragic Mode

FROM POETICS

Aristotle*

In the fourth century B.C., in the first great treatise on fiction, Aristotle defined tragedy as the imitation of an action of high importance, complete and of some amplitude; by exercising the emotions of pity and fear tragedy effects purgation of these emotions. The tragic hero is neither completely good nor completely without goodness; he is a person of importance who has a flaw through which is brought about his downfall. The tragic plot accomplishes a complication and resolution of good and evil—a reversal of fortune or situation and a discovery of the nature of that reversal. Since tragedy is concerned with ethical conflict, action is primary to it, and character is necessary only because you cannot have acts without people to perform them.

I propose to treat of Poetry in itself and of its various kinds, noting the essential quality of each; to inquire into the structure of the plot as requisite to a good poem; into the number and nature of the parts of which a poem is composed; and similarly into whatever else falls within the same inquiry. Following, then, the order of nature, let us begin with the principles which come first.

* The treatise is reprinted from the translation by S. H. Butcher in *Aristotle's Theory of Poetry and Fine Arts*, 4th edition. Copyright 1932 by Macmillan & Company, Ltd.

Epic poetry and Tragedy, Comedy also and Dithyrambic poetry, and the music of the flute and of the lyre in most of their forms, are all in their general conception modes of imitation. They differ, however, from one another in three respects, the medium, the objects, the manner or mode of imitation, being in each case distinct.

For as there are persons who, by conscious art or mere habit, imitate and represent various objects through the medium of colour and form, or again by the voice; so in the arts above mentioned,

30

taken as a whole, the imitation is produced by rhythm, language, or "harmony," either singly or combined.

Thus in the music of the flute and of the lyre, "harmony" and rhythm alone are employed; also in other arts, such as that of the shepherd's pipe, which are essentially similar to these. In dancing, rhythm alone is used without "harmony"; for even dancing imitates character, emotion, and action, by rhythmical movement.

There is another art which imitates by means of language alone, and that either in prose or verse—which verse, again, may either combine different metres or consist of but one kind—but this has hitherto been without a name. For there is no common term we could apply to the mimes of Sophron and Xenarchus and the Socratic dialogues on the one hand; and, on the other, to poetic imitations in iambic, elegiac, or any similar metre. People do, indeed, add the word "maker" or "poet" to the name of the metre, and speak of elegiac poets, or epic (that is, hexameter) poets, as if it were not the imitation that makes the poet, but the verse that entitles them all indiscriminately to the name. Even when a treatise on medicine or natural science is brought out in verse, the name of poet is by custom given to the author; and yet Homer and Empedocles have nothing in common but the metre, so that it would be right to call the one poet, the other physicist rather than poet. On the same principle, even if a writer in his poetic imitation were to combine all metres, as Chaeremon did in his Centaur, which is a medley composed of metres of all kinds, we should bring him too under the general term poet. So much then for these distinctions.

There are, again, some arts which employ all the means above mentioned,—namely, rhythm, tune, and metre. Such

are Dithyrambic and Nomic poetry, and also Tragedy and Comedy; but between them the difference is, that in the first two cases these means are all employed in combination, in the latter, now one means is employed, now another.

Such, then, are the differences of the arts with respect to the medium of imitation.

Since the objects of imitation are men in action, and these men must be either of a higher or a lower type (for moral character mainly answers to these divisions, goodness and badness being the distinguishing marks of moral differences), it follows that we must represent men either as better than in real life, or as worse, or as they are. It is the same in painting. Polygnotus depicted men as nobler than they are, Pauson as less noble, Dionysius drew them true to life.

Now it is evident that each of the modes of imitation above mentioned will exhibit these differences, and become a distinct kind in imitating objects that are thus distinct. Such diversities may be found even in dancing, flute-playing, and lyre-playing. So again in language, whether prose or verse unaccompanied by music. Homer, for example, makes men better than they are; Cleophon as they are; Hegemon the Thasian, the inventor of parodies, and Nicochares, the author of the Deiliad, worse than they are. The same thing holds good of Dithyrambs and Nomes; here too one may portray different types, as Timotheus and Philoxenus differed in representing their Cyclopes. The same distinction marks off Tragedy from Comedy; for Comedy aims at representing men as worse, Tragedy as better than in actual life.

There is still a third difference—the manner in which each of these objects may be imitated. For the medium being the same, and the objects the same, the poet may imitate by narration—in which case he can either take another personality as Homer does, or speak in his own person, unchanged—or he may present all his characters as living and moving before us.

These, then, as we said at the beginning, are the three differences which distinguish artistic imitation,—the medium, the objects, and the manner. So that from one point of view, Sophocles is an imitator of the same kind as Homer —for both imitate higher types of character; from another point of view, of the same kind as Aristophanes—for both imitate persons acting and doing. Hence, some say, the name of "drama" is given to such poems, as representing action. For the same reason the Dorians claim the invention both of Tragedy and Comedy. The claim to Comedy is put forward by the Megarians,—not only by those of Greece proper, who allege that it originated under their democracy, but also by the Megarians of Sicily, for the poet Epicharmus, who is much earlier than Chionides and Magnes, belonged to that country. Tragedy too is claimed by certain Dorians of the Peloponnese. In each case they appeal to the evidence of language. The outlying villages, they say, are by them called κῶμαι, by the Athenians δῆμοι: and they assume that Comedians were so named not from κωμάζειν, "to revel," but because they wandered from village to village (κατὰ κώμας), being excluded contemptuously from the city. They add also that the Dorian word for "doing" is δρᾶν, and the Athenian, πράττειν.

This may suffice as to the number and nature of the various modes of imitation.

Poetry in general seems to have sprung from two causes, each of them lying deep in our nature. First, the instinct of imitation is implanted in man from childhood, one difference between him and other animals being that he is the most imitative of living creatures, and through imitation learns his earliest lessons; and no less universal is the pleasure felt in things imitated. We have evidence of this in the facts of experience. Objects which in themselves we view with pain, we delight to contemplate when reproduced with minute fidelity: such as the forms of the most ignoble animals and of dead bodies. The cause of this again is, that to learn gives the liveliest pleasure, not only to philosophers but to men in general; whose capacity, however, of learning is more limited. Thus the reason why men enjoy seeing a likeness is, that in contemplating it they find themselves learning or inferring, and saying perhaps, "Ah, that is he." For if you happen not to have seen the original, the pleasure will be due not to the imitation as such, but to the execution, the colouring, or some such other cause.

Imitation, then, is one instinct of our nature. Next, there is the instinct for "harmony" and rhythm, metres being manifestly sections of rhythm. Persons, therefore, starting with this natural gift developed by degrees their special aptitudes, till their rude improvisations gave birth to Poetry.

Poetry now diverged in two directions, according to the individual character of the writers. The graver spirits imitated noble actions, and the actions of good men. The more trivial sort imitated the actions of meaner persons, at first composing satires, as the former did hymns to the gods and the praises of famous men. A poem of the satirical kind cannot indeed be put down to any author earlier than Homer; though many such writers probably there were. But from Homer onward, instances can be cited,—his own Margites, for example, and other similar compositions. The appropriate metre was also here introduced; hence the measure is still called the iambic or lampooning measure, being that in which people lampooned one another. Thus the older poets were distinguished as writers of heroic or of lampooning verse.

As, in the serious style, Homer is pre-eminent among poets, for he alone combined dramatic form with excellence of imitation, so he too first laid down the main lines of Comedy, by dramatising the ludicrous instead of writing personal satire. His Margites bears the same relation to Comedy that the Iliad and Odyssey do to Tragedy. But when Tragedy and Comedy came to light, the two classes of poets still followed their natural bent: the lampooners became writers of Comedy, and the Epic poets were succeeded by Tragedians, since the drama was a larger and higher form of art.

Whether Tragedy has as yet perfected its proper types or not; and whether it is to be judged in itself, or in relation also to the audience,—this raises another question. Be that as it may, Tragedy—as also Comedy—was at first mere improvisation. The one originated with the authors of the Dithyramb, the other with those of the phallic songs, which are still in use in many of our cities. Tragedy advanced by slow degrees; each new element that showed itself was in turn developed. Having passed through many changes, it found its natural form, and there it stopped.

Aeschylus first introduced a second actor; he diminished the importance of the Chorus, and assigned the leading part to the dialogue. Sophocles raised the number of actors to three, and added scene-painting. Moreover, it was not till late that the short plot was discarded for one of greater compass, and the grotesque diction of the earlier satyric form for the stately manner of Tragedy. The iambic measure then replaced the trochaic te-trameter, which was originally employed when the poetry was of the satyric order, and had greater affinities with dancing. Once dialogue had come in, Nature herself discovered the appropriate measure. For the iambic is, of all measures, the most colloquial: we see it in the fact that conversational speech runs into iambic lines more frequently than into any other kind of verse; rarely into hexameters, and only when we drop the colloquial intonation. The additions to the number of "episodes" or acts, and the other accessories of which tradition tells, must be taken as already described; for to discuss them in detail would, doubtless, be a large undertaking.

Comedy is, as we have said, an imitation of characters of a lower type,—not, however, in the full sense of the word bad, the Ludicrous being merely a subdivision of the ugly. It consists in some defect or ugliness which is not painful or destructive. To take an obvious example, the comic mask is ugly and distorted, but does not imply pain.

The successive changes through which Tragedy passed, and the authors of these changes, are well known, whereas Comedy has had no history, because it was not at first treated seriously. It was late before the Archon granted a comic chorus to a poet; the performers were till then voluntary. Comedy had already taken definite shape when comic poets, distinctively so called, are heard of. Who furnished it with masks, or prologues, or increased the number of actors,—these and other similar details remain unknown. As for the plot, it came originally from Sicily; but of Athenian writers Crates was the first who, abandoning the "iambic" or lampooning form, generalised his themes and plots.

Epic poetry agrees with Tragedy in so far as it is an imitation in verse of characters of a higher type. They differ, in that Epic poetry admits but one kind of metre, and is narrative in form. They differ, again, in their length: for Tragedy endeavours, as far as possible, to confine itself to a single revolution of the sun, or but slightly to exceed this limit; whereas the Epic action has no limits of time. This, then, is a second point of difference; though at first the same freedom was admitted in Tragedy as in Epic poetry.

Of their constituent parts some are common to both, some peculiar to Tragedy: whoever, therefore, knows what is good or bad Tragedy, knows also about Epic poetry. All the elements of an Epic poem are found in Tragedy, but the elements of a Tragedy are not all found in the Epic poem.

Of the poetry which imitates in hexameter verse, and of Comedy, we will speak hereafter. Let us now discuss Tragedy, resuming its formal definition, as resulting from what has been already said.

Tragedy, then, is an imitation of an action that is serious, complete, and of a certain magnitude; in language embellished with each kind of artistic ornament, the several kinds being found in separate parts of the play; in the form of action, not of narrative; through pity and fear effecting the proper purgation of these emotions. By "language embellished," I mean language into which rhythm, "harmony," and song enter. By "the several kinds in separate parts," I mean, that some parts are rendered through the medium of verse alone, others again with the aid of song.

Now as tragic imitation implies persons acting, it necessarily follows, in the first place, that Spectacular equipment will be a part of Tragedy. Next, Song and Diction, for these are the medium of imitation. By "Diction" I mean the mere metrical arrangement of the words: as for "Song," it is a term whose sense every one understands.

Again, Tragedy is the imitation of an action; and an action implies personal agents, who necessarily possess certain distinctive qualities both of character and thought; for it is by these that we qualify actions themselves, and these— thought and character—are the two natural causes from which actions spring, and on actions again all success or failure depends. Hence, the Plot is the imitation of the action:—for by plot I here mean the arrangement of the incidents. By Character I mean that in virtue of which we ascribe certain qualities to the agents. Thought is required wherever a statement is proved, or, it may be, a general truth enunciated. Every Tragedy, therefore, must have six parts, which parts determine its quality—namely, Plot, Character, Diction, Thought, Spectacle, Song. Two of the parts constitute the medium of imitation, one the manner, and three the objects of imitation. And these complete the list. These elements have been employed, we may say, by the poets to a man; in fact, every play contains Spectacular elements as well as Character, Plot, Diction, Song, and Thought.

But most important of all is the structure of the incidents. For Tragedy is an imitation, not of men, but of an action and of life, and life consists in action, and its end is a mode of action, not a quality. Now character determines men's qualities, but it is by their actions that they are happy or the reverse. Dramatic action, therefore, is not with a view to the representation of character: character comes in as subsidiary to the actions. Hence the incidents and the plot are the end of a tragedy; and the end is the chief thing of all. Again, without action there cannot be a tragedy; there may be without character. The tragedies of most of our modern poets fail in the rendering of character; and of poets in general this is often true. It is the same in painting; and here lies the difference between Zeuxis and Polygnotus. Polygnotus delineates character well: the style of Zeuxis is devoid of ethical quality. Again, if you string together a set of speeches expressive of character, and well finished in point of diction and thought, you will not produce the essential tragic effect nearly so well as with a play which, however deficient in these respects, yet has a plot and artistically constructed incidents. Besides which, the most powerful elements of emotional interest in Tragedy—Peripeteia or Reversal of the Situation, and Recognition scenes—are parts of the plot. A further proof is, that novices in the art attain to finish of diction and precision of portraiture before they can construct the plot. It is the same with almost all the early poets.

The Plot, then, is the first principle, and, as it were, the soul of a tragedy: Character holds the second place. A similar fact is seen in painting. The most beautiful colours, laid on confusedly, will not give as much pleasure as the chalk outline of a portrait. Thus Tragedy is the imitation of an action, and of the agents mainly with a view to the action.

Third in order is Thought,—that is, the faculty of saying what is possible and pertinent in given circumstances. In the case of oratory, this is the function of the political art and of the art of rhetoric: and so indeed the older poets make their characters speak the language of civic life; the poets of our time, the language of the rhetoricians. Character is that which reveals moral purpose, showing what kind of things a man chooses or avoids. Speeches, therefore, which do not make this manifest, or in which the speaker does not choose or avoid anything whatever, are not expressive of character. Thought, on the other hand, is found where something is proved to be or not to be, or a general maxim is enunciated.

Fourth among the elements enumerated comes Diction; by which I mean, as has been already said, the expression of the meaning in words; and its essence is the same both in verse and prose.

Of the remaining elements Song holds the chief place among the embellishments.

The Spectacle has, indeed, an emotional attraction of its own, but, of all the parts, it is the least artistic, and connected least with the art of poetry. For the power of Tragedy, we may be sure, is felt even apart from representation and actors. Besides, the production of spectacular effects depends more on the art of the stage machinist than on that of the poet.

These principles being established, let us now discuss the proper structure of the Plot, since this is the first and most important thing in Tragedy.

Now, according to our definition, Tragedy is an imitation of an action that is complete, and whole, and of a certain magnitude; for there may be a whole that is wanting in magnitude. A whole is that which has a beginning, a middle, and an end. A beginning is that which does not itself follow anything by causal necessity, but after which something naturally is or comes to be. An end, on the contrary, is that which itself naturally follows some other thing, either by necessity, or as a rule, but has nothing following it. A middle is that which follows something as some other thing follows it. A well constructed plot, therefore, must neither begin nor end at haphazard, but conform to these principles.

Again, a beautiful object, whether it be a living organism or any whole composed of parts, must not only have an orderly arrangement of parts, but must also be of a certain magnitude; for beauty depends on magnitude and order. Hence a very small animal organism cannot be beautiful; for the view of it is confused, the object being seen in an almost imperceptible moment of time. Nor, again, can one of vast size be beautiful; for as the eye cannot take it all in at once, the unity and sense of the whole is lost for the spectator; as for instance if there were one a thousand miles long. As, therefore, in the case of animate bodies and organisms a certain magnitude is necessary, and a magnitude which may be easily embraced in one view; so in the plot, a certain length is necessary, and a length which can be easily embraced by the memory. The limit of length in relation to dramatic competition and sensuous presentment, is no part of artistic theory. For had it been the rule for a hundred tragedies to compete together, the performance would have been regulated by the water-clock,—as indeed we are told was formerly done. But the limit as fixed by the nature of the drama itself is this: —the greater the length, the more beautiful will the piece be by reason of its size, provided that the whole be perspicuous. And to define the matter roughly, we may say that the proper magnitude is comprised within such limits, that the sequence of events, according to the law of probability or necessity, will admit of a change from bad fortune to good, or from good fortune to bad.

Unity of plot does not, as some persons think, consist in the unity of the hero. For infinitely various are the incidents in one man's life which cannot be reduced to unity; and so, too, there are many actions of one man out of which we cannot make one action. Hence the error, as it appears, of all poets who have composed a Heracleid, a Theseid, or other poems of the kind. They imagine that as Heracles was one man, the story of Heracles must also be a unity. But Homer, as in all else he is of surpassing merit, here too—whether from art or natural genius—seems to have happily discerned the truth. In composing the Odyssey he did not include all the adventures of Odysseus—such as his wound on Parnassus, or his feigned madness at the mustering of the host—incidents between which there was no necessary or probable connexion: but he made the Odyssey, and likewise the Iliad, to centre round an action that in our sense of the word is one. As therefore, in the other imitative arts, the imitation is one when the object imitated is one, so the plot, being an imitation of an action, must imitate one action and that a whole, the structural union of the parts being such that, if any one of them is displaced or removed, the whole will be disjointed and disturbed. For a thing whose presence or absence makes no visible difference, is not an organic part of the whole.

It is, moreover, evident from what has been said, that it is not the function of the poet to relate what has happened, but what may happen,—what is possible according to the law of probability or necessity. The poet and the historian differ not by writing in verse or in prose. The work of Herodotus might be put into verse, and it would still be a species of history, with metre no less than without it. The true difference is that one relates what has happened, the other what may happen. Poetry, therefore, is a more philosophical and a higher thing than history: for poetry tends to express the universal, history the particular. By the universal I mean how a person of a certain type will on occasion speak or act, according to the law of probability or necessity; and it is this universality at which poetry aims in the names she attaches to the personages. The particular is—for example—what Alcibiades did or suffered. In Comedy this is already apparent: for here the poet first constructs the plot on the lines of probability, and then inserts characteristic names;—unlike the lampooners who write about particular individuals. But tragedians still keep to real names, the reason being that what is possible is credible: what has not happened we do not at once feel sure to be possible: but what has happened is manifestly possible: otherwise it would not have happened. Still there are even some tragedies in which there are only one or two well known names, the rest being fictitious. In others, none are well known, —as in Agathon's Antheus, where incidents and names alike are fictitious, and yet they give none the less pleasure. We must not, therefore, at all costs keep to the received legends, which are the usual subjects of Tragedy. Indeed, it would be absurd to attempt it; for even subjects that are known are known only to a few, and yet give pleasure to all. It clearly follows that the poet or "maker" should be the maker of plots rather than of verses; since he is a poet because he imitates, and what he imitates are actions. And even if he chances to take an historical subject, he is none the less a poet; for there is no reason why some events that have actually happened should not conform to the law of the probable and possible, and in virtue of that quality in them he is their poet or maker.

Of all plots and actions the epeisodic are the worst. I call a plot "epeisodic" in which the episodes or acts succeed one another without probable or necessary sequence. Bad poets compose such pieces by their own fault, good poets, to please the players; for, as they write show pieces for competition, they stretch the plot beyond its capacity, and are often forced to break the natural continuity.

But again, Tragedy is an imitation not only of a complete action, but of events inspiring fear or pity. Such an effect is best produced when the events come on us by surprise; and the effect is heightened when, at the same time, they follow as cause and effect. The tragic wonder will then be greater than if they happened of themselves or by accident; for even coincidences are most striking when they have an air of design. We may instance the statue of Mitys at Argos, which fell upon his murderer while he was a spectator at a festival, and killed him. Such events seem not to be due to mere chance. Plots, therefore, constructed on these principles are necessarily the best.

Plots are either Simple or Complex, for the actions in real life, of which the plots are an imitation, obviously show a similar distinction. An action which is one and continuous in the sense above defined, I call Simple, when the change of fortune takes place without Reversal of the Situation and without Recognition.

A Complex action is one in which the change is accompanied by such Reversal, or by Recognition, or by both. These last should arise from the internal structure of the plot, so that what follows should be the necessary or probable result of the preceding action. It makes all the difference whether any given event is a case of *propter hoc* or *post hoc*.

Reversal of the Situation is a change by which the action veers round to its opposite, subject always to our rule of probability or necessity. Thus in the Oedipus, the messenger comes to cheer Oedipus and free him from his alarms about his mother, but by revealing who he is, he produces the opposite effect. Again in the Lynceus, Lynceus is being led away to his death, and Danaus goes with him, meaning to slay him; but the outcome of the preceding incidents is that Danaus is killed and Lynceus saved.

Recognition, as the name indicates, is a change from ignorance to knowledge, producing love or hate between the persons destined by the poet for good or bad fortune. The best form of recognition is coincident with a Reversal of the Situation, as in the Oedipus. There are indeed other forms. Even inanimate things of the most trivial kind may in a sense be objects of recognition. Again, we may recognise or discover whether a person has done a thing or not. But the recognition which is most intimately connected with the plot and action is, as we have said, the recognition of persons. This recognition, combined with Reversal, will produce either pity or fear; and actions producing these effects are those which, by our definition, Tragedy represents. Moreover, it is upon such situations that the issues of good or bad fortune will depend. Recognition, then, being between persons, it may happen that one person only is recognised by the other—when the latter is already known —or it may be necessary that the recognition should be on both sides. Thus Iphigenia is revealed to Orestes by the sending of the letter; but another act of recognition is required to makes Orestes known to Iphigenia.

Two parts, then, of the Plot—Reversal of the Situation and Recognition—turn upon surprises. A third part is the Scene of Suffering. The Scene of Suffering is a destructive or painful action, such as death on the stage, bodily agony, wounds and the like.

[The parts of Tragedy which must be treated as elements of the whole have been already mentioned. We now come to the quantitative parts—the separate parts into which Tragedy is divided— namely, Prologue, Episode, Exode, Choric song; this last being divided into Parode and Stasimon. These are common to all plays: peculiar to some are the songs of actors from the stage and the Commoi.

The Prologue is that entire part of a tragedy which precedes the Parode of the Chorus. The Episode is that entire part of a tragedy which is between complete choric songs. The Exode is that entire part of a tragedy which has no choric song after it. Of the Choric part the Parode is the first undivided utterance of the Chorus: the Stasimon is a Choric ode without anapaests or trochaic tetrameters: the Commos is a joint lamentation of Chorus and actors. The parts of Tragedy which must be treated as elements of the whole have been already mentioned. The quantitative parts—the separate parts into which it is divided— are here enumerated.]

As the sequel to what has already been said, we must proceed to consider what the poet should aim at, and what he should avoid, in constructing his plots; and by what means the specific effect of Tragedy will be produced.

A perfect tragedy should, as we have seen, be arranged not on the simple but on the complex plan. It should, moreover, imitate actions which excite pity and fear, this being the distinctive mark of tragic imitation. It follows plainly, in the first place, that the change of fortune presented must not be the spectacle of a virtuous man brought from prosperity to adversity: for this moves neither pity nor fear; it merely shocks us. Nor, again, that of a bad man passing from adversity to prosperity: for nothing can be more alien to the spirit of Tragedy; it possesses no single tragic quality; it neither satisfies the moral sense nor calls forth pity or fear. Nor, again, should the downfall of the utter villain be exhibited. A plot of this kind would, doubtless, satisfy the moral sense, but it would inspire neither pity nor fear; for pity is aroused by un-merited misfortune, fear by the misfortune of a man like ourselves. Such an event, therefore, will be neither pitiful nor terrible. There remains, then, the character between these two extremes,—that of a man who is not eminently good and just, yet whose misfortune is brought about not by vice or depravity, but by some error or frailty. He must be one who is highly renowned and prosperous,—a personage like Oedipus, Thyestes, or other illustrious men of such families.

A well constructed plot should, therefore, be single in its issue, rather than double as some maintain. The change of fortune should be not from bad to good, but, reversely, from good to bad. It should come about as the result not of vice, but of some great error or frailty, in a character either such as we have described, or better rather than worse. The practice of the stage bears out our view. At first the poets recounted any legend that came in their way. Now, the best tragedies are founded on the story of a few houses,—on the fortunes of Alcmaeon, Oedipus, Orestes, Meleager, Thyestes, Telephus, and those others who have done or suffered something terrible. A tragedy, then, to be perfect according to the rules of art should be of this construction. Hence they are in error who censure Euripides just because he follows this principle in his plays, many of which end unhappily. It is, as we have said, the right ending. The best proof is that on the stage and in dramatic competition, such plays, if well worked out, are the most tragic in effect; and Euripides, faulty though he may be in the general management of his subject, yet is felt to be the most tragic of the poets.

In the second rank comes the kind of tragedy which some place first. Like the Odyssey, it has a double thread of plot, and also an opposite catastrophe for the good and for the bad. It is accounted the best because of the weakness of the spectators; for the poet is guided in what he writes by the wishes of his audience. The pleasure, however, thence derived is not the true tragic pleasure. It is proper rather to Comedy, where those who, in the piece, are the deadliest enemies—like Orestes and Aegisthus—quit the stage as friends at the close, and no one slays or is slain.

Fear and pity may be aroused by spectacular means; but they may also result from the inner structure of the piece, which is the better way, and indicates a superior poet. For the plot ought to be so constructed that, even without the aid of the eye, he who hears the tale told will thrill with horror and melt to pity at what takes place. This is the impression we should receive from hearing the story of the Oedipus. But to produce this effect by the mere spectacle is a less artistic method, and dependent on extraneous aids. Those who employ spectacular means to create a sense not of the terrible but only of the monstrous, are strangers to the purpose of Tragedy; for we must not demand of Tragedy any and every kind of pleasure, but only that which is proper to it. And since the pleasure which the poet should afford is that which comes from pity and fear through imitation, it is evident that this quality must be impressed upon the incidents.

Let us then determine what are the circumstances which strike us as terrible or pitiful.

Actions capable of this effect must happen between persons who are either friends or enemies or indifferent to one another. If an enemy kills an enemy, there is nothing to excite pity either in the act or the intention,—except so far as the suffering in itself is pitiful. So again with indifferent persons. But when the tragic incident occurs between those who are near or dear to one another—if, for example, a brother kills, or intends to kill, a brother, a son his father, a mother her son, a son his mother, or any other deed of the kind is done—these are the situations to be looked for by the poet. He may not indeed destroy the framework of the received legends—the fact, for instance, that Clytemnestra was slain by Orestes and Eriphyle by Alcmaeon—but he ought to show invention of his own, and skilfully handle the traditional material. Let us explain more clearly what is meant by skilful handling.

The action may be done consciously and with knowledge of the persons, in the manner of the older poets. It is thus too that Euripides makes Medea slay her children. Or, again, the deed of horror may be done, but done in ignorance, and the tie of kinship or friendship be discovered afterwards. The Oedipus of Sophocles is an example. Here, indeed, the incident is outside the drama proper; but cases occur where it falls within the action of the play: one may cite the Alcmaeon of Astydamas, or Telegonus in the Wounded Odysseus. Again, there is a third case,— < to be about to act with knowledge of the persons and then not to act. The fourth case is > when some one is about to do an irreparable deed through ignorance, and makes the discovery before it is done. These are the only possible ways. For the deed must either be done or not done,—and that wittingly or unwittingly. But of all these ways, to be about to act knowing the persons, and then not to act, is the worst. It is shocking without being tragic, for no disaster follows. It is, therefore, never, or very rarely, found in poetry. One instance, however, is in the Antigone, where Haemon threatens to kill Creon. The next and better way is that the deed should be perpetrated. Still better, that it should be perpetrated in ignorance,

and the discovery made afterwards. There is then nothing to shock us, while the discovery produces a startling effect. The last case is the best, as when in the Cresphontes Merope is about to slay her son, but, recognising who he is, spares his life. So in the Iphigenia, the sister recognises the brother just in time. Again in the Helle, the son recognises the mother when on the point of giving her up. This, then, is why a few families only, as has been already observed, furnish the subjects of tragedy. It was not art, but happy chance, that led the poets in search of subjects to impress the tragic quality upon their plots. They are compelled, therefore, to have recourse to those houses whose history contains moving incidents like these.

Enough has now been said concerning the structure of the incidents, and the right kind of plot.

In respect of Character there are four things to be aimed at. First, and most important, it must be good. Now any speech or action that manifests moral purpose of any kind will be expressive of character: the character will be good if the purpose is good. This rule is relative to each class. Even a woman may be good, and also a slave; though the woman may be said to be an inferior being, and the slave quite worthless. The second thing to aim at is propriety. There is a type of manly valour; but valour in a woman, or unscrupulous cleverness, is inappropriate. Thirdly, character must be true to life: for this is a distinct thing from goodness and propriety, as here described. The fourth point is consistency: for though the subject of the imitation, who suggested the type, be inconsistent, still he must be consistently inconsistent. As an example of motiveless degradation of character, we have Menelaus in the Orestes: of character indecorous and inappropriate, the lament of Odysseus in the Scylla, and the speech of Melanippe: of inconsistency, the Iphigenia at Aulis,—for Iphigenia the suppliant in no way resembles her later self.

As in the structure of the plot, so too in the portraiture of character, the poet should always aim either at the necessary or the probable. Thus a person of a given character should speak or act in a given way, by the rule either of necessity or of probability; just as this event should follow that by necessary or probable sequence. It is therefore evident that the unravelling of the plot, no less than the complication, must arise out of the plot itself, it must not be brought about by the *Deus ex Machina*—as in the Medea, or in the Return of the Greeks in the Iliad. The *Deus ex Machina* should be employed only for events external to the drama,—for antecedent or subsequent events, which lie beyond the range of human knowledge, and which require to be reported or foretold; for to the gods we ascribe the power of seeing all things. Within the action there must be nothing irrational. If the irrational cannot be excluded, it should be outside the scope of the tragedy. Such is the irrational element in the Oedipus of Sophocles.

Again, since Tragedy is an imitation of persons who are above the common level, the example of good portrait-painters should be followed. They, while reproducing the distinctive form of the original, make a likeness which is true to life and yet more beautiful. So too the poet, in representing men who are irascible or indolent, or have other defects of character, should preserve the type and yet ennoble it. In this way Achilles is portrayed by Agathon and Homer.

These then are rules the poet should observe. Nor should he neglect those appeals to the senses, which, though not among the essentials, are the concomitants of poetry; for here too there is much room for error. But of this enough has been said in our published treatises.

What Recognition is has been already explained. We will now enumerate its kinds.

First, the least artistic form, which, from poverty of wit, is most commonly employed—recognition by signs. Of these some are congenital,—such as "the spear which the earth-born race bear on their bodies," or the stars introduced by Carcinus in his Thyestes. Others are acquired after birth; and of these some are bodily marks, as scars; some external tokens, as necklaces or the little ark in the Tyro by which the discovery is effected. Even these admit of more or less skilful treatment. Thus in the recognition of Odysseus by his scar, the discovery is made in one way by the nurse, in another by the swineherds. The use of tokens for the express purpose of proof—and, indeed, any formal proof with or without tokens —is a less artistic mode of recognition. A better kind is that which comes about by a turn of incident, as in the Bath Scene in the Odyssey.

Next come the recognitions invented at will by the poet, and on that account wanting in art. For example, Orestes in the Iphigenia reveals the fact that he is Orestes. She, indeed, makes herself known by the letter; but he, by speaking himself, and saying what the poet, not what the plot requires. This, therefore, is nearly allied to the fault above mentioned:—for Orestes might as well have brought tokens with him. Another similar instance is the "voice of the shuttle" in the Tereus of Sophocles.

The third kind depends on memory when the sight of some object awakens a feeling: as in the Cyprians of Dicaeogenes, where the hero breaks into tears on seeing the picture; or again in the "Lay of Alcinous," where Odysseus, hearing the minstrel play the lyre, recalls the past and weeps; and hence the recognition.

The fourth kind is by process of reasoning. Thus in the Choëphori:—"Some one resembling me has come: no one resembles me but Orestes: therefore Orestes has come." Such too is the discovery made by Iphigenia in the play of Polyidus the Sophist. It was a natural reflexion for Orestes to make, "So I too must die at the altar like my sister." So, again, in the Tydeus of Theodectes, the father says, "I came to find my son, and I lose my own life." So too in the Phineidae: the women, on seeing the place, inferred their fate:—"Here we are doomed to die, for here we were cast forth." Again, there is a composite kind of recognition involving false inference on the part of one of the characters, as in the Odysseus Disguised as a Messenger. A said < that no one else was able to bend the bow; . . . hence B (the disguised Odysseus) imagined that A would > recognise the bow which, in fact, he had not seen; and to bring about a recognition by this means—the expectation that A would recognise the bow—is false inference.

But, of all recognitions, the best is that which arises from the incidents themselves, where the startling discovery is made by natural means. Such is that in the Oedipus of Sophocles, and in the Iphigenia; for it was natural that Iphigenia should wish to dispatch a letter. These recognitions alone dispense with the artificial aid of tokens or amulets. Next come the recognitions by process of reasoning.

In constructing the plot and working it out with the proper diction, the poet should place the scene, as far as possible, before his eyes. In this way, seeing everything with the utmost vividness, as if he were a spectator of the action, he will discover what is in keeping with it, and be most unlikely to overlook inconsistencies. The need of such a rule is shown by the fault found in Carcinus. Amphiaraus was on his way from the temple. This fact escaped the observation of one who did not see the situation. On the stage, however, the piece failed, the audience being offended at the oversight.

Again, the poet should work out his play, to the best of his power, with appropriate gestures; for those who feel emotion are most convincing through natural sympathy with the characters they represent; and one who is agitated storms, one who is angry rages, with the most lifelike reality. Hence poetry implies either a happy gift of nature or a strain of madness. In the one case a man can take the mould of any character; in the other, he is lifted out of his proper self.

As for the story, whether the poet takes it ready made or constructs it for himself, he should first sketch its general outline, and then fill in the episodes and amplify in detail. The general plan may be illustrated by the Iphigenia. A young girl is sacrificed; she disappears mysteriously from the eyes of those who sacrificed her; she is transported to another country, where the custom is to offer up all strangers to the goddess. To this ministry she is appointed. Some time later her own brother chances to arrive. The fact that the oracle for some reason ordered him to go there, is outside the general plan of the play. The purpose, again, of his coming is outside the action proper. However, he comes, he is seized, and, when on the point of being sacrificed, reveals who he is. The mode of recognition may be either that of Euripides or of Polyidus, in whose play he exclaims very naturally:—"So it was not my sister only, but I too, who was doomed to be sacrificed"; and by that remark he is saved.

After this, the names being once given, it remains to fill in the episodes. We must see that they are relevant to the action. In the case of Orestes, for example, there is the madness which led to his capture, and his deliverance by means of the purificatory rite. In the drama, the episodes are short, but it is these that give extension to Epic poetry. Thus the story of the Odyssey can be stated briefly. A certain man is absent from home for many years; he is jealously watched by Poseidon, and left desolate. Meanwhile his home is in a wretched plight—suitors are wasting his substance and plotting against his son. At length, tempest-tost, he himself arrives; he makes certain persons acquainted with him; he attacks the suitors with his own hand, and is himself preserved while he destroys them. This is the essence of the plot; the rest is episode.

Every tragedy falls into two parts,—Complication and Unravelling or *Dénouement*. Incidents extraneous to the action are frequently combined with a portion of the action proper, to form the Complication; the rest is the Unravelling. By the Complication I mean all that extends from the beginning of the action to the part which marks the turning-point to good or bad fortune. The Unravelling is that which extends from the beginning of the change to the end. Thus, in the Lynceus of Theodectes, the Complication consists of the incidents presupposed in the drama, the seizure of the child, and then again < The Unravelling > extends from the accusation of murder to the end.

There are four kinds of Tragedy, the Complex, depending entirely on Reversal of the Situation and Recognition; the Pathetic (where the motive is passion), —such as the tragedies on Ajax and Ixion; the Ethical (where the motives are ethical),—such as the Phthiotides and

the Peleus. The fourth kind is the Simple. < We here exclude the purely spectacular element >, exemplified by the Phorcides, the Prometheus, and scenes laid in Hades. The poet should endeavour, if possible, to combine all poetic elements; or failing that, the greatest number and those the most important; the more so, in face of the cavilling criticism of the day. For whereas there have hitherto been good poets, each in his own branch, the critics now expect one man to surpass all others in their several lines of excellence.

In speaking of a tragedy as the same or different, the best test to take is the plot. Identity exists where the Complication and Unravelling are the same. Many poets tie the knot well, but unravel it ill. Both arts, however, should always be mastered.

Again, the poet should remember what has been often said, and not make an Epic structure into a Tragedy—by an Epic structure I mean one with a multiplicity of plots—as if, for instance, you were to make a tragedy out of the entire story of the Iliad. In the Epic poem, owing to its length, each part assumes its proper magnitude. In the drama the result is far from answering to the poet's expectation. The proof is that the poets who have dramatised the whole story of the Fall of Troy, instead of selecting portions, like Euripides; or who have taken the whole tale of Niobe, and not a part of her story, like Aeschylus, either fail utterly or meet with poor success on the stage. Even Agathon has been known to fail from this one defect. In his Reversals of the Situation, however, he shows a marvellous skill in the effort to hit the popular taste,—to produce a tragic effect that satisfies the moral sense. This effect is produced when the clever rogue, like Sisyphus, is outwitted, or the brave villain defeated. Such an event is probable in Agathon's sense of the word: "it is probable," he says, "that many things should happen contrary to probability."

The Chorus too should be regarded as one of the actors; it should be an integral part of the whole, and share in the action, in the manner not of Euripides but of Sophocles. As for the later poets, their choral songs pertain as little to the subject of the piece as to that of any other tragedy. They are, therefore, sung as mere interludes,—a practice first begun by Agathon. Yet what difference is there between introducing such choral interludes, and transferring a speech, or even a whole act, from one play to another?

It remains to speak of Diction and Thought, the other parts of Tragedy having been already discussed. Concerning Thought, we may assume what is said in the Rhetoric, to which inquiry the subject more strictly belongs. Under Thought is included every effect which has to be produced by speech, the subdivisions being,—proof and refutation; the excitation of the feelings, such as pity, fear, anger, and the like; the suggestion of importance or its opposite. Now, it is evident that the dramatic incidents must be treated from the same points of view as the dramatic speeches, when the object is to evoke the sense of pity, fear, importance, or probability. The only difference is, that the incidents should speak for themselves without verbal exposition; while the effects aimed at in speech should be produced by the speaker, and as a result of the speech. For what were the business of a speaker, if the Thought were revealed quite apart from what he says? ...

Metaphor is the application of an alien name by transference either from genus to species, or from species to genus, or from species to species, or by analogy, that is, proportion. Thus from genus to

species, as: "There lies my ship"; for lying at anchor is a species of lying. From species to genus, as: "Verily ten thousand noble deeds hath Odysseus wrought"; for ten thousand is a species of large number, and is here used for a large number generally. From species to species, as: "With blade of bronze drew away the life," and "Cleft the water with the vessel of unyielding bronze." Here ἀρύσαι, "to draw away," is used for ταμεῖν, "to cleave," and ταμεῖν again for ἀρύσαι,—each being a species of taking away. Analogy or proportion is when the second term is to the first as the fourth to the third. We may then use the fourth for the second, or the second for the fourth. Sometimes too we qualify the metaphor by adding the term to which the proper word is relative. Thus the cup is to Dionysus as the shield to Ares. The cup may, therefore, be called "the shield of Dionysus," and the shield "the cup of Ares." Or, again, as old age is to life, so is evening to day. Evening may therefore be called "the old age of the day," and old age, "the evening of life," or, in the phrase of Empedocles, "life's setting sun." For some of the terms of the proportion there is at times no word in existence; still the metaphor may be used. For instance, to scatter seed is called sowing: but the action of the sun in scattering his rays is nameless. Still this process bears to the sun the same relation as sowing to the seed. Hence the expression of the poet "sowing the god-created light." There is another way in which this kind of metaphor may be employed. We may apply an alien term, and then deny of that term one of its proper attributes; as if we were to call the shield, not "the cup of Ares," but "the wineless cup." ...

As to that poetic imitation which is narrative in form and employs a single metre, the plot manifestly ought, as in a tragedy, to be constructed on dramatic principles. It should have for its subject a single action, whole and complete, with a beginning, a middle, and an end. It will thus resemble a living organism in all its unity, and produce the pleasure proper to it. It will differ in structure from historical compositions, which of necessity present not a single action, but a single period, and all that happened within that period to one person or to many, little connected together as the events may be. For as the sea-fight at Salamis and the battle with the Carthaginians in Sicily took place at the same time, but did not tend to any one result, so in the sequence of events, one thing sometimes follows another, and yet no single result is thereby produced. Such is the practice, we may say, of most poets. Here again, then, as has been already observed, the transcendent excellence of Homer is manifest. He never attempts to make the whole war of Troy the subject of his poem, though that war had a beginning and an end. It would have been too vast a theme, and not easily embraced in a single view. If, again, he had kept it within moderate limits, it must have been over-complicated by the variety of the incidents. As it is, he detaches a single portion, and admits as episodes many events from the general story of the war—such as the Catalogue of the ships and others—thus diversifying the poem. All other poets take a single hero, a single period, or an action single indeed, but with a multiplicity of parts. Thus did the author of the Cypria and of the Little Iliad. For this reason the Iliad and the Odyssey each furnish the subject of one tragedy, or, at most, of two; while the Cypria supplies materials for many, and the Little Iliad for eight—the Award of the Arms, the Philoctetes, the Neoptolemus, the Eurypylus, the Mendicant Odysseus,

the Laconian Women, the Fall of Ilium, the Departure of the Fleet.

Again, Epic poetry must have as many kinds as Tragedy: it must be simple, or complex, or "ethical," or "pathetic." The parts also, with the exception of song and spectacle, are the same; for it requires Reversals of the Situation, Recognitions, and Scenes of Suffering. Moreover, the thoughts and the diction must be artistic. In all these respects Homer is our earliest and sufficient model. Indeed each of his poems has a twofold character. The Iliad is at once simple and "pathetic," and the Odyssey complex (for Recognition scenes run through it), and at the same time "ethical." Moreover, in diction and thought they are supreme.

Epic poetry differs from Tragedy in the scale on which it is constructed, and in its metre. As regards scale or length, we have already laid down an adequate limit:—the beginning and the end must be capable of being brought within a single view. This condition will be satisfied by poems on a smaller scale than the old epics, and answering in length to the group of tragedies presented at a single sitting.

Epic poetry has, however, a great—a special—capacity for enlarging its dimensions, and we can see the reason. In Tragedy we cannot imitate several lines of actions carried on at one and the same time; we must confine ourselves to the action on the stage and the part taken by the players. But in Epic poetry, owing to the narrative form, many events simultaneously transacted can be presented; and these, if relevant to the subject, add mass and dignity to the poem. The Epic has here an advantage, and one that conduces to grandeur of effect, to diverting the mind of the hearer, and relieving the story with varying episodes. For sameness of incident soon produces satiety, and makes tragedies fail on the stage.

As for the metre, the heroic measure has proved its fitness by the test of experience. If a narrative poem in any other metre or in many metres were now composed, it would be found incongruous. For of all measures the heroic is the stateliest and the most massive; and hence it most readily admits rare words and metaphors, which is another point in which the narrative form of imitation stands alone. On the other hand, the iambic and the trochaic tetrameter are stirring measures, the latter being akin to dancing, the former expressive of action. Still more absurd would it be to mix together different metres, as was done by Chaeremon. Hence no one has ever composed a poem on a great scale in any other than heroic verse. Nature herself, as we have said, teaches the choice of the proper measure.

Homer, admirable in all respects, has the special merit of being the only poet who rightly appreciates the part he should take himself. The poet should speak as little as possible in his own person, for it is not this that makes him an imitator. Other poets appear themselves upon the scene throughout, and imitate but little and rarely. Homer, after a few prefatory words, at once brings in a man, or woman, or other personage; none of them wanting in characteristic qualities, but each with a character of his own.

The element of the wonderful is required in Tragedy. The irrational, on which the wonderful depends for its chief effects, has wider scope in Epic poetry, because there the person acting is not seen. Thus, the pursuit of Hector would be ludicrous if placed upon the stage— the Greeks standing still and not joining in the pursuit, and Achilles waving them back. But in the Epic poem the absurdity passes unnoticed. Now the wonderful is

pleasing: as may be inferred from the fact that every one tells a story with some addition of his own, knowing that his hearers like it. It is Homer who has chiefly taught other poets the art of telling lies skilfully. The secret of it lies in a fallacy. For, assuming that if one thing is or becomes, a second is or becomes, men imagine that, if the second is, the first likewise is or becomes. But this is a false inference. Hence, where the first thing is untrue, it is quite unnecessary, provided the second be true, to add that the first is or has become. For the mind, knowing the second to be true, falsely infers the truth of the first. There is an example of this in the Bath Scene of the Odyssey.

Accordingly, the poet should prefer probable impossibilities to improbable possibilities. The tragic plot must not be composed of irrational parts. Everything irrational should, if possible, be excluded; or, at all events, it should lie outside the action of the play (as, in the Oedipus, the hero's ignorance as to the manner of Laius' death); not within the drama, —as in the Electra, the messenger's account of the Pythian games; or, as in the Mysians, the man who has come from Tegea to Mysia and is still speechless. The plea that otherwise the plot would have been ruined, is ridiculous; such a plot should not in the first instance be constructed. But once the irrational has been introduced and an air of likelihood imparted to it, we must accept it in spite of the absurdity. Take even the irrational incidents in the Odyssey, where Odysseus is left upon the shore of Ithaca. How intolerable even these might have been would be apparent if an inferior poet were to treat the subject. As it is, the absurdity is veiled by the poetic charm with which the poet invests it.

The diction should be elaborated in the pauses of the action, where there is no expression of character or thought. For, conversely, character and thought are merely obscured by a diction that is over brilliant.

With respect to critical difficulties and their solutions, the number and nature of the sources from which they may be drawn may be thus exhibited.

The poet being an imitator, like a painter or any other artist, must of necessity imitate one of three objects,—things as they were or are, things as they are said or thought to be, or things as they ought to be. The vehicle of expression is language,—either current terms or, it may be, rare words or metaphors. There are also many modifications of language, which we concede to the poets. Add to this, that the standard of correctness is not the same in poetry and politics, any more than in poetry and any other art. Within the art of poetry itself there are two kinds of faults,—those which touch its essence, and those which are accidental. If a poet has chosen to imitate something, <but has imitated it incorrectly> through want of capacity, the error is inherent in the poetry. But if the failure is due to a wrong choice—if he has represented a horse as throwing out both his off legs at once, or introduced technical inaccuracies in medicine, for example, or in any other art—the error is not essential to the poetry. These are the points of view from which we should consider and answer the objections raised by the critics.

First as to matters which concern the poet's own art. If he describes the impossible, he is guilty of an error; but the error may be justified, if the end of the art be thereby attained (the end being that already mentioned),—if, that is, the effect of this or any other part of the poem is thus rendered more striking. A case in point is the pursuit of Hector.

If, however, the end might have been as well, or better, attained without violating the special rules of the poetic art, the error is not justified: for every kind of error should, if possible, be avoided.

Again, does the error touch the essentials of the poetic art, or some accident of it? For example,—not to know that a hind has no horns is a less serious matter than to paint it inartistically.

Further, if it be objected that the description is not true to fact, the poet may perhaps reply,—"But the objects are as they ought to be": just as Sophocles said that he drew men as they ought to be; Euripides, as they are. In this way the objection may be met. If, however, the representation be of neither kind, the poet may answer,—"This is how men say the thing is." This applies to tales about the gods. It may well be that these stories are not higher than fact nor yet true to fact: they are, very possibly, what Xenophanes says of them. But anyhow, "this is what is said." Again, a description may be no better than the fact: "still, it was the fact"; as in the passage about the arms: "Upright upon their butt-ends stood the spears." This was the custom then, as it now is among the Illyrians.

Again, in examining whether what has been said or done by some one is poetically right or not, we must not look merely to the particular act or saying, and ask whether it is poetically good or bad. We must also consider by whom it is said or done, to whom, when, by what means, or for what end; whether, for instance, it be to secure a greater good, or avert a greater evil. . . .

In general, the impossible must be justified by reference to artistic requirements, or to the higher reality, or to received opinion. With respect to the requirements of art, a probable impossibility is to be preferred to a thing improbable and yet possible. Again, it may be impossible that there should be men such as Zeuxis painted. "Yes," we say, "but the impossible is the higher thing; for the ideal type must surpass the reality." To justify the irrational, we appeal to what is commonly said to be. In addition to which, we urge that the irrational sometimes does not violate reason; just as "it is probable that a thing may happen contrary to probability."

Things that sound contradictory should be examined by the same rules as in dialectical refutation—whether the same thing is meant, in the same relation, and in the same sense. We should therefore solve the question by reference to what the poet says himself, or to what is tacitly assumed by a person of intelligence.

The element of the irrational, and, similarly, depravity of character, are justly censured when there is no inner necessity for introducing them. Such is the irrational element in the introduction of Aegeus by Euripides and the badness of Menelaus in the Orestes.

Thus, there are five sources from which critical objections are drawn. Things are censured either as impossible, or irrational, or morally hurtful, or contradictory, or contrary to artistic correctness. The answers should be sought under the twelve heads above mentioned.

The question may be raised whether the Epic or Tragic mode of imitation is the higher. If the more refined art is the higher, and the more refined in every case is that which appeals to the better sort of audience, the art which imitates anything and everything is manifestly most unrefined. The audience is supposed to be too dull to comprehend unless something of their own is thrown in by the performers, who therefore indulge in restless movements. Bad flute-players twist and twirl, if they have to represent "the quoit-throw," or hustle the coryphaeus when they perform the "Scylla."

Tragedy, it is said, has this same defect. We may compare the opinion that the older actors entertained of their successors. Mynniscus used to call Callippides "ape" on account of the extravagance of his action, and the same view was held of Pindarus. Tragic art, then, as a whole, stands to Epic in the same relation as the younger to the elder actors. So we are told that Epic poetry is addressed to a cultivated audience, who do not need gesture; Tragedy, to an inferior public. Being then unrefined, it is evidently the lower of the two.

Now, in the first place, this censure attaches not to the poetic but to the histrionic art; for gesticulation may be equally overdone in epic recitation, as by Sosistratus, or in lyrical competition, as by Mnasitheus the Opuntian. Next, all action is not to be condemned—any more than all dancing—but only that of bad performers. Such was the fault found in Callippides, as also in others of our own day, who are censured for representing degraded women. Again, Tragedy like Epic poetry produces its effect even without action; it reveals its power by mere reading. If, then, in all other respects it is superior, this fault, we say, is not inherent in it.

And superior it is, because it has all the epic elements—it may even use the epic metre—with the music and spectacular effects as important accessories; and these produce the most vivid of pleasures. Further, it has vividness of impression in reading as well as in representation. Moreover, the art attains its end within narrower limits; for the concentrated effect is more pleasurable than one which is spread over a long time and so diluted. What, for example, would be the effect of the Oedipus of Sophocles, if it were cast into a form as long as the Iliad? Once more, the Epic imitation has less unity; as is shown by this, that any Epic poem will furnish subjects for several tragedies. Thus if the story adopted by the poet has a strict unity, it must either be concisely told and appear truncated; or, if it conform to the Epic canon of length, it must seem weak and watery. <Such length implies some loss of unity,> if, I mean, the poem is constructed out of several actions, like the Iliad and the Odyssey, which have many such parts, each with a certain magnitude of its own. Yet these poems are as perfect as possible in structure; each is, in the highest degree attainable, an imitation of a single action.

If, then, Tragedy is superior to Epic poetry in all these respects, and moreover, fulfils its specific function better as an art—for each art ought to produce, not any chance pleasure, but the pleasure proper to it, as already stated—it plainly follows that Tragedy is the higher art, as attaining its end more perfectly.

Thus much may suffice concerning Tragic and Epic poetry in general; their several kinds and parts, with the number of each and their differences; the causes that make a poem good or bad; the objections of the critics and the answers to these objections.

HEGEL'S THEORY OF TRAGEDY
A. C. Bradley*

Hegel examines Greek tragedy and concludes that tragedy's essence is ethical conflict. Such conflicts occur between the determining forces of the will, like family duty and duty to the state, which are justified in themselves but which err in demanding individual priority. Reconciliation of these forces results when each is reduced to its proper proportion by the force of the "ethical totality." Bradley restates Hegel's theory to include modern tragedy—a conflict, expressed in the subjective terms of a central character, between two spiritual forces (both of which may be good in themselves) that are reconciled in the "violent self-restitution of the spiritual unity." The tragic quality stems from the spiritual waste in this self-restitution.

Since Aristotle dealt with tragedy, and, as usual drew the main features of his subject with those sure and simple strokes which no later hand has rivalled,

the only philosopher who has treated it in a manner both original and searching is Hegel.[1] I propose here to give a sketch of Hegel's theory, and to add some re-

---

* The essay is reprinted from Oxford Lectures on Poetry, by A. C. Bradley, by permission of Macmillan & Co., Ltd., and St. Martin's Press, Inc. Copyright 1909 by Macmillan & Co., Ltd.
[1] See, primarily, Aesthetik, iii. 479–581, and especially 525–581. There is much in Aesthetik, i. 219–306, and a good deal in ii. 1–243, that bears on the subject. See also the section on Greek religion in Religionsphilosophie, ii. 96–156, especially 131–6, 152–6; and the references to the death of Socrates in Geschichte

der Philosophie, ii. 81 ff., especially 102–5. The works so far cited all consist of posthumous redactions of lecture-notes. Among works published by Hegel himself, the early essay on "Naturrecht" (Werke, i. 386 ff.), and Phaenomenologie d. Geistes, 320–348, 527–542, deal with or bear on Greek tragedy. See also Rechtsphilosophie, 196, note. There is a note on Wallenstein in Werke, xvii. 411–4. These references are to the second edition of the works cited, where there are two editions.

marks upon it. But I cannot possibly do justice in a sketch to a theory which fills many pages of the *Aesthetik*; which I must tear from its connections with the author's general view of poetry, and with the rest of his philosophy;[2] and which I must try to exhibit as far as possible in the language of ordinary literature. To estimate this theory, therefore, from my sketch would be neither safe nor just— all the more because, in the interest of immediate clearness, I have not scrupled to insert without warning various remarks and illustrations for which Hegel is not responsible.

On certain characteristics of tragedy the briefest reminder will suffice. A large part of the nature of this form of drama is common to the drama in all its forms; and of this nothing need be said. It will be agreed, further, that in all tragedy there is some sort of collision or conflict —conflict of feelings, modes of thought, desires, wills, purposes; conflict of persons with one another, or with circumstances, or with themselves; one, several, or all of these kinds of conflict, as the case may be. Again, it may be taken for granted that a tragedy is a story of unhappiness or suffering, and excites such feelings as pity and fear. To this, if we followed the present usage of the term, we should add that the story of unhappiness must have an unhappy end; by which we mean in effect that the conflict must close with the death of one or more of the principal characters. But this usage of the word "tragedy" is comparatively recent; it leaves us without a name for many plays, in many languages, which deal with unhappiness without ending unhappily; and

2 His theory of tragedy is connected with his view of the function of negation in the universe. No statement therefore which ignores his metaphysics and his philosophy of religion can be more than a fragmentary account of that theory.

Hegel takes the word in its older and wiser sense.

Passing on from these admitted characteristics of tragedy, we may best approach Hegel's peculiar view by observing that he lays particular stress on one of them. That a tragedy is a story of suffering is probably to many people the most obvious fact about it. Hegel says very little of this; partly, perhaps, because it is obvious, but more because the essential point to him is not the suffering but its cause; namely, the action or conflict. Mere suffering, he would say, is not tragic, but only the suffering that comes of a special kind of action. Pity for mere misfortune, like fear of it, is not tragic pity or fear. These are due to the spectacle of the conflict and its attendant suffering, which do not appeal simply to our sensibilities or our instinct of self-preservation, but also to our deeper mind or spirit (*Geist*, a word which, with its adjective, I shall translate "spirit," "spiritual," because our words "mind" and "mental" suggest something merely intellectual).

The reason why the tragic conflict thus appeals to the spirit is that it is itself a conflict of the spirit. It is a conflict, that is to say, between powers that rule the world of man's will and action—his "ethical substance." The family and the state, the bond of parent and child, of brother and sister, of husband and wife, of citizen and ruler, or citizen and citizen, with the obligations and feelings appropriate to these bonds; and again the powers of personal love and honour, or of devotion to a great cause or an ideal interest like religion or science or some kind of social welfare—such are the forces exhibited in tragic action; not indeed alone, not without others less affirmative and perhaps even evil, but still in preponderating mass. And as they form the substance of man, are common to all civilised men, and are acknowledged as powers rightfully claiming human allegiance, their exhibition in tragedy has that interest, at once deep and universal, which is essential to a great work of art.

In many a work of art, in many a statue, picture, tale, or song, such powers are shown in solitary peace or harmonious co-operation. Tragedy shows them in collision. Their nature is divine, and in religion they appear as gods; but, as seen in the world of tragic action, they have left the repose of Olympus, have entered into human wills, and now meet as foes. And this spectacle, if sublime, is also terrible. The essentially tragic fact is the self-division and intestinal warfare of the ethical substance, not so much the war of good with evil as the war of good with good. Two of these isolated powers face each other, making incompatible demands. The family claims what the state refuses, love requires what honour forbids. The competing forces are both in themselves rightful, and so far the claim of each is equally justified; but the right of each is pushed into a wrong, because it ignores the right of the other, and demands that absolute sway which belongs to neither alone, but to the whole of which each is but a part.

And one reason why this happens lies in the nature of the characters through whom these claims are made. It is the nature of the tragic hero, at once his greatness and his doom, that he knows no shrinking or half-heartedness, but identifies himself wholly with the power that moves him, and will admit the justification of no other power. However varied and rich his inner life and character may be, in the conflict it is all concentrated in one point. Antigone *is* determination to do her duty to her dead brother; Romeo is not a son or a citizen as well as a lover, he is lover pure and

simple, and his love is the whole of him.

The end of the tragic conflict is the denial of both the exclusive claims. It is not the work of chance or blank fate; it is the act of the ethical substance itself, asserting its absoluteness against the excessive pretensions of its particular powers. In that sense, as proceeding from an absolute right which cancels claims based on right but pushed into wrong, it may be called the act of "eternal justice." Sometimes it can end the conflict peacefully, and the tragedy closes with a solution. Appearing as a divine being, the spiritual unity reconciles by some adjustment the claims of the contending powers (*Eumenides*); or at its bidding one of them softens its demand (*Philoctetes*); or again, as in the more beautiful solution of the *Oedipus Coloneus*, the hero by his own self-condemnation and inward purification reconciles himself with the supreme justice, and is accepted by it. But sometimes the quarrel is pressed to extremes; the denial of the one-sided claims involves the death of one or more of the persons concerned; and we have a catastrophe. The ultimate power thus appears as a destructive force. Yet even here, as Hegel insists, the end is not without an aspect of reconciliation. For that which is denied is not the rightful powers with which the combatants have identified themselves. On the contrary, those powers, and with them the only thing for which the combatants cared, are affirmed. What is denied is the exclusive and therefore wrongful assertion of their right.

Such in outline is Hegel's main view. It may be illustrated more fully by two examples, favourites of his, taken from Aeschylus and Sophocles. Clytemnestra has murdered Agamemnon, her husband and king. Orestes, their son, is impelled by filial piety to avenge his father, and is ordered by Apollo to do so. But to kill a mother is to sin against filial piety. The spiritual substance is divided against itself. The sacred bond of father and son demands what the equally sacred bond of son and mother forbids. When, therefore, Orestes has done the deed, the Furies of his murdered mother claim him for their prey. He appeals to Apollo, who resists their claim. A solution is arrived at without a catastrophe. The cause is referred to Athene, who institutes at Athens a court of sworn judges. The votes of this court being equally divided, Athene gives her casting-vote for Orestes; while the Furies are at last appeased by a promise of everlasting honour at Athens.

In the *Antigone*, on the other hand, to Hegel the "perfect exemplar of tragedy," the solution is negative. The brother of Antigone has brought against his native city an army of foreigners bent on destroying it. He has been killed in the battle, and Creon, the ruler of the city, has issued an edict forbidding anyone on pain of death to bury the corpse. In so doing he not only dishonours the dead man, but violates the rights of the gods of the dead. Antigone without hesitation disobeys the edict, and Creon, despite the remonstrance of his son, who is affianced to her, persists in exacting the penalty. Warned by the prophet Teiresias, he gives way, but too late. Antigone, immured in a rocky chamber to starve, has anticipated her death. Her lover follows her example, and his mother refuses to survive him. Thus Antigone has lost her life through her absolute assertion of the family against the state; Creon has violated the sanctity of the family, and in return sees his own home laid in ruins. But in this catastrophe neither the right of the family nor that of the state is denied; what is denied is the absoluteness of the claim of each.

The danger of illustrations like these is that they divert attention from the principle illustrated to questions about the interpretation of particular works. So it will be here. I cannot stay to discuss these questions, which do not affect Hegel's principle; but it will be well, before going further, to remove a misunderstanding of it which is generally to be found in criticisms of his treatment of the *Eumenides* and the *Antigone*. The main objection may be put thus: "Hegel talks of equally justified powers or claims. But Aeschylus never meant that Orestes and the Furies were equally justified; for Orestes was acquitted. Nor did Sophocles mean that Antigone and Creon were equally right. And how can it have been equally the duty of Orestes to kill his mother and not to kill her?" But, in the first place, it is most important to observe that Hegel is not discussing at all what we should generally call the moral quality of the acts and persons concerned, or, in the ordinary sense, what it was their duty to do. And, in the second place, when he speaks of "equally justified" powers, what he means, and, indeed, sometimes says, is that these powers are *in themselves* justified. The family and the state, the bond of father and son, the bond of mother and son, the bond of citizenship, these are each and all, one as much as another, powers rightfully claiming human allegiance. It is tragic that observance of one should involve the violation of another. These are Hegel's propositions, and surely they are true. Their truth is quite unaffected by the fact (assuming it is one) that in the circumstances the act combining this observance of one and violation of another was morally right, or by the fact (if so it is) that one such act (say Antigone's) was morally right, and another (say Creon's) was morally wrong. It is sufficient for Hegel's principle that the violation should take place, and that we should feel its weight. We do feel it. We may approve the act of Antigone or Orestes, but in approving it we still feel that it is no light matter to disobey the law or to murder a mother, that (as we might say) there is much justice in the pleas of the Furies and of Creon, and that the *tragic* effect depends upon these facts. If, again, it is objected that the underlying conflict in the *Antigone* is not between the family and the state, but between divine and human law, that objection, if sound, might touch Hegel's interpretation,[3] but it would not affect his principle, except for those who recognise no obligation in human law; and it will scarcely be contended that Sophocles is to be numbered among them. On the other hand, it is, I think, a matter for regret that Hegel employed such words as "right," "justified," and "justice." They do not mislead readers familiar with his writings, but to others they suggest associations with criminal law, or our everyday moral judgments, or perhaps the theory of "poetic justice"; and these are all out of place in a discussion on tragedy.

Having determined in outline the idea or principle of tragedy, Hegel proceeds to give an account of some differences between ancient and modern works. In the limited time at our disposal we shall do best to confine ourselves to a selection from his remarks on the latter. For in speaking of ancient tragedy Hegel, who finds something modern in Euripides, makes accordingly but little use of him for purposes of contrast, while his main point of view as to Aeschylus and Sophocles has already appeared in the illustrations we have given of the general principle. I will only add, by way of preface, that the pages about to be

[3] I say "might," because Hegel himself in the *Phaenomenologie* uses those very terms "divine" and "human law" in reference to the *Antigone.*

summarised leave on one, rightly or wrongly, the impression that to his mind the principle is more adequately realised in the best classical tragedies than in modern works. But the question whether this really was his deliberate opinion would detain us too long from weightier matters.

Hegel considers first the cases where modern tragedy resembles ancient in dealing with conflicts arising from the pursuit of ends which may be called substantial or objective and not merely personal. And he points out that modern tragedy here shows a much greater variety. Subjects are taken, for example, from the quarrels of dynasties, of rivals for the throne, of kings and nobles, of state and church. Calderon shows the conflict of love and honour regarded as powers imposing obligations. Schiller in his early works makes his characters defend the rights of nature against convention, or of freedom of thought against prescription—rights in their essence universal. Wallenstein aims at the unity and peace of Germany; Karl Moor attacks the whole arrangement of society; Faust seeks to attain in thought and action union with the Absolute. In such cases the end is more than personal; it represents a power claiming the allegiance of the individual; but, on the other hand, it does not always or generally represent a great *ethical* institution or bond like the family or the state. We have passed into a wider world.

But secondly, he observes, in regard to modern tragedy, that in a larger number of instances such public or universal interests either do not appear at all, or, if they appear, are scarcely more than a background for the real subject. The real subject, the impelling end or passion, and the ensuing conflict, is personal,— these particular characters with their struggle and their fate. The importance given to subjectivity—this is the distinctive mark of modern sentiment, and so of modern art; and such tragedies bear its impress. A part at least of Hegel's meaning may be illustrated thus. We are interested in the personality of Orestes or Antigone, but chiefly as it shows itself in one aspect, as identifying itself with a certain ethical relation; and our interest in the personality is inseparable and indistinguishable from our interest in the power it represents. This is not so with Hamlet, whose position so closely resembles that of Orestes. What engrosses our attention is the whole personality of Hamlet in his conflict, not with an opposing spiritual power, but with circumstances and, still more, with difficulties in his own nature. No one could think of describing Othello as the representative of an ethical family relation. His passion, however much nobility he may show in it, is personal. So is Romeo's love. It is not pursued, like Posa's freedom of thought, as something universal, a right of man. Its right, if it could occur to us to use the term at all, is Romeo's right.

On this main characteristic of modern tragedy others depend. For instance, that variety of subject to which reference has just been made depends on it. For when so much weight is attached to personality, almost any fatal collision in which a sufficiently striking character is involved may yield material for tragedy. Naturally, again, characterisation has become fuller and more subtle, except in dramas which are more or less an imitation of the antique. The characters in Greek tragedy are far from being types or personified abstractions, as those of classical French tragedy tend to be: they are genuine individuals. But still they are comparatively simple and easy to understand, and have not the intricacy of the characters in Shakespeare. These, for the most part,

represent simply themselves; and the loss of that interest which attached to the Greek characters from their identification with an ethical power, is compensated by an extraordinary subtlety in their portrayal, and also by their possession of some peculiar charm or some commanding superiority. Finally, the interest in personality explains the freedom with which characters more or less definitely evil are introduced in modern tragedy. Mephistopheles is as essentially modern as Faust. The passion of Richard or Macbeth is not only personal, like that of Othello; it is egoistic and anarchic, and leads to crimes done with a full knowledge of their wickedness; but to the modern mind the greatness of the personality justifies its appearance in the position of hero. Such beings as Iago and Goneril, almost portents of evil, are not indeed made the heroes of tragedies; but, according to Hegel, they would not have been admitted in Greek tragedy at all. If Clytemnestra had been cited in objection as a parallel to Lady Macbeth, he would have replied that Lady Macbeth had not the faintest ground of complaint against Duncan, while in reading the *Agamemnon* we are frequently reminded that Clytemnestra's husband was the sacrificer of their child. He might have added that Clytemnestra is herself an example of the necessity, where one of the principal characters inspires hatred or horror, of increasing the subtlety of the drawing or adding grandeur to the evil will.

It remains to compare ancient and modern tragedy in regard to the issue of the conflict. We have seen that Hegel attributes this issue in the former to the ethical substance or eternal justice, and so accounts for such reconciliation as we feel to be present even where the end is a catastrophe. Now, in the catastrophe of modern tragedy, he says, a certain justice is sometimes felt to be present; but even then it differs from the antique justice. It is in some cases more "abstract": the end pursued by the hero, though it is not egoistic, is still presented rather as his particular end than as something rightful though partial; and hence the catastrophe appears as the reaction, not of an undivided ethical totality, but merely of the universal turning against a too assertive particular.[4] In cases, again, where the hero (Richard or Macbeth) openly attacks an ethical power and plunges into evil, we feel that he meets with justice, and only gets what he deserves; but then this justice is colder and more "criminalistic" than that of ancient tragedy. Thus even when the modern work seems to resemble the ancient in its issue, the sense of reconciliation is imperfect. And partly for this reason, partly from the concentration of our interest on individuality as such, we desire to see in the individual himself some sort of reconciliation with his fate. What shape this will take depends, of course, on the story and the character of the hero. It may appear in a religious form, as his feeling that he is exchanging his earthly being for an indestructible happiness; or again, in his recognition of the justice of his fall; or at least he may show us that, in face of the forces that crush him to death, he maintains untouched the freedom and strength of his own will.

But there remain, says Hegel, many modern tragedies where we have to attribute the catastrophe not to any kind of justice, but to unhappy circumstances and outward accidents. And then we can only feel that the individual whose merely personal ends are thwarted by mere particular circumstances and chances, pays the penalty that awaits

existence in a scene of contingency and finitude. Such a feeling cannot rise above sadness, and, if the hero is a noble soul, it may become the impression of a dreadful external necessity. This impression can be avoided only when circumstance and accident are so depicted that they are felt to coincide with something in the hero himself, so that he is not simply destroyed by an outward force. So it is with Hamlet. "This bank and shoal of time" is too narrow for his soul, and the death that seems to fall on him by chance is also within him. And so in *Romeo and Juliet* we feel that the rose of a love so beautiful is too tender to bloom in the stormswept valley of its birth. But such a feeling of reconciliation is still one of pain, an unhappy blessedness.[5] And if the situation displayed in a drama is of such a kind that we feel the issue to depend *simply* on the turn the dramatist may choose to give to the course of events, we are fully justified in our preference for a happy ending.

In this last remark (or rather in the pages misrepresented by it) Hegel, of course, is not criticising Shakespeare. He is objecting to the destiny-dramas of his own time, and to the fashionable indulgence in sentimental melancholy. Strongly as he asserted the essential function of negation throughout the universe, the affirmative power of the spirit, even in its profoundest divisions, was for him the deepest truth and the most inspiring theme. And one may see this even in his references to Shakespeare. He appreciated Shakespeare's representation of extreme forms of evil, but, even if he was fully satisfied of its justification, his personal preference lay in another direction, and while I do not doubt that he thought

---

[4] This interpretation of Hegel's "abstract" is more or less conjectural and doubtful.

[5] Hegel's meaning does not fully appear in the sentences here condensed. The "blessedness" comes from the sense of the greatness or beauty in the characters.

Hamlet a greater work than *Iphigenie*, I suspect he loved Goethe's play the best.

Most of those who have thought about this subject will agree that the ideas I have tried to sketch are interesting and valuable; but they suggest scores of questions. Alike in the account of tragedy in general, and in that of the differences between ancient and modern tragedy, everyone will find statements to doubt and omissions to regret; and scarcely one of Hegel's interpretations of particular plays will escape objection. It is impossible for me to touch on more than a few points; and to the main ideas I owe so much that I am more inclined to dwell on their truth than to criticise what seem to be defects. But perhaps after all an attempt to supplement and amend may be the best way of throwing some part of Hegel's meaning more into relief. And I will begin with the attempt to supplement.

He seems to be right in laying emphasis on the action and conflict in tragedy rather than on the suffering and misfortune. No mere suffering or misfortune, no suffering that does not spring in great part from human agency, and in some degree from the agency of the sufferer, is tragic, however pitiful or dreadful it may be. But, sufficient connection with these agencies being present, misfortune, the fall from prosperity to adversity, with the suffering attending it, at once becomes tragic; and in many tragedies it forms a large ingredient, as does the pity for it in the tragic feeling. Hegel, I think, certainly takes too little notice of it; and by this omission he also withdraws attention from something the importance of which he would have admitted at once; I mean the way in which suffering is borne. Physical pain, to take an extreme instance, is one thing: Philoctetes, bearing it, is another. And the

noble endurance of pain that rends the heart is the source of much that is best worth having in tragedy.

Again, there is one particular kind of misfortune *not* obviously due to human agency, which undoubtedly may affect us in a tragic way. I mean that kind which suggests the idea of fate. Tragedies which represent man as the mere plaything of chance or a blank fate or a malicious fate, are never really deep: it is satisfactory to see that Maeterlinck, a man of true genius, has now risen above these ideas. But, where those factors of tragedy are present which Hegel emphasises, the impression of something fateful in what we call accident, the impression that the hero not only invites misfortune by his exceptional stature and exceptional daring, but is also, if I may so put it, strangely and terribly unlucky, is in many plays a genuine ingredient in tragic effect. It is so, for example, in the *Oedipus Tyrannus*. It is so even in dramas like Shakespeare's, which exemplify the saying that character is destiny. Hegel's own reference to the prominence of accident in the plot of *Hamlet* proves it. Othello would not have become Iago's victim if his own character had been different; but still, as we say, it is an extraordinary fatality which makes him the companion of the one man in the world who is at once able enough, brave enough, and vile enough to ensnare him. In the *Antigone* itself, and in the very catastrophe of it, accident plays its part; we can hardly say that it depends solely on the characters of Creon and Antigone that the one yields just too late to save the life of the other. Now, it may be said with truth that Hegel's whole account of the ultimate power in tragedy is a rationalisation of the idea of fate, but his remarks on this particular aspect of fate are neither sufficient nor satisfactory.

His insistence on the need for some

element of reconciliation in a tragic catastrophe, and his remarks on the various forms it assumes, have the greatest value; but one result of the omissions just noticed is that he sometimes exaggerates it, and at other times rates it too low. When he is speaking of the kind of tragedy he most approves, his language almost suggests that our feeling at the close of the conflict is, or should be, one of complete reconciliation. This it surely neither is nor can be. Not to mention the suffering and death we have witnessed, the very existence of the conflict, even if a supreme ethical power is felt to be asserted in its close, remains a painful fact, and, in large measure, a fact not understood. For, though we may be said to see, in one sense, how the opposition of spiritual powers arises, something in us, and that the best, still cries out against it. And even the perception or belief that it must needs be that offences come would not abolish our feeling that the necessity is terrible, or our pain in the woe of the guilty and the innocent. Nay, one may conjecture, the feeling and the pain would not vanish if we fully understood that the conflict and catastrophe were by a rational necessity involved in the divine and eternally accomplished purpose of the world. But this exaggeration in Hegel's language, if partly due to his enthusiasm for the affirmative, may be mainly, like some other defects, an accident or lecturing. In the *Philosophy of Religion*, I may add, he plainly states that in the solution even of tragedies like the *Antigone* something remains unresolved (ii, 135).

On the other hand, his treatment of the aspect of reconciliation in modern tragedy is in several respects insufficient. I will mention only one. He does not notice that in the conclusion of not a few tragedies pain is mingled not merely with acquiescence, but with something like exultation. Is there not such a feeling at the close of *Hamlet, Othello*, and *King Lear*; and that although the end in the last two cases touches the limit of legitimate pathos? This exultation appears to be connected with our sense that the hero has never shown himself so great or noble as in the death which seals his failure. A rush of passionate admiration, and a glory in the greatness of the soul, mingle with our grief; and the coming of death, so far from destroying these feelings, appears to leave them untouched, or even to be entirely in harmony with them. If in such dramas we may be said to feel that the ultimate power is no mere fate, but a spiritual power, then we also feel that the hero was never so near to this power as in the moment when it required his life.

The last omission I would notice in Hegel's theory is that he underrates the action in tragedy of what may be called by a rough distinction moral evil rather than defect. Certainly the part played by evil differs greatly in different cases, but it is never absent, not even from tragedies of Hegel's favourite type. If it does not appear in the main conflict, it appears in its occasion. You may say that, while Iago and Macbeth have evil purposes, neither the act of Orestes nor the vengeance of the Furies, neither Antigone's breach of the edict nor even Creon's insistence on her punishment, springs from evil in them; but the situation with which Orestes or Antigone has to deal, and so in a sense the whole tragedy, arises from evil, the murder of Agamemnon, and the attempt of Polyneices to bring ruin on his native city. In fact, if we confine the title "tragedy" to plays ending with a catastrophe, it will be found difficult to name great tragedies, ancient or modern, in which evil has not directly or indirectly a prominent part. And its presence has an important bearing on the effect produced by the catastrophe. On the one hand, it deepens the sense of painful awe. The question why affirmative spiritual forces should collide is hard enough; but the question why, together with them, there should be generated violent evil and extreme depravity is harder and more painful still. But, on the other hand, the element of reconciliation in the catastrophe is strengthened by recognition of the part played by evil in bringing it about; because our sense that the ultimate power cannot endure the presence of such evil is implicitly the sense that this power is at least more closely allied with good. If it rejects the exaggerated claims of its own isolated powers, that which provokes from it a much more vehement reaction must be still more alien to its nature. This feeling is forcibly evoked by Shakespeare's tragedies, and in many Greek dramas it is directly appealed to by repeated reminders that what is at work in the disasters is the unsleeping Ate which follows an ancestral sin. If Aristotle did not in some lost part of the *Poetics* discuss ideas like this, he failed to give a complete rationale of Greek tragedy.

I come lastly to the matter I have most at heart. What I take to be the central idea in Hegel's theory seems to me to touch the essence of tragedy. And I will not assert that his own statement of it fails to cover the whole field of instances. For he does not teach, as he is often said to do, that tragedy portrays only the conflict of such ethical powers as the family and the state. He adds to these, as we have seen, others, such as love and honour, together with various universal ends; and it may even be maintained that he has provided in his general statement for those numerous cases where, according to himself, no substantial or universal ends collide, but the interest is centered

on "personalities." Nevertheless, when these cases come to be considered more fully—and, in Hegel's view they are the most characteristically modern cases— we are not satisfied. They naturally tend to appear as declensions from the more ideal ancient form; for how can a personality which represents only itself claim the interest of one which represents something universal? And further, they are sometimes described in a manner which strikes the reader, let us say, of Shakespeare, as both insufficient and misleading. Without raising, then, unprofitable questions about the comparative merits of ancient and modern tragedy, I should like to propose a restatement of Hegel's general principle which would make it more obviously apply to both.

If we omit all reference to ethical or substantial powers and interests, what have we left? We have the more general idea—to use again a formula not Hegel's own—that tragedy portrays a self-division and self-waste of spirit, or a division of spirit involving conflict and waste. It is implied in this that on *both* sides in the conflict there is a spiritual value. The same idea may be expressed (again, I think, not in Hegel's own words) by saying that the tragic conflict is one not merely of good with evil, but also, and more essentially, of good with good. Only, in saying this, we must be careful to observe that "good" here means anything that has spiritual value, not moral goodness alone,[6] and that "evil" has a similarly wide sense.

Now this idea of a division of spirit involving conflict and waste covers the tragedies of ethical and other universal powers, and it covers much besides. According to it the collision of such powers would be one kind of tragic collision, but only one. *Why* are we tragically moved

[6] Hegel himself expressly guards against this misconception.

by the conflict of family and state? Because we set a high value on family and state. Why then should not the conflict of anything else that has sufficient value affect us tragically? It does. The value must be sufficient—a moderate value will not serve; and other characteristics must be present which need not be considered here. But, granted these conditions, *any* spiritual conflict involving spiritual waste is tragic. And it is just one greatness of modern art that it has shown the tragic fact in situations of so many and such diverse kinds. These situations have not the peculiar effectiveness of the conflicts preferred by Hegel, but they may have an equal effectiveness peculiar to themselves.

Let me attempt to test these ideas by choosing a most unfavourable instance—unfavourable because the play seems at first to represent a conflict simply of good and evil, and so, according both to Hegel's statement and the proposed restatement, to be no tragedy at all: I mean *Macbeth*. What is the conflict here? It will be agreed that it does not lie between two ethical powers or universal ends, and that, as Hegel says, the main interest is in personalities. Let us take it first, then, to lie between Macbeth and the persons opposing him, and let us ask whether there is not spiritual value or good on both sides—not an equal amount of good (that is not necessary), but enough good on each to give the impression of spiritual waste. Is there not such good in Macbeth? It is not a question merely of moral goodness, but of good. It is not a question of the use made of good, but of its presence. And such bravery and skill in war as win the enthusiasm of everyone about him; such an imagination as few but poets possess; a conscience so vivid that his deed is to him beforehand a thing of terror, and, once done, condemns him to that torture of the mind on which he

lies in restless ecstasy; a determination so tremendous and a courage so appalling that, for all this torment, he never dreams of turning back, but, even when he has found that life is a tale full of sound and fury, signifying nothing, will tell it out to the end though earth and heaven and hell are leagued against him; are not these things, in themselves, good, and gloriously good? Do they not make you, for all your horror, admire Macbeth, sympathise with his agony, pity him, and see in him the waste of forces on which you place a spiritual value? It is simply on this account that he is for you, not the abstraction called a criminal who merely "gets what he deserves" (art, like religion, knows no such thing), but a tragic hero, and that his war with other forces of indubitable spiritual worth is a tragic war.[7]

It is required by the restatement of Hegel's principle to show that in the external conflict of persons there is good on both sides. It is not required that this should be true, secondly, of both sides in the conflict within the hero's soul; for the hero is only a part of the tragedy. Nevertheless in almost all cases, if not in all, it is true. It is obviously so where, as in the hero and also the heroine of the *Cid*, the contending powers in this internal struggle are love and honour. Even when love is of a quality less pure and has a destructive force, as in Shakespeare's Antony, it is clearly true. And

---

[7] The same point may be put thus, in view of that dangerous word "personality." Our interest in Macbeth may be called interest in a personality; but it is not an interest in some bare form of self-consciousness, nor yet in a person in the legal sense, but in a personality full of matter. This matter is not an ethical or universal end, but it must in a sense be universal—human nature in a particular form —or it would not excite the horror, sympathy, and admiration it does excite. Nor, again, could it excite these feelings if it were not composed largely of qualities on which we set a high value.

it remains true even where, as in Hamlet and Macbeth, the contest seems to lie, and for most purposes might conveniently be said to lie, between forces simply good and simply the reverse. This is not really so, and the tragic effect depends upon the fact. It depends on our feeling that the elements in the man's nature are so inextricably blended that the good in him, that which we admire, instead of simply opposing the evil, reinforces it. Macbeth's imagination deters him from murder, but it also makes the vision of a crown irresistibly bright. If he had been less determined, nay, if his conscience had been less maddening in its insistence that he had thrown the precious jewel of his soul irretrievably away, he might have paused after his first deed, might even have repented. Yet his imagination, his determination, and his conscience were things good. Hamlet's desire to do his duty is a good thing, but what opposes this desire is by no means simply evil. It is something to which a substantial contribution is made by the qualities we most admire in him. Thus the nature of tragedy, as seen in the external conflict, repeats itself on each side of this conflict, and everywhere there is a spiritual value in both the contending forces.

In showing that *Macbeth*, a tragedy as far removed as possible from the *Antigone* as understood by Hegel, is still of one nature with it, and equally answers to the account of tragedy proposed, it has been necessary to ignore the great difference between the two plays. But when once the common essence of all tragedies has been determined, their differences become the interesting subject. They could be distinguished according to the character of the collisions on which they are built, or of the main forces which move the principal agents. And it may well be that, other things being equal (as they never are), the

tragedy in which the hero is, as we say, a good man, is more tragic than that in which he is, as we say, a bad one. The more spiritual value, the more tragedy in conflict and waste. The death of Hamlet or Othello is, so far, more tragic than that of Macbeth, that of Macbeth than that of Richard. Below Richard stands Iago, a figure still tragic, but unfit for the hero's part; below him persons like Regan or, in the very depth, Oswald, characters no longer (at least in the dramatic sense) tragic at all. Moral evil, that is to say, so greatly diminishes the spiritual value we ascribe to the personality that a very large amount of good of some kind is required to bring this personality up to the tragic level, the destruction of evil as such being in no degree tragic. And again, it may well be that, other things being equal, the more nearly the contending forces approach each other in goodness, the more tragic is the conflict; that the collision is, so far, more tragic in the *Antigone* than in *Macbeth*, and Hamlet's internal conflict than his struggle with outward enemies and obstacles. But it is dangerous to describe tragedy in terms that even appear to exclude *Macbeth*, or to describe *Macbeth*, even casually or by implication, in terms which imply that it portrays a conflict of mere evil with mere good.

The restatement of Hegel's main principle as to the conflict would involve a similar restatement as to the catastrophe (for we need not consider here those "tragedies" which end with a solution). As before, we must avoid any reference to ethical or universal ends, or to the work of "justice" in the catastrophe. We might then simply say that, as the tragic action portrays a self-division or intestinal conflict of spirit, so the catastrophe displays the violent annulling of this division or conflict. But this statement, which might be pretty generally accepted, would represent only half of Hegel's idea, and perhaps nothing of what is most characteristic and valuable in it. For the catastrophe (if I may put his idea in my own way) has two aspects, a negative and an affirmative, and we have ignored the latter. On the one hand it is the act of a power immeasurably superior to that of the conflicting agents, a power which is irresistible and unescapable, and which overbears and negates whatever is incompatible with it. So far, it may be called, in relation to the conflicting agents,[8] necessity or fate; and unless a catastrophe affects us in ways corresponding with this aspect it is not truly tragic. But then if this were all and this necessity were merely infinite, characterless, external force, the catastrophe would not only terrify (as it should), it would also horrify, depress, or at best provoke indignation or rebellion; and these are not tragic feelings. The catastrophe, then, must have a second and affirmative aspect, which is the source of our feelings of reconciliation, whatever form they may assume. And this will be taken into account if we describe the catastrophe as the violent self-restitution of the divided spiritual unity. The necessity which acts and negates in it, that is to say, is yet

[8] In relation to *both* sides in the conflict (though it may not need to negate life in both). For the ultimate agent in the catastrophe is emphatically not the finite power of one side. It is beyond both, and, at any rate in relation to them, boundless.

of one substance with both the agents. *It* is divided against itself in them; they are *its* conflicting forces; and in restoring its unity through negation it affirms them, so far as they are compatible with that unity. The qualification is essential, since the hero, for all his affinity with that power, is, as the living man we see before us, not so compatible. He must die, and his union with "eternal justice" (which is more than "justice") must itself be "eternal" or ideal. But the qualification does not abolish what it qualifies. This is no occasion to ask how in particular, and in what various ways in various works, we feel the effect of this affirmative aspect in the catastrophe. But it corresponds at least with that strange double impression which is produced by the hero's death. He dies, and our hearts die with him; and yet his death matters nothing to us, or we even exult. He is dead; and he has no more to do with death than the power which killed him and with which he is one.

I leave it to students of Hegel to ask whether he would have accepted the criticisms and modifications I have suggested. Naturally I think he would, as I believe they rest on truth, and am sure he had a habit of arriving at truth. But in any case their importance is trifling, compared with that of the theory which they attempt to strengthen and to which they owe their existence.

THE SUBSTANCE OF
SHAKESPEAREAN TRAGEDY
A. C. Bradley*

According to Bradley, Shakespeare saw tragedy as an exceptional calamity brought upon a conspicuous person through an overweening predisposition of his character that sets in motion a complex of events leading necessarily to his doom. Shakespeare's tragic universe labors for perfection, but in bringing about great good also gives birth to great evil. This evil can be eliminated only by incurring sacrifice of the good. Bradley proposes that the mystery of such a universe is the essential spirit of the tragedy of Shakespeare.

The question we are to consider in this lecture may be stated in a variety of ways. We may put it thus: What is the substance of a Shakespearean tragedy, taken in abstraction both from its form and from the differences in point of substance between one tragedy and another? Or thus: What is the nature of the tragic aspect of life as represented by Shakespeare? What is the general fact shown now in this tragedy and now in that? And we are putting the same question when we ask: What is Shakespeare's tragic conception, or conception of tragedy?

These expressions, it should be observed, do not imply that Shakespeare himself ever asked or answered such a question; that he set himself to reflect on the tragic aspects of life, that he framed a tragic conception, and still less that, like Aristotle or Corneille, he had a theory of the kind of poetry called tragedy. These things are all possible; how far any one of them is probable we need

not discuss; but none of them is presupposed by the question we are going to consider. This question implies only that, as a matter of fact, Shakespeare in writing tragedy did represent a certain aspect of life in a certain way, and that through examination of his writings we ought to be able, to some extent, to describe this aspect and way in terms addressed to the understanding. Such a description, so far as it is true and adequate, may, after these explanations, be called indifferently an account of the substance of Shakespearean tragedy, or an account of Shakespeare's conception of tragedy or view of the tragic fact.

Two further warnings may be required. In the first place, we must remember that the tragic aspect of life is only one aspect. We cannot arrive at Shakespeare's whole dramatic way of looking at the world from his tragedies alone, as we can arrive at Milton's way of regarding things, or at Wordsworth's or at Shelley's, by examining almost any one of their important works. Speaking very broadly, one may say that these poets at their best always look at things in one light; but

* The essay is reprinted from *Shakespearean Tragedy*, by A. C. Bradley, by permission of Macmillan & Co., Ltd., and St. Martin's Press, Inc. Copyright 1905 by Macmillan & Co., Ltd.

Hamlet and *Henry IV.* and *Cymbeline* reflect things from quite distinct positions, and Shakespeare's whole dramatic view is not to be identified with any one of these reflections. And, in the second place, I may repeat that in these lectures, at any rate for the most part, we are to be content with his *dramatic* view, and are not to ask whether it corresponded exactly with his opinions or creed outside his poetry—the opinions or creed of the being whom we sometimes oddly call "Shakespeare the man." It does not seem likely that outside his poetry he was a very simple-minded Catholic or Protestant or Atheist, as some have maintained; but we cannot be sure, as with those other poets we can, that in his works he expressed his deepest and most cherished convictions on ultimate questions, or even that he had any. And in his dramatic conceptions there is enough to occupy us.

I

In approaching our subject it will be best, without attempting to shorten the path by referring to famous theories of the drama, to start directly from the facts, and to collect from them gradually an idea of Shakespearean Tragedy. And first, to begin from the outside, such a tragedy brings before us a considerable number of persons (many more than the persons in a Greek play, unless the members of the Chorus are reckoned among them); but it is pre-eminently the story of one person, the "hero,"[1] or at most of two, the "hero" and "heroine." Moreover, it is only in the love-tragedies, *Romeo and Juliet* and *Antony and Cleopatra*, that the heroine is as much the centre of the action as the hero. The rest,

[1] *Julius Caesar* is not an exception to this rule. Caesar, whose murder comes in the Third Act, is in a sense the dominating figure in the story, but Brutus is the "hero."

including *Macbeth*, are single stars. So that, having noticed the peculiarity of these two dramas, we may henceforth, for the sake of brevity, ignore it, and may speak of the tragic story as being concerned primarily with one person.

The story, next, leads up to, and includes the *death* of the hero. On the one hand (whatever may be true of tragedy elsewhere), no play at the end of which the hero remains alive is, in the full Shakespearean sense, a tragedy; and we no longer class *Troilus and Cressida* or *Cymbeline* as such, as did the editors of the Folio. On the other hand, the story depicts also the troubled part of the hero's life which precedes and leads up to his death; and an instantaneous death occurring by "accident" in the midst of prosperity would not suffice for it. It is, in fact, essentially a tale of suffering and calamity conducting to death.

The suffering and calamity are, moreover, exceptional. They befall a conspicuous person. They are themselves of some striking kind. They are also, as a rule, unexpected, and contrasted with previous happiness or glory. A tale, for example, of a man slowly worn to death by disease, poverty, little cares, sordid vices, petty persecutions, however piteous or dreadful it might be, would not be tragic in the Shakespearean sense.

Such exceptional suffering and calamity, then, affecting the hero, and—we must now add—generally extending far and wide beyond him, so as to make the whole scene a scene of woe, are an essential ingredient in tragedy and a chief source of the tragic emotions, and especially of pity. But the proportions of this ingredient, and the direction taken by tragic pity, will naturally vary greatly. Pity, for example, has a much larger part in *King Lear* than in *Macbeth*, and is directed in the one case chiefly to the hero, in the other chiefly to minor characters.

Let us now pause for a moment on the ideas we have so far reached. They would more than suffice to describe the whole tragic fact as it presented itself to the mediaeval mind. To the mediaeval mind a tragedy meant a narrative rather than a play, and its notion of the matter of this narrative may readily be gathered from Dante or, still better, from Chaucer. Chaucer's *Monk's Tale* is a series of what he calls "tragedies"; and this means in fact a series of tales *de Casibus Illustrium Virorum,*—stories of the Falls of Illustrious Men, such as Lucifer, Adam, Hercules and Nebuchadnezzar. And the Monk ends the tale of Croesus thus:

Anhanged was Cresus, the proudè kyng;
His roial tronè myghte hym nat availle.
Tragédie is noon oother maner thyng,
Ne kan in syngyng criè ne biwaille
But for that Fortune alwey wole assaile
With unwar strook the regnès that been
    proude;
For whan men trusteth hire, thanne wol
    she faille,
And covere hire brighte facè with a
    clowde.

A total reverse of fortune, coming unawares upon a man who "stood in high degree," happy and apparently secure,—such was the tragic fact to the mediaeval mind. It appealed strongly to common human sympathy and pity; it startled also another feeling, that of fear. It frightened men and awed them. It made them feel that man is blind and helpless, the plaything of an inscrutable power, called by the name of Fortune or some other name,—a power which appears to smile on him for a little, and then on a sudden strikes him down in his pride.

Shakespeare's idea of the tragic fact is larger than this idea and goes beyond it; but it includes it, and it is worth while to

observe the identity of the two in a certain point which is often ignored. Tragedy with Shakespeare is concerned always with persons of "high degree"; often with kings or princes; if not, with leaders in the state like Coriolanus, Brutus, Antony; at the least, as in *Romeo and Juliet,* with members of great houses, whose quarrels are of public moment. There is a decided difference here between *Othello* and our three other tragedies, but it is not a difference of kind. Othello himself is no mere private person; he is the General of the Republic. At the beginning we see him in the Council-Chamber of the Senate. The consciousness of his high position never leaves him. At the end, when he is determined to live no longer, he is as anxious as Hamlet not to be misjudged by the great world, and his last speech begins,

Soft you; a word or two before you go.
I have done the state some service, and
    they know it.[2]

And this characteristic of Shakespeare's tragedies, though not the most vital, is neither external nor unimportant. The saying that every death-bed is the scene of the fifth act of a tragedy has its meaning, but it would not be true if the word "tragedy" bore its dramatic sense. The pangs of despised love and the anguish of remorse, we say, are the same in a peasant and a prince; but, not to insist that they cannot be so when the prince is really a prince, the story of the prince,

[2] *Timon of Athens,* we have seen, was probably not designed by Shakespeare, but even Timon is no exception to the rule. The sub-plot is concerned with Alcibiades and his army, and Timon himself is treated by the Senate as a man of great importance. *Arden of Feversham* and *A Yorkshire Tragedy* would certainly be exceptions to the rule; but I assume that neither of them is Shakespeare's; and if either is, it belongs to a different species from his admitted tragedies. See, on this species, Symonds, *Shakspere's Predecessors,* ch. xi.

the triumvir, or the general, has a greatness and dignity of its own. His fate affects the welfare of a whole nation or empire; and when he falls suddenly from the height of earthly greatness to the dust, his fall produces a sense of contrast, of the powerlessness of man, and of the omnipotence—perhaps the caprice—of Fortune or Fate, which no tale of private life can possibly rival.

Such feelings are constantly evoked by Shakespeare's tragedies,—again in varying degrees. Perhaps they are the very strongest of the emotions awakened by the early tragedy of *Richard II.*, where they receive a concentrated expression in Richard's famous speech about the antic Death, who sits in the hollow crown

That rounds the mortal temples of a king,

grinning at his pomp, watching till his vanity and his fancied security have wholly encased him round, and then coming and boring with a little pin through his castle wall. And these feelings, though their predominance is subdued in the mightiest tragedies, remain powerful there. In the figure of the maddened Lear we see

A sight most pitiful in the meanest
  wretch,
Past speaking of in a king;

and if we would realise the truth in this matter we cannot do better than compare with the effect of *King Lear* the effect of Tourgénief's parallel and remarkable tale of peasant life, A *King Lear of the Steppes.*

II

A Shakespearean tragedy as so far considered may be called a story of exceptional calamity leading to the death of a man in high estate. But it is clearly much more than this, and we have now to regard it from another side. No amount of calamity which merely befell a man, descending from the clouds like lightning, or stealing from the darkness like pestilence, could alone provide the substance of its story. Job was the greatest of all the children of the east, and his afflictions were well-nigh more than he could bear; but even if we imagined them wearing him to death, that would not make his story tragic. Nor yet would it become so, in the Shakespearean sense, if the fire, and the great wind from the wilderness, and the torments of his flesh were conceived as sent by a supernatural power, whether just or malignant. The calamities of tragedy do not simply happen, nor are they sent; they proceed mainly from actions, and those the actions of men.

We see a number of human beings placed in certain circumstances; and we see, arising from the co-operation of their characters in these circumstances, certain actions. These actions beget others, and these others beget others again, until this series of inter-connected deeds leads by an apparently inevitable sequence to a catastrophe. The effect of such a series on imagination is to make us regard the sufferings which accompany it, and the catastrophe in which it ends, not only or chiefly as something which happens to the persons concerned, but equally as something which is caused by them. This at least may be said of the principal persons, and, among them, of the hero, who always contributes in some measure to the disaster in which he perishes.

This second aspect of tragedy evidently differs greatly from the first. Men, from this point of view, appear to us primarily as agents, "themselves the authors of their proper woe"; and our fear and pity, though they will not cease or diminish, will be modified accordingly. We are now to consider this second aspect, remembering that it too is only one aspect, and additional to the first, not a substitute for it.

The "story" or "action" of a Shakespearean tragedy does not consist, of course, solely of human actions or deeds; but the deeds are the predominant factor. And these deeds are, for the most part, actions in the full sense of the word; not things done " 'tween asleep and wake," but acts or omissions thoroughly expressive of the doer,—characteristic deeds. The centre of the tragedy, therefore, may be said with equal truth to lie in action issuing from character, or in character issuing in action.

Shakespeare's main interest lay here. To say that it lay in *mere* character, or was a psychological interest, would be a great mistake, for he was dramatic to the tips of his fingers. It is possible to find places where he has given a certain indulgence to his love of poetry, and even to his turn for general reflections; but it would be very difficult, and in his later tragedies perhaps impossible, to detect passages where he has allowed such freedom to the interest in character apart from action. But for the opposite extreme, for the abstraction of mere "plot" (which is a very different thing from the tragic "action"), for the kind of interest which predominates in a novel like *The Woman in White*, it is clear that he cared even less. I do not mean that this interest is absent from his dramas; but it is subordinate to others, and is so interwoven with them that we are rarely conscious of it apart, and rarely feel in any great strength the half-intellectual, half-nervous excitement of following an ingenious complication. What we do feel strongly, as a tragedy advances to its close, is that the calamities and catastrophe follow inevitably from the deeds of men,

and that the main source of these deeds is character. The dictum that, with Shakespeare, "character is destiny" is no doubt an exaggeration, and one that may mislead (for many of his tragic personages, if they had not met with peculiar circumstances, would have escaped a tragic end, and might even have lived fairly untroubled lives); but it is the exaggeration of a vital truth.

This truth, with some of its qualifications, will appear more clearly if we now go on to ask what elements are to be found in the "story" or "action," occasionally or frequently, beside the characteristic deeds, and the sufferings and circumstances, of the persons. I will refer to three of these additional factors.

1. Shakespeare, occasionally and for reasons which need not be discussed here, represents abnormal conditions of mind; insanity, for example, somnambulism, hallucinations. And deeds issuing from these are certainly not what we called deeds in the fullest sense, deeds expressive of character. No; but these abnormal conditions are never introduced as the origin of deeds of any dramatic moment. Lady Macbeth's sleepwalking has no influence whatever on the events that follow it. Macbeth did not murder Duncan because he saw a dagger in the air: he saw the dagger because he was about to murder Duncan. Lear's insanity is not the cause of a tragic conflict any more than Ophelia's; it is, like Ophelia's, the result of a conflict; and in both cases the effect is mainly pathetic. If Lear were really mad when he divided his kingdom, if Hamlet were really mad at any time in the story, they would cease to be tragic characters.

2. Shakespeare also introduces the supernatural into some of his tragedies; he introduces ghosts, and witches who have supernatural knowledge. This supernatural element certainly cannot in most

cases, if in any, be explained away as an illusion in the mind of one of the characters. And further, it does contribute to the action, and is in more than one instance an indispensable part of it: so that to describe human character, with circumstances, as always the *sole* motive force in this action would be a serious error. But the supernatural is always placed in the closest relation with character. It gives a confirmation and a distinct form to inward movements already present and exerting an influence; to the sense of failure in Brutus, to the stifled workings of conscience in Richard, to the half-formed thought or the horrified memory of guilt in Macbeth, to suspicion in Hamlet. Moreover, its influence is never of a compulsive kind. It forms no more than an element, however important, in the problem which the hero has to face; and we are never allowed to feel that it has removed his capacity or responsibility for dealing with this problem. So far indeed are we from feeling this, that many readers run to the opposite extreme, and openly or privately regard the supernatural as having nothing to do with the real interest of the play.

3. Shakespeare, lastly, in most of his tragedies allows to "chance" or "accident" an appreciable influence at some point in the action. Chance or accident here will be found, I think, to mean any occurrence (not supernatural, of course) which enters the dramatic sequence neither from the agency of a character, nor from the obvious surrounding circumstances.[3] It may be called an accident, in this sense, that Romeo never got the Friar's message about the potion, and that Juliet did not awake from her long

sleep a minute sooner; an accident that Edgar arrived at the prison just too late to save Cordelia's life; an accident that Desdemona dropped her handkerchief at the most fatal of moments; an accident that the pirate ship attacked Hamlet's ship, so that he was able to return forthwith to Denmark. Now this operation of accident is a fact, and a prominent fact, of human life. To exclude it *wholly* from tragedy, therefore, would be, we may say, to fail in truth. And, besides, it is not merely a fact. That men may start a course of events but can neither calculate nor control it, is a *tragic* fact. The dramatist may use accident so as to make us feel this; and there are also other dramatic uses to which it may be put. Shakespeare accordingly admits it. On the other hand, any *large* admission of chance into the tragic sequence[4] would certainly weaken, and might destroy, the sense of the causal connection of character, deed, and catastrophe. And Shakespeare really uses it very sparingly. We seldom find ourselves exclaiming, "What an unlucky accident!" I believe most readers would have to search painfully for instances. It is, further, frequently easy to see the dramatic intention of an accident; and some things which look like accidents have really a connection with character, and are therefore not in the full sense accidents. Finally, I believe it will be found that almost all the prominent accidents occur when the action is well advanced and the impression of the causal sequence is too firmly fixed to be impaired.

Thus it appears that these three elements in the "action" are subordinate, while the dominant factor consists in deeds which issue from character. So that, by way of summary, we may now

[3] Even a deed would, I think, be counted an "accident," if it were the deed of a very minor person whose character had not been indicated; because such a deed would not issue from the little world to which the dramatist had confined our attention.

[4] Comedy stands in a different position. The tricks played by chance often form a principal part of the comic action.

alter our first statement, "A tragedy is a story of exceptional calamity leading to the death of a man in high estate," and we may say instead (what in its turn is one-sided, though less so), that the story is one of human actions producing exceptional calamity and ending in the death of such a man.[5]

Before we leave the "action," however, there is another question that may usefully be asked. Can we define this "action" further by describing it as a conflict?

The frequent use of this idea in discussions on tragedy is ultimately due, I suppose, to the influence of Hegel's theory on the subject, certainly the most important theory since Aristotle's. But Hegel's view of the tragic conflict is not only unfamiliar to English readers and difficult to expound shortly, but it had its origin in reflections on Greek tragedy and, as Hegel was well aware, applies only imperfectly to the works of Shakespeare.[6] I shall, therefore, confine myself to the idea of conflict in its more general form. In this form it is obviously applicable to Shakespearean tragedy; but it is vague, and I will try to make it more precise by putting the question, Who are the combatants in this conflict?

Not seldom the conflict may quite naturally be conceived as lying between two persons, of whom the hero is one; or, more fully, as lying between two parties or groups, in one of which the hero is the leading figure. Or if we prefer to speak (as we may quite well do if we know what we are about) of the passions, tendencies, ideas, principles, forces, which animate these persons or groups, we may

say that two of such passions or ideas, regarded as animating two persons or groups, are the combatants. The love of Romeo and Juliet is in conflict with the hatred of their houses, represented by various other characters. The cause of Brutus and Cassius struggles with that of Julius, Octavius and Antony. In *Richard II.* the King stands on one side, Bolingbroke and his party on the other. In *Macbeth* the hero and heroine are opposed to the representatives of Duncan. In all these cases the great majority of the *dramatis personae* fall without difficulty into antagonistic groups, and the conflict between these groups ends with the defeat of the hero.

Yet one cannot help feeling that in at least one of these cases, *Macbeth*, there is something a little external in this way of looking at the action. And when we come to some other plays this feeling increases. No doubt most of the characters in *Hamlet, King Lear, Othello*, or *Antony and Cleopatra* can be arranged in opposed groups;[7] and no doubt there is a conflict; and yet it seems misleading to describe this conflict as one *between these groups*. It cannot be simply this. For though Hamlet and the King are mortal foes, yet that which engrosses our interest and dwells in our memory at least as much as the conflict between them, is the conflict *within* one of them. And so it is, though not in the same degree, with *Antony and Cleopatra* and

---

[5] It may be observed that the influence of the three elements just considered is to strengthen the tendency, produced by the sufferings considered first, to regard the tragic persons as passive rather than as agents.

[6] An account of Hegel's view may be found in the *Hibbert Journal* for July, 1904.

[7] The reader, however, will find considerable difficulty in placing some very important characters in these and other plays. I will give only two or three illustrations. Edgar is clearly not on the same side as Edmund, and yet it seems awkward to range him on Gloster's side when Gloster wishes to put him to death. Ophelia is in love with Hamlet, but how can she be said to be of Hamlet's party against the King and Polonius, or of their party against Hamlet? Desdemona worships Othello, yet it sounds odd to say that Othello is on the same side with a person whom he insults, strikes and murders.

even with *Othello*; and, in fact, in a certain measure, it is so with nearly all the tragedies. There is an outward conflict of persons and groups, there is also a conflict of forces in the hero's soul; and even in *Julius Caesar* and *Macbeth* the interest of the former can hardly be said to exceed that of the latter.

The truth is, that the type of tragedy in which the hero opposes to a hostile force an undivided soul, is not the Shakespearean type. The souls of those who contend with the hero may be thus undivided; they generally are; but, as a rule, the hero, though he pursues his fated way, is, at least at some point in the action, and sometimes at many, torn by an inward struggle; and it is frequently at such points that Shakespeare shows his most extraordinary power. If further we compare the earlier tragedies with the later, we find that it is in the latter, the maturest works, that this inward struggle is most emphasised. In the last of them, *Coriolanus*, its interest completely eclipses towards the close of the play that of the outward conflict. *Romeo and Juliet*, *Richard III.*, *Richard II.*, where the hero contends with an outward force, but comparatively little with himself, are all early plays.

If we are to include the outer and the inner struggle in a conception more definite than that of conflict in general, we must employ some such phrase as "spiritual force." This will mean whatever forces act in the human spirit, whether good or evil, whether personal passion or impersonal principle; doubts, desires, scruples, ideas—whatever can animate, shake, possess, and drive a man's soul. In a Shakespearean tragedy some such forces are shown in conflict. They are shown acting in men and generating strife between them. They are also shown, less universally, but quite as characteristically, generating disturbance and even conflict in the soul of the hero. Treasonous ambition in Macbeth collides with loyalty and patriotism in Macduff and Malcolm: here is the outward conflict. But these powers or principles equally collide in the soul of Macbeth himself: here is the inner. And neither by itself could make the tragedy.[8]

We shall see later the importance of this idea. Here we need only observe that the notion of tragedy as a conflict emphasises the fact that action is the centre of the story, while the concentration of interest, in the greater plays, on the inward struggle emphasises the fact that this action is essentially the expression of character.

III

Let us turn now from the "action" to the central figure in it; and, ignoring the characteristics which distinguish the heroes from one another, let us ask whether they have any common qualities which appear to be essential to the tragic effect.

One they certainly have. They are exceptional beings. We have seen already that the hero, with Shakespeare, is a person of high degree or of public importance, and that his actions or sufferings are of an unusual kind. But this is not all. His nature also is exceptional, and generally raises him in some respect much above the average level of humanity. This does not mean that he is an eccentric or a paragon. Shakespeare never drew monstrosities of virtue; some of his heroes are

[8] I have given names to the "spiritual forces" in *Macbeth* merely to illustrate the idea, and without any pretension to adequacy. Perhaps, in view of some interpretations of Shakespeare's plays, it will be as well to add that I do not dream of suggesting that in any of his dramas Shakespeare imagined two abstract principles or passions conflicting, and incorporated them in persons; or that there is any necessity for a reader to define for himself the particular forces which conflict in a given case.

far from being "good"; and if he drew eccentrics he gave them a subordinate position in the plot. His tragic characters are made of the stuff we find within ourselves and within the persons who surround them. But, by an intensification of the life which they share with others, they are raised above them; and the greatest are raised so far that, if we fully realise all that is implied in their words and actions, we become conscious that in real life we have known scarcely any one resembling them. Some, like Hamlet and Cleopatra, have genius. Others, like Othello, Lear, Macbeth, Coriolanus, are built on the grand scale; and desire, passion, or will attains in them a terrible force. In almost all we observe a marked one-sidedness, a predisposition in some particular direction; a total incapacity, in certain circumstances, of resisting the force which draws in this direction; a fatal tendency to identify the whole being with one interest, object, passion, or habit of mind. This, it would seem, is, for Shakespeare, the fundamental tragic trait. It is present in his early heroes, Romeo and Richard II., infatuated men, who otherwise rise comparatively little above the ordinary level. It is a fatal gift, but it carries with it a touch of greatness; and when there is joined to it nobility of mind, or genius, or immense force, we realise the full power and reach of the soul, and the conflict in which it engages acquires that magnitude which stirs not only sympathy and pity, but admiration, terror, and awe.

The easiest way to bring home to oneself the nature of the tragic character is to compare it with a character of another kind. Dramas like *Cymbeline* and the *Winter's Tale*, which might seem destined to end tragically, but actually end otherwise, owe their happy ending largely to the fact that the principal characters fail to reach tragic dimensions. And, conversely, if these persons were put in the place of the tragic heroes, the dramas in which they appeared would cease to be tragedies. Posthumus would never have acted as Othello did; Othello, on his side, would have met Iachimo's challenge with something more than words. If, like Posthumus, he had remained convinced of his wife's infidelity, he would not have repented her execution; if, like Leontes, he had come to believe that by an unjust accusation he had caused her death, he would never have lived on, like Leontes. In the same way the villain Iachimo has no touch of tragic greatness. But Iago comes nearer to it, and if Iago had slandered Imogen and had supposed his slanders to have led to her death, he certainly would not have turned melancholy and wished to die. One reason why the end of the *Merchant of Venice* fails to satisfy us is that Shylock is a tragic character, and that we cannot believe in his accepting his defeat and the conditions imposed on him. This was a case where Shakespeare's imagination ran away with him, so that he drew a figure with which the destined pleasant ending would not harmonise.

In the circumstances where we see the hero placed, his tragic trait, which is also his greatness, is fatal to him. To meet these circumstances something is required which a smaller man might have given, but which the hero cannot give. He errs, by action or omission; and his error, joining with other causes, brings on him ruin. This is always so with Shakespeare. As we have seen, the idea of the tragic hero as a being destroyed simply and solely by external forces is quite alien to him; and not less so is the idea of the hero as contributing to his destruction only by acts in which we see no flaw. But the fatal imperfection or error, which is never absent, is of different kinds and degrees. At one extreme stands the excess and precipitancy of Romeo, which scarcely, if at all, diminish our regard for him; at the other the murderous ambition of Richard III. In most cases the tragic error involves no conscious breach of right; in some (*e.g.* that of Brutus or Othello) it is accompanied by a full conviction of right. In Hamlet there is a painful consciousness that duty is being neglected; in Antony a clear knowledge that the worse of two courses is being pursued; but Richard and Macbeth are the only heroes who do what they themselves recognise to be villainous. It is important to observe that Shakespeare does admit such heroes,[9] and also that he appears to feel, and exerts himself to meet, the difficulty that arises from their admission. The difficulty is that the spectator must desire their defeat and even their destruction; and yet this desire, and the satisfaction of it, are not tragic feelings. Shakespeare gives to Richard therefore a power which excites astonishment, and a courage which extorts admiration. He gives to Macbeth a similar, though less extraordinary, greatness, and adds to it a conscience so terrifying in its warnings and so maddening in its reproaches that the spectacle of inward torment compels a horrified sympathy and awe which balance, at the least, the desire for the hero's ruin.

The tragic hero with Shakespeare, then, need not be "good," though generally he is "good" and therefore at once wins sympathy in his error. But it is necessary that he should have so much of greatness that in his error and fall we may be vividly conscious in the possibilities of human nature.[10] Hence, in

the first place, a Shakespearean tragedy is never, like some miscalled tragedies, depressing. No one ever closes the book with the feeling that man is a poor mean creature. He may be wretched and he may be awful, but he is not small. His lot may be heart-rending and mysterious, but it is not contemptible. The most confirmed of cynics ceases to be a cynic while he reads these plays. And with this greatness of the tragic hero (which is not always confined to him) is connected, secondly, what I venture to describe as the centre of the tragic impression. This central feeling is the impression of waste. With Shakespeare, at any rate, the pity and fear which are stirred by the tragic story seem to unite with, and even merge in, a profound sense of sadness and mystery, which is due to this impression of waste. "What a piece of work is man," we cry; "so much more beautiful and so much more terrible than we knew! Why should he be so if this beauty and greatness only tortures itself and throws itself away?" We seem to have before us a type of the mystery of the whole world, the tragic fact which extends far beyond the limits of tragedy. Everywhere, from the crushed rocks beneath our feet to the soul of man, we see power, intelligence, life and glory, which astound us and seem to call for our worship. And everywhere we see them perishing, devouring one another and destroying themselves, often with dreadful pain, as though they came into being for no other end. Tragedy is the typical form of this mystery, because that greatness of soul which it exhibits oppressed, conflicting and destroyed, is the highest existence in our view. It forces the mystery upon us, and it makes us realise so vividly the worth of that which is wasted that we cannot possibly seek comfort in the reflection that all is vanity.

[9] Aristotle apparently would exclude them.
[10] Richard II. is perhaps an exception, and I must confess that to me he is scarcely a tragic character, and that, if he is nevertheless a tragic figure, he is so only because his fall from prosperity to adversity is so great.

IV

In this tragic world, then, where individuals, however great they may be and however decisive their actions may appear, are so evidently not the ultimate power, what is this power? What account can we give of it which will correspond with the imaginative impressions we receive? This will be our final question.

The variety of the answers given to this question shows how difficult it is. And the difficulty has many sources. Most people, even among those who know Shakespeare well and come into real contact with his mind, are inclined to isolate and exaggerate some one aspect of the tragic fact. Some are so much influenced by their own habitual beliefs that they import them more or less into their interpretation of every author who is "sympathetic" to them. And even where neither of these causes of error appears to operate, another is present from which it is probably impossible wholly to escape. What I mean is this. Any answer we give to the question proposed ought to correspond with, or to represent in terms of the understanding, our imaginative and emotional experience in reading the tragedies. We have, of course, to do our best by study and effort to make this experience true to Shakespeare; but, that done to the best of our ability, the experience is the matter to be interpreted, and the test by which the interpretation must be tried. But it is extremely hard to make out exactly what this experience is, because, in the very effort to make it out, our reflecting mind, full of everyday ideas, is always tending to transform it by the application of these ideas, and so to elicit a result which, instead of representing the fact, conventionalises it. And the consequence is not only mistaken theories; it

is that many a man will declare that he feels in reading a tragedy what he never really felt, while he fails to recognise what he actually did feel. It is not likely that we shall escape all these dangers in our effort to find an answer to the question regarding the tragic world and the ultimate power in it.

It will be agreed, however, first, that this question must not be answered in "religious" language. For although this or that *dramatis persona* may speak of gods or of God, of evil spirits or of Satan, of heaven and of hell, and although the poet may show us ghosts from another world, these ideas do not materially influence his representation of life, nor are they used to throw light on the mystery of its tragedy. The Elizabethan drama was almost wholly secular; and while Shakespeare was writing he practically confined his view to the world of non-theological observation and thought, so that he represents it substantially in one and the same way whether the period of the story is pre-Christian or Christian.[11] He looked at this "secular" world most intently and seriously; and he painted it, we cannot but conclude, with entire fidelity, without the wish to enforce an opinion of his own, and, in essentials, without regard to anyone's hopes, fears, or beliefs. His greatness is largely due to this fidelity in a mind of extraordinary power; and if, as a private person, he had a religious faith, his tragic view can hardly have been in contradiction with this faith, but must have been included in it, and supplemented, not abolished, by additional ideas.

Two statements, next, may at once be made regarding the tragic fact as he represents it: one, that it is and remains to us something piteous, fearful and

[11] I say substantially; but the concluding remarks on *Hamlet* will modify a little the statements above.

mysterious; the other, that the representation of it does not leave us crushed, rebellious or desperate. These statements will be accepted, I believe, by any reader who is in touch with Shakespeare's mind and can observe his own. Indeed such a reader is rather likely to complain that they are painfully obvious. But if they are true as well as obvious, something follows from them in regard to our present question.

From the first it follows that the ultimate power in the tragic world is not adequately described as a law or order which we can see to be just and benevolent,—as, in that sense, a "moral order": for in that case the spectacle of suffering and waste could not seem to us so fearful and mysterious as it does. And from the second it follows that this ultimate power is not adequately described as a fate, whether malicious and cruel, or blind and indifferent to human happiness and goodness: for in that case the spectacle would leave us desperate or rebellious. Yet one or other of these two ideas will be found to govern most accounts of Shakespeare's tragic view or world. These accounts isolate and exaggerate single aspects, either the aspect of action or that of suffering; either the close and unbroken connection of character, will, deed and catastrophe, which, taken alone, shows the individual simply as sinning against, or failing to conform to, the moral order and drawing his just doom on his own head; or else that pressure of outward forces, that sway of accident, and those blind and agonised struggles, which, taken alone, show him as the mere victim of some power which cares neither for his sins nor for his pain. Such views contradict one another, and no third view can unite them; but the several aspects from whose isolation and exaggeration they spring are both present in the fact, and a view which would be true to the fact and to the whole of our imaginative experience must in some way combine these aspects.

Let us begin, then, with the idea of fatality and glance at some of the impressions which give rise to it, without asking at present whether this idea is their natural or fitting expression. There can be no doubt that they do arise and that they ought to arise. If we do not feel at times that the hero is, in some sense, a doomed man; that he and others drift struggling to destruction like helpless creatures borne on an irresistible flood towards a cataract; that, faulty as they may be, their fault is far from being the sole or sufficient cause of all they suffer; and that the power from which they cannot escape is relentless and immovable, we have failed to receive an essential part of the full tragic effect.

The sources of these impressions are various, and I will refer only to a few. One of them is put into words by Shakespeare himself when he makes the player-king in *Hamlet* say:

Our thoughts are ours, their ends none
   of our own;

"their ends" are the issues or outcomes of our thoughts, and these, says the speaker, are not our own. The tragic world is a world of action, and action is the translation of thought into reality. We see men and women confidently attempting it. They strike into the existing order of things in pursuance of their ideas. But what they achieve is not what they intended; it is terribly unlike it. They understand nothing, we say to ourselves, of the world on which they operate. They fight blindly in the dark, and the power that works through them makes them the instrument of a design which is not theirs. They act freely, and yet their action binds them hand and foot. And it makes no difference whether they meant well or ill. No one could mean better than Brutus, but he contrives misery for his country and death for himself. No one could mean worse than Iago, and he too is caught in the web he spins for others. Hamlet, recoiling from the rough duty of revenge, is pushed into blood-guiltiness he never dreamed of, and forced at last on the revenge he could not will. His adversary's murders, and no less his adversary's remorse, bring about the opposite of what they sought. Lear follows an old man's whim, half generous, half selfish; and in a moment it looses all the powers of darkness upon him. Othello agonises over an empty fiction, and, meaning to execute solemn justice, butchers innocence and strangles love. They understand themselves no better than the world about them. Coriolanus thinks that his heart is iron, and it melts like snow before a fire. Lady Macbeth, who thought she could dash out her own child's brains, finds herself hounded to death by the smell of a stranger's blood. Her husband thinks that to gain a crown he would jump the life to come, and finds that the crown has brought him all the horrors of that life. Everywhere, in this tragic world, man's thought, translated into act, is transformed into the opposite of itself. His act, the movement of a few ounces of matter in a moment of time, becomes a monstrous flood which spreads over a kingdom. And whatsoever he dreams of doing, he achieves that which he least dreamed of, his own destruction.

All this makes us feel the blindness and helplessness of man. Yet by itself it would hardly suggest the idea of fate, because it shows man as in some degree, however slight, the cause of his own undoing. But other impressions come to aid it. It is aided by everything which makes us feel that a man is, as we say, terribly

unlucky; and of this there is, even in Shakespeare, not a little. Here come in some of the accidents already considered, Juliet's waking from her trance a minute too late, Desdemona's loss of her handkerchief at the only moment when the loss would have mattered, that insignificant delay which cost Cordelia's life. Again, men act, no doubt, in accordance with their characters; but what is it that brings them just the one problem which is fatal to them and would be easy to another, and sometimes brings it to them just when they are least fitted to face it? How is it that Othello comes to be the companion of the one man in the world who is at once able enough, brave enough, and vile enough to ensnare him? By what strange fatality does it happen that Lear has such daughters and Cordelia such sisters? Even character itself contributes to these feelings of fatality. How could men escape, we cry, such vehement propensities as drive Romeo, Antony, Coriolanus, to their doom? And why is it that a man's virtues help to destroy him, and that his weakness or defect is so intertwined with everything that is admirable in him that we can hardly separate them even in imagination?

If we find in Shakespeare's tragedies the source of impressions like these, it is important, on the other hand, to notice what we do *not* find there. We find practically no trace of fatalism in its more primitive, crude and obvious forms. Nothing, again, makes us think of the actions and sufferings of the persons as somehow arbitrarily fixed beforehand without regard to their feelings, thoughts and resolutions. Nor, I believe, are the facts ever so presented that it seems to us as if the supreme power, whatever it may be, had a special spite against a family or an individual. Neither, lastly, do we receive the impression (which, it must be observed, is not purely fatalistic) that a family, owing to some hideous crime or impiety in early days, is doomed in later days to continue a career of portentous calamities and sins. Shakespeare, indeed, does not appear to have taken much interest in what we now call heredity, or to have attached much importance to it.

What, then, is this "fate" which the impressions already considered lead us to describe as the ultimate power in the tragic world? It appears to be a mythological expression for the whole system or order, of which the individual characters form an inconsiderable and feeble part; which seems to determine, far more than they, their native dispositions and their circumstances, and, through these, their action; which is so vast and complex that they can scarcely at all understand it or control its workings; and which has a nature so definite and fixed that whatever changes take place in it produce other changes inevitably and without regard to men's desires and regrets. And whether this system or order is best called by the name of fate or no,[12] it can hardly be denied that it does appear as the ultimate power in the tragic world, and that it has such characteristics as these. But the name "fate" may be intended to imply something more—to imply that this

[12] I have raised no objection to the use of the idea of fate, because it occurs so often both in conversation and in books about Shakespeare's tragedies that I must suppose it to be natural to many readers. Yet I doubt whether it would be so if Greek tragedy had never been written; and I must in candour confess that to me it does not often occur while I am reading, or when I have just read, a tragedy of Shakespeare. Wordsworth's lines, for example, about

poor humanity's afflicted will
Struggling in vain with ruthless destiny

do not represent the impression I receive; much less do images which compare man to a puny creature helpless in the claws of a bird of prey. The reader should examine himself closely on this matter.

order is a blank necessity, totally regardless alike of human weal and of the difference between good and evil or right and wrong. And such an implication many readers would at once reject. They would maintain, on the contrary, that this order shows characteristics of quite another kind from those which made us give it the name of fate, characteristics which certainly should not induce us to forget those others, but which would lead us to describe it as a moral order and its necessity as a moral necessity.

V

Let us turn, then, to this idea. It brings into the light those aspects of the tragic fact which the idea of fate throws into the shade. And the argument which leads to it in its simplest form may be stated briefly thus: "Whatever may be said of accidents, circumstances and the like, human action is, after all, presented to us as the central fact in tragedy, and also as the main cause of the catastrophe. That necessity which so much impresses us is, after all, chiefly the necessary connection of actions and consequences. For these actions we, without even raising a question on the subject, hold the agents responsible; and the tragedy would disappear for us if we did not. The critical action is, in greater or less degree, wrong or bad. The catastrophe is, in the main, the return of this action on the head of the agent. It is an example of justice; and that order which, present alike within the agents and outside them, infallibly brings it about, is therefore just. The rigour of its justice is terrible, no doubt, for a tragedy is a terrible story; but, in spite of fear and pity, we acquiesce, because our sense of justice is satisfied."

Now, if this view is to hold good, the "justice" of which it speaks must be at once distinguished from what is called "poetic justice." "Poetic justice" means that prosperity and adversity are distributed in proportion to the merits of the agents. Such "poetic justice" is in flagrant contradiction with the facts of life, and it is absent from Shakespeare's tragic picture of life; indeed, this very absence is a ground of constant complaint on the part of Dr. Johnson. Δράσαντι παθεῖν, "the doer must suffer"—this we find in Shakespeare. We also find that villainy never remains victorious and prosperous at the last. But an assignment of amounts of happiness and misery, an assignment even of life and death, in proportion to merit, we do not find. No one who thinks of Desdemona and Cordelia; or who remembers that one end awaits Richard III. and Brutus, Macbeth and Hamlet; or who asks himself which suffered most, Othello or Iago; will ever accuse Shakespeare of representing the ultimate power as "poetically" just.

And we must go further. I venture to say that it is a mistake to use at all these terms of justice and merit or desert. And this for two reasons. In the first place, essential as it is to recognise the connection between act and consequence, and natural as it may seem in some cases (e.g. Macbeth's) to say that the doer only gets what he deserves, yet in very many cases to say this would be quite unnatural. We might not object to the statement that Lear deserved to suffer for his folly, selfishness and tyranny; but to assert that he deserved to suffer what he did suffer is to do violence not merely to language but to any healthy moral sense. It is, moreover, to obscure the tragic fact that the consequences of action cannot be limited to that which would appear to us to follow "justly" from them. And, this being so, when we call the order of the tragic world just, we are either using the word in some vague and unexplained sense, or we are

going beyond what is shown us of this order, and are appealing to faith.

But, in the second place, the ideas of justice and desert are, it seems to me, in *all* cases—even those of Richard III. and of Macbeth and Lady Macbeth—untrue to our imaginative experience. When we are immersed in a tragedy, we feel towards dispositions, actions, and persons such emotions as attraction and repulsion, pity, wonder, fear, horror, perhaps hatred; but we do not *judge*. This is a point of view which emerges only when, in reading a play, we slip, by our own fault or the dramatist's, from the tragic position, or when, in thinking about the play afterwards, we fall back on our everyday legal and moral notions. But tragedy does not belong, any more than religion belongs, to the sphere of these notions; neither does the imaginative attitude in presence of it. While we are in its world we watch what is, seeing that so it happened and must have happened, feeling that it is piteous, dreadful, awful, mysterious, but neither passing sentence on the agents, nor asking whether the behaviour of the ultimate power towards them is just. And, therefore, the use of such language in attempts to render our imaginative experience in terms of the understanding is, to say the least, full of danger.[13]

Let us attempt then to re-state the idea

[13] It is dangerous, I think, in reference to all really good tragedies, but I am dealing here only with Shakespeare's. In not a few Greek tragedies it is almost inevitable that we should think of justice and retribution, not only because the *dramatis personae* often speak of them, but also because there is something essential about the tragic problem itself. The poet treats the story in such a way that the question, Is the hero doing right or wrong? is almost forced upon us. But this is not so with Shakespeare. *Julius Caesar* is probably the only one of his tragedies in which the question suggests itself to us, and this is one of the reasons why that play has something of a classic air. Even here, if we ask the question, we have no doubt at all about the answer.

that the ultimate power in the tragic world is a moral order. Let us put aside the ideas of justice and merit, and speak simply of good and evil. Let us understand by these words, primarily, moral good and evil, but also everything else in human beings which we take to be excellent or the reverse. Let us understand the statement that the ultimate power or order is "moral" to mean that it does not show itself indifferent to good and evil, or equally favourable or unfavourable to both, but shows itself akin to good and alien from evil. And, understanding the statement thus, let us ask what grounds it has in the tragic fact as presented by Shakespeare.

Here, as in dealing with the grounds on which the idea of fate rests, I choose only two or three out of many. And the most important is this. In Shakespearean tragedy the main source of the convulsion which produces suffering and death is never good: good contributes to this convulsion only from its tragic implication with its opposite in one and the same character. The main source, on the contrary, is in every case evil; and, what is more (though this seems to have been little noticed), it is in almost every case evil in the fullest sense, not mere imperfection but plain moral evil. The love of Romeo and Juliet conducts them to death only because of the senseless hatred of their houses. Guilty ambition, seconded by diabolic malice and issuing in murder, opens the action in *Macbeth*. Iago is the main source of the convulsion in *Othello*; Goneril, Regan and Edmund in *King Lear*. Even when this plain moral evil is not the obviously prime source within the play, it lies behind it: the situation with which Hamlet has to deal has been formed by adultery and murder. *Julius Caesar* is the only tragedy in which one is even tempted to find an exception to this rule. And the inference is obvious.

If it is chiefly evil that violently disturbs the order of the world, this order cannot be friendly to evil or indifferent between evil and good, any more than a body which is convulsed by poison is friendly to it or indifferent to the distinction between poison and food.

Again, if we confine our attention to the hero, and to those cases where the gross and palpable evil is not in him but elsewhere, we find that the comparatively innocent hero still shows some marked imperfection or defect,—irresolution, precipitancy, pride, credulousness, excessive simplicity, excessive susceptibility to sexual emotions, and the like. These defects or imperfections are certainly, in the wide sense of the word, evil, and they contribute decisively to the conflict and catastrophe. And the inference is again obvious. The ultimate power which shows itself disturbed by this evil and reacts against it, must have a nature alien to it. Indeed its reaction is so vehement and "relentless" that it would seem to be bent on nothing short of good in perfection, and to be ruthless in its demand for it.

To this must be added another fact, or another aspect of the same fact. Evil exhibits itself everywhere as something negative, barren, weakening, destructive, a principle of death. It isolates, disunites, and tends to annihilate not only its opposite but itself. That which keeps the evil man[14] prosperous, makes him succeed, even permits him to exist, is the good in him (I do not mean only the obviously "moral" good). When the evil in him masters the good and has its way, it destroys other people through him, but it also destroys *him*. At the close of the

[14] It is most essential to remember that an evil man is much more than the evil in him. I may add that in this paragraph I have, for the sake of clearness, considered evil in its most pronounced form; but what is said would apply, *mutatis mutandis*, to evil as imperfection, etc.

struggle he has vanished, and has left behind him nothing that can stand. What remains is a family, a city, a country, exhausted, pale and feeble, but alive through the principle of good which animates it; and, within it, individuals who, if they have not the brilliance or greatness of the tragic character, still have won our respect and confidence. And the inference would seem clear. If existence in an order depends on good, and if the presence of evil is hostile to such existence, the inner being or soul of this order must be of one nature with good.

These are aspects of the tragic world at least as clearly marked as those which, taken alone, suggest the idea of fate. And the idea which they in their turn, when taken alone, may suggest, is that of an order which does not indeed award "poetic justice," but which reacts through the necessity of its own "moral" nature both against attacks made upon it and against failure to conform to it. Tragedy, on this view, is the exhibition of that convulsive reaction; and the fact that the spectacle does not leave us rebellious or desperate is due to a more or less distinct perception that the tragic suffering and death arise from collision, not with a fate or blank power, but with a moral power, a power akin to all that we admire and revere in the characters themselves. This perception produces something like a feeling of acquiescence in the catastrophe, though it neither leads us to pass judgment on the characters nor diminishes the pity, the fear, and the sense of waste, which their struggle, suffering and fall evoke. And, finally, this view seems quite able to do justice to those aspects of the tragic fact which give rise to the idea of fate. They would appear as various expressions of the fact that the moral order acts not capriciously or like a human being, but from the necessity of its nature, or, if we prefer the phrase, by

general laws,—a necessity or law which of course knows no exception and is as "ruthless" as fate.

It is impossible to deny to this view a large measure of truth. And yet without some amendment it can hardly satisfy. For it does not include the whole of the facts, and therefore does not wholly correspond with the impressions they produce. Let it be granted that the system or order which shows itself omnipotent against individuals is, in the sense explained, moral. Still—at any rate for the eye of sight—the evil against which it asserts itself, and the persons whom this evil inhabits, are not really something outside the order, so that they can attack it or fail to conform to it; they are within it and a part of it. It itself produces them,—produces Iago as well as Desdemona, Iago's cruelty as well as Iago's courage. It is not poisoned, it poisons itself. Doubtless it shows by its violent reaction that the poison *is* poison, and that its health lies in good. But one significant fact cannot remove another, and the spectacle we witness scarcely warrants the assertion that the order is responsible for the good in Desdemona, but Iago for the evil in Iago. If we make this assertion we make it on grounds other than the facts as presented in Shakespeare's tragedies.

Nor does the idea of a moral order asserting itself against attack or want of conformity answer in full to our feelings regarding the tragic character. We do not think of Hamlet merely as failing to meet its demand, of Antony as merely sinning against it, or even of Macbeth as simply attacking it. What we feel corresponds quite as much to the idea that they are *its* parts, expressions, products; that in their defect or evil *it* is untrue to its soul of goodness, and falls into conflict and collision with itself; that, in making them suffer and waste themselves, *it* suffers and wastes itself; and that when, to save its life and regain peace from this intestinal struggle, it casts them out, it has lost a part of its own substance,—a part more dangerous and unquiet, but far more valuable and nearer to its heart, than that which remains,—a Fortinbras, a Malcolm, an Octavius. There is no tragedy in its expulsion of evil: the tragedy is that this involves the waste of good.

Thus we are left at last with an idea showing two sides or aspects which we can neither separate nor reconcile. The whole or order against which the individual part shows itself powerless seems to be animated by a passion for perfection: we cannot otherwise explain its behaviour towards evil. Yet it appears to engender this evil within itself, and in its effort to overcome and expel it it is agonised with pain, and driven to mutilate its own substance and to lose not only evil but priceless good. That this idea, though very different from the idea of a blank fate, is no solution of the riddle of life is obvious; but why should we expect it to be such a solution? Shakespeare was not attempting to justify the ways of God to men, or to show the universe as a Divine Comedy. He was writing tragedy, and tragedy would not be tragedy if it were not a painful mystery. Nor can he be said even to point distinctly, like some writers of tragedy, in any direction where a solution might lie. We find a few references to gods or God, to the influence of the stars, to another life: some of them certainly, all of them

perhaps, merely dramatic—appropriate to the person from whose lips they fall. A ghost comes from Purgatory to impart a secret out of the reach of its hearer—who presently meditates on the question whether the sleep of death is dreamless. Accidents once or twice remind us strangely of the words, "There's a divinity that shapes our ends." More important are other impressions. Sometimes from the very furnace of affliction a conviction seems borne to us that somehow, if we could see it, this agony counts as nothing against the heroism and love which appear in it and thrill our hearts. Sometimes we are driven to cry out that these mighty or heavenly spirits who perish are too great for the little space in which they move, and that they vanish not into nothingness but into freedom. Sometimes from these sources and from others comes a presentiment, formless but haunting and even profound, that all the fury of conflict, with its waste and woe, is less than half the truth, even an illusion, "such stuff as dreams are made on." But these faint and scattered intimations that the tragic world, being but a fragment of a whole beyond our vision, must needs be a contradiction and no ultimate truth, avail nothing to interpret the mystery. We remain confronted with the inexplicable fact, or the no less inexplicable appearance, of a world travailing for perfection, but bringing to birth, together with glorious good, an evil which it is able to overcome only by self-torture and self-waste. And this fact or appearance is tragedy.

THE TRAGIC FORM
Richard B. Sewall*

Sewall is concerned first with the question—does there exist a definable form of tragedy? Can we talk about it as a genre? Second, what are the characteristics of its form? He develops a definition of the tragic structure as one that accomplishes a moment of "higher vision" in a restless, interminable, and paradoxical struggle between good and evil, in the suffering and the passions of which tragic man is transfigured.

A discussion of tragedy is confronted at the outset with the strenuous objections of Croce, who would have no truck with the genres. "Art is one," he wrote in his famous Britannica article,[1] "and cannot be divided." For convenience, he would allow the division of Shakespeare's plays into tragedies, comedies, and histories, but he warned of the dogmatism that lay in any further refining of distinctions. He made a special point of tragedy, which as usual was the fighting issue. No artist, he said, will submit to the servitude of the traditional definition: that a tragedy must have a subject of a certain kind, characters of a certain kind, and a plot of a certain kind and length. Each work of art is a world in itself, "a creation, not a reflection, a monument, not a document." The concepts of aesthetics do not exist "in a transcendent region" but only in innumerable specific works. To ask of a given work "is it a tragedy?" or "does it obey the laws of tragedy?" is irrelevant and impertinent.

Although this may be substituting one dogmatism for another, there is sense in it. Nothing is more dreary than the textbook categories; and their tendency, if carried too far, would rationalize art out of existence. The dilemma is one of critical means, not ends: Croce would preserve tragedy by insuring the autonomy of the artist; the schoolmen would preserve it by insuring the autonomy of the form.

But the dilemma is not insurmountable, as Eliot and a number of others have pointed out. There is a life-giving relationship between tradition and the individual talent, a "wooing both ways" (in R. P. Blackmur's phrase) between the form which the artist inherits and the new content he brings to it. This wooing both ways has been especially true of the development of tragedy, where values have been incremental, where (for instance) each new tragic protagonist is in some degree a lesser Job and each new tragic work owes an indispensable element to the Greek idea of the chorus. So I should say that, provided we can get beyond the stereotypes Croce seems to have had in mind, we should continue to talk about tragedy, to make it grow in meaning, impel more artists, and attract

* The essay is reprinted from Essays in Criticism, Vol. IV, No. 4 (1954), by permission of the author and Basil Blackwell and Mott, Ltd. Copyright 1954 by Basil Blackwell and Mott, Ltd.

[1] Eleventh edition, article "Aesthetics."

a greater and more discerning audience.

But we must first get a suitable idea of form. Blackmur's article[2] from which I have just quoted provides, I think, a useful suggestion. It is the concept of "theoretic form," which he distinguishes from technical or "executive" form. "Technical form," he writes, "is our means of getting at . . . and then making something of, what we feel the form of life itself is: the tensions, the stresses, the deep relations and the terrible disrelations that inhabit them. . . . This is the form that underlies the forms we merely practice. . . ." This (and here Croce's full concept of form is more adequately represented) is "what Croce means by theoretic form for feeling, intuition, insight, what I mean by the theoretic form of life itself." Discussion of the "form" of tragedy in this sense need be neither prescriptive nor inhibiting, but it may define a little more precisely a vital area of thought and feeling.

Here is the kind of situation in which such a discussion might be helpful: Two years ago, in *Essays in Criticism* (October 1952), Miss K. M. Burton defended what she called the "political tragedies" of Ben Jonson and George Chapman as legitimate tragedies, although non-Aristotelian. *Sejanus* was perhaps the clearest case in point. Herford and Simpson, in their commentary, had set the play down as at best "the tragedy of a satirist," a "proximate" tragedy, with no tragic hero and with no cathartic effect. "Whatever effect [Jonson] aimed at," they wrote, "it was not the purifying pity excited by the fatal errors of a noble nature." Miss Burton's reply lay in her concept of political tragedy. She saw Jonson's tragic theme as "the manner in which evil

penetrates the political structure." The "flaw" that concerned him lay "within the social order," and whatever purifying pity we feel would come from contemplating the ordeal of society, not the fatal errors of a noble nature. The play for her had "tragic intensity"; it was both "dramatic, and a tragedy."

Whether one agrees with her or not, the question, despite Croce, is out: "Is the play a tragedy?" And many others follow. Can there be a tragedy without a tragic hero? Can "the social order" play his traditional role? Is catharsis the first, or only, or even a reliable test? In a recent article, Professor Pottle wrote, "I shall be told Aristotle settled all that." And added, "I wish he had." The disagreement on *Sejanus* is symptomatic. F. L. Lucas once pointed out that (on much the same issues) Hegel thought only the Greeks wrote true tragedy; and I. A. Richards, only Shakespeare. Joseph Wood Krutch ruled out the moderns, like Hardy, Ibsen and O'Neill; and Mark Harris ruled them in.[3] The question arises about every new "serious" play or novel; we seem to care a great deal about whether it is, or is not, a tragedy.

I have little hope of settling all this, but I am persuaded that progress lies in the direction of theoretic form, as Blackmur uses the term. Is it not possible to bring the dominant feelings, intuitions, insights that we meet in so-called tragic writings into some coherent relationship to which the word "form" could be applied without too great violence? This is not to tell artists what to do, nor to set up strict *a priori* formulae, nor to legislate among the major genres. The problem of evaluating the total excel-

---

2 "The Loose and Baggy Monsters of Henry James: Notes on the Underlying Classic Form in the Novel," *Accent*, Summer, 1951; see also Eliseo Vivas, "Literature and Knowledge," *Sewanee Review*, Autumn, 1952.

3 F. A. Pottle, "Catharsis," *Yale Review*, Summer, 1951; F. L. Lucas, *Tragedy in Relation to Aristotle's Poetics*, N.Y., 1928; Joseph Wood Krutch, *The Modern Temper*, N.Y., 1929; Mark Harris, *The Case for Tragedy*, N.Y., 1932.

lence of a given work involves much more than determining its status as a tragedy, or as a "proximate" tragedy, or as a nontragedy. It involves, among other things, the verbal management within the work and the ordering of the parts. Furthermore, our discussion need not imply the superiority of tragedy over comedy (certainly not as Dante conceived of comedy) or over epic, although, if we look upon these major forms as presenting total interpretations of life, the less inclusive forms (lyric, satire) would seem to occupy inferior categories. But as we enter the world of any play or novel to which the term tragedy is at all applicable, we may well judge it by what we know about the possibilities of the form, without insisting that our judgment is absolute. If, set against the full dimensions of the tragic form, Jonson's *Sejanus* or Hemingway's *A Farewell to Arms* (for instance) reveal undeveloped possibilities or contrary elements, we can still respect their particular modes of expression.

In indicating these dimensions of tragedy, I shall be mindful of Unamuno's warning[4] that tragedy is not a matter, ultimately, to be systematized. He speaks truly, I think, about "the tragic sense of life." He describes it as a subphilosophy, "more or less formulated, more or less conscious," reaching deep down into temperament, not so much "flowing from ideas as determining them." It is the sense of ancient evil, of the mystery of human suffering, of the gulf between aspiration and achievement. It colours the tragic artist's vision of life (his theoretic form) and gives his works their peculiar shade and tone. It speaks, not the language of systematic thought, but through symbolic action, symbol and figure, diction and image, sound and rhythm. Such a recognition should precede any attempt to talk "systematically" about tragedy, while not denying the value of the attempt itself.

Two more comments remain to be made about method. The first is the problem of circular evidence,[5] the use of tragedies to define tragedy. I am assuming that we can talk meaningfully about a body of literature which reveals certain generic qualities and which can be distinguished from the body of literature called comedy, epic, satire, or the literature of pathos. My purpose is to isolate these qualities and to refer to the works themselves as illustrations rather than proof.

The second comment involves the problem of affectivism, which is the problem of catharsis: "This play is a tragedy because it makes me feel thus and so." As Max Scheler puts it, this method would bring us ultimately to the contemplation of our own ego. Thus, I would reverse the order of F. L. Lucas's discussion, which assumes that we must know what tragedy does before we can tell what it is: "We cannot fully discuss the means," Lucas wrote, "until we are clear about the ends." It is true that the usual or "scientific" way is to define natures by effects, which are observable. But rather than found a definition of tragedy on the infinite variables of an audience's reactions, I would consider first the works themselves as the "effects" and look in them for evidences of an efficient cause: a world-view, a form that "underlies the forms we merely practice." What are the generic qualities of these effects? Do they comprise a "form"? I think they do; and for convenience I shall use the term from the start as if I had already proved its legitimacy.

---

[4] *The Tragic Sense of Life*, tr. J. E. C. Flitch, London, 1921, pp. 17–18.

[5] Cf. Max Scheler, "On the Tragic," *Cross Currents*, Winter, 1954. This is a selection from Scheler's *Vom Umsturtz der Werte*, Vol. I (1923), tr. Bernard Stambler.

Basic to the tragic form is its recognition of the inevitability of paradox, of unresolved tensions and ambiguities, of opposites in precarious balance. Like the arch, tragedy never rests—or never comes to rest, with all losses restored and sorrows ended. Problems are put and pressed, but not solved. An occasional "happy ending," as in *The Oresteia* or *Crime and Punishment*, does not mean a full resolution. Though there may be intermittences, there is no ultimate discharge in that war. Although this suggests formlessness, as it must in contrast with certain types of religious orthodoxy or philosophical system, it would seem the essence of the tragic form. Surely it is more form than chaos. For out of all these tensions and paradoxes, these feelings, intuitions, insights, there emerges a fairly coherent attitude towards the universe and man. Tragedy makes certain distinguishable and characteristic affirmations, as well as denials, about (1) the cosmos and man's relation to it; (2) the nature of the individual and his relation to himself; (3) the individual in society.

1. *The tragic cosmos.* In using the term cosmos to signify a theory of the universe and man's relation to it, I have, of course, made a statement about tragedy: that tragedy affirms a cosmos of which man is a meaningful part. To be sure, the characteristic locale of tragedy is not the empyrean. Tragedy is primarily humanistic. Its focus is an event in this world; it is uncommitted as to questions of ultimate destiny, and it is nonreligious in its attitude toward revelation. But it speaks, however vaguely or variously, of an order that transcends time, space and matter.[6] It assumes man's connection with some supersensory or supernatural, or metaphysical being or principle, whether it be the Olympians, Job's Jehovah or the Christian God; Fate, Fortune's Wheel, the "elements" that Lear invoked, or Koestler's "oceanic sense," which comes in so tentatively (and pathetically) at the end of *Darkness at Noon.* The first thing that tragedy says about the cosmos is that, for good or ill, it *is*; and in this respect tragedy's theoretic opposite is naturalism or mechanism. Tragedy is witness (secondly) to the cosmic mystery, to the "wonderful" surrounding our lives; and in literature the opposite of tragedy is not only writing based upon naturalistic theory but also upon the four-square, "probable"[7] world of satire and rationalistic comedy. Finally, what distinguishes tragedy from other forms which bespeak this cosmic sense—for tragedy of course is not unique in this—is its peculiar and intense preoccupation with the *evil* in the universe, whatever it is in the stars that compels, harasses, and bears man down. Tragedy wrestles with the evil of the mystery— and the mystery of the evil. And the contest never ends.

But, paradoxically, its view of the cosmos is what sustains tragedy. Tragedy discerns a principle of goodness that coexists with the evil. This principle need be nothing so pat as The Moral Order, the "armies of unalterable law," and it is nothing so sure as the orthodox Christian God. It is nearer the folk sense that justice exists somewhere in the universe, or what Nietzsche describes as the orgiastic, mystical sense of oneness, of life as "indestructibly powerful and pleasurable." It may be a vision of some transcendent beauty and dignity against which the present evil may be seen as evil and the welter as welter. This is what keeps tragedy from giving up the whole

6 Cf. Susan Taubes, "The Nature of Tragedy," *Review of Metaphysics,* December 1953.

7 The "wonderful" and the "probable" are the basic categories in Albert Cook's distinction between tragedy and comedy (*The Dark Voyage and the Golden Mean,* Cambridge, Mass., 1949, Chap. I).

human experiment, and in this respect its opposite is not comedy or satire but cynicism and nihilism, as in Schopenhauer's theory of resignation. The "problem of the good" plays as vital a part in tragedy as the "problem of evil." It provides the living tension without which tragedy ceases to exist.

Thus tragedy contemplates a universe in which man is not the measure of all things. It confronts a mystery. W. Macneile Dixon[8] pointed out that tragedy started as "an affair with the gods"; and the extent to which literature has become "secularized and humanized," he wrote, is a sign of its departure from (to use our present term) the tragic form. While agreeing with him as to the tendency, one may question the wholesale verdict which he implies. The affair with the gods has not, in the minds of all our artists, been reduced to an affair with the social order, or the environment, or the glands. But certainly where it becomes so, the muse of tragedy walks out; the universe loses its mystery and (to invoke catharsis for a moment) its terror.

The terms "pessimism" and "opti-

[8] *Tragedy*, London, 1924. The extent of my indebtedness to this book, and to the other discussions of tragedy mentioned in this paper, is poorly indicated by such passing references as this. Since observations on tragedy and the theory of tragedy appear in innumerable discussions of particular authors, eras, and related critical problems, a complete list would be far too cumbersome. Among them would be, surely, the standard work of A. C. Bradley and Willard Farnham on Shakespearean tragedy; C. M. Bowra and Cedric Whitman on Sophocles; W. L. Courtney, *The Idea of Tragedy*, London, 1900; Maxwell Anderson, *The Essence of Tragedy*, Washington, 1939; Northrop Frye, "The Archetypes of Literature," *Kenyon Review*, Winter, 1951; Moody Prior, *The Language of Tragedy*, N.Y., 1947; and Herbert Weisinger, *Tragedy and the Paradox of the Fortunate Fall*, Michigan State College Press, 1953, which makes rich use of the archaeological and mythographic studies of the origin of tragedy (Cornford, Harrison, Murray). I am indebted, also, to my colleague Laurence Michel for frequent conversations and helpful criticism.

mism" in the view of the universe as conceived in the tragic form, do not suggest adequate categories, as Nietzsche first pointed out.[9] Tragedy contains them both, goes beyond both, illuminates both, but comes to no conclusion. Tragedy could, it is true, be called pessimistic in its view of the evil in the universe as unremitting and irremediable, the blight man was born for, the necessary condition of existence. It is pessimistic, also, in its view of the overwhelming proportion of evil to good and in its awareness of the mystery of why this should be —the "unfathomable element" in which Ahab foundered. But it is optimistic in what might be called its vitalism, which is in some sense mystical, not earthbound; in its faith in a cosmic good; in its vision, however fleeting, of a world in which all questions could be answered.

2. *Tragic man.* If the tragic form asserts a cosmos, some order behind the immediate disorder, what does it assert about the nature of man, other than that he is a being capable of cosmic affinities? What is tragic man as he lives and moves on this earth? Can he be distinguished meaningfully from the man of comedy, satire, epic or lyric? How does he differ from "pathetic man" or "religious man"? or from man as conceived by the materialistic psychologies? Tragic man shares some qualities, of course, with each of these. I shall stress differences in the appropriate contexts.

Like the cosmos which he views, tragic man is a paradox and a mystery. He is no child of God; yet he feels himself more than a child of earth. He is not the plaything of Fate, but he is not entirely free. He is "both creature and creator" (in Niebuhr's phrase)—"fatefully free and freely fated" (in George Schrader's). He recognizes "the fact of guilt"

[9] See also Reinhold Niebuhr, *Beyond Tragedy*, London, 1938.

while cherishing the "dream of innocence" (Fiedler), and he never fully abandons either position. He is plagued by
the ambiguity of his own nature and of
the world he lives in. He is torn between
the sense in common sense (which is
the norm of satire and rationalistic, or
corrective, comedy) and his own uncommon sense. Aware of the just but irreconcilable claims within and without,
he is conscious of the immorality of his
own morality and suffers in the knowledge of his own recalcitrance.

The dynamic of this recalcitrance is
pride. It sustains his belief, however hum-
bled he may become by later experience,
in his own freedom, in his innocence,
and in his uncommon sense. Tragic man
is man at his most prideful and independent, man glorying in his humanity.
Tragic pride, like everything else about
tragedy, is ambiguous; it can be tainted
with arrogance and have its petty side;
but it is not to be equated with sin or
weakness. The Greeks feared it when it
threatened the gods or slipped into arrogance, but they honoured it and even
worshipped it in their heroes. It was the
common folk, the chorus, who had no
pride, or were "flawless."[10] The chorus
invariably argue against pride, urging caution and moderation, because they know
it leads to suffering; but tragedy as such
does not prejudge it.

While many of these things, again,
might be said of other than tragic man, it
is in the peculiar nature of his suffering,
and in his capacity for suffering and ap-
propriating his suffering, that his distinguishing quality lies. For instance (to
ring changes on the Cartesian formula),
tragic man would not define himself, like
the man of corrective comedy or satire:
"I think, therefore I am"; nor like the

man of achievement (epic): "I act, or
conquer, therefore I am"; nor like the
man of sensibility (lyric): "I feel, therefore I am"; nor like the religious man:
"I believe, therefore I am." Although he
has all these qualities (of thought,
achievement, sensibility, and belief) in
various forms and degrees, the essence of
his nature is brought out by suffering: "I
suffer, I will to suffer, I learn by suffering;
therefore I am." The classic statement, of
course, is Aeschylus's: "Wisdom comes
alone through suffering" (Lattimore's
translation); perhaps the most radical is
Dostoevski's: "Suffering is the sole origin
of consciousness."[11]

This is not to say that only tragic man
suffers or that he who suffers is tragic.
Saints and martyrs suffer and learn by
suffering; Odysseus suffered and learned;
Dante suffered and learned on his journey
with Virgil. But tragic man, I think, is
distinguishable from these others in the
nature of his suffering as conditioned by
its source and locus, in its characteristic
course and consequences (that is, the
ultimate disaster and the "knowledge" it
leads to), and in his intense preoccupation with his own suffering.

But to consider these matters in turn
and to illustrate them briefly:

I have already suggested the main
sources and locus of tragic man's suffering. He suffers because he is more than
usually sensitive to the "terrible disrelations" he sees about him and experiences
in himself. He is more than usually aware
of the mighty opposites in the universe
and in man, of the gulf between desire
and fulfilment, between what is and what
should be. This kind of suffering is suffering on a high level, beyond the reach
of the immature or brutish, and for ever
closed to the extreme optimist, the ex-

[10] Cf. Arthur Miller, "Tragedy and the Common Man," New York *Times*, February 27th,
1949.

[11] *Notes from Underground*, tr. B. G. Guer-
ney.

treme pessimist,[12] or the merely indifferent. It was Job on the ash-heap, the prototype of tragic man, who was first struck by the incongruity between Jehovah's nature and His actions, between desert and reward in this life; and it was he who first asked, not so much for a release from physical suffering as a reasonable explanation of it. But above all, the source of tragic suffering is the sense, in the consciousness of tragic man, of simultaneous guilt and guiltlessness. Tillich called tragedy "a mixture of guilt and necessity." If tragic man could say, "I sinned, therefore I suffer" or "He (or They or God) sinned, therefore I suffer," his problem would be resolved, and the peculiar poignancy of his suffering would be removed. If he felt himself entirely free or entirely determined, he would cease to be tragic. But he is neither—he is, in short, a paradox and mystery, the "riddle of the world."

To draw further distinctions: The element of guilt in tragic suffering distinguishes it from the pathetic suffering of the guiltless and from the suffering of the sentimentalist's bleeding heart. On the other hand, tragic man's sense of fate, and of the mystery of fate, distinguishes his suffering from the suffering (which is little more than embarrassment) of the man of corrective comedy and satire. The suffering of the epic hero has little of the element of bafflement or enigma; it is not, characteristically, spiritual suffering. The Christian in his suffering can confess *total* guilt and look to the promise of redemption through grace.[13] The martyr seeks suffering, accepts it gladly, "glories in tribulation." Tragic man knows nothing of grace and never glories in his suffering. Although he may come to

acquiesce in it partly and "learn" from it (a stage I shall discuss below), his characteristic mood is resentment and dogged endurance. He has not the stoic's patience, although this may be part of what he learns. Characteristically, he is restless, intense, probing and questioning the universe and his own soul (Job, Lear, Ahab). It is true that, from Greek tragedy to tragedy written in the Christian era (Shakespeare and beyond) emphasis shifts from the universe to the soul, from the cosmic to the psychological. But Prometheus had an inner life; Antigone, for all her composure, suffered an ultimate doubt; Oedipus suffered spiritually as he grew to understand the dark ambiguities in his own nature. And we should be mistaken if we tried to interpret the divine powers in the plays of Shakespeare simply as "allegorical symbols for psychological realities."[14]

Tragic man, then, placed in a universe of irreconcilables, acting in a situation in which he is both innocent and guilty, and peculiarly sensitive to the "cursèd spite" of his condition, suffers. What in the tragic view is the characteristic course of this suffering and what further aspects of tragic man are revealed by it? The tragic form develops, not only the partial outlines of a cosmology and a psychology, but of an ethic.

3. *Tragic man and society*. The tragic sufferer may now be viewed in his social and moral relationships. In the tragic world there are several alternatives. A man can default from the human condition—"Curse God and die"—and bring his suffering to an end; he can endure and be silent; he can turn cynic. Tragic man understands these alternatives, feels their attractions, but chooses a different way. Rising in his pride, he protests: he pits himself in some way against whatever, in the heavens above and in the

[12] Cf. William Van O'Connor, *Climates of Tragedy*, Baton Rouge, La., 1943.
[13] Cf. Karl Jaspers, *Tragedy Is Not Enough*, tr. Reiche, Moore, Deutsch; Boston, 1952.

[14] Susan Taubes, *op. cit.*, p. 196.

earth beneath, seems to him to be wrong, oppressive, or personally thwarting. This is the hero's commitment, made early or late, but involving him necessarily in society and in action—with Prometheus and Antigone early, with Hamlet late. What to the orthodox mind would appear to be the wisdom or folly, the goodness or badness, of the commitment is not, in the beginning, the essence of the matter. In the first phase of his course of suffering, the hero's position may be anarchic, individual, romantic. Herein tragedy tests all norms—as, by contrast, satire,[15] comedy, or epic tend to confirm them. The commitment may even be expressed in what society knows as a crime, but, as with tragic pride (of which the commitment is in part the expression), tragedy does not prejudge it. Thus it is said that tragedy studies "the great offenders," and Dostoevski sought among criminals and outcasts for his greatest spiritual discoveries. But the commitment must grow in meaning to include the more-than-personal. Ultimately, and ideally, the tragic hero stands as universal man, speaking for all men. The tragic sufferer, emerging from his early stage of lament or rebellion (Job's opening speech; the first scenes of Prometheus; Lear's early bursts of temper), moves beyond the "intermittences" of his own heart and makes a "pact with the world that is unremitting and sealed."[16]

Since the commitment cannot lead in the direction of escape or compromise, it must involve head-on collision with the forces that would oppress or frustrate. Conscious of the ambiguities without and within, which are the source of his peculiar suffering, tragic man accepts the conflict. It is horrible to do it, he says,

but it is more horrible to leave it undone. He is now in the main phase of his suffering—the "passion."[17]

In his passion he differs from the rebel, who would merely smash; or the romantic hero, who is not conscious of guilt; or the epic hero, who deals with emergencies rather than dilemmas. Odysseus and Aeneas, to be sure, face moral problems, but they proceed in a clear ethical light. Their social norms are secure. But the tragic hero sees a sudden, unexpected evil at the heart of things that infects all things. His secure and settled world has gone wrong, and he must oppose his own ambiguous nature against what he loves. Doing so involves total risk, as the chorus and his friends remind him. He may brood and pause, like Hamlet, or he may proceed with Ahab's fury; but proceed he must.

He proceeds, suffers, and in his suffering "learns." This is the phase of "perception." Although it often culminates in a single apocalyptic scene, a moment of "recognition," as in *Oedipus* and *Othello*, it need not be separate in time from the passion phase. Rather, perception is all that can be summed up in the spiritual and moral change that the hero undergoes from first to last and in the similar change wrought by his actions or by his example in those about him.

For the hero, perception may involve an all-but-complete transformation in character, as with Lear and Oedipus; or a gradual development in poise and self-mastery (Prometheus, Hamlet); or the softening and humanizing of the hard outlines of a character like Antigone's. It may appear in the hero's change from

[15] Cf. Maynard Mack, "The Muse of Satire," *Yale Review*, Spring, 1952.

[16] Wallace Fowlie, "Swann and Hamlet: A Note on the Contemporary Hero," *Partisan Review*, 1942.

[17] Cf. Francis Fergusson, *The Idea of a Theatre*, Princeton, N.J., 1949, Chap. 1, "The Tragic Rhythm of Action." Fergusson translates Kenneth Burke's formulation "*Poiema, Pathema, Mathema*" into "Purpose, Passion, Perception." (See *A Grammar of Motives*, pp. 38 ff.) Cf. also Susan Taubes, *op. cit.*, p. 199.

moody isolation and self-pity to a sense of his sharing in the general human condition, of his responsibility for it and to it. This was one stage in Lear's pilgrimage ("I have ta'en too little care of this") and as far as Dostoevski's Dmitri Karamazov ever got. In all the manifestations of this perception there is an element of Hamlet's "readiness," of an acceptance of destiny that is not merely resignation. At its most luminous it is Lear's and Oedipus's hard-won humility and new understanding of love. It may transform or merely inform, but a change there must be.

And it is more, of course, than merely a moral change, just as the hero's problem is always more than a moral one. His affair is still with the gods. In taking up arms against the ancient cosmic evil, he transcends the human situation, mediating between the human and the divine. It was Orestes's suffering that, in the end, made the heavens more just. In the defeat or death which is the usual lot of the tragic hero, he becomes a citizen of a larger city, still defiant but in a new mood, a "calm of mind," a partial acquiescence. Having at first resented his destiny, he has lived it out, found unexpected meanings in it, carried his case to a more-than-human tribunal. He sees his own destiny, and man's destiny, in its ultimate perspective.

But the perception which completes the tragic form is not dramatized solely through the hero's change, although his pilgrimage provides the traditional tragic structure.[18] The full nature and extent of the new vision is measured also by what happens to the other figures in the total symbolic situation—to the hero's antagonists (King Creon, Claudius, Iago); to his opposites (the trimmers and hangers-on, the Osrics); to his approximates (Ismene, Horatio, Kent, the Chorus). Some he moves, some do not change at all. But his suffering must make a difference somewhere outside himself. After Antigone's death the community (even Creon) reforms around her; the "new acquist" at the end of *Samson Agonistes* is the common note, also, at the end of the Shakespearean tragedies. For the lookers-on there is no sudden rending of the veil of clay, no triumphant assertion of The Moral Order. There has been suffering and disaster, ultimate and irredeemable loss, and there is promise of more to come. But all who are involved have been witness to new revelations about human existence, the evil of evil and the goodness of good. They are more "ready." The same old paradoxes and ambiguities remain, but for the moment they are transcended in the higher vision.

---

[18] Indeed, it has been pointed out that, in an age when the symbol of the hero as the dominating centre of the play seems to have lost its validity with artist and audience, the role is taken over by the artist himself, who is his own tragic hero. That is, "perception" is conveyed more generally, in the total movement of the piece and through all the parts. The "pact with the world" and the suffering are not objectified in a hero's ordeal but seem peculiarly the author's. This quality has been noted in Joyce's *Ulysses*; Berdiaev saw it in Dostoevski; Hardy, Conrad, Faulkner are examples that come to mind. At any rate, the distinction may be useful in determining matters of tone, although it is not clear cut, as distinctions in tone seldom are. But it is one way of pointing to the difference between the tragic tone and the Olympian distance of Meredithian comedy, the harmony of the final phase of Dantesque comedy, or the ironic detachment of satire. Nietzsche spoke of the difference between the Dionysian (or tragic) artist and "the poet of the dramatized epos . . . the calm, unmoved embodiment of Contemplation, whose wide eyes see the picture before them" (*Birth of Tragedy* in *Works*, ed. O. Levy, Edinburgh and London, 1909, III, p. 96).

TRAGEDY: DOSTOEVSKI TO FAULKNER
Richard B. Sewall*

Sewall here considers the possibility of writing tragedy in drama or in fiction in our time. Reflecting the pessimistic and deterministic tone of certain philosophers, from Darwin to Freud, modern writers tend to produce what Sewall terms the "drama of pathos" rather than genuine tragedy. He sees their failure as a failure to embrace the full tragic vision, a thinness and timidity rather than lack of insight or denial of the human spirit.

Literature since Dostoevski that would report faithfully the dire aspects of the human condition has often been appalling witness to the truth of his prophecy. "After Dostoievsky's heroes," wrote Berdyaev,[1] "there is the unforeseeable twentieth century with its promise of a cultural crisis and the end of an era in the world's history." Especially in the two postwar periods, disorientation and violence in human affairs have been the major testimony. Writers such as Ibsen, Conrad, Hardy, Dreiser had reduced the possibility of freedom and transcendence to a minimum. They presented the human struggle against so bleak a cosmic or social background that effort seemed puny indeed in the face of what Conrad called "the fiendish and appalling joke" that is man's lot in the universe—Ivan's irony carried to the bitterest conclusion and redeemed only (in Conrad, for instance) by occasional individual sensitivity to the problem, an increased awareness of the need for human solidarity and responsibility, or (in Ibsen)

of the necessity of clinging to the maximal ideal, however futile.[2] "What makes mankind tragic," wrote Conrad,[3] "is not that they are victims of nature, it is that they are conscious of it.... As soon as you know of your slavery, the pain, the

* The essay is reprinted from *The Vision of Tragedy*, by Richard B. Sewall, Chapter 12, by permission of Yale University Press. Copyright 1959 by Yale University Press.

[1] *Dostoievsky*, p. 75.

[2] See Konstantin Reichardt, "Tragedy of Idealism: Henrik Ibsen," in *Tragic Themes in Western Literature*.

[3] In a letter to R. B. Cunninghame Graham, Jan. 31, 1898 (G. Jean-Aubry, *Joseph Conrad, Life and Letters*, Garden City, Doubleday Page, 1927, 2, 226). Conrad's novels and letters abound in remarks that reveal a view ranging from a subtragic pessimism to a view which, by counterthrust of spirit, is redeemed for tragedy. He may speak (in *Lord Jim*) of the "fiendish joke" of existence, of the "burlesque meanness" of the "Dark Powers," and have Marlow say of Jim's case, "There was not the thickness of a sheet of paper between the rightness and the wrongness of their affair." Again, at one point he suspects that "the aim of creation cannot be ethical at all." In another letter to Cunninghame Graham he writes: "Life knows us not and we do not know life.... Faith is a myth and beliefs shift like mists on the shore: thoughts vanish: words once pronounced, die: and the memory of yesterday is as shadowy as the hope of tomorrow.... And yet he can regard life as "a spectacle for awe, love, admiration, or hate ... but ... never for despair." (Quoted by W. Macneile Dixon, *The Human Situation*, New York, Longmans, Green, 1937, p. 239.) Morton D. Zabel's Introduction to *The Portable Conrad* (1952) is a sensitive treatment of this central aspect of Conrad's thought.

anger, the strife—the tragedy begins. . . ." Subsequently the grim Freudian image showed man as slave to the subrational and subconscious, a being who entertained merely "the illusion of psychic freedom";[4] and the Marxist view pronounced man slave to the great impersonal and external forces of history.[5]

[4] Sigmund Freud, A General Introduction to Psychoanalysis (Garden City Publishing Co., 1943), p. 45. Stanley Edgar Hyman's article, "Freud and the Climate of Tragedy," Partisan Review, Spring 1956, which touches our study at many points, makes a sharp distinction between the "gloomy, stoic, and essentially tragic" Freudian view and the "optimistic and meliorative" (p. 201) interpretation of it by the "revisionists," Horney, Fromm, and Sullivan, who see man (says Hyman) as "fundamentally good, innocent, and unfallen" (p. 207). But in declaring his belief that "the writings of Sigmund Freud once again make a tragic view possible for the modern mind" (p. 201), he seems to be identifying the tragic view with the "gloomy" and the "stoic." The "discovery," or "perception," of tragedy is to him merely man's awakening to the grim facts of his own nature and to the fact that life "is nasty, brutish, and short" (p. 214). This, says Hyman, is what "the great philosophers and the great tragic writers have always said." His strictures upon the revisionists are well taken in regard to tragedy. In their brand of "cultural determinism" in which "whatever is is no individual's fault" (p. 211), tragedy is impossible. But the great tragic writers have said more about life, of course, than that it is nasty, brutish, and short. The crux of the matter, I think, is Freud's view of psychic freedom as illusory. Later in A General Introduction (p. 252) he writes: "But man's craving for grandiosity is now suffering the third and most bitter blow [after Copernicus and Darwin] from present-day psychological research which is endeavouring to prove to the 'ego' of each one of us that he is not even the master in his own house, but that he must remain content with the veriest scraps of information about what is going on unconsciously in his own mind." If man is not in some degree the master in his own house, who can be held responsible for anything, where is guilt, and where is tragedy?

[5] What happens to tragedy under statism of any kind is well illustrated in George Orwell's 1984 (New York, Harcourt, Brace, 1949), p. 31, where the protagonist reminisces in this vein about his mother's death: "The thing that now suddenly struck Winston was that his mother's death, nearly thirty years ago, had been tragic and sorrowful in a way that was no longer possible. Tragedy, he perceived, belonged to the

During the decade of the twenties, many observers declared tragedy bankrupt in the general devaluation. In 1924, Macneile Dixon saw no hope for any more "tragedy of the center," by which he meant tragedy (like the Greek and the Elizabethan) which posited freedom and a cosmic order—the "affair with the gods." In 1929 Joseph Wood Krutch's famous essay, "The Tragic Fallacy,"[6] denied the possibility of tragedy in the modern world, from which (he wrote) "both the Glory of God and the Glory of Man have departed. . . . Our cosmos may be farcical or it may be pathetic but it has not the dignity of tragedy and we cannot accept it as such." In the critical skirmish that followed Krutch's essay, his assumptions about tragedy were challenged; but the bulk of contemporary "tragic" fiction, both before and after, tended to confirm his views.

But perhaps not for the reasons he alleged: the death of God and the debasement of man in his own eyes—"the enfeeblement [in Krutch's phrase] of the human spirit." "The best that we can

ancient time, to a time when there were still privacy, love, and friendship, and when the members of a family stood by one another without needing to know the reason. . . . [His mother] had sacrificed herself to a conception of loyalty that was private and unalterable. . . . Today there were fear, hatred, and pain, but no dignity of emotion, no deep or complex sorrows."

[6] In The Modern Temper (New York, Harcourt, Brace, 1929), ch. 5. A vigorous reply to this essay came in Mark Harris, The Case for Tragedy, New York, G. P. Putnam's Sons, 1932. Questioning Krutch's "absolute" requirements for tragedy, Harris set up a sociological, or relativistic, theory based on the concept of the democratic "representative individual" (p. 163), whose values the audience shares. The "tragic response" is elicited when these values are jeopardized. Although demonstrating effectively that Krutch had not the last word in this controversy, Harris' theory depends too much, I think, on the "response" of the audience. It speaks more of what tragedy does than what it is. He does not question the nature of the values shared by hero and audience.

achieve," he wrote, "is pathos and the most we can do is feel sorry for ourselves." Granted that the bent of history, especially in the era in which Krutch wrote, was away from tragedy: the disillusioning effects of the first World War, described by Hemingway, for instance, in the weariness and cynicism of *The Sun Also Rises*; or on the other hand the shallow optimisms of the postwar boom (as crippling to tragedy as despair), of technology, and the promises of the social and psychiatric sciences. Granted that contemporary heroes often lack "nobility," actions "magnitude," and that a prevalent tone is despair: "I don't think, I operate," said Rinaldi in *A Farewell to Arms*. Granted also that pathos is a dominant mood in many contemporary would-be tragedies. Indeed, "the drama of pathos" has recently been declared a unique achievement of our theater—and a positive achievement, so the argument runs, of dignity and significance comparable to the tragic achievement of the Greeks and Elizabethans.[7] And granted, finally, the unsettling effects of modern philosophic views of time and space, so that the artist, sensitive to the relativities of his time, and feeling himself estopped

from timeless truth, sees himself justified only in snatching a moment from the flux and rendering it vivid in his fictions.

But our era has produced not only artists who saw all this and in the way of Zola (and Thomas Middleton) reported it "without prejudice, without personality" but some who saw around and above it. Indeed, the very attempt to fictionalize it, to give form to the despair and the pity and the flux, is a gesture toward tragedy; it is the first phase of the gesture, or action, of tragedy as we have earlier defined it. In this sense, as it has been said of Joyce's *Ulysses*, many a modern artist is his own tragic hero.[8] The values of tragedy have not disappeared, even if they no longer are embodied in the traditional symbolic figure of the tragic hero. They have been scattered, relocated, distributed. A less dogmatic view than Krutch's would see no blanket capitulation among modern writers. The perceptions are there—even of the nobility, dignity, and magnitude which Krutch found wanting—but he is right that they have nowhere found the synthesis and full development of a realized form.

Apparently there is no want of will on the part of the artists themselves. Although it may be little more than an interesting cultural phenomenon, or of

---

[7] Preston T. Roberts, Jr., "Bringing Pathos into Focus," *University of Chicago Magazine*, Feb. 1954, p. 7: "The first and most distinguishing mark of modern plays is their pathos." The Greek plays, like *Oedipus*, says Roberts, are preoccupied with "what is simply and purely tragic about life," and "Christian plays like *King Lear*" with "what is redemptive or more than tragic in life...." A *Streetcar Named Desire* and *Death of a Salesman* are typical modern plays "distinguished by their absorption with what is pathetic or less than tragic and incapable of redemption in experience. They seem to be peculiarly concerned with those aspects of experience which lie below the conscious mind or active will...." The question, of course, is what *is* "simply and purely tragic." Does Roberts mean that there is no redemption of any kind in *Oedipus*, and is the idea of redemption so powerful in *Lear* as to raise it "above" tragedy? I hope my previous analyses have made my answers to these questions clear.

[8] F. L. Lucas, in *Tragedy in Relation to Aristotle's Poetics* (pp. 57–8), makes this point: "Complaining of the want of great personalities in this play or that, they [the critics] forgot the author. For the characters may be poor in spirit and feeble in desire, and the play remain tragic in spite of it, if we feel that the author is himself none of these things and has never cheated or paltered in his picture of men as they are." I am doubtful how far one can carry this view without accepting mere reportage, however stark and "honest," as tragedy. If all his characters are "poor in spirit and feeble in desire," how and where can the author dramatize the transcendence, the perception, the "knowledge" indispensable to the full vision of tragedy? Tragedy cannot stop with the realist's picture of men "as they are."

autobiographical meaning only, it is clear that even in this period of the alleged dearth of tragedy artists have consciously striven to realize the form according to whatever notion it was they entertained of it. Neither Hardy nor Conrad called their novels "tragedies," but Hardy had a coherent theory of tragedy, viewed man's lot as "tragic,"[9] and Conrad frequently called his characters and situations "tragic." Perhaps, like Ibsen who, after one abortive self-styled verse tragedy (*Catilina*), called his subsequent work "dramas" or "social dramas," Hardy and Conrad realized that their view of man's fate fell too far short of the full tragic affirmation to warrant calling their novels tragedies. Hardy's universe was much like Conrad's "fiendish joke," and he (though less so than Conrad) saw scant value in suffering. ("Error and chance," said Hardy, "rule the world, not justice.") But Dreiser wrote what he called *An American Tragedy*; and O'Neill called himself "a bit of a poet, who has labored ... to see the transfiguring nobility of tragedy, in as near the Greek sense as one can grasp it" and set out to "develop a tragic expression in terms of transfigured modern values."[10] Hemingway

made no such claims (although he once called A *Farewell to Arms* his *Romeo and Juliet*), nor did Fitzgerald; but serious and not unwarranted claims to "genuine tragedy" have been made for them by others. Latterly, in a flurry of interest in the idea of tragedy since World War II, dramatists such as Arthur Miller and Tennessee Williams, articulate about their craft, have freely discussed their own works in the context of traditional tragedy.[11] And it may be significant of a

9 See Helen Garwood, *Thomas Hardy: An Illustration of the Philosophy of Schopenhauer* (Philadelphia, The John C. Winston Co., 1911), ch. 3, for a perceptive exposition of Hardy's views on tragedy. The quoted remarks on Hardy in the following paragraphs are from her study. In general, Hardy saw no tragedy where the individual is able to help himself; there is "tragedy," he felt, only when the individual is helpless and blameless, a victim of the "blind irrationality" of the universe. "So we get characters," writes Helen Garwood, "who are not aggressive nor strenuous, who seldom take the initiative, who do not demand much, who do not challenge life, who scarcely aim at all, much less at the stars ... and above all [are] capable of endurance. Placed, against their will, in a world not to their liking, they are resigned to it and will make the best of it" (p. 68).

10 See Sophus Keith Winther, *Eugene O'Neill: A Critical Study* (New York, Random

House, 1934), p. 220, who quotes the passage from Arthur Hobson Quinn's *History of the American Drama* (New York, F. S. Crofts, 1943), 2, 199. The extent to which O'Neill succeeded in achieving in his plays "the transfiguring nobility of tragedy" has been variously argued. See for instance Herbert Muller's sympathetic but, in the end, dissenting view in his section on O'Neill in *The Spirit of Tragedy* (New York, Alfred A. Knopf, 1956), pp. 311–19. "He was in fact," writes Muller, "closer in spirit to Greek tragedy than any other modern dramatist. His high aim may therefore make one more painfully aware of his limitations, both as thinker and as poet." Muller points in a general way to some of these limitations—the "sometimes limp" colloquial dialogue, the "sometimes crude" and labored psychology stemming from "a secondhand Freudianism learned by rote." They are more specifically illustrated in Doris M. Alexander's study of *Mourning Becomes Electra* (the play which invites most immediate comparison with Greek tragedy) in "Psychological Fate in *Mourning Becomes Electra*," *PMLA*, Dec. 1953.

11 I have already referred to Miller's essay on "Tragedy and the Common Man." He made another statement of his ideas on tragedy in "The 'Salesman' Has a Birthday," *New York Times Theater Section*, Feb. 5, 1950. See also his Introduction to *Arthur Miller's Collected Plays*, New York, Viking Press, 1957, where he makes some pungent remarks on academic definitions of tragedy. Of *Death of a Salesman* he says: "I set out not to 'write a tragedy' in this play, but to show the truth as I saw it. However, some of the attacks upon it as a pseudo-tragedy contain ideas so misleading, and in some cases so laughable, that it might be in place here to deal with them" (p. 31). It might be said that any writer, at this late date, who sets out to "write a tragedy" is as vulnerable as the critic who attacks a play because "it is not a tragedy." The crux of the matter is the nature of the truth revealed in the play, and one may properly ask whether it is "tragic," or

resurgent spirit that the critics seem (for better or worse) more than ever concerned with the label. About every new serious play or novel the question is asked, "Is it a tragedy?" Indeed, the will to tragedy seems so great on both sides of the footlights that there is a general turn toward short cuts. Arthur Miller defends his "common man" as a fitting protagonist in genuine tragedy, and Brooks Atkinson finds Williams' *Summer and Smoke* "a tragedy because its heroine has a noble spirit."[12] In academic circles there is a notable increase (on both sides of the desk) of interest in tragedy and the idea of the tragic—perhaps symptomatic (among students) of a disoriented generation reaching for forgotten values, for a vision of life free from dogma, tonic and positive, however precarious; and (among teachers) of the perennial desire to set the problem of form and meaning in literature in its ultimate perspective—this time by way of an ancient discipline that has latterly known some neglect.[13]

And there has been no want of realization, however partial and fragmented, of genuine tragic values. Hardy is not "dispiriting" in the sense in which cynicism is dispiriting; he depicts people who "refuse to be dwarfed into sluggishness." The stars may shine down on Egdon Heath coldly and impersonally, but they are beautiful. Life is presented in his novels as neither "little, nor cheap, nor easily found out." Ibsen's attitude toward his generation was tragic in many ways; and however he fails to evoke "the original terror" in his dramatic situations, he is acutely conscious of the problem—"tragic" up to a certain point—of the gifted or idealistic individual in the face of a hostile and uncomprehending society. Both Heyst and Lord Jim of Conrad's stories achieved tragic "victories," transcending the pasts which threatened their moral maturity and freedom. If Dreiser and O'Neill misunderstood the Greek idea of fate to imply a denial of human freedom as complete as Marx's and Freud's, their characters have occasional glimpses beyond their bondage; they are sometimes capable (like Clyde Griffiths and Lavinia Mannon) of being schooled in suffering, or (like the wrangling Tyrones) of showing honesty, moral

---

"pseudo-tragic," or something else. For now, it is enough to say that these are questions that seem to be of increasing concern to us, and it is well that it is so. To my knowledge, Tennessee Williams has never discussed his craft as fully as Miller, but see his brief prefatory notes to *The Glass Menagerie*, Norfolk, Conn., 1949, and *27 Wagons Full of Cotton*, Norfolk, Conn., 1953. Above all, see Elia Kazan's notes on *A Streetcar Named Desire* in *Directing the Play*, ed. Toby Cole and Helen Chinoy (New York, Bobbs-Merrill, 1953): "This is like a classic tragedy," writes Kazan. "Blanche is Medea or someone pursued by the Harpies, the Harpies being *her own nature*" (p. 301).

[12] Atkinson reviewed Williams' play in the *New York Times*, April 25, 1952.

[13] Perhaps, among other reasons, because of the influence on teaching of the methods introduced by I. A. Richards' *Practical Criticism* (1930) and the development of the New Criticism? This was true, certainly, in many academic communities in America. In some quarters the current interest in tragedy is seen as a reaction against the so-called formalistic approach, with its sharp focus on the inner harmonies and structure of the single work, particularly the

lyric poem. Herbert Muller makes this a minor polemical theme of his *The Spirit of Tragedy*, though he makes exceptions: "The language of a poem is a continuous reference to things outside itself. Its meaning is never intact, self-contained, self-explanatory. Hence a sensitive reader like Cleanth Brooks, who is most insistent on the necessity of staying inside the poem, is usually carried further afield than most readers just because he finds poetry more profoundly suggestive" (p. 13). The danger, of course, is that the student of tragedy, concerned as it is with such momentous issues, may go too far afield and forget that he is dealing with works of art. The two disciplines are complementary—or should be. The "tragic analysis" as I have tried to illustrate it in this book—its focus on "the vision of evil: the vision of the good"—is never complete until the last metaphor and the last structural relationship are explored for their full meaning.

courage, and love which transcend self and the wreckage of their lives. Fitzgerald's Gatsby cherished an ideal, however meretricious; died for it; and brought his choric observer (Nick Carraway) to a new "moral attention." Hemingway's Frederick Henry ends in stoical despair (his universe, too, is "a dirty trick"), but not before he has learned to love— "I don't love," he told the priest at first —and has been moved by pressures of his tragic situation to thoughts, even religious ones, that point to realities beyond the sense of "nothingness" in which he leaves his Catherine's deathbed. Koestler's Rubashov in Lubyanka (*Darkness at Noon*) finally capitulates to the will of the party, but not before he has hearkened to the all-but-forgotten "first person singular" whose reality he denied through forty years of party discipline. He sees the stars shine above the turrets of his prison; perceives what he calls (after Freud?) "the oceanic sense" as the neglected dimension of his party's thinking and as ultimately denying the Marxist promise; and comes (before his capitulation) to Faustus' terrifying realization: "What about the infinite?"

None of these insights, however bracing, will make a tragedy. They are incidental, not powerful enough in their contexts to establish what Henry Myers called the "equivalence" of the good and evil necessary to tragedy. Nor are they incorporated in forms (Conrad is perhaps the closest) which do justice to the full dimensions of tragedy as they have been marked out by the artists of the tradition. Tragedy (as we have seen), coming at the maturity of a culture, has traditionally put to the test of action *all* the formulations, philosophical and religious, which man has shored up against his ruins. It sees man in all his relationships—to the cosmos, to society, to himself—and in all his possibilities as well as limitations. It sees the present evil not only in terms of the past but endurable in terms of the future, and all these phases are made effective in the progressing dialectic of the action. (This is no prescription for tragedy; it is simply a statement of what has been done.) In view of all these concerns, what seems most obvious about contemporary tragic writing is not so much its lack of insight or its denial of the human spirit but its thinness, its timidity, its failure to pursue the full implications of its genuine insights. The insights remain as insights only, incapable of maintaining the tension of the tragic drama. (A tragedy is not a tragedy simply because its heroine has a "noble spirit" or its hero intimations of the infinite.) And so, more often than not, the potential tragedy ends as a single-voiced expression of lyric pathos or stoic despair.

CHAPTER 3

Comic Mode

FROM AN ESSAY ON COMEDY
George Meredith[*]

Meredith distinguishes what he calls comedy from satire, irony, and humor. Comedy is the spirit of moderation, the spirit of sanity and reason. The comic spirit observes the rigidity and incongruity of mankind from a position of high detachment. It is primarily intellectual rather than emotional, but at times it is so serious that merely the introduction of intense sympathy would be enough to turn comedy to tragedy.

... You may estimate your capacity for comic perception by being able to detect the ridicule of them you love without loving them less; and more by being able to see yourself somewhat ridiculous in dear eyes, and accepting the correction their image of you proposes.

Each one of an affectionate couple may be willing, as we say, to die for the other, yet unwilling to utter the agreeable word at the right moment; but if the wits were sufficiently quick for them to perceive that they are in a comic situation, as affectionate couples must be when they quarrel, they would not wait for the moon or the almanac, or a Dorine, to bring back the flood-tide of tender feelings, that they should join hands and lips.

If you detect the ridicule, and your kindliness is chilled by it, you are slipping into the grasp of Satire.

If, instead of falling foul of the ridiculous person with a satiric rod, to make him writhe and shriek aloud, you prefer to sting him under a semi-caress, by which he shall in his anguish be rendered dubious whether indeed anything has hurt him, you are an engine of Irony.

If you laugh all round him, tumble him, roll him about, deal him a smack, and drop a tear on him, own his likeness to you, and yours to your neighbor, spare him as little as you shun, pity him as much as you expose, it is a spirit of Humor that is moving you.

* The selection is reprinted from *An Essay on Comedy and the Uses of the Comic Spirit*, Charles Scribner's Sons, 1897.

The comic, which is the perceptive, is the governing spirit, awakening and giving aim to these powers of laughter, but it is not to be confounded with them; it enfolds a thinner form of them, differing from satire in not sharply driving into the quivering sensibilities, and from humor in not comforting them and tucking them up, or indicating a broader than the range of this bustling world to them.

Fielding's Jonathan Wild presents a case of this peculiar distinction, when that man of eminent greatness remarks upon the unfairness of a trial in which the condemnation has been brought about by twelve men of the opposite party; for it is not satiric, it is not humorous; yet it is immensely comic to hear a guilty villain protesting that his own "party" should have a voice in the law. It opens an avenue into villains' ratiocination. And the comic is not canceled though we should suppose Jonathan to be giving play to his humor. (I may have dreamed this, or had it suggested to me, for, on referring to *Jonathan Wild*, I do not find it.) Apply the case to the man of deep wit, who is ever certain of his condemnation by the opposite party, and then it ceases to be comic, and will be satiric.

The look of Fielding upon Richardson is essentially comic. His method of correcting the sentimental writer is a mixture of the comic and the humorous. Parson Adams is a creation of humor. But both the conception and the presentation of Alceste and of Tartuffe, of Célimène and Philaminte, are purely comic, addressed to the intellect; there is no humor in them, and they refresh the intellect they quicken to detect their comedy, by force of the contrast they offer between themselves and the wiser world about them—that is to say, society, or that assemblage of minds whereof the comic spirit has its origin.

Byron had splendid powers of humor, and the most poetic satire that we have example of, fusing at times to hard irony. He had no strong comic sense, or he would not have taken an anti-social position, which is directly opposed to the comic; and in his philosophy, judged by philosophers, he is a comic figure by reason of this deficiency. "*Sobald er reflectirt ist er ein Kind*" [As soon as he reflects, he is a child], Goethe says of him. Carlyle sees him in this comic light, treats him in the humorous manner.

The satirist is a moral agent, often a social scavenger, working on a storage of bile.

The ironist is one thing or another, according to his caprice. Irony is the humor of satire; it may be savage, as in Swift, with a moral object, or sedate, as in Gibbon, with a malicious. The foppish irony fretting to be seen, and the irony which leers, that you shall not mistake its intention, are failures in satiric effort pretending to the treasures of ambiguity.

The humorist of mean order is a refreshing laugher, giving tone to the feelings, and sometimes allowing the feelings to be too much for him; but the humorist of high has an embrace of contrasts beyond the scope of the comic poet.

Heart and mind laugh out at Don Quixote, and still you brood on him. The juxtaposition of the knight and squire is a comic conception, the opposition of their natures most humorous. They are as different as the two hemispheres in the time of Columbus, yet they touch, and are bound in one, by laughter. The knight's great aims and constant mishaps, his chivalrous valiancy exercised on absurd objects, his good sense along the high road of the craziest of expeditions, the compassion he plucks out of derision, and the admirable figure he preserves while stalking through the frantically grotesque and burlesque assailing him, are in the loftiest moods of humor, fusing the tragic sentiment with the comic narrative. The stroke of the great humorist is world-wide, with lights of tragedy in his laughter.

Taking a living great, though not creative, humorist to guide our description: the skull of Yorick is in his hands in our seasons of festival; he sees visions of primitive man capering preposterously under the gorgeous robes of ceremonial. Our souls must be on fire when we wear solemnity, if we would not press upon his shrewdest nerve. Finite and infinite flash from one to the other with him, lending him a two-edged thought that peeps out of his peacefullest lines by fits, like the lantern of the fire-watcher at windows, going the rounds at night. The comportment and performances of men in society are to him, by the vivid comparison with their mortality, more grotesque than respectable. But ask yourself: "Is he always to be relied on for justness?" He will fly straight as the emissary eagle back to Jove at the true Hero. He will also make as determined a swift descent upon the man of his wilful choice, whom we cannot distinguish as a true one. This vast power of his, built up of the feelings and the intellect in union, is often wanting in proportion and in discretion. Humorists touching upon history or society are given to be capricious. They are, as in the case of Sterne, given to be sentimental; for with them the feelings are primary, as with singers. Comedy, on the other hand, is an interpretation of the general mind, and is for that reason of necessity kept in restraint. The French lay marked stress on *mesure et goût* [measure and taste], and they own how much they owe to Molière for leading them in simple justness and taste. We can teach them many things; they can teach us in this.

The comic poet is in the narrow field, or enclosed square, of the society he depicts; and he addresses the still narrower enclosure of men's intellects, with reference to the operation of the social world upon their characters. He is not concerned with beginnings or endings or surroundings, but with what you are now weaving. To understand his work and value it, you must have a sober liking of your kind, and a sober estimate of our civilized qualities. The aim and business of the comic poet are misunderstood, his meaning is not seized nor his point of view taken, when he is accused of dishonoring our nature and being hostile to sentiment, tending to spitefulness and making an unfair use of laughter. Those who detect irony in comedy do so because they choose to see it in life. Poverty, says the satirist, "has nothing harder in itself than that it makes men ridiculous." But poverty is never ridiculous to comic perception until it attempts to make its rags conceal its bareness in a forlorn attempt at decency, or foolishly to rival ostentation. Caleb Balderstone, in his endeavor to keep up the honor of a noble household in a state of beggary, is an exquisitely comic character. In the case of "poor relatives," on the other hand, it is the rich, whom they perplex, that are really comic; and to laugh at the former, not seeing the comedy of the latter, is to betray dullness of vision. Humorist and satirist frequently hunt together as ironists in pursuit of the grotesque, to the exclusion of the comic. That was an affecting moment in the history of the Prince Regent, when the First Gentleman of Europe burst into tears at a sarcastic remark of Beau Brummell's on the cut of his coat. Humor, satire, irony, pounce on it altogether as their common prey. The Comic Spirit eyes, but does not touch, it. Put into action, it would be farcical. It is too gross for comedy.

Incidents of a kind casting ridicule on

our unfortunate nature, instead of our conventional life, provoke derisive laughter, which thwarts the comic idea. But derision is foiled by the play of the intellect. Most of doubtful causes in contest are open to comic interpretation, and any intellectual pleading of a doubtful cause contains germs of an idea of comedy.

The laughter of satire is a blow in the back or the face. The laughter of comedy is impersonal and of unrivaled politeness, nearer a smile—often no more than a smile. It laughs through the mind, for the mind directs it; and it might be called the humor of the mind.

One excellent test of the civilization of a country, as I have said, I take to be the flourishing of the comic idea and comedy; and the test of true comedy is that it shall awaken thoughtful laughter.

If you believe that our civilization is founded in common sense (and it is the first condition of sanity to believe it), you will, when contemplating men, discern a Spirit overhead; not more heavenly than the light flashed upward from glassy surfaces, but luminous and watchful; never shooting beyond them, nor lagging in the rear; so closely attached to them that it may be taken for a slavish reflex, until its features are studied. It has the sage's brows, and the sunny malice of a faun lurks at the corners of the half-closed lips drawn in an idle wariness of half-tension. That slim feasting smile, shaped like the long-bow, was once a big round satyr's laugh, that flung up the brows like a fortress lifted by gunpowder. The laugh will come again, but it will be of the order of the smile, finely-tempered, showing sunlight of the mind, mental richness rather than noisy enormity. Its common aspect is one of unsolicitous observation, as if surveying a full field and having leisure to dart on its chosen morsels, without any fluttering eagerness.

Men's future upon earth does not attract it; their honesty and shapeliness in the present does; and whenever they wax out of proportion, overblown, affected, pretentious, bombastical, hypocritical, pedantic, fantastically delicate; whenever it sees them self-deceived or hoodwinked, given to run riot in idolatries, drifting into vanities, congregating in absurdities, planning short-sightedly, plotting dementedly; whenever they are at variance with their professions, and violate the unwritten but perceptible laws binding them in consideration one to another; whenever they offend sound reason, fair justice; are false in humility or mined with conceit, individually, or in the bulk; the Spirit overhead will look humanely malign, and cast an oblique light on them, followed by volleys of silvery laughter. That is the Comic Spirit.

Not to distinguish it is to be bull-blind to the spiritual, and to deny the existence of a mind of man where minds of men are in working conjunction.

You must, as I have said, believe that our state of society is founded in common sense, otherwise you will not be struck by the contrasts the Comic Spirit perceives, or have it to look to for your consolation. You will, in fact, be standing in that peculiar oblique beam of light, yourself illuminated to the general eye as the very object of chase and doomed quarry of the thing obscure to you. But to feel its presence, and to see it, is your assurance that many sane and solid minds are with you in what you are experiencing; and this of itself spares you the pain of satirical heat, and the bitter craving to strike heavy blows. You share the sublime of wrath, that would not have hurt the foolish, but merely demonstrate their foolishness. Molière was contented to revenge himself on the critics of the *École des Femmes* by writing the *Critique de l'École des Femmes*, one of the wisest as well as the playfullest of studies in criticism. A perception of the Comic Spirit gives high fellowship. You become a citizen of the selecter world, the highest we know of in connection with our old world, which is not supermundane. Look there for your unchallengeable upper class! You feel that you are one of this our civilized community, that you cannot escape from it, and would not if you could. Good hope sustains you; weariness does not overwhelm you; in isolation you see no charms for vanity; personal pride is greatly moderated. Nor shall your title of citizenship exclude you from worlds of imagination or of devotion. The Comic Spirit is not hostile to the sweetest song-fully poetic. Chaucer bubbles with it; Shakespeare overflows; there is a mild moon's ray of it (pale with super-refinement through distance from our flesh and blood planet) in *Comus*. Pope has it, and it is the daylight side of the night half-obscuring Cowper. It is only hostile to the priestly element when that, by baleful swelling, transcends and overlaps the bounds of its office; and then, in extreme cases, it is too true to itself to speak, and veils the lamp—as, for example, the spectacle of Bossuet over the dead body of Molière, at which the dark angels may, but men do not, laugh.

We have had comic pulpits, for a sign that the laughter-moving and the worshipful may be in alliance; I know not how far comic, or how much assisted in seeming so by the unexpectedness and the relief of its appearance; at least they are popular—they are said to win the ear. Laughter is open to perversion, like other good things; the scornful and the brutal sorts are not unknown to us; but the laughter directed by the Comic Spirit is a harmless wine, conducing to sobriety in the degree that it enlivens. It enters you like fresh air into a study, as when one of the sudden contrasts of the comic idea floods the brain like reassuring daylight. You are cognizant of the true kind by feeling that you take it in, savor it, and have what flowers live on, natural air for food. That which you give out—the joyful roar—is not the better part; let that go to good-fellowship and the benefit of the lungs. Aristophanes promises his auditors that, if they will retain the ideas of the comic poet carefully, as they keep dried fruits in boxes, their garments shall smell odoriferous of wisdom throughout the year. The boast will not be thought an empty one by those who have choice friends that have stocked themselves according to his directions. Such treasuries of sparkling laughter are wells in our desert. Sensitiveness to the comic laugh is a step in civilization. To shrink from being an object of it is a step in cultivation. We know the degree of refinement in men by the matter they will laugh at, and the ring of the laugh; but we know likewise that the larger natures are distinguished by the great breadth of their power of laughter, and no one really loving Molière is refined by that love to despise or be dense to Aristophanes, though it may be that the lover of Aristophanes will not have risen to the height of Molière. Embrace them both, and you have the whole scale of laughter in your breast. Nothing in the world surpasses in stormy fun the scene in the *Frogs*, when Bacchus and Xanthias receive their thrashings from the hands of businesslike Acacus, to discover which is the divinity of the two by his imperviousness to the mortal condition of pain, and each, under the obligation of not crying out, makes believe that his horrible bellow—the god's "*iou! iou!*" being the lustier—means only the stopping of a sneeze, or horsemen sighted, or the prelude to an invocation to some deity, and the slave contrives that the god shall get the bigger lot of blows. Passages of Rabelais, one or two in *Don Quixote,* and the supper "in the manner of the ancients" in *Peregrine Pickle,* are of a similar cataract of laughter. But it is not illuminating; it is not the laughter of the mind. Molière's laughter, in his purest comedies, is ethereal—as light to our nature, as color to our thoughts. The *Misanthrope* and the *Tartuffe* have no audible laughter, but the characters are steeped in the comic spirit. They quicken the mind through laughter, from coming out of the mind; and the mind accepts them because they are clear interpretations of certain chapters of the Book lying open before us all. Between these two stand Shakespeare and Cervantes, with the richer laugh of heart and mind in one; with much of the Aristophanic robustness, something of Molière's delicacy.

The laughter heard in circles not pervaded by the comic idea will sound harsh and soulless, like versified prose, if you step into them with a sense of the distinction. You will fancy you have changed your habitation to a planet remoter from the sun. You may be among powerful brains, too. You will not find poets—or but a stray one, overworshiped. You will find learned men undoubtedly, professors, reputed philosophers, and illustrious dilettanti. They have in them, perhaps, every element composing light, except the comic. They read verse, they discourse of art; but their eminent faculties are not under that vigilant sense of a collective supervision, spiritual and present, which we have taken note of. They build a temple of arrogance; they speak much in the voice of oracles; their hilarity, if it does not dip in grossness, is usually a form of pugnacity.

Insufficiency of sight in the eye looking outward has deprived them of the eye that should look inward. They have never weighed themselves in the delicate balance of the comic idea, so as to obtain a suspicion of the rights and dues of the world; and they have, in consequence, an irritable personality. A very learned English professor crushed an argument in a political discussion by asking his adversary angrily. "Are you aware, Sir, that I am a philologer?"

The practice of polite society will help in training them, and the professor on a sofa, with beautiful ladies on each side of him, may become their pupil and a scholar in manners without knowing it; he is at least a fair and pleasing spectacle to the comic Muse. But the society named polite is volatile in its adorations, and to-morrow will be petting a bronzed soldier, or a black African, or a prince, or a spiritualist; ideas cannot take root in its ever-shifting soil. It is besides addicted in self-defence to gabble exclusively of the affairs of its rapidly revolving world, as children on a whirli-go-round bestow their attention on the wooden horse or cradle ahead of them, to escape from giddiness and preserve a notion of identity. The professor is better out of a circle that often confounds by lionizing, sometimes annoys by abandoning, and always confuses. The school that teaches gently what peril there is lest a cultivated head should still be coxcomb's, and the collisions which may befall high-soaring minds, empty or full, is more to be recommended than the sphere of incessant motion supplying it with material. . . .

FROM LAUGHTER
Henri Bergson*

Laughter is caused by seeing the human being as a machine, according to Bergson—it is the "mechanical encrusted on the living." The three principal means of creating the comic are repetition, inversion, and reciprocal interference of series. The comic character is generally comic in proportion to his ignorance of himself. In developing these and other axioms of comedy, Bergson investigates both the psychology of laughter and its application to literature.

...To sum up, whatever be the doctrine to which our reason assents, our imagination has a very clear-cut philosophy of its own: in every human form it sees the effort of a soul which is shaping matter, a soul which is infinitely supple and perpetually in motion, subject to no law of gravitation, for it is not the earth that attracts it. This soul imparts a portion of its winged lightness to the body it animates: the immateriality which thus passes into matter is what is called gracefulness. Matter, however, is obstinate and resists. It draws to itself the ever-alert activity of this higher principle, would fain convert it to its own inertia and cause it to revert to mere automatism. It would fain immobilise the intelligently varied movements of the body in stupidly contracted grooves, stereotype in permanent grimaces the fleeting expressions of the face, in short imprint on the whole person such an attitude as to make it appear immersed and absorbed in the materiality of some mechanical occupation instead of ceaselessly renew-

ing its vitality by keeping in touch with a living ideal. Where matter thus succeeds in dulling the outward life of the soul, in petrifying its movements and thwarting its gracefulness, it achieves, at the expense of a body, an effect that is comic. If, then, at this point we wish to define the comic by comparing it with its contrary, we should have to contrast it with gracefulness even more than with beauty. It partakes rather of the unsprightly than of the unsightly, of *rigidness* rather than of *ugliness*.

We will now pass from the comic element in *forms* to that in *gestures* and *movements*. Let us at once state the law which seems to govern all the phenomena of this kind. It may indeed be deduced without any difficulty from the considerations stated above.

The attitudes, gestures and movements of the human body are laughable in exact proportion as that body reminds us of a mere machine....

Something mechanical encrusted on the living will represent a cross at which we must halt, a central image from which the imagination branches off in different directions. What are these directions? There appear to be three main ones. We will follow them one after the other, and then continue our onward course.

1. In the first place, this view of the mechanical and the living dovetailed into each other makes us incline towards the vaguer image of *some rigidity or other* applied to the mobility of life, in an awkward attempt to follow its lines and counterfeit its suppleness. Here we perceive how easy it is for a garment to become ridiculous. It might almost be said that every fashion is laughable in some respect. Only, when we are dealing with the fashion of the day, we are so accustomed to it that the garment seems, in our mind, to form one with the individual wearing it. We do not separate them in imagination. The idea no longer occurs to us to contrast the inert rigidity of the covering with the living suppleness of the object covered: consequently, the comic here remains in a latent condition. It will only succeed in emerging when the natural incompatibility is so deepseated between the covering and the covered that even an immemorial association fails to cement this union: a case in point is our head and top hat. Suppose, however, some eccentric individual dresses himself in the fashion of former times our attention is immediately drawn to the clothes themselves; we absolutely distinguish them from the individual, we say that the latter *is disguising himself,*— as though every article of clothing were not a disguise!—and the laughable aspect of fashion comes out of the shadow into the light. . . .

Let us go on to society. As we are both in and of it, we cannot help treating it as a living being. Any image, then, suggestive of the notion of a society disguising itself, or of a social masquerade, so to speak, will be laughable. Now, such a notion is formed when we perceive anything inert or stereotyped, or simply ready-made, on the surface of living

society. There we have rigidity over again, clashing with the inner suppleness of life. The ceremonial side of social life must, therefore, always include a latent comic element, which is only waiting for an opportunity to burst into full view. It might be said that ceremonies are to the social body what clothing is to the individual body: they owe their seriousness to the fact that they are identified, in our minds, with the serious object with which custom associates them, and when we isolate them in imagination, they forthwith lose their seriousness. For any ceremony, then, to become comic, it is enough that our attention be fixed on the ceremonial element in it, and that we neglect its matter, as philosophers say, and think only of its form. Every one knows how easily the comic spirit exercises its ingenuity on social actions of a stereotyped nature, from an ordinary prize-distribution to the solemn sitting of a court of justice. Any form or formula is a ready-made frame into which the comic element may be fitted.

To sum up, then, we have one and the same effect, which assumes ever subtler forms as it passes from the idea of an artificial *mechanisation* of the human body, if such an expression is permissible, to that of any substitution whatsoever of the artificial for the natural. A less and less rigorous logic, that more and more resembles the logic of dreamland, transfers the same relationship into higher and higher spheres, between increasingly immaterial terms, till in the end we find a mere administrative enactment occupying the same relation to a natural or moral law that a ready-made garment, for instance, does to the living body. We have now gone right to the end of the first of the three directions we had to follow. Let us turn to the second and see where it will lead us.

2. Our starting-point is again "some-

thing mechanical encrusted upon the living." Where did the comic come from in this case? It came from the fact that the living body became rigid, like a machine. Accordingly, it seemed to us that the living body ought to be the perfection of suppleness, the ever-alert activity of a principle always at work. But this activity would really belong to the soul rather than to the body. It would be the very flame of life, kindled within us by a higher principle and perceived through the body, as though through a glass. When we see only gracefulness and suppleness in the living body, it is because we disregard in it the elements of weight, of resistance, and, in a word, of matter; we forget its materiality and think only of its vitality, a vitality which we regard as derived from the very principle of intellectual and moral life. Let us suppose, however, that our attention is drawn to this material side of the body; that, so far from sharing in the lightness and subtlety of the principle with which it is animated, the body is no more in our eyes than a heavy and cumbersome vesture, a kind of irksome ballast which holds down to earth a soul eager to rise aloft. Then the body will become to the soul what, as we have just seen, the garment was to the body itself—inert matter dumped down upon living energy. The impression of the comic will be produced as soon as we have a clear apprehension of this putting the one on the other. And we shall experience it most strongly when we are shown the soul *tantalised* by the needs of the body: on the one hand, the moral personality with its intelligently varied energy, and, on the other, the stupidly monotonous body, perpetually obstructing everything with its machine-like obstinacy. The more paltry and uniformly repeated these claims of the body, the more striking will be the result. But that is only a matter of degree, and the general

law of these phenomena may be formulated as follows: *Any incident is comic that calls our attention to the physical in a person, when it is the moral side that is concerned.*

Why do we laugh at a public speaker who sneezes just at the most pathetic moment of his speech? Where lies the comic element in this sentence, taken from a funeral speech and quoted by a German philosopher: "He was virtuous and plump"? It lies in the fact that our attention is suddenly recalled from the soul to the body. Similar instances abound in daily life. . . . Now, we have a speaker whose most eloquent sentences are cut short by the twinges of a bad tooth; now, one of the characters who never begins to speak without stopping in the middle to complain of his shoes being too small, or his belt too tight, etc. A *person embarrassed by his body* is the image suggested to us in all these examples. . . .

3. Let us then return, for the last time, to our central image—something mechanical encrusted on something living. Here, the living being under discussion was a human being, a person. A mechanical arrangement, on the other hand, is a thing. What, therefore, incited laughter, was the momentary transformation of a person into a thing, if one considers the image from this standpoint. Let us then pass from the exact idea of a machine to the vaguer one of a thing in general. We shall have a fresh series of laughable images which will be obtained by taking a blurred impression, so to speak, of the outlines of the former and will bring us to this new law: *We laugh every time a person gives us the impression of being a thing.* . . .

Let us, then, start with the games of a child, and follow the imperceptible process by which, as he grows himself, he makes his puppets grow, inspires them with life, and finally brings them to an ambiguous state in which, without ceasing to be puppets, they have yet become human beings. We thus obtain characters of a comedy type. And upon them we can test the truth of the law of which all our preceding analyses gave an inkling, a law in accordance with which we will define all broadly comic situations in general. *Any arrangement of acts and events is comic which gives us, in a single combination, the illusion of life and the distinct impression of a mechanical arrangement.*

1. *The Jack-in-the-box.*—As children we have all played with the little man who springs out of his box. You squeeze him flat, he jumps up again. Push him lower, and he shoots up still higher. Crush him down beneath the lid, and often he will send everything flying. It is hard to tell whether or not the toy itself is very ancient, but the kind of amusement it affords belongs to all time. It is a struggle between two stubborn elements, one of which, being simply mechanical, generally ends by giving in to the other, which treats it as a plaything. A cat playing with a mouse, which from time to time she releases like a spring, only to pull it up short with a stroke of her paw, indulges in the same kind of amusement. . . .

Let us scrutinise more closely the image of the spring which is bent, released, and bent again. Let us disentangle its central element, and we shall hit upon one of the usual processes of classic comedy,—*repetition.*

Why is it there is something comic in the repetition of a word on the stage? No theory of the ludicrous seems to offer a satisfactory answer to this very simple question. Nor can an answer be found, so long as we look for the explanation of an amusing word or phrase in the phrase or word itself, apart from all it suggests to us. Nowhere will the usual method prove to be so inadequate as here. With the exception, however, of a few special instances to which we shall recur later, the repetition of a word is never laughable in itself. It makes us laugh only because it symbolises a special play of moral elements, this play itself being the symbol of an altogether material diversion. It is the diversion of the cat with the mouse, the diversion of the child pushing back the Jack-in-the-box, time after time, to the bottom of his box—but in a refined and spiritualised form, transferred to the realm of feelings and ideas. Let us then state the law which we think defines the main comic varieties of word-repetition on the stage: *In a comic repetition of words we generally find two terms: a repressed feeling which goes off like a spring, and an idea that delights in repressing the feeling anew. . . .*

2. *The Dancing-jack.*—There are innumerable comedies in which one of the characters thinks he is speaking and acting freely, and consequently, retains all the essentials of life, whereas, viewed from a certain standpoint, he appears as a mere toy in the hands of another, who is playing with him. The transition is easily made, from the dancing-jack which a child works with a string, to Géronte and Argante manipulated by Scapin. Listen to Scapin himself: "The *machine* is all there," and again: "Providence has brought them into my net," etc. Instinctively, and because one would rather be a cheat than be cheated, in imagination at all events, the spectator sides with the knaves, and for the rest of the time, like a child who has persuaded his playmate to lend him his doll, he takes hold of the strings himself and makes the marionette come and go on the stage as he pleases. But this latter condition is not indispensable; we can remain outside the pale of what is taking place if only

we retain the distinct impression of a mechanical arrangement. This is what happens whenever one of the characters vacillates between two contrary opinions, each in turn appealing to him, as when Panurge asks Tom, Dick and Harry whether or not he ought to get married. Note that, in such a case, a comic author is always careful to *personify* the two opposing decisions. For, if there is no spectator, there must at all events be actors to hold the strings.

All that is serious in life comes from our freedom. The feelings we have matured, the passions we have brooded over, the actions we have weighed, decided upon and carried through, in short, all that comes from us and is our very own, these are the things that give life its ofttimes dramatic and generally grave aspect. What, then, is requisite to transform all this into a comedy? Merely to fancy that our seeming freedom conceals the strings of a dancing-jack, and that we are, as the poet says,

> . . . humble marionettes
> The wires of which are pulled by Fate.

So there is not a real, a serious, or even a dramatic scene that fancy cannot render comic by simply calling forth this image. Nor is there a game for which a wider field lies open.

3. *The Snow-ball.*—The farther we proceed in this investigation into the methods of comedy, the more clearly we see the part played by childhood's memories. These memories refer, perhaps, less to any special game than to the mechanical device of which that game is a particular instance. The same general device, moreover, may be met with in widely different games, just as the same operatic air is found in many different arrangements and variations. What is here of importance and is retained in the

mind, what passes by imperceptible stages from the games of a child to those of a man, is the mental diagram, the skeleton outline of the combination, or, if you like, the abstract formula of which these games are particular illustrations. Take, for instance, the rolling snow-ball, which increases in size as it moves along. We might just as well think of toy soldiers standing behind one another. Push the first and it tumbles down on the second, this latter knocks down the third, and the state of things goes from bad to worse until they all lie prone on the floor. . . .

Life presents itself to us as evolution in time and complexity in space. Regarded in time, it is the continuous evolution of a being ever growing older; it never goes backwards and never repeats itself. Considered in space, it exhibits certain coexisting elements so closely interdependent, so exclusively made for one another, that not one of them could, at the same time, belong to two different organisms: each living being is a closed system of phenomena, incapable of interfering with other systems. A continual change of aspect, the irreversibility of the order of phenomena, the perfect individuality of a perfectly self-contained series: such, then, are the outward characteristics—whether real or apparent is of little moment—which distinguish the living from the merely mechanical. Let us take the counterpart of each of these: we shall obtain three processes which might be called *repetition, inversion,* and *reciprocal interference of series.* Now, it is easy to see that these are also the methods of light comedy, and that no others are possible.

As a matter of fact, we could discover them, as ingredients of varying importance, in the composition of all the scenes we have just been considering, and, *a fortiori,* in the children's games, the mechanism of which they reproduce. The requisite analysis would, however, delay us too long, and it is more profitable to study them in their purity by taking fresh examples. Nothing could be easier, for it is in their pure state that they are found, both in classic comedy and in contemporary plays.

1. *Repetition.*—Our present problem no longer deals, like the preceding one, with a word or a sentence repeated by an individual, but rather with a situation, that is, a combination of circumstances, which recurs several times in its original form and thus contrasts with the changing stream of life. Everyday experience supplies us with this type of the comic, though only in a rudimentary state. Thus, you meet a friend in the street whom you have not seen for an age; there is nothing comic in the situation. If, however, you meet him again the same day, and then a third and a fourth time, you may laugh at the "coincidence." Now, picture to yourself a series of imaginary events which affords a tolerably fair illusion of life, and within this ever-moving series imagine one and the same scene reproduced either by the same characters or by different ones: again you will have a coincidence, though a far more extraordinary one. Such are the repetitions produced on the stage. . . .

2. *Inversion.*—This second method has so much analogy with the first that we will merely define it without insisting on illustrations. Picture to yourself certain characters in a certain situation: if you reverse the situation and invert the *rôles*, you obtain a comic scene. The double rôôôô ôôôôô in *Lơ Voyơgơ de M. I'ơr richon* belongs to this class. There is no necessity, however, for both the identical scenes to be played before us. We may be shown only one, provided the other is really in our minds. Thus, we laugh at the prisoner at the bar lecturing the magistrate; at a child presuming to teach its parents; in a word, at everything that comes under the heading of "topsyturvydom." . . .

3. We have dwelt at considerable length on repetition and inversion; we now come to the *reciprocal interference of series.* This is a comic effect, the precise formula of which is very difficult to disentangle, by reason of the extraordinary variety of forms in which it appears on the stage. Perhaps it might be defined as follows: A *situation is invariably comic when it belongs simultaneously to two altogether independent series of events and is capable of being interpreted in two entirely different meanings at the same time.* . . .

We will not carry any further this analysis of the methods of light comedy. Whether we find reciprocal interference of series, inversion, or repetition, we see that the objective is always the same— to obtain what we have called a *mechanisation* of life. You take a set of actions and relations and repeat it as it is, or turn it upside down, or transfer it bodily to another set with which it partially coincides—all these being processes that consist in looking upon life as a repeating mechanism, with reversible action and interchangeable parts. Actual life is comedy just so far as it produces, in a natural fashion, actions of the same kind; consequently, just so far as it forgets itself, for were it always on the alert, it would be ever-changing   continuity,   irreversible progress, undivided unity. And so the ludicrous in events may be defined as absentmindedness in things, just as the ludicrous in an individual character always results from some fundamental absentmindedness in the person, as we have already intimated and shall prove later on. This absentmindedness in events, however, is exceptional. Its results are slight. At any rate it is incurable, so that it is useless to laugh at it. Therefore the idea would never have occurred to any one of exaggerating absentmindedness, of converting it into a system, and creating an art for it, if laughter were not always a pleasure, and mankind did not pounce upon the slightest excuse for indulging in it. This is the real explanation of light comedy, which holds the same relation to actual life as does a jointed dancing-doll to a man walking,—being, as it is, an artificial exaggeration of a natural rigidity in things. The thread that binds it to actual life is a very fragile one. It is scarcely more than a game which, like all games, depends on a previously accepted convention. Comedy in character strikes far deeper roots into life. . . .

To sum up, whether a character is good or bad is of little moment; granted he is unsociable, he is capable of becoming comic. We now see that the seriousness of the case is of no importance either: whether serious or trifling, it is still capable of making us laugh, provided that care be taken not to arouse our emotions. Unsociability in the performer and insensibility in the spectator—such, in a word, are the two essential conditions. There is a third, implicit in the other two, which so far it has been the aim of our analysis to bring out.

This third condition is automatism. We have pointed it out from the outset of this work, continually drawing attention to the following point: what is essentially laughable is what is done automatically. In a vice, even in a virtue, the comic is that element by which the person unwittingly betrays himself—the involuntary gesture or the unconscious remark. . . .

And so we come back, by a roundabout way, to the double conclusion we reached in the course of our investigations. On the one hand, a person is never ridiculous except through some mental attribute resembling absentmindedness, through something that lives upon him without forming part of his organism, after the fashion of a parasite; that is the reason this state of mind is observable from without and capable of being corrected. But, on the other hand, just because laughter aims at correcting, it is expedient that the correction should reach as great a number of persons as possible. This is the reason comic observation instinctively proceeds to what is general. It chooses such peculiarities as admit of being reproduced, and consequently are not indissolubly bound up with the individuality of a single person,—a possibly common sort of uncommonness, so to say, —peculiarities that are held in common. By transferring them to the stage, it creates works which doubtless belong to art in that their only visible aim is to please, but which will be found to contrast with other works of art by reason of their generality, and also of their scarcely confessed or scarcely conscious intention to correct and instruct. So we were probably right in saying that comedy lies midway between art and life. It is not disinterested as genuine art is. By organising laughter, comedy accepts social life as a natural environment; it even obeys an impulse of social life. And in this respect it turns its back upon art, which is a breaking away from society and a return to pure nature. . . .

FROM OUR NEW SENSE OF THE COMIC
Wylie Sypher*

Through its connection with the deepest strivings of the unconscious mind, through a linking of its contradictions with the contradictions of modern life, comedy rather than tragedy is seen by Sypher as the expressive mode of our time.

Doubtless Meredith and Bergson were alike wearied by the "heavy moralizings" of the nineteenth century, with its "terrific tonnage," and thus sought relief in comedy of manners. For both really confine their idea of comedy within the range of comedy of manners; and they have given us our finest, most sensitive theory of that form. Comedy, says Bergson, is a game—a game that imitates life. And in writing the introduction to *The Egoist*, Meredith thinks of this game as dealing with human nature in the drawing room "where we have no dust of the struggling outer world, no mire, no violent crashes." The aftertaste of laughter may be bitter, Bergson grants, but comedy is itself only "a slight revolt on the surface of social life." Its gaiety happens like froth along a beach, for comedy looks at man from the outside: "It will go no farther."

For us, today, comedy goes a great deal farther—as it did for the ancients with their cruel sense of the comic. Indeed, to appreciate Bergson and Meredith we must see them both in a new perspective, now that we have lived amid the "dust and crashes" of the twentieth century

and have learned how the direst calamities that befall man seem to prove that human life at its depths is inherently absurd. The comic and the tragic views of life no longer exclude each other. Perhaps the most important discovery in modern criticism is the perception that comedy and tragedy are somehow akin, or that comedy can tell us many things about our situation even tragedy cannot. At the heart of the nineteenth century Dostoevsky discovered this, and Søren Kierkegaard spoke as a modern man when he wrote that the comic and the tragic touch one another at the absolute point of infinity—at the extremes of human experience, that is. . . .

Our comedy of manners is a sign of desperation. Kafka's novels are a ghastly comedy of manners showing how the awkward and hopelessly maladroit hero, K, is inexorably an "outsider" struggling vainly somehow to "belong" to an order that is impregnably closed by some inscrutable authority. Kafka transforms comedy of manners to pathos by looking, or feeling, from the angle of the alien soul. He treats comedy of manners from the point of view of Dostoevsky's "underground man," and his heroes are absurd because their efforts are all seen from below, and from within. In his notebooks Kafka described the anxiety with which his characters try to bear up under a perpetual judgment life passes upon them: "Watching, fearing, hoping, the answer steals round the question, peers despairingly in her enigmatic face, follows her through the maddest paths, that is, the paths leading farthest away from the answer." Kafka is a modern Jeremiah laughing in feverish merriment, prophetically writing the incredible—the depraved—comedy of our concentration camps, which are courts where the soul of contemporary man undergoes an absurd Trial by Ordeal. His comedy reaches the stage of the inarticulate, as tragedy does when Lear frets about the button. . . .

In his notebooks Kafka explained that he wanted to exaggerate situations until everything becomes clear. Dostoevsky has this sort of comic clarity—a frightening clarity of the grotesque, reducing life, as totally as tragedy, by means of a perspective that foreshortens everything, to absurdity. From this perspective, which is often Goya's or Picasso's, man looks puppetlike, and his struggles diminish to pathos. For example, in the closing pages of *The Brothers Karamazov* when Ilusha is buried, Snegiryov runs distracted about the corpse of his boy, strewing flowers on the coffin, scattering morsels of bread for sparrows on the little grave. These scenes cause a laughter so raw that it brings grimaces hardly to be distinguished from tragic response. The force of this comic "shock" is like the "qualm" stirred by tragedy; it can disorient us, "disturb" us as confusingly as tragic calamity. Melville's tormented Captain Ahab sets his course headlong "outward," driven on by the modern "delight in foundering." Like Conrad's character Kurtz, he is a madman in the grip of "merciless logic for a futile purpose." We are now more sensitive to these absurd calamities than to tragic recognitions. We appreciate

Rouault, who sees man as a Clown. In its style Picasso's giant Guernica, that premonition of total war, is a shocking comic strip in black and white, showing how the ridiculous journalese of painting can be an idiom for modern art. . . .

No doubt the tragic experience reaches deeply down into the "interruptions" of conscious life, conjuring up our grim disinherited selves and expressing the "formless" intimations of archaic fear and archaic struggle. But in an artist like Dostoevsky the comic experience can reach as deeply down, perhaps because the comic artist begins by accepting the absurd, "the improbable," in human existence. Therefore he has less resistance than the tragic artist to representing what seems incoherent and inexplicable, and thus lowers the threshold of artistic perception. After all, comedy, not tragedy, admits the disorderly into the realm of art; the grotesque depends upon an irrational focus. Ours is a century of disorder and irrationalism.

Is it any wonder that along with our wars, our machines, and our neuroses we should find new meanings in comedy, or that comedy should represent our plight better than tragedy? For tragedy needs the "noble," and nowadays we seldom can assign any usable meaning to "nobility." The comic now is more relevant, or at least more accessible, than the tragic. As Mephisto explains to God, one cannot understand man unless one is able to laugh: "For man must strive, and striving, he must err." . . .

The mirth of the disenchanted and frustrated idealist, frenzied by his sense of the impassable distance between what might be and what is, reaches its shrillest pitch in Nietzsche, the scorpion-philosopher, exempt from every middle-class code, whose revolt is, unlike Bergson's comedy of "slight revolt on the surface of social life," savage. Nietzsche is able to transvalue all social values by pain, disgust, fury. This sickly laughter of the last romantics is the most confused and destructive mirth Western man has ever allowed himself. It has all the pessimism which Bergson chose not to consider. Rimbaud's laugh is a symptom of anguish and a glimpse· into the abyss of the self. It is a terrifying scorn, a shameless expense of lust, an eruption of the pleasure-principle in a world where pleasure is denied. Nietzsche's laughter is a discharge far more "posssessed" than the Freudian sexual release.

So Bergson's analysis of laughter is incomplete, which may explain why he thinks comedy works only from "the outside." Comedy may, in fact, not bring laughter at all; and certain tragedies may make us laugh hysterically. It was Shelley who found the comedy in *King Lear* to be "universal, ideal, and sublime." Ben Jonson himself noted "Nor is the moving of laughter always the end of comedy." When Coleridge lectured on *Hamlet* and *Lear* he pointed out that terror is closely joined with what is ludicrous, since "The laugh is rendered by nature itself the language of extremes, even as tears are." Thus *Hamlet* "will be found to touch on the verge of the ludicrous," because "laughter is equally the expression of extreme anguish and horror as of joy." The grimace of mirth resembles the grimace of suffering; comic and tragic masks have the same distortion. Today we know that a comic action sometimes yields tragic values. In Balzac's *human comedy* (*Comédie humaine*) we meet Old Goriot and Cousin Pons, those heroes of misery.

If we have no satisfactory definition of laughter, neither do we have any satisfactory definition of comedy. Indeed, most of the theories of laughter and comedy fail precisely because they oversimplify a situation and an art more complicated than the tragic situation and art. Comedy seems to be a more pervasive human condition than tragedy. Often we are, or have been, or could be, Quixotes or Micawbers or Malvolios, Benedicks or Tartuffes. Seldom are we Macbeths or Othellos. Tragedy, not comedy, limits its field of operation and is a more closely regulated form of response to the ambiguities and dilemmas of humanity. The comic action touches experience at more points than tragic action. We can hardly hope that our various definitions of comedy will be more compatible than our definitions of laughter; yet each of the many definitions has its use in revealing the meanings of comedy. Bergson's alone will not suffice, or Meredith's either; and they both will mean more when seen against the full spectrum of comic values.

Ordinarily we refer to "high" and "low" comedy; but we cannot speak of "low" tragedy. All tragedy ought to be "high." There are, of course, various orders of tragic action, such as *drame* and "heroic tragedy"; however, as tragedy falls away from its "high" plane it tends to become something else than tragedy. Tragedy is indeed "an achievement peculiarly Greek"—and needs a special view of man's relation to the world. But comedy thrives everywhere and fearlessly runs the gamut of effects from "high" to "low" without diminishing its force or surrendering its values or even jeopardizing them. Once Mme. de Staël said: "Tragedies (if we set aside some of the masterpieces) require less knowledge of the human heart than comedies." What a strange opinion! Yet which of Shakespeare's plays really shows a more profound knowledge of the hearts of fathers and children: *Lear*, or *Henry IV*, 1 and 2, and *Henry V*? Is not the crisis luridly overstated in *Lear* and met with greater insight in the figures of Henry IV, Hal,

Hotspur, and Falstaff? Can we honestly claim that Shakespeare reveals more about life in the tragedy of Lear than in the conflicts between Henry and his wild son? Are not many of the problems raised in the great tragedies solved in the great comedies? . . .

As we move "up" the scale of comic action, the mechanisms become more complex but no more "comic." Physical mishaps, pratfalls, and loud collisions are the crudest products of Bergson's comic "automatism." It is hard to distinguish these pleasures from our glee at physical deformity; and here we detect the cruelty inherent in comedy, which may perhaps be another form of the cruelty inherent in tragic disaster. Essentially our enjoyment of physical mishap or deformity springs from our surprise and delight that man's motions are often absurd, his energies often misdirected. This is the coarsest, most naïve, comedy of manners. Another sort of mechanical comedy is the farce—mistaken identities, coincidences, mistimings—which can be a very complicated engine of plot devices. In this range of comedy the characters need only be puppets moved from the outside, as events require. There is the right key to the wrong door, or the wrong key to the right door; and it does not matter very much who is inside, provided it is the unexpected figure. In these comic vehicles fate takes the guise of happy or unhappy chance, which is, of course, only a tidy arrangement of improbable possibilities. On this sort of artificial framework comedy displays some of its most glittering designs. . . .

But it is more than a parterre of devices: it is a drama played by those odd, lovable Shakespearean creatures for whom Bergson seems to have so little feeling—they are "characters" in the British sense of the word. Berowne and Don Armado are among them, and they inhabit the higher domain of comedy where we meet Fielding's Squire Western, Chaucer's Monk, Cervantes' Quixote, Sterne's Uncle Toby, and Dickens' Sam Weller. Such persons cannot exist in the dry seclusion of farce. They require the mellow neighborhood of a comedy of humors which gathers into its action spirits of strong and perverse disposition and convincing weight. These characters thrive at more genial latitudes than Ben Jonson allowed them in his comedy of humors, which was too harshly satiric. English literature is, as Taine said, the native province of these unruly creatures whose life blood pulses richly, whose features are odd, and whose opinions, gestures, vices, and habits control the mechanism of the plot in which they happen to be cast. Indeed, such dispositions may temper the whole climate in which events happen and constantly threaten to wreck the tight logic of a fiction. Mercutio and Benedick are incorrigible fellows of this sort. We never take seriously the action in which they have a role; but we take them seriously. They live for us as Falstaff lives; for Falstaff is more than a sack of guts. He moves the whole play from within; he is a temperamental as well as an anatomical grotesque.

These "characters" realized in depth stand at the threshold of "high" comedy, which is really a transformation of comedy of manners. Whenever a society becomes self-conscious about its opinions, codes, or etiquette, comedy of manners may serve as a sort of philosophic engine called "comedy of ideas." Frail as they are, and known best in their moments of raillery, Millamant and Mirabell raise Congreve's *Way of the World* to a bolder order of comedy of manners: "Let us," says Millamant to Mirabell, "be as strange as if we had been married a great while, and as well bred as if we were not married at all." The edge of this comedy is sharpened by sanity as well as verbal wit, and, as Meredith clearly saw, Molière magnified comedy of manners to the dimensions of a criticism of life. Our most provoking social critic is Shaw, although Pirandello soars farther into a crystalline sphere of ideas. The world of Aristophanes could have been shaped only in the sophisticated theatre of an Athens that had begun to examine its own conventions. Aristophanes is like Erasmus or Gide, who serve as the intellectual conscience of a nervous and self-scrutinizing society where all is not now so well as it might be or has been or seems to be.

At the radiant peak of "high" comedy —a peak we can easily sight from Meredith's essay—laughter is qualified by tolerance, and criticism is modulated by a sympathy that comes only from wisdom. Just a few writers of comedy have gained this unflinching but generous perspective on life, which is a victory over our absurdities but a victory won at a cost of humility, and won in a spirit of charity and enlightenment. Besides Shakespeare in, perhaps, *The Tempest*, one might name Cervantes and Henry James and Jane Austen, or Thomas Mann in his *Magic Mountain*, when pliable, diseased Claudia yields carelessly to the stricken Hans Castorp in a scene where the grimness of human life, its folly and its error, are seen clearly and with a perverse tenderness: *"Petit bourgeois!"* she says to him—*"Joli bourgeois à la petite tache humide."* For they both know that the body, love, and death are all three the same thing, and that the flesh is sickness and desire, and life only a fever in matter. This is how "high" comedy chastens men without despair, without rancor, as if human blunders were seen from a godlike distance, and also from within the blundering self. The deep humiliation

and reassurance in Don Quixote's madness and recovery, with his resignation, detachment, and self-awareness, are all confirmed by the experience of Shakespeare's Benedick—to whom Meredith appealed. After proving himself as foolish as the rest of the world, Benedick comes to a vision of the human condition: "For man is a giddy thing, and this is my conclusion." Benedick speaks without bitterness, bias, or pride; and has learned, like Hans Castorp, to accept the insufficiency of man without being damaged.

So the range of comedy is more embracing than the range of tragedy; and if tragedy occurs at some middle point in ethical life where failure is weighed against man's nobility of spirit, comedy ventures out into the farther extremes of experience in both directions, toward the bestial or "obscene," and at the other end of the spectrum toward the insane heroics of Nietzsche or the vision of Prospero, who sees sin as the last mistake of all our many mistakes, dispelled before our clearer reason whenever hate seems more absurd than charity.

We may prefer one theory of comedy to another; but we shall find it hard to get along without the other. In *Winter's Tale*, Autolycus meditates on his lot: "I am courted now with a *double occasion*." The phrase is useful, for comedy is built upon double occasions, double premises, double values. "Nothing human is alien to me," says the character in Terence. Nothing human is alien to comedy. It is an equivocal art. If we now have trouble isolating comedy from tragedy, this is not because comedy and tragedy are identical, but rather because comedy often intersects the orbit of tragic action without losing its autonomy. Instead, comedy in its own right, boldly and illogically, lays claim to some of the values that traditionally are assigned to tragedy alone. Think, for example, of Henry James's "Beast In the Jungle," which really is comedy of manners suddenly consumed in the flame of Marcher's grief that he has lost May forever through his own selfishness. Here is comedy seen ruthlessly "from within" as Bergson did not allow. Marcher is a fool —but a sinister fool, an egoist far more barbaric than Meredith's sleek Sir Willoughby Patterne. And James's London, a society of genteel manners and frail nerves, is a scene where savage eyes glare behind the social simper.

FROM THE BOUNDARIES OF COMEDY
L. J. Potts[*]

Potts, in a discussion of drama, distinguishes comedy from farce, which lacks significance; from satire, which is subjective, idealistic, and rejects the nature that comedy accepts; and from the problem play, which is dominated by moral intent.

... If comedy is bounded on one side by tragedy, tragicomedy, and sentimental drama, its neighbours on the other side are satire, farce, and the "problem" play. Of these, farce is the simplest and least important; I will therefore discuss it only very briefly.

Analysing the Titania-Bottom scene[1] in Chapter II, I found an element of farce in it; and I defined farce very roughly as physical sensationalism of a ludicrous kind, bearing the same relationship to comedy as melodrama bears to tragedy. More simply, and perhaps more accurately, it might be described as comedy with the meaning left out; which is as much as to say, with the comedy left out. Cassell's Dictionary defines it as "a short dramatic work in which the action is trivial and the sole purpose is to excite mirth"; and this indicates the main difference between it and comedy, in which the mirth is a means to an end. Thus, though farce is not comedy, comedy can contain farce, just as wine can have bubbles, though effervescence is not a generic quality of wine. Moreover farce, like soda-water, flushes and tickles without satisfying, and one does not need a discriminating palate to respond to it. Since its *sole* purpose is to excite mirth it is most likely to confine itself to merely physical situations, such as the fantasy of a man with a donkey's head on him. But clowning too is an art, and there have been clowns of genius; so there is a genius in literary clowning. Sterne possessed it, among his other qualities; the scene in *Tristram Shandy* where the hot chestnut shoots across the table and lands in the lap of Phutatorius without his noticing it is high farce. Perhaps it is also farce rather than comedy when the Shandys' baby is christened Tristram by mistake for Trismegistus, to the annoyance of his father; a *mere* pun without any meaning might be called farcical.

But it is of little use drawing out the distinction between farce and comedy into definitions and examples, because everything depends on the response of

[*] The selection is reprinted from *Comedy*, by L. J. Potts, by permission of Hillary House Ltd. Copyright 1949 by Hillary House Ltd.
[1] A *Midsummer Night's Dream*, III, i.

the reader or spectator. In practice one can never say with confidence "this is comedy; that is farce." If I think a "comedy" lacks significance, however funny its separate episodes may be, I call it a farce; if I can see in it a significance of the kind indicated in this book I call it comedy. For me *The Importance of Being Earnest* is a farce, and *The Second Shepherds' Play* a comedy. Again, Dickens does not seem to me a writer of comedies; though it is hard to exclude Sam Weller, Betsy Trotwood, and Mr. Micawber from any list of English comic characters, the ludicrous scenes in which they appear have the arbitrariness of farce, with sometimes a strong vein of sentimentality or satire. Lastly, the presence of farcical episodes or elements in real comedy complicates the distinction in practice beyond all possibility of unravelling. For example, the mistaken identities in *Twelfth Night* are a traditional device derived from late Greek comedy, through Latin comedy; yet in themselves they are farcical rather than comic. Such devices are well in keeping with a comic plot, because they contribute to a general atmosphere of fantasy in which the comic spirit can have a freer play, since it releases the characters from any pressure of relentless or inevitable circumstance.

The distinction between satire and comedy is also difficult to draw, though not for the same reason; for here there is an essential incompatibility. But as I explained in the first chapter, satire is not a clearly defined species of literature. Indeed, it originated in deliberately *formless* writing: the word means "hotch-potch." The Latin *satura* took at least two distinct forms; the more persistent was no more than an essay in verse. Quite early in its history it was used largely for invective, and from this historical accident the modern sense of the word

is derived. What that sense is, is far from clear. It is not *mere* invective. It involves some kind of distortion: it caricatures its object, as in *MacFlecknoe:* or compares it to something ridiculous or of ill repute, or contemptible, as usually in Pope; or stands it on its head as Samuel Butler stood Victorian England in *Erewhon:* or merely drenches it in wit as the other Samuel Butler drenched the Seventeenth-century Puritans. One way of attacking a class of men would be to put a representative of the class into a play or novel, and give him a discreditable rôle in it; in Mr. Shaw's excellent comedy, *The Philanderer,* Paramore is a satire on doctors. All Peacock's novels are on the borderline between comedy and satire: perhaps in a no-man's-land. Burlesque is in a similar no-man's-land. *Joseph Andrews* begins as a burlesque of Richardson's *Pamela:* it is markedly satirical at first, but as Parson Adams becomes more prominent and Fielding's prejudice against Richardson subsides into the background, it turns into comedy. Is *The Rape of the Lock* a satirical comedy or a humorous satire? Clearly the answer depends on Pope's intention in writing the poem, which is not quite clear: unfortunately very little value can ever be placed on his own statements about his aims or motives. In this border-country it is impossible to tell simply by the effect of a book whether the author is hostile or detached: he may even not know it himself, if he is a good artist. I am disposed to give Pope the credit of having fallen in love with the scene he was depicting in this poem, and of having looked at it with the truthful vision of the comic artist, rather than with the jaundiced if penetrating eye of malice. One may draw a distinction between some of Ben Jonson's plays (for example *Cynthia's Revels* and *The Poetaster*), which are a mixture of self-advertisement and satire, and his comic masterpieces, *Volpone, The Alchemist,* and *Bartholomew Fair:* yet I should hardly object to the description of *Volpone* as a satire against avarice.

In spite of all this common ground, comedy and satire cannot in the last analysis be reconciled. The comic writer need not spare anything in nature, but he must not fall out with Nature herself. The satirist writes only from his own feelings; the comic writer must partly go outside his own feelings, to a conception of nature. Their techniques are in part interchangeable; but in idea they conflict. The distinction between them has something in common with the distinction between madness and sanity. Of course I do not mean to imply that all satirists are mad, or even potentially mad. Dryden and his contemporary Samuel Butler (the author of *Hudibras*) were the sanest of writers; so much so that their satire borders on comedy. But the satirist either deliberately eschews for an immediate purpose, or is helplessly cut off by his temperament from, that interplay between a man's self and the world outside him in which the life of the mind consists. The madman is, and the satirist becomes for artistic purposes, purely subjective in standpoint. The sane man is more or less capable of mental detachment; and it is by his power of detachment, or his willingness to exercise it, that the comic writer is distinguished from the satirist. Great satirists are of course more than merely angry, bitter, or disappointed men; they are usually baffled idealists. They compare life as it is with life as they would have it to be; and being unable or unwilling to reconcile the two, they attack that which is the less dear to them. But you cannot be in this position if the centre in which you take your stand is the norm; for the norm is always, by definition, reconcilable with the real. It

is perhaps nowhere to be found in nature, but it is everywhere latent. Swift's Houyhnhnms are the symbols of an ideal; but they are utterly abnormal.

To return once more to Titania and Bottom. I suggested that in their love scene Shakespeare was symbolising one aspect of the curious love of eternity for the productions of time: we have fairy minds, but they are tied to the distracting, inconvenient, and sometimes grotesque behaviour of our bodies. So too the ideal and the earthy are linked together in the ludicrous and pathetic partnership of Don Quixote and Sancho Panza. Both these great comedies weigh aspiring fancy and earth-bound nature in the finest balance. Our greatest satirist, Swift, also sets them against each other in sharp relief. But his imagination cannot harmonise them; for him there is no love between time and eternity. This brings to light the fundamental difference between comedy and satire. Comedy accepts life and human nature: sometimes with a light heart, as in *A Midsummer Night's Dream,* sometimes rather sadly as in *Don Quixote,* but always with the good sense that comes from clear vision and understanding. Satire, on the other hand, does not accept; it rejects and aims at destruction; and therefore it must either direct its aim at the unnatural, or if (as in the fourth book of *Gulliver's Travels*) it is extended to the essentials of life, it undoes its effect and becomes futile. I conclude that comedy, as well as tragedy, is not only in a different class from satire, but in a higher class; and that when a satirist develops into a comic writer his mind has become more mature and his work more truthful.

I have said that we classify a work as satirical in virtue of its immediate purpose, and that satire is distinguished from comedy by a deliberate and *ad hoc,* or an inherent and constitutional, lack of balance. The distinction between comedy and "problem" fiction is somewhat similar. Comedy sees men as units in a society composed of similar units, and judges them accordingly. The comic dramatist does not usually give judgment himself, but he presents the evidence for a judgment by his audience; that is both better policy and better art. In order to do this he must understand human nature at least sufficiently to convince us that he knows what he is talking about, and he must be able to depict character in speech and action. But he is not only a psychologist with dramatic imagination, he is also (if only indirectly) a critic of life; and that means that if he is to do his work well he must not only know how people behave, but also have a standard of behaviour. In the best comedy these two sides, the psychological and the moral, are nicely balanced. The characters must be recognisably human, or the moral will most likely misfire. On the other hand, the dramatist must have a philosophy of life, or the play, however truthful in its detail, will lack significance and coherence, and will therefore be both dull and undramatic. This applies also to the novel, but for convenience I will discuss the question in terms of drama.

A very little philosophy will suffice to support a comedy, if it is well constructed, lively in its characterisation and incident, and well written; and for this kind of play there is a convenient name —we call it a "light" comedy. Such are the comedies of Fletcher, which were popular throughout the Seventeenth Century: they have not kept the stage, but at least one of them, *Rule a Wife and Have a Wife*, would be worth a revival. I suppose *She Stoops to Conquer* is a light comedy; though whether a comedy is "light" or "low" or "high" must often be a matter of opinion. All these kinds of play are within the boundaries of comedy.

But a play whose human interest is merely general and not particular cannot I think properly be called a comedy. It might be (and indeed sometimes is) said that such a play, concentrating on morality or politics to the exclusion of psychology is not a drama at all, but a sermon or tract. Is not a play without interesting characters like an animal without blood or breath—a still-born infant? But there are such plays, and famous ones too. A medieval morality play is peopled by abstractions; and strange as the allegorical way of writing is to the Twentieth Century, *Everyman* has not lost its dramatic appeal. And another example of drama without substantial character interest is the modern Problem Play, which, in contradistinction to both comedy and tragedy, treats the situations that arise in society simply as moral or political problems, in the abstract and without reference to the idiosyncracies of human nature. There was a vogue for such plays at the end of the Nineteenth and the beginning of the Twentieth Centuries; Galsworthy's plays belong to this class, though he called some of them comedies. But there are earlier problem plays. If we regard Shakespeare's *Measure for Measure* as a play about puritanism, and his *Troilus and Cressida* as a play about the disintegration of society in the later stages of a war, they might be classed as problem plays; characters like Isabella and Ulysses seem to owe their dramatic force to the abstractions for which they stand.

While the subject of a problem play is of intense public interest, the audience, with their minds full of their own concern in it, may be prepared to overlook its dramatic limitations; in perspective it is apt to look unreal—even more artificial and remote from life than the allegorical incidents of the *Fairy Queen*, which have at least the imagination of a poet to support them. (So, of course, by the way, have *Measure for Measure* and *Troilus and Cressida*.) But there is one condition which can give to a problem play a limited permanent interest. If the problem is complicated enough it can support a play without either psychological or emotional depth. Place a set of characters in complicated (and therefore particularised) circumstances, and they will come to life on that account alone. But no amount of ingenuity can by itself turn problem fiction into either tragedy or comedy.

Just on the other side of the boundary is the comedy of ideas. There is no reason why comedy, or for that matter tragedy, should not concern itself with social problems; but they must do so in a way compatible with their distinct natures and purposes. In theory this territory is fairly easy to map out, even if there is a difference of opinion about the side of the frontier on which any given play should be placed. Take a "problem"—say war, or heredity. If the situation is conceived as fatal—as a dilemma or disaster in which the characters are caught without hope of escape—the result is tragedy. If it is conceived as a setting for the display of character, so that the dramatist can throw a special light on a number of human types, or imaginary persons, by showing how they all react to or are influenced by a common factor in social history, the result is comedy. If on the other hand it is conceived simply as a situation, with no aim but to make the situation clear, the result is a problem play. I will give two sets of examples to illustrate these distinctions; they will, like all such examples, be hypothetical, because they depend on our interpretation of each separate work. But it does not matter; the point is as well illustrated by a hypothesis as by a known fact. In *Antony and Cleopatra* war is fatal to Antony; he knows that if he drifts or is manoeuvred

into war with Caesar he will surely be destroyed. And he knows also that if he stays with Cleopatra there will be war. Then "Antony must leave her utterly." "Never, he will not." This is the plot of the tragedy. In *Arms and the Man,* on the other hand, Mr. Shaw does not make his war disastrous to anybody; he merely uses it to show up the pathetic vanity and egoism of Sergius, the shrewd good-natured insignificance of Major Petkoff, the man-hunting duplicity of Raina, and the stolid and efficient romanticism of Bluntschli. It is true that he has a thesis about war—roughly, that chocolate is more useful to a soldier than bullets; but in this, as in all his best plays, he is more interested in his characters and their points of view (especially the latter), than in the thesis. He knows that human nature constantly upsets the best theories, and he is wise enough to delight in the knowledge. After all, it is Sergius who wins the battle, by disregarding all the rules of modern warfare, as Bluntschli ruefully admits. Lastly, let us suppose that *Troilus and Cressida* has no deeper purpose than I suggested in the last paragraph but one; that the central theme of the play is contained in the famous speech of Ulysses about degree, or more dramatically in the demoralisation indicated by the dry factual line, "Hector was gone, but Helen was not up," and in the snarls of Thersites. There are ingredients of both tragedy and comedy, as surely there must be in any comprehensive picture of war; but the play as a whole will not fit into either category, and it will fit into that of the problem play. Another, and clearer, example of a problem play about war is Jean Giraudoux's *La Guerre de Troie n'aura pas lieu.*

To take the other example, heredity. This factor in human life impressed itself on the greatest European dramatist of the Nineteenth Century, Ibsen, so power-

fully that it threw a tragic cast over the whole of his view of life. *Ghosts,* although it has much of the concern with a removable social evil proper to problem drama, is a tragedy, because its plot is founded on the notion that life is irresistibly determined, and can in spite of valiant effort be ruined, by it. This is a prominent theme of many of Ibsen's other tragedies—*The Wild Duck,* for example. Mr. Shaw, also a dramatist keenly sensitive to the current ideas of the late Nineteenth Century and especially to the impact of biology on ethics, a great admirer of Ibsen moreover, can never really bring himself to crush the individuality out of his characters in the ruthless manner of Ibsen. In the crisis of *Major Barbara* the fate of the heroine is in a sense determined by her heredity; she cannot resist the lure of power, and shows herself a true daughter of Undershaft, and for that matter also of Lady Britomart. But Stephen is of the same parentage and so is Sarah; and they show it in the most widely different ways, for of course heredity, though it is a problem, need not land us in fatalism. When, therefore, Barbara makes her choice, we feel it to be a real choice, taken jointly by her and Cusins of their free will and made possible by their individual temperaments. Lastly, *The Way of All Flesh,* Samuel Butler's famous *roman à thèse* (the class of novel equivalent to the problem play) is an attempt to present life in terms of biology, with no other purpose than to induce in his readers a biological approach to human character and conduct, or more specifically to education.

I am glad to end this book by these references to Bernard Shaw. He is sometimes described as a problem playwright rather than a comic dramatist. Certainly some of his plays—*Widowers' Houses,* for example, at one end, *The Apple Cart* at the other—are problem plays. But I prefer to accept his own claim, in the preface to the 1934 collection of his plays, that he is "a classic writer of comedies" and that his purpose is "to chasten morals with ridicule." His characters talk a great deal about the problems of the world they and he live in, but he lets them have their separate say, and we learn more from them about the vagaries of human thought and character than about the problems they discuss. Few of our dramatists have a more impressive list of comedies to their credit than, say, *Arms and the Man, Candida, Caesar and Cleopatra, Major Barbara, Androcles and the Lion, Pygmalion,* and *St. Joan.*

CHAPTER 4

Lyric Mode

FROM LYRIC POETRY
Harold DeWolf Fuller*

Fuller considers inadequate the usual attempts to define a lyric by such attributes as musical verse, natural imagery, and subjective emotion. He turns instead to such criteria as "lyric form" and "lyric sentiment or coloring," impossible to isolate from the nature of poetry.

Lyric poetry has in large measure been spared from the blight of over-zealous scholarship by the difficulty to define it. There used to be a legend at a certain university that only two beings in the world knew what lyric poetry was, God and Professor ——; and that God wouldn't tell, and Professor —— couldn't tell. Other forms of literature have been searched and classified according to the well-known prescription for the study of types. But the lyric has presented a smiling defiance to such treatment. It has a piquant quality like life itself, springing up where least expected, a flower in a cranny. Formerly it was thought sufficient to divide poetry into

* The selection is reprinted by permission of the publishers from *Essays in Memory of Barrett Wendell*, Cambridge, Mass.: Harvard University Press, Copyright, 1926, by the President and Fellows of Harvard College.

epic, dramatic, and lyric. What was not the first two was, generally speaking, the last. This was a good enough working basis.

Recently scholars have taken to looking at the lyric more narrowly. Professor E. B. Reed gives the following definition: "All songs, all poems following classic lyric forms; all short poems expressing the writer's moods and feelings in rhythm that suggests music, are to be considered lyrics." Difficulty arose when Professor Reed attempted to enforce his tests. He accepted sonnets because some of them, notably in the days of Elizabeth, have been set to music; yet Wordsworth's genius was styled unlyrical because "he has not left us a single song." And the book shows many other curious instances of selection and exclusion. Professor F. E. Schelling's volume on "The English Lyric" adds nothing new to the foregoing statements. "The primary conception involved in the term 'lyric,'" he says, "has always to do with song; and it is the song-like quality of the lyric that falls most conspicuously into contrast with the epic or telling quality of narrative verse.... So, too, the lyric is concerned with the poet, his thoughts, his emotions, his moods, and his passions.... With the lyric subjective poetry begins. The latest to match his skill with this elusive type is Mr. Ernest Rhys,[1] the editor of Everyman's Library: "Lyrical, it may be said, implies a form of musical utterance in words governed by overmastering emotion and set free by a powerfully concordant rhythm. So soon as narrator or playwright, carried out of the given medium of personal feeling, begins to dilate individually on the theme, that moment he or she surely tends to grow lyrical." The musical test, it will be noted, is abandoned in the second sentence, where Mr. Rhys applies his definition; and, unless one must infer that personal feeling in verse inevitably draws upon music, it is of little practical use. The looseness of Mr. Rhys's conception is quite typical of his practice. Beginning with early forms which were certainly sung, he later accepts sonnets and certain dramatic soliloquies; but as if feeling guilty over his small use of the musical requirement, he periodically refers to an underlying "singing mode," "singing idiom," or "hidden note." The early portion of the volume has to do with metrical developments, especially the transition from alliterative verse to rhyming schemes, and with the flexibility bestowed on English poetry by borrowings from the French. As the book progresses, its treatment may be described as scarcely more than literary history.

[1] Ernest Rhys, *Lyric Poetry.*

I

I have no desire to hazard a new definition but merely wish to consider whether the scope of lyric poetry is not immensely different from that usually assigned to it. All may admit that the lyric and song originated in much the same impulse—the desire to express personal, often inarticulate, feeling; and that the two may at times still be closely allied. It would require no magic rod to strike a gush of song from the lyrics of Burns, or from the light stanzas scattered through Shakespeare's dramas, even if the particular airs to which they were set had been forgotten. But this is very different from implying such an accompaniment for all pieces that commonly pass as lyrics. The discussion will be forwarded by a glance at certain developments in music itself. Such is its present state that critics would probably be as perplexed to agree on what is meant by "lyric" in music as others are to say what the word conveys as regards verse. Whereas formerly lyric music must above all else have melody, some composers, notably Debussy, are now depending instead on harmony, coloring. When he wishes to describe the play of moonlight on the water, Debussy resorts to a series of tinkles broken by syncopated glissandos and mingled with something like whispers. His "Reflet dans l'eau" shows an entirely different treatment from Nevin's woodland sketches. Both men have essayed to speak for nature. The latter has made her tuneful, and in any age would be accounted a true lyrist; Debussy, accepting certain features of nature as in themselves the embodiment of lyric sentiment, has been content to decorate, to sophisticate. He has replaced melody—one of the traditional marks of the lyric—by dexterous harmony; and through this "programme" variety of music has carried the lyric into close association with other musical types.

Manifestly, then, those critics who stick for a musical basis of the lyric should distinguish the kind of music meant. "Lycidas" suggests music no more strongly than many portions of "Paradise Lost," or, if so, does not recall the pure melodies which critics would still unite in terming lyrical. Nor can much significance be extracted from the fact that the sonnet owes its form to a combination of stanzas which usually went with song, or that in some instances the sonnet itself has received a musical arrangement. Certainly within the last three centuries composers of sonnets could never have had the thought of music in mind; and only such supersensitive ears as Mr. Rhys's could possibily discover a "hidden note" of song at the bottom of, say, Shakespeare's lines beginning

Let me not to the marriage of true minds Admit impediments.

If they convey any note, it is Milton's epic organ tone. One might go further and say that they are less lyrical as regards pure sound than Macbeth's memorable lament after hearing that his wife is dead. If by "musical basis" critics would mean melodious song, they would have little difficulty in classification, though this would exclude the majority of selections found in the "Golden Treasury."

In endeavoring to hold to a conception of the ancient Greeks we have really confused their ideas. They recognized the kinship of the lyric and song, though they did not use it as a strict test, but also the more general relation of poetry and music. If lyric verse was sung, so were the epic and large portions of the drama, and the instrument of accompaniment might, at least in the first two instances,

be the same, the lyre. Yet it is true that to most minds to-day the lyric appears to have a prior claim to a musical alliance. Partly this is because it is the only one of the three poetic divisions which continues to be set to music—a thoroughly arbitrary distinction. But more especially it is because the beginnings of poetry, like the beginnings of music, were "lyrical," in the sense that they fell easily into the jingle of song. This must have been the reason for the style, "lyric Apollo," to characterize the god of poetry and music, who was rooted in their ancient traditions. And down the centuries lyric verse and lyric music have furnished enough examples of early uncomplicated melodies to keep the two, in human instincts, subtly bound together. "O my luve's like, a red, red rose" has not advanced far in rhythm beyond poetry, in an elementary stage, which, of course, only heightens its homely freshness. The movement of Keats's "Ode to a Grecian Urn" has no such implication, and though it might set an ancient Greek to chanting, it does not so affect us moderns. In retaining, despite the inconsistencies of our practice, a musical basis exclusively for the lyric, we are but emphasizing the stream of, as it were, primordial poetry which still runs through it, though it also runs through the drama and epic in less degree. It is heard now and again in "Samson Agonistes" and in Homer's episode of Nausicaa.

II

I have referred to a present tendency in lyrical music to replace melody by skilful harmony playing over choice aspects of nature. Something much akin to this has long been operative in lyric poetry. Offhand one would not think of turning to Petrarch for an illustration. Coming on the heels of the troubadours, whose songs he laid under heavy contribution, he would surely seem to give the strongest reinforcement to the musical test. Nearly always there is music in his language, and some of his stanzas were obviously intended to be sung. But here again the test is not decisive, for his sonnets are no more melodious than parts of Chaucer's narrative, such as the lines

And smalë foulës maken melodye
That slepen al the night with open eye,

or than much of the "Divine Comedy." In the hands of all three authors poetry of whatever type still betrayed its twin-birth with music.

Petrarch's greatest influence on others came undoubtedly from his peculiar use of nature. It was not original with him, but his expertness gave it the widest currency, and then and there created the nature cult which still has adherents. In illustrating his love for Laura he connected her with nature's treasury. Her curls were tossed by the gentlest breeze, the laurel was instinct with her presence, the stars gained in lustre by resembling her eyes, her footsteps consecrated the meadows, the flowers that brushed her were an inspiration henceforth, and a stream once visited by her thereafter murmured music. Sappho had furnished charming natural settings, but it was left to Petrarch to bring nature and love into fusion. French and English caught up his manner until no mistress was worthy if unattended by nature's store of tenderest fragrances, colors, and sounds. The insincerity of many of these writers does not remove the fact that nature was then made an almost indispensable accompaniment of what passed as lyric poetry. The thought of music might be absent from the poet, but nature must in some fashion serve him. From continual use in this way certain natural features came

to have an almost independent lyric value, especially the stars, the dawn, a stream, and flowers. Though the vogue of flower poems, such as Spenser, Shakespeare, and Milton yielded to, was enhanced by a special sentiment which each flower acquired, their main effect was the sheer beauty bestowed by long lyric associations. And in a more general way Spenser and later Thomson were content to rest the value of whole lyric stanzas upon a lovely array of sweet natural details.

Nor has the practice been neglected by more modern writers. In the case of "Fiona Macleod" it attained the proportions of a naturalistic *rêve*. Individual details of nature had received from centuries of poetic use (so we may suppose he felt) such an accumulation of emotional value that merely to pronounce their names was enough to furnish a lyric background; much after the manner of any catalogue of ships which, ever since Homer's famous list, has been apt to start in the mind a reminiscence of epic poetry. In not a few of his poems William Sharp gives little more than an enumeration of these alleged lyric features, as in the following lines:

There is in everything an undertone . . .
Those clear in soul are also clear in sight,
And recognize in a white cascade's flash
The roar of mountain torrents, and the
    wail
Of multitudinous waves on barren sands,
The song of skylark at the flush of dawn,
A mayfield all ablaze with king-cups
    gold,
The clamour musical of culver wings
Beating the soft air of a dewy dusk,
The crescent moon far voyaging thro'
    darked skies,
And Sirius throbbing in the distant
    south,
A something deeper than mere audible
And visible sensations.

Sharp's tendency—which is shared by many, among them Maeterlinck, I suspect—to see a "rainbow of feeling" in any nosegay of nature is most similar, it must be admitted, to Debussy's way of imputing subtle, fleeting emotions to his formless chromatics. I have pursued this speculation to illustrate the danger of exalting a poetical accompaniment, whether it be song or nature, to a test of type.

III

The other test usually employed to mark off lyric poetry is personal, subjective emotion. Like many other words that come trippingly from the tongue, these are meaningless unless strictly interpreted. Taken to signify merely the language of feeling, as they generally are, they lead nowhere. Is Horace's pleasant quarrel with Lydia, is many a pretty trifle by Austin Dobson, subjective emotion simply because both poets have used words of the heart? Was Robert Herrick subjective when he chaffered in the conventional conceits of his day? Are we to ignore the fact that the troubadours had a special motive for proclaiming a Blanche or a Diana to be a nonpareil? And there is the whole class of so-called lyrics which retouch ancient mythology, such as the Anacreontic of Cupid stung by a bee, whose sentiments are artificial by the nature of the case. Are they, too, subjective? But even when held to denote the poet's expression of his own sincere feeling, as I construe it, the subjective test furnishes no simple rule of thumb; for how shall we be sure when a poet is feigning?

There is, for instance, the sonnet sequence of Thomas Watson, which he openly declared to be merely an exercise in a fashion of the day. Now, oddly enough, it sounds in parts not less sincere than similar works of his time: and probably other writers, if pressed, would have had to confess that they, too, were merely playing at a game. Nor is it reasonable to accept, as Professor Reed would do, a sonnet as being necessarily a truer chart of an author's own sentiments than are various lines in a play. If there was a Dark Lady, who shall say that the views on life and death in "Hamlet" were not in part the poet's own? If there is a ring of sincerity in the lines of Sonnet LIV:

O! how much more doth beauty beauteous seem
By that sweet ornament which truth doth give!

it appears to be present also in:

There's a divinity that shapes our ends,
Rough-hew them how we will.

In attempting to reach a man through his works one has to penetrate the veil of art, whatever the form of the poem chosen. In any case, the author reacts *poetically* upon a given theme or situation, and unless the poetical equation is clearly understood, a critic would be rash to say that here the poet's heart lies bare. Take an individual sonnet unconnected with a sequence or a literary vogue. Its metrical arrangement, especially in the Italian form, and its requirements of balance, climax, and point are too complex, within such small compass, to be adjusted readily to a poet's feeling without causing some sacrifice to art. Milton, determined to speak his mind on the atrocity at Piemont, in the sonnet commencing

Avenge, O Lord, Thy slaughtered saints,

almost broke down the sonnet structure, employing a loose construction suggestive of Biblical utterance. Even while we marvel at the happy result, the impression obtrudes that here the art of the sonnet received the smallest toll on record. In some other sonnets, Milton, supreme poet that he was, so mastered the medium he worked in as to make his perceptions seem spontaneous; and Keats undoubtedly had similar success. But this does not mean that the poetical equation is not present for the critic to solve.

The mechanism of a sonnet may be thought of as an alembic which distils a poet's sentiments. Its effect is too subtle to be often detected by the critic. Yet any one who has written a sonnet (as who hasn't?) realizes that the mood in the finished product is apt to differ from the original conception, and that the transforming power of art is operative when least we think of it. The predicament of the lyrist who would be sincere may be illustrated by a modern tendency in the drama. The desire to represent life on the stage exactly as it is brings the finicky realist face to face with certain insurmountable conditions of dramatic construction. There is the element of time. Try as he will, he cannot make the stage square with life. Crises do not form with the celerity of stage convention, and in numerous other respects the dramatist of things as they are has to admit himself balked.

This directing power of artistic form increases, naturally, according to the intricacy of the type used. A drama or epic may impose a large number of external conditions, and quite conceal the author's own feelings. They are there, nevertheless, and could be sifted out if the laws of artistic construction were accurately known. By contrast, the lyric in general puts few restraints upon the poet. Particularly in open stanzas he would seem to have a good chance to express his

very self. The language of Wordsworth's "I Wandered Lonely as a Cloud" is so simple and direct as to leave no doubt that it came straight from the heart. But between the extremes represented by this poem and by such an impersonal performance as an Æschylean play the degree of subjectivity varies so much, whatever the literary form, as to make personal feeling a tricky test of type. It is hard, for instance, to imagine Wordsworth concealing his own feeling even in a drama. And Schiller's "Wilhelm Tell" is in many portions as close an index of his feeling as is his simplest lyric.

IV

Francis Palgrave, searching for a principle of selection for his "Golden Treasury," held the term lyrical "to imply that each poem shall turn upon a single thought, feeling, or situation." He ignored the tests of music and personal emotion and included in his collection eminent poems of supposedly single and continuous inspiration, in a word, all varieties of relatively short poems. The soundness of his definition might be disputed on the ground that, Poe's well-known views notwithstanding, "Paradise Lost" is the embodiment of but a single mood, albeit a huge mood. Yet if slightly arbitrary, Palgrave's distinction, which is based mainly on extent rather than on kind, is immensely convenient in practice; and I know of no other which would be usable for an anthology.

Looked at in the light of what has been said, the poems in Palgrave's collection show, it is true, certain characteristics which grow out of their brevity. Admitting that even a small structure, like a sonnet, has its artistic alchemy, it naturally lacks the resources of poetic works of considerable compass. Why is it, for instance, that Desdemona's simple utterance, "If you say so, I hope you will not kill me," is supreme poetry? It is because these prosaic words are released from a situation which has been long preparing and which in itself is surcharged with imagination. Not being included in a plot, the lyric as defined by Palgrave must depend much upon its surface value— upon graceful conceits, poignant turns of thought, choice of detail, and the piquancy of its seeming artlessness. It obviously has not the artistic framework to support any large measure of sentences which, save for the metre, are prose. So no one can conceive of a short poem including the following passage from "All's Well that Ends Well":

O! were that all. I think not on my
    father;
And these great tears grace his
    remembrance more
Than those I shed for him. What was
    he like?
I have forgot him: my imagination
Carries no favour in 't but Bertram's.
I am undone: there is no living, none,
If Bertram be away.

Yet in their proper place in the play these lines are effective. Not that the short lyric's appeal is always superficial. Though superficial in artistry, it has in general been occupied with ideas and feelings as old and deeply planted as life itself. Thus the simple line, "Gather ye rosebuds while ye may," symbolizes a fundamental tragedy. And only the slightest poetic heightening is absolutely required when the theme is a lyric standby, owing to the carrying power of the implicit sentiment.

But richness of surface, though usually an essential of the short poem, is not a safe distinction. Poets like Shelley would never have been satisfied, even when writing drama, with anything less than a succession of individually glowing lines; and

Milton and Shakespeare, while not given to Shelley's excess of fancy, resorted to figures in many instances where another might have used plain, dignified language, trusting to the poetic structure to carry it. Shakespeare has, indeed, many passages in his plays which bear a striking resemblance to poems generally accepted as lyric. Take Macbeth's lament, previously referred to:

She should have died hereafter;
There would have been time for such a
    word.
To-morrow, and to-morrow, and
    to-morrow,
Creeps in this petty pace from day to
    day
To the last syllable of recorded time,
And all our yesterdays have lighted fools
The way to dusty death. Out, out, brief
    candle!
Life's but a walking shadow, a poor
    player
That struts and frets his hour upon the
    stage
And then is heard no more: it is a tale
Told by an idiot, full of sound and fury,
Signifying nothing.

Is this less "lyric" in effect than the following lines of similar content in Pindar's eighth Pythian Ode?

In a little moment groweth up the delight of men; yea and in like sort falleth it to the ground, when a doom adverse hath shaken it.
Things of a day—what are we, and what not? Man is as a dream of shadows.

Even if we were to go back to the test of subjective emotion, Macbeth's words would still qualify as lyric. The sharp situation in which they are uttered makes them appear to be entirely the expression of personal feeling.

It is quite possible that the lyric, except in Palgrave's practical use of the term, means little more than a poetic quality. It comes close to signifying what is conveyed by the vague phrase "pure poetry." That is to say, when poetry is manifestly functioning effectively—namely, distinguishing itself from prose—it is lyric. This condition is not prescribed necessarily by brevity, though it is obviously more difficult to sustain poetry at great length. On the other hand, a plot may at times furnish a lyric, or poetic, intensity hard to attain in a short poem. Shakespeare and Milton, superb poets that they were, contrived to be almost constantly lyric even while they were, respectively, dramatic and epic. . . .

FROM THE "LYRIC"
Kenneth Burke*

Burke analyzes a conventional definition of the lyric and considers its implications in a series of fragmentary comments exploring the problem of definition itself.

Definition

A short complete poem, elevated or intense in thought and sentiment, expressing and evoking a unified attitude towards a momentous situation more or less explicitly implied—in diction harmonious and rhythmical, often but not necessarily rhymed—the structure lending itself readily to a musical accompaniment strongly repetitive in quality; the gratification of the whole residing in the nature of the work as an ordered summation of emotional experience otherwise fragmentary, inarticulate, and unsimplified.

Comments

"A short, complete poem." Insofar as a fragment of a larger work can be excerpted and offered as a lyric, it must meet these tests of brevity and completeness, to be a *perfect* lyric. Lyrics can, however, have a function over and above their completeness. Thus, recall Aristotle's observation that the earlier writers of tragedy used choral songs as integral parts of the action, whereas later these became merely intercalary pieces, having no more to do with the plot of one play than of another.

"Elevated or intense." "Intense" because even a mood of sullenness or vindictiveness would be a fit subject for a lyric. Sometimes maybe even "dense" would be the word, or "condensed." Maybe "dense" would serve to cover both "elevated" and "intense."

"Thought and sentiment." The contemporary stress upon the purely *sensory* nature of the lyric image makes this part of the formula look a bit quaint? But let's recover the whole process here by disclosing the "sentiments" implicit in the "sensations," and the "thoughts" implicit in the "sentiments." True, in one poet's poem of a few lines, such a search may be tenuous, or the findings hard to establish beyond question. But if the critic can gauge the particular poet's language by the study of other poems by the same

* The selection is reprinted from "Three Definitions" in *The Kenyon Review*, Vol. XIII (1951), by permission of the author.

poet using the same terms, an entire "philosophy" can be evolved.

"Expressing and evoking." We might bring the two steps together in the one word "communicating." But the lyric, at least the subjective lyric, in contrast with the drama, tends to be first an outcry, and second a persuasion. Hence, our preference for splitting into two aspects the single use of a communicative medium.

"A unified attitude." The "lyric attitude," as vs. the "dramatic act." Attitude as gesture, as posture. Think of it in the most plastic sense. As with the statue of a man on horseback, being heroic, in a public park (the scene integral to the gesture and posture not being there at all). Strictly speaking, an attitude is by its very nature "unified." Even an attitude of hesitancy or internal division is "unified" in the formal sense, if the work in its entirety rounds out precisely that.

Attitude "towards a momentous situation." Are we being too tricky here, in this word "momentous"? We wanted a word that connoted the significant, outstanding, distinct, or distinguished. "Momentous" would seem to do this, in meaning "of moment." But there are also suggestions of the "momentary" in the word (hence involving us by another route in the lyric "arrest"). We could think here also of the ways in which Hegel might divide an idea into "moments," and thereby we also verge upon the "motivational."

Situation "more or less explicitly implied." That is, the lyric attitude implies *some* kind of situation. The situation may be the vaguest sort: The poet stands alone by the seashore while the waves are rolling in; or, the poet is separated from his beloved; or, the poet is old, remembering his youth—etc. Or the situation may be given in great detail. Indeed, a lyric may be, on its face, but

a listing of descriptive details specifying a scene—but these *images* are all manifestations of a single *attitude* (attitude being incipient act, and image implying attitude towards the thing imaged).

"In diction harmonious and rhythmical, often but not necessarily rhymed." The formula would accommodate both strict and free verse, as it should.

"The structure lending itself readily to a musical accompaniment strongly repetitive in nature." This part of the definition involves ultimately something so idealistic (rather than realistic) as "tendencies" or "trends." Hence, maybe this should be out. It implies definition in terms of "ideal paradigm," as with our account of the five acts in a Shakespearean tragedy. . . .

Similarly, could we legitimately be to this extent "idealistic" in our definition: Could we say that the lyric "tends ideally" to be of such a nature as would adapt it to rondolike musical forms; hence, it would have stanzas varying in sense though metrically similar, and built about a recurrent refrain. It could be studied as a departure from this "*Urform*," or archetype. But it need not preserve such a structure explicitly, to qualify as a lyric.

"The gratification of the whole residing in the nature of the work as an ordered summation of emotional experience otherwise fragmentary, inarticulate, and unsimplified." This "gratification" (or "lyric pleasure") would correspond to the "catharsis" of "pity, fear, and like emotions" (named by Aristotle as the tragic pleasure). An attitude is a summing-up (as were all the details of an actual experience to terminate in an attitude of cheerfulness or gloom on our part). But, as compared with the order in the poem, wherein things fall together felicitously, the experiences reflected there are "fragmentary, inarticulate, and unsimplified."

One colleague, erroneously hearing the last word as "simplified," gave us a further insight into the problems of definition at this point. Presumably he was thinking of the experience in art as more complex than the experiences in life. There is certainly a sense in which this can be so: The reader of the poem must "make allowances" for the fact that the poem is an artifact, its moods artificial— and in this respect the poem could be called less "simple" than the actual attitudes it imitates. But when calling the poem a simplification and life outside the poem unsimplified, we have in mind the sense of unity (order) supplied by the poem. Croce would give the name of "catharsis" to such transcending of emotional matter by artistic form, or "expression."

FROM THE FACES OF THE POET
George T. Wright[*]

Wright distinguishes lyric from dramatic on the basis of the identity of the speaker. In a lyric there is an implicit poet and a speaker or persona through whom the poet addresses an audience much as a character in drama speaks to other characters and to an audience.

...As soon as we recognize that in all poems it is a persona, not a poet, who speaks the actual words, we can see the fundamental dramatic character even of lyric verse. In noting this character we seem almost to be effecting an identity between two opposite poles of literary production. For although every speaker in a play is, for the duration of his speech, a lyric self, a presenter of a point of view, dramatic form requires that one speaker's person be confronted with another. In their "pure" forms the lyric presents one speaker, the drama more than one. We call lyrical, therefore, those dramas in which one character (with his point of view) so predominates that his confrontations of other characters seem falsified: the meetings with other personae are merely opportunities for their spiritual domination by the hero.

Similarly, the lyric is or becomes dramatic when it presents not a single point of view but a struggle between conflicting points of view. The deliberate placing of a distance between the poet and his lyric persona effectively dramatizes the substance of the poem. But, however accustomed we may be to the more direct lyric in which the thoughts or feelings of the poet, or of the characters he represents, are stated with unambiguous explicitness, art is formal, and there must always be a distance, minimized or emphasized, between the maker of the poem and the persons in the poem. Poetry, dramatic or lyric, does not present fragments of human experience, but formalized versions of it. The actions represented do not really take place; the persons, including the "I," do not exist outside

* The selection is reprinted from *The Poet in the Poem*, by George T. Wright, by permission of the University of California Press. Copyright 1960 by the University of California Press.

the poem, or at least do not exist in the same way. Characters in literature have no extension in space or time beyond the limits of the work in which they appear; they have, on the other hand, a kind of extendability, a symbolic dimension, that the matter-of-fact persons of our acquaintance do not have. Together with the literary context in which they appear, they objectively represent something larger than any group of persons in actual life can ever objectively represent. That is, in "real life" we ascribe to persons a typicality or a symbolic function that they do not really have; there is no such thing as a typical American or a man of the people outside our speculations, there are only various men. In a novel or poem, however, the typicality of a man is objectively there, placed intentionally by the writer for us to see; his symbolic function, like his symbolic context, is an inseparable part of him.

The literary character is thus a formalization of our experience of actual human beings, as the literary context in which he appears is a formalization of more general human experience. And this is true for the lyric as well as for the drama. The frequent modern practice of making a clear distinction between a poet and his personae draws attention to the facts that art is formal and that a work of art—even a lyric poem—in which the poet is, as Wallace Stevens writes, "too exactly himself" is in danger of not being art at all. Stevens goes on:

We do not say ourselves like that in
    poems.
We say ourselves in syllables that rise
From the floor, rising in speech we do
    not speak.

[CPWS, 311]

We do not say anything directly, least of all ourselves. If we want to say our-selves, we make a formal structure whose import will be *us*. . . .

In drama the first persona addresses a second and may talk about a third. When the second speaks, he becomes the first persona, and his interlocutor becomes the second, for whoever speaks *is* the first persona and whoever is spoken to is the second. The third may become the second by being addressed or the first by speaking, and the first two may become the third if they are referred to by other speakers. The personae of the stage, like the persons of ordinary life, shift their grammatical roles, and the audience takes in the action first from one point of view, then from another, grasping the "I-ness" of each persona at the same time as it regards each of them from outside as a "he." For the persona, the mask, the person, is a role, a point of view, which any man may assume; the different *personae* of grammar and the stage are roles among which a man may move.

But while the *dramatis personae* alternate as speakers, each of them represents a fairly consistent point of view, a role or part that is signalized by the mask and parallel devices of costume, gesture, and speech. On the stage these points of view, these attitudes, find themselves in conflicts (to be in relation is to be in conflict) with one another, conflicts that are sometimes in the foreground of the action (as in the I-you of dialogue), sometimes in the background (he, she, it, they). The conflict among points of view, however, is complicated by the implied comment on all the points of view which the playwright makes from his omniscient point of view (somewhat as the judge in the courtroom triad resolves the conflict between two other persons). In this process the writer relegates all the masks and all the surface action of the play to third-person position. The discretion with which he selects certain points of view for presentation, and his skill in arranging and controlling them, give to each of them in turn a deeper significance, for in any final analysis the meaning of each presented point of view, of each person, is formulable only with reference to the total hypostasis, the structure of meaning which the play as a whole represents: the playwright's voice, his deepest lyrical person, *his* point of view.

For there are always two levels of speech in a work of literature—that on which the characters speak to each other, to themselves, to an implied audience, or to God, and that on which the writer speaks to us. In the lyric poem more than in any other genre these levels tend to become confused. We can sense rather easily the presence of the two levels in a fairly formal lyric, say a love sonnet. On the surface we can read the following personae:

1st person: singer of love song.
2d person: singer's mistress.
3d person: singer's love for mistress.

On the deeper level of the poem the poet talks to us:

1st person: composer of song.
2d person: we as readers or hearers.
3d person: human passion, one aspect of the human world.

Even if the poet is in love to distraction, the poem is always finally addressed to us. Beyond the plot, beyond the characters, even beyond any expressed didactic statements, the writer is telling us something, giving us his view of life or of some part of life. But such a view, requiring for its full formulation these particular events, situations, emotions, and tones, can never be expressed by any "I" within the poem. The poet's point of view is always larger than that of his "I," for the "I," like the other surface materials of

the poem, is only a conventional element in a symbolic context that serves as the formal expression of the poet's view of reality. If the point of view of the poet is not larger than that of his "I," what we have is not a poem but transcribed and polished talk, a fragment of *a* human dialogue instead of a stylization of *the* human dialogue.

All this holds true for the lyric as well as for other, apparently less "personal," kinds of literature. We tend to think of the lyric as stating "directly" the poet's feelings or thoughts; but, in fact, definitions of the lyric by reference to its content are mostly recent. J. E. Spingarn tells us:

. . . during the Renaissance there was no systematic lyric theory. Those who discussed it at all gave most of their attention to its formal structure, its style, and especially the conceit it contained. . . . [For them] the real question at issue . . . is merely that of external form.[1]

And Raymond Macdonald Alden writes:

. . . the word lyric is used both in a general and a more particular sense, having gradually been extended from its original meaning—a poem to be *sung* by a single singer —to include all poetry expressing *subjectively* the emotion of the poet or those whom he represents.[2]

The more formal definition—"a poem to be *sung* by a single singer"—shows us how clearly the lyric is to be contrasted with the drama, in which several "singers" take part. From this point of view lyric might include epic and, more loosely, all fiction not actually dramatized on a stage, for even in those stories told in turn by different characters a single voice, pre-

[1] *A History of Literary Criticism in the Renaissance* (New York, 1899), pp. 58–59.
[2] *An Introduction to Poetry* (New York, 1909), p. 55.

sumably that of the author, is the voice we hear throughout.

But even if we accept in spirit the restriction of "lyric" to those poems that express "*subjectively* the emotion of the poet or those whom he represents," we find that the poems themselves do not express anything subjectively but the poet's view of life, the feelings that are communicated on the second and deeper level of the poem. On the immediate and literal level the poem presents *objectively* "the emotion of the poet or those whom he represents." If it were not so, the poem would not be a poem. As in the drama, as in fiction, the action of the lyric must function as a trope, a figure, a mask, an affirmation in symbolic terms of whatever it is that the poet, most deeply, is telling us. The speech of literature is different in kind from that of ordinary talk, and the lyric, no less than the drama, is a stylized abstraction of the human dialogue, not an instance of it.

But precisely what is a poetic persona? In spite of frequent references to the term in modern criticism, how it functions in poems is still far from clear. Most of those who speak of personae and masks treat them as evasions or obfuscations of the self rather than as revelations of more significant aspects of reality. Discussions of Swift or of Blake sometimes imply that the use of masks represents a lapse of the writer's integrity, that the author is "hiding," and that the device of the persona is at best dubiously poetic. Such writers usually try to "get behind" the masks to "the man," to the historical human being whose beliefs, education, prejudices, and impressions belie the masks and throw light on the "real" meaning of the work. Research along this line has the merit of all biographical inquiry directed toward the illumination of

literature, but it often overlooks or distorts the specific literary purposes that the mask is designed not to evade but to fulfill. Only very recently have a small number of articles and books begun to examine the use of personae as a satirical or ironic technique; yet, although at least one persona is present in every work of literature, modern criticism contains hardly a remark on the use of personae as a fundamental literary device.[3]

Literature is made up of words, composed by writers and spoken by personae. In some works the distinction between poet and speaker is obvious; in others it seems an extravagance to call attention to a distinction so thin that it can hardly be said to exist. Its existence is nevertheless a matter of fact. The persona may share much with his creator—a point of view, an attitude toward life, certain historical circumstances, certain intellectual qualities; but the persona is part of the poem, and the poet exists outside it. The author dies; the persona has a permanently potential existence, realized whenever the work in which he appears is read. However skillfully the poet may try to effect an identity between himself and his persona, the task is hopeless, for he and what he has created exist on different

[3] The best direct theoretical discussions of personae appear in William B. Ewald's *The Masks of Jonathan Swift* (Cambridge, Mass., 1954), Rebecca Price Parkin's *The Poetic Workmanship of Alexander Pope* (Minneapolis, 1955), and Maynard Mack's "The Muse of Satire," *Yale Review*, XLI (Autumn, 1951), 80–92. Hugh Kenner's *The Poetry of Ezra Pound* (London, 1951) and H. H. Watt's *Ezra Pound and the Cantos* (London, 1951) include studies of Pound's personae; Warren Ramsey's *Jules Laforgue and the Ironic Inheritance* (New York, 1953) studies Laforgue's "voices"; Richard Ellmann's *Yeats: The Man and the Masks* (New York, 1948) and *The Identity of Yeats* (New York, 1954) examine Yeats's multiple poses and their implications. These, along with Robert Langbaum's *The Poetry of Experience* (New York, 1957), which bears on the subject at every point, are valuable to any student of personae.

metaphysical levels. Mainly because the speaker is in the poem, not behind it—though he may be behind the events of the poem, not in them—he cannot quite be identified with the maker of the whole poem, speaker and all. The speaker is wholly a product, and only apparently a source. . . .

Throughout the long tradition of the English lyric down to the Romantic era, the persona of poems maintains a fairly consistent identity. When the troubadours of Provence sent jongleurs to sing their songs for them, they established a tradition that the lyric followed for many centuries. The practice is again reminiscent of drama: as the playwright composes words for the actor to speak through a mask, so the lyric poet composes a song for the jongleur to sing. The jongleur is the lyric persona, and he sings through masks of his own, the different roles—lover, mourner, panegyrist—which compound his role as singer. As the origins of the tradition become obscured, the disparity between singer and poet decreases, and the lyric persona comes to be identifiable as singer or poet, or poet as singer. Nevertheless, the sense in which the persona is a poet must be carefully discriminated. The "I" of most English lyric poems is identified by his vocation of song, not by his physical and social existence as a man. The lyric persona is man singing, man as composer or singer of songs.

When he turns his music to specific human activities and events, and takes on more specific human modifications in order to play his roles, the singer does not forget that he *is* a singer. The several conventional kinds of lyrics place the singer in relation to conventional subjects —to love, to death, to his country. And what he says of these subjects will conform largely to the audience's expecta-

tions derived from experience of other singers; through song the singer confirms and deepens the audience's conceptions of love or death. Thus, a love sonnet does not present man in love, but man singing of love; an elegy is not a presentation of man feeling about death, but of man singing about death. The poet appears not as man undergoing experiences but as man singing about his experiences. The Renaissance lyric persona repeatedly refers to himself as a poet or singer, in effect as man in his role of celebrant of human reality. Herrick's well-known lines exceed others only in articulateness:

I sing of brooks, of blossoms, birds, and
    bowers:
Of April, May, of June, and July flowers.
I sing of May-poles, hock-carts, wassails,
    wakes,
Of bridegrooms, brides, and of their
    bridal cakes.
I write of youth, of love, and have
    access
By these, to sing of cleanly wantonness.

This, as Herrick tells us in its title, is the "argument" of his work, and it is the argument, too, of the traditional lyric. The poet is a singer. Whatever else he is remains irrelevant. He never, or very rarely, appears as a full man, participating in all the variety of life as other men do, with private interests and private business of his own. His only business is song; whatever he celebrates, he celebrates in his role as singer. For brooks and blossoms unsung are different from brooks and blossoms sung. The singing of them is an assertion of their value, a transportation of them into a dimension peculiar to the sung. . . .

Other recognizable genres employ singers in other recognizable roles. The singer of patriotic songs is a patriot; the singer of dirges is a mourner; the singer of reflective poems is a reflective man. Every conventional kind largely defines, and is largely defined by, the role of the singer; which comes first is hard to say, for the two work together. As the poem is all words, the words define simultaneously the singer and the nature of his present activity; a role itself *is* a kind of conduct rather than a kind of man. The assumption of any role is an act of limitation and compression; it is a means to the focusing of human intelligence on a specific category of human experience. As the poem does not cover all of life, so the "I" is not the singer in all his possible human roles. But both, along with other poetic elements, are narrowed: the "I" to denote the singer in the specific role of lover or mourner, the subject matter to love or death, the tone to certain limits appropriate to both subject and speaker, the diction to certain similarly appropriate limits. Within these bounds the poet can range widely; almost every conceivable attitude toward love and death can be and has been taken. But conventions tend to make possible the more concrete renderings of feelings about any subject. No singer is all men in all moods, as no poem tells all about life. As each poem defines itself in its progress, so it defines and limits its singer as well. Every poem that emerges as satirical excludes from its coverage an acceptance of man as straightforwardly meditative; every poem consistently nonsatirical excludes from its coverage satirical man. The speaker's role and the genre define themselves together and are recognizable in terms of similar roles and genres that readers have already met. . . .

Since the confusion about the identity of the speaker revolves around the possible denotations of the word "I" and the inevitable use of an "I" in literary art,

it is not surprising that when the external conditions of the Provençal division of labor between poet and singer were forgotten,[4] the lyric "I" gradually came to stand more and more for the poet himself. In fact, it is doubtful if in practice the poet ever completely detaches himself from his persona. Although the "I" is fundamentally a singer, a mask through which the poet examines reality, the poet necessarily draws from his own experience in establishing the song of his singer. And because in any linguistic symbolism the word "I" is a center of ambiguity, even the poet may become understandably confused as to who it is that actually speaks his poems. Thus Herrick, in the rest of the poem quoted above, goes on listing the matter of his song, but in the last two lines becomes something more than a singer:

I sing of dews, of rains, and piece by piece
Of balm, of oil, of spice, and ambergris.
I sing of times trans-shifting: and I write
How roses first came red, and lilies white.
I write of groves, of twilights, and I sing
The court of Mab, and of the Fairy King.
I write of hell; I sing (and ever shall)
Of heaven, and hope to have it after all.

All the persona's activity until the last two lines is present-tense activity, for his office requires him only to sing or to write (the offices of poet and singer clearly merge as singer and writer become almost interchangeable). Under the conditions of the lyric as an apostrophe, as a naming of subjects in song, the present tense is perfectly appropriate. The celebration of the parts of the world is a subjection of

---

[4] Such a division is, of course, common and almost inevitable wherever the lyric tradition is oral.

them to the magic process of poetry, through which they become things sung, different from things unsung. The singer in the poem, through the pure apostrophe, also acquires the agelessness, the elemental stylization, of what he sings —the world, in fact, is pure song. But the agelessness suffers a jar in the penultimate line when the singer refers to his future intentions. As they are still confined to his role of singer, they do not violently disturb the picture. But the last line quite destroys the view of the singer which we have so far built up, or rather

conveys the persona from the dimension of a mask to the dimension of actual life:

> I sing (and ever shall)
> Of heaven, and hope to have it after all.

"After all" does not mean "after a career of singing," but "after my life as a man." Heaven is not for singers, but for men. And our realization that this singer is not man singing but *a* man singing alters our interpretation of the whole poem. A man, not a singer, has been speaking all the time. . . .

FROM THE NATURE OF
METAPHYSICAL POETRY
Herbert Read*

Read avers that, whatever else it may be, a lyric is "simply a perception." Conceptual though metaphysical poetry is, "it is no less 'emotional' than lyrical poetry"—it is, in fact, "the emotional apprehension of thought."

An examination of the many diverse theories of poetry current since the romantic revival of a hundred years ago would reveal unanimity on one point at least. Rhetoric and thought have been expended, often with ingenious results, on the manner and style of poetry—on questions of the necessity of metre and rhyme, on the relative merits of the ode and sonnet, and on such external subjects as the propriety of realism or the ethical confusions of romanticism. But the poetry thus generously treated approximates in every case to that type known as the lyric; if it is not exactly a lyric, it is a "lyrical passage" from some

other kind of poem. In short, poetry has been identified with lyricism. There is, of course, a very good reason for this universal confusion, and my first intention is to make it distinct.

The etymological significance of the word *lyric* is largely lost, but generally it now connotes that quality in writing which we may for the moment be content to call "emotional." A lyric poem has in addition certain formal characteristics, such as brevity, simplicity, and directness, and for this reason it is commonly held that a good poem cannot be long, or that a long poem can only be good "in parts." It may further be noted that those poems the world agrees to call lyrical are exclusively concerned with the record of sensibility—of direct sensibility, as in

* This selection is reprinted from *Reason and Romanticism*, by Herbert Read, by permission of Faber and Faber Ltd. Copyright 1926 by Faber and Faber Ltd.

"The Solitary Reaper," or of those vaguer reactions of direct sensibility that are "the bliss of solitude." Some lyric poets are sensible of the beauty of the actual phenomenon, others are sensible of the ideal associations of phenomena. But they agree, and it is essential to bear this in mind, in deriving their emotions from a direct awareness of the world—of its women, its flowers, its atmospheres, and its subtleties.

The occasionality of such emotional awareness has resulted in the practice, and then in the theory, of an emotional unity in the poem. An emotion is fleeting and must be seized in its uniqueness; all elements that do not contribute to its expression must be rigorously excluded: clarity, succinctness, simplicity —these are the virtues of the lyric, and, in modern minds, of all poetry. All the elaborate rules, and even all the revolts against any rules, exemplified in modern poetry, have their origin in the peculiar needs of the lyric.

The occasionality of the lyric does not, however, deprive it of a more general utility; a lyric is simply a perception, and all thought is based primarily on perceptions. From the accumulation of selected perceptions, expressed as lyrics, it is obvious that a general view of life may be constructed, and this general view may possess great ethical and aesthetic value. But it will remain a view, a *Weltanschauung;* it cannot become metaphysical until it is converted into concepts. But, in the mind of the modern theorist, to convert perceptions (*i.e.,* emotional perceptions) into concepts is to destroy their poetic quality. In reality, however, such a result is by no means inevitable.

Let us examine more carefully the use of the word *emotion* in this connection. I gather from the critics who have established the lyrical standard of poetry that they use the word in its general psychological sense. Even in psychology any exact scientific use of the word is difficult, as McDougall has shown;[1] and while our critics do not normally expect poetry to embody or inspire primary emotions like anger or fear, the emotions they do demand of poetry differ in degree rather than in kind from these. The tenderness expressed and induced by a lyric may even be so influential as to cause a "lump in the throat," even as fear is accompanied by certain visceral disturbances; and physiology may yet identify and classify the various glandular excretions and their appropriate lyrical responses. Nor am I disposed to deny that the state of attention or contemplation induced by metaphysical poetry may not also have its basis in some material agitation of the human cortex or glandular system. But the business of the literary critic is to identify the mental rather than the physiological significance of the material in his hands, and in this sense a more useful distinction can be made in the content of the emotions; though immediately we desert the field of a material science we are driven to the use of inexact terms. But terms are inexact only because they mean different things to different people: to those who are willing to understand, they can convey an exact meaning; and, when I contrast the abstract and the concrete contents of emotions, I do not thereby imply that an abstract content is something vague and indefinable. To the scientific poet, as to the scientific philosopher, abstract conceptions have their exactitudes. With this understanding, I may distinguish the concrete character of the content of the lyric, which in its purest state is concerned with the direct awareness of phenomenal environment, from the abstract

[1] *Social Psychology,* chap. iii.

character of what I am going to call metaphysical poetry.

Metaphysical poetry is abstract because, like metaphysics, it deals with concepts. But, as poetry, it is no less "emotional" than lyrical poetry—though, since the emotion is differently manifested, it is a question whether that state of vivid contemplation inspired by metaphysical poetry had not better be described by another word. For my present purpose I do not think so, for it is necessary at all costs to maintain a nexus between lyrical poetry and metaphysical poetry in the word *poetry*; and since I despise all distinctions based on the technique or *décor* of poetry, I prefer to justify this nexus in the word *emotion*, which denotes a common foundation in physical fact. Later I shall illustrate the actual character of metaphysical poetry. For the present I will define it as the emotional apprehension of thought—or, to use words suggested by Dante, as thought transmuted into vision:

e il pensamento in sogno transmutai.

...In reality very few of the metaphysical school were metaphysical in any sense, and the name only adds confusion to literary criticism. Their characteristics—"stranger than seven antiquaries' studies"—are well enough known; and their faults have been ably summarized and controverted by Johnson in his *Life of Cowley*. But the quality that was really distinctive in the experiments of Donne and some of his followers Johnson missed altogether; all that he could grudgingly allow to "this race of authors" was a virtuous erudition: "To write on their plan it was at least necessary to read and think." In this way he did considerable injustice to Donne, as is shown by the quotations he uses, which never represent the Donne that appeals to a modern mind. In Donne we do as a matter of fact find the first consciousness of felt thought, and his compasses and mandrakes are small matters in comparison to this. The new consciousness is so incidental that at first it seems accidental; but it continues to be incidental, not only in the metaphysical school, but in others that came after them, and we must ascribe its rarity to its difficulty. It begins to be present in lines like the following:

Earths hollownesses, which the worlds
    lungs are,
Have no more wind than the upper valt
    of aire.
We can nor lost friends, nor sought foes
    recover,
But meteorlike, save that we move not,
    hover.
Onely the Calenture together drawes
Deare friends, which meet dead in great
    fishes jawes.[2]

It may be asked: what metaphysics is there in a passage like this? The only answer is that only a metaphysician could have written it. Only a mind habituated to thought would visualize its thoughts in precisely that way. Donne's metaphors, even when they are most "poetical," are still a part of his thought:

All their proportion's lame, it sinkes, it
    swels.
For of Meridians, and Parallels
Man hath weav'd out a net, and this net
    throwne,
Upon the Heavens, and now they are his
    owne.
Loth to goe up the hill, or labour thus
To go to heaven, we make heaven come
    to us.
We spur, we reine the starres, and in
    their race
They're diversely content t'obey our
    pace.

[2] From *The Calme*, Oxford Edition, 1912, p. 178.

But keepes the earth her round
  proportion still?
Doth not a Tenarif, or higher Hill
Rise so high like a Rocke, that one
  might thinke
The floating Moone would shipwracke
  there, and sinke?[3]

Poorer poets bring lights into their
rooms, but Donne, like all true metaphysical poets, strikes fire in the very
process of his reasoning.

If we turn to a contemporary of
Donne's—to George Chapman—we discover an even better augury of what the
metaphysical poet might be. It would, in
fact, be difficult to exaggerate the wealth
of possibilities that came into existence
with Chapman's individual poetry; but
after Chapman came Milton, destroying
this indigenous growth. Although a contemporary of Donne's, Chapman was not
at the time often associated with Donne;
he was not considered one of the metaphysical school—which shows, indeed,
how prone contemporary opinion is to
judge authors by their superficies: Donne
by his conceits and Chapman by his
"full and heightened style." When we get
to the essence of these authors we find in
Donne a mind poised at the exact turn of
the course of philosophy—drawing his
inspiration right back from scholastic
sources, and yet at the same time eagerly
surveying the new future promised by
the science of Copernicus and Galileo.
Chapman, on the other hand, is in a
remarkable degree the forerunner of humanist philosophy—of Hume and Spinoza in particular. He is aware, above all
things, of "the consent and sacred harmony of life." He brings ethics even into
his title-page (e.g., *Caesar and Pompey:
A Roman Tragedy*, declaring their
Warres. Out of whose events is evicted
this proposition: *Only a just man is a*

[3] From *An Anatomie of the World: The
First Anniversary*, Oxford Edition, pp. 239–40.

freeman). And his theory of tragedy, as
expressed in the dedication of *The Revenge of Bussy D'Ambois*, is more definitely didactic than Aristotle's even, and
more uncompromising than Dante's
theory of poetry: "And for the authenti-
cal truth of either person or action, who
(worth the respecting) will expect it in
a poem, whose subject is not truth, but
things like truth? Poor envious souls they
are that cavil at truth's want in these
natural fictions; material instruction, ele-
gant and sententious excitation to virtue,
and deflection from her contrary, being
the soul, limbs, and limits of an au-
thentical tragedy." But who, in reading
The Revenge of Bussy D'Ambois, pauses
for an instant conscious of the boredom
of its ethical purpose? It is, on the contrary, one of the most sustained poetic
dramas in English literature. But the
poetry is not "easy";[4] it is musical, like
lyrical poetry, but it has an opacity, or
"charged" effect, characteristic of all
good metaphysical poetry; as though behind each word lurked considerable processes of thought:

And know ye all...
That in this one thing all the discipline
Of manners and of manhood is
  contained;
A man to join himself with th' Universe
In his main sway, and make (in all
  things fit)
One with that All, and go on, round
  as it;
Not plucking from the whole his
  wretched part,
And into straits, or into nought revert,
Wishing the complete Universe might
  be
Subject to such a rag of it as he;
But to consider great Necessity,

[4] It is important, in this connection, to remember the dedicatory epistle to Ovid's *Banquet of Sense*, which embodies Chapman's very
direct affirmations on the subject of his metaphysical poetry.

All things as well refract as voluntary
Reduceth to the prime celestial cause,
Which he that yields to with a man's
   applause,
And cheek by cheek goes, crossing it no
   breath,
But, like God's image, follows to the
   death,
That man is truly wise. . . .

. . . Milton, in his later phase, perhaps did more to destroy the true tradition of metaphysical poetry than any other agent. His thought was a system apart from his poetic feeling, and in the violence wrought by his too forceful fashion he almost crushed the life out of an only too subtle advance of human consciousness. He did not think poetically, but merely expounded thought in verse: psychologically he was conscious all the time of a dualism—on the one side the thought to be expounded, on the other side the poetic mould into which his thought had to be smelted. The true metaphysical poet is conscious of no such dualism: his thought is in its very process poetical. This distinction so briefly expressed may seem a trifle upon which to dismiss so established a reputation as Milton's is in this particular sphere, and it must be admitted that the whole matter needs careful analysis and consideration; for the present I prefer not to endanger a good cause by enlisting a doubtful ally. Shelley, too, I prefer to leave unquoted: his sentiments were too vague to bring him within the scientific definition of philosophy underlying the assumptions of this essay; and when he meant to be metaphysical he was merely mystical. As for Browning, he was neither mystical nor metaphysical, and I am not sure that it would not be legitimate to say that he was just wordy. It may be admitted, however, that he has very definite claims to be considered as a psychological poet; and if "Bishop Blougram's Apology" is not so good of its kind as is Cavalcanti's canzone beginning "L'ardente fiamma della fiera pesta" (it is not so sincere), yet "Bishop Blougram" and parts of *The Ring and the Book* and certain of the *Parleyings* are good enough to establish the *genre* in its own rights. But the *genre* is definitely psychological, consisting of the analysis of motives and personalities, and differing entirely from the metaphysical, which should confine itself to the statement of ideas. Leibniz has defined an intelligent author as one who includes the most reality in the least possible compass,[5] and it would be difficult to improve on this definition. And in that case it is difficult to see how psychological poetry, which is descriptive, can compete with metaphysical poetry, which is synthetic. It is for this reason, if for no other, that Wordsworth tends to emerge out of the immediate welter of his epoch with something more of solidity than we can associate with the merely descriptive evocations of his contemporaries. In fact, I might go a long way to find a better example of metaphysical poetry than certain lines from the fragment of *The Recluse*:

. . . I must tread on shadowy ground,
   must sink
Deep—and, aloft ascending, breathe in
   worlds
To which the heaven of heavens is but
   a veil.
All strength—all terror, single or in
   bands,
That ever was put forth in personal
   form;
Jehovah—with his thunder, and the
   choir
Of shouting Angels, and the empyreal
   thrones—
I pass them unalarmed. Not Chaos, not
The darkest pit of lowest Erebus,

5 *Discourse on Metaphysics,* § v.

Nor aught of blinder vacancy, scooped
  out
By help of dreams, can breed such fear
  and awe
As fall upon us when we look
Into our Minds, into the Mind of Man,
My haunt, and the main region of my
  song.

        ...if I oft
Must turn elsewhere—to travel near the
  tribes
And fellowships of man, and see ill
  sights
Of madding passion, mutually inflamed:
Must hear Humanity, in fields and
  groves
Pipe solitary anguish; or must hang
Brooding over the fierce confederate
  storm
Of sorrow, barricadoed evermore
Within the walls of Cities; may these
  sounds
Have their authentic comment,—that
  even these
Hearing, I be not downcast or forlorn!

The first part of this quotation is a
gesture, and it may be advanced that as
such it comes dangerously near to being
rhetorical. But rhetoric is only repre-
hensible when it is hollow, as it mostly
is; when it is compact with thought, as
this rhetoric of Wordsworth's is, it is
powerful beyond any other mode of expression. Blake recoiled in horror from
three of these lines: he saw in them a
rebellion against the very basis of humanistic religion. And if to-day we can
no longer share Blake's apprehension, we
can instead appreciate the profundity, the
intellectual significance, and the emotional power of these verses. The second
part of the quotation does not lack something of such qualities also, but I use it
rather with the special intention of illus-

trating how words like "confederate" and
"authentic comment" can be lifted from
their prosaic origins and made the very
keywords of a poetic vigour.

With Wordsworth the metaphysical
tradition in English poetry for the time
being ends. The possibility of recovering
this lost tradition remains to be considered.

I began by defining metaphysical
poetry as the emotional apprehension of
thought, and I am not sure that I can do
better than leave the definition simply
so, trusting that the quotations I have
meanwhile made use of may quite sufficiently illustrate my meaning. It has
been seen very noticeably, I hope, that
a degree of economy is implied in the
word "apprehension"—that economy of
thought, in fact, breeds its corresponding
intensity, which is to be identified with
the poetry itself. More anxiously I hope
that it has been seen in exactly what
sense the epithet "emotional" has been
used. Now that my illustrative matter
is complete, as far as may reasonably
be allowed, "emotional apprehension"
should appear as a fairly "hard," even
as a necessarily "dry," process. It is important beyond everything, in this era of
emotional or "commonsense" philosophies, not to confuse this mental process
in which emotion is the product of
thought, with that other vaguer, easier
process, which is the emotionalization of
thought, or thought as the product of
emotion. Metaphysical poetry is determined logically: its emotion is a joy that
comes with the triumph of the reason,
and is not a simple instinctive ecstasy.
It is, finally, but the precise statement of
such abstractions as the poet derives from
his experience. Perhaps, in the scholastic
sense, it is the poetry of universals. . . .

PART II

PERSPECTIVES AND TECHNIQUES

THE CATEGORIES in this section have established themselves in critical theory as "isms" that at one time or another have developed out of significant literary schools or movements, each one assimilating experience according to a certain viewpoint and rendering it in literature according to some correspondent method. There is, for instance, the ethics and correspondent esthetics of classicism, and the epistemology and correspondent esthetics of romanticism. Even realism, surrealism, and symbolism, which appear to be simply techniques, have been coupled with philosophical or ideological cults. The categories are, of course, analytically neat and conceal the complex interrelationships that exist among them in practice. The following essays are themselves indicative of this.

CHAPTER 5

Classicism

FROM THE GROUNDS OF CRITICISM IN POETRY
John Dennis

Dennis propounds the eighteenth-century neoclassical doctrine that the end of poetry is to "bring mankind from irregularity, extravagance, and confusion, to rule and order. . . ." The subordinate end is pleasure; the final end is instruction.

THAT POETRY IS TO BE ESTABLISH'D, BY LAYING DOWN THE RULES

That an art, so divine in its institution, is sunk and profan'd, and miserably debas'd, is a thing that is confess'd by all. But since poetry is fallen from the excellence which it once attain'd to, it must be fallen either by the want of parts, or want of industry, or by the errors of its professors. But that it cannot be for want of parts, we have shewn clearly in the advancement of modern poetry; nor can it be suppos'd to be for want of industry, since so many of its professors have no other dependance. It remains then that it must have fallen by their errors, and for want of being guided right. Since therefore 'tis for want of

knowing by what rules they ought to proceed, that poetry is fallen so low, it follows then that it is the laying down of those rules alone, that can re-establish it. In short, poetry is either an art, or whimsy and fanaticism. If it is an art, it follows that it must propose an end to it self, and afterwards lay down proper means for the attaining that end: for this is undeniable, that there are proper means for the attaining of every end, and those proper means in poetry we call the rules. Again, if the end of poetry be to instruct and reform the world, that is, to bring mankind from irregularity, extravagance, and confusion, to rule and order, how this should be done by a thing that is in it self irregular and extravagant, is difficult to be conceiv'd. Besides, the work of every reasonable creature must

143

derive its beauty from regularity; for reason is rule and order, and nothing can be irregular either in our conceptions or our actions, any further than it swerves from rule, that is, from reason. As man is the more perfect, the more he resembles his Creator; the works of man must needs be more perfect, the more they resemble his Maker's. Now the works of God, tho infinitely various, are extremely regular.

The universe is regular in all its parts, and it is to that exact regularity that it owes its admirable beauty. The microcosm owes the beauty and health both of its body and soul to order, and the deformity and distempers of both to nothing but the want of order. Man was created, like the rest of the creatures, regular, and as long as he remain'd so, he continu'd happy; but as soon as he fell from his primitive state, by transgressing order, weakness and misery was the immediate consequence of that universal disorder that immediately follow'd in his conceptions, in his passions and actions.

The great design of arts is to restore the decays that happen'd to human nature by the Fall, by restoring order: The design of logick is to bring back order, and rule, and method to our conceptions, the want of which causes most of our ignorance, and all our errors. The design of moral philosophy is to cure the disorder that is found in our passions, from which proceeds all our unhappiness, and all our vice; as from the due order that is seen in them, comes all our virtue and all our pleasure. But how should these arts re-establish order, unless they themselves were regular? Those arts that make the senses instrumental to the pleasure of the mind, as painting and musick, do it by a great deal of rule and order: Since therefore poetry comprehends the force of all these arts of logick, of ethicks, of eloquence, of painting, of musick; can any thing be more ridiculous than to imagine, that poetry it self should be without rule and order?

What Poetry Is, and That It Attains Its End by Exciting of Passion

We have said above, that as poetry is an art, it must have a certain end, and that there must be means that are proper for the attaining that end, which means are otherwise call'd the rules: But that we may make this appear the more plainly, let us declare what poetry is. Poetry then is an art, by which a poet excites passion (and for that very cause entertains sense) in order to satisfy and improve, to delight and reform the mind, and so to make mankind happier and better: from which it appears that poetry has two ends, a subordinate, and a final one; the subordinate one is pleasure, and the final one is instruction.

First, the subordinate end of poetry is to please, for that pleasure is the business and design of poetry is evident; because poetry, unless it pleases, nay and pleases to a height, is the most contemptible thing in the world. Other things may be borne with if they are indifferent, but poetry, unless it is transporting, is abominable: nay, it has only the name of poetry, so inseparable is pleasure from the very nature of the thing.

But, *Secondly*, the final end of poetry is to reform the manners: as poetry is an art, instruction must be its final end; but either that instruction must consist in reforming the manners, or it cannot instruct at all, and consequently be an art; for poetry pretends to no other instruction as its final end. But since the final end of poetry is to reform the manners, nothing can be according to the true art of it, which is against religion, or which runs counter to moral virtue, or to the true politicks, and to the liberty of mankind: and every thing which is against the last, tends to the corruption and destruction of mankind; and consequently every thing against the last, must be utterly inconsistent with the true art of poetry.

Now the proper means for poetry, to attain both its subordinate and final end, is by exciting passion.

1st, the subordinate end of poetry, which is to please, is attain'd by exciting passion, because every one who is pleas'd is mov'd, and either desires, or rejoices, or admires, or hopes, or the like. As we are mov'd by pleasure which is happiness, to do every thing we do, we may find upon a little reflection, that every man is incited by some passion or other, either to action, or to contemplation; and passion is the result either of action or of contemplation, as long as either of them please; and the more either of them pleases, the more they are attended with passion. The satisfaction that we receive from geometry it self, comes from the joy of having found out truth, and the desire of finding more. And the satiety that seizes us upon too long a lecture, proceeds from nothing but from the weariness of our spirits, and consequently from the cessation or the decay of those two pleasing passions. But,

2dly, poetry attains its final end, which is the reforming the minds of men, by exciting of passion. And here I dare be bold to affirm, that all instruction whatever depends upon passion. The moral philosophers themselves, even the dryest of them, can never instruct and reform, unless they move; for either they make vice odious and virtue lovely, or they deter you from one by the apprehension of misery, or they incite you to the other by the happiness they make you expect from it; or they work upon your shame,

or upon your pride, or upon your indignation. And therefore poetry instructs and reforms more powerfully than philosophy can do, because it moves more powerfully: And therefore it instructs more easily too. For whereas all men have passions, and great passions of one sort or another; and whereas those passions will be employ'd, and whatever way they move, they that way draw the man; it follows, that philosophy can instruct but hardly, because it moves but gently: for the violent passions not finding their account in those faint emotions, begin to rebel and fly to their old objects; whereas poetry, at the same time that it instructs us powerfully, must reform us easily; because it makes the very violence of the passions contribute to our reformation. For the generality of mankind are apparently sway'd by their passions, nay, and perhaps the very best and wisest of them. The greatest philosophers and the greatest princes are influenc'd by their favourites, and so are the wisest magistrates. And 'tis for this reason that not only the devil, who must be suppos'd to understand human nature, corrupts mankind by their passions; (for temptation is nothing but the inclining men to such and such actions, by the raising such and such passions in them) but God himself, who made the soul, and best understands its nature, converts it by its passions. For whereas philosophy pretends to correct human passions by human reason, that is, things that are strong and ungovernable, by something that is feeble and weak; poetry by the force of the passion, instructs and reforms the reason: which is the design of the true religion, as we have shewn in another place. So that we have here already laid down one great rule, necessary for the succeeding in poetry: for since it can attain neither its subordinate nor its final end, without exciting of passion, it follows, that where there is nothing which directly tends to the moving of that, there can be no poetry; and that consequently a poet ought to contrive every thing in order to the moving of passion, that not only the fable, the incidents and characters, but the very sentiments and the expressions, ought all to be design'd for that. For since poetry pleases and instructs us more even than philosophy it self, only because it moves us more, it follows, that the more poetry moves, the more it pleases and instructs: and it is for this reason that tragedy, to those who have a taste of it, is both more pleasing and more instructing than comedy. And this naturally brings us to the dividing poetry into the greater and the less.

1. The greater poetry is an art by which a poet justly and reasonably excites great passion, that he may please and instruct; and comprehends epick, tragick, and the greater lyrick poetry.

2. The less poetry is an art by which a poet excites less passion for the foremention'd ends; and includes in it comedy and satire, and the little ode, and elegiack and pastoral poems. . . .

A DISSERTATION UPON POETRY
Samuel Johnson

In this eighteenth-century discussion of what makes a poet, Dr. Johnson has his fictional figure Imlac, the court poet, define somewhat puritanically the neoclassical ideal of poetry. Poetry, declares Imlac, must depict the general and the universal; it "does not number the streaks of the tulip, or describe the different shades of verdure in the forest." Instead, it strives after "general properties and large appearances." The essay is the tenth chapter of *Rasselas*.

"Wherever I went, I found that poetry was considered as the highest learning, and regarded with a veneration somewhat approaching to that which man would pay to the angelic nature. And yet it fills me with wonder that, in almost all countries, the most ancient poets are considered as the best: whether it be that every other kind of knowledge is an acquisition gradually attained, and poetry is a gift conferred at once; or that the first poetry of every nation surprised them as a novelty, and retained the credit by consent which it received by accident at first; or whether, as the province of poetry is to describe nature and passion, which are always the same, the first writers took possession of the most striking objects for description and the most probable occurrences for fiction, and left nothing to those that followed them, but transcription of the same events, and new combinations of the same images. Whatever be the reason, it is commonly observed that the early writers are in possession of nature, and their followers of art; that the first excel in strength and invention, and the latter in elegance and refinement.

"I was desirous to add my name to this illustrious fraternity. I read all the poets of Persia and Arabia, and was able to repeat by memory the volumes that are suspended in the mosque of Mecca. But I soon found that no man was ever great by imitation. My desire of excellence impelled me to transfer my attention to nature and to life. Nature was to be my subject, and men to be my auditors: I could never describe what I had not seen; I could not hope to move those with delight or terror, whose interests and opinions I did not understand.

"Being now resolved to be a poet, I saw everything with a new purpose; my sphere of attention was suddenly magnified; no kind of knowledge was to be overlooked. I ranged mountains and deserts for images and resemblances, and pictured upon my mind every tree of the forest and flower of the valley. I observed with equal care the crags of the rock and the pinnacles of the palace. Sometimes I wandered along the mazes of the rivulet, and sometimes watched the changes of the summer clouds. To a poet nothing can be useless. Whatever is beautiful, and whatever is dreadful, must be familiar to his imagination; he must be conversant with all that is awfully vast or elegantly little. The plants of the garden, the animals of the wood, the minerals of the earth, and meteors of the sky, must all concur to store his mind with inexhaustible variety: for every idea is useful for the enforcement or decoration of moral or religious truth; and he who knows most will have most power of diversifying his scenes, and of gratifying his reader with remote allusions and unexpected instruction.

"All the appearances of nature I was therefore careful to study, and every country which I have surveyed has contributed something to my poetical powers."

"In so wide a survey," said the prince, "you must surely have left much unobserved. I have lived till now within the circuit of these mountains, and yet cannot walk abroad without the sight of something which I have never beheld before, or never heeded."

"The business of a poet," said Imlac, "is to examine, not the individual, but the species; to remark general properties and large appearances; he does not number the streaks of the tulip, or describe the different shades in the verdure of the forest. He is to exhibit in his portraits of nature such prominent and striking features as recall the original to every mind, and must neglect the minuter discriminations, which one may have remarked and another have neglected, for those characteristics which are alike obvious to vigilance and carelessness.

"But the knowledge of nature is only half the task of a poet; he must be acquainted likewise with all the modes of life. His character requires that he estimate the happiness and misery of every condition; observe the power of all the passions in all their combinations, and trace the changes of the human mind, as they are modified by various institutions and accidental influences of climate or custom, from the sprightliness of infancy to the despondence of decrepitude. He must divest himself of the prejudices of his age or country; he must consider right and wrong in their abstracted and invariable state; he must disregard present laws and opinions, and rise to general and transcendental truths, which will always be the same. He must, therefore, content himself with the slow progress of his name, contemn the applause of his own time, and commit his claims to the justice of posterity. He must write as the interpreter of nature and the legislator of mankind, and consider himself as presiding over the thoughts and manners of future generations, as a being superior to time and place.

"His labour is not yet at an end; he must know many languages and many sciences; and, that his style may be worthy of his thoughts, must by incessant practice familiarize to himself every delicacy of speech and grace of harmony."

THE CLASSIC AND
NEO-CLASSIC PREMISES
W. J. Bate*

Bate examines the purpose and approach of classicism (or *humanism*—which, he says, is in a certain sense almost another word for *classicism*) to show that it views man's "intellectual and moral nature as ideally the same." He consequently emphasizes "ethical 'reason' " as distinctive of human nature and as the "means of gaining insight into the ideal and of comprehending the standard or end which this ideal comprises." He then proceeds to demonstrate what happened to these basic tenets in the hands of the eighteenth-century English neoclassicists.

Conceptions of the nature and purpose of art closely parallel man's conceptions of himself and of his destiny. For art, in one of its primary functions, is the interpreter of values, and aesthetic criticism, when it rises above mere technical analysis, attempts to grasp and estimate these values in order to judge the worth of the interpretation. The period which is often called the European Enlightenment—a period which extends roughly from the middle of the seventeenth century through the close of the eighteenth—is in this sense the transitional meeting-ground between two dominant epochs of modern thinking.

The earlier portion of the Enlightenment marks the final subsiding of the European Renaissance: it comprises the consolidation and in some respects the extreme development of the values it inherited. Concluding as it did a Renaissance of extraordinary intellectual activity, it possessed ready at hand a body of conceptions which had been widely urged in philosophical and scientific writing and brilliantly exemplified in all the arts. Much of its inheritance consisted of a collective system of values to which—because of the lack of any more specific or generally accepted term—the broad and chameleon-like word "humanism" has often been applied. The word may be easily disputed. But whatever term we apply to it, this general outlook or system of values is one which largely permeated classical thought, and also received some qualification and re-direction by Christian elements in the later Middle Ages and the Renaissance. Though indefinite and even vague in a few of its exterior ramifications, it was always unified in its fundamental purpose and approach: it viewed man's intellectual and moral nature as ideally the same, and it assumed as its goal the evolution of the total man in accordance with that view. It especially emphasized man's ethical "reason" as his own distinctive nature, and as the means of gaining insight into the ideal and of com-

* The essay is reprinted by permission of the publishers from Walter Jackson Bate, *From Classic to Romantic: Premises of Taste in Eighteenth-Century England*, Cambridge, Mass.: Harvard University Press, Copyright, 1946, by the President and Fellows of Harvard College.

prehending the standard or end which this ideal comprises. Humanism, as it is used in this special sense, is almost another word for classicism itself. Similarly, the codification of some of the means and premises which Renaissance humanism postulated for the attainment or portrayal of this standard, the carrying to an extreme conclusion of others, and the inevitable counteractions to which this codification gave rise, may, in a general sense, be said to comprise neo-classicism as an historical phenomenon. And within these codifications and reactions the various neo-classic conceptions of taste largely reside.

I

On a journey through France with the Thrales, Dr. Johnson, while the scenery was being admired, impatiently retorted: "A blade of grass is always a blade of grass, whether in one country or another. ... Men and women are my subjects of inquiry; let us see how these differ from those we have left behind." The statement is reminiscent of that made by Socrates to Phaedrus, as the two reclined on the bank of the Ilyssus: "I am a lover of knowledge; and the men who dwell in the city are my teachers, and not the trees or the country." Such sentiments would have elicited at least some agreement from any classicist, even a less sternly ethical one than was Socrates or Johnson. The absence or the depreciation of the landscape in Greek and Roman art is no historical accident: whether the classical artist sought to portray physical or moral beauty, his attention was directed to its existence and its ideal potentiality in the human being. Similarly, to Michelangelo and Raphael, and to the enormous group of artists which pivots about them, the landscape was of merely complementary interest. As late as

1719 the Abbé du Bos could write, with reasonable representativeness:

The finest landskip, were it even Titian's or Caraccio's, does not affect us. ... The most knowing painters have been so thoroughly convinced of this truth, that it is rare to find any *mere* landskips of theirs without an intermixture of figures. They have therefore thought proper to people them, as it were, by introducing into their pieces a subject composed of several personages, whereof the action might be capable of moving, and consequently of engaging us.[1]

The classical direction of art to human actions and potentialities mirrors the traditional humanistic stress upon moral knowledge and cultivation rather than upon the scientific investigation of the external world. The classical moralist, without being narrowly dogmatic, might still dissent from the view of a recent scientist who took issue with Terence's statement, *Homo sum, humani nil a me alienum puto*—"I am a man, and consider nothing that is human to be foreign to me"—and who thought it should be altered to read: "I am a space-time event, and I deem nothing that is a space-time event to be foreign to me." "Our business here," said Locke, humanistic even in his empiricism, "is not to know all things, but those which concern our conduct." A fair number of early eighteenth-century satires, of which that in *Gulliver's Travels* on the Academy of Lagado is the preëminent example, rest upon this conviction. The activities with which the Academy was occupied—extracting sunbeams out of cucumbers, condensing air into a tangible substance, making gunpowder from ice, attempting to plot the date of the sun's eventual extinction—are instanced by Swift to signify an amoral

[1] *Critical Reflections on Poetry, Painting, and Music* (tr. Thomas Nugent, 1748), I, 44.

tendency to be "curious and conceited in matters where we have least concern, and for which we are least adapted either by study or nature." Gulliver's Houyhnhnm master, in the fourth voyage, found it strange that "a creature pretending to *Reason*" should devote himself much to "natural philosophy"; and he concluded that, if mankind were not destroyed through the growing horror of war, such an indiscriminate devotion would only "multiply our original wants," and then lead us "to spend our whole lives in vain endeavours to supply them by our own inventions."

To Dr. Johnson, again, only the study of man's ideals and conduct deserves to be called "intercourse with intellectual nature":

The knowledge of external nature, and the sciences which that knowledge requires or includes, are not the great or frequent business of the human mind. Whether we provide for action or conversation, . . . the first requisite is the religious and moral knowledge of right and wrong; the next is an acquaintance with the history of mankind, and with those examples which may be said to embody truth, and prove by events the reasonableness of opinions. . . . We are perpetually moralists, but we are geometricians only by chance. Our intercourse with intellectual nature is necessary; our speculations upon matter are voluntary, and at leisure.[2]

Consequently, as Johnson elsewhere stated, "He who thinks reasonably must think morally." To the classicist, indeed, any rational evaluation of the beautiful was, in the widest implication of the word, a moral one, which simultaneously transcended and gauged or controlled the worth of strictly aesthetic feelings or reactions; nor would the classicist have taken very seriously Poe's attack on those

[2] *Life of Milton, Works* (1820), IX, 91.

who attempt "to reconcile the obstinate oils and waters of Poetry and Truth."

With such a direction and aim assumed for art, the classical and Renaissance conception of the poet as a teacher of moral excellence was a logical conclusion. "For what ought we to admire the poet?" asked Aristophanes; and his answer was "because the poet makes better men." The good can be conceived and then taught only by the good; and the insistence of Cicero, Quintilian, and others that the orator must first of all be a good man was repeatedly applied to the poet in Renaissance and eighteenth-century criticism. Again, since his concern is man, the poet must be versed in the customs and manners of men, not as they are found under local and temporary conditions, but as they mirror the immutable principles and aspirations of human beings throughout history. The constancy of the basic working of human nature is stressed in most early eighteenth-century writing. A characteristic contention is an article in the *British Magazine* (1760) which has as its subject the "similitude of genius" in Horace, Boileau, and Pope as indicative of "that ingenious observation of Plutarch, that Nature delights in reproducing the same characters." Or, similarly, Richard Hurd, in his "Discourse on Poetical Imitation," defends apparent imitation of earlier works on the basis that both the passions and manners are "constant in their effects," and successive writers must necessarily deal with much the same situations.

The profit gained from history is ethical in that it furnishes aid in estimating what is general and what is merely accidental. "History's chief use," said Hume, "is only to discover the constant and universal principles of human nature." In the *Tour to the Hebrides,* Boswell records Monboddo as stating: "The story of manners is the most valuable. I never set a high value on any other history":

Johnson. "Nor I; and therefore I esteem biography, as giving us what comes near to ourselves. . . ." *Boswell.* "But in the course of general history, we find manners. In wars, we see the dispositions of people, their degrees of humanity, and other particulars." *Johnson.* "Yes; but then you must take all the facts to get this, and it is but a little you get." *Monboddo.* "And it is that little which makes history valuable."[3]

The long and hearty duration of classical antiquity's experience with society, and the brilliant interpretation which it evolved, made both the history of its experience and the study of its verdicts of primary value to the artist's comprehension of man's ideal and general nature; and the authority of antiquity, as a consequence, was continually upheld. John Dennis censured Pope's failure to state more precisely from what the ideal of man's nature is to be taken; and he added that Horace had not merely told his readers that the principal source of good writing is moral learning, but had "pointed to the very Books where they might find that moral Philosophy"—that is, the works of Plato.

The prevalence of didactic art in the late seventeenth and early eighteenth centuries, and the frequent employment in criticism of purely didactic values, are a somewhat extreme development of this premise. Aristotle had stated that the subject of poetry, though necessarily ethical in purpose, was less the exposition of moral theory than the revelation of "the manners of men"; and Renaissance critics, as in Scaliger's admonition that

[3] (Edd. Pottle and Bennett, 1936), p. 55.

"the poet teaches character through *actions,*" generally reiterated this distinction. Joseph Trapp, lecturing at Oxford early in the eighteenth century, stressed the ethical end of poetry as illustrative and not as didactically explanatory; and a similar emphasis is not uncommon in other English critics of the day. But in practice, and somewhat in precept, the late seventeenth century increasingly inclined towards the didactic direction which Roman poetry, proceeding from an ethical standpoint, had also taken. The unhesitating adoption of the verse-essay by Boileau, Pope, and a plentiful number of other writers is symptomatic of the evolution; and the same may be said to some extent of the pronounced contemporary rise of verse-satire, which, Dryden maintained, "is of the nature of moral philosophy, as being instructive." The famous attack on the *Immorality and Profaneness of the English Stage* (1698) by Jeremy Collier, who regarded criticism as irresponsible and even harmful if it did not put into practice the moral considerations it extolled, was only a vigorous application of the precepts of Boileau, Rapin, Dacier, and indeed the bulk of Renaissance and eighteenth-century critics. Scaliger, although Aristotle had thought differently, had emphasized the necessity of portraying, in the drama, the reward of virtue and the punishment of vice; D'Aubignac and others considered this "the most indispensable rule of dramatic poetry"; and the occasional critical premium throughout the eighteenth century on "poetic justice"—which was given its name by Thomas Rymer, and which had as many opponents as it had adherents—exemplifies an extreme development and subsequent petrification of the broad humanistic conception of the poet's ethical function.

II

Arising from the classical assumption that man's reason and his moral nature are one is the belief that character can be justly formed and guided only by a genuine insight into the universal, and by the rational grasp of the decorum, measure, and standard which characterize the ideal. The portrayal of the universal in art—the exhibition, in other words, of the general in the particular, of the one in the many—can achieve permanent success only if the particulars employed are reasonably common to the experience of cultivated mankind throughout successive generations. Indeed, the most pervasive single tendency of almost all classicism may be defined, as Mr. Santayana has said, by the phrase "the idealization of the familiar." The achievement of this goal may utilize various means; but they are in all cases related directly to man, and are based upon man's common intellectual, aesthetic, and moral experience and interest. The representation of familiar examples of character; the embodiment of the ideal potentialities of the human figure, as in classical and Renaissance sculpture; the illustration of the working of primary and elementary feelings and passions, divorced from situations peculiar only to a specific locality or time; the delineation of the progress and objective significance of those climactic occurrences of destiny, especially death, which are common to all, and of the manner in which human reactions to such occurrences most fully and nobly reveal themselves; and, above all, the expression in such types, postures, attitudes, exertions, or passions, of those laws and indeed heroic ideals which are manifested and held by the most exemplary in all ages and places:—the employment, depiction, and idealization of

these form the province and purpose of classical art.

A corollary of this dedication to the elementary and primary had always been, in classical thought, an emphasis on clarity of expression. To the ancient rhetoricians, such as Cicero and Quintilian, one of the first requisites of art had been lucidity and immediacy of communication. And the widespread preoccupation of Restoration and early eighteenth-century British critics with simplicity of style, the attacks on complicated metaphor by such writers as Thomas Sprat, John Eachard, and Lord Lansdowne, the stress on the employment of an idiom and of stylistic devices which, from long sanction and use, had become intimately and prevalently known, the growing disfavor with which "metaphysical" verse was viewed, the common attitude towards poetry as a branch of rhetoric, the painstaking attempt by later critics to outline concretely the means by which clarity of diction, metaphor, and sentence-structure might be attained—often accompanied by appeal to the authority of classical rhetoricians—such tendencies, though they reveal other intentions as well, are a neo-classic reassertion of the importance of the familiar as far as stylistic values are concerned.

"*Truth* in poetry," said Hurd, paraphrasing Horace, "means such an expression as conforms to the general nature of things: *falsehood*, that which, however suitable to the particular instance in view, doth yet not correspond to such *general nature*. And the classical aesthetic values of unity, simplicity, and the natural and harmonious adaptation of parts to the whole are founded upon a confidence in the truth and grandeur of ordered generality. They may be said to stand opposed, for example, to the romantic cherishing of the surprise in variety, the wonder and mystery in contemplating the strange and occasionally the grotesque, which attend upon an indiscriminate amusement and transitory delight in the particular.

This emphasis on the stripping of all that is extraneous and accidental in the portrayal of the familiar is not to be confused, of course, with the intention of "naturalism." To the classicist, "naturalism," especially in its more extreme form, could be only a partial view of phenomena. Its essentially empirical standpoint, that is, would display a disregard of those fundamental realities which only the ideal can signify and declare; and, to take but one instance, the classicist postulated as a general rule that the writing of tragedy could have little success without a judicious selection of the characters portrayed. The feelings and thoughts of the character can be participated in and can be said to have significance only in proportion as the character himself is capable of feeling and thinking. Oedipus, Antigone, Prometheus, and Lear are tragic characters; Wordsworth's Betty Foy, "the idiot mother of the idiot boy," or Harry Gill, who is continually cold and whose "teeth chatter, chatter still," are hapless enough beings, but they have hardly the significance of Hamlet. "How shall our attention," said the Abbé du Bos, "be engaged by a picture representing a peasant driving a couple of beasts along the highway?" Such a picture "may possibly amuse us some few moments, and may even draw from us an applause of the artist's abilities in imitating, but can never raise any emotion or concern." Painters of genuine insight do not picture

a man going along the highroad, or ... a woman carrying fruit to market; they commonly present us with figures that *think*, in order to make us think; they paint men

hurried with passions, to the end that ours may also be raised, and our attention fixed by this very agitation.[4]

The naturalistic writer, it is true, attempts to approach the norm, and to discard the adventitious; but at least the more extreme naturalist may be said, in a sense, to assume the lowest as the norm, and to view whatever is better as an unexpected if happy gain or as helpful to "progress"; while the classicist conceives the highest as the norm, and regards whatever falls below, not as "natural," but as corruption. The difference resides in the interpretation of "nature." To the naturalist, nature is inevitably what he empirically judges as reality, in which any human idealization discovered is not inherent or actual but either something superimposed, something simply displayed as a psychological reaction of human beings under given circumstances, or at best something useful or desirable for the social, scientific, and humanitarian betterment of mankind. The various shades of meaning in the use of the word "nature" in English neo-classic thought have been sufficiently traced, especially by Mr. Lovejoy, and need not be recapitulated here. It is sufficient to state that in general the classical conception of nature, from the Greeks to almost the middle of the eighteenth century, is that central idea and form which the particular struggles to attain; and when Aristotle defined poetry as an "imitation of nature," he did not mean the indiscriminate copying of any individual, but rather the selective imitation of what is general and representative in man. Dennis condemned Pope for not defining "nature" in as unmistakably plain detail as Horace, who

[4] *Reflections*, I, 42, 44–45.

makes it as clear as the Sun, what it is to follow Nature in giving us a draught of human Life, and of the manners of Men, and that is, not to draw after particular Men, who are but Copies and imperfect Copies of the great universal Pattern; but to consult that innate Original, and that universal Idea, which the Creator has fix'd in the minds of ev'ry reasonable Creature.[5]

"What is natural," said Grotius, "we must judge by those in whom nature is *least* corrupt"; and those who serve as concrete if not wholly ideal standards for the natural are "those who are most civilized." The conception of "nature" as the ultimate standard, as the essential meaning and final aim of life, underlies the classical conviction that the end of art is the revelation to man and the rational, ethical inculcation in him of that ideal perfection of which, in a degree varying according to his own character, he as a particular is only a faulty image.

III

In its devotion to the rationally conceived ideal, classicism is opposed not only to the naturalistic but to any other conception of art which can be designated as personal or local—to the conception of art, in other words, as sheer emotional experience for its own sake, as intellectual amusement, or as propaganda. It views the mere stimulation of emotional excitement and the unschooled liberation of impulses as at best a temporary narcotic, the awakening from which inevitably brings in its train —as some later aspects of European romanticism were perhaps to illustrate —a dichotomy of mind and feeling, and a dissatisfaction based not so much on intellectual conviction and criticism as on mere insecurity of feeling.

[5] *Reflections upon a Late Rhapsody Called an Essay upon Criticism* (1711), p. 31.

From the universal character of its ethical standpoint, classicism draws a marked distinction between centrality and diversity, between man's unified rational grasp of his ideal nature, and his peripheral and independent development, as a particular, of the impulses and reactions which comprise what is occasionally called his personality. Indeed, classicism assumes that only through the former can genuine individual fulfillment be found. For it regards man's feelings as by themselves helpless, blind, and eminently susceptible to dictation of some sort. They are not, that is, free to determine themselves, but are inevitably led by something else: they are subject to whatever is in closest or most vital proximity to them—whether it be a rationally determined end which is vividly and firmly held in the mind, or whether, if this end be lacking, it be merely whatever external environment chance may offer. It is in this respect that Dr. Johnson could state, with complete practicality: "Whatever withdraws us from the power of our senses, whatever makes the past, the distant, or the future predominate over the present, advances us in the dignity of thinking beings." True individual freedom accrues in the channeling of man's responses towards an end which reason conceives to transcend the local and temporary; its opposite exists when such a formative and determining conception is lacking, and habit is established through chance, fashion, local custom, or individual caprice.

Classicism does not subscribe, therefore, to the belief that man's feelings and responses are themselves inherently good —a belief which was to underlie at least some romantic assumptions towards the close of the eighteenth century. And just as art itself is inadequate when it is conditoned largely by the customs and opinions of a transitory society, or when its primary purpose is to serve either as an emotional narcotic or as an esoteric exercise of ingenuity; similarly, in the role of the artist as propagandist, as an indulger in subjective sensibility, or as the mere craftsman, there is much that fails to attain and indeed obstruct what, in the classical sense, a man should be.

To rest a determination of values upon the feelings, the floating inclinations, or the varying empirically-held opinions of particular individuality is to rest it upon the most fluid of foundations. For the abandonment of the centrally ideal by empirical relativism not only results in a conflict of predilections from man to man, but, as Irving Babbitt so frequently insisted, in conflict and change within even the same man. Its probable consequence, of which European art and thought of the past century contain frequent instances, may be typified by D. H. Lawrence's rather confused assertion: "I am many men. . . . Who are you? How many selves have you? And which of these selves do you want to be?"; and the classicist might question whether an even more ultimate conclusion was not exemplified in a recent poem which begins with the declaration "I am four monkeys," and concludes with the question "How many monkeys are you?" Against the fluidity and relativism of either personal or else local and fashionable predilection, classicism places universal "nature" as that centripetal and "just standard" which, said Pope, is "at once the source, and end, and test of art," and which also comprises, in its broad ethical character, "the source, and end, and test" of all that may be called the ideal of man.

"Besides the purging of the passions," said Thomas Rymer, poetry infuses order and justness of comprehension into the mind simply by its reflection, in the form and outline of its own structure, of "that constant order, that harmony

and beauty of Providence."[6] For the very nature of the universal, in its transcendence and control over the accidental and specific, exemplifies order and harmony; and the living exhibition of order and the persuasive infiltration of it into man's moral and mental character are both a vital aspect of the means by which art simultaneously "delights and teaches," and also an end for which it performs these functions. It is ethical in furnishing both the process and the aim.

With the same assumption, the notable classical discussions, such as that in Plato's *Republic*, of the fundamental importance of music in the ethical inculcation of order, measure, and harmony, are occasionally repeated and applied with historical pertinence in neo-classic criticism. Characteristic is a book by the opponent of Shaftesbury, John Brown, one of the purposes of which is to illustrate that, in past cultures, "As every change of Manners influenced their Music, so by a reciprocal Action, every Considerable Change of Music influenced their Manners." When music had attained in Greece a sufficiently high development in order and universality of form, it was rightly esteemed, said Brown, as

a *necessary Accomplishment:* And an Ignorance of this Art was regarded as a capital Defect. Of this we have an Instance, even in Themistocles himself, who was upbraided with his Ignorance in Music. The whole Country of *Cynaethe* laboured under a parallel Approach: And all the enormous *Crimes* committed there, were attributed by the neighbouring States to the *Neglect of Music.*—What wonder? For according to the Delineation here given of ancient Greek Music, their ignorance implied a general Deficiency in

[6] *The Tragedies of the Last Age, Considered and Examined by the Practice of the Ancients and by the Common Sense of All Ages* (1678), p. 140.

the three great articles of a social Education, *Religion, Morals,* and *Polity.*[7]

The classical doctrine of exemplifying order in art often finds a humanistically Christian expression in eighteenth-century criticism as it had even more frequently in the Renaissance. "The great Design of Arts," Dennis maintained, "is to restore the Decays that happen'd to human Nature by the Fall, by restoring Order"; and "if the end of Poetry," he added, "be to instruct and reform the World, that is, to bring Mankind from Irregularity, Extravagance, and Confusion, to Rule and Order, how this should be done by a thing that is in itself irregular and extravagant, is difficult to be conceiv'd."[8] Poetry, as Aristotle had pointed out, possesses a more general truth than does history, and presents, in its selection and form, a model or imitation of more valid pertinence. And the representation of order being an aesthetic end, it must, as Charles Gildon said, "have certain Means of attaining that End, which are the *Rules of Art.*"

IV

The primary rule may perhaps be defined as decorum. In Aristotelian and indeed most classical use of the term, decorum consists in the simultaneous "preservation and ennobling of the type" —in a faithful adherence to a probability of manners and language in the dramatic character and, at the same time, in a deepening of the import of this probability by disclosing its connection, not merely with temporary or social law, but with that which reason conceives as universal and ideal. Decorum, especially

in neo-classic thought, was occasionally developed to certain conclusions and conventions which were perhaps as contradictory to the general rule of decorum as any other excess would be. Thus, the insistence on the unity and probability of a character's actions found a somewhat extreme ramification in the theory of the "ruling passion," which was perhaps more widespread in neo-classic precept, if not practice, than in the Renaissance. Yet the theory of the "ruling passion" was hardly universal; and the moderate issue which Dryden took with it was by no means unique:

A character, or that which distinguishes one man from all others, cannot be supposed to consist of one particular virtue, or vice, or passion only; but 'tis a composition of qualities which are not contrary to one another in the same person; thus, the same man may be liberal and valiant, but not liberal and covetous . . . yet it is still to be observed, that the virtue, vice, or passion, ought to be shown in every man, as predominant over all the rest.[9]

A similar rather confined application of the rule of decorum was frequently made in respect to rank or condition: even Dryden, for example, states that "when a poet has given the dignity of a king to one of his persons, in all his actions and speeches that person must discover majesty, magnanimity, and jealousy of power, because these are suitable to the general manners of a king"; and similar assertions are a commonplace throughout eighteenth-century European criticism. Still, such an application though rather absurd, as Johnson pointed out, when measured against a broader interpretation of decorum—cannot appear as an extreme aberration when one recalls that many of the social distinctions of

[7] *Dissertation on the Rise, Union, and Power, the Progessions, Separations, and Corruptions of Poetry and Music* (1763), pp. 126–127.
[8] *Grounds of Criticism in Poetry* (1704), chap. ii.

[9] *Preface to Troilus and Cressida, Essays* (ed. Ker, 1926), I, 215.

classical and Renaissance life had, in a sense, something of an intellectual justification in that underlying conception of "degree" and order which the aesthetic principles of classicism and neo-classicism also reflect.

The rule and order of decorum are of special importance in the total formation and unraveling of the outline or plot of action in dramatic or epic poetry. "The manners, in a poem," said Dryden, "are understood to be those inclinations, whether natural or acquired, which move and carry us to actions, good, bad, or indifferent . . . ; or which incline the persons to such or such actions." If several inclinations or actions, for example, have a common source in their past, they are immanent in that past; and again, since that source is perpetuated, as it were, in the subsequent inclinations or actions to which it gives rise, those resulting phenomena have a degree of immanence in each other.

With its goal of rendering vital the probability and ideal meaning which compose decorum, art seeks to declare the unity of this immanence; it attempts, in other words, to descry and exhibit the order and law disclosed in the interweaving of past, present, and future, of event and inclination, of action and ideal. It was earlier stated that, in the classical conception, the very nature of unity or order presupposes for its delineation an ordered approach, an approach, in fact, which necessitates *rule*. "If the rules be well considered," Dryden quotes from Rapin, "we shall find them to be made only to reduce Nature into method, to trace her step by step, and not to suffer the least mark to escape us: 'tis only by these, that probability . . . is maintained, which is the soul of poetry."[10] The interplay of action,

motive, and event in the *Iliad*, as might be expected, is summarized and extolled with special frequency, and usually with the purpose of illustrating, as Gildon says, that "this productive Chain of Incidents, in the *Iliad*, could not be formed without admirable Art and Design; and consequently, by such Rules as no Man since has ever been able to alter for the better." The often unfavorable attitude in neo-classic criticism towards many of the more exuberant romances of the Renaissance was largely conditioned by the importance attributed to a simple but closely interwoven unity of action. The ordered construction of the *Iliad*, for example, presents a strong contrast with the lack of it in such a poem as Spenser's *Faerie Queene*, which D'Avenant regarded as a dream "such as Poets and Painters, by being over-studious, may have in the beginning of Feavers," and which even neo-classic admirers of Spenser, like John Hughes, thought hopelessly "distracting" in its "want of Unity."

Among the dramatic rules formulated as subordinate and contributory to the broad governing rule of decorum, the most preëminent, and later the most controversial, were the famous "unities." It is characteristic of the empiricism which he accelerated, and which a century later gave support to the frequent romantic concern with the individual particular, that Thomas Hobbes should have considered the design and plot of a poem as less important than the language; and it is equally characteristic that Dryden should have censured him for doing so:

Mr. Hobbes, in the preface to his own bald translation of the *Iliad* (studying poetry as he did mathematics, when it was too late) . . . begins the praise of Homer where he should have ended it. He tells us that the first beauty of an epic poem con-

[10] *Preface to Troilus and Cressida, Essays*, I, 213.

sists in diction; that is, in the choice of words, and harmony of numbers. Now the words are the colouring of the work, which, in the order of nature, is last to be considered. The design, the disposition, manners, and the thoughts, are all before it.[11]

It is the "*Fable or Plot,*" states Rymer, "which all conclude to be the *Soul* of a *Tragedy;* which, with the *Ancients,* is always found to be a *reasonable Soul;* but *with us,* for the most part, a *brutish....*"[12] "The most beautiful colors laid on without proportion," Aristotle had said, "will not give as much pleasure as the chalk outline of a portrait." The neo-classic doctrine of the "unities," which are frequently compared with "proportion" in painting, constitutes a rather exaggerated offshoot and codification of the classical emphasis on the order and probability of interrelation in the total structure of plot or outline.

Aristotle had mentioned the importance of a "unity of action"—a coherence and order, as a single whole, of events and conclusion. As for the unities of "place" and of "time," he said nothing at all about the former; and, about the latter, he merely observed that, in Greek poetry, the length of time elapsing in the action of dramatic tragedy differs from that of the epic: "For tragedy endeavors, as far as possible, to confine itself to a single revolution of the sun, or but slightly to exceed this limit; whereas the action of the epic has no limit of time." Aristotle's tentative statement about the customary practice of Greek tragedy was hardened into a rule in the first half of the sixteenth century by the Italian critic Giraldi Cintio: within another two or three generations, the restriction to a single day of the time of action in the

drama had become a prevalent rule of decorum; and some critics, like Minturno, basing their deduction on the time covered in the *Iliad* and the *Aeneid,* attempted to restrict the action of the epic to a year.

Similarly, in the latter half of the sixteenth century, another Italian, Castelvetro, formulated the rule of the "unity of place" on the ground that, since its action takes place before our eyes, the drama would lose all verisimilitude, all probability, if a change of place were made in the course of it. Castelvetro became so enamored of the unities of time and place, and perhaps also of the prospect of the ingenuity which would be necessary to satisfy them, that he considered the one unity upon which Aristotle had insisted—the unity of action—as quite secondary, and as merely a convenient means of helping to fulfill the requirements of the other two! Within a hundred years after Castelvetro, the unity of place, like that of time, had achieved as much vogue and as much ingenuity of application as even he could have desired. But by the middle of the eighteenth century, these two unities were taken with less seriousness than is sometimes supposed; and Johnson was not alone in regarding them as giving "more trouble to the poet, than pleasure to the auditor," and in considering a drama that observed them "as an elaborate curiosity, as the product of superfluous and ostentatious art, by which is shewn rather, what is possible, than what is necessary."

V

It is the inherent order and proportion of the whole which comprises, in Pope's words, "the naked nature, and the living grace":

---

[11] Preface to the *Fables, Essays,* II, 252.
[12] *Tragedies of the Last Age,* p. 4.

'Tis not the lip, or eye, we beauty call,
But the joint force and full result of all.

Aristotle's emphasis on plot rather than on the portrayal of particular characters —his insistence, in other words, that man be revealed through the instrumentality of ordered actions rather than that events be shown through the medium of the feelings and identities of particular men—may be said to illustrate the classical conviction that poetry should seek less to arouse and give voice to the personal associations and feelings of the observer than to guide them, and to impose upon them a finished ideal. The representation of the human being in classical sculpture or painting has a similar end: it does not, by the portrayal of individual "expression" in its model, seek to evoke images from past experiences and thus appeal to the affections and associations of the beholder, but rather, by an imitation of the ideal, to form and control those affections and associations. Such a purpose is ethical in the very broadest sense of the word: for the classical attempt to embody, in plot, design, rhythm, or visual proportion, an "imitation" of the fundamental order and decorum of the universal is not to be viewed as "abstraction" but rather as "integration" and completion; it aspires to present an ideal end and a finished totality which the distinctive "expression" of the model, as a particular, cannot give.

Individual portraiture in painting or sculpture, for example, necessarily diverts art from the whole to only a specific performance and to an incomplete disclosure of one's personal identity. Classical sculpture, on the other hand, does not essay very often the piecemeal and miscellaneous expression of isolated actions, or of such single facets of individual character as would necessarily result from the representation of a given act, position, or facial feature. It endeavors, rather, to picture, in the light of an ideal, the total capacity of the human figure, and to endow it with that completeness which would have originally been formed and determined only by multifarious and rounded activities. It seeks to offer a concluded and integrated synthesis of all ideal human aspects, which, since they cannot be articulated in single performances without the exclusion of some of them and the loss of completeness and unison, are presented, as it were, potentially rather than kinetically, and as in perpetual readiness rather than in active execution.

Xenophon records Socrates as saying that "It is the business of the sculptor to represent in bodily form the energies of the spirit." The spirit, the ideal, is neither a means nor a reaction: it is an end, a fruition. It signifies the *ethos* or "character"—which is eternal and changeless—rather than the *pathos* or "feeling," which is passing and in flux. And from the revelation of the potentialities of this fruition, of this changeless *ethos*, and from the subduing and disciplining of these potentialities to the consonance and decorum of the ideal, arise the inherent finality, the repose and serenity, which are the properties of classical sculpture, architecture, and writing. "We are lovers of beauty," said Pericles of the Athenians, but of beauty "in its *frugal* forms." Similarly, music deserves to be specified as integrated rather than abstract when it becomes classical: when, disregarding appeal to subjective mood or transitory fashion, it weaves a disciplined structure from simple chords and melodies, and, combining with freedom and spontaneity a rational decorum of selection and design, renders audible and definite the potentialities of that proportion and form which alone may be said to constitute the universal in music.

Beneath the classical conception of the ideal and of the essential order, rule, and harmony which characterize it, is, of course, a general conviction in the absoluteness of divine law. The humanistic watchword for the knowledge of this law, as Mr. Bush's lectures on humanism have shown,[13] is *sapientia*, which Cicero defined as the knowledge of "the bonds of union between divinity and man and the relations of man to man." It had been the invaluable contribution of the Greek Sophists to illustrate that the material world, without exception, is characterized by continual flux; and as eighteenth and nineteenth-century empiricism itself, pursuing its logical evolution, was at length to conclude, the forces which dominate or issue from the material world are equally changing. To the "humanist," therefore,—in the sense in which the word has been used in this chapter—the law to which man by his intrinsic nature is subjected is not to be confused with the forces, intelligible or unintelligible, which appear to operate in the phenomenal and animal world, or with such compulsions or necessities as appear to play upon the individual man when he is considered as an atom in social dynamics. Indeed, the humanistic contention is that man possesses an end of his own; that his distinctive privilege consists in his ability to conceive the character of this ideal end; and that for man to be "natural" does not mean for him to live in accordance with what he judges the phenomenal world to be, as both romantic primitivism and empirical science were, in their varying ways, to encourage him to do—but rather to manifest the absolute and centrally unified "nature," the joint ethical and ra-

[13] *The Renaissance and English Humanism* (Toronto: 1939), chap. ii.

tional fruition, which is at once his obligation and prerogative to fulfill. For the grasping of the nature of this ideal, and for comprehending its ethical import, Renaissance humanistic thought, in the main, had assumed three means, the complete employment of any one of which necessarily involved the employment of the others.

The philosophical conception of the universal was given its original formulation, of course, by Plato; and from the specific issues raised by him, almost all the extensions, re-applications, and contradictions of the theory of universals take their distinctive direction. The history of European philosophy, Mr. Whitehead has said, is "a series of footnotes to Plato." Certainly, since the delineation of most arguments proving the existence and character of the ideal is essentially a recapitulation of the bulk of classical thought, humanistic writers of the Renaissance continually emphasized the importance of classical authority. Even in such a figure as Montaigne, "the vagabondage and egotism," as one critic has said, "are more or less superficial. What we find under the surface is a fairly firm conviction, based on the Greek, and especially the Latin, classics, as to what the true man should be." Again, the humanistic conception of what comprises "natural law" —the law, order, and character, that is to say, of the universal—was strongly interwoven with Christian elements: in this sense, it continues, of course, a widespread tendency of medieval thought; and the complete indebtedness of Grotius to Aquinas and the Spanish Thomists, as Mr. Chroust has shown, is an outstanding example.

Lastly, and like classicism itself, Renaissance humanism placed its confidence in that faculty which alone distinguishes man from lower creation, and which may be designated as "reason." The belief that, with the removal of "reason," not man but only animal is left may seem obvious to the point of being banal; yet the neglect or actual discarding of this commonplace was to plunge European philosophy, by the close of the eighteenth century, into a disunity which was without parallel in its entire history, and from which it has shown no genuine sign of emergence.

I affirm [said Erasmus], that, as the instinct of the dog is to hunt, of the bird to fly, of the horse to gallop, so the natural bent of man is to philosophy and right and conduct. . . . What is the proper nature of man? Surely it is to live the life of reason, for reason is the peculiar prerogative of man.[14]

From the moral exercise of this faculty, aided by classical authority and religious purpose, insight into the universal may be attained; and the grasp of the absolute standard which that insight affords is, for the humanist, the sure and indeed the only means of estimating the simultaneously real, beautiful, and good, and of evaluating the material reflection of these universals in both human ethics and art.

To know the ideally good with genuine conviction is to insure the fulfillment of it in judgment and act. Humanism, from Plato through the Renaissance, in general subscribes to the contention that what may be called the "will" is dependent upon the "reason," and is determined by it. To know the good is to do it: not to do it arises from a misapprehension of precisely what the good is; it may arise, for example, from the belief that another course of action is preferable or at least more pleasant for oneself—a belief which

[14] De Pueris Instituendis, in Erasmus Concerning the Aim and Method of Education (ed. Woodward, Cambridge, 1904), p. 190.

implies an ignorant confusion of the good with pleasure. The prevalence and strength of this ethical principle in later medieval and Renaissance thought may be illustrated by the fact that the word "dunce" was coined in honor of the extreme followers of Duns Scotus, whose philosophy of "voluntarism" maintained that the will is not dependent at all upon the reason. In the opinion of many of the opponents of Scotus, to say that the will was independent of a rational guide was not, in the final analysis, to maintain that the will was "free": it was rather to admit as an ultimate conclusion that the will is so completely determined by the chain of fluctuating forces and circumstances in the material world that ethical judgment of motives is impossible. Indeed, the will is free only *through* its dependence on the intellect. Because the will follows the intellectual conviction of what is good—and such a conviction implies not an acquiescent half-conception but a firm and vital grasp of the good—all evaluation and all ethical action which proceeds from that evaluation are, in the traditional phrase, *sub ratione boni*.

VI

The exercise of reason, therefore, and the proper use by it of experience, of classical philosophy, and of humanistic studies in general, result in forming the temper and tone of character, the standard of judgment, purposes, and conduct, and the subsequent abidance by that standard, which together constitute the fulfillment of man's "nature." Thus Erasmus could insist that "Nature hath endued man with knowledge of liberal sciences and a fervent desire of knowledge: which thing as it doth most specially withdraw man's wit from all beastly wildness, so hath it a special grace *to get and knit together love and friendship.*"[15]

Such a fulfillment of his ideal "nature" will not suffer a man to incline towards whatever would deprive him of the companionship of the noble and the rationally good in art or conduct. He carries within him his own standard not as a dogma to which to adhere in letter, but as a living intuition; indeed Plato and Aristotle would not have understood the divorce between reason and intuition which seventeenth-century mathematical rationalism was to encourage and European romanticism was generally to accept.

The man who possesses this insight, at once rational and moral, is to be considered, Aristotle had maintained, as the arbiter in all questions of aesthetic taste and of ethics. With Renaissance humanists, and especially with those neo-classic critics, such as Dennis, who are relatively close to the humanistic spirit, this contention is increasingly applied with historical pertinence as well: rational determination of the absolute and ideally good in taste and morality is to be facilitated and made more authoritative by the study of the preferences and the conduct of the best in all ages, and especially in classical antiquity.

Some indication was earlier given of the more radical ramifications in Renaissance and neo-classic criticism of the classical and humanistic principles of decorum, of proportion, and of the ethical purpose of the poet. Similarly, from the humanistic emphasis upon reason as man's distinctive faculty and as his means of contact with the universe, there arise in the Renaissance and culminate in neo-classicism an optimism, based on a confidence in the order of the universe and in man's ability to conceive and abide by that order, and also, with an accompanying trust that only "method" is needed to arrive at and reflect that order, a widespread interest in method itself. "From heavenly harmony," wrote Dryden, "this universal frame began"; and as reason underlies the law and order of nature, human reason is an extension and mirroring of that universal harmony. "Nature," said Dennis, paraphrasing D'Aubignac, is "that Rule and Order and Harmony which we find in the visible Creation," while "Reason is the very same throughout the invisible Creation. For Reason is Order and the Result of Order."[16] Not to conceive and act aright is simply a failure to perceive, by rational means, the nature of order: "nothing can be irregular either in our Conceptions or our Actions, any further than it swerves from Rule, that is, from Reason."[17] Consequently, as Pope stated,

All Nature is but art, unknown to thee;
All chance, direction, which thou canst
    not see;
All discord, harmony not understood;
All partial evil, universal good.

Renaissance humanism had been characterized by faith based upon reason. The eighteeenth century, Mr. Whitehead has said, is "an age of reason based upon faith"—"a faith in the order of nature," of the universal frame.[18] The statement is especially an adequate definition of the movement which was known as Deism, and which was peculiarly indicative of a prevailing temper of the Enlightenment. It is true not only of such thorough-going rationalists as Samuel Clarke, John Toland, or Matthew Tindal, who strove to make their

[15] *Against War* (ed. Einstein, Boston: 1907), pp. 8–9.

[16] *Advancement and Reformation of Modern Poetry* (1701), pp. [14–15].

[17] *Grounds of Criticism in Poetry* (1704), p. 5.

[18] *Science and the Modern World* (1925), p. 83.

blueprints of the universe "reasonably" and even mathematically demonstrable. Its reflection is strong even in the "moral sense" deists such as Shaftesbury and his prolific following: characteristic are the very names of such Shaftesburyan poems as Henry Brooke's *Universal Beauty* (1728–1735), John Gilbert Cooper's *The Power of Harmony* (1745), James Harris's *Concord* (1751), and a bevy of other poems with such titles as *Order* or *Design and Beauty*. It is significant that the English neo-classic figures who most strenuously combat this easy optimism—Swift, Bishop Butler, and Johnson—are men who are at once distinguished by an intense religious conviction and by a genuinely classical conception of the problem of evil inherent in the empirical world.

Accompanying the optimistic generalization that the "rules" which reason discovers are "nature methodized," was an essentially unclassical interest in "method" itself. The exemplification of this interest may be generally described as twofold. It is shown in a somewhat excessive and increasingly academic investigation of the rules which should comprise method, and in an attempt to apply them, whether in aesthetics, morality, or theology, with almost mathematical precision. A further manifestation, above all in British empiricism, was a growing attention to the nature of the reasoning and "methodizing" faculty itself—a tendency which, by the middle of the eighteenth century, was to culminate in a marked skepticism about both reason and method, and was therefore to furnish an argumentative basis for romanticism. Many of the varying English neo-classic conceptions of what constitutes aesthetic judgment, except where they are directly classical in origin, may be said to have been largely determined by the paths which the investigation of "method" pursued. In addition, an inevitable antagonism to this excessive methodizing became increasingly marked, with a resulting emphasis upon feeling; but this emphasis was to receive small philosophical support until its mighty ally, British psychological empiricism, abandoned "reason" for subjective "sentiment."

FROM THE TERMS CLASSIC AND ROMANTIC
Irving Babbitt[*]

Babbitt maintains that the classical ideal derives from the concepts of a "general nature, a core of normal experience." "Having decided what is normal either for man or some particular class of man, the classicist takes this normal 'nature' for his model and proceeds to imitate it. . . . Whatever in conduct or character is duly restrained and proportionate with reference to the model is said to observe decorum." Finally, Babbitt makes a distinction between the genuine decorum—the form—of the true classic, and the artificial decorum—the formalism—of the neoclassical literature of France and eighteenth-century England.

[*] The selection is reprinted from Chapter I of *Rousseau and Romanticism*, by Irving Babbitt, by permission of Houghton Mifflin Company. Copyright 1919 by Houghton Mifflin Company.

The words classic and romantic, we are often told, cannot be defined at all, and even if they could be defined, some would add, we should not be much profited. But this inability or unwillingness to define may itself turn out to be only one aspect of a movement that from Rousseau to Bergson has sought to discredit the analytical intellect—what Wordsworth calls "the false secondary power by which we multiply distinctions." However, those who are with Socrates rather than with Rousseau or Wordsworth in this matter, will insist on the importance of definition, especially in a chaotic era like the present; for nothing is more characteristic of such an era than its irresponsible use of general terms. Now to measure up to the Socratic standard, a definition must not be abstract and metaphysical, but experimental; it must not, that is, reflect our opinion of what a word should mean, but what it actually has meant. Mathematicians may be free at times to frame their own definitions, but in the case of words like classic and romantic, that have been used innumerable times, and used not in one but in many countries, such a method is inadmissible. One must keep one's eye on actual usage. One should indeed allow for a certain amount of freakishness in this usage. Beaumarchais, for example, makes classic synonymous with barbaric.[1] One may disregard an occasional aberration of this kind, but if one can find only confusion and inconsistency in all the main uses of words like classic and romantic, the only procedure for those who speak or write in order to be understood is to banish the words from their vocabulary.

Now to define in a Socratic way two things are necessary: one must learn to see a common element in things that are apparently different and also to dis-

[1] See his *Essai sur le genre dramatique sérieux.*

criminate between things that are apparently similar. A Newton, to take the familiar instance of the former process, saw a common element in the fall of an apple and the motion of a planet; and one may perhaps without being a literary Newton discover a common element in all the main uses of the word romantic as well as in all the main uses of the word classic; though some of the things to which the word romantic in particular has been applied seem, it must be admitted, at least as far apart as the fall of an apple and the motion of a planet. The first step is to perceive the something that connects two or more of these things apparently so diverse, and then it may be found necessary to refer this unifying trait itself back to something still more general, and so on until we arrive, not indeed at anything absolute— the absolute will always elude us—but at what Goethe calls the original or underlying phenomenon (*Urphänomenon*). A fruitful source of false definition is to take as primary in a more or less closely allied group of facts what is actually secondary—for example, to fix upon the return to the Middle Ages as the central fact in romanticism, whereas this return is only symptomatic; it is very far from being the original phenomenon. Confused and incomplete definitions of romanticism have indeed just that origin —they seek to put at the centre something that though romantic is not central but peripheral, and so the whole subject is thrown out of perspective.

My plan then is to determine to the best of my ability, in connection with a brief historical survey, the common element in the various uses of the words classic and romantic; and then, having thus disposed of the similarities, to turn to the second part of the art of defining and deal, also historically, with the differences. For my subject is not romanticism in general, but only a particular type of romanticism, and this type of romanticism needs to be seen as a recoil, not from classicism in general, but from a particular type of classicism. . . .

Because the classicism against which romanticism rebelled was inadequate it does not follow that every type of classicism suffers from a similar inadequacy. The great movement away from imaginative unrestraint towards regularity and good sense took place in the main under French auspices. In general the French have been the chief exponents of the classic spirit in modern times. They themselves feel this so strongly that a certain group in France has of late years inclined to use interchangeably the words classicist and nationalist. But this is a grave confusion, for if the classic spirit is anything at all it is in its essence not local and national, but universal and human. To be sure, any particular manifestation of classicism will of necessity contain elements that are less universal, elements that reflect merely a certain person or persons, or a certain age and country. This is a truth that we scarcely need to have preached to us; for with the growth of the historical method we have come to fix our attention almost exclusively on these local and relative elements. The complete critic will accept the historical method but be on his guard against its excess. He will see an element in man that is set above the local and the relative; he will learn to detect this abiding element through all the flux of circumstance; in Platonic language, he will perceive the One in the Many.

Formerly, it must be admitted, critics were not historical enough. They took to be of the essence of classicism what was merely its local coloring, especially the coloring it received from the French of the seventeenth century. If we wish to distinguish between essence and accident in the classic spirit we must get behind the French of the seventeenth century, behind the Italians of the sixteenth century who laid the foundations of neo-classical theory, behind the Romans who were the immediate models of most neo-classicists, to the source of classicism in Greece. Even in Greece the classic spirit is very much implicated in the local and the relative, yet in the life of no other people perhaps does what is universal in man shine forth more clearly from what is only local and relative. We still need, therefore, to return to Greece, not merely for the best practice, but for the best theory of classicism; for this is still found in spite of all its obscurities and incompleteness in the Poetics of Aristotle. If we have recourse to this treatise, however, it must be on condition that we do not, like the critics of the Renaissance, deal with it in an abstract and dogmatic way (the form of the treatise it must be confessed gave them no slight encouragement), but in a spirit akin to Aristotle's own as revealed in the total body of his writings—a spirit that is at its best positive and experimental.

Aristotle not only deals positively and experimentally with the natural order and with man so far as he is a part of this order, but he deals in a similar fashion with a side of man that the modern positivist often overlooks. Like all the great Greeks Aristotle recognizes that man is the creature of two laws: he has an ordinary or natural self of impulse and desire and a human self that is known practically as a power of control over impulse and desire. If man is to become human he must not let impulse and desire run wild, but must oppose to everything excessive in his ordinary self, whether in thought or deed or emotion, the law of measure. This insistence on restraint and proportion is rightly taken to be of the essence not merely of the Greek spirit but of the classical spirit in general. The norm or standard that is to set bounds to the ordinary self is got at by different types of classicists in different ways and described variously: for example, as the human law, or the better self, or reason (a word to be discussed more fully later), or nature. Thus when Boileau says, "Let nature be your only study," he does not mean outer nature, nor again the nature of this or that individual, but representative human nature. Having decided what is normal either for man or some particular class of men the classicist takes this normal "nature" for his model and proceeds to imitate it. Whatever accords with the model he has thus set up he pronounces natural or probable, whatever on the other hand departs too far from what he conceives to be the normal type or the normal sequence of cause and effect he holds to be "improbable" and unnatural or even, if it attains an extreme of abnormality, "monstrous." Whatever in conduct or character is duly restrained and proportionate with reference to the model is said to observe decorum. Probability and decorum are identical in some of their aspects and closely related in all.[2] To recapitulate, a general nature, a core of normal experience, is affirmed by all classicists. From this central affirmation derives the doctrine of imitation, and from imitation in turn the doctrines of probability and decorum.

But though all classicists are alike in insisting on nature, imitation, probability

---

[2] The French Academy discriminates in its *Sentiments sur le Cid* between two types of probability, "ordinary" and "extraordinary." Probability in general is more especially reserved for action. In the domain of action "ordinary" probability and decorum run very close together. It is, for example, both indecorus and improbable that Chimène in the *Cid* should marry her father's murderer.

and decorum, they differ widely, as I have already intimated, in what they understand by these terms. Let us consider first what Aristotle and the Greeks understand by them. The first point to observe is that according to Aristotle one is to get his general nature not on authority or second hand, but is to disengage it directly for himself from the jumble of particulars that he has before his eyes. He is not, says Aristotle, to imitate things as they are, but as they ought to be. Thus conceived imitation is a creative act. Through all the welter of the actual one penetrates to the real and so succeeds without ceasing to be individual in suggesting the universal. Poetry that is imitative in this sense is, according to Aristotle, more "serious" and "philosophical" than history. History deals merely with what has happened, whereas poetry deals with what may happen according to probability or necessity. Poetry, that is, does not portray life literally but extricates the deeper or ideal truth from the flux of circumstance. One may add with Sydney that if poetry is thus superior to history in being more serious and philosophical it resembles history and is superior to philosophy in being concrete.

The One that the great poet or artist perceives in the Many and that gives to his work its high seriousness is not a fixed absolute. In general the model that the highly serious man (δ $\sigma\pi\text{ου}\delta\alpha\tilde{\iota}\text{ος}$) imitates and that keeps his ordinary self within the bounds of decorum is not to be taken as anything finite, as anything that can be formulated once for all. This point is important for on it hinges every right distinction not merely between the classic and the romantic, but between the classic and the pseudo-classic. Romanticism has claimed for itself a monopoly of imagination and infinitude, but on closer examination, as I hope to show later, this claim, at least so far as genuine classicism is concerned, will be found to be quite unjustified. For the present it is enough to say that true classicism does not rest on the observance of rules or the imitation of models but on an immediate insight into the universal. Aristotle is especially admirable in the account he gives of this insight and of the way it may manifest itself in art and literature. One may be rightly imitative, he says, and so have access to a superior truth and give others access to it only by being a master of illusion. Though the great poet "breathes immortal air," though he sees behind the shows of sense a world of more abiding relationships, he can convey his vision not directly but only imaginatively. Aristotle, one should observe, does not establish any hard and fast opposition between judgment and imagination, an opposition that pervades not only the neo-classical movement but also the romantic revolt from it. He simply affirms a supersensuous order which one can perceive only with the help of fiction. The best art, says Goethe in the true spirit of Aristotle, gives us the "illusion of a higher reality." This has the advantage of being experimental. It is merely a statement of what one feels in the presence of a great painting, let us say, or in reading a great poem.

After this attempt to define briefly with the help of the Greeks the classical spirit in its essence we should be prepared to understand more clearly the way in which this spirit was modified in neo-classical times, especially in France. The first thing that strikes one about the classicism of this period is that it does not rest on immediate perception like that of the Greeks but on outer authority. The merely dogmatic and traditional classicist gave a somewhat un-Greek meaning to the doctrines of nature and imitation. Why imitate nature directly, said Scali-

ger, when we have in Virgil a second nature? Imitation thus came to mean the imitation of certain outer models and the following of rules based on these models. Now it is well that one who aims at excellence in any field should begin by a thorough assimilation of the achievements of his great predecessors in this field. Unfortunately the neo-classical theorist tended to impose a multitude of precepts that were based on what was external rather than on what was vital in the practice of his models. In so far the lesson of form that the great ancients can always teach any one who approaches them in the right spirit degenerated into formalism. This formalistic turn given to the doctrine of imitation was felt from the outset to be a menace to originality; to be incompatible, and everything hinges at last on this point, with the spontaneity of the imagination. There was an important reaction headed by men like Boileau, within the neo-classical movement itself, against the oppression of the intuitive side of human nature by mere dogma and authority, above all against the notion that "regularity" is in itself any guarantee of literary excellence. A school of rules was succeeded by a school of taste. Yet even to the end the neo-classicist was too prone to reject as unnatural or even monstrous everything that did not fit into one of the traditional pigeon-holes. One must grant, indeed, that much noble work was achieved under the neo-classical dispensation, work that shows a genuine insight into the universal, but it is none the less evident that the view of the imagination held during this period has a formalistic taint.

This taint in neo-classicism is due not merely to its dogmatic and mechanical way of dealing with the doctrine of imitation but also to the fact that it had to reconcile classical with Christian dogma; and the two antiquities, classical and

Christian, if interpreted vitally and in the spirit, were in many respects divergent and in some respects contradictory. The general outcome of the attempts at reconciliation made by the literary casuists of Italy and France was that Christianity should have a monopoly of truth and classicism a monopoly of fiction. For the true classicist, it will be remembered, the two things are inseparable—he gets at his truth through a veil of fiction. Many of the neo-classicists came to conceive of art as many romanticists were to conceive of it later as a sort of irresponsible game or play, but they were, it must be confessed, very inferior to the romanticists in the spontaneity of their fiction. They went for this fiction as for everything else to the models, and this meant in practice that they employed the pagan myths, not as imaginative symbols of a higher reality—it is still possible to employ them in that way—but merely in Boileau's phrase as "traditional ornaments" (*ornements reçus*). The neo-classicist to be sure might so employ his "fiction" as to inculcate a moral; in that case he is only too likely to give us instead of the living symbol, dead allegory; instead of high seriousness, its caricature, didacticism. The traditional stock of fiction became at last so intolerably trite as to be rejected even by some of the late neo-classicists. "The rejection and contempt of fiction," said Dr. Johnson (who indulged in it himself on occasion) "is rational and manly." But to reject fiction in the larger sense is to miss the true driving power in human nature—the imagination. Before concluding, however, that Dr. Johnson had no notion of the rôle of the imagination one should read his attack on the theory of the three unities[3] which was later to be turned to account by the romanticists.

Now the three unities may be defended

[3] In his *Preface* to Shakespeare.

on an entirely legitimate ground—on the ground namely that they make for concentration, a prime virtue in the drama; but the grounds on which they were actually imposed on the drama, especially in connection with the Quarrel of the Cid, illustrate the corruption of another main classical doctrine, that of probability or verisimilitude. In his dealings with probability as in his dealings with imitation, the neo-classical formalist did not allow sufficiently for the element of illusion. What he required from the drama in the name of probability was not the "illusion of a higher reality," but strict logic or even literal deception. He was not capable of a poetic faith, not willing to suspend his disbelief on passing from the world of ordinary fact to the world of artistic creation. Goethe was thinking especially of the neo-classical French when he said: "As for the French, they will always be arrested by their reason. They do not recognize that the imagination has its own laws which are and always must be problematic for the reason."

It was also largely under French influence that the doctrine of decorum, which touches probability at many points, was turned aside from its true meaning. Decorum is in a way the peculiar doctrine of the classicist, is in Milton's phrase "the grand masterpiece to observe." The doctrines of the universal and the imitation of the universal go deeper indeed than decorum, so much deeper that they are shared by classicism with religion. The man who aspires to live religiously must no less than the humanist look to some model set above his ordinary self and imitate it. But though the classicist at his best meditates, he does not, like the seeker after religious perfection, see in meditation an end in itself but rather a support for the mediatory virtues, the virtues of the man who would live to the best advantage in this world rather than renounce it; and these virtues may be said to be summed up in decorum. For the best type of Greek humanist, a Sophocles let us say, decorum was a vital and immediate thing. But there enters into decorum even from the time of the Alexandrian Greeks, and still more into French neo-classical decorum, a marked element of artificiality. The all-roundness and fine symmetry, the poise and dignity that come from working within the bounds of the human law, were taken to be the privilege not of **man** in general but of a special social class. Take for instance verbal decorum: the French neo-classicists assumed that if the speech of poetry is to be noble and highly serious it must coincide with the speech of the aristocracy. As Nisard puts it, they confused nobility of language with the language of the nobility. Decorum was thus more or less merged with etiquette, so that the standards of the stage and of literature in general came to coincide, as Rousseau complains, with those of the drawing-room. More than anything else this narrowing of decorum marks the decline from the classic to the pseudo-classic, from form to formalism. . . .

ROMANTICISM AND CLASSICISM
T. E. Hulme*

T. E. Hulme asserts the superiority of the classical over the romantic attitude. The romantic is dedicated to the vague and the infinite, the classical to the exact depiction of the world as it is. The former sees man as an "infinite reservoir," the latter sees him as fixed and limited, constant in nature.

I want to maintain that after a hundred years of romanticism, we are in for a classical revival, and that the particular weapon of this new classical spirit, when it works in verse, will be fancy. And in this I imply the superiority of fancy—not superior generally or absolutely, for that would be obvious nonsense, but superior in the sense that we use the word good in empirical ethics—good for something, superior for something. I shall have to prove then two things, first that a classical revival is coming, and, secondly, for its particular purposes, fancy will be superior to imagination.

So banal have the terms Imagination and Fancy become that we imagine they must have always been in the language. Their history as two differing terms in the vocabulary of criticism is comparatively short. Originally, of course, they both mean the same thing; they first began to be differentiated by the German writers on aesthetics in the eighteenth century.

I know that in using the words "classic" and "romantic" I am doing a dangerous thing. They represent five or six different kinds of antitheses, and while I may be

* The essay is reprinted from *Speculations: Essays on Humanism and the Philosophy of Art*, by T. E. Hulme, edited by Herbert Read. Reprinted by permission of Harcourt, Brace & World, Inc. Copyright 1924 by Harcourt, Brace, and Company, Inc.

using them in one sense you may be interpreting them in another. In this present connection I am using them in a perfectly precise and limited sense. I ought really to have coined a couple of new words, but I prefer to use the ones I have used, as I then conform to the practice of the group of polemical writers who make most use of them at the present day, and have almost succeeded in making them political catchwords. I mean Maurras, Lasserre and all the group connected with *L'Action Française*.

At the present time this is the particular group with which the distinction is most vital. Because it has become a party symbol. If you asked a man of a certain set whether he preferred the classics or the romantics, you could deduce from that what his politics were.

The best way of gliding into a proper definition of my terms would be to start with a set of people who are prepared to fight about it—for in them you will have no vagueness. (Other people take the infamous attitude of the person with catholic tastes who says he likes both.)

About a year ago, a man whose name I think was Fauchois gave a lecture at the Odéon on Racine, in the course of which he made some disparaging remarks about his dullness, lack of invention and the rest of it. This caused an immediate riot: fights took place all over the house; several people were arrested and imprisoned, and the rest of the series of lectures took place with hundreds of gendarmes and detectives scattered all over the place. These people interrupted because the classical ideal is a living thing to them and Racine is the great classic. That is what I call a real vital interest in literature. They regard romanticism as an awful disease from which France had just recovered.

The thing is complicated in their case by the fact that it was romanticism that made the revolution. They hate the revolution, so they hate romanticism.

I make no apology for dragging in politics here; romanticism both in England and France is associated with certain political views, and it is in taking a concrete example of the working out of a principle in action that you can get its best definition.

What was the positive principle behind all the other principles of '89? I am talking here of the revolution in as far as it was an idea; I leave out material causes—they only produce the forces. The barriers which could easily have resisted or guided these forces had been previously rotted away by ideas. This always seems to be the case in successful changes; the privileged class is beaten only when it has lost faith in itself, when it has itself been penetrated with the ideas which are working against it.

It was not the rights of man—that was a good solid practical war-cry. The thing which created enthusiasm, which made the revolution practically a new religion, was something more positive than that. People of all classes, people who stood to lose by it, were in a positive ferment about the idea of liberty. There must have been some idea which enabled them to think that something positive could come out of so essentially negative a thing. There was, and here I get my definition of romanticism. They had been taught by Rousseau that man was by nature good, that it was only bad laws and customs that had suppressed him. Remove all these and the infinite possibilities of man would have a chance. This is what made them think that something positive could come out of disorder, this is what created the religious enthusiasm. Here is the root of all romanticism: that man, the individual, is an infinite reservoir of possibilities; and if you can so rearrange society by the destruction of oppressive order then these possibilities will have a chance and you will get Progress.

One can define the classical quite clearly as the exact opposite to this. Man is an extraordinarily fixed and limited animal whose nature is absolutely constant. It is only by tradition and organisation that anything decent can be got out of him.

This view was a little shaken at the time of Darwin. You remember his particular hypothesis, that new species came into existence by the cumulative effect of small variations—this seems to admit the possibility of future progress. But at the present day the contrary hypothesis makes headway in the shape of De Vries's mutation theory, that each new species comes into existence, not gradually by the accumulation of small steps, but suddenly in a jump, a kind of sport, and that once in existence it remains absolutely fixed. This enables me to keep the classical view with an appearance of scientific backing.

Put shortly, these are the two views, then. One, that man is intrinsically good, spoilt by circumstance; and the other that he is intrinsically limited, but disciplined by order and tradition to something fairly decent. To the one party man's nature is like a well, to the other like a bucket. The view which regards man as a well, a reservoir full of possibilities, I call romantic; the one which regards him as a very finite and fixed creature, I call the classical.

One may note here that the Church has always taken the classical view since the defeat of the Pelagian heresy and the adoption of the sane classical dogma of original sin.

It would be a mistake to identify the classical view with that of materialism. On the contrary it is absolutely identical with the normal religious attitude. I should put it in this way: That part of the fixed nature of man is the belief in the Deity. This should be as fixed and true for every man as belief in the existence of matter and in the objective world. It is parallel to appetite, the instinct of sex, and all the other fixed qualities. Now at certain times, by the use of either force or rhetoric, these instincts have been suppressed—in Florence under Savonarola, in Geneva under Calvin, and here under the Roundheads. The inevitable result of such a process is that the repressed instinct bursts out in some abnormal direction. So with religion. By the perverted rhetoric of Rationalism, your natural instincts are suppressed and you are converted into an agnostic. Just as in the case of the other instincts, Nature has her revenge. The instincts that find no right and proper outlet in religion must come out in some other way. You don't believe in a God, so you begin to believe that man is a god. You don't believe in Heaven, so you begin to believe in a heaven on earth. In other words, you get romanticism. The concepts that are right and proper in their own sphere are spread over, and so mess up, falsify and blur the clear outlines of human experience. It is like pouring a pot of treacle over the dinner table. Romanticism then, and this is the best definition I can give of it, is spilt religion.

I must now shirk the difficulty of saying exactly what I mean by romantic and classical in verse. I can only say that it means the result of these two attitudes towards the cosmos, towards man, in so far as it gets reflected in verse. The romantic, because he thinks man infinite, must always be talking about the infinite; and as there is always the bitter contrast between what you think you ought to be able to do and what man actually can, it always tends, in its later stages at any rate, to be gloomy. I really can't go any further than to say it is the reflection of these two temperaments, and point out examples of the different spirits. On the one hand I would take such diverse people as Horace, most of the Elizabethans and the writers of the Augustan age, and on the other side Lamartine, Hugo, parts of Keats, Coleridge, Byron, Shelley and Swinburne.

I know quite well that when people think of classical and romantic in verse, the contrast at once comes into their mind between, say, Racine and Shakespeare. I don't mean this; the dividing line that I intend is here misplaced a little from the true middle. That Racine is on the extreme classical side I agree, but if you call Shakespeare romantic, you are using a different definition to the one I give. You are thinking of the difference between classic and romantic as being merely one between restraint and exuberance. I should say with Nietzsche that there are two kinds of classicism, the static and the dynamic. Shakespeare is the classic of motion.

What I mean by classical in verse, then, is this. That even in the most imaginative flights there is always a holding back, a reservation. The classical poet never forgets this finiteness, this limit of man. He remembers always that he is mixed up with earth. He may jump, but he always returns back; he never flies away into the circumambient gas.

You might say if you wished that the whole of the romantic attitude seems to crystallise in verse round metaphors of flight. Hugo is always flying, flying over abysses, flying up into the eternal gases. The word infinite in every other line.

In the classical attitude you never seem to swing right along to the infinite nothing. If you say an extravagant thing which does exceed the limits inside which you know man to be fastened, yet there is always conveyed in some way at the end an impression of yourself standing outside it, and not quite believing it, or consciously putting it forward as a flourish. You never go blindly into an atmosphere more than the truth, an atmosphere too rarefied for man to breathe for long. You are always faithful to the conception of a limit. It is a question of pitch; in romantic verse you move at a certain pitch of rhetoric which you know, man being what he is, to be a little high-falutin. The kind of thing you get in Hugo or Swinburne. In the coming classical reaction that will feel just wrong. For an example of the opposite thing, a verse written in the proper classical spirit, I can take the song from Cymbeline beginning with "Fear no more the heat of the sun." I am just using this as a parable. I don't quite mean what I say here. Take the last two lines:

Golden lads and lasses must,
Like chimney sweepers come to dust.

Now, no romantic would have ever written that. Indeed, so ingrained is romanticism, so objectionable is this to it, that people have asserted that these were not part of the original song.

Apart from the pun, the thing that I think quite classical is the word lad. Your modern romantic could never write that. He would have to write golden youth, and take up the thing at least a couple of notes in pitch.

I want now to give the reasons which make me think that we are nearing the end of the romantic movement.

The first lies in the nature of any convention or tradition in art. A particular convention or attitude in art has a strict analogy to the phenomena of organic life. It grows old and decays. It has a definite period of life and must die. All the possible tunes get played on it and then it is exhausted; moreover its best period is its youngest. Take the case of the extraordinary efflorescence of verse in the Elizabethan period. All kinds of reasons have been given for this—the discovery of the new world and all the rest of it. There is a much simpler one. A new medium had been given them to play with—namely, blank verse. It was new and so it was easy to play new tunes on it.

The same law holds in other arts. All the masters of painting are born into the world at a time when the particular tradition from which they start is imperfect. The Florentine tradition was just short of full ripeness when Raphael came to Florence, the Bellinesque was still young when Titian was born in Venice. Landscape was still a toy or an appanage of figure-painting when Turner and Constable arose to reveal its independent power. When Turner and Constable had done with landscape they left little or nothing for their successors to do on the same lines. Each field of artistic activity is exhausted by the first great artist who gathers a full harvest from it.

This period of exhaustion seems to me to have been reached in romanticism. We shall not get any new efflorescence of verse until we get a new technique, a new convention, to turn ourselves loose in.

Objection might be taken to this. It might be said that a century as an organic unity doesn't exist, that I am being deluded by a wrong metaphor, that I am treating a collection of literary people as if they were an organism or state department. Whatever we may be in other things, an objector might urge, in literature in as far as we are anything at all —in as far as we are worth considering —we are individuals, we are persons, and as distinct persons we cannot be subordinated to any general treatment. At any period at any time, an individual poet may be a classic or a romantic just as he feels like it. You at any particular moment may think that you can stand outside a movement. You may think that as an individual you observe both the classic and the romantic spirit and decide from a purely detached point of view that one is superior to the other.

The answer to this is that no one, in a matter of judgment of beauty, can take a detached standpoint in this way. Just as physically you are not born that abstract entity, man, but the child of particular parents, so you are in matters of literary judgment. Your opinion is almost entirely of the literary history that came just before you, and you are governed by that whatever you may think. Take Spinoza's example of a stone falling to the ground. If it had a conscious mind it would, he said, think it was going to the ground because it wanted to. So you with your pretended free judgment about what is and what is not beautiful. The amount of freedom in man is much exaggerated. That we are free on certain rare occasions, both my religion and the views I get from metaphysics convince me. But many acts which we habitually label free are in reality automatic. It is quite possible for a man to write a book almost automatically. I have read several such products. Some observations were recorded more than twenty years ago by Robertson on reflex speech, and he found that in certain cases of dementia, where the people were quite unconscious so far as the exercise of reasoning went, that very intelligent answers were given to a succession of questions on politics and such matters. The meaning of these questions could not possibly have been understood. Language here acted after the manner of a reflex. So that certain extremely complex mechanisms, subtle enough to imitate beauty, can work by themselves—I certainly think that this is the case with judgments about beauty.

I can put the same thing in slightly different form. Here is a question of a conflict of two attitudes, as it might be of two techniques. The critic, while he has to admit that changes from one to the other occur, persists in regarding them as mere variations to a certain fixed normal, just as a pendulum swing. I admit the analogy of the pendulum as far as movement, but I deny the further consequence of the analogy, the existence of the point of rest, the normal point.

When I say that I dislike the romantics, I dissociate two things: the part of them in which they resemble all the great poets, and the part in which they differ and which gives them their character as romantics. It is this minor element which constitutes the particular note of a century, and which, while it excites contemporaries, annoys the next generation. It was precisely that quality in Pope which pleased his friends, which we detest. Now, anyone just before the romantics who felt that, could have predicted that a change was coming. It seems to me that we stand just in the same position now. I think that there is an increasing proportion of people who simply can't stand Swinburne.

When I say that there will be another classical revival I don't necessarily anticipate a return to Pope. I say merely that now is the time for such a revival. Given people of the necessary capacity, it may be a vital thing; without them we may get a formalism something like Pope. When it does come we may not even recognise it as classical. Although it will be classical it will be different because it has passed through a romantic period. To take a parallel example: I remember being very surprised, after seeing the Post Impressionists, to find in

Maurice Denis's account of the matter that they consider themselves classical in the sense that they were trying to impose the same order on the mere flux of new material provided by the impressionist movement, that existed in the more limited materials of the painting before.

There is something now to be cleared away before I get on with my argument, which is that while romanticism is dead in reality, yet the critical attitude appropriate to it still continues to exist. To make this a little clearer: For every kind of verse, there is a corresponding receptive attitude. In a romantic period we demand from verse certain qualities. In a classical period we demand others. At the present time I should say that this receptive attitude has outlasted the thing from which it was formed. But while the romantic tradition has run dry, yet the critical attitude of mind, which demands romantic qualities from verse, still survives. So that if good classical verse were to be written tomorrow very few people would be able to stand it.

I object even to the best of the romantics. I object still more to the receptive attitude. I object to the sloppiness which doesn't consider that a poem is a poem unless it is moaning or whining about something or other. I always think in this connection of the last line of a poem of John Webster's which ends with a request I cordially endorse:

End your moan and come away.

The thing has got so bad now that a poem which is all dry and hard, a properly classical poem, would not be considered poetry at all. How many people now can lay their hands on their hearts and say they like either Horace or Pope? They feel a kind of chill when they read them.

The dry hardness which you get in the classics is absolutely repugnant to them. Poetry that isn't damp isn't poetry at all. They cannot see that accurate description is a legitimate object of verse. Verse to them always means a bringing in of some of the emotions that are grouped round the word infinite.

The essence of poetry to most people is that it must lead them to a beyond of some kind. Verse strictly confined to the earthly and the definite (Keats is full of it) might seem to them to be excellent writing, excellent craftsmanship, but not poetry. So much has romanticism debauched us, that, without some form of vagueness, we deny the highest.

In the classic it is always the light of ordinary day, never the light that never was on land or sea. It is always perfectly human and never exaggerated: man is always man and never a god.

But the awful result of romanticism is that, accustomed to this strange light, you can never live without it. Its effect on you is that of a drug.

There is a general tendency to think that verse means little else than the expression of unsatisfied emotion. People say: "But how can you have verse without sentiment?" You see what it is: the prospect alarms them. A classical revival to them would mean the prospect of an arid desert and the death of poetry as they understand it, and could only come to fill the gap caused by that death. Exactly why this dry classical spirit should have a positive and legitimate necessity to express itself in poetry is utterly inconceivable to them. What this positive need is, I shall show later. It follows from the fact that there is another quality, not the emotion produced, which is at the root of excellence in verse. Before I get to this I am concerned with a negative thing, a theoretical point, a prejudice that stands in the way and is really at the bottom of this reluctance to understand classical verse.

It is an objection which ultimately I believe comes from a bad metaphysic of art. You are unable to admit the existence of beauty without the infinite being in some way or another dragged in.

I may quote for purposes of argument, as a typical example of this kind of attitude made vocal, the famous chapters in Ruskin's *Modern Painters*, Vol. II, on the imagination. I must say here, parenthetically, that I use this word without prejudice to the other discussion with which I shall end the paper. I only use the word here because it is Ruskin's word. All that I am concerned with just now is the attitude behind it, which I take to be the romantic.

Imagination cannot but be serious; she sees too far, too darkly, too solemnly, too earnestly, ever to smile. There is something in the heart of everything, if we can reach it, that we shall not be inclined to laugh at.... Those who have so pierced and seen the melancholy deeps of things, are filled with intense passion and gentleness of sympathy. (Part III, Chap. III, §9.)

There is in every word set down by the imaginative mind an awful undercurrent of meaning, and evidence and shadow upon it of the deep places out of which it has come. It is often obscure, often half-told; for he who wrote it, in his clear seeing of the things beneath, may have been impatient of detailed interpretation; for if we choose to dwell upon it and trace it, it will lead us always securely back to that metropolis of the soul's dominion from which we may follow out all the ways and tracks to its farthest coasts. (Part III, Chap. III, §5.)

Really in all these matters the act of judgment is an instinct, an absolutely unstateable thing akin to the art of the tea taster. But you must talk, and the only language you can use in this matter is that of analogy. I have no material clay to mould to the given shape; the only thing which one has for the purpose, and which acts as a substitute for it, a kind of mental clay, are certain metaphors modified into theories of aesthetic and rhetoric. A combination of these, while it cannot state the essentially unstateable intuition, can yet give you a sufficient analogy to enable you to see what it was and to recognise it on condition that you yourself have been in a similar state. Now these phrases of Ruskin's convey quite clearly to me his taste in the matter.

I see quite clearly that he thinks the best verse must be serious. That is a natural attitude for a man in the romantic period. But he is not content with saying that he prefers this kind of verse. He wants to deduce his opinion like his master, Coleridge, from some fixed principle which can be found by metaphysic.

Here is the last refuge of this romantic attitude. It proves itself to be not an attitude but a deduction from a fixed principle of the cosmos.

One of the main reasons for the existence of philosophy is not that it enables you to find truth (it can never do that) but that it does provide you a refuge for definitions. The usual idea of the thing is that it provides you with a fixed basis from which you can deduce the things you want in aesthetics. The process is the exact contrary. You start in the confusion of the fighting line, you retire from that just a little to the rear to recover, to get your weapons right. Quite plainly, without metaphor this—it provides you with an elaborate and precise language in which you really can explain definitely what you mean, but what you want to say is decided by other things. The ultimate reality is the hurly-burly, the struggle; the metaphysic is an adjunct to clear-headedness in it.

To get back to Ruskin and his objection to all that is not serious. It seems to me that involved in this is a bad metaphysical aesthetic. You have the metaphysic which in defining beauty or the nature of art always drags in the infinite. Particularly in Germany, the land where theories of aesthetics were first created, the romantic aesthetes collated all beauty to an impression of the infinite involved in the identification of our being in absolute spirit. In the least element of beauty we have a total intuition of the whole world. Every artist is a kind of pantheist.

Now it is quite obvious to anyone who holds this kind of theory that any poetry which confines itself to the finite can never be of the highest kind. It seems a contradiction in terms to them. And as in metaphysics you get the last refuge of a prejudice, so it is now necessary for me to refute this.

Here follows a tedious piece of dialectic, but it is necessary for my purpose. I must avoid two pitfalls in discussing the idea of beauty. On the one hand there is the old classical view which is supposed to define it as lying in conformity to certain standard fixed forms; and on the other hand there is the romantic view which drags in the infinite. I have got to find a metaphysic between these two which will enable me to hold consistently that a neo-classic verse of the type I have indicated involves no contradiction in terms. It is essential to prove that beauty may be in small, dry things.

The great aim is accurate, precise and definite description. The first thing is to recognise how extraordinarily difficult this is. It is no mere matter of carefulness; you have to use language, and language is by its very nature a communal thing; that is, it expresses never the exact thing but a compromise—that which is common to you, me and everybody. But each man sees a little differently, and to get out clearly and exactly what he does see, he must have a terrific struggle with language, whether it be with words or the technique of other arts. Language has its own special nature, its own conventions and communal ideas. It is only by a concentrated effort of the mind that you can hold it fixed to your own purpose. I always think that the fundamental process at the back of all the arts might be represented by the following metaphor. You know what I call architect's curves—flat pieces of wood with all different kinds of curvature. By a suitable selection from these you can draw approximately any curve you like. The artist I take to be the man who simply can't bear the idea of that "approximately." He will get the exact curve of what he sees whether it be an object or an idea in the mind. I shall here have to change my metaphor a little to get the process in his mind. Suppose that instead of your curved pieces of wood you have a springy piece of steel of the same types of curvature as the wood. Now the state of tension or concentration of mind, if he is doing anything really good in this struggle against the ingrained habit of the technique, may be represented by a man employing all his fingers to bend the steel out of its own curve and into the exact curve which you want. Something different to what it would assume naturally.

There are then two things to distinguish, first the particular faculty of mind to see things as they really are, and apart from the conventional ways in which you have been trained to see them. This is itself rare enough in all consciousness. Second, the concentrated state of mind, the grip over oneself which is necessary in the actual expression of what one sees. To prevent one falling into the conventional curves of ingrained technique, to hold on through infinite detail and

trouble to the exact curve you want. Wherever you get this sincerity you get the fundamental quality of good art without dragging in infinite or serious.

I can now get at that positive fundamental quality of verse which constitutes excellence, which has nothing to do with infinity, with mystery or with emotions.

This is the point I aim at, then, in my argument. I prophesy that a period of dry, hard, classical verse is coming. I have met the preliminary objection founded on the bad romantic aesthetic that in such verse, from which the infinite is excluded, you cannot have the essence of poetry at all.

After attempting to sketch out what this positive quality is, I can get on to the end of my paper in this way: That where you get this quality exhibited in the realm of the emotions you get imagination, and that where you get this quality exhibited in the contemplation of finite things you get fancy.

In prose as in algebra concrete things are embodied in signs or counters which are moved about according to rules, without being visualised at all in the process. There are in prose certain type situations and arrangements of words, which move as automatically into certain other arrangements as do functions in algebra. One only changes the X's and the Y's back into physical things at the end of the process. Poetry, in one aspect at any rate, may be considered as an effort to avoid this characteristic of prose. It is not a counter language, but a visual concrete one. It is a compromise for a language of intuition which would hand over sensations bodily. It always endeavours to arrest you, and to make you continuously see a physical thing, to prevent you gliding through an abstract process. It chooses fresh epithets and fresh metaphors, not so much because they are new, and we are tired of the old, but because the old cease to convey a physical thing and become abstract counters. A poet says a ship "coursed the seas" to get a physical image, instead of the counter word "sailed." Visual meanings can only be transferred by the new bowl of metaphor; prose is an old pot that lets them leak out. Images in verse are not mere decoration, but the very essence of an intuitive language. Verse is a pedestrian taking you over the ground, prose—a train which delivers you at a destination.

I can now get on to a discussion of two words often used in this connection, "fresh" and "unexpected." You praise a thing for being "fresh." I understand what you mean, but the word besides conveying the truth conveys a secondary something which is certainly false. When you say a poem or drawing is fresh, and so good, the impression is somehow conveyed that the essential element of goodness is freshness, that it is good because it is fresh. Now this is certainly wrong, there is nothing particularly desirable about freshness *per se*. Works of art aren't eggs. Rather the contrary. It is simply an unfortunate necessity due to the nature of language and technique that the only way the element which does constitute goodness, the only way in which its presence can be detected externally, is by freshness. Freshness convinces you, you feel at once that the artist was in an actual physical state. You feel that for a minute. Real communication is so very rare, for plain speech is unconvincing. It is in this rare fact of communication that you get the root of aesthetic pleasure.

I shall maintain that wherever you get an extraordinary interest in a thing, a great zest in its contemplation which carries on the contemplator to accurate description in the sense of the word accurate I have just analysed, there you have sufficient justification for poetry. It must be an intense zest which heightens a thing out of the level of prose. I am using contemplation here just in the same way that Plato used it, only applied to a different subject; it is a detached interest. "The object of aesthetic contemplation is something framed apart by itself and regarded without memory or expectation, simply as being itself, as end not means, as individual not universal."

To take a concrete example, I am taking an extreme case. If you are walking behind a woman in the street, you notice the curious way in which the skirt rebounds from her heels. If that peculiar kind of motion becomes of such interest to you that you will search about until you can get the exact epithet which hits it off, there you have a properly aesthetic emotion. But it is the zest with which you look at the thing which decides you to make the effort. In this sense the feeling that was in Herrick's mind when he wrote "the tempestuous petticoat" was exactly the same as that which in bigger and vaguer matters makes the best romantic verse. It doesn't matter an atom that the emotion produced is not of dignified vagueness, but on the contrary amusing; the point is that exactly the same activity is at work as in the highest verse. That is the avoidance of conventional language in order to get the exact curve of the thing.

I have still to show that in the verse which is to come, fancy will be the necessary weapon of the classical school. The positive quality I have talked about can be manifested in ballad verse by extreme directness and simplicity, such as you get in "On Fair Kirkconnel Lea." But the particular verse we are going to get will be cheerful, dry and sophisticated, and here the necessary weapon of the positive quality must be fancy.

Subject doesn't matter; the quality in

it is the same as you get in the more romantic people.

It isn't the scale or kind of emotion produced that decides, but this one fact: Is there any real zest in it? Did the poet have an actually realised visual object before him in which he delighted? It doesn't matter if it were a lady's shoe or the starry heavens.

Fancy is not mere decoration added on to plain speech. Plain speech is essentially inaccurate. It is only by new metaphors, that is, by fancy, that it can be made precise.

When the analogy has not enough connection with the thing described to be quite parallel with it, where it overlays the thing it described and there is a certain excess, there you have the play of fancy—that I grant is inferior to imagination.

But where the analogy is every bit of it necessary for accurate description in the sense of the word accurate I have previously described, and your only objection to this kind of fancy is that it is not serious in the effect it produces, then I think the objection to be entirely invalid. If it is sincere in the accurate sense, when the whole of the analogy is necessary to get out the exact curve of the feeling or thing you want to express—there you seem to me to have the highest verse, even though the subject be trivial and the emotions of the infinite far away.

It is very difficult to use any terminology at all for this kind of thing. For whatever word you use is at once sentimentalised. Take Coleridge's word "vital." It is used loosely by all kinds of people who talk about art, to mean something vaguely and mysteriously significant. In fact, vital and mechanical is to them exactly the same antithesis as between good and bad.

Nothing of the kind; Coleridge uses it in a perfectly definite and what I call

dry sense. It is just this: A mechanical complexity is the sum of its parts. Put them side by side and you get the whole. Now vital or organic is merely a convenient metaphor for a complexity of a different kind, that in which the parts cannot be said to be elements as each one is modified by the other's presence, and each one to a certain extent is the whole. The leg of a chair by itself is still a leg. My leg by itself wouldn't be.

Now the characteristic of the intellect is that it can only represent complexities of the mechanical kind. It can only make diagrams, and diagrams are essentially things whose parts are separate one from another. The intellect always analyses—when there is a synthesis it is baffled. That is why the artist's work seems mysterious. The intellect can't represent it. This is a necessary consequence of the particular nature of the intellect and the purposes for which it is formed. It doesn't mean that your synthesis is ineffable, simply that it can't be definitely stated.

Now this is all worked out in Bergson, the central feature of his whole philosophy. It is all based on the clear conception of these vital complexities which he calls "intensive" as opposed to the other kind which he calls "extensive," and the recognition of the fact that the intellect can only deal with the extensive multiplicity. To deal with the intensive you must use intuition.

Now, as I said before, Ruskin was perfectly aware of all this, but he had no such metaphysical background which would enable him to state definitely what he meant. The result is that he has to flounder about in a series of metaphors. A powerfully imaginative mind seizes and combines at the same instant all the important ideas of its poem or picture, and while it works with one of them, it is at the same instant working with and modifying all in their relation to it and never losing sight of their bearings on each other—as the motion of a snake's body goes through all parts at once and its volition acts at the same instant in coils which go contrary ways.

A romantic movement must have an end of the very nature of the thing. It may be deplored, but it can't be helped —wonder must cease to be wonder.

I guard myself here from all the consequences of the analogy, but it expresses at any rate the inevitableness of the process. A literature of wonder must have an end as inevitably as a strange land loses its strangeness when one lives in it. Think of the lost ecstasy of the Elizabethans. "Oh my America, my new found land," think of what it meant to them and of what it means to us. Wonder can only be the attitude of a man passing from one stage to another, it can never be a permanently fixed thing.

PRELIMINARY PROBLEMS
Yvor Winters[*]

Some aspects of Winters' modern classicism appear in his assertion that the rational content of language cannot be extinguished, that there is a relationship in poetry between concept and feeling —the relationship, he calls it, "of motive to emotion." This relationship must be appropriate and satisfactory, and the judgment of whether it is or not is a moral one, since through a poem we are "judging representative acts."

FIRST PROBLEM

Is it possible to say that Poem A (one of Donne's *Holy Sonnets*, or one of the poems of Jonson or of Shakespeare) is better than Poem B (Collins' *Ode to Evening*) or vice versa?

If not, is it possible to say that either of these is better than Poem C (*The Cremation of Sam Magee*, or something comparable)?

If the answer is no in both cases, then any poem is as good as any other. If this is true, then all poetry is worthless; but this obviously is not true, for it is contrary to all our experience.

If the answer is yes in both cases, then there follows the question of whether

the answer implies merely that one poem is better than another for the speaker, or whether it means that one poem is intrinsically better than another. If the former, then we are impressionists, which is to say relativists; and are either mystics of the type of Emerson, or hedonists of the type of Stevens and Ransom. If the latter, then we assume that constant principles govern the poetic experience, and that the poem (as likewise the judge) must be judged in relationship to those principles. It is important, therefore, to discover the consequences of assuming each of these positions.

If our answer to the first question is no and to the second yes, then we are asserting that we can distinguish between those poems which are of the canon and those which are not, but that within the canon all judgment is impossible. This

* This essay is reprinted from *In Defense of Reason*, by Yvor Winters, by permission of the publisher, Alan Swallow. Copyright 1947, 1960, by Yvor Winters.

view, if adopted, will require serious elucidation, for on the face of it, it appears inexplicable. On the other hand, one cannot deny that within the canon judgment will become more difficult, for the nearer two poems may be to the highest degrees of excellence, the harder it will be to choose between them. Two poems, in fact, might be so excellent that there would be small profit in endeavoring to say that one was better, but one could arrive at this conclusion only after a careful examination of both.

Second Problem

If we accept the view that one poem can be regarded as better than another, the question then arises whether this judgment is a matter of inexplicable intuition, or whether it is a question of intuition that can be explained, and consequently guided and improved by rational elucidation.

If we accept the view that the judgment in question is inexplicable, then we are again forced to confess ourselves impressionists and relativists, unless we can show that the intuitions of all men agree at all times, or that the intuitions of one man are invariably right and those of all others wrong whenever they differ. We obviously can demonstrate neither of these propositions.

If we start, then, with the proposition that one poem may be intrinsically superior to another, we are forced to account for differences of opinion regarding it. If two critics differ, it is possible that one is right and the other wrong, more likely that both are partly right and partly wrong, but in different respects: neither the native gifts nor the education of any man have ever been wholly adequate to many of the critical problems he will encounter, and no two men are

ever the same in these respects or in any others. On the other hand, although the critic should display reasonable humility and caution, it is only fair to add that few men possess either the talent or the education to justify their being taken very seriously, even of those who are nominally professional students of these matters.

But if it is possible by rational elucidation to give a more or less clear account of what one finds in a poem and why one approves or disapproves, then communication between two critics, though no doubt imperfect, becomes possible, and it becomes possible that they may in some measure correct each other's errors and so come more near to a true judgment of the poem.

Third Problem

If rational communication about poetry is to take place, it is necessary first to determine what we mean by a poem.

A poem is first of all a statement in words.

But it differs from all such statements of a purely philosophical or theoretical nature, in that it has by intention a controlled content of feeling. In this respect, it does not differ from many works written in prose, however.

A poem differs from a work written in prose by virtue of its being composed in verse. The rhythm of verse permits the expression of more powerful feeling than is possible in prose when such feeling is needed, and it permits at all times the expression of finer shades of feeling.

A poem, then, is a statement in words in which special pains are taken with the expression of feeling. This description is merely intended to distinguish the poem from other kinds of writing; it is not offered as a complete description.

Fourth Problem

What, however, are words?

They are audible sounds, or their visual symbols, invented by man to communicate his thoughts and feelings. Each word has a conceptual content, however slight; each word, exclusive, perhaps, of the particles, communicates vague associations of feeling.

The word *fire* communicates a concept; it also connotes very vaguely certain feelings, depending on the context in which we happen to place it—depending, for example, on whether we happen to think of a fire on a hearth, in a furnace, or in a forest. These feelings may be rendered more and more precise as we render the context more and more precise; as we come more and more near to completing and perfecting our poem.

Fifth Problem

But if the poem, as compared to prose, pays especial attention to feeling, are we to assume that the rational content of the poem is unimportant to its success?

The rational content cannot be eliminated from words; consequently the rational content cannot be eliminated from poetry. It is there. If it is unsatisfactory in itself, a part of the poem is unsatisfactory; the poem is thus damaged beyond argument. If we deny this, we must surely explain ourselves very fully.

If we admit this, we are faced with another problem: is it conceivable that rational content and feeling-content may both be perfect, and yet that they may be unrelated to each other, or imperfectly related? To me this is inconceivable, because the emotional content of words is generated by our experience with the conceptual content, so that a relationship is necessary.

This fact of the necessity of such rela-tionship may fairly return us for a moment to the original question: whether imperfection of rational content damages the entire poem. If there is a necessary relationship between concept and feeling, and concept is unsatisfactory, then feeling must be damaged by way of the relationship.

Sixth Problem

If there is a relationship between concept and feeling, what is the nature of that relationship?

To answer this, let us return to the basic unit, the word. The concept represented by the word, motivates the feeling which the word communicates. It is the concept of fire which generates the feelings communicated by the word, though the sound of the word may modify these feelings very subtly, as may other accidental qualities, especially if the word be used skillfully in a given context. The accidental qualities of a word, however, such as its literary history, for example, can only modify, cannot essentially change, for these will be governed ultimately by the concept; that is, *fire* will seldom be used to signify *plum-blossom*, and so will have few opportunities to gather connotations from the concept, *plum-blossom*. The relationship, in the poem, between rational statement and feeling, is thus seen to be that of motive to emotion.

Seventh Problem

But has not this reasoning brought us back to the proposition that all poems are equally good? For if each word motivates its own feeling, because of its intrinsic nature, will not any rational statement, since it is composed of words, motivate the feeling exactly proper to it?

This is not true, for a good many

reasons, of which I shall enumerate only a few of the more obvious. In making a rational statement, in purely theoretical prose, we find that our statement may be loose or exact, depending upon the relationships of the words to each other. The precision of a word depends to some extent upon its surroundings. This is true likewise with respect to the connotations of words. Two words, each of which has several usably close rational synonyms, may reinforce and clarify each other with respect to their connotations or they may not do so.

Let me illustrate with a simple example from Browning's *Serenade at the Villa:*

So wore night; the East was gray,
    White the broad-faced hemlock flowers.

The lines are marred by a crowding of long syllables and difficult consonants, but they have great beauty in spite of the fault. What I wish to point out, for the sake of my argument, is the relationship between the words *wore* and *gray.* The verb *wore* means literally that the night passed, but it carries with it connotations of exhaustion and attrition which belong to the condition of the protagonist; and grayness is a color which we associate with such a condition. If we change the phrase to read: "Thus night passed," we shall have the same rational meaning, and a meter quite as respectable, but no trace of the power of the line: the connotation of *wore* will be lost, and the connotation of *gray* will remain merely in a state of ineffective potentiality. The protagonist in seeing his feeling mirrored in the landscape is not guilty of motivating his feeling falsely, for we know his general motive from the poem as a whole; he is expressing a portion of the feeling motivated by the total situation through a more or less common psychological phenomenon. If the poem were

such, however, that we did not know why the night *wore* instead of *passed,* we should have just cause for complaint; in fact, most of the strength of the word would probably be lost. The second line contains other fine effects, immediately with reference to the first line, ultimately with reference to the theme; I leave the reader to analyze them for himself, but he will scarcely succeed without the whole poem before him.

Concepts, as represented by particular words, are affected by connotations due to various and curious accidents. A word may gather connotations from its use in folk-poetry, in formal poetry, in vulgar speech, or in technical prose: a single concept might easily be represented by four words with these distinct histories; and any one of the words might prove to be proper in a given poetic context. Words gain connotation from etymological accidents. Something of this may be seen in the English word *outrage,* in which is commonly felt, in all likelihood, something associated with *rage,* although there is no rage whatever in the original word. Similarly the word *urchin,* in modern English, seldom connotes anything related to hedgehogs, or to the familiars of the witches, by whose intervention the word arrived at its modern meaning and feeling. Yet the connotation proper to any stage in the history of such a word might be resuscitated, or a blend of connotations effected, by skillful use. Further, the connotation of a word may be modified very strongly by its function in the metrical structure, a matter which I shall discuss at length in connection with the theories of Ransom.

This is enough to show that exact motivation of feeling by concept is not inherent in any rational statement. Any rational statement will govern the general possibilities of feeling derivable from it, but the task of the poet is to adjust feeling to motive precisely. He has to select words containing not only the right relationships within themselves, but the right relationships to each other. The task is very difficult; and this is no doubt the reason why the great poetry of a great poet is likely to be very small in bulk.

EIGHTH PROBLEM

Is it not possible, however, to escape from this relationship of motive to emotion by confining ourselves very largely to those words which denote emotion: love, envy, anger, and the like?

This is not possible, for these words, like others, represent concepts. If we should confine ourselves strictly to such a vocabulary, we should merely write didactic poetry: poetry about love in general, or about anger in general. The emotion communicated would result from our apprehension of the ideas in question. Such poetry is perfectly legitimate, but it is only one kind of poetry, and it is scarcely the kind which the Romantic theorist is endeavoring to define.

Such poetry has frequently been rendered particular by the use of allegory. The playful allegorizing of minor amoristic themes which one encounters in the Renaissance and which is possibly descended from certain neo-Platonic elements in medieval poetry may serve as illustration. Let us consider these and the subsequent lines by Thomas Lodge:

Love in my bosom like a bee
  Doth suck his sweet,
Now with his wings he plays with me,
  Now with his feet.

Love itself is a very general idea and might include many kinds of experience; the idea is limited by this allegory to the sentimental and sensual, but we still have an idea, the subdivision of the original idea, and the feeling must be appropriate to the concept. The concept is rendered concrete by the image of Cupid, whose actions, in turn, are rendered visible by comparison to the bee: it is these actions which make the poem a kind of anticipatory meditation on more or less sensual love, a meditation which by its mere tone of expression keeps the subject in its proper place as a very minor one. Sometimes the emphasis is on the mere description of the bee, sometimes on the description of Cupid, sometimes on the lover's feeling; but the feeling motivated in any passage is governed by this emphasis. The elements, once they are united in the poem, are never really separated, of course. In so far as the poet departs from his substantial theme in the direction of mere bees and flowers, he will achieve what Ransom calls irrelevance; but if there is much of this the poem will be weakened. Whether he so departs or not, the relation of motive to emotion must remain the same, within each passage. I have discussed this problem in my essay on Ransom.

A common romantic practice is to use words denoting emotions, but to use them loosely and violently, as if the very carelessness expressed emotion. Another is to make a general statement, but seem to refer it to a particular occasion, which, however, is never indicated: the poet thus seems to avoid the didactic, yet he is not forced to understand the particular motive. Both these faults may be seen in these lines from Shelley:

Out of the day and night
A joy has taken flight;
  Fresh spring, and summer, and winter
    hoar,
Move my faint heart with grief, but with
    delight
  No more—oh, never more.

The poet's intention is so vague, however, that he achieves nothing but stereotypes of a very crude kind.

The Romantics often tried other devices. For example, it would be possible to write a poem on fear in general, but to avoid in some measure the effect of the purely didactic by illustrating the emotion along the way with various experiences which might motivate fear. There is a danger here, though it is merely a danger, that the general idea may not dominate the poem, and that the poem may thus fall apart into a group of poems on particular experiences. There is the alternative danger, that the particular quality of the experiences may be so subordinated to the illustrative function of the experiences, that within each illustration there is merely a stereotyped and not a real relationship of motive to feeling: this occurs in Collins' *Ode to Fear*, though a few lines in the Epode come surprisingly to life. But the methods which I have just described really offer no semblance of an escape from the theory of motivation which I am defending.

Another Romantic device, if it is conscious enough to be called a device, is to offer instead of a defensible motive a false one, usually culled from landscape. This kind of writing represents a tacit admission of the principle of motivation which I am defending, but a bad application of the principle. It results in the kind of writing which I have called pseudo-reference in my volume, *Primitivism and Decadence*. One cannot believe, for example, that Wordsworth's passions were charmed away by a look at the daffodils, or that Shelley's were aroused by the sight of the leaves blown about in the autumn wind. A motive is offered, and the poet wants us to accept it, but we recognize it as inadequate. In such a poem there may be fragments of good description, which motivate a feeling more or less purely appropriate to the objects described, and these fragments may sustain our liking for the poem: this happens in Collins' *Ode to Evening*; but one will find also an account of some kind of emotion essentially irrelevant to the objects described, along with the attempt, more or less explicit, to deduce the emotion from the object.

There remains the method of the Post-Romantics, whether French Symbolists or American Experimentalists: the method of trying to extinguish the rational content of language while retaining the content of association. This method I have discussed in *Primitivism and Decadence*, and I shall discuss it again in this book.

NINTH PROBLEM

The relationship in the poem of rational meaning to feeling we have seen to be that of motive to emotion; and we have seen that this must be a satisfactory relationship. How do we determine whether such a relationship is satisfactory? We determine it by an act of moral judgment. The question then arises whether moral judgments can be made, whether the concept of morality is or is not an illusion.

If morality can be considered real, if a theory of morality can be said to derive from reality, it is because it guides us toward the greatest happiness which the accidents of life permit: that is, toward the fullest realization of our nature, in the Aristotelian or Thomistic sense. But is there such a thing, abstractly considered, as full realization of our nature?

To avoid discussion of too great length, let us consider the opposite question: is there such a thing as obviously unfulfilled human nature? Obviously there is. We need only turn to the feeble-minded, who cannot think and so cannot perceive or feel with any clarity; or to the insane, who sometimes perceive and feel with great intensity, but whose feelings and perceptions are so improperly motivated that they are classed as illusions. At slightly higher levels, the criminal, the dissolute, the unscrupulously selfish, and various types of neurotics are likely to arouse but little disagreement as examples.

Now if we are able to recognize the fact of insanity—if in fact we are forced to recognize it—that is, the fact of the obvious maladjustment of feeling to motive, we are forced to admit the possibility of more accurate adjustment, and, by necessary sequence, of absolutely accurate adjustment, even though we admit the likelihood that most people will attain to a final adjustment but very seldom indeed. We can guide ourselves toward such an adjustment in life, as in art, by means of theory and the critical examination of special instances; but the final act of judgment is in both life and art a unique act—it is a relationship between two elements, the rational understanding and the feeling, of which only one is classificatory and of which the other has infinite possibilities of variation.

Tenth Problem

If the final act of adjustment is a unique act of judgment, can we say that it is more or less right, provided it is demonstrably within the general limits prescribed by the theory of morality which has led to it? The answer to this question is implicit in what has preceded; in fact the answer resembles exactly that reached at the end of the first problem examined. We can say that it is more or less nearly right. If extreme deviation from right judgment is obvious,

then there is such a thing as right judgment. The mere fact that life may be conducted in a fairly satisfactory manner, by means of inaccurate judgment within certain limits, and that few people ever bother to refine their judgment beyond the stage which enables them to remain largely within those limits, does not mean that accurate judgment has no reality. Implicit in all that has preceded is the concept that in any moral situation, there is a right judgment as an ultimate possibility; that the human judge, or actor, will approximate it more or less nearly; that the closeness of his approximation will depend upon the accuracy of his rational understanding and of his intuition, and upon the accuracy of their interaction upon each other.

Eleventh Problem

Nothing has thus far been said about human action, yet morality is supposed to guide human action. And if art is moral, there should be a relationship between art and human action.

The moral judgment, whether good, bad, or indifferent, is commonly the prelude and instigation to action. Hastily or carefully, intelligently or otherwise, one arrives at some kind of general idea of a situation calling for action, and one's idea motivates one's feeling: the act results. The part played by will, or the lack of it, between judgment and act, the possibility that action may be frustrated by some constitutional or habitual weakness or tendency, such as cowardice or a tendency to anger, in a person of a fine speculative or poetic judgment, are subjects for a treatise on ethics or psychology; a treatise on poetry stops with the consideration of the speculative judgment, which reaches its best form and expression in poetry. In the situations of daily life, one does not, as a rule, write a poem before acting: one makes a more rapid and simple judgment. But if the poem does not individually lead to a particular act, it does not prevent action. It gives us a better way of judging representative acts than we should otherwise have. It is thus a civilizing influence: it trains our power of judgment, and should, I imagine, affect the quality of daily judgments and actions.

TWELFTH PROBLEM

What, then, is the nature of the critical process?

It will consist (1) of the statement of such historical or biographical knowledge as may be necessary in order to understand the mind and method of the writer; (2) of such analysis of his literary theories as we may need to understand and evaluate what he is doing; (3) of a rational critique of the paraphrasable content (roughly, the motive) of the poem; (4) of a rational critique of the

feeling motivated—that is, of the details of style, as seen in language and technique; and (5) of the final act of judgment, a unique act, the general nature of which can be indicated, but which cannot be communicated precisely, since it consists in receiving from the poet his own final and unique judgment of his matter and in judging that judgment. It should be noted that the purpose of the first four processes is to limit as narrowly as possible the region in which the final unique act is to occur.

In the actual writing of criticism, a given task may not require all of these processes, or may not require that all be given equal emphasis; or it may be that in connection with a certain writer, whether because of the nature of the writer or because of the way in which other critics have treated him previously, one or two of these processes must be given so much emphasis that others must be neglected for lack of space. These are practical matters to be settled as the occasions arise.

FROM CLASSIC, ROMANTIC AND MODERN
Jacques Barzun[*]

Barzun examines the classic and romantic perspectives as a basis for the claims, sound and unsound, which each makes against the other in the twentieth century.

I

Two conclusions have so far emerged from our concern with romanticism. One

* The essay is Chapter III, "The Classic Objection," reprinted from *Classic, Romantic and Modern*, by Jacques Barzun, by permission of Little, Brown and Co.–Atlantic Monthly Press. Copyright © 1943, 1961 by Jacques Barzun.

is that it is a complex movement, whose direct connection with any doctrine in our own day cannot be asserted offhand or lightheartedly. The other is that romanticism has to do with creating a new society different from its immediate forerunner. Since we ourselves are living in an epoch of travail, perhaps of creation, and since there is fear of what some are pleased to call a new romanticism, we must, before going further, attend to the pre- or anti-romantic outlook; the old order which romanticism left behind when it repudiated—as the phrase goes —classicism and rationalism.

Given the native absolutism of the human mind, we may take it for granted that every epoch looks for unity—unity within the human breast and unity in the institutions sheltering man. Now the straightest path to unity is to choose from all possible ways of living those that seem to the ruling powers most profitable, most sensible, most general; and to enforce these as a code for public and private behavior. The laws soon give rise to attitudes by which any man may shape his feelings, and this in turn brings about a ready understanding among men. For no matter how arbitrary, conventions are useful and can be relied upon in proportion as they are held inviolable.

Such a system produces stability in the state and with it all the attributes of the static: fixed grandeur, dignity, authority, and high polish; while in the individual it produces morality and peace by showing him that values are rooted in the universe, rather than dependent upon his fallible and changing judgment. This, I take it, is the view of life properly called "classical," irrespective of whether it is enforced upon Europe under Louis XIV, or advocated anywhere today by the proponents of a new or old order. It is an attractive view and it draws out the best in those who make themselves its master-builders. It calls for intelligence, discipline, unselfish renunciation of private desires, a sense of social solidarity, and punctilious behavior towards other members of one's own caste.

From these premises, it follows that everything the romanticist thinks and does is wrong: far from taking the short cut to unity and peace, he insists on the reality of double-mindedness and self-contradiction. He denies the beauty and fitness of the conventions that bind men together and prefers the loose human diversity. Sharply aware of his own desires, he argues that the social rule is oppressive and unjust, so that he becomes, potentially at least, an anarchist. Being an anarchist in an anarchical world, he places a high value on effort, strife, energy. He is therefore in the position of constantly bewailing a condition for which he is solely to blame: Having refused all help from social conventions, his art, philosophy, and religion are bound to remain diversified, many-shaped, chaotic—hence unsatisfying.

This, I believe, is a fair copy of the classic objection—classic because it has been so often uttered and because it has been uttered in the name of classicism. In common speech, certainly, the sentiments aroused by the word "classical" are those of repose and serenity, while the connotations of "romantic" suggest restlessness and disorder. It is perhaps inevitable that something of these associations should always cling to these two words; but it is desirable for the moment to make a conscious effort at forgetting them, in order to look upon both classicism and romanticism historically. Instead of two neatly paired abstractions, of two contrasted ideals falling into familiar formulas, consider classicism and romanticism as recurring facts. Let us try moreover to imagine some concrete case for every generality and to generalize from the examples we are about to take up.

For the contrast I began by describing is obviously and falsely heightened. It takes the abstract perfection of classicism and matches it with the concrete imperfection of romanticism. If the comparison were historically fair, we should properly expect the men of a classical age to be as completely happy as it is possible for humans to be; and we should expect the men of a romantic age to kill themselves en masse, like lemmings. But this has not happened. The wails of the classical gentlemen about existence differ in tone, but not in subject matter, from those of the romanticists; and beneath the difference in tone we shall find certain facts which afford a better test of cultural meanings than the routine antitheses about *the* classicist and *the* romanticist.

To begin with, the opponents of romanticism are strong on generalities but rather weak on particular cases. This is indeed consistent with the other tastes that make them prefer classicism. It is because they are bewildered by romanticist concreteness and diversity that they seek refuge in the simplicity which classicism achieves by generalizing and abstracting. And here comes the pragmatic test: how far can abstracting and generalizing be carried as a device for organizing society? Clearly some unity of opinion, some common ground, is indispensable to every social order. Romanticism does not deny it, either in theory or in practice. The romanticists may have defied certain conventions, but they did not go about naked. They praised originality but they did not talk each in his own private language. Still, let us suppose for the sake of argument that on the basis of some degree of uniformity one desires to abstract and generalize, so as to build a stable classical order. One decrees that Man is a clothed creature, whose proper, because logical, language is French, and whose destiny is to live according to the Christian religion under an hereditary monarchy. How far can one go without meeting some actual instance that defies the universal rule? The world being what it is, not very far.

There are then two courses to follow: one is to remove the exception by pretending that it does not count; the other is to remove it by enforcing conformity.

The reasoning here proposed is not so fantastic as it seems. It is neither a straw man nor an imaginary instance, but simply one feature of the historic ideal embodied in seventeenth-century French classicism. The absolutist temper of that century removed the "exception" of the unclothed man by calling him a savage "who does not count," while the unorthodox habit of speaking a foreign tongue was removed by declaring French the universal language and successfully imposing it on all Europe.

This suggests that if a just comparison is to be made with the historic romanticists, we must look not at a theoretical classicism found in books or fancied in ancient Greece, but at an actual classicism found at work in modern history. This is another way of saying that we must look behind the Versailles façade of the Age of Louis XIV, with its alliance between an absolute monarchy and an absolute church, and assess the work of the half-century 1661–1715, which established a new order and succeeded in enforcing it upon manners, behavior, language, art, and thought. This classical age followed appropriately upon a period of political disorders, national disunity, and dynastic troubles. Once established, it entered upon a career of territorial aggrandizement and it spread its culture by snobbery and force of arms to the rest of Europe. The pattern of conformity came to England with the restored Stuarts who had lived in exile at the French court; and everywhere in the following century it evolved into a cosmopolitan classicism, during which its ideals became less and less compelling or productive, until the ground was cleared for the romantic revival.

To sketch in this way the career of a modern classicism is to treat it as it were from outside. Within, the first important fact confronting us is that classicism must begin by making, by manufacturing, its unity. Then, when this artificial unity has been enforced long enough to have become habitual, classicism is sure that it has been found ready-made in nature. This explains why the classical period used the two words Reason and Nature interchangeably, and why the romanticists, in repudiating classical Reason, had to give Nature an entirely different meaning.

What lent support to the seventeenth-century view that reason and nature are one is that the classical scheme of society coincided with a great scientific epoch; an epoch, moreover, specializing upon the one branch of science most congenial to the classical temper. I mean mathematics. For mathematics also abstracts and generalizes and yields simplicity and certainty while appearing to find these ready-made in nature. Seeing the beautiful demonstrations of Descartes and Newton as they explained the heavens with their coordinates, the great classical minds sought to rival this perfection and simplicity on earth. Philosophers used the geometrical method to arrive at moral and religious truth; social scientists reduced government to mechanics; the tragic muse imitated the tight deductive gait of Euclid; and I am not merely playing upon words when I say that poetry itself adopted one common meter as if scientific accuracy depended upon it. In all the imponderables of life, conduct, and art, the test was no longer the flexible, "Is it good, true, or beautiful for such and such a purpose?" but "Is it correct?"

As the classicists are wont to boast, the tremendous pressure of all these restrictions and rigidities produced some magnificent expressions of human genius.

Racine and Boileau, Dryden, Swift, and Pope, Lully, Rameau, and Handel, the English portraitists and the French landscape school, created an abundance of great works to which we return with ever-renewed pleasure and admiration.

Yet there is to this brilliant period a darker and a neglected side. It is surely no accident that Pascal's *Thoughts*, written at the height of classicism, but undermining it, should begin with a distinction between the geometrical mind and the intuitive. Pascal's actual phrase to express the latter is *esprit de finesse*, which means the ability to distinguish and deal with concrete things, with living beings, as against the geometrician's ability to manipulate abstractions and definitions of the nonexistent. The geometrician's universe is articulate, colorless, and clear-cut; the *esprit de finesse* on the contrary sees the color, continuity, and indefiniteness of things. The *esprit de finesse*, in short, is the instrument of romanticist perception, though romanticism does not necessarily begin and end in the realm of concrete detail.

The two types of mind contrasted by Pascal are alike capable of subtlety and greatness, but the geometrician works in a closed universe, limited by his own axioms and definitions; the romanticist works in an open universe, limited by concrete imperfections—imperfections which have not all been charted, which may change, and which need not be the same for all men. Classicism is geometrical in its assumption that human shortcomings must be disregarded in order to be corrected, correctness being stated in the form of an exact rule. Romanticism is *finesse* in the belief that exactitude is only a guide to thought, less important than fact, and never worthy of receiving human sacrifices. Classicism is therefore stability within known limits; romanticism is expansion within limits known and unknown.

An enforced choice at this point would, it is true, probably still incline us toward the classical as meeting more nearly the requirements of such a wayward creature as man. Since man wants certainty and stability, it seems better to have known limits and known ways of moving towards them. As a seventeenth-century English poet, Robert Herrick, phrased it under the title *Rules for Our Reach:*—

Men must have bounds how farre to
walk; for wc
Are made farre worse by lawless liberty.

But there is a great doubt concealed within the safer choice: does a geometrical order yield stability when imposed on life? The question can perhaps be answered by comparing this same seventeenth century with the agreeable fictions that are current about it. Modern critics who are avowed enemies of our century and the last, yearn for the classical order as having given to the best men full scope, high honors, and true peace. Under classical rules, they say, the artist is not a rebel at war with society and his public; he satisfies a settled taste and is a willing supporter of the established regime. Under classical morality, the good man is reasonably happy; he is not, as with us, driven by the chaos of manners and codes into morbid guilt and fanatical efforts at reform. Lastly, under classical religion, the human mind finds an unshakable embodiment of its own permanent values, making impossible that modern freakishness or irresponsibility of belief which turns every man into a puzzle or threat to every other man and robs the state of all cohesiveness. In a word, the classical order acts as an infallible balance wheel to steady the human emotions.

Yet on looking at the classical centuries in biographical detail, one is struck by the amount and kind of ill-repressed human feeling beneath the crust of serenity and politeness. The number of converts to the forbidden religion of tears, self-mortification, and enthusiasm which goes by the name of Pietism was considerable. They include Pascal, Racine, and Fénelon. The names of Mme. Guyon and of the convent of Port-Royal will suggest many more; and a famous chapter in Voltaire's *Age of Louis XIV* tells us in a satirical vein about the unhappy quarrels and tribulations of those the historian mocks as fools and bigots. Far from keeping a religious balance, Louis XIV and Mme. de Maintenon themselves ended their reign as extremists in superstition and devoutness, an excess which swung the early eighteenth century into libertinism and atheism.

As for the standard comparison between the classical geniuses, thoroughly in harmony with their age, and the romantic rebels divorced from their society, it is simply not true. To take France alone, the first case we meet is Corneille's compulsory retirement after his quarrel with the Academy. Some may feel that Corneille was a belated romanticist harking back to the Renaissance. We must then recall Racine's struggles with his critics and the cabals which cut off his career at thirty-eight. Another genius, La Fontaine, was forgiven his nonconformity only because he seemed a child, a "natural," who loved the woods, and would not be acclimated to the only classical life—city life. Molière himself, supposedly the great interpreter of classical moderation and social sense, harbored a dissenter within. It was the dissenter who created the Alceste of the *Misanthrope* in his own image, who maintained the tradition of popular speech against refined diction, and whose death robbed the world of a projected satire on the highest classical product, the courtier.

The poets were not alone in feeling out of joint with the times. What we find among the philosophers, from Descartes to Voltaire, is one long story of persecution and flight from authority, only a little less violent than the harrying out of the Huguenots after the Revocation of the Edict of Nantes.

Because of the force of authority in all departments of classic life, it has become a commonplace that the romantic cry for freedom reveals an egotist. We take it for granted that the classic ego is silent if not subdued. But this is mere forgetfulness on our part. Compare the prefaces of Boileau, a classicist, with those of Victor Hugo, a romanticist. Contrary to your expectations, you will find that whereas Hugo is chiefly concerned with the principles of the artistic battle he is waging, Boileau seems to be interested only in reporting the praise that has been lavished on him and in disputing the statements of fault-finding critics. Hugo is "objective," historical-minded, occasionally grandiloquent; Boileau is "subjective," autobiographical, downright pettish. Or again, turn to Racine's prefaces—there are usually two to each play, the first rather grumpy and quarrelsome about the play's reception, which was seldom satisfactory; the second more complacent, because, after all, Racine knows what he is worth.

I am not saying, of course, that Racine and Boileau were egomaniacs. I believe rather that the reason their egotism seems so personal and small is to be found in the very nature of the classical scheme of things. It is the worst of the classicist beliefs that all true judgments are absolute and universal. As the King rules, so is the law. By extension, what is decreed by that vague abstraction, polite society, must be correct; for standards are common and public and there

is no such thing as individual taste. In reality the polite world is a single cabal or critic. Hence any attack on an artist is fraught for him with grave consequences. Unless repelled it may mean ostracism, because society pretends to be unanimous. In any case it means battle, which explains the fate of Corneille and Racine, and the narrow escapes of Molière and La Fontaine. Indeed, the story of Poussin's or Bernini's misadventures with officialdom, and the function of the Royal Academy under the dictatorship of the First Painter to the King, Charles Lebrun, form a tale of coercion, jealousy, subservience, and war against all but mediocre talents, such as must give pause to the most sanguine neoclassicists. Pascal himself was not secure in his private retreat from a classical church and state jealous of all individualism.

In other words, the classical hierarchy maintains an unruffled front behind which all the fighting passions of men go on just as usual. But these passions take an especially heavy toll because there is no legitimate shelter in some other group —a second, or third, or fourth party— based on diverse interests and tastes. For the artist, the classic society is like a disunited family that is compelled to live together in a single room. There is hatred but no fair field for it. At the same time the issues lack magnitude; they are personalities. To read the memoirs of Saint-Simon gives one a painful impression of frivolity, even of immaturity at the root of the system. His admirably drawn figures are like schoolboys, kicking and cuffing one another under the table while the royal master is not looking.

II

These conflicts of authority and individual wills are not peculiar to classicism; only their form, and the pretense that no conflict is there. All of which naturally brings up the classical antithesis between Reason and Emotion. With its bent towards social unanimity how does classicism cope with man's emotions? Classicism does not of course deny their existence. It merely says that for the sake of decency certain feelings only can be exhibited—pleasure, amusement, ridicule, surprise, a few others—and these in their mildest form. For the same reason, gestures, fervor, eccentricity, must be suppressed, so that the social stage—the salon or the court—shall be peopled by human beings whose contacts will resemble those of perfectly smooth and well-lubricated ball bearings. With this ideal, incidentally, go some admirable rules of conversation which it would be well for modern man to meditate. But the trouble with the social device of repression throughout is, again, that there is no outlet, no elsewhere, for the force generated by pressure to expend itself, either harmlessly or productively.

This force, it may be said, has no right to intrude itself on society's attention. It is for the individual to dispose of it, since it is, by definition, irrational. More than that, it is *the* Irrational. Granted. But it is precisely called the Irrational because it cannot be argued out of existence, "it" being the blind and resistless force that we call life. Abstract reason is here simply irrelevant. Rather we must look for the socially accepted channels that may help drain off these energies. Whether admitted or concealed, these channels exist.

What investment, so to speak, could the classic century make of its fund of unreasoning passion? Taking for granted the ancient tradition of love-making, we discover several other institutions for expressing emotion. One excellent object of enthusiasm was the person of the King. Whoever thinks the romanticists worshiped heroes foolishly had better see

for himself how much time and effort went into deifying the *Roi Soleil*. Certainly there is no extravagance in the nineteenth century comparable to the folly uttered and acted out when Louis XIV crossed the Rhine in 1672. One would suppose he had actually fought a battle and built a bridge like Caesar. His virtue, his grandeur, his words, his appetite, his form—nothing seemed too slight to deserve exaggeration. Perhaps the nation was worshiping itself through the King: it was a time of aggressive imperialism; the fact remains that it was hero-worship, and concentrated upon a non-hero.

At all times, in spite of his title of Most Christian Majesty, the monarch was reverenced—and painted and sculptured—as a pagan emperor-god, and the state followed imperial precedent by exacting (or purchasing) from its most brilliant talents the most profuse expressions of praise. The King could see his figure reflected from every wall and outlined in every square. In an Academy presumably devoted to letters, it was customary rather than strange to hear a new appointee—often an ecclesiastic who had never published a line—signalize the cultural greatness of the regime by saying:—

What have I been doing thus far? Why have I spent so much time admiring in Antiquity examples of virtue which I deemed without equal? Our age has gathered them all up, greater and more pure, in the person of the monarch to whom Heaven has subjected us for our greater happiness . . . [and to whom we owe] a great state better organized in all its parts, order more solidly established . . . our frontiers more gloriously extended, our enemies more promptly conquered, our neighbors put in greater fear or respect towards us, . . . everywhere a more perfect union between the Head and the Members. . . .

All these great and wonderful qualities

. . . united in him whom we have the honor to obey . . . will henceforth furnish me with a nobler object for my admiration and my studies, and a fitter subject for my praise than any of those I have found in ancient history.

Though the pension system will account for much of this adulation, we must remember that even without bribes flattery is a binding medium between the layers of classical society. For in its effect upon the emotions the theory of rank serves a double purpose. According to it, each man is absolutely better and nobler than the man below him, hence energy can go into emulation, *noblesse oblige* —and social climbing. But at the same time, the single code common to all men of honor restores a kind of equality and releases a certain amount of passion, by giving egotism an outlet through the point of honor.

King-worship, love-making, intrigue, etiquette, dueling, will certainly take up a good deal of slack in the sphere of the irrational, but there were still other socially approved channels for feeling in the seventeenth century. The playhouse —not quite so orderly then as now—was one. Watching public executions was another, a pastime which in eighteenth-century England degenerated into the worship of the highwayman. The life of leisure and the constraints of politeness encouraged pleasures that were violent and exhausting. Sport embraced gaming, hunting, and the playing of murderous practical jokes; not to mention lavish entertainment, which was often so extravagant that the expense ruined the host if the King did not rescue him in return. In all these it is not the thing itself, but the lengths to which it is carried that is a significant comment on "reason."

Such were the energetic manifestations of feeling tolerated under classicism. There were also more passive ones. The literature of the seventeenth century, we must not forget, was not limited to the high tragedies and comedies that we still read. The age consumed a great quantity of long-winded romances about Grecian heroes, shepherds and shepherdesses, swooning lovers, and marvelous adventures. Books like *The Great Cyrus* and the *Astrea* were not read by the lower classes but by the aristocracy; they were not confined to France but were translated or imitated abroad. Parlor games grew out of such reading, and nature imitated art to the pitch that Molière records in *Les Précieuses Ridicules*.

Lastly, classicism had to recognize, though perhaps it did not relish, two flaws of temperament that we are likely to forget in speaking of classical balance. One was melancholy, a familiar yet half-hidden manifestation of the strength of the feelings. The other was vindictiveness. We should like to know more about the settled sadness of the moralist La Rochefoucauld, whose melancholy, as he tells us, came not only from his constitution, "but from elsewhere." We ought also to ponder the strange irresoluteness of Dryden's faith, the true source of Swift's "savage indignation," and the mental depression which the young Alexander Pope suffered during his four years at Binfield. Perhaps Pope recovered by main strength of Newtonian reason. Certain it is that in *The Dunciad* he discharged passion enough for a lifetime. Yet characteristically this passion was the undiluted one of hatred, turned upon men whose crime was either to have offended him or to have remained lowly and poor. Finally, in the supposed paragon of sound eighteenth-century common sense, Dr. Johnson, emotional troubles and the fear of death were so deeply implanted that a sympathetic critic can only describe him as "melancholy almost to madness, radically wretched, diseased, indolent," and unpredictable in his actions.

Historic classicism is therefore not the blessed epoch that some modern critics like to imagine. Without taking Pope or Racine or Dr. Johnson as typical—for they are the finest products of the age and its best recommendation—we can nevertheless infer something from so much covert rebellion, hate, and misery. The least we can infer is that classicism does not necessarily bring peace to the individual and stability to the state. Making "admirable rules" is one thing; enforcing them, another; and still another, having them enforced upon oneself by the eternal knaves and fools whom Racine suffered or Pope pickled in vinegar.

If it is objected that the facts I have presented are only the by-products of a fine distillation, I fully agree. No one should argue that classicist art, philosophy, or science are diminished by stating the conditions under which they were created. Nor is personal taste involved. I for one enthusiastically admire many of the seventeenth-century masters, and am not so foolish as to think less of Johnson as a critic because he showed psychiatric symptoms. The argument is not about the undisputable merits of classical genius; the argument is about the feelings and behavior of representative classicists, and the political, social, moral, and esthetic forms within which they worked. The point is quite simple: the usual comparison between classic and romantic depicts a wonderfully ordered greenhouse as the nursery of the former and a desperate battleground as the ungrateful soil of the latter. That comparison is false.

More than that, the catchword "tradition," which is monopolized by the pro-

ponents of classical order, helps to conceal the important fact that seventeenth-century classicism was nearly everywhere a break with European national traditions and a return to an imaginary Graeco-Roman past. It was just such another "break" as that of the Renaissance before, and Romanticism after. Classicism naturally borrowed from the Renaissance, but looked upon itself as civilized order replacing barbaric chaos. Quite specifically, the French classicists were asserting their independence from the Italians who had been their masters during the previous century and a half. But whether in politics or art, nothing could be further from the *ancient* classic spirit than the products of seventeenth- and eighteenth-century Europe.

To be sure, poets, painters, and academic critics ceaselessly invoked the ancients and pretended to follow them humbly, but the rules they tried to respect and enforce upon one another were as arbitrary and as "original" as those of any "revolting" romantic. It is precisely because modern classicism was an original creation, and not a copy, that it deserves to be called great. It differed from romanticism in seeking greatness through the adoption of common forms which it tried to make exclusive. In this sense it is "traditional" and resembles other periods of thoroughgoing orthodoxy—including the earlier phases of ancient civilizations—where individualism in art, action, or belief is sternly repressed.

Pro-classical critics are wont to say of some romanticist they half admire, "If only he had had discipline!" It would be easy to retort of a classicist, "If only he had been let alone by rule-ridden mediocrities!" Both statements are antihistorical. The choice does not exist, for artists find themselves inspired or crushed by institutions which they are not alone in making. That is why it is important to know what is achieved when the general will produces a classical order, and at what cost. To suppose that one can have classicism without authoritarianism is like supposing that one can have braking power without friction. Conversely, romanticism is not simply love of ease or impatient rebellion. It is a different way of fulfilling human wants after the breakdown of an attempt at eternal order.

III

The question of human wants brings us back from historic to *intrinsic* classicism, for a second look at the classical meanings of Reason, Nature, and Feeling. The classic objection to romantic psychology is that it accepts an inner dualism—the "two souls in one breast" which publicists in wartime like to think especially German, if only because it is exemplified in Goethe's *Faust*. In romanticism, the two souls can be variously interpreted. I have chosen as most basic man's double consciousness of power and weakness. Another expression of the feeling is the Christian awareness of grace and sin. A third is the conflict between man's sense of values and his knowledge that nature is indifferent, this last being another form of Pascal's loneliness in the eternal silent spaces.

The classicist view of man's mind also recognizes the split but makes it fall in a different place. Following one of Plato's myths, it sees the soul as a charioteer driving a team of wild horses. The charioteer is Reason, the wild horses are the emotions. Some emotions are good, some evil; the driver is of the same sort as the good. Classic man is a kind of Centaur— man above and horse beneath. Now, one of the features of classical Reason is that

it can be put into words and become common property. Hence a society can be built which embodies Reason and helps each individual to drive his equipage on the straight road of duty and decency.

So natural is this psychological metaphor that we still speak of reason and emotion as opposites, we use the Head and the Heart as images of rival powers. Even when we repeat Pascal's phrase "The heart has its reasons which the reason does not know" we tend to mistake its meaning and to use it as an equivalent of: "It is sometimes good to do something which our judgment disapproves." We go so far in our slipshod use of words on this subject that we commonly characterize certain people as "emotional," as if they were cursed with pure emotion, or with more emotion than others. Freudian psychology is doing something to correct this error by pointing out how deceptive is the calm of so-called repressed personalities. The task is difficult because common speech imputes the wish to go beserk to anyone who challenges the classic figure of the charioteer.

Fortunately, in this same classical seventeenth century there lived a philosopher of blameless and even stoical life, who can act as a character witness for the anti-classical view of emotion. I refer to Spinoza, and to his demonstration that the only way the human mind can conquer an emotion is by attaching its thought to another and stronger emotion. According to Spinoza, Reason is not a charioteer; it does not play the role of a guardian angel pushing back the demons into the pit; reason is but a guide, always moved by some emotion and pointing to an object. By effort and training, ideas can be detached from one deep-lying motive and reattached to another. As William James showed, will power consists in the ability to sustain an idea against its competitors from within the stream of thought. It is imagination plus attention. Hence there is never an emotion without an idea, nor an idea without an emotion. In the so-called reasonable man there is an awareness of motives and consequences which gives the impression that reason is wholly aloof from passion; but this is an illusion —the illusion upon which classicism builds its society.

This corrected view of the human passions explains why it is not sufficient to know the good in order to achieve it. It explains why copybook maxims always seem empty words until "something hits us." If this is true, we should cease to qualify a man or a mob as "emotional" when what we mean is that the ideas of the one or the other are crude, over-simple, and destructive. If we ever come to feel this difference clearly enough to change our clichés, we shall know that it takes as much emotion to solve a differential equation as it does to write a sonnet, and we shall stop speaking of "cold reason" and its counterpart, the "hot fit of inspiration," as if the categories of the plumber would suit the psychologist.

Spinoza is a doubly telling witness, for it so happens that, like Pascal, he was neglected by his classical age and rediscovered by the romantics. On the point we have been discussing, they all saw alike, and what they saw was not a need to glorify emotion or to give up thinking; it was something much more subtle and important, namely, the need to find organic unity within the human animal— the mind harmoniously expressing the demands of the feelings. Pascal who said "The whole duty of man is to think well"; Spinoza who said that the freedom of man lay in concentrating his passions on a proper object; the romanticists who

said that the highest development of the self was true morality—all agreed that the task was one of reconciling the two souls as a prelude to social harmony. Blake put it with his usual forthrightness when he denied "that energy, called evil, is alone from the body; and that reason, called good, is alone from the soul." Contrary to the charioteer theory, he asserted that "energy is the only life and is from the body; and reason is the bound or outward circumference of energy."

It is urged against this view of reason and emotion that it sets men no common goal, and that the romanticists in particular did not seem to agree on the good life. Shall a man be a saint or a civil engineer, a gentleman of leisure or a social reformer? The disagreement exists, but it may point to an eternal feature in the world of men—its pluralism. In any case, Romanticism declined to be deceived by the sleight-of-hand with which classicism pretends that the truth has been found and can be handed to each shareholder in its limited-liability company. Classicism forgets that its truth has not been found but made; that its social order does not represent concurring wills but is imposed by a caste; and that its boasted reason is mere maxims of prudence, useful in their place, but incapable of stilling forever the diverse claims that men do in fact make upon life, and make good. There is, in short, as much weakness in mankind as classicism sees and tries to conceal, but there is also much more power than it allows room for.

In calling classicist reason "maxims of prudence," I mean that they are negative commandments, whose application to life can only be mechanical, since they fail to recognize temperamental differences among individuals and the organic bond between feeling and thought. Too

much ignored in the seventeenth century, this bond was rediscovered in the
eighteenth. The men of the Enlightenment did not underrate the irrational,
but they still dealt with it abstractly.
Voltaire's *Candide* is a complete demonstration that the world is largely the
product of impulse. But of what use is
the maxim "Cultivate your garden" except to a wise old man like the author,
who has indulged his passions for many
a year before prescribing this capsule of
wisdom? Surely it is rank unreason to
expect of the youth Candide, at the beginning of the book, that he should cultivate his garden instead of the lovely
Cunégonde's acquaintance.

The difference, then, between classical
man and romanticist on the point of
irrationalism lies wholly in a difference
of judgment and intellectual bias. It is
not a factual difference. Nothing can be
more false than to represent the rationalist as natively able to get on without trouble from his feelings, or even
as wishing to forget them. Those who
have tried to palm off this picture of a
rationalist superman might be surprised
if one asked, "Who was the first great
French writer to say that the passions
were all good?" They would certainly
shout "Rousseau" with one voice, but
the correct answer is Descartes, who concludes his *Treatise on the Passions* with
that blanket approval. His rationalism
lay in recommending a "simple method"
for controlling these all-good energies.
Hume, too, saw very clearly that "without passion, no idea has any force": and
the psychologist Hartley was far from
ignorant of the importance of the sexual
passion in shaping human character. But
they all believed in a simple common
rule of reason, almost a recipe, for maintaining equilibrium and keeping not
only the individual but society static.
When reason itself suggested that

society might stand in need of improvement, what did classicism offer on the
perplexing subject of social change?
Nothing, unless we adapt the words that
Pope applied to fashions:—

Be not the first by whom the new are
    tried,
Nor yet the last to lay the old aside.

In other words, let a romanticist begin.
Let Columbus discover America: the
classicist will come when de luxe passage
has been provided. In truth, under classicism, innovation and discovery cannot
be underwritten by society, because they
are destructive, venturesome, uncertain;
and because all the necessary forms and
truths are known. Classicism assumes its
own highest perfection and the individual who departs from it does so at his
own risk. Rousseau is accordingly compelled to define genius as that which
has the power to create from nothing,
and to add that only fiery souls ever accomplish anything.

But why should there be creation and
social change? Because although the
great classical word is "restraint," classicism is impotent to restrain the forces
that keep society alive. In the eighteenth
century, the most perfect of neo-classical
ages, the stirrings of unchanneled emotion were the most tangible force disrupt-
ing the old order. No sooner had
"civilization" reached its high point, as
all agreed, than restlessness set in and the
South Sea islands began to seem a better
world. Throughout Europe new interests
developed in popular ballads, in Gothic
architecture, in natural scenery, in sentimental stories, in informal gardens, in
tales of horror and mystery, in the Celtic
and Germanic literatures as against the
Graeco-Roman—all having the common
feature of a pleasing *irregularity*.

All these new tastes were at first affectations, for things which have been formerly neglected can only be taken up by a conscious steeling of the person against public censure. The innovator has to pretend that faddishness is a merit, and the new does not sit as lightly upon him as upon his successors. The modern connoisseur of cathedrals is a man like any other, but the first gentleman to like Gothic architecture made himself ridiculous by building false ruins.

The significant fact is that the new taste was for pleasing irregularity. Each innovation was just another fad, but all together amounted to a shift in outlook. The results were to mark an epoch not only in art and society, but in political forms and natural science. What happened in these four realms may be summed up in the words which apply particularly to science: it was a Biological Revolution. The term says plainly enough that the absolute reign of physics and mathematics was over, and with it the dominance of the Reason patterned upon these two sciences. By the end of the eighteenth century new branches of knowledge—the sciences of man—had come of age: anthropology, ethnology, and zoology were offering new facts, new analogies, new modes of thought. Cartesian and Newtonian mechanics were taken for granted; the new principle was vitalism and the new theory, evolution. The mechanical materialism which had threatened to overcome all rival philosophies was in full retreat.

The clearest manifestations of this unexpected reversal are to be found in the careers of three famous rationalists—David Hume in England; Diderot in France; Lessing in Germany. All three had won fame by battling for the Enlightenment, for Deism, for the classical view of art and life. But by dint of sticking to their method and leaving nothing untouched by it, they dethroned Reason

herself—Reason, that is, with a capital R, the Reason of the eighteenth century. A curious parallel unites the last thoughts of these men—they are consigned in dialogues, all three posthumously published. Hume's *Dialogues concerning Natural Religion* undermined Deism, and did so by means of biological comparisons and suggestions, including the notion of the survival of the fittest. In France, Diderot adopted the evolutionism of Buffon and Bordeu and became a virtual pantheist. At the same time, in his extraordinary dialogue, *Rameau's Nephew*, he plumbed the irrational depths of a human specimen chosen as if on purpose to disprove that man is a machine and to forecast the dilemmas of the romanticists.

It was Goethe who first drew Diderot's masterpiece to the world's attention. Meantime, Lessing in Germany had been having conversations with a young publicist named Jacobi, of which the burden was Lessing's enthusiastic adherence to Spinoza's psychology and Spinoza's religion. When Jacobi published an account of these conversations it caused a scandal throughout Germany: the philosophy of the Enlightenment had been dealt a mortal blow.

Why should this be so? What does biology imply that mechanics does not? It implies that life is an element and not merely a combination of dead parts. It implies organic structure and organic function. It implies that the primary reality is the individual and not either the parts of which he is made or the artificial groupings which he may enter into. This is, in a word, individualism. Within the individual, the motive power is, as its name reveals, emotion. Consciousness and intelligence remain at the top of the hierarchy of values but they are not disembodied or centered upon themselves. They serve larger interests, which are those of life itself—the survival of the individual and of the species.

Survival in turn suggests that the first law of the universe is not thought but action. As Goethe has Faust say, "In the beginning was"—not the Word, or Thought, but "the Deed." Action means effort, energy, possibly strife and certainly risk. The world is a world of novelty, in which changing situations cannot always be met by rules previously learned, though imagination can foresee and forearm the creature, who thereby becomes also an agent of creation. But imagination and creation carry with them no guarantee of success. The sustaining principle in man and his new world is therefore not reason—which is merely the already acquired and codified experience—but faith, which is hope plus the power of hope to realize itself. Why this power should work as it does is a mystery. It is the mystery at the heart of nature, which reason can guess at but not pluck out. When successful, man's reason—man's sense of power—is justified, and equally justified when he fails is his sense of weakness: in denying neither he has become a romanticist.

As a romanticist, his task is to reconcile the contraries within him by finding some entity outside himself vast enough to hold all his facts. He has become once again a religious thinker. For religion is more than a description of the Unseen. It is a theory of energy—the energy that animates nature and that animates him. To the romanticist, religion is no longer a superstition or a bald statement that the universe must have a First Cause; religion is an intellectual and emotional necessity. As Pascal said, man must wager on the existence of God, "because he is embarked." In the romantic period, man wagered on the existence of the Catholic or Protestant God, on pantheism, on art, on science, on the national state, on the future of mankind: but in all the pattern is the same. The solutions differ in concrete particulars only because salvation is ultimately individual.

With these premises, classicism—at least in its old form—cannot subsist. It had built a shelter for man on too narrow an enclosure. It had supposed society to be static, emotions compressible, and novelty needless. It had selected what seemed to it best and truest and most eternal—monarchy, orthodoxy, courtly etiquette, mathematics, and rules of art and of morality so simple that their universality could be deemed self-evident. But what had it selected these elements from? Clearly from a previous romanticism, that of the sixteenth-century Renaissance, an age of exploration and creation.

That is why, when classicism had twinges, they were like pre-natal recollections of romanticism. When Corneille drew his heroes, they were medieval knights and religious martyrs in seventeenth-century dilemmas. When Molière drew Alceste, the prospect of retiring to the country did not frighten the so-called misanthrope, but only the coquette and the flatterers he left behind. When Racine was melancholy, he wrote a simple song in which he says he feels two souls within his breast, two men struggling with each other; and on hearing the song Louis XIV is reported to have leaned over to Mme. de Maintenon and said, "How well I know these two men!" In short, the protection and certainty that classicism gave were only temporary. It is no discredit to the genius or the strength of the classicists that it should have been so. It is merely a reflection on their self-knowledge, and a damaging flaw in the anti-romantics' classic objection, that they should mistake the man-made and temporary for what is given and permanent.

CHAPTER 6

Romanticism

FROM ON THE SUBLIME
Longinus*

The treatise of Longinus (213–273 A.D.) is remarkable for the fact that of all the literary studies from antiquity it is the only one extant whose viewpoint resembles that of criticism after the mid-eighteenth century in its concern with the psychological relationship between literature and readers, with emotion and impression, with the organic nature of expression, with image and metaphor as a source of esthetic energy.

First of all, we must raise the question whether there is such a thing as an art of the sublime or lofty. Some hold that those are entirely in error who would bring such matters under the precepts of art. A lofty tone, says one, is innate, and does not come by teaching; nature is the only art that can compass it. Works of nature are, they think, made worse and altogether feebler when wizened by the rules of art. 2. But I maintain that this will be found to be otherwise if it be observed that, while nature as a rule is free and independent in matters of passion and elevation, yet is she wont not to act at random and utterly without system. Further, nature is the original and vital underlying principle in all cases, but system can define limits and fitting seasons, and can also contribute the safest rules for use and practice. Moreover, the expression of the sublime is more exposed to danger when it goes its own way without the guidance of knowledge, —when it is suffered to be unstable and unballasted,—when it is left at the mercy of mere momentum and ignorant audacity. It is true that it often needs the spur, but it is also true that it often needs the curb. 3. Demosthenes expresses the view, with regard to human life in general, that good fortune is the greatest of blessings, while good counsel, which occupies the second place, is hardly inferior in im-

* The selection is from Longinus, *On the Sublime*, translated and edited by W. Rhys Roberts, Cambridge University Press, 1899. Reprinted by permission of Cambridge University Press.

portance, since its absence contributes inevitably to the ruin of the former. This we may apply to diction, nature occupying the position of good fortune, art that of good counsel. Most important of all, we must remember that the very fact that there are some elements of expression which are in the hands of nature alone, can be learnt from no other source than art. If, I say, the critic of those who desire to learn were to turn these matters over in his mind, he would no longer, it seems to me, regard the discussion of the subject as superfluous or useless. . . .

Quell they the oven's far-flung splendour-
  glow!
Ha, let me but one hearth-abider mark—
One flame-wreath torrent-like I'll whirl on
  high;
I'll burn the roof, to cinders shrivel it!—
Nay, now my chant is not of noble strain.[1]

Such things are not tragic but pseudo-tragic—"flamewreaths," and "belching to the sky," and Boreas represented as a "flute-player," and all the rest of it. They are turbid in expression and confused in imagery rather than the product of intensity, and each one of them, if examined in the light of day, sinks little by little from the terrible into the contemptible. But since even in tragedy, which is in its very nature stately and prone to bombast, tasteless tumidity is unpardonable, still less, I presume, will it harmonise with the narration of fact. 2. And this is the ground on which the phrases of Gorgias of Leontini are ridiculed when he describes Xerxes as the "Zeus of the Persians" and vultures as "living tombs." So is it with some of the expressions of Callisthenes which are not sublime but high-flown, and still more with those of Cleitarchus, for the man is frivolous and blows, as Sophocles has it,

On pigmy hautboys: mouthpiece have they
  none.[2]

Other examples will be found in Amphicrates and Hegesias and Matris, for often when these writers seem to themselves to be inspired they are in no true frenzy but are simply trifling. 3. Altogether, tumidity seems particularly hard to avoid. The explanation is that all who aim at elevation are so anxious to escape the reproach of being weak and dry that they are carried, as by some strange law of nature, into the opposite extreme. They put their trust in the maxim that "failure in a great attempt is at least a noble error." 4. But evil are the swellings, both in the body and in diction, which are inflated and unreal, and threaten us with the reverse of our aim; for nothing, say they, is drier than a man who has the dropsy. While tumidity desires to transcend the limits of the sublime, the defect which is termed puerility is the direct antithesis of elevation, for it is utterly low and mean and in real truth the most ignoble vice of style. What, then, is this puerility? Clearly, a pedant's thoughts, which begin in learned trifling and end in frigidity. Men slip into this kind of error because, while they aim at the uncommon and elaborate and most of all at the attractive, they drift unawares into the tawdry and affected. 5. A third, and closely allied, kind of defect in matters of passion is that which Theodorus used to call *parenthyrsus*. By this is meant unseasonable and empty passion, where no passion is required, or immoderate, where moderation is needed. For men are often carried away, as if by intoxication, into displays of emotion which are not caused by the nature of the subject, but are purely personal and wearisome. In consequence they seem to hearers who

[1] *Aeschylus.*—Translated by A. S. Way. . . .

[2] *Sophocles.*—Translated by A. S. Way. . . .

are in no wise affected to act in an ungainly way. And no wonder; for they are beside themselves, while their hearers are not. But the question of the passions we reserve for separate treatment. . . .

There are, it may be said, five principal sources of elevated language. Beneath these five varieties there lies, as though it were a common foundation, the gift of discourse, which is indispensable. First and most important is the power of forming great conceptions, as we have elsewhere explained in our remarks on Xenophon. Secondly, there is vehement and inspired passion. These two components of the sublime are for the most part innate. Those which remain are partly the product of art. The due formation of figures deals with two sorts of figures, first those of thought and secondly those of expression. Next there is noble diction, which in turn comprises choice of words, and use of metaphors, and elaboration of language. The fifth cause of elevation—one which is the fitting conclusion of all that have preceded it—is dignified and elevated composition. Come now, let us consider what is involved in each of these varieties, with this one remark by way of preface, that Caecilius has omitted some of the five divisions, for example, that of passion. 2. Surely he is quite mistaken if he does so on the ground that these two, sublimity and passion, are a unity, and if it seems to him that they are by nature one and inseparable. For some passions are found which are far removed from sublimity and are of a low order, such as pity, grief and fear; and on the other hand there are many examples of the sublime which are independent of passion, such as the daring words of Homer with regard to the Aloadae, to take one out of numberless instances,

Yea, Ossa in fury they strove to upheave on Olympus on high,
With forest-clad Pelion above, that thence they might step to the sky.[3]

And so of the words which follow with still greater force:—

Ay, and the deed had they done.[4]

3. Among the orators, too, eulogies and ceremonial and occasional addresses contain on every side examples of dignity and elevation, but are for the most part void of passion. This is the reason why passionate speakers are the worst eulogists, and why, on the other hand, those who are apt in encomium are the least passionate. 4. If, on the other hand, Caecilius thought that passion never contributes at all to sublimity, and if it was for this reason that he did not deem it worthy of mention, he is altogether deluded. I would affirm with confidence that there is no tone so lofty as that of genuine passion, in its right place, when it bursts out in a wild gust of mad enthusiasm and as it were fills the speaker's words with frenzy. . . .

Images, moreover, contribute greatly, my young friend, to dignity, elevation, and power as a pleader. In this sense some call them mental representations. In a general way the name of *image* or *imagination* is applied to every idea of the mind, in whatever form it presents itself, which gives birth to speech. But at the present day the word is predominantly used in cases where, carried away by enthusiasm and passion, you think you see what you describe, and you place it before the eyes of your hearers. 2. Further, you will be aware of the fact that an image has one purpose with the

[3] *Odyss.* XI. 315, 316.
[4] *Odyss.* XI. 317.

orators and another with the poets, and that the design of the poetical image is enthralment, of the rhetorical—vivid description. Both, however, seek to stir the passions and the emotions.

Mother!—'beseech thee, hark not thou on me
Yon maidens gory-eyed and snaky-haired!
Lo there!—lo there!—they are nigh—they leap on me![5]

And:

Ah! she will slay me! whither can I fly?[6]

In these scenes the poet himself saw Furies, and the image in his mind he almost compelled his audience also to behold. 3. Now, Euripides is most assiduous in giving the utmost tragic effect to these two emotions—fits of love and madness. Herein he succeeds more, perhaps, than in any other respect, although he is daring enough to invade all the other regions of the imagination. Notwithstanding that he is by nature anything but elevated, he forces his own genius, in many passages, to tragic heights, and everywhere in the matter of sublimity it is true of him (to adopt Homer's words) that

The tail of him scourgeth his ribs and his flanks to left and to right,
And he lasheth himself into frenzy, and spurreth him on to the fight.[7]

... Further, with regard to the number of metaphors to be employed, Caecilius seems to assent to the view of those who lay it down that not more than two, or at the most three, should be ranged together in the same passage. Demosthenes is, in fact, the standard in this as in other matters. The proper time for using meta-

phors is when the passions roll like a torrent and sweep a multitude of them down their resistless flood. 2. "Men," says he, "who are vile flatterers, who have maimed their own fatherlands each one of them, who have toasted away their liberty first to Philip and now to Alexander, who measure happiness by their belly and their lowest desires, and who have overthrown that liberty and that freedom from despotic mastery which to the Greeks of an earlier time were the rules and standards of good."[8] Here the orator's wrath against the traitors throws a veil over the number of the tropes. 3. In the same spirit, Aristotle and Theophrastus point out that the following phrases serve to soften bold metaphors— "as if," and "as it were," and "if one may so say," and "if one may venture such an expression"; for the qualifying words mitigate, they say, the audacity of expression. 4. I accept that view, but still for number and boldness of metaphors I maintain, as I said in dealing with figures, that strong and timely passion and noble sublimity are the appropriate palliatives. For it is the nature of the passions, in their vehement rush, to sweep and thrust everything before them, or rather to demand hazardous turns as altogether indispensable. They do not allow the hearer leisure to criticise the number of the metaphors because he is carried away by the fervour of the speaker. 5. Moreover, in the treatment of commonplaces and in descriptions there is nothing so impressive as a number of tropes following close one upon the other. It is by this means that in Xenophon the anatomy of the human tabernacle is magnificently depicted, and still more divinely in Plato. Plato says that its head is a citadel; in the midst, between the head and the breast, is built the neck like some isthmus. The vertebrae, he says, are

[5] Eurip. Orest. 255.
[6] Eurip. Iph. in T. 291.
[7] Il. XX. 170, 1.

[8] Dem. de Cor. 296.

fixed beneath like pivots. Pleasure is a bait which tempts men to ill, the tongue the test of taste; the heart is the knot of the veins and the wellspring of the blood that courses round impetuously, and it is stationed in the guard-house of the body. The passages by which the blood races this way and that he names alleys. He says that the gods, contriving succour for the beating of the heart (which takes place when dangers are expected, and when wrath excites it, since it then reaches a fiery heat), have implanted the lungs, which are soft and bloodless and have pores within, to serve as a buffer, in order that the heart may, when its inward wrath boils over, beat against a yielding substance and so escape injury. The seat of the desires he compared to the women's apartments in a house, that of anger to the men's. The spleen he called the napkin of the inward parts, whence it is filled with secretions and grows to a great and festering bulk. After

this, the gods canopied the whole with flesh, putting forward the flesh as a defence against injuries from without, as though it were a hair-cushion. The blood he called the fodder of the flesh. "In order to promote nutrition," he continues, "they irrigated the body, cutting conduits as in gardens, in order that, with the body forming a set of tiny channels, the streams of the veins might flow as from a never-failing source." When the end comes, he says that the cables of the soul are loosed like those of a ship, and she is allowed to go free.[9] Examples of a similar nature are to be found in a never-ending series. But those indicated are enough to show that figurative language possesses great natural power, and that metaphors contribute to the sublime; and at the same time that it is impassioned and descriptive passages which rejoice in them to the greatest extent....

[9] Plato, *Tim.* 65 c–85 e.

FROM AN ESSAY ON THE GENIUS AND WRITINGS OF POPE
Joseph Warton

Warton's eighteenth-century essay represents a post-neoclassical, early romantic reconsideration of the nature of poetry. In it Warton develops the empirical thesis that a "minute enumeration of circumstances judiciously selected" to strike the imagination with lively pictures produces the most moving poetry. Epithets should be particular and pictural instead of general and indiscriminate as, unfortunately, some of Pope's are. Poetry should introduce moral sentences and instructions in an oblique and indirect manner from descriptions leading to some reflection upon moral life.

... The influences and effects of peace, and its consequence, a diffusive commerce, are expressed by selecting such circumstances as are best adapted to strike the imagination by lively pictures; the selection of which chiefly constitutes true poetry. An historian, or prose-writer, might say, "Then shall the most distant nations croud into my port": a poet sets before your eyes "the ships of uncouth form," that shall arrive in the Thames.[1]

And *feather'd* people croud my wealthy side;
And *naked* youths, and *painted* chiefs, admire
Our speech, our colour, and our strange *attire*.

And the benevolence and poetry of the succeeding wish are worthy admiration.

Till the freed Indians, in their native groves,
Reap their own fruits, and woo their sable loves;
Peru once more a race of kings behold,
And other Mexicos be roof'd with gold.[2]

The two epithets, *native* and *sable*, have peculiar elegance and force; and as Peru was particularly famous for its long succession of Incas, and Mexico for many magnificent works of massy gold, there is great propriety in fixing the restoration of the grandeur of each to that object for which each was once so remarkable.

The group of allegorical personages that succeeds the last mentioned lines, are worthy the pencil of Rubens or Julio Romano: it may, perhaps, however, be wished that the epithets *barbarous* (discord,) *mad*, (ambition,) *hateful*, (envy,)[3] had been particular and picturesque, instead of general and indiscriminating; though it may possibly be urged, that, in describing the dreadful inhabitants of the portal of hell, Virgil has not always used such adjuncts and epithets as a painter or statuary might work after; he says only *ultrices curæ, mortiferum bellum, mala mentis gaudia*; particularly, *malesuada* is only applied to *fames*, instead of a word that might represent the meagre and

ghastly figure intended. I make no scruple of adding, that in this famous passage, Virgil has exhibited no images so lively and distinct, as these living figures painted by Pope, each of them with their proper insignia and attributes:

——*envy* her own snakes shall feel,
And *persecution* mourn his broken wheel:
There *faction* roar, *rebellion* bite her chain,
And gasping *furies* thirst for blood in vain[4]

A person of no small rank has informed me, that Mr. Addison was inexpressibly chagrined at this noble conclusion of *Windsor Forest*, both as a politician and as a poet. As a politician, because it so highly celebrated that treaty of peace which he deemed so pernicious to the liberties of Europe; and as a poet, because he was deeply conscious that his own *Campaign*, that gazette in rhyme, contained no strokes of such genuine and sublime poetry as the conclusion before us.

It is one of the greatest and most pleasing arts of descriptive poetry, to introduce moral sentences and instructions in an oblique and indirect manner, in places where one naturally expects only painting and amusement. We have virtue, as Pope remarks,[5] put upon us by surprize, and are pleased to find a thing where we should never have looked to meet with it. I must do a pleasing English poet the justice to observe, that it is this particular art that is the very distinguishing excellence of *Cooper's-Hill*; throughout which, the descriptions of places, and images raised by the poet, are still tending to some hint, or leading into some reflection, upon moral life, or political institution; much in the same manner as the real sight of such scenes and prospects is apt to give the mind a composed

---

[1] Pope, *Windsor Forest*, l. 400 ff.
[2] L. 409.
[3] L. 411 ff.

[4] L. 419 ff.
[5] *Iliad*. B. 16. in the notes: l. 465.

turn, and incline it to thoughts and contemplations that have a relation to the object. This is the great charm of the incomparable *Elegy* written in a Country Church-Yard. Having mentioned the rustic monuments and simple epitaphs of the swains, the amiable poet falls into a very natural reflection:

For who, to dumb forgetfulness a prey,
This pleasing anxious being e'er resign'd.
Left the warm precincts of the chearful day,
Nor cast one longing, ling'ring look behind?

Of this art Pope has exhibited some specimens in the poem we are examining, but not so many as might be expected from a mind so strongly inclined to a moral way of writing. After speaking of hunting the hare, he immediately subjoins, much in the spirit of Denham,

Beasts urg'd by us their fellow-beasts pursue,
And learn of man each other to undo.[6]

Where he is describing the tyrannies formerly exercised in this kingdom,

Cities laid waste, they storm'd the dens and caves,

He instantly adds, with an indignation becoming a true lover of liberty,

For wiser brutes were backward to be slaves.[7]

But I am afraid our author, in the following passage, has fallen into a fault rather uncommon in his writings, a reflection that is very far-fetched and forced;

Here waving groves a chequer'd scene display,
And part admit, and part exclude the day;
As some coy nymph her lover's warm address

Nor quite indulges, nor can quite repress.[8]

Bohours would rank this comparison among false thoughts and Italian conceits; such particularly as abound in the works of Marino. The fallacy consists in giving design and artifice to the wood, as well as to the coquette; and in putting the light of the sun and the warmth of a lover on a level.

A pathetic reflection, properly introduced into a descriptive poem, will have greater force and beauty, and more deeply interest a reader, than a moral one. When Pope, therefore, has described a pheasant shot, he breaks out into a very masterly exclamation;

Ah! what avail his glossy varying dyes,
His purple crest, and scarlet-circled eyes,
The vivid green his shining plumes unfold,
His painted wings, and breast that flames with gold.[9]

This exquisite picture heightens the distress, and powerfully excites the commiseration of the reader. Under this head, it would be unpardonable to omit a capital, and, I think, one of the most excellent examples extant, of the beauty here intended, in the third Georgic of Virgil.[10] The poet having mournfully described a steer struck with a pestilence, and falling down dead in the middle of his work, artfully reminds us of his former services;

Quid labor aut benefacta juvant? Quid vomere terras Invertisse graves?[11]
[What good labor and service—to have turned the heavy earth with a plow?]

---

[6] L. 123. But a critic of taste objected to me the use of the word *undo;* and of the word *backward* in a subsequent line.
[7] L. 50.

[8] L. 17.
[9] L. 115.
[10] L. 525.
[11] By the epithet *graves,* Virgil insinuates, after his manner, the difficulty and laboriousness of the work.

This circumstance would have been sufficient, as it raised our pity from a motive
of gratitude; but with this circumstance
the tender Virgil was not content; what
he adds, therefore, of the natural unde-
viating temperance of the animal, who
cannot have contracted disease by excess,
and who for that reason deserved a better
fate, is moving beyond compare:

——Atqui non Massica Bacchi
Munera, non illis epulæ nocuere repostæ!
Frondibus, et victu pascuntur simplicis
 herbæ;
Pocula sunt fontes liquidi atque exercita
 cursu
Flumina, nec somnos abrumpit cura salu-
 bris.

[And yet these creatures are never debilitated by the Massic wine of Bacchus or
excessive feasts; they feed on simple grass,
their cups are flowing springs and streams
that hasten on their course, and anxiety
does not trouble their healthy sleep.]

... It would be unpardonable to conclude these remarks on descriptive poesy,
without taking notice of the *Seasons* of
Thomson, who had peculiar and powerful talents for this species of composition.
Let the reader, therefore, pardon a digression, if such it be, on his merits and
character.

Thomson was blessed with a strong
and copious fancy; he hath enriched
poetry with a variety of new and original
images, which he painted from nature itself, and from his own actual observations: his descriptions have, therefore, a
distinctness and truth, which are utterly
wanting to those of poets who have only
copied from each other, and have never
looked abroad on the objects themselves.
Thomson was accustomed to wander
away into the country for days, and for

weeks, attentive to "each rural sight,
each rural sound"; while many a poet,
who has dwelt for years in the Strand,
has attempted to describe fields and
rivers, and generally succeeded accordingly. Hence that nauseous repetition of
the same circumstances; hence that disgusting impropriety of introducing what
may be called a set of hereditary images,
without proper regard to the age, or climate, or occasion, in which they were
formerly used. Though the diction of the
Seasons is sometimes harsh and inharmo-
nious, and sometimes turgid and obscure,
and though, in many instances, the numbers are not sufficiently diversified by
different pauses, yet is this poem, on the
whole, from the numberless strokes of
nature in which it abounds, one of the
most captivating and amusing in our
language; and which, as its beauties are
not of a transitory kind, as depending on
particular customs and manners, will ever
be perused with delight. The scenes of
Thomson are frequently as wild and
romantic as those of Salvator Rosa, varied
with precipices and torrents, and "castled
cliffs," and deep vallies, with piny mountains, and the gloomiest caverns. Innumerable are the little circumstances in his
descriptions, totally unobserved by all his
predecessors. What poet hath ever taken
notice of the leaf, that, towards the end
of autumn,

Incessant rustles from the mournful grove,[12]
Oft startling such as, studious, walk below.
And slowly circles through the waving air?

Or who, in speaking of a summer evening, hath ever mentioned

The quail that clamours for his running
 mate?

Or the following natural image at the
same time of the year?

[12] L. 1004.

Wide o'er the thistly lawn, as swells the breeze,
A whitening shower of vegetable down
Amusive floats.[13] . . .

In what other poet do we find the silence and expectation that precedes an April shower insisted on, as in ver. 165 of *Spring?* Or where,

The stealing shower is scarce to patter heard,
By such as wander through the forest walks,
Beneath th' umbrageous multitude of leaves.[14]

How full, particular, and picturesque, is this assemblage of circumstances that attend a very keen frost in a night of winter!

Loud rings the frozen earth, and hard reflects
A double noise; while at his evening watch
The village dog deters the nightly thief;
The heifer lows; the distant water-fall
Swells in the breeze; and with the hasty tread
Of traveller, the hollow-sounding plain
Shakes from afar.[15]

In no one subject are common writers more confused and unmeaning, than in their descriptions of rivers, which are generally said only to wind and to murmur, while their qualities and courses are seldom accurately marked. Examine the exactness of the ensuing description, and consider what a perfect idea it communicates to the mind.

Around th' adjoining brook, that purls along
The vocal grove, now fretting o'er a rock,
Now scarcely moving through a reedy pool,
Now starting to a sudden stream, and now
Gently diffus'd into a limpid plain;

A various groupe the herds and flocks compose,
Rural confusion.[16]

A groupe worthy the pencil of Giacomo da Bassano, and so minutely delineated, that he might have worked from this sketch:

On the grassy bank
Some ruminating lie; while others stand
Half in the flood, and often bending sip
The circling surface. . . .

He adds, that the ox, in the middle of them,

From his sides
The troublous insects lashes, to his sides
Returning still.[17]

A natural circumstance, that, to the best of my remembrance, hath escaped even the natural Theocritus. Nor do I recollect that any poet hath been struck with the murmurs of the numberless insects that swarm abroad at the noon of a summer's day: as attendants of the evening, indeed, they have been mentioned;

Resounds the living surface of the ground:
Nor undelightful is the ceaseless hum
To him who muses through the woods at noon;
Or drowsy shepherd, as he lies reclin'd
With half-shut eyes.[18]

But the novelty and nature we admire in the descriptions of Thomson, are by no means his only excellencies; he is equally to be praised for impressing on our minds the effects, which the scene delineated would have on the present spectator or hearer. Thus having spoken of the roaring of the savages in a wilderness of

[13] L. 1657.
[14] L. 176.
[15] *Winter*, l. 731.

[16] *Summer*, l. 479.
[17] *Summer*, l. 485 ff.
[18] *Summer*, l. 280.

Africa, he introduces a captive, who, though just escaped from[19] prison and slavery under the tyrant of Morocco, is so terrified and astonished at the dreadful uproar, that

The wretch half wishes for his bonds again.

Thus also having described a caravan lost and overwhelmed in one of those whirlwinds that so frequently agitate and lift up the whole sands of the desert, he finishes his picture by adding, that,

In Cairo's crouded streets,[20]
Th' impatient merchant, wondering waits in vain,
And Mecca saddens at the long delay.

And thus, lastly, in describing the pestilence that destroyed the British troops at the siege of Carthagena, he has used a circumstance inimitably lively, pictur-

esque and striking to the imagination; for he says, that the admiral not only heard the groans of the sick that echoed from ship to ship, but that he also pensively stood, and listened at midnight to the dashing of the waters, occasioned by throwing the dead bodies into the sea;

Heard, nightly, plung'd into the sullen waves,
The frequent corse....[21]

A minute and particular enumeration of circumstances judiciously selected, is what chiefly discriminates poetry from history, and renders the former, for that reason, a more close and faithful representation of nature than the latter. And if our poets would accustom themselves to contemplate fully every object, before they attempted to describe it, they would not fail of giving their readers more new and more complete images than they generally do....

[19] *Summer*, l. 935.
[20] L. 976.

[21] L. 1047.

FROM ON THE DISCRIMINATION OF ROMANTICISMS
Arthur O. Lovejoy*

Lovejoy's thesis is that there is not one perspective, theory, or practice identifiable as romanticism but several, often contradictory in their elements—gothicism vs. naturalism, primitivism vs. transcendentalism, simplicity vs. irony, detailed particularities vs. supersensible reality and illusion.

...There is no hope of clear thinking on the part of the student of modern literature, if—as, alas! has been repeatedly done by eminent writers—he vaguely hypostatizes the term, and starts with the

presumption that "Romanticism" is the heaven-appointed designation of some single real entity, or type of entities, to be found in nature. He must set out from the simple and obvious fact that there are various historic episodes or movements to which different historians of our own or other periods have, for one reason or

* The selection is reprinted from *Essays in the History of Ideas*, by Arthur O. Lovejoy, by permission of The Johns Hopkins Press. Copyright 1948 by The Johns Hopkins Press.

another, given the name. There is a movement which began in Germany in the seventeen-nineties—the only one which has an indisputable title to be called Romanticism, since it invented the term for its own use. There is another movement which began pretty definitely in England in the seventeen-forties. There is a movement which began in France in 1801. There is another movement which began in France in the second decade of the century, is linked with the German movement, and took over the German name. There is the rich and incongruous collection of ideas to be found in Rousseau. There are numerous other things called Romanticism by various writers whom I cited at the outset. The fact that the same name has been given by different scholars to all of these episodes is no evidence, and scarcely even establishes a presumption, that they are identical in essentials. There may be some common denominator of them all; but if so, it has never yet been clearly exhibited, and its presence is not to be assumed *a priori*. In any case, each of these so-called Romanticisms was a highly complex and usually an exceedingly unstable intellectual compound; each, in other words, was made up of various unit-ideas linked together, for the most part, not by any indissoluble bonds of logical necessity, but by alogical associative processes, greatly facilitated and partly caused, in the case of the Romanticisms which grew up after the appellation "Romantic" was invented, by the congenital and acquired ambiguities of the word. And when certain of these Romanticisms have in truth significant elements in common, they are not necessarily the same elements in any two cases. Romanticism A may have one characteristic presupposition or impulse, X, which it shares with Romanticism B, another characteristic, Y, which it shares with

Romanticism C, to which X is wholly foreign. In the case, moreover, of those movements or schools to which the label was applied in their own time, the contents under the label sometimes changed radically and rapidly. At the end of a decade or two you had the same men and the same party appellation, but profoundly different ideas. As everyone knows, this is precisely what happened in the case of what is called French Romanticism. It may or may not be true that, as M. A. Viatte has sought to show,[1] at the beginning of this process of transformation some subtle leaven was already at work which made the final outcome inevitable; the fact remains that in most of its practically significant sympathies and affiliations of a literary, ethical, political, and religious sort, the French "Romanticism" of the eighteen-thirties was the antithesis of that of the beginning of the century.

But the essential of the second remedy is that each of these Romanticisms— after they are first thus roughly discriminated with respect to their representatives or their dates—should be resolved, by a more thorough and discerning analysis than is yet customary, into its elements —into the several ideas and aesthetic susceptibilities of which it is composed. Only after these fundamental thought-factors or emotive strains in it are clearly discriminated and fairly exhaustively enumerated, shall we be in a position to judge of the degree of its affinity with other complexes to which the same name has been applied, to see precisely what tacit preconceptions or controlling motives or explicit contentions were common to any two or more of them, and wherein they manifested distinct and divergent tendencies.

[1] *Le Catholicisme chez les Romantiques,* 1922.

Of the needfulness of such analytic comparison and discrimination of the Romanticisms let me attempt three illustrations.

1. In an interesting lecture before the British Academy a few years since, Mr. Edmund Gosse described Joseph Warton's youthful poem, *The Enthusiast*, written in 1740, as the first clear manifestation of "the great romantic movement, such as it has enlarged and dwindled down to our day. . . . Here for the first time we find unwaveringly emphasized and repeated what was entirely new in literature, the essence of romantic hysteria. *The Enthusiast* is the earliest expression of complete revolt against the classical attitude which had been sovereign in all European literature for nearly a century. So completely is this expressed by Joseph Warton that it is extremely difficult to realize that he could not have come under the fascination of Rousseau, . . . who was not to write anything characteristic until ten years later."[2] Let us, then, compare the ideas distinctive of this poem with the conception of *romantische Poesie* formulated by Friedrich Schlegel and his fellow-Romanticists in Germany after 1796. The two have plainly certain common elements. Both are forms of revolt against the neoclassical aesthetics; both are partly inspired by an ardent admiration for Shakespeare; both proclaim the creative artist's independence of "rules." It might at first appear, therefore, that these two Romanticisms, in spite of natural differences of phraseology, are identical in essence—are separate outcroppings of the same vein of metal, precious or base, according to your taste.

But a more careful scrutiny shows a contrast between them not less important

—indeed, as it seems to me, more important—than their resemblance. The general theme of Joseph Warton's poem (of which, it will be remembered, the subtitle is "The Lover of Nature") is one which had been a commonplace for many centuries: the superiority of "nature" to "art." It is a theme which goes back to Rabelais's contrast of Physis and Antiphysie. It had been the inspiration of some of the most famous passages of Montaigne. It had been attacked by Shakespeare. Pope's *Essay on Man* had been full of it. The "natural" in contrast with the artificial meant, first of all, that which is not man-made; and within man's life, it was supposed to consist in those expressions of human nature which are most spontaneous, unpremeditated, untouched by reflection or design, and free from the bondage of social convention. "Ce n'est pas raison," cried Montaigne, "que l'art gagne le point d'honneur sur notre grande et puissante mêre Nature. Nous avons tant rechargé la beauté et richesse de ses ouvrages par nos inventions, que nous l'avons tout à fait étouffée." [It is not right that art should be honored above our great and powerful mother Nature. We have so much overloaded the beauty and richness of her works by our inventions that we have completely strangled her.] There follows the *locus classicus* of primitivism in modern literature, the famous passage on the superiority of wild fruits and savage men over those that have been "bastardized" by art.[3]

Warton, then, presents this ancient theme in various aspects. He prefers to

2 "Two Pioneers of Romanticism," *Proc. Brit. Acad.*, 1915, pp. 146–8.

3 *Essais*, I, 31. There is a certain irony in the fact that the sort of naturalism here expressed by Montaigne was to be the basis of a Shakespeare-revival in the eighteenth century. For Shakespeare's own extreme antipathy to the passage is shown by the fact that he wrote two replies to it—a humorous one in *The Tempest*, a serious and profound one in *The Winter's Tale*.

all the beauties of the gardens of Versailles

> Some pine-topt precipice
> Abrupt and shaggy.

He rhetorically inquires:

> Can Kent design like Nature?

He laments

> That luxury and pomp . . .
> Should proudly banish Nature's simple
> charms.

He inquires why "mistaken man" should deem it nobler

> To dwell in palaces and high-roof'd halls
> Than in God's forests, architect supreme?

All this, if I may be permitted the expression, was old stuff. The principal thing that was original and significant in the poem was that Warton boldly applied the doctrine of the superiority of "nature" over conscious art to the theory of poetry:

> What are the lays of artful Addison,
> Coldly correct, to Shakespeare's warblings
> wild?

That Nature herself was wild, untamed, was notorious, almost tautological; and it was Shakespeare's supposed "wildness," his non-conformity to the conventional rules, the spontaneous freedom of his imagination and his expression, that proved him Nature's true pupil.

Now this aesthetic inference had not, during the neo-classical period, ordinarily been drawn from the current assumption of the superiority of nature to art. The principle of "following nature" had in aesthetics usually been taken in another, or in more than one other, of the several dozen senses of the sacred word.[4] Yet in other provinces of thought an analogous inference had long since and repeatedly been suggested. From the first the fashion of conceiving of "nature" (in the sense in which it was antithetic to "art") as norm had made for antinomianism, in some degree or other —for a depreciation of restraint, for the ideal of "letting yourself go." There seems to be an idea current that an antinomian temper was, at some time in the eighteenth century, introduced into aesthetic theory and artistic practise by some Romanticist, and that it thence speedily spread to moral feeling and social conduct.[5] The historic sequence is precisely the opposite. It was Montaigne again— not usually classified as a Romanticist— who wrote:

J'ai pris bien simplement et crûment ce précepte ancien: "que nous ne saurions faillir à suivre Nature." . . . Je n'ai pas corrigé, comme Socrate, par la force de la raison, mes complexions naturelles, je n'ai aucunement troublé, par art, mon inclination; je me laisse aller comme je suis venu; je ne combats rien.[6]

[I have simply taken without embellishment the ancient precept that we cannot fail in following Nature. I have not corrected, as did Socrates, my natural complexions by force of reason; I have in no way disturbed my inclinations by art; I let myself go as I have come; I do not fight anything.]

It was Pope who asked:

[4] This is not rhetorical exaggeration; more than sixty different senses or applications of the notion of "nature" can be clearly distinguished.
[5] So apparently Mr. Gosse: "When the history of the [Romantic] school comes to be written, there will be a piquancy in tracing an antinomianism down from the blameless Warton to the hedonist essays of Oscar Wilde and the frenzied anarchism of the futurists" (*op. cit.*, 15).
[6] *Essais*, III. 12.

Can that offend great Nature's God
Which Nature's self inspires?

and who spoke of

Wild Nature's vigor working at the root

as the source of the passions in which all the original and vital energies of men are contained.

Aside from a certain heightening of the emotional tone, then, the chief novelty of Warton's poem lay in its suggesting the application of these ideas to a field from which they had usually been curiously and inconsistently excluded, in its introduction of antinomianism, of a rather mild sort, into the conception of poetic excellence.[7] But this extension was obviously implicit from the outset in the logic of that protean "naturalism" which had been the most characteristic and potent force in modern thought since the late Renaissance; it was bound to be made by somebody sooner or later. Nor was Warton's the first aesthetic application of the principle; it had already been applied to an art in the theory and practice of which eighteenth-century Englishmen were keenly interested—the art of landscape design. The first great revolt against the neo-classical aesthetics was not in literature at all, but in gardening; the second, I think, was in architectural taste; and all three were inspired by the same ideas.[8] Since, the "artful Addison" had observed, "artificial works receive a greater advantage from their

resemblance of such as are natural," and since Nature is distinguished by her "rough, careless strokes," the layer-out of gardens should aim at "an artificial rudeness much more charming than that neatness and elegancy usually met with."[9] This horticultural Romanticism had been preached likewise by Sir William Temple, Pope, Horace Walpole, Batty Langley, and others, and ostensibly exemplified in the work of Kent, Brown, and Bridgman. Warton in the poem in question describes Kent as at least doing his best to imitate in his gardens the wildness of Nature:

He, by rules unfettered, boldly scorns
Formality and method; round and square
Disdaining, plans irregularly great.

It was no far cry from this to the rejection of the rules in the drama, to a revulsion against the strait-laced regularity and symmetry of the heroic couplet, to a general turning from convention, formality, method, artifice, in all the arts.

There had, however, from the first been a curious duality of meaning in the antithesis of "nature" and "art"—one of the most pregnant of the long succession of confusions of ideas which make up much of the history of human thought. While the "natural" was, on the one hand, conceived as the wild and spontaneous and "irregular," it was also conceived as the simple, the naïve, the unsophisticated. No two words were more fixedly associated in the mind of the sixteenth, seventeenth, and early eighteenth centuries than "Nature" and "simple." Consequently the idea of preferring nature to custom and to art usually carried with it the suggestion of a program of simplification, of reform by elimination; in other words, it implied

---

[7] The title of the poem and some elements of its thought and feeling—especially its note of religious "enthusiasm" for "Nature" in the sense of the visible universe—are akin to, and probably derivative from, Shaftesbury's *Moralists*. But in Shaftesbury there is no opposition of "nature" to "art" and no antinomian strain, either ethical or aesthetic; "decorum," "order," "balance," and "proportion" are among his favorite words.

[8] Cf. the essay on "The First Gothic Revival," etc., above. [Another essay in the collection.]

[9] *Spectator*, No. 144.

primitivism. The "natural" was a thing you reached by going back and by leaving out. And this association of ideas— already obvious in Montaigne, in Pope, and scores of other extollers of "Nature" —is still conspicuous in Warton's poem. It was the "bards of old" who were "fair Nature's friends." The poet envies

The first of men, ere yet confined
In smoky cities.

He yearns to dwell in some

Isles of innocence from mortal view
Deeply retired beneath a plantane's shade,
Where Happiness and Quiet sit enthroned,
With simple Indian swains.

For one term of the comparison, then, I limit myself, for brevity's sake, to this poem to which Mr. Gosse has assigned so important a place in literary history. There were, of course, even in the writings of the elder Warton, and still more in other phenomena frequently called "Romantic," between the 1740's and the 1790's, further elements which cannot be considered here. There is observable, for example, in what it has become the fashion to classify as the early phases of English Romanticism, the emergence of what may be called gothicism, and the curious fact of its partial and temporary fusion with naturalism. It is one of the interesting problems of the analytic history of ideas to see just how and why naturalism and gothicism became allied in the eighteenth century in England, though little, if at all, in France. But for the present purpose it suffices to take *The Enthusiast* as typical, in one especially important way, of a great deal of the so-called Romanticism before the seventeen-nineties—a Romanticism, namely, which, whatever further characteristics it may have had, was based

upon naturalism (in the sense of the word which I have indicated) and was associated with primitivism of some mode or degree.

2. For in this fundamental point this earlier "Romanticism" differed essentially from that of the German aesthetic theorists and poets who chose the term "Romantic poetry" as the most suitable designation for their own literary ideals and program. The latter "Romanticism" is in its very essence a denial of the older naturalistic presuppositions, which Warton's poem had manifested in a special and somewhat novel way. The German movement, as I have elsewhere shown, received its immediate and decisive impetus from Schiller's essay *On Naïve and Sentimental Poetry*; and what it derived from that confused work was the conviction that "harmony with nature," in any sense which implied an opposition to "culture," to "art," to reflection and self-conscious effort, was neither possible nor desirable for the modern man or the modern artist. The *Frühromantiker* [early romantic] learned from Schiller, and partly from Herder, the idea of an art which should look back no more to the primitive than to the classical—the notions of which, incidentally, Schiller had curiously fused—for its models and ideals; which should be the appropriate expression, not of a *natürliche* [natural] but of a *künstliche Bildung* [artistic culture]; which, so far from desiring simplification, so far from aiming at the sort of harmony in art and life which is to be attained by the method of leaving out, should seek first fullness of content, should have for its program the adequate expression of the entire range of human experience and the entire reach of the human imagination. For man, the artificial, Friedrich Schlegel observed, *is* "natural." "Die Abstraktion ist ein

künstlicher Zustand. Dies ist kein Grund gegen sie, denn es ist dem Menschen gewiss natürlich, sich dann und wann auch in künstliche Zustände zu versetzen." [Abstraction is an artificial condition. That is no argument against it, for it is certainly natural for the human being to transplant himself into artificial situations now and then.] And again: "Eine nur im Gegensatz der Kunst und Bildung natürliche Denkart soll es gar nicht geben."[There is not to be a way of thinking which is completely natural except in contrast to art and culture.] To be unsophisticated, to revert to the mental state of "simple Indian swains," was the least of the ambitions of a German Romantic—though, since the unsophisticated is one type of human character, his art was not, at least in theory, indifferent even to that. The Shakespeare whom he admired was no gifted child of nature addicted to "warblings wild." Shakespeare, said A. W. Schlegel, is not "eine blindes wildlaufendes Genie" [a blind genius, running wild]; he had "a system in his artistic practise and an astonishingly profound and deeply meditated one." The same critic seems to be consciously attacking either Joseph Warton's or Gray's famous lines about Shakespeare when he writes: "Those poets whom it is customary to represent as carefree nurslings of nature, without art and without schooling, if they produce works of genuine excellence, give evidence of exceptional cultivation (*Kultur*) of their mental powers, of practised art, of ripely pondered and just designs." The greatness of Shakespeare, in the eyes of *these* Romantics, lay in his *Universalität*, his sophisticated insight into human nature and the many-sidedness of his portrayal of character; it was this, as Friedrich Schlegel said, that made him "wie der Mittelpunkt der romantischen Kunst" [like the central point of Romantic art]. It may be added that another trait of the Romanticism found by Mr. Gosse in Joseph Warton, namely, the feeling that didactic poetry is not poetic, was also repudiated by early German Romanticism: "How," asked F. Schlegel again, "can it be said that ethics (*die Moral*) belongs merely to philosophy, when the greatest part of poetry relates to the art of living and to the knowledge of human nature?"[10]

The difference, then, I suggest, is more significant, more pregnant, than the likeness between these two Romanticisms. Between the assertion of the superiority of "nature" over conscious "art" and that of the superiority of conscious art over mere "nature"; between a way of thinking of which primitivism is of the essence and one of which the idea of perpetual self-transcendence is of the essence; between a fundamental preference for simplicity—even though a "wild" simplicity—and a fundamental preference for diversity and complexity; between the sort of ingenuous naïveté characteristic of *The Enthusiast* and the sophisticated subtlety of the conception of romantic irony: between these the antithesis is one of the most radical that modern thought and taste have to show. I don't deny anyone's right to call both these things Romanticism, if he likes; but I cannot but observe that the fashion of giving both the same name has led to a good deal of unconscious falsification of the history of ideas. The elements of the one Romanticism tend to be read into the other; the nature and profundity of the oppositions between them tend to be overlooked; and the relative importance of the different changes of preconcep-

[10] Quotations in this paragraph from F. Schlegel are from *Athenaeum*, II, 1, p. 29; III, 1, p. 12; I, 2, p. 68; III, 1, p. 19. Those from A. W. Schlegel have already been cited by Marie Joachimi, *Weltanschauung der Romantik*, 179–183.

tions in modern thought, and of susceptibilities in modern taste, tends to be wrongly estimated. I shall not attempt to cite here what seem to me examples of such historical errors; but the sum of them is, I think, far from negligible.

Between the "Romanticism" which is but a special and belated manifestation of the naturalism that had flourished since the Renaissance (and before it) and the "Romanticism" which began at the end of the eighteenth century in Germany (as well as that which appeared a little later in France) there is another difference not less significant. This is due to the identification of the meaning of "Romantic" in the later movement with "Christian"—and mainly with the medieval implications of that term. This was not the central idea in the original notion of "Romantic poetry" as conceived by Friedrich Schlegel. Primarily, as I have elsewhere tried to show,[11] the adjective meant for him and the entire school "das eigentümlich Moderne" [that which is peculiarly modern] in contrast with "das eigentümlich Antike." But it early occurred to him that the principal historic cause of the supposed radical differentiation of modern from classical art could lie only in the influence of Christianity. He wrote in 1796, before his own conversion to what he had already defined as the "Romantic," *i.e.*, modern, point of view:

So lächerlich und geschmacklos sich dieses Trachten nach dem Reich Gottes in der christlichen Poesie offenbaren möchte; so wird es dem Geschichtsforscher doch eine sehr merkwürdige Erscheinung, wenn er gewahr wird, dass eben dieses Streben, das absolut Vollkommene und Unendliche zu realisiren, eine unter dem unaufhörlichen Wechsel der Zeiten und bei der grössten Verschiedenheit der Völker bleibende

Eigenschaft dessen ist, was man mit dem besten Rechte modern nennen darf.[12]

[No matter how ridiculously and tastelessly this striving toward the realm of God may be revealed in Christian poetry, it nonetheless becomes a noteworthy phenomenon for the historian, when he realizes that this striving to realize absolute perfection and absolute infinity is, amid the ceaseless change of times and the great difference between peoples, an enduring quality of that which one may justly call modern.]

When, after reading Schiller's essay, Schlegel himself became a devotee of those aesthetic ideals which he had previously denounced, he wrote (1797):

Nachdem die vollendete natürliche Bildung der Alten entschieden gesunken, und ohne Rettung ausgeartet war, ward durch den Verlust der endlichen Realität und die Zerrüttung vollendeter Form ein Streben nach unendlicher Realität veranlasst, welches bald allgemeiner Ton des Zeitalters wurde.[13]

[After the perfect, natural culture of the ancients had definitely declined and had degenerated beyond salvation, the loss of finite reality and the disintegration of perfect form caused a striving toward infinite reality which soon generally became the tone of the age.]

"Romantic" art thus came to mean— for one thing—an art inspired by or expressive of some idea or some ethical temper supposed to be essential in Christianity. "Ursprung und Charakter der ganzen neuern Poesie lässt sich so leicht aus dem Christentume ableiten, dass man die romantische eben so gut die christliche nennen könnte"[14] [The origin

[11] Cf. the essay on "The Meaning of Romantic," etc.

[12] Review of Herder's *Humanitätsbriefe*; in Minor, *Fr. Schlegel, 1794–1802.*

[13] Vorrede, *Die Griechen und Römer*, in Minor, *op. cit.*, I, 82.

[14] *Vorschule der Aesthetik*, I, Programm V, § 23.

and character of all modern poetry can be so easily traced back to Christianity that Romantic could just as well be called Christian], said Richter in 1804, repeating what had by that time become a commonplace. But the nature of the essentially Christian, and therefore essentially Romantic, spirit was variously conceived. Upon one characteristic of it there was, indeed, rather general agreement among the German Romanticists: the habit of mind introduced by Christianity was distinguished by a certain insatiability; it aimed at infinite objectives and was incapable of lasting satisfaction with any goods actually reached. It became a favorite platitude to say that the Greeks and Romans set themselves limited ends to attain, were able to attain them, and were thus capable of self-satisfaction and finality; and that modern or "romantic" art differed from this most fundamentally, by reason of its Christian origin, in being, as Schiller had said, a *Kunst des Unendlichen* [art of the infinite]. "Absolute Abstraktion, Vernichtung des Jetzigen, Apotheose der Zukunft, dieser eigentlich bessern Welt!; dies ist der Kern des Geheisses des Christentums" [Absolute abstraction, abrogation of the present, apotheosis of the future, of this truly better world!: this is the core of Christianity's calling], declared Novalis. In its application to artistic practice this "apotheosis of the future" meant the ideal of endless progress, of "eine progressive Universalpoesie" [a progressive world-poetry] in the words of Fr. Schlegel's familiar definition, it implied the demand that art shall always go on bringing new provinces of life within its domain and achieving ever fresh and original effects. But anything which was, or was supposed to be, especially characteristic of the Christian *Weltanschauung* [world-view] tended to become a part of the current connotation

of "Romantic," and also a part of the actual ideals of the school. Preoccupation with supersensible realities and a feeling of the illusoriness of ordinary existence was thus often held to be a distinctive trait of Romantic art, on the ground that Christianity is an otherworldly religion: "in der christlichen Ansicht," said A. W. Schlegel, "die Anschauung des Unendlichen hat das Endliche vernichtet; das Leben ist zur Schattenwelt und zur Nacht geworden"[15] [in the Christian view, contemplation of infinity has nullified the finite; life has become a shadow world, has become night]. Another recognized characteristic of Christianity, and therefore of the "Romantic," was ethical dualism, a conviction that there are in man's constitution two natures ceaselessly at war. The Greek ideal, in the elder Schlegel's words, was "volkommene Eintracht und Ebenmass aller Kräfte, natürliche Harmonie. Die Neueren hingegen sind zum Bewusstsein der inneren Entzweiung gekommen, welche ein solches Ideal unmöglich macht"[16] [complete concord and proportion of all powers, natural harmony. Those who followed, those of later times, on the other hand, have come to a consciousness of the inner schism which makes such an ideal impossible]. Directly related to this, it was perceived, was the "inwardness" of Christianity, its preoccupation with "the heart" as distinguished from the outward act, its tendency to introspection; and hence, as Mme de Stael and others observed, "modern" or "Romantic" art has discovered, and has for its peculiar province, the inexhaustible realm of the inner life of man:

Les anciens avaient, pour ainsi dire, une âme corporelle, dont tous les mouvements

---

[15] *Vorlesungen über dramatische Kunst und Literatur*, 1809–11, in *Werke*, 1846, V, 16. Cf. also Novalis's *Hymnen an die Nacht*.
[16] *Op. cit.*, V, 17.

étaient forts, directs, et conséquents; il n'en est pas de même du coeur humain développé par le christianisme: les modernes ont puisé dans le repentir chrétien l'habitude de se replier continuellement sur eux-mêmes. Mais, pour manifester cette existence tout intérieure, il faut qu'une grande variété dans les faits présente sous toutes les formes les nuances infinies de ce qui se passe dans l'âme.[17]

[The Ancients had, in a manner of speaking, a corporeal soul whose movements were strong, direct, and logical; it is not the same for the human heart as it developed under Christianity: the Moderns have acquired through Christian repentance the habit of continually turning inward upon themselves. But, in order to manifest this completely interior existence, a great variety of facts must present in all forms the infinite nuances of what takes place in the soul.]

It is one of the many paradoxes of the history of the word, and of the controversies centering about it, that several eminent literary historians and critics of our time have conceived the moral essence of Romanticism as consisting in a kind of "this-worldliness" and a negation of what one of them has termed "the Christian and classical dualism." Its most deplorable and dangerous error, in the judgment of these critics, is its deficient realization of the "civil war in the cave" of man's soul, its belief in the "natural goodness" of man. They thus define "Romanticism" in terms precisely opposite to those in which it was often defined by the writers who first called their own ideals "Romantic"; and this fashion, I cannot but think, has done a good deal to obscure the palpable and important historical fact that the one "Romanticism" which (as I have said) has an indisputable title to the name was conceived by those writers as a rediscovery and revival, for better or worse,

[17] *De l'Allemagne,* Pt. II, chap. XI.

of characteristically Christian modes of thought and feeling, of a mystical and otherworldly type of religion, and a sense of the inner moral struggle as the distinctive fact in human experience—such as had been for a century alien to the dominant tendencies in "polite" literature. The new movement was, almost from the first, a revolt against what was conceived to be paganism in religion and ethics as definitely as against classicism in art. The earliest important formulation of its implications for religious philosophy was Schleiermacher's famous *Reden* (1799) addressed "to the cultivated contemners of religion," a work profoundly—sometimes, indeed, morbidly—dualistic in its ethical temper. Christianity, declares Schleiermacher, is *durch und durch polemisch* [militant through and through]; it knows no truce in the warfare of the spiritual with the natural man, it finds no end in the task of inner self-discipline. And the *Reden,* it must be remembered, were (in the words of a German literary historian) "greeted by the votaries of Romanticism as a gospel."

Now it is not untrue to describe the ethical tendency of the "Romanticism" which had its roots in naturalism—that is, in the assumption of the sole excellence of what in man is native, primitive, "wild," attainable without other struggle than that required for emancipation from social conventions and artificialities—as anti-dualistic and essentially non-moral. This aspect of it can be seen even in the poem of the "blameless Warton," when he describes the life of the state of nature for which he yearns. But as a consequence of the prevalent neglect to discriminate the Romanticisms, the very movement which was the beginning of a deliberate and vigorous insurrection against the naturalistic assumptions that had been potent, and usually dominant, in modern thought for more than three centuries, is actually treated as if it were a continuation of that tendency. Thesis and antithesis have, partly through accidents of language and partly through a lack of careful observation on the part of historians of literature, been called by the same name, and consequently have frequently been assumed to be the same thing. An ideal of ceaseless striving towards goals too vast or too exacting ever to be wholly attained has been confused with a nostalgia for the untroubled, because unaspiring, indolent, and unselfconscious life of the man of nature. Thus one of the widest and deepest-reaching lines of cleavage in modern thought has been more or less effectually concealed by a word.

3. This cleavage between naturalistic and anti-naturalistic "Romanticism" crosses national lines; and it manifestly cuts, so to say, directly through the person of one great writer commonly classed among the initiators of the Romantic movement in France. The author of the *Essai sur les révolutions* and of the earlier-written parts of *Atala* may perhaps properly be called a Romantic; the author of the later-written parts of the latter work and of the *Génie du Christianisme* may perhaps properly be called a Romantic; but it is obvious that the word has, in most important respects, not merely different but antithetic senses in these two applications of it to the same person. Chateaubriand before 1799 represented in some sort the culmination of the naturalistic and primitivistic Romanticism of which Mr. Gosse sees the beginning in Joseph Warton; he had not only felt intensely but had even gratified the yearning to live "with simple Indian swains." That the Chateaubriand of 1801 represents just as clearly a revolt against this entire tendency is sufficiently

evident from the repudiation of primitivism in the first preface to *Atala*:

Je ne suis point, comme M. Rousseau, un enthousiaste des sauvages; . . . je ne crois point que la *pure nature* soit la plus belle chose du monde. Je l'ai toujours trouvée fort laide partout où j'ai eu occasion de la voir. . . . Avec ce mot de nature on a tout perdu.[18]

[I am not at all, as is Monsieur Rousseau, enthusiastic about savages; I do not believe at all that pure nature is the most beautiful thing in the world. I have always found her very ugly wherever I have had the occasion to see her. With this word Nature we have lost everything.]

Thus the magic word upon which the whole scheme of ideas of the earlier writing had depended is now plainly characterized as the fruitful source of error and confusion that it was. And in his views about the drama the Chateaubriand of 1801 was opposed *both* to the movement represented by *The Enthusiast* and to the German Romanticism of his own time. Shakespeare was (though mainly, as we have seen, for differing reasons) the idol of both; but Chateaubriand in his *Essai sur la littérature anglaise*[19] writes of Shakespeare in the vein, and partly in the words, of Voltaire and Pope. In point of natural genius, he grants, the English dramatist was without a peer in his own age, and perhaps in any age: "je ne sais si jamais homme a jeté des regards plus profonds sur la nature humaine" [I do not know if ever a man has cast deeper glances into human nature]. But Shakespeare knew almost nothing of the requirements of the drama as an art:

[18] On the two strains in *Atala*, cf. Chinard, *L'Exotisme américain dans l'oeuvre de Chateaubriand*, 1918, ch. ix.
[19] The section on Shakespeare was published in April, 1801 (*Mélanges politiques et littéraires*, 1854, pp. 390 ff.).

Il faut se persuader d'abord qu' écrire est un art; que cet art a nécessairement ses genres, et que chaque genre a ses règles. Et qu'on ne dise pas que les genres et les règles sont arbitraires; ils sont nés de la nature même; l'art a seulement séparé ce que la nature a confondu. . . . On peut dire que Racine, dans toute l'excellence de son art, est plus naturel que Shakespeare.

[One must first convince oneself that writing is an art, that this art necessarily has genres, and that each genre has its rules. And let no one say that the genres and the rules are arbitary. They are born of nature itself; art has only separated what nature has mingled. One can say that Racine, in all the excellence of his art, is more natural than Shakespeare.]

Chateaubriand here, to be sure, still finds the standard of art in "nature"; but it is "nature" in the sense of the neo-classical critics, a sense in which it is not opposed, but equivalent, to an art that rigorously conforms to fixed rules. And the "great literary paradox of the partisans of Shakespeare," he observes, is that their arguments imply that "there are *no* rules of the drama," which is equivalent to asserting "that an art is not an art." Voltaire rightly felt that "by banishing all rules and returning to *pure nature*, nothing was easier than to equal the *chefs-d'oeuvre* of the English stage"; and he was well advised in recanting his earlier too enthusiastic utterances about Shakespeare, since he saw that "en relevant les beautés des barbares, il avait séduit des hommes qui, comme lui, ne sauraient séparer l'alliage de l'or" [by picking out the beauties of primitive art, he had seduced those men who, like himself, were unable to separate the alloy from the gold]. Chateaubriand regrets that "the *Cato* of Addison is no longer played" and that consequently "on ne se délasse au théâtre anglais des mon-

struosités de Shakespeare que par les horreurs d'Otway" [one only finds relief, in the English theater, from the monstrosities of Shakespeare in the horrors of Otway]. "Comment," he exclaims, "ne pas gémir de voir une nation éclairée, et qui compte parmi ses critiques les Pope et les Addison, de la voir s'extasier sur le portrait de l'apothicaire dans *Roméo et Juliette*. C'est le burlesque le plus hideux et le plus dégoûtant." [How can one not groan to see an enlightened nation, and one which counts among its critics a Pope and an Addison, go into ecstasy over the portrait of the apothecary in Romeo and Juliet. It is a most hideous and disgusting burlesque]. The entire passage might almost have been written with Warton's poem in mind, so completely and methodically does this later "Romanticist" controvert the aesthetic principles and deride the enthusiasm of the English "Romanticist" of 1740. It is worth noting, also, that Chateaubriand at this time thinks almost as ill of Gothic architecture as of Shakespeare and of *la pure nature*:

Une beauté dans Shakespeare n'excuse pas ses innombrables défauts: un monument gothique peut plaire par son obscurité et la difformité même de ses proportions, mais personne ne songe á bâtir un palais sur son modèle.[20]

[The beautiful in Shakespeare may not excuse his innumerable faults: a Gothic monument may give pleasure because of its obscurity and the very deformity of its proportions, but no one would think to build a palace after such a model.]

[20] It is somewhat difficult to reconcile this with the eloquent passage on the Gothic church in the *Génie du Christianisme* (V, Ch. 8); yet even there, while ascribing to the Gothic style "une beauté qui lui est particulière" [a beauty all its own], Chateaubriand also refers to its "proportions barbares" [primitive proportions].

We have, then, observed and compared—very far from exhaustively, of course, yet in some of their most fundamental and determinative ideas—three "Romanticisms." In the first and second we have found certain common elements, but still more significant oppositions; in the second and third we have found certain other common elements, but likewise significant oppositions. But between the first and third the common elements are very scanty; such as there are, it could, I think, be shown, are not the same as those subsisting between either the first and second or the second and third; and in their ethical preconceptions and implications and the crucial articles of their literary creeds, the opposition between them is almost absolute.

All three of these historic episodes, it is true, are far more complex than I have time to show. I am attempting only to illustrate the nature of a certain procedure in the study of what is called Romanticism, to suggest its importance, and to present one or two specific results of the use of it. A complete analysis would qualify, without invalidating, these results, in several ways. It would (for one thing) bring out certain important connections between the revolt against the neo-classical aesthetics (common to two of the episodes mentioned) and other aspects of eighteenth-century thought. It would, again, exhibit fully certain *internal* oppositions in at least two of the Romanticisms considered. For example, in German Romanticism between 1797 and 1800 there grew up, and mainly from a single root, both an "apotheosis of the future" and a tendency to retrospection —a retrospection directed, not, indeed, towards classical antiquity or towards the primitive, but towards the medieval. A belief in progress and a spirit of reaction were, paradoxically, joint offspring of the same idea, and were nurtured for a time in the same minds. But it is just these internal incongruities which make it most of all evident, as it seems to me, that any attempt at a *general* appraisal even of a single chronologically determinate Romanticism—still more, of "Romanticism" as a whole—is a fatuity. When a Romanticism has been analyzed into the distinct "strains" or ideas which compose it, the true philosophic affinities and the eventual practical influence in life and art of these several strains will usually be found to be exceedingly diverse and often conflicting. It will, no doubt, remain abstractly possible to raise the question whether the preponderant effect, moral or aesthetic, of one or another large movement which has been called by the name was good or bad. But that ambitious inquiry cannot even be legitimately begun until a prior task of analysis and detailed comparison—of the sort that I have attempted here to indicate—has been accomplished. And when this has been done, I doubt whether the larger question will seem to have much importance or meaning. What will then appear historically significant and philosophically instructive will be the way in which *each* of these distinguishable strains has worked itself out, what its elective affinities for other ideas, and its historic consequences, have shown themselves to be. The categories which it has become customary to use in distinguishing and classifying "movements" in literature or philosophy and in describing the nature of the significant transitions which have taken place in taste and in opinion, are far too rough, crude, undiscriminating—and none of them so hopelessly so as the category "Romantic." It is not any large *complexes* of ideas, such as that term has almost always been employed to designate, but rather certain simpler, diversely combinable, intellectual and emotional components of such complexes, that are the true elemental and dynamic factors in the history of thought and of art; and it is with the genesis, the vicissitudes, the manifold and often dramatic interactions of these, that it is the task of the historian of ideas in literature to become acquainted.

FROM ON WORDSWORTH AND THE LOCKE TRADITION
Basil Willey[*]

The effect of mechanical philosophy upon poetry was to put mythology out of style; the poet explained the workings of the universe in abstract instead of mythological terms. Wordsworth had to "animise the 'real' world, the 'universe of death' that the 'mechanical' system of philosophy had produced, but without either using an exploded mythology or fabricating a new one." He did this by means of imagination working on sense-perceived objects.

I

The manner in which the triumph of the mechanical philosophy affected poetry can be illustrated, I think, by comparing a representative serious poem of the earlier eighteenth century, Pope's *Essay on Man*, with *Paradise Lost* as representing the previous century. It has been pointed out that there is no Satan in Pope's poem. From one standpoint this fact merely exemplifies Pope's optimistic "philosophy." With the characteristic desire of his time to explain, and to explain favourably, Pope unquestioningly makes his poem a theodicy, a vindication of an order of things in which evil appears, but only appears, to exist. To "explain" evil is almost necessarily to explain it away. But taking a more general view, one is struck by the

absence, in Pope's poem, of any sort of mythological machinery. In giving pointed expression to the real beliefs of his time, Pope instinctively adopts an explanatory method. It would have been unthinkable in Pope's time that a serious poet should have used any such machinery, or even an allegorical convention, for such a purpose. Mythologies, including the Christian, were now felt to be exploded; what may have been "true" in them is that part which can be conceptually or intellectually stated. Milton, as we have seen, although himself a considerable rationaliser, could still employ the concrete symbols of the faith without feeling that he was deliberately utilising what was fictitious. God and Satan were real beings to him, as well as "principles." But though Pope and his contemporaries were debarred by their intellectual climate from using any great system of commonly-accepted symbols, as Dante and Milton could, they could still employ mythological material for

[*] The selection is reprinted from *The Seventeenth Century Background*, by Basil Willey (New York: Columbia University Press, 1942), Chapter XII, pp. 296–306, by permission of Columbia University Press.

oher purposes, as Pope did in the *Rape of the Lock*, for example. They could use it consciously, for technical convenience and for purposes of "delight." It is in this manner that the mythologies of the ancient world are generally used by eighteenth century poets. These poets employ their personifications and their other mythological apparatus in full awareness that they are "fiction." They are "fictions" of proved evocative power and of long association with poetic experience, and they can thus still be made use of to assist in producing poetry out of the dead-matter of modernity. But fictions they are still felt to be, and they cannot therefore be used with full conviction. Their employment involves the deliberate exploitation of obsolete modes of feeling, a conscious disregard of contemporary truth-standards. It was, one may suppose, his sense of this situation which made Johnson dislike *Lycidas* and Gray's *Odes*.

As a consequence of these developments it was inevitable that when a major poet again appeared he should be "left alone, seeking the visible world." No existing mythology could express the "real," as the "real" was now felt to be. A final effort had been made, by Erasmus Darwin, to enlist poetry under the banner of science by describing the Loves of the Plants with all the apparatus of "poetical machinery," but of this unholy alliance it would be hard to say whether it was more degrading to science or to poetry. The new poet must therefore either make poetry out of the direct dealings of his mind and heart with the visible universe, or he must fabricate a genuine new mythology of his own (not necessarily rejecting all old material in so doing). Keats and Shelley often follow the second of these methods; Wordsworth typically follows the first.

Wordsworth's relation to the "scientific" tradition is not quite simple. In a sense he is in violent reaction against it, and yet it conditioned much of his poetic experience. What he owed to it was his instinctive repudiation of any concrete mythology. His poetry was "scientific" in that his interest lay in the free relations between the mind of man and the universe to which, he believes, it is "so exquisitely fitted." According to him, we "build up the being that we are" by "deeply drinking-in the soul of things." That is, there must be no abstractions, no symbols, no myths, to stand between the mind and its true object. In so far as it was the abstract world-picture (the world as "machine") of the seventeenth century natural philosophers which had exploded the mythologies, Wordsworth may be said to have owed to them (as well as to his own temperament) his root-assumption that truth could only be achieved by "making verse deal boldly with substantial things." Wordsworth was the kind of poet who could only have appeared at the end of the eighteenth century, when mythologies were exploded, and a belief in the visible universe as the body of which God was the soul alone remained. In this sense his beliefs can be viewed as data furnished to him by a tradition; in this sense he, as well as Dante, may be said to have employed his sensibility within a framework of received beliefs. But his debt to tradition, unlike Dante's, was a negative one; he owed to it his *deprivation* of mythology, his aloneness with the universe. His more positive beliefs, those by which he appears in reaction against the scientific tradition, were built up by him out of his own poetic experiences, and it is this which makes him representative of the modern situation—the situation in which beliefs are made out of poetry rather than poetry out of beliefs. To animise the "real" world, the "universe of death" that the "mechanical" system of philosophy had produced, but to do so without either using an exploded mythology or fabricating a new one, this was the special task and mission of Wordsworth. Wordsworth's conviction that the human mind was capable of this task was the most important of his "positive" beliefs, and this belief he owed chiefly to his own experiences. It is this which distinguishes his "deism" from that of, for instance, Thomson's *Seasons*, to which it bears an obvious superficial resemblance. For Thomson, as for Pope, mythologies were almost as "unreal" as for Wordsworth, but their positive belief, their Deism (in so far as they genuinely held it), was "intellectually" held, and it consequently appears in poetry mainly as rhetoric. The poetry exists to decorate, to render agreeable, a set of abstract notions; and these abstractions have been taken over, as truth, from the natural philosophers—from Descartes, Newton, Locke, or Leibnitz. Wordsworth's beliefs, on the other hand, were largely the formulation of his own dealings with "substantial things"; they were held intellectually only because they had first been "proved upon the pulses." That the result of his "dealings" was not a *Divine Comedy* or a *Paradise Lost* was due, we may say, to the scientific movement and the sensationalist philosophy of Locke and Hartley; that the result was not an *Essay on Man*, a *Seasons*, or a *Botanic Garden* was due to himself. For it was the "visible world," no abstract machine, that Wordsworth sought; and he felt that mechanical materialism had substituted a "universe of death for that which moves with light and life instinct, actual, divine, and true."[1] The belief that Wordsworth constructed out of his experiences was a belief in the capacity of the mind to co-operate with

[1] *Prelude*, xiv. 160.

this "active universe," to contribute something of its own to it in perceiving it, and not, as sensationalism taught, merely to receive, passively, impressions from without. It was this belief, or the experiences upon which the belief was based, which encouraged him to hope that poetry might be delivered from the fetters of the mechanical tradition without being allowed to fall into disrepute as "unreal" or "fanciful."

Of this belief, as intellectually formulated, there are many explicit statements in Wordsworth's poetry, especially in the *Prelude*, as well as in his prose. There is, for example, the passage on the child (the "inmate of this active universe"):

For feeling has to him imparted power
That through the growing faculties of sense
Doth like an agent of the one great Mind
Create, creator and receiver both,
Working but in alliance with the works
Which it beholds.[2]

In a later passage of the same Book he distinguishes the true creative power from arbitrary fancy:

A plastic power
Abode with me, a forming hand, at times
Rebellious, acting in a devious mood,
A local spirit of his own, at war
With general tendency, but, for the most,
Subservient strictly to external things
With which it communed.[3]

The classic "locus" is in the Preface to the *Excursion*, where in deliberately Miltonic language he has been claiming more than epic dignity for his own subject-matter:[4]

Paradise, and groves
Elysian, Fortunate Fields—*why should they be*
A *history only of departed things,*

[2] *Prelude*, ii. 254.
[3] *Ibid.*, 362.
[4] The italics are the author's.

Or a mere fiction of what never was?
For the discerning intellect of Man,
When wedded to this goodly universe
In love and holy passion, shall find these
A simple produce of the common day.
—I, long before the blissful hour arrives,
Would chant in lonely peace the spousal verse
Of this great consummation:—and, *by words*
Which speak of nothing more than what we are,
Would I arouse the sensual from their sleep
Of Death, and win the vacant and the vain
To noble raptures; while my voice proclaims
How exquisitely the individual Mind to the external World
Is fitted, and how exquisitely too—
Theme this but little heard of among men—
The external World is fitted to the Mind;
And the Creation (by no lower name
Can it be called) *which they with blended might*
Accomplish.

The famous "Fancy-Imagination" distinction of Wordsworth and Coleridge, and their followers, may best be understood as arising from the existence in them of the particular "belief-state" I have tried to indicate. The fact-world of modern scientific consciousness was the primary datum. In this "inanimate cold world" "objects, *as* objects, are essentially fixed and dead."[5] But just as a "known and familiar landscape" may be transmuted by moonlight or "accidents of light and shade,"[6] so, owing to the bond between nature and the soul of man, this dead world may be brought to life by the modifying colours of the "imagination." Of the *imagination*, for this is the faculty which works the required magic without producing what is now felt to be "fictitious." Where there is consciousness of fiction, it is the *fancy*

that has been at work. The test of the "imaginative," as distinct from the "imaginary," is that external objects shall have been coloured by the poet's own mood, or made the symbol of it; that the plastic power shall have been exercised, but kept "subservient strictly to external things." Modifications *so* wrought, values *so* ascribed to the fact-world, have a reality-status which is unassailable, because they are psychological in origin; they spring, that is, from states of mind, of which the "reality" cannot be questioned.

Wordsworth's belief in the possibility of this creation which the mind and the universe may "with blended might accomplish" was, I have suggested, largely built up out of his own poetic experience. One need only consider a number of passages in which Wordsworth has commemorated those of his experiences which he felt to be most significant, to see that they are generally occasions on which he had (for the most part unconsciously at the time) exerted the "visionary," the "plastic" power upon some external object. In the celebrated "spots of time" passage at the end of Book XII. of the *Prelude*,[7] he says explicitly that of all the recollections which hold for him a "renovating virtue," he values most those which record moments of the greatest self-activity, those which "give knowledge to what point, and how, the mind is lord and master, outward sense the obedient servant of her will"; recollections, that is, which show the mind "not prostrate, overborne, as if the mind herself were nothing, a mere pensioner on outward forms—" (as in sensationalist philosophy), but in its native dignity, creating significance in alliance with external things. It is unfortunately true that Wordsworth frequently *dis-*

[5] Coleridge, *Biog. Lit.*, ch. xiii. (vol. i. p. 202 in Shawcross).

[6] Phrases from the opening of ch. xiv. of *Biog. Lit.*

[7] Lines 208–286.

cusses his experiences, and states the results which his intellect has extracted from them, instead of communicating them to us. The modern reader demands the experience, and cares little or nothing what metaphysical or psychological principle they are supposed to exemplify. This criticism is perhaps applicable to the passage in Book XII. to which I have referred, for Wordsworth there avows his inability to communicate the "visionary dreariness" which then invested the moor, the lonely pool, and the woman with the pitcher, although the knowledge that his imagination had been strong enough to impart the visionary quality to the scene was his reason for valuing the recollection. But he has given enough examples of his sensibility in action for us to see that its workings were independent of, and antecedent to, the formulation of the belief. When (to take a few illustrations at random):

> a gentle shock of mild surprise
> Has carried far into his heart the voice
> Of mountain torrent;[8]

when he saw the Leech-Gatherer pace

> About the weary moors continually,
> Wandering about alone and silently;[9]

when the Highland woman's greeting seemed

> a sound
> Of something without place or bound;[10]

when

> the high spear-grass on that wall
> By mist and silent rain-drops silvered o'er,
> As once I passed, into my heart conveyed
> So still an image of tranquillity,

[8] *Prelude*, v. 382.
[9] *Stepping Westward*, verse 2.
[10] *Resolution and Independence*, stanza xix.

> So calm and still, and looked so beautiful
> Among the uneasy thoughts which filled my mind,[11]

these experiences, and many another that could be collected from his best poetry, depended upon no special beliefs (and of course no beliefs are needed by the reader in order to share them to the full). It was out of the repetition of these imaginative moments that the belief arose; the belief itself was the intellectual formulation of what they seemed to mean. It must be recognised, nevertheless, that the formulation, once made (no doubt with Coleridge's assistance), gave added importance to the recollected "moments," the "spots of time," and that Wordsworth would probably not have conducted his *recherche du temps perdu* with such eagerness and such conviction if he had not so formulated it.

II

Wordsworth's poetic activity, then, was largely conditioned by the "reality-standards" of his time, which left him alone with the visible universe. But his "creative sensibility" had taught him that he was not alone with an "inanimate cold world," but with an "active universe," a universe capable of being moulded and modified by the "plastic power" which abode within himself. As long as he could be a poet, this belief in the bond between man and nature was valid. Poetry becomes, with Wordsworth, the record of moments of "ennobling interchange of action from within and from without";[12] it takes on, in fine, a *psychological* aspect. "There is scarcely one of my poems," Wordsworth wrote to Lady Beaumont, "which does not aim

[11] *Excursion*, i. 943.
[12] *Prelude*, xiii. 375.

to direct the attention to some moral sentiment, or to some general principle, or law of thought, or of our intellectual constitution."[13]

I have emphasised this "aloneness" of Wordsworth with the universe, because I think it marks his position in the history of "poetry and beliefs," and because it seems to determine the quality of much of his work. Centuries of intellectual development had now brought · matters to this, that if poetry were still to be made, it must be made by the sheer unaided power of the individual poet. And what was it that he must make? A record of successes; of successful imaginative dealings with the world of eye and ear. And what was to be the criterion of success? That plastic power shall have been exerted upon the "vulgar forms of every day," but in such a way that there shall be no departure from "nature's living images." The midnight storm may grow darker in presence of the poet's eye, the visionary dreariness, the consecration, may be spread over sea or land, but the transforming power must work "subservient strictly to external things"; there must be intensification without distortion. Fact and value were to be combined in this "fine balance of truth in observing, with the imaginative faculty in modifying, the object observed." But what sort of "truth" may be claimed for the creation which world and mind "with blended might accomplish"?—for, that poetry is "the most philosophic of all writing," that "its

object is truth," is Wordsworth's profound conviction.[14] I suppose the answer would be, "psychological" truth; that is to say, the poetry is faithfully expressive of certain states of consciousness. Of the two elements of which these states are composed, fact and value, Wordsworth is equally sure of both. He is sure of the fact, because he knows no man has observed it more intently; he is sure of the value, because this was intuitively apprehended in himself, it came from within. He is no less sure of the truth of the resulting creation, because it had been experienced as a modification of his own consciousness. But it was only as long as his mind was dealing thus nakedly with observed fact that Wordsworth could feel this conviction of truthfulness. Any translation of his experience into myth, personification or fable, though not necessarily always culpable, is inevitably a lapse towards a lower level of truth, a fall, in fact, from imagination to fancy. Poetry exists to transform, to make this much-loved earth more lovely; and in former times men could express their sense of fact, without misgiving, in mythologies. But since the coming of the enlightened age this was becoming almost impossible. The efforts of eighteenth century poets to vitalise the dead matter of the Cartesian universe by using the symbols of an outworn mythology had ended in fiasco, and the abandonment of the symbols, at any rate for a time, became a necessity. . . .

[13] In *Wordsworth's Lit. Crit.*, p. 51.

[14] *Lyrical Ballads*, Pref., p. 25 in *Wordsworth's Lit. Crit.*

THE REALITY OF PERCEPTION
S. T. Coleridge*

Coleridge here sketches the different notions of reality underlying on the one hand the doctrine of materialism and on the other the doctrine of idealism. These realities are conveniently termed *objective* and *subjective*. The former attributes a reality to objects "independent of the mind that perceives them." Idealism, however, declares "the material and corporeal world to be wholly subjective, that is, to exist only as far as it is perceived." Thus, for the idealist the distinction between subjective and objective disappears, and all reality becomes subjective. These distinctions may be considered in conjunction with Wordsworth's "mighty world of eye and ear,—both what they half create, And what perceive," and with romantic subjectivism generally.

... Lastly, when we contradistinguish the Mind or the percipient power from that which it perceives, the former has been (very conveniently, I think) entitled the subject and the latter the object.

Hence the mind may be defined as a subject which is its own object. And hence those who attribute a reality to bodies and to material phenomena, independent of the mind that perceives them, and yet assert equally an independent reality of the mind itself, namely those who believe in both immaterial and corporeal substances, or in the language of the day, in soul and body both, would define the body as merely and purely objective; while an idealist,[1] would declare the material and corporeal world to be wholly subjective, that is, to exist

only as far as it is perceived. In other words, he, the idealist, concedes a real existence to one of the two terms only— to the *natura naturans*, in Berkeley's language, to God, and to the finite minds on which it acts, the natura naturata, or the bodily world, being the result, even as the tune between the wind and the Aeolian harp. I remember when I was yet young this fancy struck me wonderfully, and here are some verses I wrote on the subject:

And what if all of animated nature
Be but organic Harps diversely framed
That tremble into thought, as o'er them sweeps
Plastic and vast, one intellectual Breeze
At once the Soul of each and God of all.

Now in and from this last view, that of the idealists I mean, arises the difficulty and perplexity of our metaphysical vocabulary. As long as the *subject*, that is the percipient, was opposed to the *object*, namely the thing perceived, all was clear. Again, in considering the finite

---

* The selection is reprinted from *The Philosophical Lectures of Samuel Taylor Coleridge*, edited by Kathleen Coburn, by permission of Philosophical Library. Copyright 1949 by Philosophical Library.

[1] NB. 25: or what is called a Berkleian tho', as we have seen, the doctrine was taught & fully developed more than 2000 years before Bishop Berkley [sic] was born.

mind or soul as self-percipient, or a subject capable of becoming an immediate object to itself, but incapable of being an immediate object to any one other finite subject, there would be no great difficulty. A man's thoughts are known only to God and himself, as reduced, as a rule, to a general formula—for the convenience of reasoning—as we use marks and letters in algebra. But when not only the mind's self-consciousness, but all other things perceived by it, are regarded as modifications of itself, as disguised but actual modes of self-perception, then the whole ground of the difference between subject and object appears gone. All is subject, and the sole distinction is: first, between that which not only is, but is thought of by us as being such, and that which indeed truly *is* so no less than the former, but which we think of as being the contrary. By way of illustration: man contemplates the image of his friend. Not only his recollection of the friend is in his mind, but he contemplates it as such; but when his friend is present, though according to the idealist that impression is as much in his mind as the former, he yet considers it to be external and independent of himself. Secondly, the distinction between that which all men are, by the common necessity, constrained so to imagine, and that which is accidental and individual—as for instance all men in a sane state are compelled to see the objects which all others at least see around them, as compared with the man who, in a fever or delirium, blends objects which no man else perceives—so that one of the older idealists will state the subject according to his view of it, that when we are awake we have a dream in common, when asleep every man has a dream of his own; that is, when we are awake we have a world in common and when we are asleep every man has a world of his own—

We have only to reverse this order of thought, and we shall have the opposite result, that of the materialist. All here is merged in the objective, as the former in the subjective, and this reduced, as before, into the general and permanent and the particular and transitory. The thought[2] of a table,[3] according to the materialist differs from the table itself, not by essential invisibility or by being essentially imponderable, but only because this portion of the brain is too thin and subtle to be perceptible of weight, and it is truly owing to the defect of our organs that we cannot weigh our thoughts or measure our perceptions. Henceforward therefore "objective" acquired two meanings, the first being the reality of any thing, outwardly correspondent to our perception or notion[4] thereof, independent of the perception itself, and the second, meaning the universality of the perception as arising out of inherent laws of human nature in opposition to the accidental state of any one individual percipient. That grass is green is an instance of the former; that it appears yellow to a man in the jaundice (if such be the fact) would be an instance of the latter.

Still, most serious difficulties started, and have been stated with incomparable clearness by Lord Bacon in his *Novum Organum*. It is thus: that the human understanding itself is but an individuality in nature, having its own peculiar organization,[5] and modifying all objects, even its own form of self-consciousness, no less than the forms seen as external, by its own peculiar appropriate perspective. In the language of our British Plato, there are not only Idols of the Den,

---

[2] NB. 25: "and image" was inserted here and then crossed out.

[3] The reporter wrote "tale" here and below.

[4] The reporter wrote "motions."

[5] NB. 25: idiosyncrasy or peculiar organism.

the Theatre, and the Market Place—the Idols or delusions of our passions, of our imagination, and of custom and habit, but Idols of the race. And consequently the utmost that rational conviction can amount to is, not that this or that is true by any inherent necessity, but only that it is true for man, that he is[6] compelled so to perceive and so to conceive, and the deductions thus drawn can be questioned only by those who admit themselves to be deranged—that is, not in the same order with their

fellow-men. To what an extent this position has been carried by ancient and modern sceptics it will be sufficient that I remind you by one observation of Mr. Hume's in the *Essays* in the form in which they first appeared: namely, that if spiders had been theologians[7] they would have been under the necessity of concluding that the world had been spun; and that— <but a philosophical lecture will be no excuse for repeating blasphemy—and I stop>[8] though a philosopher <*said it*>.

[6] NB. 25: by the very mechanism of his nature. (Coleridge obviously wished to avoid any misunderstanding that he was fighting on the enemy's side by using this phrase.)

[7] The report reads: theologicians.
[8] MS. Egerton 3057 gives substantially the same reading as the NB. and therefore I insert it, though there is no gap in the report.

PREFACE TO THE *LYRICAL BALLADS*
William Wordsworth

Wordsworth's poetic canon requires of poetry the following: "a selection of the real language of men in a state of vivid sensation" —a language "arising out of repeated experience"; feeling "modified and directed by our thoughts," which are "the representatives of all our past feelings"; feeling that gives importance to action and situation rather than action and situation that give importance to feeling; sensations and objects related, according to "the primary laws of our nature," through "the manner in which we associate ideas"; truth as "our visible friend," palpably material; knowledge that connects us with our fellow beings. The essay appeared as a preface to the 1800 edition of *Lyrical Ballads*.

The first Volume of these Poems has already been submitted to general perusal. It was published, as an experiment, which, I hoped, might be of some use to ascertain, how far, by fitting to metrical arrangement a selection of the real language of men in a state of vivid sensation, that sort of pleasure and that quantity of pleasure may be imparted, which a Poet may rationally endeavour to impart.

I had formed no very inaccurate esti-

mate of the probable effect of those Poems: I flattered myself that they who should be pleased with them would read them with more than common pleasure: and, on the other hand, I was well aware, that by those who should dislike them, they would be read with more than common dislike. The result has differed from my expectation in this only, that a greater number have been pleased than I ventured to hope I should please.

Several of my Friends are anxious for the success of these Poems, from a belief, that, if the views with which they were composed were indeed realised, a class of Poetry would be produced, well adapted to interest mankind permanently, and not unimportant in the quality, and in the multiplicity of its moral relations: and on this account they have advised me to prefix a systematic defence of the theory upon which the Poems were written. But I was unwilling to undertake the task, knowing that on this occasion the Reader would look coldly upon my arguments, since I might be suspected of having been principally influenced by the selfish and foolish hope of *reasoning* him into an approbation of these particular Poems: and I was still more unwilling to undertake the task, because, adequately to display the opinions, and fully to enforce the arguments, would require a space wholly disproportionate to a preface. For, to treat the subject with the clearness and coherence of which it is susceptible, it would be necessary to give a full account of the present state of the public taste in this country, and to determine how far this taste is healthy or depraved; which, again, could not be determined, without pointing out in what manner language and the human mind act and re-act on each other, and without retracing the revolutions, not of literature alone, but likewise of society itself. I have therefore altogether declined to enter regularly upon this defence; yet I am sensible, that there would be something like impropriety in abruptly obtruding upon the Public, without a few words of introduction, Poems so materially different from those upon which general approbation is at present bestowed.

It is supposed, that by the act of writing in verse an Author makes a formal engagement that he will gratify certain known habits of association; that he not only thus apprises the Reader that certain classes of ideas and expressions will be found in his book, but that others will be carefully excluded. This exponent or symbol held forth by metrical language must in different eras of literature have excited very different expectations: for example, in the age of Catullus, Terence, and Lucretius, and that of Statius or Claudian; and in our own country, in the age of Shakespeare and Beaumont and Fletcher, and that of Donne and Cowley, or Dryden, or Pope. I will not take upon me to determine the exact import of the promise which, by the act of writing in verse, an Author in the present day makes to his reader: but it will undoubtedly appear to many persons that I have not fulfilled the terms of an engagement thus voluntarily contracted. They who have been accustomed to the gaudiness and inane phraseology of many modern writers, if they persist in reading this book to its conclusion, will, no doubt, frequently have to struggle with feelings of strangeness and awkwardness: they will look round for poetry, and will be induced to inquire by what species of courtesy these attempts can be permitted to assume that title. I hope therefore the reader will not censure me for attempting to state what I have proposed to myself to perform; and also (as far as the limits of a preface will permit) to explain some of the chief reasons which have determined me in the choice of my purpose: that at least he may be spared any unpleasant feeling of disappointment, and that I myself may be protected from one of the most dishonourable accusations which can be brought against an Author; namely, that of an indolence which prevents him from endeavouring to ascertain what is his duty, or, when his duty is ascertained, prevents him from performing it.

The principal object, then, proposed in

these Poems was to choose incidents and situations from common life, and to relate or describe them, throughout, as far as was possible in a selection of language really used by men, and, at the same time, to throw over them a certain colouring of imagination, whereby ordinary things should be presented to the mind in an unusual aspect; and, further, and above all, to make these incidents and situations interesting by tracing in them, truly though not ostentatiously, the primary laws of our nature: chiefly, as far as regards the manner in which we associate ideas in a state of excitement. Humble and rustic life **was** generally chosen, because, in that condition, the essential passions of the heart find a better soil in which they can attain their maturity, are less under restraint, and speak a plainer and more emphatic language; because in that condition of life our elementary feelings coexist in a state of greater simplicity, and, consequently, may be more accurately contemplated, and more forcibly communicated; because the manners of rural life germinate from those elementary feelings, and, from the necessary character of rural occupations, are more easily comprehended, and are more durable; and, lastly, because in that condition the passions of men are incorporated with the beautiful and permanent forms of nature. The language, too, of these men has been adopted (purified indeed from what appear to be its real defects, from all lasting and rational causes of dislike or disgust) because such men hourly communicate with the best objects from which the best part of language is originally derived; and because, from their rank in society and the sameness and narrow circle of their intercourse, being less under the influence of social vanity, they convey their feelings and notions in simple and unelaborated expressions. Accordingly, such a language,

arising out of repeated experience and regular feelings, is a more permanent, and a far more philosophical language, than that which is frequently substituted for it by Poets, who think that they are conferring honour upon themselves and their art, in proportion as they separate themselves from the sympathies of men, and indulge in arbitrary and capricious habits of expression, in order to furnish food for fickle tastes, and fickle appetites, of their own creation.[1]

I cannot, however, be insensible to the present outcry against the triviality and meanness, both of thought and language, which some of my contemporaries have occasionally introduced into their metrical compositions; and I acknowledge that this defect, where it exists, is more dishonourable to the Writer's own character than false refinement or arbitrary innovation, though I should contend at the same time, that it is far less pernicious in the sum of its consequences. From such verses the Poems in these volumes will be found distinguished at least by one mark of difference, that each of them has a worthy *purpose*. Not that I always began to write with a distinct purpose formally conceived; but habits of meditation have, I trust, so prompted and regulated my feelings, that my descriptions of such objects as strongly excite those feelings, will be found to carry along with them a *purpose*. If this opinion be erroneous, I can have little right to the name of a Poet. For all good poetry is the spontaneous overflow of powerful feelings: and though this be true, Poems to which any value can be attached were never produced on any variety of subjects but by a man who, being possessed of more than usual organic sensibility, had

[1] It is worth while here to observe, that the affecting parts of Chaucer are almost always expressed in language pure and universally intelligible even to this day.

also thought long and deeply. For our continued influxes of feeling are modified and directed by our thoughts, which are indeed the representatives of all our past feelings; and, as by contemplating the relation of these general representatives to each other, we discover what is really important to men, so, by the repetition and continuance of this act, our feelings will be connected with important subjects, till at length, if we be originally possessed of much sensibility, such habits of mind will be produced, that, by obeying blindly and mechanically the impulses of those habits, we shall describe objects, and utter sentiments, of such a nature, and in such connection with each other, that the understanding of the Reader must necessarily be in some degree enlightened, and his affections strengthened and purified.

It has been said that each of these poems has a purpose. Another circumstance must be mentioned which distinguishes these Poems from the popular Poetry of the day; it is this, that the feeling therein developed gives importance to the action and situation, and not the action and situation to the feeling.

A sense of false modesty shall not prevent me from asserting, that the Reader's attention is pointed to this mark of distinction, far less for the sake of these particular Poems than from the general importance of the subject. The subject is indeed important! For the human mind is capable of being excited without the application of gross and violent stimulants; and he must have a very faint perception of its beauty and dignity who does not know this, and who does not further know, that one being is elevated above another, in proportion as he possesses this capability. It has therefore appeared to me, that to endeavour to produce or enlarge this capability is one of the best services in which, at any period,

a Writer can be engaged; but this service, excellent at all times, is especially so at the present day. For a multitude of causes, unknown to former times, are now acting with a combined force to blunt the discriminating powers of the mind, and, unfitting it for all voluntary exertion, to reduce it to a state of almost savage torpor. The most effective of these causes are the great national events which are daily taking place, and the increasing accumulation of men in cities, where the uniformity of their occupations produces a craving for extraordinary incident, which the rapid communication of intelligence hourly gratifies. To this tendency of life and manners the literature and theatrical exhibitions of the country have conformed themselves. The invaluable works of our elder writers, I had almost said the works of Shakespeare and Milton, are driven into neglect by frantic novels, sickly and stupid German Tragedies, and deluges of idle and extravagant stories in verse.—When I think upon this degrading thirst after outrageous stimulation, I am almost ashamed to have spoken of the feeble endeavour made in these volumes to counteract it; and, reflecting upon the magnitude of the general evil, I should be oppressed with no dishonourable melancholy, had I not a deep impression of certain inherent and indestructible qualities of the human mind, and likewise of certain powers in the great and permanent objects that act upon it, which are equally inherent and indestructible; and were there not added to this impression a belief that the time is approaching when the evil will be systematically opposed, by men of greater powers, and with far more distinguished success.

Having dwelt thus long on the subjects and aim of these Poems, I shall request the Reader's permission to apprise him of a few circumstances relating to their *style*, in order, among other reasons, that he may not censure me for not having performed what I never attempted. The Reader will find that personifications of abstract ideas rarely occur in these volumes; and are utterly rejected, as an ordinary device to elevate the style, and raise it above prose. My purpose was to imitate, and, as far as possible, to adopt the very language of men; and assuredly such personifications do not make any natural or regular part of that language. They are, indeed, a figure of speech occasionally prompted by passion, and I have made use of them as such; but have endeavoured utterly to reject them as a mechanical device of style, or as a family language which Writers in metre seem to lay claim to by prescription. I have wished to keep the Reader in the company of flesh and blood, persuaded that by so doing I shall interest him. Others who pursue a different track will interest him likewise; I do not interfere with their claim, but wish to prefer a claim of my own. There will also be found in these volumes little of what is usually called poetic diction; as much pains has been taken to avoid it as is ordinarily taken to produce it; this has been done for the reason already alleged, to bring my language near to the language of men; and further, because the pleasure which I have proposed to myself to impart, is of a kind very different from that which is supposed by many persons to be the proper object of poetry. Without being culpably particular, I do not know how to give my Reader a more exact notion of the style in which it was my wish and intention to write, than by informing him that I have at all times endeavoured to look steadily at my subject; consequently, there is I hope in these Poems little falsehood of description, and my ideas are expressed in language fitted to their respective importance. Something

must have been gained by this practice, as it is friendly to one property of all good poetry, namely, good sense: but it has necessarily cut me off from a large portion of phrases and figures of speech which from father to son have long been regarded as the common inheritance of Poets. I have also thought it expedient to restrict myself still further, having abstained from the use of many expressions, in themselves proper and beautiful, but which have been foolishly repeated by bad Poets, till such feelings of disgust are connected with them as it is scarcely possible by any art of association to overpower.

If in a poem there should be found a series of lines, or even a single line, in which the language, though naturally arranged, and according to the strict laws of metre, does not differ from that of prose, there is a numerous class of critics, who, when they stumble upon these prosaisms, as they call them, imagine that they have made a notable discovery, and exult over the Poet as over a man ignorant of his own profession. Now these men would establish a canon of criticism which the Reader will conclude he must utterly reject, if he wishes to be pleased with these volumes. And it would be a most easy task to prove to him, that not only the language of a large portion of every good poem, even of the most elevated character, must necessarily, except with reference to the metre, in no respect differ from that of good prose, but likewise that some of the most interesting parts of the best poems will be found to be strictly the language of prose when prose is well written. The truth of this assertion might be demonstrated by innumerable passages from almost all the poetical writings, even of Milton himself. To illustrate the subject in a general manner, I will here adduce a short composition of Gray, who was at the head of those who, by their reasonings, have attempted to widen the space of separation betwixt Prose and Metrical composition, and was more than any other man curiously elaborate in the structure of his own poetic diction.

In vain to me the smiling mornings shine,
And reddening Phoebus lifts his golden fire:
The birds in vain their amorous descant join,
Or cheerful fields resume their green attire.
These ears, alas! for other notes repine;
A *different object do these eyes require;*
My lonely anguish melts no heart but mine,
And in my breast the imperfect joys expire;
Yet morning smiles the busy race to cheer,
And new-born pleasure brings to happier men;
The fields to all their wonted tribute bear;
To warm their little loves the birds complain.
I *fruitless mourn to him that cannot hear,*
And weep the more because I weep in vain.

It will easily be perceived, that the only part of this Sonnet which is of any value is the lines printed in Italics; it is equally obvious, that, except in the rhyme, and in the use of the single word "fruitless" for fruitlessly, which is so far a defect, the language of these lines does in no respect differ from that of prose.

By the foregoing quotation it has been shown that the language of Prose may yet be well adapted to Poetry; and it was previously asserted, that a large portion of the language of every good poem can in no respect differ from that of good Prose. We will go further. It may be safely affirmed, that there neither is, nor can be, any *essential* difference between the language of prose and metrical composition. We are fond of tracing the resemblance between Poetry and Painting, and, accordingly, we call them Sisters: but where shall we find bonds of connection sufficiently strict to typify the affinity betwixt metrical and prose composition? They both speak by and to the same organs; the bodies in which both of them are clothed may be said to be of the same substance, their affections are kindred, and almost identical, not necessarily differing even in degree; Poetry[2] sheds no tears "such as Angels weep," but natural and human tears; she can boast of no celestial ichor that distinguishes her vital juices from those of prose; the same human blood circulates through the veins of them both.

If it be affirmed that rhyme and metrical arrangement of themselves constitute a distinction which overturns what has just been said on the strict affinity of metrical language with that of prose, and paves the way for other artificial distinctions which the mind voluntarily admits, I answer that the language of such Poetry as is here recommended is, as far as is possible, a selection of the language really spoken by men; that this selection, wherever it is made with true taste and feeling, will of itself form a distinction far greater than would at first be imagined, and will entirely separate the composition from the vulgarity and meanness of ordinary life; and, if metre be superadded thereto, I believe that a dissimilitude will be produced altogether sufficient for the gratification of a rational mind. What other distinction would we have? Whence is it to come? And where is it to exist? Not, surely, where the Poet speaks through the mouths of his characters: it cannot be necessary here, either for elevation of style, or any of its

[2] I here use the word "Poetry" (though against my own judgment) as opposed to the word Prose, and synonymous with metrical composition. But much confusion has been introduced into criticism by this contradistinction of Poetry and Prose, instead of the more philosophical one of Poetry and Matter of Fact, or Science. The only strict antithesis to Prose is Metre; nor is this, in truth, a *strict* antithesis, because lines and passages of metre so naturally occur in writing prose, that it would be scarcely possible to avoid them, even were it desirable.

supposed ornaments: for, if the Poet's subject be judiciously chosen, it will naturally, and upon fit occasion, lead him to passions the language of which, if selected truly and judiciously, must necessarily be dignified and variegated, and alive with metaphors and figures. I forbear to speak of an incongruity which would shock the intelligent Reader, should the Poet interweave any foreign splendour of his own with that which the passion naturally suggests: it is sufficient to say that such addition is unnecessary. And, surely, it is more probable that those passages, which with propriety abound with metaphors and figures, will have their due effect, if, upon other occasions where the passions are of a milder character, the style also be subdued and temperate.

But, as the pleasure which I hope to give by the Poems now presented to the Reader must depend entirely on just notions upon this subject, and, as it is in itself of high importance to our taste and moral feelings, I cannot content myself with these detached remarks. And if, in what I am about to say, it shall appear to some that my labour is unnecessary, and that I am like a man fighting a battle without enemies, such persons may be reminded, that, whatever be the language outwardly holden by men, a practical faith in the opinions which I am wishing to establish is almost unknown. If my conclusions are admitted, and carried as far as they must be carried if admitted at all, our judgments concerning the works of the greatest Poets both ancient and modern will be far different from what they are at present, both when we praise, and when we censure: and our moral feelings influencing and influenced by these judgments will, I believe, be corrected and purified.

Taking up the subject, then, upon general grounds, let me ask, what is meant by the word Poet? What is a Poet? To whom does he address himself? And what language is to be expected from him?—He is a man speaking to men: a man, it is true, endowed with more lively sensibility, more enthusiasm and tenderness, who has a greater knowledge of human nature, and a more comprehensive soul, than are supposed to be common among mankind; a man pleased with his own passions and volitions, and who rejoices more than other men in the spirit of life that is in him; delighting to contemplate similar volitions and passions as manifested in the goings-on of the Universe, and habitually impelled to create them where he does not find them. To these qualities he has added a disposition to be affected more than other men by absent things as if they were present; an ability of conjuring up in himself passions, which are indeed far from being the same as those produced by real events, yet (especially in those parts of the general sympathy which are pleasing and delightful) do more nearly resemble the passions produced by real events, than anything which, from the motions of their own minds merely, other men are accustomed to feel in themselves:—whence, and from practice, he has acquired a greater readiness and power in expressing what he thinks and feels, and especially those thoughts and feelings which, by his own choice, or from the structure of his own mind, arise in him without immediate external excitement.

But whatever portion of this faculty we may suppose even the greatest Poet to possess, there cannot be a doubt that the language which it will suggest to him, must often, in liveliness and truth, fall short of that which is uttered by men in real life, under the actual pressure of those passions, certain shadows of which the Poet thus produces, or feels to be produced, in himself.

However exalted a notion we would wish to cherish of the character of a Poet, it is obvious, that while he describes and imitates passions, his employment is in some degree mechanical, compared with the freedom and power of real and substantial action and suffering. So that it will be the wish of the Poet to bring his feelings near to those of the persons whose feelings he describes, nay, for short spaces of time, perhaps, to let himself slip into an entire delusion, and even confound and identify his own feelings with theirs; modifying only the language which is thus suggested to him by a consideration that he describes for a particular purpose, that of giving pleasure. Here, then, he will apply the principle of selection which has been already insisted upon. He will depend upon this for removing what would otherwise be painful or disgusting in the passion; he will feel that there is no necessity to trick out or to elevate nature: and, the more industriously he applies this principle, the deeper will be his faith that no words, which *his* fancy or imagination can suggest, will be to be compared with those which are the emanations of reality and truth.

But it may be said by those who do not object to the general spirit of these remarks, that, as it is impossible for the Poet to produce upon all occasions language as exquisitely fitted for the passion as that which the real passion itself suggests, it is proper that he should consider himself as in the situation of a translator, who does not scruple to substitute excellencies of another kind for those which are unattainable by him; and endeavours occasionally to surpass his original, in order to make some amends for the general inferiority to which he feels that he must submit. But this would be to en-

courage idleness and unmanly despair. Further, it is the language of men who speak of what they do not understand; who talk of Poetry as of a matter of amusement and idle pleasure; who will converse with us as gravely about a *taste* for Poetry, as they express it, as if it were a thing as indifferent as a taste for rope-dancing, or Frontiniac or Sherry. Aristotle, I have been told, has said, that Poetry is the most philosophic of all writing: it is so: its object is truth, not individual and local, but general, and operative; not standing upon external testimony, but carried alive into the heart by passion; truth which is its own testimony, which gives competence and confidence to the tribunal to which it appeals, and receives them from the same tribunal. Poetry is the image of man and nature. The obstacles which stand in the way of the fidelity of the Biographer and Historian, and of their consequent utility, are incalculably greater than those which are to be encountered by the Poet who comprehends the dignity of his art. The Poet writes under one restriction only, namely, the necessity of giving immediate pleasure to a human Being possessed of that information which may be expected from him, not as a lawyer, a physician, a mariner, an astronomer, or a natural philosopher, but as a Man. Except this one restriction, there is no object standing between the Poet and the image of things; between this, and the Biographer and Historian, there are a thousand.

Nor let this necessity of producing immediate pleasure be considered as a degradation of the Poet's art. It is far otherwise. It is an acknowledgment of the beauty of the universe, an acknowledgment the more sincere, because not formal, but indirect; it is a task light and easy to him who looks at the world in the spirit of love: further, it is a homage paid to the native and naked dignity of man, to the grand elementary principle of pleasure, by which he knows, and feels, and lives, and moves. We have no sympathy but what is propagated by pleasure: I would not be misunderstood; but wherever we sympathise with pain, it will be found that the sympathy is produced and carried on by subtle combinations with pleasure. We have no knowledge, that is, no general principles drawn from the contemplation of particular facts, but what has been built up by pleasure, and exists in us by pleasure alone. The Man of science, the Chemist and Mathematician, whatever difficulties and disgusts they may have had to struggle with, know and feel this. However painful may be the objects with which the Anatomist's knowledge is connected, he feels that his knowledge is pleasure; and where he has no pleasure he has no knowledge. What then does the Poet? He considers man and the objects that surround him as acting and re-acting upon each other, so as to produce an infinite complexity of pain and pleasure; he considers man in his own nature and in his ordinary life as contemplating this with a certain quantity of immediate knowledge, with certain convictions, intuitions, and deductions, which from habit acquire the quality of intuitions; he considers him as looking upon this complex scene of ideas and sensations, and finding everywhere objects that immediately excite in him sympathies which, from the necessities of his nature, are accompanied by an overbalance of enjoyment.

To this knowledge which all men carry about with them, and to these sympathies in which, without any other discipline than that of our daily life, we are fitted to take delight, the Poet principally directs his attention. He considers man and nature as essentially adapted to each other, and the mind of man as naturally the mirror of the fairest and most interesting properties of nature. And thus the Poet, prompted by this feeling of pleasure, which accompanies him through the whole course of his studies, converses with general nature, with affections akin to those, which, through labour and length of time, the Man of science has raised up in himself, by conversing with those particular parts of nature which are the objects of his studies. The knowledge both of the Poet and the Man of science is pleasure; but the knowledge of the one cleaves to us as a necessary part of our existence, our natural and unalienable inheritance; the other is a personal and individual acquisition, slow to come to us, and by no habitual and direct sympathy connecting us with our fellow-beings. The Man of science seeks truth as a remote and unknown benefactor; he cherishes and loves it in his solitude: the Poet, singing a song in which all human beings join with him, rejoices in the presence of truth as our visible friend and hourly companion. Poetry is the breath and finer spirit of all knowledge; it is the impassioned expression which is in the countenance of all Science. Emphatically may it be said of the Poet, as Shakespeare hath said of man, "that he looks before and after." He is the rock of defence for human nature; an upholder and preserver, carrying everywhere with him relationship and love. In spite of difference of soil and climate, of language and manners, of laws and customs: in spite of things silently gone out of mind, and things violently destroyed; the Poet binds together by passion and knowledge the vast empire of human society, as it is spread over the whole earth, and over all time. The objects of the Poet's thoughts are everywhere; though the eyes and senses of man are, it is true, his favourite guides, yet he will follow wheresoever he can find an atmosphere of sensation in which to move his wings. Poetry is the first and last of all knowledge—it is as immortal as the heart of man. If the labours of Men of science should ever create any material revolution, direct or indirect, in our condition, and in the impressions which we habitually receive, the Poet will sleep then no more than at present; he will be ready to follow the steps of the Man of science, not only in those general indirect effects, but he will be at his side, carrying sensation into the midst of the objects of the science itself. The remotest discoveries of the Chemist, the Botanist, or Mineralogist, will be as proper objects of the Poet's art as any upon which it can be employed, if the time should ever come when these things shall be familiar to us, and the relations under which they are contemplated by the followers of these respective sciences shall be manifestly and palpably material to us as enjoying and suffering beings. If the time should ever come when what is now called science, thus familiarised to men, shall be ready to put on, as it were, a form of flesh and blood, the Poet will lend his divine spirit to aid the transfiguration, and will welcome the Being thus produced, as a dear and genuine inmate of the household of man.—It is not, then, to be supposed that any one, who holds that sublime notion of Poetry which I have attempted to convey, will break in upon the sanctity and truth of his pictures by transitory and accidental ornaments, and endeavour to excite admiration of himself by arts, the necessity of which must manifestly depend upon the assumed meanness of his subject.

What has been thus far said applies to Poetry in general; but especially to those parts of composition where the Poet speaks through the mouths of his characters; and upon this point it appears to authorise the conclusion that there are few persons of good sense, who would not allow that the dramatic parts of composition are defective, in proportion as they deviate from the real language of nature, and are coloured by a diction of the Poet's own, either peculiar to him as an individual Poet or belonging simply to Poets in general; to a body of men who, from the circumstance of their compositions being in metre, it is expected will employ a particular language.

It is not, then, in the dramatic parts of composition that we look for this distinction of language; but still it may be proper and necessary where the Poet speaks to us in his own person and character. To this I answer by referring the Reader to the description before given of a Poet. Among the qualities there enumerated as principally conducing to form a Poet, is implied nothing differing in kind from other men, but only in degree. The sum of what was said is, that the Poet is chiefly distinguished from other men by a greater promptness to think and feel without immediate external excitement, and a greater power in expressing such thoughts and feelings as are produced in him in that manner. But these passions and thoughts and feelings are the general passions and thoughts and feelings of men. And with what are they connected? Undoubtedly with our moral sentiments and animal sensations, and with the causes which excite these; with the operations of the elements, and the appearances of the visible universe; with storm and sunshine, with the revolutions of the seasons, with cold and heat, with loss of friends and kindred, with injuries and resentments, gratitude and hope, with fear and sorrow. These, and the like, are the sensations and objects which the Poet describes, as they are the sensations of other men, and the objects which interest them. The Poet thinks and feels in the spirit of human passions. How, then, can his language differ in any material degree from that of all other men who feel vividly and see clearly? It might be *proved* that it is impossible. But supposing that this were not the case, the Poet might then be allowed to use a peculiar language when expressing his feelings for his own gratification, or that of men like himself. But Poets do not write for Poets alone, but for men. Unless therefore we are advocates for that admiration which subsists upon ignorance, and that pleasure which arises from hearing what we do not understand, the Poet must descend from this supposed height; and, in order to excite rational sympathy, he must express himself as other men express themselves. To this it may be added, that while he is only selecting from the real language of men, or, which amounts to the same thing, composing accurately in the spirit of such selection, he is treading upon safe ground, and we know what we are to expect from him. Our feelings are the same with respect to metre; for, as it may be proper to remind the Reader, the distinction of metre is regular and uniform, and not, like that which is produced by what is usually called poetic diction, arbitrary, and subject to infinite caprices upon which no calculation whatever can be made. In the one case, the Reader is utterly at the mercy of the Poet, respecting what imagery or diction he may choose to connect with the passion; whereas, in the other, the metre obeys certain laws, to which the Poet and Reader both willingly submit because they are certain, and because no interference is made by them with the passion, but such as the concurring testimony of ages has shown to heighten and improve the pleasure which co-exists with it.

It will now be proper to answer an obvious question, namely, Why, professing these opinions, have I written in verse? To this, in addition to such answer as is included in what has been already said, I reply, in the first place, Because, however I may have restricted myself, there is still left open to me what confessedly constitutes the most valuable object of all writing, whether in prose or verse; the great and universal passions of men, the most general and interesting of their occupations, and the entire world of nature before me—to supply endless combinations of forms and imagery. Now, supposing for a moment that whatever is interesting in these objects may be as vividly described in prose, why should I be condemned for attempting to superadd to such description the charm which, by the consent of all nations, is acknowledged to exist in metrical language? To this, by such as are yet unconvinced, it may be answered that a very small part of the pleasure given by Poetry depends upon the metre, and that it is injudicious to write in metre, unless it be accompanied with the other artificial distinctions of style with which metre is usually accompanied, and that, by such deviation, more will be lost from the shock which will thereby be given to the Reader's associations than will be counterbalanced by any pleasure which he can derive from the general power of numbers. In answer to those who still contend for the necessity of accompanying metre with certain appropriate colours of style in order to the accomplishment of its appropriate end, and who also, in my opinion, greatly underrate the power of metre in itself, it might, perhaps, as far as relates to these Volumes, have been almost sufficient to observe, that poems are extant, written upon more humble subjects, and in a still more naked and simple style, which have continued to give pleasure from generation to generation. Now, if nakedness and simplicity be a defect, the fact here mentioned affords a strong presumption that poems somewhat less naked and simple are capable of affording pleasure at the present day; and, what I wished *chiefly* to attempt, at present, was to justify myself for having written under the impression of this belief.

But various causes might be pointed out why, when the style is manly, and the subject of some importance, words metrically arranged will long continue to impart such a pleasure to mankind as he who proves the extent of that pleasure will be desirous to impart. The end of Poetry is to produce excitement in coexistence with an overbalance of pleasure; but, by the supposition, excitement is an unusual and irregular state of the mind; ideas and feelings do not, in that state, succeed each other in accustomed order. If the words, however, by which this excitement is produced be in themselves powerful, or the images and feelings have an undue proportion of pain connected with them, there is some danger that the excitement may be carried beyond its proper bounds. Now the co-presence of something regular, something to which the mind has been accustomed in various moods and in a less excited state, cannot but have great efficacy in tempering and restraining the passion by an intertexture of ordinary feeling, and of feeling not strictly and necessarily connected with the passion. This is unquestionably true; and hence, though the opinion will at first appear paradoxical, from the tendency of metre to divest language, in a certain degree, of its reality, and thus to throw a sort of half-consciousness of unsubstantial existence over the whole composition, there can be little doubt but that more pathetic situations and sentiments, that is, those which have a greater proportion of pain connected with them, may be endured in metrical composition, especially in rhyme, than in prose. The metre of the old ballads is very artless;

yet they contain many passages which would illustrate this opinion; and, I hope, if the following Poems be attentively perused, similar instances will be found in them. This opinion may be further ilustrated by appealing to the Reader's own experience of the reluctance with which he comes to the re-perusal of the distressful parts of "Clarissa Harlowe," or the "Gamester"; while Shakespeare's writings, in the most pathetic scenes, never act upon us, as pathetic, beyond the bounds of pleasure—an effect which, in a much greater degree than might at first be imagined, is to be ascribed to small, but continual and regular impulses of pleasurable surprise from the metrical arrangement.—On the other hand (what it must be allowed will much more frequently happen) if the Poet's words should be incommensurate with the passion, and inadequate to raise the Reader to a height of desirable excitement, then, (unless the Poet's choice of his metre has been grossly injudicious) in the feelings of pleasure which the Reader has been accustomed to connect with metre in general, and in the feeling, whether cheerful or melancholy, which he has been accustomed to connect with that particular movement of metre, there will be found something which will greatly contribute to impart passion to the words, and to effect the complex end which the Poet proposes to himself.

If I had undertaken a systematic defence of the theory here maintained, it would have been my duty to develope the various causes upon which the pleasure received from metrical language depends. Among the chief of these causes is to be reckoned a principle which must be well known to those who have made any of the Arts the object of accurate reflection; namely, the pleasure which the mind derives from the perception of similitude in dissimilitude. This principle is the great spring of the activity of our minds, and their chief feeder. From this principle the direction of the sexual appetite, and all the passions connected with it, take their origin: it is the life of our ordinary conversation; and upon the accuracy with which similitude in dissimilitude, and dissimilitude in similitude are perceived, depend our taste and our moral feelings. It would not be a useless employment to apply this principle to the consideration of metre, and to show that metre is hence enabled to afford much pleasure, and to point out in what manner that pleasure is produced. But my limits will not permit me to enter upon this subject, and I must content myself with a general summary.

I have said that poetry is the spontaneous overflow of powerful feelings: it takes its origin from emotion recollected in tranquillity: the emotion is contemplated till, by a species of reaction, the tranquillity gradually disappears, and an emotion, kindred to that which was before the subject of contemplation, is gradually produced, and does itself actually exist in the mind. In this mood successful composition generally begins, and in a mood similar to this it is carried on; but the emotion, of whatever kind, and in whatever degree, from various causes, is qualified by various pleasures, so that in describing any passions whatsoever, which are voluntarily described, the mind will, upon the whole, be in a state of enjoyment. If Nature be thus cautious to preserve in a state of enjoyment a being so employed, the Poet ought to profit by the lesson held forth to him, and ought especially to take care, that, whatever passions he communicates to his Reader, those passions, if his Reader's mind be sound and vigorous, should always be accompanied with an overbalance of pleasure. Now the music of harmonious metrical language, the sense of difficulty

overcome, and the blind association of pleasure which has been previously received from works of rhyme or metre of the same or similar construction, an indistinct perception perpetually renewed of language closely resembling that of real life, and yet, in the circumstance of metre, differing from it so widely—all these imperceptibly make up a complex feeling of delight, which is of the most important use in tempering the painful feeling always found intermingled with powerful descriptions of the deeper passions. This effect is always produced in pathetic and impassioned poetry; while, in lighter compositions, the ease and gracefulness with which the Poet manages his numbers are themselves confessedly a principal source of the gratification of the Reader. All that it is *necessary* to say, however, upon this subject, may be effected by affirming, what few persons will deny, that, of two descriptions, either of passions, manners, or characters, each of them equally well executed, the one in prose and the other in verse, the verse will be read a hundred times where the prose is read once.

Having thus explained a few of my reasons for writing in verse, and why I have chosen subjects from common life, and endeavoured to bring my language near to the real language of men, if I have been too minute in pleading my own cause, I have at the same time been treating a subject of general interest; and for this reason a few words shall be added with reference solely to these particular poems, and to some defects which will probably be found in them. I am sensible that my associations must have sometimes been particular instead of general, and that, consequently, giving to things a false importance, I may have sometimes written upon unworthy subjects; but I am less apprehensive on this account, than that my language may frequently have suffered from those arbitrary connections of feelings and ideas with particular words and phrases, from which no man can altogether protect himself. Hence I have no doubt, that, in some instances, feelings, even of the ludicrous, may be given to my Readers by expressions which appeared to me tender and pathetic. Such faulty expressions, were I convinced they were faulty at present, and that they must necessarily continue to be so, I would willingly take all reasonable pains to correct. But it is dangerous to make these alterations on the simple authority of a few individuals, or even of certain classes of men; for where the understanding of an Author is not convinced, or his feelings altered, this cannot be done without great injury to himself: for his own feelings are his stay and support; and, if he set them aside in one instance, he may be induced to repeat this act till his mind shall lose all confidence in itself, and become utterly debilitated. To this it may be added, that the critic ought never to forget that he is himself exposed to the same errors as the Poet, and, perhaps, in a much greater degree: for there can be no presumption in saying of most readers, that it is not probable they will be so well acquainted with the various stages of meaning through which words have passed, or with the fickleness or stability of the relations of particular ideas to each other; and, above all, since they are so much less interested in the subject, they may decide lightly and carelessly.

Long as the Reader has been detained, I hope he will permit me to caution him against a mode of false criticism which has been applied to Poetry, in which the language closely resembles that of life and nature. Such verses have been triumphed over in parodies, of which Dr. Johnson's stanza is a fair specimen:—

> I put my hat upon my head
> And walked into the Strand,
> And there I met another man
> Whose hat was in his hand.

Immediately under these lines let us place one of the most justly-admired stanzas of the "Babes in the Wood."

> These pretty Babes with hand in hand
> Went wandering up and down;
> But never more they saw the Man
> Approaching from the Town.

In both these stanzas the words, and the order of the words, in no respect differ from the most unimpassioned conversation. There are words in both, for example, "the Strand," and "the Town," connected with none but the most familiar ideas; yet the one stanza we admit as admirable, and the other as a fair example of the superlatively contemptible. Whence arises this difference? Not from the metre, not from the language, not from the order of the words; but the *matter* expressed in Dr. Johnson's stanza is contemptible. The proper method of treating trivial and simple verses, to which Dr. Johnson's stanza would be a fair parallelism, is not to say, this is a bad kind of poetry, or, this is not poetry; but, this wants sense; it is neither interesting in itself, nor can *lead* to anything interesting; the images neither originate in that sane state of feeling which arises out of thought, nor can excite thought or feeling in the Reader. This is the only sensible manner of dealing with such verses. Why trouble yourself about the species till you have previously decided upon the genus? Why take pains to prove that an ape is not a Newton, when it is self-evident that he is not a man?

One request I must make of my reader, which is, that in judging these Poems he would decide by his own feelings genuinely, and not by reflection upon what will probably be the judgment of others. How common is it to hear a person say, I myself do not object to this style of composition, or this or that expression, but, to such and such classes of people it will appear mean or ludicrous! This mode of criticism, so destructive of all sound unadulterated judgment, is almost universal: let the Reader then abide, independently, by his own feelings, and, if he finds himself affected, let him not suffer such conjectures to interfere with his pleasure.

If an Author, by any single composition, has impressed us with respect for his talents, it is useful to consider this as affording a presumption, that on other occasions where we have been displeased, he, nevertheless, may not have written ill or absurdly; and further, to give him so much credit for this one composition as may induce us to review what has displeased us, with more care than we should otherwise have bestowed upon it. This is not only an act of justice, but, in our decisions upon poetry especially, may conduce, in a high degree, to the improvement of our own taste; for an *accurate* taste in poetry, and in all the other arts, as Sir Joshua Reynolds has observed, is an *acquired* talent, which can only be produced by thought and a long-continued intercourse with the best models of composition. This is mentioned, not with so ridiculous a purpose as to prevent the most inexperienced Reader from judging for himself (I have already said that I wish him to judge for himself); but merely to temper the rashness of decision, and to suggest, that, if Poetry be a subject on which much time has not been bestowed, the judgment may be erroneous; and that, in many cases, it necessarily will be so.

Nothing would, I know, have so effectually contributed to further the end which I have in view, as to have shown of what kind the pleasure is, and how that pleasure is produced, which is confessedly produced by metrical composition essentially different from that which I have here endeavoured to recommend: for the Reader will say that he has been pleased by such composition; and what more can be done for him? The power of any art is limited; and he will suspect, that, if it be proposed to furnish him with new friends, that can be only upon condition of his abandoning his old friends. Besides, as I have said, the Reader is himself conscious of the pleasure which he has received from such composition, composition to which he has peculiarly attached the endearing name of Poetry; and all men feel an habitual gratitude, and something of an honourable bigotry, for the objects which have long continued to please them: we not only wish to be pleased, but to be pleased in that particular way in which we have been accustomed to be pleased. There is in these feelings enough to resist a host of arguments; and I should be the less able to combat them successfully, as I am willing to allow, that, in order entirely to enjoy the Poetry which I am recommending, it would be necessary to give up much of what is ordinarily enjoyed. But, would my limits have permitted me to point out how this pleasure is produced, many obstacles might have been removed, and the Reader assisted in perceiving that the powers of language are not so limited as he may suppose; and that it is possible for poetry to give other enjoyments, of a purer, more lasting, and more exquisite nature. This part of the subject has not been altogether neglected, but it has not been so much my present aim to prove, that the interest excited by some other kinds of poetry is less vivid, and less worthy of the nobler powers of the mind, as to offer reasons for presuming, that if my purpose were fulfilled, a species of poetry would be produced, which is genuine poetry; in its nature well adapted to interest mankind permanently, and likewise important in the multiplicity and quality of its moral relations.

From what has been said, and from a perusal of the Poems, the Reader will be able clearly to perceive the object which I had in view: he will determine how far it has been attained; and, what is a much more important question, whether it be worth attaining: and upon the decision of these two questions will rest my claim to the approbation of the Public.

FROM CHANGING METAPHORS OF MIND
M. H. Abrams[*]

Abrams discusses the change that took place during the eighteenth and nineteenth centuries in concepts of the "role played by the mind in perception." He traces this change through "a mutation of metaphors almost exactly parallel" to it in discourses on the nature of art. The shift, for example, from the notion of imitation to that of expression appears in a shift from the image of the mind as a mirror to the images of the fountain or the lamp, which picture the mind in perception as "active rather than inertly receptive, and as contributing to the world in the very process of perceiving the world." The romantics substituted for the world-as-mechanism—the "inanimate cold world"—the "inert world of both empirical philosophy and of common sense," the world-as-organism—" a warm world united with the life of man."

The change from imitation to expression, and from the mirror to the fountain, the lamp, and related analogues, was not an isolated phenomenon. It was an integral part of a corresponding change in popular epistemology—that is, in the concept of the role played by the mind in perception which was current among romantic poets and critics. And the movement from eighteenth- to early nineteenth-century schemes of the mind and its place in nature is indicated by a mutation of metaphors almost exactly parallel to that in contemporary discussions of the nature of art.

The various physical analogues which make up the ground plans or conceptual schemes for those "modes of inmost being," as Coleridge called them, which "can not be conveyed save in symbols of time and space,"[1] are sometimes explicitly formulated. At other times they merely intimate their existence by the structure of the metaphors with which men refer to the mental processes. To elucidate the nature of sense-perception, memory, and thought, Plato, for example, appealed to the reflection of images in a

[1] *Biographia Literaria*, II, 120.

mirror, as well as to paintings, the writing of characters in the pages of a book, and the stamping of impressions into a wax plate.[2] Aristotle also said that the receptions of sense "must be conceived of as taking place in the way in which a piece of wax takes on the impress of a signet-ring without the iron or gold."[3] Thus John Locke—who more than any philosopher established the stereotype for the popular view of the mind in the eighteenth century—was able to levy upon a long tradition of ready-made parallels in giving definition to his view of the mind in perception as a passive receiver for images presented ready-formed from without. The mind in Locke's *Essay* is said to resemble a mirror which fixes the objects it reflects.[4] Or (suggesting the *ut pictura poesis* of the aesthetics of that period) it is a *tabula rasa* on which sensations write or paint themselves.[5] Or (employing the analogy of the *camera obscura*, in which the light,

entering through a small aperture, throws an image of the external scene on the wall) external and internal senses are said to be "the windows by which light is let into this *dark room*."

For, methinks, the understanding is not much unlike a closet wholly shut from light, with only some little openings left, to let in external visible resemblances, or ideas of things without: would the pictures coming into such a dark room but stay there, and lie so orderly as to be found upon occasion, it would very much resemble the understanding of a man, in reference to all objects of sight, and the ideas of them.[6]

Alternatively, the mind is a "waxed tablet" into which sensations, like seals, impress themselves.[7]

The analogies for the mind in the writings of both Wordsworth and Coleridge show a radical transformation. Varied as these are, they usually agree in picturing the mind in perception as active rather than inertly receptive, and as contributing to the world in the very process of perceiving the world. Wordsworth's *Prelude*, as completed in 1805, provides us with an anthology of mental schema whose properties are in accord with the initial plan of that poem, which, as Coleridge said more than three decades later, was, "I believe, partly suggested by me. . . . He was to treat man as man—a subject of eye, ear, touch, and taste, in contact with external nature, and informing the senses from the mind, and not compounding a mind out of the senses."[8] The thirteenth book of that poem ends,

---

[2] E.g. *Thaeatetus* 191–5, 206; *Philebus* 38–40; *Timaeus* 71–2.

[3] *De anima* II. ii. 424[a]

[4] Locke, *Essay Concerning Human Understanding*, ed. A. C. Fraser (Oxford, 1894), I, 142–3 (II, i, 25): "In this part the understanding is merely passive. . . . These simple ideas, when offered to the mind, the understanding can no more refuse to have, nor alter when they are imprinted, nor blot them out and make new ones itself, than a mirror can refuse, alter, or obliterate the images or ideas which the objects set before it do therein produce." The comparison of the mind, or at least the "phantasy," to a mirror had been common in the Renaissance; see, e.g., George Puttenham, *The Arte of English Poesie*, in *Elizabethan Critical Essays*, ed. G. G. Smith (Oxford, 1904), II, 20; and Bacon's discussion of this analogue in his passage on the Idols of the mind, *De Augmentis*, v, iv.

[5] *Essay Concerning Human Understanding*, I, 121 (II, i, 2): "Let us then suppose the mind to be, as we say, white paper, void of all characters, without any ideas." See Locke's earlier draft, *An Essay Concerning the Understanding*, ed. Benjamin Rand (Cambridge, Mass., 1931), p. 61: The soul "at first is perfectly *rasa tabula*, quite void. . . ."

[6] Ibid. pp. 211–12 (II, xi, 17).

[7] Ibid. I, 48n, and 49. Cf. D. F. Bond, "Neo-Classic Theory of the Imagination," *ELH*, IV (1937), p. 248.

[8] *Table Talk and Omniana of Samuel Taylor Coleridge* (Oxford, 1917), p. 188; 21 July 1832. Cf. ibid. p. 361 (1812): "The mind makes the sense, far more than the senses make the mind."

in fact, with the manifestation of "a new world," ruled by laws

Which do both give it being and maintain
A balance, an ennobling interchange
Of action from without and from within;
The excellence, pure function, and best
    power
Both of the object seen, and eye that sees.

... Most frequently, however, the mind is imaged by romantic poets as projecting life, physiognomy, and passion into the universe. The mere postulation of an animate universe was no novelty; Isaac Newton's ubiquitous God, constituting duration and space and sustaining by his presence the laws of motion and gravitation, and the World-Soul of the ancient Stoics and Platonists, are often to be found dwelling amicably together in the nature-poetry of the eighteenth century. What is distinctive in the poetry of Wordsworth and Coleridge is not the attribution of a life and soul to nature, but the repeated formulation of this outer life as a contribution of, or else as in constant reciprocation with, the life and soul of man the observer. This same topic was also central in the literary theory of these writers, where it turns up repeatedly in their discussions of the subject matter of poetry, their analyses of the imaginative process, and their debates on poetic diction and the legitimacy of personification and allied figures of speech.

The reason for this common concern of the early nineteenth-century philosophy of nature and of art is not hard to find. It was an essential part of the attempt to revitalize the material and mechanical universe which had emerged from the philosophy of Descartes and Hobbes, and which had been recently dramatized by the theories of Hartley and the French mechanists of the latter eight-

eenth century. It was at the same time an attempt to overcome the sense of man's alienation from the world by healing the cleavage between subject and object, between the vital, purposeful, value-full world of private experience and the dead postulated world of extension, quantity, and motion. To establish that man shares his own life with nature was to reanimate the dead universe of the materialists, and at the same time most effectively to tie man back into his milieu.

The persistent objective of Coleridge's formal philosophy was to substitute "life and intelligence ... for the philosophy of mechanism, which, in everything that is most worthy of the human intellect, strikes *Death*." And the life transfused into the mechanical motion of the universe is one with the life in man: in nature, he wrote in 1802, "everything has a life of its own, and ... we are all *One Life*."[9] A similar idea constitutes the leitmotif of Wordsworth's *Prelude*. In a crucial passage, for example, Wordsworth describes how the infant in his mother's arms, seeing a world "irradiated" by a sense of her love, comes to feel at home in the universe.

No outcast he, bewildered and depressed:
Along his infant veins are interfused
The gravitation and the filial bond
Of nature that connect him with the world.

But more is achieved than the mere linkage of feeling; the child becomes integral with the external world by the strongest of all bonds, through participating in its very creation and so sharing with it attributes of his own being. Through the faculties of sense, the mind creates—

[9] To Wordsworth, 30 May 1815, *Letters*, II, 648–9; to W. Sotheby, 10 Sept. 1802, ibid. I, 403–4.

Creator and receiver both,
Working but in alliance with the works
Which it beholds.[10]

The culmination of this process of domiciliation came in his seventeenth year when, by a process he opposes to "analytic industry," he found not only his senses and feelings but his life allied to an all-pervasive life in nature, and with bliss ineffable,

. . . felt the sentiment of Being spread
O'er all that moves and all that seemeth still.

This experience of the one life within us and abroad cancels the division between animate and inanimate, between subject and object—ultimately, even between object and object, in that climactic all is one of the mystical trance-state,

   then, when the fleshly ear,
O'ercome by humblest prelude of that
 strain,
Forgot her functions, and slept undisturbed.[11]

[10] *The Prelude* (1850 ed.), II, 232–60.
[11] Ibid. ll. 382–418. Cf. ibid. (1805 ed.), VIII, 623–30; and see Stallknecht, *Strange Seas of Thought*, Chap. III. It is relevant to consider here the extraordinary weight that other romantic poets, as well as Coleridge and Wordsworth, placed on the experience of *Einfühlung*, or loss of distinction between self and external scene. E.g., Shelley, "On Life," *Literary and Philosophical Criticism*, p. 56: "Those who are subject to the state called reverie, feel as if their nature were dissolved into the surrounding universe, or as if the surrounding universe were absorbed into their being. They are conscious of no distinction." And Byron, *Childe Harold's Pilgrimage*, III, lxxii: "I live not in myself, but I become Portion of that around me"; "the soul can flee, And with the sky, the peak, and the heaving plain Of ocean, or the stars, mingle, and not in vain." And ibid, IV, clxxviii: "I steal From all I may be, or have been before, To mingle with the Universe." Keats was exceptional, in that he felt an identification rather with individual things, such as sparrows and people, than with the total landscape; see the familiar passages in his *Letters*, ed. M. B. Forman (3d ed.; Oxford, 1948), pp. 69, 227–8, 241.

Wordsworth here refers to his relation with nature in terms of "filial bonds"; we must add the remarkable passage from the conclusion to the first book of *The Recluse* in which he replaces the familial by conjugal metaphors. That great undertaking, the intended crown of his poetic career, he announces in unmistakable terms, is to be a "spousal verse"—a prodigious prothalamion celebrating the marriage of mind and nature, the consummation of the marriage, and the consequent creation (or procreation?) of a living perceptual world. "Paradise, groves Elysian, Fortunate Fields—"

   the discerning intellect of Man,
When wedded to this goodly universe
In love and holy passion, shall find these
A simple produce of the common day.
—I, long before the blissful hour arrives,
Would chant, in lonely peace, the spousal
 verse
Of this great consummation:—, and, by
 words
Which speak of nothing more than what
 we are,
Would I arouse the sensual from their sleep
Of Death, and win the vacant and the vain
To noble raptures; while my voice proclaims
How exquisitely the individual Mind
(And the progressive powers perhaps no less
Of the whole species) to the external World
Is fitted:—and how exquisitely, too—
Theme this but little heard of among men—
The external World is fitted to the Mind;
And the creation (by no lower name
Can it be called) which they with blended
 might
Accomplish:—this is our high argument.[12]

Two of the greatest and most representative poems of the early nineteenth century, Wordsworth's "Intimations of

[12] Included in the Preface to *The Excursion* (1814), ll. 47–71. The barely submerged analogy in this passage, by the way, presents an interesting parallel to cabalistic and other esoteric theories of the sexual generation of the world.

Immortality" and Coleridge's "Dejection," turn on the distinction between data and addenda in sense experience. In both poems, the theme concerns an apparent change in the objects of sense, and is developed in terms of mental schemes which analogize the mind to something which is at once projective and capable of receiving back the fused product of what it gives and what is given to it. Wordsworth's "Ode" employs, with dazzling success, the familiar optical metaphors of light and of radiant objects —lamps and stars. His problem is one of a loss of "celestial light" and "glory" from meadow, grove, and stream. The solution inheres in the figure (not uncommon, as we know, in Neoplatonic theologians) of the soul as "our life's star," "trailing clouds of glory" at its rising, but gradually, in the westward course of life, fading "into the light of common day," though leaving behind recollections which "Are yet the fountainlight of all our day."[13] But if maturity has its loss of "splendor in the grass, of glory in the flower," it has its compensating gains, and the mind, though altered, retains its power of radiant give-and-take with the external world:

The clouds that gather round the setting sun
Do take a sober coloring from an eye
That hath kept watch o'er man's mortality.

Coleridge's "Dejection," on the other hand, memorializes not merely an alteration but the utter loss of the reciprocating power of the mind, leaving it a death-in-life as a passive receptor of the inanimate

[13] Culverwel, e.g., joins the familiar concept of the first-order stars as angelic existences with the figure of the fountain of light: The Creator "fill'd the *highest part* of the World with those *Stars* of the *first Magnitude,* I mean those *Orient* and *Angelic Beings,* that dwell so near the *fountain of Light,* and continually drink in the *Beams of Glory*. . . ." (*The Cambridge Platonists,* ed. Campagnac, p. 283.)

visible scene. In the short third and fourth stanzas, in which Coleridge five times iterates the dependence of nature's life on the inner life of man, he strikes the full diapason of metaphors for the active and contributive mind, some familiar, others seemingly of his own invention. The mind is a fountain, a source of light, the generator of a cloud that conveys life-giving rain, a musical voice like that of a wind-harp whose echo mingles with the sounds of outer origin; there is even the suggestion of a Wordsworthian marriage with nature. And the fifth stanza, proposing "joy" as the indispensable inner condition for the "effluence" and return of life, most subtly recapitulates all these figures, optical, acoustical, meteorological, and marital:

Joy, Lady! is the spirit and the power,
Which, wedding Nature to us, gives in
    dower
  A new Earth and new Heaven,
Undreamt of by the sensual and the proud—
Joy is the sweet voice, Joy the luminous
    cloud—
  We in ourselves rejoice!
And thence flows all that charms or ear or
    sight,
  All melodies the echoes of that voice,
All colours a suffusion from that light.

But it is not until the resolution in the closing stanza, when Coleridge prays that the Lady to whom the poem is addressed may retain the power he has lost, that we come upon the crowning metaphor of an eddy. The figure implies a ceaseless and circular interchange of life between soul and nature in which it is impossible to distinguish what is given from what received:

To her may all things live, from pole to pole,
Their life the eddying of her living soul!

This version of the perceptual mind as projecting life and passion into the world it apprehends is the one which most approximates the concurrent formulations of the mind active in the highest poetic composition—as Coleridge implies when he says, in "Dejection," that the failure of his power to project "the passion and the life" marks the failure also of his "genial spirits" and his "shaping spirit of imagination." We may say, then, by way of summary, that in the theory of Coleridge (partly though not consistently paralleled by that of Wordsworth) the primary and already creative act of perception yields the "inanimate cold world" of the ever-anxious crowd. This coincides roughly with the inert world of both empirical philosophy and of common sense, which is perceived only in so far as it serves our practical interests and aims. This world includes Peter Bell's yellow primrose, but nothing more; daffodils set moving by the breeze, but neither gleeful nor dancing; the moon radiant in a bare sky—with the proviso that it is not the moon but the poet who "doth with delight look round him when the heavens are bare." The subsequent and higher act of re-creation, among its other functions, by projecting its own passion and life, transforms the cold inanimate world into a warm world united with the life of man, and by that same act, converts matter-of-fact into matter-of-poetry —and according to Coleridge's conception, into the highest poetry, because it is the product of the "secondary imagination."

We must not leave the subject of the romantic analogues of mind without citing one that was Coleridge's favorite, and destined to alter more drastically the conceptions of mind, art, and the universe than all the apparatus of lamps, fountains, and wind-harps we have come upon thus far. This was the archetype (potentially present in the Platonist's figure of the "seeds of light" in the mind) representing the mind not as a physical object or artifact, but as a living plant, growing out into its perception. To mental mechanism, Coleridge often and explicitly opposes the concept of life and growth. In a central passage of *The Statesman's Manual*, Coleridge discovers "correspondences and symbols" of the highest faculty of man in the growth of a plant and its power to assimilate outer elements to which its respiration has already made contribution. Looking at a plant in a flowery meadow, he says, "I feel an awe, as if there were before my eyes the same power as that of the reason—the same power in a lower dignity, and therefore a symbol established in the truth of things."

Lo!—with the rising sun it commences its outward life and enters into open communion with all the elements, at once assimilating them to itself and to each other. At the same moment it strikes its roots and unfolds its leaves, absorbs and respires, steams forth its cooling vapour and finer fragrance, and breathes a repairing spirit, at once the food and tone of the atmosphere, into the atmosphere that feeds it. Lo!—at the touch of light how it returns an air akin to light, and yet with the same pulse effectuates its own secret growth, still contracting to fix what expanding it had refined.[14]

In any period, the theory of mind and the theory of art tend to be integrally related and to turn upon similar analogues, explicit or submerged. To put the matter schematically: for the representative eighteenth-century critic, the perceiving mind was a reflector of the external world; the inventive process consisted in a re-

[14] *Lay Sermons*, ed. Derwent Coleridge (3d ed.; London, 1852), pp. 75–7. Coleridge added in a note that this passage "might properly form the conclusion of a disquisition on the spirit . . . without reference to any theological dogma. . . ."

assembly of "ideas" which were literally images, or replicas of sensations; and the resulting art work was itself comparable to a mirror presenting a selected and ordered image of life. By substituting a projective and creative mind and, consonantly, an expressive and creative theory of art, various romantic critics reversed the basic orientation of all aesthetic philosophy. Consider now the further innovative possibilities in Cole-

ridge's archetypal plant. Through this perspective, Coleridge saw the mind as growing into its percepts, conceived of the activity of the poetic imagination as differing from this vital, self-determining, assimilative process in degree rather than kind, and thus was able to envision the product of artistic genius as exhibiting the mode of development and the internal relations of an organic whole. But that is a subject for a later chapter.

FROM ROMANTICISM AS A MODERN TRADITION
Robert Langbaum*

Modern romanticism is a reaction within the tradition of eighteenth-century empiricism, correcting the latter's concept of reality as particles of matter moving in space, claiming that it is "*matter* which is the abstraction, the mere theoretical concept derived from an analysis of experience," whereas "the life of things" is "what we perceive at the moment when experience is immediate and unanalyzed." Thus, romanticism is essentially "a doctrine of experience, an attempt to salvage on science's own empiric grounds the validity of the individual perception against scientific abstractions," and out of the subjectivity of this perception to discover a new objectivity in form, a new condition of experience and idea.

... Although one dreads reopening at this late date the quarrel over the definition of romanticism, it nevertheless remains impossible to talk long about modern literature without employing, whether explicitly or implicitly, some working definition of the term. Such a working definition can, I think, be achieved at the lowest common denominator of agreement, once we distinguish between romanticism as a permanently

recurring characteristic of personalities and artistic periods, and romanticism as that unprecedented shift of mind and sensibility which began in the latter eighteenth century. In the first sense, romanticism is one pole of the eternal alternation between emotion and intellect, freedom and discipline. In the second, it is the attempt of modern man to reintegrate fact and value after having himself rejected, in the experience of the Enlightenment, the old values. Post-Enlightenment romanticism does, to be sure, make use of emotion and freedom,

* This selection is reprinted from *The Poetry of Experience*, by Robert Langbaum. © Copyright 1957 by Robert Langbaum. Reprinted by permission of Random House, Inc.

but only as means incidental to the main and, as far as one can make out, historically unique purpose of the movement, which is not in the end to reject intellect and discipline but to renew them by empirical means.

Post-Enlightenment romanticism is historically unique just to the extent that it uses for its reconstructive purpose the same scientific or empirical method which is itself unique to the modern world. Like the scientist's hypothesis, the romanticist's formulation is evolved out of experience and is continually tested against experience. The difference is that the scientist's experiment is a selected and analysed experience, whereas experience for the romanticist is even more empiric because less rationalized. It is what happens before selection and analysis take place. Romanticism is in this sense not so much a reaction against eighteenth-century empiricism as a reaction within it, a corrected empiricism. It is, as Mill suggested, the necessary corrective for the skeptical analytic intellect.

Thus the empiricist Locke, spelling out the philosophical implications of Newton's physics, says that the world of our ordinary perception is largely illusory, that the only objective reality consists of particles of matter moving in space. He gives us a world without aesthetic, moral or spiritual significance. Against such a world-view, the romanticist protests by appealing not to tradition but to his own concrete experience of nature, his own insight into "the life of things." It is *matter* which is the abstraction, the mere theoretical concept derived from an analysis of experience; whereas "the life of things" is what we perceive at the moment when experience is immediate and unanalysed.

"An atom," says Blake, is "a thing which does not exist."[1] For Blake, the "form" or "image," the object not in itself but as perceived, is the concrete fact. The object in itself is an abstraction, a rationalization after the fact, what Blake calls the "memory of an image," which is less certain than the "perception of an image." Wordsworth makes the same point in *The Tables Turned*. "We murder to dissect," he complains, meaning that nature is a living organism and you lose its truth, which is its life, once you analyse it. Goethe makes the same complaint in *Faust*:

The man who wants to know
organic truth and describe it well
seeks first to drive the living spirit out;
he's got the parts in hand there,
it's merely the breath of life that's lacking.[2]

The romanticist is not against science. He is merely trying to limit the applicability of its findings. He is objecting to what Whitehead, in *Science and the Modern World*, calls the Fallacy of Misplaced Concreteness—the fallacy by which the eighteenth century mistook an analysis of reality, made because the intellect is too weak to comprehend it as a whole, for the concrete totality by which we must live. "To thee," says Wordsworth to Coleridge in *The Prelude*:

Science appears but what in truth she is,
Not as our glory and our absolute boast,
But as a succedaneum and a prop
To our infirmity. No officious slave

[1] To George Cumberland, 12 April 1827, *Poetry and Prose*, ed. Geoffrey Keynes (London: Nonesuch Press, 1939), p. 927. See also Northrop Frye, *Fearful Symmetry: A Study of William Blake* (Princeton: Princeton University Press, 1947), Chap. I, "The Case Against Locke."

[2] Part I, "Faust's Study," trans. C. F. MacIntyre (Norfolk, Conn.: New Directions, 1949), p. 60.

Art thou of that false secondary power
By which we multiply distinctions, then
Deem that our puny boundaries are things
That we perceive, and not that we have
    made.

(II, 211–19)

"A man, born and bred in the so-called
exact sciences," says Goethe, "will, on
the height of his analytical reason, not
easily comprehend that there is also
something like an exact concrete imagination."[3] This "exact concrete imagination"
Goethe employed not only for his poetry
but for his scientific investigations as
well.

Goethe used the same faculty for
poetry and science because reality resided
for him in what he called the "symbol,"
by which he meant not a mere cipher
for an abstract idea but the particular
with its ideal meaning complete within
it. Goethe's "symbol," like Blake's
"form" or "image," is what really exists
because it is both real and ideal. It is
"the living revelation of the unfathomable" which can be comprehended only
by what is itself unfathomable, "and the
only truly unfathomable faculty of man
is love."[4] Romanticism is both idealistic
and realistic in that it conceives of the
ideal as existing only in conjunction with
the real and the real as existing only in
conjunction with the ideal. The two are
brought into conjunction only in the act
of perception when the higher or
imaginative rationality brings the ideal
to the real by penetrating and possessing the external world as a way of knowing both itself and the external world.

[3] Quoted in Erich Heller, *The Disinherited
Mind* (Cambridge: Bowes and Bowes, 1952),
p. 26.

[4] Heller (p. 86), who cites the Goethean
word *Anschauung*, which means "the mental
process by which we spontaneously grasp,
through observation aided by intuition, a thing
in its wholeness. Goethe uses it as the opposite
of analysis" (p. 58).

"The great significance of Goethe in
the history of the European mind," says
Heller, "lies in the fact that he is the
last great poet who lived and worked in
a continual effort to save the life of
poetry *and* the poetry of life."[5] Heller
is not entirely right. For while it is true
that no poet after Goethe dared intrude
into the scientists' own realm, the effort
to save the poetry of life, at least in the
cultural realm, has continued into our
own day along with the effort to save the
life of poetry. In both efforts, the
imagination has been the instrument of
revelation; while the revelation itself has
been that living organic reality which the
imagination perceives through immediate
experience of the external world. Such
naturalistic revelation provides the living
waters out of which the modern literary
movement, from Goethe's time to our
own, has sprung and to which it has continually returned for refreshment in its
effort to restore the spiritual possibility
in the post-Enlightenment world.

But why should immediate experience
yield a living reality? Because the act of
knowing spontaneously and completely
is an act of imaginative projection into
the external object, an act of identification with the object; so that the living
consciousness perceived in the object is
our own. If, in other words, the act of
knowing analytically requires that we
"murder" the object, treating it as something unlike ourselves, something un-
alive; the act of knowing organically
requires that we imbue the object with
life, finding in it the counterpart of our
own consciousness.

In *Movements of Thought in the Nineteenth Century*, George Mead describes
romantic thought as a way of knowing
through playing roles. "For Descartes, I
am conscious and therefore exist; for
the romanticist, I am conscious of my-

[5] P. 25.

self and therefore this self, of which I am conscious, exists and with it the objects it knows."[6] Descartes establishes the self on empiric grounds, but has to deduce the object. The romanticist, on the other hand, by projecting himself into the object, playing its role, knows himself in the object. He therefore knows both himself and the object empirically, through the reciprocal process of experience or self-objectification. Farther than this the doctrine of concrete experience cannot go. To know an object, the romanticist must *be* it.

The development of the role-playing or projective attitude of mind can, I think, be attributed to both the historical and psychological moment when the eighteenth-century iconoclastic purpose changes direction to turn into the nineteenth-century reconstructive purpose. For the free-wheeling critical intellect becomes the sympathetic intellect once, unfettered by traditional values, it tries to construct new ones by giving itself in an experimental spirit to every possibility, excluding none. There remains, however, the hard-headed critical awareness that the self is something other than the object, that the identification has been deliberately undertaken and is only temporary. It is this combination of nineteenth-century sympathy with eighteenth-century critical awareness that explains the role-playing attitude. For whether the romanticist projects himself into the past, nature, or another person, he never forgets that he is playing a role. The result is that the experience makes him more acutely aware than ever of his own modernity and his own distinctness from the external world. The process of experience is for the romanticist a process of self-realization, of a constantly expanding discovery of the self through

[6] Ed. M. H. Moore (Chicago: Chicago University Press, 1944), pp. 82–83.

discoveries of its imprint on the external world. Faust, in embarking on his career of experience, says that pleasure is not his purpose. He will close his heart, he says,

to no future pain. I mean to enjoy
in my innermost being all that is offered to
  mankind,
to seize the highest and the lowest,
to mix all kinds of good and evil,
and thus expand my Self till it includes
the spirit of all men—and, with them,
I shall be ruined and perish in the end.[7]

How, then, does this lead to values? The romanticist discovers through experience the empiric ground for values. He does this by giving himself so completely to each object that the object is allowed to generate its own laws, creating the values compatible with its fullest existence. But since the romanticist finds in the object the values he puts there, he finds also the objectification of at least one aspect of the values compatible with his own fullest existence. The romanticist's sympathy with the object leads to an illumination of beauty and truth in the object—an illumination which involves at the same time an experience of recognition, recognition of this beauty and truth as values he has known potentially all along in himself. As an experience, the illumination is undeniably valid. But once the perception of value is abstracted from the immediate experience and formulated for application elsewhere, it becomes mere theory and therefore problematical. The formulation remains useful, however, as long as it returns us to experience, as long as we earn it, to paraphrase Faust, every day anew.

The romanticist is thus always in the process of formulating values, although he never arrives at a final formulation.

[7] Part I, "Faust's Study," p. 55.

Like Faust's, his career of experience ends not logically, with the formulated truth, but naturalistically, with death. What he does achieve, however, as a positive accomplishment, is an expanding potentiality for formulating values, an expanding area of sympathy and insight out of which values of increasing refinement can emerge and to which they can return.

Faust spends the whole poem evolving the law by which his actions are to be judged. His formulations evolve because he senses at each point that his understanding of the experience is inadequate to his total apprehension of it. He does not in the end articulate a general law, but the fact that he does finally arrive at his perfect moment indicates what is confirmed by his salvation after death, that his whole career of experience, even the harm done to Margaret, even the fact that his final bliss is based on a delusion, is justified by the necessity for self-realization, for self-discovery and self-development. Of course, he has known this intuitively from the start, which is why he continually rejects Mephistopheles' too facile formulation of his actions as merely evil. His career bears out the Lord's prediction in the Prologue:

A good man, struggling in his darkness, will always be aware of the true course.[8]

In his total apprehension the good man will be aware of the true course, but his reason will at each point make a temporarily inadequate interpretation of the facts. For in making new values the romanticist employs two modes of apprehension, sympathy and judgment—sympathy being always ahead of judgment, and certain whereas judgment is problematical.

Once we understand that we are in-

[8] Part I, "Faust's Study," p. 4.

terested in romanticism not as a recurring phenomenon but as that movement in thought and art which followed the eighteenth century, it is not difficult to agree, in defining romanticism, on those qualities which could have occurred only after the eighteenth century. Nor is it difficult to account for most of those qualities as determined by the attempt to answer the central question posed by the Enlightenment—the question of tradition, of how, after the collapse of the traditional authority for values, to find and justify new values. It is when we think of romanticism as an attempt to answer this question, as in large measure literature's answer to science, that we can understand it as essentially a doctrine of experience, an attempt to salvage on science's own empiric grounds the validity of the individual perception against scientific abstractions.

The advantage of understanding romanticism in its post-Enlightenment character, as a doctrine of experience, is that we understand it as the movement which unites us to the last century instead of separating us from it. For we are still children of the Enlightenment. We are still trying to mark out a path through the wilderness bequeathed us by the Enlightenment; we are still seeking values in a world where neither tradition nor science offers much assistance to that end. If anything, the wilderness has grown wilder since the last century. Time, two world wars and universal social upheaval have removed us even farther from the traditional past; while the spread of technological culture has given science an increasing dominion over our lives. To bridge the increased gap between knowledge and value we ought to require, if our reasoning thus far has been correct, an even more extreme and articulated romanticism. The question even arises whether in the post-Enlightenment world, in a scientific and democratic age, literature, whatever its program, can be anything but romantic in the sense I mean. Are not, after all, even our new classicisms and new Christian dogmatisms really romanticisms in an age which simply cannot supply the world-views such doctrines depend on, so that they become, for all their claims to objectivity, merely another opinion, the objectification of somebody's personal view?

It would hardly be necessary to insist on this line of continuity with the nineteenth century, were it not that the rejection of romanticism has been the issue with which the twentieth-century literary movement, especially in poetry, has declared its independence of its nineteenth-century predecessor. The main charges against romantic poetry have been that it is subjective, that it is sentimental, that its diction is inflated, and that it lacks form. In regard to the first charge I have, I believe, already said enough to indicate that it is an historical mistake to accuse the romanticists of subjectivism. It is to misunderstand the *direction* of romantic thought. For subjectivity was not the program but the inescapable condition of romanticism. No sooner had the eighteenth century left the individual isolated within himself—without an objective counterpart for the values he sensed in his own will and feelings—than romanticism began as a movement toward objectivity, toward a new principle of connection with society and nature through the imposition of values on the external world. Wordsworth wrote *The Prelude*, the model in English of the subjective or autobiographical poem, not because he believed in autobiographical poetry but in order to prepare himself for a long philosophical poem treating of the "mind of man." He wrote it because he felt as yet inadequate to the objective

undertaking, out of "real humility": "Here, at least, I hoped that to a certain degree I should be sure of succeeding, as I had nothing to do but describe what I had felt and thought."[9]

The whole conscious concern with objectivity as a *problem*, as something to be achieved, is in fact specifically romantic. Objectivity presented no problem to an age of faith like the Middle Ages, which considered the object and its value as equally *given*. Nor did it present a problem to a critical and rationalist age like the Enlightenment, the whole point of which was to undermine the established order of values by driving a wedge between the object and its value. It was the romanticists with their new reconstructive purpose who, starting with an inherited split between object and value and wanting to heal the breach, saw objectivity as desirable and as difficult to achieve. When subjectivity came to be called a disease (*la maladie du siècle*), the Romantic period had begun. "Look you, the end of this disease is death!" said Goethe,[10] who as early as 1774 sought to deliver himself from the disease by writing *Werther*. The complaint continued throughout the next century into our own. Goethe had his Faust pass through the *sickness* (subjectivity) of Part I in order to achieve the *health* (objectivity) of Part II. Coleridge suffered from subjectivity:

> Such punishments, I said, were due
> To natures deepliest stained with sin,—
> For aye entempesting anew
> The unfathomable hell within.[11]

[9] To Sir George Beaumont, 1 May 1805, *The Early Letters of William and Dorothy Wordsworth (1787–1805)*, ed. Ernest de Selincourt (Oxford: Clarendon Press, 1935), p. 489.
[10] Quoted in Karl Viëtor, *Goethe the Poet* (Cambridge, Mass.: Harvard University Press, 1949), p. 28.
[11] *The Pains of Sleep*.

Byron, "the wandering outlaw of his own dark mind," tried to exorcise the devil of subjectivity with the laughter of *Don Juan*. Carlyle preached Work as an escape from subjectivity. Arnold found in his own *Empedocles* the example of what was wrong with modern poetry—that it deals with situations

in which the suffering finds no vent in action; in which a continuous state of mental distress is prolonged, unrelieved by incident, hope, or resistance; in which there is everything to be endured, nothing to be done.[12]

And in our own time a militant insistence upon objectivity characterizes the leading critical doctrines: Yeats' *mask*, that the poet must not write about himself but about the antithesis of himself; Eliot's *catalyst*, that the poet acts like a catalyst to bring the poetic elements into combination but remains himself outside the poem; and Eliot's *objective correlative*, that emotion cannot be stated as a description of subjectivity but must be presented through

a set of objects, a situation, a chain of events which shall be the formula of that *particular* emotion; such that when the external facts, which must terminate in sensory experience, are given, the emotion is immediately evoked . . . this is precisely what is deficient in *Hamlet*. Hamlet (the man) is dominated by an emotion which is inexpressible, because it is in *excess* of the facts as they appear.[13]

[12] Preface to the 1853 edition of his *Poems* (London: Oxford University Press, 1945), pp. 2–3.

[13] "Hamlet," *Selected Essays* (London: Faber and Faber), p. 145; (New York: Harcourt, Brace), pp. 124–25. For the *catalyst*, see "Tradition and the Individual Talent" in the same volume. For Yeats' doctrine of the *mask*, see T. R. Henn, *The Lonely Tower* (London: Methuen, 1950), and Richard Ellman, *Yeats: The Man and The Masks* (New York: Macmillan, 1948).

One is reminded here of Arnold's strictures on *Empedocles*.

It should be clear, then, that the desire to overcome subjectivity and achieve objectivity is by no means peculiar to the twentieth century, but has determined the direction of poetic development since the end of the Enlightenment. Certain twentieth-century poets have, it is true, tried to escape the post-Enlightenment condition by attaching their poetry to dogmas. Yeats with his cosmology of cones and gyres, Eliot with his Anglo-Catholicism, the Auden circle of the 'thirties with their Marxism, all sought to create for their poetry the external condition enjoyed by the Middle Ages and the Renaissance. By positing an objective order of values, they sought to make their poetry not so much an externalization of their own minds as an imitation of an external system of ideas.

Yeats, for example, once he had established his cosmology, was not in his own view making metaphors but, like Dante, describing objectivity. Yet Yeats can hardly be said to have succeeded in his aim, since his cosmology remained after all a private one; while the Auden circle, in renouncing Marxism, have admitted the failure of their aim. Eliot apparently rests secure on the rock of Christian dogma, but his success is no less characteristic of the romantic movement than the failure of the others. For if the others failed because of the romantic condition, he has apparently succeeded in accordance with the romantic prescription—in having intellectually worked his way back from the Enlightenment, in having achieved the goal of the romantic quest for commitment. His poetry is romantic in that it gives a history of that quest and is more consistent in its autobiographical development than any poetry in English since Wordsworth's.

Once we grant that the return to objectivity is a purpose distinctive of the literature since the Enlightenment, then the poetry of the last one hundred and seventy-five years or so can be understood as belonging to a single developing tradition in which the romantic idea, far from having been rejected, is being perpetually realized through isolation from incidental accretions—from eighteenth-century accretions in the nineteenth-century, and from nineteenth-century accretions in the twentieth. It is, for example, as eighteenth-century accretions that we can explain the sentimentalism and inflated diction of which romantic poetry has been accused.

Sentimentalism is an eighteenth-century phenomenon in that it belongs to Locke's world where the push and pull of atoms was considered the only reality. In such a world the individual fell back upon the feelings, but with the fundamental acknowledgment that they did not reflect reality. Even today sentimentalism flourishes among the so-called Philistines—in just those circles, that is, where the Lockian world-view persists, where respect for beauty is at its lowest and the *real* is equated with the ugly and mechanistic, with whatever is antithetical to human wishes. But the romanticists were prepared precisely to take up the issue that the sentimentalists were content to let lie. They were out to transform reality, to show that it had no existence apart from the emotional apprehension of it. It is where the romantic transformation does not come off, where emotion remains opposed to an object that will not yield it back, that a poem falls into sentimentalism or bathos. But the point is that sentimentalism is the failure of romantic poetry, not its characteristic. The sentimental poem has not achieved the romantic fusion, it has been unable to win out over the eighteenth century....

For it is with form as with objectivity; at the same time that the romanticists broke away from both, they were also preoccupied to a degree unknown before with working back to both. Goethe was for most of his career a professed classicist, who sought to emulate in his poetry the abstraction and pure formalism of Greek sculpture; and we owe to German romanticism generally the unprecedented glorification of Greece in modern times. It is too often forgotten that romanticism was as much responsible for a Greek as for a medieval revival, the former having had as a matter of fact the more widespread and enduring effect. It should also be remembered that the Greek interest of most nineteenth-century literary men was in the formal aspects of Greek aesthetics, as distinguished from the Renaissance interest in the Greek ethos. For the Renaissance, Greece offered an alternative way of life to Christian culture (Shelley's Greek interest was in this respect Renaissance); but for the nineteenth century, Greece came to represent objectivity and form as opposed to modern subjectivity and naturalism. Toward the end of the century, the aesthetic capital shifted for some people from Greece to Byzantium or Japan, because they found as they moved eastward a more extreme stylization.

Yeats' *Sailing to Byzantium* is less a reaction against Keats' *Ode on a Grecian Urn* than it is a more extreme articulation of Keats' essential idea. Where Keats sees in the formal perfection of Greek plastic art an idealization of nature, Yeats sees in the two-dimensional golden abstractness of the Byzantine mosaics a rejection of nature. The difference is of degree not kind. Both poets recognize the Lockian split between the real and the ideal, and both see that the artist must transform the real into the ideal. The difference is in the amount of transformation which each considered necessary. Yeats required a more radical transformation because he saw the split as wider. The fact that Yeats had to turn Keats' recognition of the split between art and nature into a belligerently anti-naturalistic position is a sign that his is, if anything, the more extreme romanticism, the more radical solution of the more radical problem.

For if romanticism gave rise to the poetry of artlessness, spontaneity, and sincerity, to the "spasmodic" poets, Whitman and free verse; it also gave rise, and this has been its more enduring contribution, to Keats, the pre-Raphaelites, and the aesthetic and symbolist movements, to the poetry of art, even of artifice and insincerity. The doctrine of insincerity that characterized the aesthetic movement is a sign of the connection of that movement with romanticism and the doctrine of sincerity. Neither would have been conceivable as classical doctrine. The classical poet could afford to distinguish between the subjectivity of his lyric poetry and the objectivity of his narrative and dramatic poetry, because he had no trouble being objective when he wanted to be. It is only when meaning is in the epistemological sense a personal creation that the distinction between the subjective and objective statement breaks down and the poet feels it necessary to mask the subjective origin of his idea, to expend art to objectify it. *Insincerity* together with its offshoot Yeats' *mask*, in fact the whole literary attempt since the late nineteenth century to escape from personality, have created a literature in which sincerity and autobiography are encoded, written backwards.[14]

[14] For a discussion of the aesthetic movement's doctrine of insincerity in connection with Yeats' doctrine of the mask, see Ellman, *Yeats: The Man and the Masks*, Chap. IV.

We would therefore require, to talk intelligently about the form of romantic poetry, a theory which could account for both the artlessness and the artifice, the sincerity and the insincerity, the subjectivity and the objectivity, of poetry since the Enlightenment. We would require, in other words, a theory to connect the poetry of the nineteenth and twentieth centuries, to connect romanticism with the so-called reactions against it. We are now in a position to advance such a theory. For having seen the poetry which set out to be different from romantic poetry, we can find in the core that remains unchanged the essential idea of romanticism. That essential idea is, I would suggest, the doctrine of experience—the doctrine that the imaginative apprehension gained through immediate experience is primary and certain, whereas the analytic reflection that follows is secondary and problematical. The poetry of the nineteenth and twentieth centuries can thus be seen in connection as a poetry of experience—a poetry constructed upon the deliberate disequilibrium between experience and idea, a poetry which makes its statement not as an idea but as an experience from which one or more ideas can be abstracted as problematical rationalizations.

Much could be learned from the isolation of a poetry of experience. It would reveal for the first time, in addition to the distinctively romantic sensibility and subject matter which we already know, a distinctively romantic form in poetry —a form of which the potentials are realized in the so-called reactions against romantic poetry, in the dramatic monologues of the Victorians and the symbolist poems of the moderns. Such a form, furthermore, if it were treated as a way of meaning, a way of establishing the validity of a poetic statement, would become the best index of a distinctively modern tradition. What better sign can there be, after all, of a culture's real belief than the principle by which it establishes the validity of its statements of value? And what better sign can there be of its coherence than the fact that it can make such statements, statements combining its unspoken convictions on the nature of truth, goodness and beauty? Form is a better index of a tradition than subject matter in that subject matter is often controversial; it is often an index of what people think they believe, whereas form is an index of what is believed too implicitly to be discussed.

Since a new culture, like a new art, looks disorderly until we discover its principle of order, and since the principle which gives order to a culture is intimately related to the principle which gives order to its art, the critic who finds the latter principle is by implication at least helping to find the former. If in addition to isolating the poetry of experience as a form, as a way of establishing in an anti-dogmatic and empiricist age a truth based on the disequilibrium between experience and idea, he could show that there emerges from this deliberate disequilibrium a correspondingly new moral and aesthetic symmetry—he would have suggested at least one line of coherence by which to discern in the bewildering heterogeneity of modern culture a distinctively modern tradition. Such a tradition would present a curious paradox in that it would have been created out of the rejection of tradition and the preoccupation with its loss. We would find that the artists and thinkers of the last one hundred and seventy-five years or so have, in proclaiming the freedom of modern life, actually laid down new rules for it, that they have, in proclaiming its meaninglessness and disunity, formulated for it a new meaning and a new unity.[15]

[15] The work of counting up the cultural treasure of the nineteenth and twentieth centuries and formulating from it a modern tradition may well fall upon the now emerging literary generation—a generation already recognizable as more critical than creative just because we of that generation have, I think, been rendered silent by our reverence for the immediate past, by our sense of having inherited a modern tradition, of having to master an impressive canon of modern "classics" before we can speak out in our own right.

CHAPTER 7

Realism

REALISM VERSUS ROMANTICISM
William Dean Howells*

Howells demands that literature contain "honest, wholesome, every-day" detail and depict accurately the phenomena of the real, matter-of-fact world. The realist "cannot look upon human life and declare this thing or that thing unworthy of notice, any more than the scientist can declare a fact of the material world beneath the dignity of his inquiry." The romantic "ideal" is a falsified image of man; romanticism lies about life, whereas realism portrays "men and women as they are, actuated by the motives and the passions in the measure we all know." The realistic novelist has a moral duty "not to sentimentalize and falsify the actual."

...The young writer who attempts to report the phrase and carriage of every-day life, who tries to tell just how he has heard men talk and seen them look, is made to feel guilty of something low and unworthy by the stupid people who would like to have him show how Shakespeare's men talked and looked, or Scott's, or Thackeray's, or Balzac's, or Hawthorne's, or Dickens's; he is instructed to idealize his personages, that is, to take the life-likeness out of them, and put the book-likeness into them. He is approached in the spirit of the wretched pedantry into which learning, much or little, always decays when it withdraws itself and stands apart from experience in an attitude of imagined superiority, and which would say with the same confidence to the scientist: "I see that you are looking at a grasshopper there which you have found in the grass, and I suppose you intend to describe it. Now don't waste your time and sin against culture in that way. I've got a grasshopper here, which has been

* The selection is from Chapter II of *Criticism and Fiction*, by William Dean Howells, Harper and Brothers, 1892.

evolved at considerable pains and expense out of the grasshopper in general; in fact, it's a type. It's made up of wire and card-board, very prettily painted in a conventional tint, and it's perfectly indestructible. It isn't very much like a real grasshopper, but it's a great deal nicer, and it's served to represent the notion of a grasshopper ever since man emerged from barbarism. You may say that it's artificial. Well, it is artificial; but then it's ideal too; and what you want to do is to cultivate the ideal. You'll find the books full of my kind of grasshopper, and scarcely a trace of yours in any of them. The thing that you are proposing to do is commonplace; but if you say that it isn't commonplace, for the very reason that it hasn't been done before, you'll have to admit that it's photographic."

As I said, I hope the time is coming when not only the artist, but the common, average man, who always "has the standard of the arts in his power," will have also the courage to apply it, and will reject the ideal grasshopper wherever he finds it, in science, in literature, in art, because it is not "simple, natural, and honest," because it is not like a real grasshopper. But I will own that I think the time is yet far off, and that the people who have been brought up on the ideal grasshopper, the heroic grasshopper, the impassioned grasshopper, the self-devoted, adventureful, good old romantic card-board grasshopper, must die out before the simple, honest, and natural grasshopper can have a fair field. I am in no haste to compass the end of these good people, whom I find in the mean time very amusing. It is delightful to meet one of them, either in print or out of it—some sweet elderly lady or excellent gentleman whose youth was pastured on the literature of thirty or forty years ago—and to witness the con-

fidence with which they preach their favorite authors as all the law and the prophets. They have commonly read little or nothing since, or, if they have, they have judged it by a standard taken from these authors, and never dreamed of judging it by nature; they are destitute of the documents in the case of the later writers; they suppose that Balzac was the beginning of realism, and that Zola is its wicked end; they are quite ignorant, but they are ready to talk you down, if you differ from them, with an assumption of knowledge sufficient for any occasion. The horror, the resentment, with which they receive any question of their literary saints is genuine; you descend at once very far in the moral and social scale, and anything short of offensive personality is too good for you; it is expressed to you that you are one to be avoided, and put down even a little lower than you have naturally fallen.

These worthy persons are not to blame; it is part of their intellectual mission to represent the petrifaction of taste, and to preserve an image of a smaller and cruder and emptier world than we now live in, a world which was feeling its way towards the simple, the natural, the honest, but was a good deal "amused and misled" by lights now no longer mistakable for heavenly luminaries. They belong to a time, just passing away, when certain authors were considered authorities in certain kinds, when they must be accepted entire and not questioned in any particular. Now we are beginning to see and to say that no author is an authority except in those moments when he held his ear close to Nature's lips and caught her very accent. These moments are not continuous with any authors in the past, and they are rare with all. Therefore I am not afraid to say now that the greatest classics are sometimes not at all great, and that we can profit by them only when we hold them, like our meanest contemporaries, to a strict accounting, and verify their work by the standard of the arts which we all have in our power, the simple, the natural and the honest.

Those good people, those curious and interesting if somewhat musty back-numbers, must always have a hero, an idol of some sort, and it is droll to find Balzac, who suffered from their sort such bitter scorn and hate for his realism while he was alive, now become a fetich in his turn, to be shaken in the faces of those who will not blindly worship him. But is it no new thing in the history of literature: whatever is established is sacred with those who do not think. At the beginning of the century, when romance was making the same fight against effete classicism which realism is making to-day against effete romanticism, the Italian poet Monti declared that "the romantic was the cold grave of the Beautiful," just as the realistic is now supposed to be. The romantic of that day and the real of this are in certain degree the same. Romanticism then sought, as realism seeks now, to widen the bounds of sympathy, to level every barrier against aesthetic freedom, to escape from the paralysis of tradition. It exhausted itself in this impulse; and it remained for realism to assert that fidelity to experience and probability of motive are essential conditions of a great imaginative literature. It is not a new theory, but it has never before universally characterized literary endeavor. When realism becomes false to itself, when it heaps up facts merely, and maps life instead of picturing it, realism will perish too. Every true realist instinctively knows this, and it is perhaps the reason why he is careful of every fact, and feels himself bound to express or to indicate its meaning at the risk of over-moralizing. In life he finds nothing insignificant; all tells for destiny and character; nothing that God has made is contemptible. He cannot look upon human life and declare this thing or that thing unworthy of notice, any more than the scientist can declare a fact of the material world beneath the dignity of his inquiry. He feels in every nerve the equality of things and the unity of men; his soul is exalted, not by vain shows and shadows and ideals, but by realities, in which alone the truth lives. In criticism it is his business to break the images of false gods and misshapen heroes, to take away the poor silly toys that many grown people would still like to play with. He cannot keep terms with Jack the Giant-killer or Puss in Boots, under any name or in any place, even when they reappear as the convict Vautrec, or the Marquis de Montrivaut, or the Sworn Thirteen Noblemen. He must say to himself that Balzac, when he imagined these monsters, was not Balzac, he was Dumas; he was not realistic, he was romantic.

REALISM AND THE
AEGIS OF SCIENCE
William Van O'Connor[*]

O'Connor regards *realism* as an ambiguous term. To define it is difficult, for if we say it is "the desire to tell the truth," we can point to dozens of artists who have maintained this as their goal. Moreover, "the realism of Howells is not that of James, Hamlin Garland, or Stephen Crane." To all so-called realistic writers, however, realism signified an actual correspondence, ascertainable through the methods of science, between reality and the fictional account of it.

As a critical term, "realism" is not very useful. It does suggest the exclusion of a certain type of subject matter, such as fantasy, utopias, tales of Gothic horror, and the like. In the latter part of the nineteenth century it meant, more specifically, opposition to tales in which "girls were shrinkingly modest and yet brave in emergencies," as well as opposition to novels like *Ben Hur* and *Uncle Tom's Cabin*. (Henry James said that American readers of fiction had not made up their minds whether the truth could be told, and Howells said that truth "unvarnished" is "almost the rarest thing in an Anglo-Saxon book.") But to say what realism *is*, is quite another matter. The realism of Howells is not the realism of James or Hamlin Garland or Stephen Crane. Common to all of them was the desire to tell the truth, but each of them was likely to discover reality in different forms and to search for his truth in diverse sources. The following passage from Howells' *Criticism and Fiction* is

* The essay is reprinted from *An Age of Criticism, 1900–1950*, by William Van O'Connor, by permission of Henry Regnery Company. Copyright 1952 by Henry Regnery Company.

his version of what the eyes of the honest critic should see:

In life he finds nothing insignificant; all tells for destiny and character; nothing that God has made is contemptible. He cannot look upon human life and declare this thing or that thing unworthy of notice, any more than the scientist can declare a fact of the material world beneath the dignity of his inquiry. He feels in every nerve the equality of things and the unity of men; his soul is exalted, not by vain shows and shadows and ideals, but by realities, in which alone the truth lives.

In the passage are echoes from Emerson and the latter's reverence for each object in the living world. Obviously Crane would not have formulated his understanding of the concept of realism in any such idealistic or genteel terms. The truth about the complexity of the problem of realism was put neatly by James in "The Art of Fiction": "Humanity is immense, and reality has a myriad forms; the most one can affirm is that some of the flowers of fiction have the odor of it, and others have not; as for telling you in advance how your nosegay should be composed, that is another affair."

Some of James's contemporaries, however, believed that by drawing upon the truths of science, or those which science would eventually furnish, the artist could know in advance how a literary work should be composed, how reality could be caught and fixed. They were, of course, living in a period in which for many science had become the religion of reason; and even for those who saw it in a different light the prestige of scientific modes of thought was necessarily high. One frequently finds critics trying to model their own methodology on the methodology of science (or what they think the methodology to be) or trying to establish as literary ideals the ideals of the scientist.

Surprisingly enough, one finds that even a man like Howells could be so awed on occasion by what he understood to be scientific methodology that he could abjure his right to make judgments about literary worth. Apparently, his desire to be of his age, and therefore scientific, induced him to make comments that contradict the position he takes when expressing himself as the genteel idealist that at heart he was. There is a contradiction, for instance, between his emphasis on a genteel morality and his comments on the function of scientific criticism. He was willing to have expressions of the "beast man" dropped from literature, "as they were long ago dropped from the talk of decent people." On the other hand, he sometimes wrote of literature as being the inevitable product of milieu. The function of the critic, he once said, was to report on what he found. "There is a measure of the same absurdity in his trampling on a poem, a novel, or an essay that does not please him as in the botanist grinding a plant underfoot because he does not find it pretty." It should be his concern "rather to identify the species and then explain how and where the specimen is imperfect and irregular." When he was not being so fashionably scientific Howells could state his doubt that formlessness, whatever its roots or causes, should be accepted as inevitable. "Something, it seems to me, may be contained and kept alive in formality, but in formlessness everything spills and wastes away. This is what I find the fatal defect of our American Ossian, Walt Whitman, whose way is where artistic madness lies." But this conflict, however minor in Howells, is an important clue to the minds of his critic contemporaries. The appeal for a realistic literature was frequently made on the ground that it was scientific.

II

The battle waged, and finally won, over the excesses of Emile Zola's naturalism—the battle which helped make it possible to write the truth rather than make-believe—was conducted largely on the grounds of its being scientific. The translation of Nana[1] in 1880 had been called obscene, sordid, and nauseous. Magazines like The Literary World and The Atlantic Monthly had scoffed at Zola's claim in Le roman expérimental (1881) that he was like the medical scientist concerned with the sickness of man socially in order to help restore him to health; the former said Zola's interest "must be that of a man of science watching with abhorrent fascination some hideous larva crawling in the filth of a dung hill," and the latter assumed that any French novelist claiming "to have purpose with a capital P" undoubtedly "intends to be particularly

[1] See A. J. Salvan, Zola aux Etats Unis (Providence, R.I., Brown Univ. Press, 1943).

indecent." (The battle was won partly, of course, by the sympathies Zola aroused through his support of Alfred Dreyfus. Whereas *L'assommoir* had been violently decried for its low life and moral contagion, later books, such as *La terre*, *L'argent*, and *La débâcle* were read as painful accounts that were moral in intention and ignored by respectable people at their peril. Zola won new respect in 1898 with his famous letter *J'accuse*, in Dreyfus's behalf. It is obvious, *The Nation* said, that he is "a devoted champion of civil justice." When he died in 1902, Zola, by and large, was treated with respect by the literary commentators.) Zola and his followers made their appeal for acceptance on the grounds that they were scientific writers. One of the key statements in *Le roman expérimental*, translated by Belle Sherman in 1893, is this: "The experimental novelist is therefore the one who accepts the proven facts, who points out in man and in society the mechanism of the phenomena over which science is mistress, and who does not interpose his personal sentiments, except in the phenomena whose determinism is not yet settled...." The tone of the whole essay is suggested by this: "The metaphysical man is dead; our whole territory is transformed by the advent of the physiological man." In his private notes Zola had written for his own guidance: "Study men as simple elements and note the reactions," and: "What matters most to me is to be purely naturalistic, purely physiological. Instead of having principles (royalism, Catholicism) I shall have laws (heredity, atavism)." Men and women are subject to inexorable and indifferent laws, economic, social, and biological. The American novelists who were or seem to have been influenced by Zola stress his objectivity and cool disinterestedness. Frank Norris, for ex-

ample, said "no one could be a writer until he could regard life and people, and the world in general, from objective points of view—until he could remain detached, outside, maintain the unswerving attitude of the observer." But most of them managed, thanks to evolution as treated by Herbert Spencer, to maintain a romantic optimism about the future of mankind collectively despite the rank hopelessness of the individual caught and crushed by the dramatic inexorable forces.[2]

McTeague and *Vandover and the Brute* are indebted to Zola for specific scenes as well as doctrine; the respect for hereditary influences, the preoccupation with disease, especially nervous diseases, character rigorously determined by environment, a liking for brutal and violent scenes, huge primitive men and healthy, vigorous women, the careful accumulation of detail to establish an air of actuality, and so forth. "Terrible things must happen," Norris wrote in *The Responsibilities of the Novelist* (1903), "to the characters of the Naturalistic tale.... Everything is extraordinary, imaginative, grotesque even, with a vague note of terror quivering throughout like the vibration of an ominous and low pitched diapason." But Norris knew that naturalistic fiction was not a transcript of life; it was a peculiar kind of adventure story. To write such stories, it helped to be able to think of modern businessmen as de-

[2] For accounts of the somewhat contradictory theories of the naturalists, see C. C. Walcott, "The Naturalism of Vandover and the Brute," *Forms of Modern Fiction*, ed. William Van O'Connor (Minneapolis, Univ. of Minnesota Press, 1948); Robert Spiller, "Toward Naturalism in Fiction," *Literary History of the United States*, pp. 1016–38; and, Malcolm Cowley, " 'Not Men': A Natural History of American Naturalism," *Kenyon Review*, IX (Summer 1947), 414–35, and his "Naturalism in American Literature," *Evolutionary Thought in America*, ed. Stow Persons (New Haven, Yale Univ. Press, 1950).

scendants of the aggressive Anglo-Saxons carrying out their fighting instincts, not in war, but in trade. Occasionally Norris could talk of the real struggles of the poor, of economic inequality and social injustices, and he could write of the need for the novelist to have a purpose. But Norris was primarily concerned, it seems, to write good stories. The aesthetic principles of the naturalistic school, as he chose to interpret them, served him. Naturalism, Norris noted with perceptiveness, "is a form of romanticism, not an inner circle of realism." Zola's laws, as Norris knew, were not absolutes; they were factors, partial truths that the artist exaggerated and stylized for his aesthetic purposes. By calling them laws and appealing thereby to the prestige of science the stories took on a greater air of reality.

Perhaps the critic who best summed up Zola's importance, and at the same time suggested why the search for realism was in the air, was Harry Thurston Peck in "Emile Zola," done for *The Bookman* in 1902 and later published in *Studies in Several Literatures* (1909). Peck said that Zola's assertions about the novelist writing as a scientist were long since "whistled down the wind." No one cares, he said, what theory or fancied theory helped make his novels possible. Peck also gave a neat summary of realism, the movement which had burst into the intensities, the efflorescence, called naturalism. Realism is a phenomenon as old as Euripides among the Greeks and Petronius among the Romans. It usually follows a period of romanticizing, as the picaresque tales followed the chivalrous romances, or as Henry Fielding followed the sentimentalities of Samuel Richardson. The present movement, he pointed out, may be seen in Stendhal or Rousseau, men who perceived the power in the naked truth. "Realism, however, was not a creation or a rediscovery by any one particular man.

Its germ was in the air.... Democracy in politics, rationalism in theology, materialism in philosophy and realism in literature, are very closely linked together." Even in Chateaubriand, the so-called father of romanticism, and in Victor Hugo one finds strong evidences of the developments later to be called realism and naturalism. The general drift of the realistic movement begins with Stendhal, carries through Balzac, the Goncourts, and "reaches absolute perfection with *Madame Bovary*.... Realism, as such, can never go beyond what Flaubert carefully wrought for us in this one exquisitely-finished etching, of which every line is bitten out as by an acid upon metal, and of which, in consequence, the sombre memory can never die." Flaubert brings the movement to its perfection. "After Flaubert came Zola—not to work further miracles in the name of Realism, but to give Realism a new development and to call it Naturalism."

Like Peck, many critics felt that the scientific movements were related to attempts to write truthfully, realistically. In 1904, Brander Matthews in "Literature in the New Century" listed some of the ways in which science had already influenced the writing of literature. Ibsen found in "the doctrine of heredity a modern analogy of the ancient Greek idea of fate"; *Ghosts* has something of the inexorable inevitability found in the tragedy of Sophocles. The doctrine of evolution has altered our theory of literary history; Brunetière "has shown us most convincingly how the several literary forms—the lyric, the oration, the epic, with its illegitimate descendant, the modern novel in prose—may cross-fertilize each other from time to time, and also how the casual hybrids that result are ever struggling to revert to their own species." Disinterestedness, an ideal of scientists, makes for a "lofty curiosity" in the search for knowledge, "helps the creative artist to strive for a more classic directness and simplicity" and to abhor the "freakish and abnormal." Respect for science means respect for "the reign of law; it establishes the strength of the social bond, and thereby, for example, it aids us to see that, altho romance is ever young and ever true, what is known as 'neo-romanticism,' with its reckless assertion of individual whim, is anti-social, and therefore probably immoral."

Matthews warned, however, that although the study of science could give the writer a sense of actuality it might tempt him, already had tempted him in fact, "to dwell unduly on the mere machinery of human motive and to aim not at a rich portrayal of the actions of men and women, but at an arid analysis of the mechanism of their impulses." Matthews was also aware of what we have come to call "scientism"; he quoted Thomas Huxley's warning that history tells us it is the "customary fate of new truths to begin as heresies, and to end as superstitions."

Vida Scudder, writing as an orthodox Christian, had devoted a part of *The Life of the Spirit in the Modern English Poets* (1895) to asking whether the influence of science is an unmixed good. If it is, she replies, it is hard to explain why it is accompanied by influences "which tend insidiously to destroy the life of poetry by robbing it of its characteristic powers." The love of fact and of minute observation restricts the imagination and encourages a confined art. How else, she asks, explain the preoccupation with sordid facts and with a "dismal fatalism." But there were many critics, unlike Vida Scudder, who had the utmost faith in the powers of science to unlock the secrets of art and to improve its very nature.

With more critics than not, the appeal

to science meant that reality could be seen, understood, and stated in literary and critical terms. We find that the concept of evolution was to unlock the secrets of literary history; that a knowledge of scientific laws would eventually enable the novelist to control his plot as he would a reaction in chemistry; that to know the factors operating in a milieu was to know the character of the literary work produced in it; and that the acceptance of a scientific milieu meant the end of romantic make-believe and the writing of a literature in which objectivity, a cool disinterestedness, and an understanding of scientific laws would make it possible to tell *the* truth.

III

Although no one has yet published a full-scale study of the influence of Hippolyte Taine on American literature, both fiction[3] and criticism, the frequency with which his name is mentioned and his works referred to in critical studies[4] suggests that the influence was broad and deep. At least five Americans translated one or another of his works, and one of them, John Durand, translated several.

William Morton Payne, as already suggested, held Taine in great respect. He had republished in *Little Leaders* (1895) the editorial article in which he had commemorated Taine as a brilliant exemplar of the "scientific method in historical

[3] Hamlin Garland, for example, acknowledged how important to him Taine's *History of English Literature* had been, and Edward Eggleston said Taine's *History of Art in the Netherlands* led him to employ local manners and local speech in his fiction.

[4] In their *An Introduction to the Methods and Materials of Literary Criticism* (1899), C. M. Gayley and F. N. Scott said: "The brilliancy of Taine's style and the glib simplicity of his system, have made his theories better known in this country than those of any other foreign writer."

criticism." Payne admits that many observers had pointed to limitations in Taine's method. Even so, the "tendency of modern criticism is unquestionably towards a scientific method; in history and philosophy it has already reached such a basis; that in art and literature it will eventually come to such a basis we may hardly doubt." A scientific method "must show itself productive of similar results when employed by many different observers, and it must fulfill the supreme test of enabling us to forecast the future with certainty." Literature depends, according to Taine, on the *race, moment,* and *milieu* that produced it, and is, therefore, rigorously determined. Virtue and vice, like vitriol and sugar, he had said, are the products of material causes.

Anyone who attempts to study Taine's influence will undoubtedly have a difficult job separating the strands of his influence from those deriving from earlier social critics. That literature cannot be wholly understood by a reader who knows little or nothing of the milieu in which it was written was implicit in J. C. Herder's *Ideen* (1784–91); also, Mme de Staël in *On Literature Considered in Relation with Social Institutions* (1800) had claimed that romanticism and Protestantism go together because both exalt the individual, whereas classicism and Catholicism go together because both respect formal discipline and exalt tradition. But Taine enlarged the conceptions of Herder and Mme de Staël, codified them, and made them explicit in his formula. The formula, modified or qualified, has been widely influential. Taine belonged also to a world that prided itself on its scientific realism, its positivism. It had an awesome respect for the powers of environment and heredity. Zola, following Taine, had attempted to find a scientific way to write novels.

Subsequent criticism and scholarship have tended to reduce Taine's triad to milieu, but under that to include social, political, and climatic environment as well as nationalism, regionalism, and traditionalism. Even biographical studies in which an author is investigated in psychological terms tend to be subsumed under milieu studies. Taine's shadow hovers in the background. How much he contributed to the *Zeitgeist* and how much he was himself a product of it seems difficult to decide. A simpler matter is to restate what some of the critics consciously borrowed, accepted, or rejected after reading his work.

Sainte-Beuve was among the first to state the general criticism that has been directed against Taine's formula: "After every allowance is made for general and particular elements and circumstances, there remains place and space enough around men of talent to give them every freedom of moving and turning." Interestingly enough, we have in some detail Henry James's reaction to Taine. He reviewed H. Van Laun's translation of *History of English Literature* (published 1864; translated 1871) for *The Atlantic Monthly*. James appreciated the "massive work" but he was not unaware of its limitations. "[Taine's] aim," James said, "has been to establish the psychology of the people. . . . It is a picture of the English intellect, with literary examples and allusions in evidence. . . . Its purpose is to discover in the strongest features of the strongest works the temper of the race and time, which involves a considerable neglect not only of works but of features." In an aside, James observes that Taine's triad has "lately been reiterated to satiety." But the will to method, James implies, is an invitation to oversimplifications. "The truth for M. Taine lies stored up, as one might say, in great lumps and blocks, to be released and detached by a few lively hammer blows; while for Sainte-Beuve it was a diffused and imponderable essence, as vague as carbon in the air which nourishes vegetation, and, like it, to be disengaged by patient chemistry . . . and we cannot but think his frank provisional empiricism more truly scientific than M. Taine's premature philosophy. One may enjoy many incidental judgments if one neglects to hold Taine to his premises. There is a constantly visible hiatus between his formula and his application of it." Taine, as James implied, had an inordinate haste to reach conclusions.

Some American readers of Taine were less critical than James. Hamilton Wright Mabie made proper acknowledgment in his *Short Studies in Literature* (1893) to the critical genius of Winckelmann, Lessing, Goethe, and Sainte-Beuve before making his bow to Taine. His chapters on race, surroundings, and time, despite their genteel tone, are further evidences of his acceptance of Taine as a master critic. Lewis E. Gates, in whose class at Harvard the young Frank Norris wrote *Vandover and the Brute*, published an article in *The Nation* the year Taine died in which he called the *History* "a magnificent achievement and a work of the greatest possible significance." Gates was primarily an impressionist, but in his article, which he republished in *Studies and Appreciations* (1900), he said that Taine "stands as the one great representative of scientific method in the study of literature." Similarly, in the Introduction written for the 1900 edition of the *History*, J. Scott Clark said that scholars owed a great deal to Taine. Hitherto they had spent their time writing vague generalities about a writer, but now, thanks to Taine, "the movement toward a true scientific method is already begun." Fred Lewis Pattee's *A History of American Literature* (1896) had, according to the

Introduction, at least an avowed intention of following Taine's method. The actual debt to Taine seems slight. Bliss Perry's *The American Mind*, published a number of years later, is profoundly indebted to Taine's method. In "Race, Nation and Book," the opening chapter, Perry says that whatever racial homogeneity develops or has developed will be an amalgam of all our immigrant peoples and their multiple traditions; each work will have a regional or local as well as a national character; certain writers will have European models, others will write out of their feeling about the political aspects of the American mores; and some will appear almost to have escaped the time spirit. These possibilities should be kept in mind by anyone looking for the representative character of American books. Perry himself concludes that the "most characteristic American writing" is a "citizen literature,"[5] the "*Federalist*, and Garrison's editorials and Grant's *Memoirs*." It is not the "self-conscious literary performances of a Poe or a Hawthorne." Perry has chapters on American idealism and individualism and fellowship. Perry's observations, despite the genteel tone which tends, incidentally, to belie his thesis, are useful in the way a sociologist's or cultural historian's observations would be useful. That his thesis and method are not adequate to his subject, literary criticism, becomes evident when he is forced to treat the work of Poe or Hawthorne as "performances." Perry's book augurs Vernon Louis Parrington's *Main Currents in American Thought*. The study of literature is the study of milieu. In Perry's thesis, citizen literature is both the more admirable and

[5] In *The Atlantic Monthly* for May 1901, J. D. Logan had found American prose part of a "citizen literature," the chief characteristic of which is vigor and "manliness."

the more characteristic part of the milieu. The status of the work as literature is largely irrelevant.

There were, of course, a few voices like James's raised in warning against any too wholehearted acceptance or too narrow application of Taine's method, but almost always his critics acknowledged that his had been a major contribution to modern criticism. In *The Masters of Modern French Criticism* (1912), Irving Babbitt said that Taine possessed a great capacity for generalizing but added that Taine usually pushed his generalizations too far. Also, according to Babbitt, there was little evidence in Taine's criticism of any very deep spiritual or aesthetic insight. Brownell's *Criticism* (1914) furnished perhaps a fairer view of Taine's virtues and limitations. Brownell said that, following Taine, it was impossible to see a purely belletristic approach to literature as other than antiquated. But Brownell was aware of two tendencies that inhered in Taine's method:

It tends generally to impose its historical theory on the literary and esthetic facts, to discern their historical rather than their essential character; and, as inelastically applied, at all events, it tends specifically to accept its "documents" as final rather than as the very *subjects* of its concern.

Taine's method of inferring characteristics of a milieu as they are evident in a piece of literature and of explaining the nature of the literature in terms of what it takes from the milieu is now a commonly accepted practice in the study of literature. Even when unacknowledged or forgotten, the influence of Taine has been very great. The influence of Brunetière, on the other hand, was for the most part only temporary, a part of the fascination caused by the concept of evolution.

IV

The doctrine of evolution, wrote William Morton Payne, in "American Literary Criticism and the Doctrine of Evolution,"[6] is the master key to the secrets of nature and human life. Evolution has given us a new geology, a new anthropology, a new sociology, a new psychology, a new sense of brotherhood, and other boons. Has it, Payne asks, given us a new literary criticism? Yes, it has given us a scientific criticism to replace classical or judicial criticism (Boileau) and romantic criticism which exhibits the character of the work being discussed (Sainte-Beuve). Scientific criticism, like other intellectual disciplines in the new era, seeks to understand by asking how the phenomenon, the literary work, came about: the work is studied in its antecedents, the conditions under which the artist developed, the opinions current at the time, the psychological and physical peculiarities of the writer, and so forth. Taine and Brunetière best exemplify such criticism. Taine, a pre-Darwinian, was scientific in that he studied literature as a product of race and environment, but it remained for Brunetière to add evolution to the formula, to make it "scientific in the most modern sense."

Brunetière (who had visited the United States in 1897) had written the Preface for an English translation of *Manuel de l'histoire de la littérature* in which he tried to summarize the virtues in his new method. Payne quotes the following passage with little or no realization that Brunetière was far too willing to let analogy run riot:

A given variety of literature, the English drama of the sixteenth century, or the French comedy of the seventeenth century,

[6] *International Monthly*, II (July 1900), 26–46 and 127–53.

or the English novel of the eighteenth century is in process of development slowly organizing itself under the double influence of the interior and exterior environment. . . . Suddenly, and without its being possible to give the reason, a Shakespeare, a Molière, or a Richardson appears, and forthwith not only is the variety modified, but new species have come into being: psychological drama, the comedy of character, the novel of manners. . . . It is in vain that the older species attempt to struggle; their fate is sealed in advance. The successors of Richardson, Molière, and Shakespeare copy these unattainable models until, their fecundity being exhausted—and by their fecundity I mean their aptitude for struggling with kindred and rival species—the imitation is changed into a routine which becomes a source of weakness, impoverishment, and death for the species. I shall not easily be persuaded that this manner of considering the history of literature or art is calculated to detract from the originality of great artists or great writers. . . . Other advantages could be enumerated, but this is the principal: the combination or conciliation of "hero-worship," as understood by Emerson or Carlyle, with the doctrine of slowly operating influences and the action of contemporary circumstances.

Awed by the concept of biological evolution, Brunetière, and Payne with him, made far too much of this thesis and neglected to consider many of the ways in which analogies from biological evolution do *not* work in discussion of literary history: certain literary works forgotten or dead for generations or centuries may suddenly reproduce. So-called "hybrid" forms like the novel or tragicomedy do reproduce their kind. And neither of these hybrids has shown any tendency to revert to either of its parent species. Further, no one can say whether Pope or Gray or Shakespeare is more characteristic of the English as a racial type, and even if one could, there is no accompanying formula for judging literary worth.

Payne was an egregious voice of the new age, willing to see final and absolute answers in the latest forms of knowledge, but he was hardly alone in his enthusiasm.

Aristotle, Horace, and most of the Renaissance critics had said that the "astonishing" and the "marvellous" are necessary attributes of literature, but Hjalmar Boyesen, studying the evolution of the German novel, *Essays on German Literature* (1892), was prepared in the name of the spirit of science to give up any such nonsense. "Fortunately, the beneficent scientific movement of recent years has revealed and is revealing to a constantly increasing number of men the true logic of existence, and teaching them to order their lives in accordance with certain ascertainable laws which will govern them either with or without their consent." What these laws are, Boyesen does not say. He does suggest, however, that the acceptance of the scientific spirit leads one to prefer the normal to the unusual. Those who rid themselves of their unscientific feelings will undoubtedly "prefer Thackeray to Dickens, and perhaps Turgenieff to both." They could not be induced to read detective stories (of the "astonishing" variety) "and they have at heart more respect even for Zola than for some of his sentimental *confrères*." The German novel, he says, has evolved, progressed from a concern with the miraculous to the probable and normal. The novelist of today puts this question regarding the incidents of his plot: "Are they likely to happen?" The novelist of the future, however, will be satisfied with nothing less than assurance that "his premises given nothing else could have happened."[7]

[7] Boyesen, of course, was not alone in his narrow determinism. Theodore Dreiser, as he recalls in *A Book About Myself*, discovered very early in the 1890's Herbert Spencer's *Synthetic*

If Boyesen could allow his faith in the ultimate powers of science to suggest an inevitable and rigorous determinism, he could, on the other hand, see that the novel of the future should more than likely require the complexity of form necessary to refract and evoke a sense of the complexities of society:

Evolution, according to one of the several definitions presented by Herbert Spencer, is a development from the homogeneous to the heterogeneous, and if the novel is to keep pace with life, it must necessarily be subject to the same development; it must, in its highest form, convey an impression of the whole complex machinery of the modern state and society, and, by implication at least, make clear the influences and surroundings which fashioned the hero's character and thus determined his career. To explain all these things in explicit language would, of course, require an encyclopedia, but there are yet other ways of making them present to the reader's consciousness. Thus in Thackeray's "The Newcombes," "Pendennis," and "Vanity Fair," we seem to hear the rush and roar of the huge city in which the scene is laid. The vigorous blood of the nineteenth century throbs and pul-

Philosophy (First Principles). Spencer, Dreiser wrote, "quite blew me, intellectually, to bits." After such knowledge he could believe only this: "Of one's ideals, struggles, deprivations, sorrows and joys, it could only be said that they were chemic compulsions, something for which for some inexplicable but unimportant reason responded to and resulted from the hope of pleasure and the fear of pain. Man was a mechanism, undevised and uncreated, and a badly and carelessly driven one at that."

sates through every scene and chapter, and we have a subconsciousness of the noisy metropolitan life even in the quietest domestic episodes.

In the latter part of the quotation Boyesen is saying pretty much what James said in "The Art of Fiction": that one knows the whole pattern from the suggestive detail, but it is interesting that Boyesen introduces the name of Herbert Spencer as authority for part of his statement.

V

Advocates of the spirit of realism found themselves looking into the relationship between realism and the life of the common man and therefore of democracy and socialism. Perhaps the realism of a critic like Howells is best explored in such terms. It is nonetheless true that many of the advocates of realism in criticism, as well as in fiction, frequently made their appeals in the name of science. More specifically, they made their appeals through such terms and concepts as environment, heredity, determinism, evolution, and objectivity. Sometimes the appeals are to analogies that are irrelevant to literary considerations. When not employed irrelevantly or reductively, however, a number of the concepts introduced by scientific-minded critics make for useful insights, and they also give one a sense of dealing with reality as it appears to the twentieth-century mind.

FROM WHAT IS REALISM?

Harry Levin*

Levin observes the shifting and ambiguous history, nature, and concepts of realism, its extension into the quasi-scientific approach of naturalism, and its questionable projection into surrealism or "superrealism."

...So much is clear, as Karl Mannheim has said: "Realism means different things in different contexts." Its would-be historians may well be deterred by the object-lesson of Lord Acton's uncompleted *History of Liberty*. But students of literature have the measurable advantage of working from texts as well as contexts, and Erich Auerbach's *Mimesis* has lately shown what stylistic analysis can do, when trained upon the descriptive techniques of selected authors from Homer to Virginia Woolf. When Professor Auerbach finds no formula for the presentation of actuality (*dargestellte Wirklichkeit*) in different languages at different epochs, he impressively documents our need for assuming a relativistic point of view. Possibly an absolute standard could be set up in the plastic arts, where the actual object can be directly compared with its artistic treatment. Yet even there the realism seems to be a matter of degree, varying with choice of subject and emphasis on detail. Even when we speak of "photographic reproduction," we cannot take for granted its objectivity. The very phrase *trompe-l'œil* gives it away. The camera's eye is relatively less subjective than the eye of the beholder; yet it was photography which opened the way for impressionistic

* The selection is reprinted from "What Is Realism?" by Harry Levin, in *Comparative Literature*, Vol. III (1951), by permission of the author.

painting, which in turn has angled and composed and highlighted the art of the photographer.

Perhaps, like students of the diverging "romanticisms," we should pluralize our subject; but we should not, like some of them, allow divergences to obscure a fundamental impetus. Art has continually adapted itself to man's changing conceptions of reality—that is to say, his successive adjustments to society and nature. In a static culture, where his position is fixed and his world-view unchanging, expression is likely to be conventionalized. But Occidental culture has been dynamic, and its arts have endeavored to keep pace with its accelerating changes. This distinction, which is broadly exemplified in the contrast between East and West, sharply emerged from the Iconoclastic Controversy, when Eastern orthodoxy prescribed a rigid convention while Western artists were free to move toward secularization, individuality, realism—from the symbolic, in short, to the representational. Now if, as Aristotle maintains, art springs from the interplay of two complementary instincts, μίμησις [imitation] and ἁρμονία [harmony or form], there are times when the imitation of nature predominates and other times when it is subordinated to the imposition of a pattern. When Plato condemned poetry for its unreality (in the most idealistic and paradoxical sense of that term), Aristotle proposed a compromise in the name of poetic truth and higher reality, and thence handed on the doctrine of verisimilitude to the neoclassical critics.

Meanwhile the sphere of the probable expanded, while much that the ancients regarded as universal was seen by the moderns to be more limited. Against such limitations romanticism protested, when Wordsworth and Coleridge set out to write about lower ranks of society and stranger wonders of nature than classicism seemed willing to recognize. Not that the classicists excluded realism, but they relegated it to the comic stage; comedy was the *imago veritatis*, and the common man was no hero but a figure of fun. The medium that most completely mirrors the increasing stature of the middle class has been, of course, the major vehicle of literary realism, the novel. The novel originated, with a characteristic gesture, by repudiating its mediaeval predecessor; the picaresque tale overtook the knightly romance; and Cervantes, by pitting the daily realities of the developing city against the chivalric ideals of the declining castle, provided an archetype for all novelists and future realists. "La rivalité du monde réel et de la représentation que nous nous en faisons" [The rivalry between the real world and the representation of it that we create]—this might be a French critic's description of *Don Quixote*. It happens to be André Gide's description of what his novelist is attempting in *Les Faux-monnayeurs*.

Conversely, looking backward from Gide, we can see how every great novel has attempted—*mutatis mutandis*—to distinguish what is real from what is counterfeit. Defoe's narrations, he invariably assured his readers, are not fiction but fact; and Diderot pointedly entitled one of his stories *Ceci n'est pas un conte* [This Is Not a Story]. To convince us of his essential veracity, the novelist must always be disclaiming the fictitious and breaking through the encrustations of the literary. "La vraie éloquence se moque de l'éloquence" [True eloquence laughs at eloquence]. It is no coincidence that, from Rabelais to Jane Austen, so many realists have begun as parodists; it has even been argued, by Viktor Shklovsky, that parody is the basis of the novelistic form. We must not assume that, because it is polymorphous, the novel is formless; nor that writers very easily or spontaneously express themselves in a realistic mode. "No more literary school than the realists has ever existed," as George Moore, their leading British apologist, allowed. But we must first go—as Moore did—to France, where most of the problems of modern literature have been formulated, if we would track the critical usage down to its historical context. (If we would trace it to its metaphysical chrysalis, we should have to look even farther back to Germany, to Schiller's *Über naive und sentimentalische Dichtung*, where antique *Realismus* is contrasted with the idealistic outlook of the romantics.)

The earliest applications of the term that we encounter in the *New English Dictionary* are cited from Emerson in 1856 and Ruskin in 1857: the first is roughly synonymous with "materialism," the second with "grotesquerie," and both are decidedly pejorative. In France, on the other hand, the latter year marks the trial and vindication of *Madame Bovary*—a date as important for realism as the *première* of *Hernani* is for romanticism. The relationship between the two movements, as we acknowledge more and more, is continuous rather than antithetical. The realism of the romanticists has its dialectical counterpart in the romanticism of the realists, and it would be hard to say under which category we should classify *La Chartreuse de Parme* or *Les Misérables*. As early as 1826, investigation has shown, *le romantisme* and *le réalisme* echoed interchangeably through contemporary periodicals. But in the phrase of its journalistic fugleman, Champfleury, realism was one of "those religions in -ism" which came into the world in 1848. Its preparation had been technical as well as ideological; it profited from Daguerre's epoch-making invention, which entered the public domain in 1839, as well as from Houssaye's history of Flemish painting published in 1846. It reached its artistic climax when Courbet, whose paintings were rejected by the Salon of 1855, set up his own exhibition of these solidly executed studies in humble life, which he called his *Pavillon du Réalisme*.

The critic Duranty summed up objectives when he called for "the exact, complete, and sincere reproduction of the social milieu in which we live." His little magazine, *Réalisme*, coincided with a collection of essays under the same title, brought out by Champfleury in 1857. By then the catchword was becoming popular; even M. Prudhomme, the bourgeois incarnate, could sign his letters with assurances of his "distinguished consideration and realism." However, Duranty believed that the realists were too individualistic to establish a school, while Champfleury considered them transitional and expected them to give way before another movement in thirty years. Within half that time, in the 1870s, Zola was putting out manifestoes for naturalism. Where the older group had posthumously venerated Balzac, the naturalists paid homage to Flaubert, but he remained indifferent to schools and slogans. When Zola amiably admitted that these were devices to gain publicity for younger writers, he scarcely did justice

to the grimmer implications of the newer term—the boundless distance between Robinson Crusoe's easy control over his environment and the crushed victims of Hardy's cosmic irony or Dreiser's chemical determinism.

Naturalism found its inspiration in science rather than art, its exemplar in Darwin rather than Courbet. In contrast to the accumulation of things, the jumbled catalogues of realism, its objects were meticulously selected and related through the chain of cause and effect. Seeking to complete the process of identification between literature and life, it conceived a book as a *document humain* [human document] and a play as a *tranche de vie* [slice of life]. But Zola's novels were experimental in quite a different sense from the physiological experimentation of Claude Bernard. Their twofold aim is reflected in their subtitle: *Histoire naturelle et sociale d'une famille sous le Second Empire* [*Natural and Social History of a Family Under the Second Empire*]. As natural history, they demonstrate nothing; they simply illustrate the obsolescent theories of Zola's scientific contemporaries. Their social story is something else again, combining the exposure of bureaucracy with a plea for the underdog, each volume covering another field of documentation. Zola, writing in retrospect, gave voice to the political opposition that the Second Empire vainly tried to silence. Similarly in Russia, under the tsars, in spite of censorship, suppression, and regimentation, writers were able to lodge their protest against an even more autocratic régime. Perhaps because Russians had to live a lie, as Turgenev suggested, their novels were so intensely devoted to truth.

Into the second half of the nineteenth century, realists and naturalists carried augmenting burdens of social criticism and humanitarian sympathy. The brothers Goncourt, for all their aristocratic tastes, furthered the advance of proletarian fiction; they urged, in the preface to *Germinie Lacerteux*, the right of the lower class to a novel of its own. The spread of democracy, the rise in the standard of living, the exploitation of typography and literacy brought pressure for further extensions of the literary franchise. Hence Harriet Beecher Stowe announced that *Uncle Tom's Cabin* (*or Life among the Lowly*) would treat a theme "hitherto ignored by the associations of polite and refined society." Politeness and refinement inevitably hold a vested interest in the *status quo*, which is loudly outraged by the depiction of uncomfortable facts and ignoble existences, and would outlaw them by invoking the ambiguous sanction of universality. Official and academic sponsorship, reducing the dynamic to the static, produce what William Dean Howells termed "a petrification of taste." Resistance is no less inevitable than movement, and repeats itself over the years. Just as Brunetière deprecated the naturalistic school, just as the disillusioned novels of the First World War were attacked by propagandists for the Second, so the hired moralists of *Life* magazine have latterly been editorializing against *From Here to Eternity* and *The Naked and the Dead*.

None the less realism, heralded by romanticism and continued by naturalism, has been the animating current of nineteenth-century literature. Today it no longer operates as an *avant-garde*; it has acquired tradition and even academies. Watchwords continue to become outmoded and novelties must be rediscovered again and again; the naturists supersede the naturalists and the verists yield to self-proclaimed veritists; and yet the real thing seems even more remote than before. Can it be that this progression, which has moved on so rapidly from generation to generation, is slowing down to an impasse? The next step, to judge from *surréalisme* (or "superrealism"), seems to be less a new projection of the old realism than a sharp reaction against it—against representation in favor of symbolism. Such landmarks as Joyce's *Ulysses*, pointing in two directions, lead forward—or is it backward?—via psychology toward fantasy and myth. The technological obsolescence of the novel itself is predictable in an era when fiction can hardly keep up with fact, when the reporter turns novelist and the novelist turns reporter, when the instinct for imitation is more efficiently satisfied by journalism, radio, film, and above all television. Within the abstracted realm now left to the purer arts, it may be that the instinct for harmony—for order, degree, and arrangement—will again prevail. . . .

CHAPTER 8

Naturalism

FROM THE EXPERIMENTAL NOVEL
Emile Zola*

Zola equates the methods of the experimental or naturalistic novelist with the methods of the research scientist working out a hypothesis. "Experiment is an observation instigated for the purpose of verification." The novelist must first observe the facts of nature, form a hypothesis about them, then set about working out his hypothesis "until the mechanism of the passion, taken to pieces and set up again by him, acts according to the fixed laws of nature."

...The first question which presents itself is this: Is experiment possible in literature, in which up to the present time observation alone has been employed?

Claude Bernard discusses observation and experiment at great length. There exists, in the first place, a very clear line of demarcation, as follows: "The name of 'observer' is given to him who applies the simple or complex process of investigation in the study of phenomena which he does not vary, and which he gathers, consequently, as nature offers them to him; the name of 'experimentalist' is given to him who employs the simple and complex process of investigation to vary or modify, for an end of some kind, the natural phenomena, and to make them appear under circumstances and conditions in which they are not presented by nature." For instance, astronomy is a science of observation, because you cannot conceive of an astronomer acting upon the stars; while chemistry is an experimental science, as the chemist acts upon nature and modifies it. This, according to Claude Bernard, is the only true and important distinction which separates the observer from the experimentalist.

I cannot follow him in his discussion of the different definitions given up to

* The selection is from *The Experimental Novel and Other Essays*, by Emile Zola, translated by Belle M. Sherman, 1893.

the present time. As I have said before, he finishes by coming to the conclusion that experiment is but provoked observation. I repeat his words: "In the experimental method the search after facts, that is to say, investigation, is always accompanied by a reason, so that ordinarily the experimentalist makes an experiment to confirm and verify the value of an experimental idea. In this case you can say that experiment is an observation instigated for the purpose of verification."

To determine how much observation and experimenting there can be in the naturalistic novel, I only need to quote the following passages:

The observer relates purely and simply the phenomena which he has under his eyes. . . . He should be the photographer of phenomena, his observation should be an exact representation of nature. . . . He listens to nature and he writes under its dictation. But once the fact is ascertained and the phenomenon observed, an idea or hypothesis comes into his mind, reason intervenes, and the experimentalist comes forward to interpret the phenomenon. The experimentalist is a man who, in pursuance of a more or less probable, but anticipated, explanation of observed phenomena, institutes an experiment in such a way that, according to all probability, it will furnish a result which will serve to confirm the hypothesis or preconceived idea. The moment that the result of the experiment manifests itself, the experimentalist finds himself face to face with a true observation which he has called forth and which he must ascertain, as all observation, without any preconceived idea. The experimentalist should then disappear, or rather transform himself instantly into the observer, and it is not until after he has ascertained the absolute results of the experiment, like that of an ordinary observation, that his mind comes back to reasoning, comparing, and judging whether the experimental hypothesis is verified or invalidated by these same results.

The mechanism is all there. It is a little complicated, it is true, and Claude Bernard is led on to say:

When all this passes into the brain of a savant who has given himself up to the study of a science as complicated as medicine still is, then there is such an entanglement between the result of observation and what belongs to experiment that it will be impossible and, besides, useless to try to analyze, in their inextricable *mélange*, each of these terms.

In one word, it might be said that observation "indicates" and that experiment "teaches."

Now, to return to the novel, we can easily see that the novelist is equally an observer and an experimentalist. The observer in him gives the facts as he has observed them, suggests the point of departure, displays the solid earth on which his characters are to tread and the phenomena to develop. Then the experimentalist appears and introduces an experiment, that is to say, sets his characters going in a certain story so as to show that the succession of facts will be such as the requirements of the determinism of the phenomena under examination call for. Here it is nearly always an experiment *"pour voir"* [for the sake of seeing], as Claude Bernard calls it. The novelist starts out in search of a truth. I will take as an example the character of the Baron Hulot, in *Cousine Bette*, by Balzac. The general fact observed by Balzac is the ravages that the amorous temperament of a man makes in his home, in his family, and in society. As soon as he has chosen his subject, he starts from known facts; then he makes his experiment, and exposes Hulot to a series of trials, placing him amid certain surroundings in order to exhibit how the complicated machinery of his passions works. It is then evident that there is not only observation there, but that there is also experiment; as Balzac does not remain satisfied with photographing the facts collected by him, but interferes in a direct way to place his character in certain conditions, and of these he remains the master. The problem is to know what such a passion, acting in such a surrounding and under such circumstances, would produce from the point of view of an individual and of society; and an experimental novel, *Cousine Bette*, for example, is simply the report of the experiment that the novelist conducts before the eyes of the public. In fact, the whole operation consists in taking facts in nature, then in studying the mechanism of these facts, acting upon them by the modification of circumstances and surroundings without deviating from the laws of nature. Finally, you possess knowledge of the man, scientific knowledge of him, in both his individual and social relations.

Doubtless we are still far from certainties in chemistry and even physiology. Nor do we know any more the reagents which decompose the passions, rendering them susceptible of analysis. Often, in this essay, I shall recall in similar fashion this fact, that the experimental novel is still younger than experimental medicine, and the latter is but just born. But I do not intend to exhibit the acquired results, I simply desire to clearly expose a method. If the experimental novelist is still groping in the most obscure and complex of all the sciences, this does not prevent this science from existing. It is undeniable that the naturalistic novel, such as we understand it today, is a real experiment that a novelist makes on man by the help of observation.

Besides, this opinion is not only mine, it is Claude Bernard's as well. He says in one place: "In practical life men but make experiments on one another." And again, in a more conclusive way, he expresses the whole theory of the experimental novel:

When we reason on our own acts we have a certain guide, for we are conscious of what we think and how we feel. But if we wish to judge of the acts of another man, and know the motives which make him act, that is altogether a different thing. Without doubt we have before our eyes the movements of this man and his different acts, which are, we are sure, the modes of expression of his sensibility and his will. Further, we even admit that there is a necessary connection between the acts and their cause; but what is this cause? We do not feel it, we are not conscious of it, as we are when it acts in ourselves; we are therefore obliged to interpret it, and to guess at it, from the movements which we see and the words which we hear. We are obliged to check off this man's actions one by the other; we consider how he acted in such a circumstance, and, in a word, we have recourse to the experimental method.

All that I have spoken of further back is summed up in this last phrase, which is written by a savant.

I shall still call your attention to another illustration of Claude Bernard, which struck me as very forcible: "The experimentalist is the examining magistrate of nature." We novelists are the examining magistrates of men and their passions.

But see what splendid clearness breaks forth when this conception of the application of the experimental method to the novel is adequately grasped and is carried out with all the scientific rigor which the matters permits today. A contemptible reproach which they heap upon us naturalistic writers is the desire to be solely photographers. We have in vain declared that we admit the necessity of an artist's possessing an individual temperament and a personal expression; they continue to reply to us with these imbecile arguments, about the impossibility of being strictly true, about the necessity of arranging facts to produce a work of art of any kind. Well, with the application of the experimental method to the novel that quarrel dies out. The idea of experiment carried with it the idea of modification. We start, indeed, from the true facts, which are our indestructible basis; but to show the mechanism of these facts it is necessary for us to produce and direct the phenomena; this is our share of invention, here is the genius in the book. Thus without having recourse to the questions of form and of style, which I shall examine later, I maintain even at this point that we must modify nature, without departing from nature, when we employ the experimental method in our novels. If we bear in mind this definition, that "observation indicates and experiment teaches," we can even now claim for our books this great lesson of experiment.

The writer's office, far from being lessened, grows singularly from this point of view. An experiment, even the most simple, is always based on an idea, itself born of an observation. As Claude Bernard says: "The experimental idea is not arbitrary, nor purely imaginary; it ought always to have a support in some observed reality, that is to say, in nature." It is on this idea and on doubt that he bases all the method. "The appearance of the experimental idea," he says further on, "is entirely spontaneous and its nature absolutely individual, depending upon the mind in which it originates; it is a particular sentiment, a *quid proprium*, which constitutes the originality, the invention, and the genius of each one." Further, he makes doubt the great scientific lever. "The doubter is the true savant; he doubts only himself and his interpretations; he believes in science; he even admits in the experimental sciences a criterion or a positive principle, the determinism of phenomena, which is absolute in living beings as in inanimate bodies." Thus, instead of confining the novelist within narrow bounds, the experimental method gives full sway to his intelligence as a thinker, and to his genius as a creator. He must see, understand, and invent. Some observed fact makes the idea start up of trying an experiment, of writing a novel, in order to attain to a complete knowledge of the truth. Then when, after careful consideration, he has decided upon the plan of his experiment, he will judge the results at each step with the freedom of mind of a man who accepts only facts conformable to the determinism of phenomena. He set out from doubt to reach positive knowledge; and he will not cease to doubt until the mechanism of the passion, taken to pieces and set up again by him, acts according to the fixed laws of nature. There is no greater, no more magnificent work for the human mind. We shall see, further on, the miseries of the scholastics, of the makers of systems, and those theorizing about the ideal, compared with the triumph of the experimentalists.

I sum up this first part by repeating that the naturalistic novelists observe and experiment, and that all their work is the offspring of the doubt which seizes them in the presence of truths little known and phenomena unexplained, until an experimental idea rudely awakens their genius some day, and urges them to make an experiment, to analyze facts, and to master them.

. . . Let us clearly define now what is meant by an experimental novelist. Claude Bernard gives the following definition of an artist: "What is an artist? He is a man who realizes in a work of art an idea or a sentiment which is personal to him." I absolutely reject this definition. On this basis if I represented a man as walking on his head, I should have made a work of art, if such happened to be my personal sentiments. But in that case I should be a fool and nothing else. So one must add that the personal feeling of the artist is always subject to the higher law of truth and nature. We now come to the question of hypothesis. The artist starts out from the same point as the savant; he places himself before nature, has an idea apriori, and works according to this idea. Here alone he separates himself from the savant, if he carries out his idea to the end without verifying its truth by the means of observation and experiment. Those who make use of experiment might well be called experimental artists; but then people will tell us that they are no longer artists, since such people regard art as the burden of personal error which the artist has put into his study of nature. I contend that the personality of the writer should only appear in the idea apriori and in the form, not in the infatuation for the false. I see no objection, besides, to its showing in the hypothesis, but it is necessary to clearly understand what you mean by these words.

It has often been said that writers ought to open the way for savants. This is true, for we have seen in *L'Introduction* that hypothesis and empiricism precede and prepare for the scientific state which is established finally by the experimental method. Man commenced by venturing certain explanations of phenomena, the poets gave expression to their emotions, and the savants ended by mastering hypotheses and fixing the truth. Claude Bernard always assigns the role of pioneers to the philosophers. It is a very noble role, and today it is the writers who should assume it and who should endeavor to fill it worthily. Only

let it be well understood that each time that a truth is established by the savants the writers should immediately abandon their hypothesis to adopt this truth; otherwise they will remain deliberately in error without benefiting anyone. It is thus that science, as it advances, furnishes to us writers a solid ground upon which we should lean for support, to better enable us to shoot into new hypotheses. In a word, every phenomenon, once clearly determined, destroys the hypothesis which it replaces, and it is then necessary to transport your hypothesis one step further into the new unknown which arises. I will take a very simple example in order to make myself better understood; it has been proved that the earth revolves around the sun; what would you think of a poet who should adopt the old belief that the sun revolves around the earth? Evidently the poet, if he wishes to risk a personal explanation of any fact, should choose a fact whose cause is not already known. This, then, illustrates the position hypothesis should occupy for experimental novelists; we must accept determined facts, and not attempt to risk about them our personal sentiments, which would be ridiculous, building throughout on the territory that science has conquered; then before the unknown, but only then, exercising our intuition and suggesting the way to science, free to make mistakes, happy if we produce any data toward the solution of the problem. Here I stand at Claude Bernard's practical program, who is forced to accept empiricism as a necessary forerunner. In our experimental novel we can easily risk a few hypotheses on the questions of heredity and surroundings, after having respected all that science knows today about the matter. We can prepare the ways, we can furnish the results of observation, human data which may prove very useful. A great lyrical poet has written lately that our century is a century of prophets. Yes, if you wish it; only let it be well understood that these prophets rely neither upon the irrational nor the supernatural. If the prophets thought best to bring up again the most elementary notions, to serve up nature with a strange religious and philosophical sauce, to hold fast to the metaphysical man, to confound and obscure everything, the prophets, notwithstanding their genius in the matter of style, would never be anything but great gooses ignorant whether they would get wet if they jumped into the water. In our scientific age it is a very delicate thing to be a prophet, as we no longer believe in the truths of revelation, and in order to be able to foresee the unknown we must begin by studying the known.

The conclusion to which I wish to come is this: If I were to define the experimental novel I should not say, as Claude Bernard says, that a literary work lies entirely in the personal feeling, for the reason that in my opinion the personal feeling is but the first impulse. Later nature, being there, makes itself felt, or at least that part of nature of which science has given us the secret, and about which we have no longer any right to romance. The experimental novelist is therefore the one who accepts proven facts, who points out in man and in society the mechanism of the phenomena over which science is mistress, and who does not interpose his personal sentiments, except in the phenomena whose determinism is not yet settled, and who tries to test, as much as he can, this personal sentiment, this idea apriori, by observation and experiment.

I cannot understand how our naturalistic literature can mean anything else. I have only spoken of the experimental novel, but I am fairly convinced that the same method, after having triumphed in history and in criticism, will triumph everywhere, on the stage and in poetry even. It is an inevitable evolution. Literature, in spite of all that can be said, does not depend merely upon the author; it is influenced by the nature it depicts and by the man whom it studies. Now if the savants change their ideas of nature, if they find the true mechanism of life, they force us to follow them, to precede them even, so as to play our role in the new hypotheses. The metaphysical man is dead; our whole territory is transformed by the advent of the physiological man. No doubt "Achilles' Anger," "Dido's Love," will last forever on account of their beauty; but today we feel the necessity of analyzing anger and love, of discovering exactly how such passions work in the human being. This view of the matter is a new one; we have become experimentalists instead of philosophers. In short, everything is summed up in this great fact: the experimental method in letters, as in the sciences, is in the way to explain the natural phenomena, both individual and social, of which metaphysics, until now, has given only irrational and supernatural explanations.

FROM A NATURAL HISTORY OF AMERICAN NATURALISM
Malcolm Cowley*

Cowley attempts in this essay to define and trace the origins and
character of American naturalism and finally to form a judgment
of the contribution of naturalistic writers to American literature.
His rejection of naturalism is based on the argument that in its
purest doctrinal form it removed human responsibility entirely
and through an amoral determinism or behaviorism asserted that
"conditions, not men, were at fault."

There have been too many unfruitful
arguments over naturalism in American
fiction. Now that the movement has
flourished for half a century, we can
forget to attack or defend it and instead
can look back in an objective or naturalistic spirit at the work of the many
authors it has inspired. We can note
that their line extends from Norris and
the early Dreiser through Farrell and
Steinbeck. We can describe their principles, note how these were modified in
practice, and finally try to reach some
judgment of their literary remains.

Naturalism has been defined in two
words as pessimistic determinism and
the definition is true so far as it goes.
The naturalistic writers were all deter-
minists in that they believed in the
omnipotence of abstract forces. They
were pessimists so far as they believed
that men and women were absolutely incapable of shaping their own destinies.
They regarded the individual as "a pawn
on a chessboard"; the phrase recurs time
and again in their novels. They felt
that he could not achieve happiness by
any conscious decision and that he re-

ceived no earthly or heavenly reward for
acting morally; man was, in Dreiser's
words, "the victim of forces over which
he has no control."

In some of his moods, Frank Norris
carried this magnification of forces and
minification of persons to an even greater
extreme. "Men were nothings, mere ani-
malculae, mere ephemerides that flut-
tered and fell and were forgotten
between dawn and dusk," he said in the
next-to-last chapter of *The Octopus*.
"Men were naught, life was naught;
FORCE only existed—FORCE that
brought men into the world, FORCE
that made the wheat grow, FORCE that
garnered it from the soil to give place
to the succeeding crop." But Norris, like
several other naturalists, was able to
combine this romantic pessimism about
individuals with romantic optimism
about the future of mankind. "The individual suffers, but the race goes on," he
said at the very end of the novel. "An-
nixter dies, but in a far distant corner of
the world a thousand lives are saved.
The larger view always and through all
shams, all wickednesses, discovers the
Truth that will, in the end, prevail, and
all things, surely, inevitably, resistlessly
work together for good." This was, in its
magniloquent way, a form of the belief

* The selection is reprinted from *Evolutionary Thought in America*, edited by Stow Persons, by permission of Yale University Press.
Copyright 1950 by Yale University Press.

in universal progress announced by Herbert Spencer, but it was also mingled with native or Emersonian idealism, and it helped to make naturalism more palatable to Norris' first American readers.

Zola had also declared his belief in human perfectibility, in what he called "a constant march toward truth"; and it was from Zola rather than Spencer or any native sources that Norris had borrowed most of his literary doctrines. Zola described himself as "a positivist, an evolutionist, a materialist." In his working notes, which Norris of course had never seen, but which one might say that he divined from the published text of the novels, Zola had indicated some of his aims as a writer. He would march through the world observing human behavior as if he were observing the forms of animal life. "Study men as simple elements and note the reactions," he said. And again, "What matters most to me is to be purely naturalistic, purely physiological. Instead of having principles (royalism, Catholicism) I shall have laws (heredity, atavism)." And yet again, "Balzac says that he wishes to paint men, women and things. I count men and women as the same, while admitting their natural differences, and *subject men and women to things*." In that last phrase, which Zola underlined, he expressed the central naturalistic doctrine: that men and women are part of nature and subject to the same indifferent laws.

The principal laws, for Zola, were those of heredity, which he assumed to be as universal and unchanging as the second law of thermodynamics. He fixed upon the hereditary weakness of the Rougon-Macquart family as a theme that would bind together his vast series of novels. Suicide, alcoholism, prostitution, and insanity were all to be explained as the result of the same hereditary taint.

"Vice and virtue," he said, "are products like vitriol and sugar." Norris offered the same explanation for the brutality of McTeague. "Below the fine fabric of all that was good in him," Norris said, "ran the foul stream of hereditary evil, like a sewer. The vices and sins of his father and of his father's father, to the third and fourth and five hundredth generation, tainted him. The evil of an entire race flowed in his veins. Why should it be? He did not desire it. Was he to blame?" Others of the naturalistic school, and Norris himself in his later novels, placed some emphasis on environmental forces. When Stephen Crane sent a copy of *Maggie* to the Reverend Thomas Dixon, he wrote on the flyleaf: "It is inevitable that this book will greatly shock you, but continue, pray, with great courage to the end, for it tries to show that environment is a tremendous thing and often shapes lives regardlessly. If I could prove that theory, I would make room in Heaven for all sorts of souls (notably an occasional street girl) who are not confidently expected to be there by many excellent people." Maggie, the victim of environment, was no more to blame for her transgressions than McTeague, the victim of hereditary evil. Nobody was to blame in this world where men and women are subject to the laws of things.

A favorite theme in naturalistic fiction is that of the beast within. As the result of some crisis—usually a fight, a shipwreck, or an expedition into the Arctic —the veneer of civilization drops or is stripped away and we are faced with "the primal instinct of the brute struggling for its life and for the life of its young." The phrase is Norris', but it might have been written by any of the early naturalists. When evolution is treated in their novels, it almost always takes the opposite form of devolution or degeneration. It is seldom that the hero evolves toward a superhuman nature, as in Nietzsche's dream; instead he sinks backward toward the beasts. Zola set the fashion in *L'Assommoir* and *La Bête humaine* and Norris followed him closely in the novel he wrote during his year at Harvard, *Vandover and the Brute*. Through yielding to his lower instincts, Vandover loses his humanity; he tears off his clothes, paddles up and down the room on his hands and feet and snarls like a dog.

A still earlier story, *Lauth*, was written at the University of California after Norris had listened to the lectures of Professor Joseph Le Conte, the famous evolutionist. The action takes place in medieval Paris, where Lauth, a student at the Sorbonne, is mortally wounded in a brawl. A doctor brings him back to life by pumping blood into his veins, but the soul had left the body and does not return. Without it, Lauth sinks back rapidly through the various stages of evolution: he is an ape, then a dog, then finally "a horrible shapeless mass lying upon the floor. It lived, but lived not as do the animals or the trees, but as the protozoa, the jellyfish, and those strange lowest forms of existence wherein the line between vegetable and animal cannot be drawn." That might have been taken as a logical limit to the process of devolution; but Jack London, who was two parts naturalist, if he was also one part socialist and three parts hack journalist, tried to carry the process even further, into the realm of inanimate nature. Here, for example, is the description of a fight in *Martin Eden*:

Then they fell upon each other, like young bulls, in all the glory of youth, with naked fists, with hatred, with desire to hurt, to maim, to destroy. All the painful, thousand years' gains of man in his upward climb through creation were lost. Only the electric light remained, a milestone on the path of the great human adventure. Martin and Cheese-Face were two savages, of the stone age, of the squatting place and the tree refuge. They sank lower and lower into the muddy abyss, back into the dregs of the raw beginnings of life, striving blindly and chemically, as atoms strive, as the star-dust of the heavens strives, colliding, recoiling, and colliding again and eternally again.

It was more than a metaphor when London said that men were atoms and star dust: it was the central drift of his philosophy. Instead of moving from the simple to the complex, as Herbert Spencer tells us that everything does in this world, the naturalists kept moving from the complex to the simple, by a continual process of reduction. They spoke of the nation as "the tribe," and a moment later the tribe became a pack. Civilized man became a barbarian or a savage, the savage became a brute and the brute was reduced to its chemical elements. "Study men as simple elements," Zola had said; and many years later Dreiser followed his advice by presenting love as a form of electromagnetism and success in life as a question of chemical compounds; thus he said of his brother Paul that he was "one of those great Falstaffian souls who, for lack of a little iron or sodium or carbon dioxide in his chemical compost, was not able to bestride the world like a Colossus."

There was a tendency in almost all the naturalistic writers to identify social laws with biological or physical laws. For Jack London, the driving force behind human events was always biology—"I mean," says his autobiographical hero, Martin Eden, "the real interpretative biology, from the ground up, from the laboratory and the test tube and the vitalized inorganic right on up to the widest esthetic and social generalizations." London believed that such biological principles as natural selection and the survival of the fittest were also the laws of human society. Thomas Hardy often spoke as if men's destinies were shaped by the physical sciences. He liked to say that his characters were doomed by the stars in their courses; but actually they were doomed by human conflicts or by the still Puritan conventions of middle-class England. Norris fell into the same confusion between the physical and the social world when he pictured the wheat as "a huge Niagara ... flowing from West to East." In his novels wheat was not a grain improved by men from various wild grasses and grown by men to meet human needs; it was an abstract and elemental force like gravity. "I corner the wheat!" says Jadwin, the hero of *The Pit.* "Great heavens, it is the wheat that has cornered me." Later, when he is ruined by the new grain that floods the market, Jadwin thinks to himself,

The Wheat had grown itself: demand and supply, these were the two great laws that the Wheat obeyed. Almost blasphemous in his effrontery, he had tampered with these laws, and roused a Titan. He had laid his puny human grasp upon Creation and the very earth herself, the great mother, feeling the touch of the cobweb that the human insect had spun, had stirred at last in her sleep and sent her omnipotence moving through the grooves of the world, to find and crush the disturber of her appointed courses.

Just as the wheat itself had grown, so, in the first volume of Norris' trilogy, the Pacific and Southwestern Railroad had built itself. This octopus that held a state in its tentacles was beyond human control. Even Shelgrim, the president of the railroad, was merely the agent of a superhuman force. At the end of the novel he gives a lecture to Presley which overwhelms the poet and leaves him feeling that it rang "with the clear reverberation of truth." "You are dealing with forces," Shelgrim says, "when you speak of Wheat and the Railroads, not with men. There is the Wheat, the supply. It must be carried to the People. There is the demand. The Wheat is one force, the Railroad, another, and there is the law that governs them—supply and demand. Men have little to do with the whole business." If the two forces came into conflict—if the employees of the railroad massacred the wheat ranchers and robbed them of their land—then Presley should "blame conditions, not men."

The effect of naturalism as a doctrine is to subtract from literature the whole notion of human responsibility. "Not men" is its constant echo. If naturalistic stories had tragic endings, these were not to be explained by human wills in conflict with each other or with fate; they were the blind result of conditions, forces, physical laws, or nature herself. "There was no malevolence in Nature," Presley reflects after meeting the railroad president. "Colossal indifference only, a vast trend toward appointed goals. Nature was, then, a gigantic engine, a vast, cyclopean power, huge, terrible, a leviathan with a heart of steel, knowing no compunction, no forgiveness, no tolerance; crushing out the human atom standing in its way, with nirvanic calm." Stephen Crane had already expressed the same attitude toward nature in a sharper image and in cleaner prose. When the four shipwrecked men in *The Open Boat* are drifting close to the beach but are unable to land because of the breakers, they stare at a windmill that is like "a giant standing with its back to the plight of the ants. It represented in a degree, to the correspondent, the serenity of nature amid the struggles of the individual—nature in the wind, and nature in the visions of men. She did not seem cruel to him, then, nor beneficent, nor treacherous, nor wise. But she was indifferent, flatly indifferent."

These ideas about nature, science, and destiny led to the recurrent use of words and phrases by which early naturalistic fiction can be identified. "The irony of fate" and "the pity of it" are two of the phrases; "pawns of circumstance" is another. The words that appear time and again are "primitive," "primordial" (often coupled with "slime"), "prehensile," "apelike," "wolflike," "brute" and "brutal," "savage," "driving," "conquering," "blood" (often as an adjective), "master" and "slave" (also as adjectives), "instinct" (which is usually "blind"), "ancestor," "huge," "cyclopean," "shapeless," "abyss," "biological," "chemic" and "chemism," "hypocrisy," "taboo," "unmoral." Time and again we read that "The race is to the swift and the battle to the strong." Time and again we are told about "the law of claw and fang," "the struggle for existence," "the blood of his Viking ancestors," and "the foul stream of hereditary evil." "The veneer of civilization" is always being "stripped away," or else it "drops away in an instant." The characters in early naturalistic novels "lose all resemblance to humanity," reverting to "the abysmal brute." But when they "clash together like naked savages," or even like atoms and star dust, it is always the hero who "proves himself the stronger"; and spurning his prostrate adversary he strides forward to seize "his mate, his female." "Was he to blame?" the author asks his readers; and always he answers, "Conditions, not men, were at fault." . . .

In writing their novels, most of the naturalists pictured themselves as expressing a judgment of life that was scientific, dispassionate, and, to borrow one of their phrases, completely unmoral; but a better word for their attitude would be "rebellious." Try as they would, they could not remain merely observers. They had to revolt against the moral standards of their time; and the revolt involved them more or less unconsciously in the effort to impose new standards that would be closer to what they regarded as natural laws. Their books are full of little essays or sermons addressed to the reader; in fact they suggest a naturalistic system of ethics complete with its vices and virtues. Among the vices those most often mentioned are hypocrisy, intolerance, conventionality, and unwillingness to acknowledge the truth. Among the virtues perhaps the first is strength, which is presented as both a physiological and a moral quality; it implies the courage to be strong in spite of social restraints. A second virtue is naturalness, that is, the quality of acting in accordance with one's nature and physical instincts. Dreiser's Jennie Gerhardt was among the first of the purely natural heroines in American literature, but she had many descendants. A third virtue is complete candor about the world and oneself; a fourth is pity for others; and a fifth is tolerance, especially of moral rebellion and economic failure. Most of the characters presented sympathetically in naturalistic novels are either the victors over moral codes which they defy (like Cowperwood in *The Financier* and Susan Lenox in the novel by David Graham Phillips about her fall and rise) or else victims of the economic struggle, paupers and drunkards with infinitely more wisdom than the respectable citizens who avoid them. A great deal of naturalistic writing, including the early poems of Edwin Arlington Robinson, is an eloquent hymn to loneliness and failure as the destiny, in America, of most superior men.

There are other qualities of American naturalism that are derived not so much from historical conditions as from the example of the two novelists whom the younger men regarded as leaders or precursors. Norris first and Dreiser after him fixed the patterns that the others would follow.

Both men were romantic by taste and temperament. Although Norris was a disciple of Zola's, his other favorite authors belonged in one way or another to the romantic school; they included Froissart, Scott, Dickens, Dumas, Hugo, Kipling, and Stevenson. Zola was no stranger in that company, Norris said; on one occasion he called him "the very head of the Romanticists."

Terrible things must happen [he wrote], to the characters of the naturalistic tale. They must be twisted from the ordinary, wrenched from the quiet, uneventful round of everyday life and flung into the throes of a vast and terrible drama that works itself out in unleashed passions, in blood and sudden death.... Everything is extraordinary, imaginative, grotesque even, with a vague note of terror quivering throughout like the vibration of an ominous and low-pitched diapason.

Norris himself wished to practice naturalism as a form of romance, instead of taking up what he described as the "harsh, loveless, colorless, blunt tool called Realism." Dreiser in his autobiographical writings often refers to his own romantic temper. "For all my modest repute as a realist," he says, "I seem, to my self-analyzing eyes, somewhat more of a romanticist." He speaks of himself in his youth as "a creature of slow and uncertain response to anything practical, having an eye to color, romance, beauty. I was but a half-baked poet, romancer,

dreamer." The other American naturalists were also romancers and dreamers in their fashion, groping among facts for the extraordinary and even the grotesque. They believed that men were subject to natural forces, but they felt those forces were best displayed when they led to unlimited wealth, utter squalor, collective orgies, blood, and sudden death.

Among the romantic qualities they tried to achieve was "bigness" in its double reference to size and intensity. They wanted to display "big"—that is, intense—emotions against a physically large background. Bigness was the virtue that Norris most admired in Zola's novels. "The world of M. Zola," he said, "is a world of big things; the enormous, the formidable, the terrible, is what counts; no teacup tragedies here." In his own novels, Norris looked for big themes; after his trilogy on Wheat, he planned to write a still bigger trilogy on the three days' battle of Gettysburg, with one novel devoted to the events of each day. The whole notion of writing trilogies instead of separate novels came to be connected with the naturalistic movement, although it was also adopted by the historical romancers. Before Norris there had been only one planned trilogy in serious American fiction: *The Littlepage Manuscripts*, written by James Fenimore Cooper a few years before his death; it traces the story of a New York state landowning family through a hundred years and three generations. After Norris there were dozens of trilogies, with a few tetralogies and pentalogies: to mention some of the better known, there were Dreiser's trilogy on the career of a financier, T. S. Stribling's trilogy on the rise of a poor-white family, Dos Passos' trilogy on the United States from 1900 to 1930, James T. Farrell's trilogy on Studs Lonigan and Eugene O'Neill's trilogy of plays, *Mourning Becomes*

Electra. Later O'Neill set to work on a trilogy of trilogies, a drama to be complete in nine full-length plays. Farrell wrote a pentalogy about the boyhood of Danny O'Neill and then attacked another theme that would require several volumes, the young manhood of Bernard Clare. Trilogies expanded into whole cycles of novels somehow related in theme. Thus, after the success of *The Jungle,* which had dealt with the meat-packing industry in Chicago, Upton Sinclair wrote novels on other cities (Denver, Boston) and other industries (oil, coal, whisky, automobiles); finally he settled on a character, Lanny Budd, whose adventures were as endless as those of Tarzan or Superman. Sinclair Lewis dealt one after another with various trades and professions: real estate, medicine, divinity, social service, hotel management, and the stage; there was no limit to the subjects he could treat, so long as his readers' patience was equal to his own. . . .

The naturalistic writers of all countries preferred an objective or scientific approach to their material. As early as 1864 the brothers Goncourt had written in their journal, "The novel of today is made with documents narrated or selected from nature, just as history is based on written documents." A few years later Zola defined the novel as a scientific experiment; its purpose, he said in rather involved language, was to demonstrate the behavior of given characters in a given situation. Still later Norris advanced the doctrine "that no one could be a writer until he could regard life and people, and the world in general, from the objective point of view —until he could remain detached, outside, maintain the unswerving attitude of the observer." The naturalists as a group not only based their work on current scientific theories, but tried to copy scientific methods in planning their novels. They were writers who believed, or claimed to believe, that they could deliberately choose a subject for their work instead of being chosen by a subject; that they could go about collecting characters as a biologist collected specimens; and that their fictional account of such characters could be as accurate and true to the facts as the report of an experiment in the laboratory.

It was largely this faith in objectivity that led them to write about penniless people in the slums, whom they regarded as "outside" or alien subjects for observation. Some of them began with a feeling of contempt for the masses. Norris during his college years used to speak of "the canaille" and often wished for the day when all radicals could be "drowned on one raft." Later this pure contempt developed into a contemptuous interest, and he began to spend his afternoons on Polk Street, in San Francisco, observing with a detached eye the actions of what he now called "the people." The minds of the people, he thought, were simpler than those of persons in his own world; essentially these human beings were animals, "the creatures of habit, the playthings of forces," and therefore they were ideal subjects for a naturalistic novel. Some of the other naturalists revealed the same rather godlike attitude toward workingmen. Nevertheless they wrote about them, a bold step at a time when most novels dealt only with ladies, gentlemen, and faithful retainers; and often their contemptuous interest was gradually transformed into sympathy.

Their objective point of view toward their material was sometimes a pretense that deceived themselves before it deceived others. From the outside world they chose the subjects that mirrored their own conflicts and obsessions. Crane, we remember, said his purpose in writing *Maggie* was to show "that environment is a tremendous thing and often shapes lives regardlessly." Yet, on the subjective level, the novel also revealed an obsessive notion about the blamelessness of prostitutes that affected his career from beginning to end; it caused a series of scandals, involved him in a feud with the vice squad in Manhattan and finally led him to marry the madam of a bawdy house in Jacksonville. Norris' first novel, *Vandover and the Brute,* is an apparently objective study of degeneration, but it also mirrors the struggles of the author with his intensely Puritan conscience; Vandover is Norris himself. He had drifted into some mild dissipations and pictured them as leading to failure and insanity. Dreiser in *Sister Carrie* was telling a story based on the adventures of one of his sisters; that explains why Carrie Meeber in the novel is "Sister" Carrie, even though her relatives disappear after the first few pages. "My mind was a blank except for the name," Dreiser said when explaining how he came to write the novel. "I had no idea who or what she was to be. I have often thought that there was something mystic about it, as if I were being used, like a medium." In a sense he was being used by his own memories, which had become subconscious. There was nothing mystic to Upton Sinclair about his fierce emotion in writing *The Jungle;* he knew from the beginning that he was telling his own story. "I wrote with tears and anguish," he says in his memoirs,

pouring into the pages all that pain which life had meant to me. Externally, the story had to do with a family of stockyards workers, but internally it was the story of my own family. Did I wish to know how the poor suffered in Chicago? I had only to recall the previous winter in a cabin, when we had only cotton blankets, and cowered shivering in our separate beds. . . . Our little boy was

down with pneumonia that winter, and nearly died, and the grief of that went into the book.

Indeed, there is personal grief and fury and bewilderment in all the most impressive naturalistic novels. They are at their best, not when they are scientific or objective, in accordance with their own theories, but when they are least naturalistic, most personal and lyrical. . . .

This scientific weakness of naturalism involves a still greater literary weakness, for it leads to a conception of man that makes it impossible for naturalistic authors to write in the tragic spirit. They can write about crimes, suicides, disasters, the terrifying, and the grotesque; but even the most powerful of their novels and plays are case histories rather than tragedies in the classical sense. Tragedy is an affirmation of man's importance; it is "the imitation of noble action," in Aristotle's phrase; and the naturalists are unable to believe in human nobility. "We write no tragedies today," said Joseph Wood Krutch in his early book, *The Modern Temper,* which might better have been called "The Naturalistic Temper." "If the plays and novels of today deal with littler people and less mighty emotions it is not because we have become interested in commonplace souls and their unglamorous adventures but because we have come, willy-nilly, to see the soul of man as commonplace and its emotions as mean." But Krutch was speaking only for those who shared the naturalistic point of view. There are other doctrines held by modern writers that make it possible to endow their characters with human dignity. Tragic novels and plays have been written in these years by Christians, Communists, humanists, and even by existentialists, all of whom believe in different fashions and degrees that men can shape their own fates. . . .

THE NATURALISM OF
VANDOVER AND THE BRUTE
C. C. Walcutt[*]

In this examination of Frank Norris' *Vandover and the Brute*, the question is raised as to the possibility that the naturalistic perspective may furnish a background for modern tragedy. Consequently, Walcutt is interested in determining whether Vandover is defeated by abstract and impersonal forces or by some moral flaw within himself.

Attempts to explain and define the naturalistic movement and to account. for the "naturalistic" novel have not yet dissipated the fog that hangs over the problem. The vapor, on the contrary, thickens apace and now shows traces of deadly gamma rays from which critics flee. The source of this trouble is the fact that the word *naturalism* now uncovers four or five quite different and often independent trains of ideas, which undergo still further transformations when they appear in what are called naturalistic novels. My purpose here is to indicate some of the scientific, social, and ethical ideas which have been associated with naturalism; to suggest some of the differences between intellectual concepts and the novels in which such concepts are somehow "expressed"; and to illustrate these generalizations in so far as they apply to a particular early naturalistic novel. I want to show that although naturalism can be philosophically defined as materialistic monism, such a definition does not describe or "account" for what is called a naturalistic novel.

The theory says that Being is One,

accessible to man as the material universe, which evinces consistent cause-and-effect relationships that he can observe and translate into laws. This belief leads to the rejection of older systems of theology, ethics, and politics—for which new data are now to be found in the order of Nature. From this beginning, naturalistic thought moves in various directions. For example:

1. Man is good: society is the culprit responsible for man's unhappiness. Or it may be said that tradition is the culprit. Here tradition means the devices by which unenlightened men—men who have not *progressed* to the understanding of their true place in Nature—have preserved the unjust social order in which they are prosperous and powerful.

2. Traditional Christian ethics are "naturally" right (the mythology is incidental) but have not yet been socially realized because of man's ignorance of nature and natural law. Thus man has been confused by his belief in demons, miracles, and dogma; he has not known himself physically (witness the history of medicine) and so has not achieved a proper conception of his "natural" need to live according to the Christian ethic. Furthermore, his struggle with nature for subsistence has produced a social order

* The essay is reprinted from *Forms of Modern Fiction* edited by William Van O'Connor. The University of Minnesota Press, Minneapolis. Copyright 1948 by the University of Minnesota.

in which security and individual development are not available to all. Hence the age-old conflict of man against man, in which only a few could succeed; and hence the *physical* impossibility of making the Christian ethic prevail. Science promises an understanding of man and an abundance of the physical necessaries of life, through which the ideals of justice, equality, freedom, and brotherhood will become social realities.

3. Transcendentalism is a great stone in the same arch. Nature is the visible embodiment of Spirit. Man ascends into oneness with Spirit through his understanding of Nature, not through revelation or authority. Thoreau's successful quest for peace through intuition was achieved by a devoted, contemplative examination of Nature: "God himself culminates in the present moment, and will never be more divine in the lapse of all the ages. And we are enabled to apprehend at all what is sublime and noble only by the perpetual instilling and drenching of the reality that surrounds us." Transcendentalism motivates Whitman's early delight in the phenomenal world:

You have waited, you always wait, you dumb, beautiful ministers, [phenomena]
We receive you with free sense at last, and are insatiate henceforward . . .
    ("Crossing Brooklyn Ferry," 1856)

It underlies the tragic quest of Ahab: "All visible objects, man, are but as pasteboard masks. But in each event—in the living act, the undoubted deed, there, some unknown but still reasoning thing puts forth the mouldings of its features from behind the unreasoning mask" (*Moby Dick*, Chapter XXXVI). It underlies Emerson's definition of Fate as "unpenetrated causes," which, penetrated, will become sources of power and steps toward the realization of the "Beautiful Necessity" by which law and freedom become identical. All these nineteenth-century trends in American thought are on the way toward scientific materialism and are still frequently involved in it, though their presence is not identified by novelists and social theorists who consider themselves to be operating on "scientific" or naturalistic premises.

4. Transcendentalism anticipates the Spencerian philosophy of evolution, which sees man's ceaseless struggle and change as an aspect of the Natural Order by which all forms ascend through higher and higher levels of excellence. Truth and right emerge and "improve" by necessity. Emerson frequently refers to the "aspiration" in Nature: "Striving to be man, the worm/Mounts through all the spires of form." But Spencer was an ardent conservative. He opposed on principle any and all legislative or governmental interference with the natural evolutionary process. The ruthless methods of business he defended as promoting the survival of the fittest. Other Darwinians, like Kropotkin and Lester Ward, dwelt upon the cooperative activities of animals and the fact that many forms of flora and fauna throve best when, as under domestication, they were freed from the struggle for survival. Socialists of course maintained versions of this position. Huxley returned to a sort of dualism by affirming that social and ethical good were to be achieved through man's opposition to the processes of nature. Ethical conduct, Huxley said, was not to be traced to a naturalistic cause.[1] Thus from transcendentalism, through Spencer, Kropotkin, and Huxley, we find such a variety of social applications of naturalistic theory that we have no single program or attitude that can

[1] See Richard Hofstadter, *Social Darwinism in American Thought 1860–1915*, Philadelphia, 1945.

with any confidence be asserted to characterize or control the "naturalistic" novel.

5. Resting on the belief that science shows man to be only an accident and an incident in a cosmic order that is moving toward eventual lifeless rest (entropy) is the "ethic" of ruthless self-expression: man must give vent to his energies and die, for there is no meaningful moral order by which he should be controlled. The superman, who enjoys as many avatars as Vishnu, appears, in some naturalistic novels, as the vehicle of this ethic. The brute superman of fiction is several steps from Nietzsche's conception. Nietzsche denounced *mediocrity*, which he conceived to be fostered by Christianity, determinism, socialism, business enterprise, and Prussian militarism. He wanted greatness of spirit, perfection; but when he had rejected traditional values (the "slave morality" of Christianity) he found himself in an ethical void. It is not, therefore, surprising that others who were already in an ethical void from the effects of naturalistic theory should have invoked his writings to justify ruthless and violent selfishness. When Jack London wrote *The Sea Wolf* (1903) and his earlier tales of Yukon violence, Nietzsche had not been translated into English. London was a devoted Spencerian who could have seen the inevitable and beatific processes of evolution being promoted through these grim struggles for survival. Yet some years later he revealed at once a familiarity with Nietzsche's term and an ignorance of his intent by referring to Wolf Larsen (the Sea Wolf) as a superman. To cap this confusion, London was a socialist. It is quite impossible to *deduce* what he was trying to do in his novels. We can only examine the novels.

6. Attitudes toward the mind reveal the growth of naturalistic theory. In 1865 Émile Zola read Claude Bernard's *Intro-duction à l'étude de la medicine expérimentale* and straightway concluded that the study of physiology was the first step toward the study of psychology. Medicine, said Bernard, had been an art but now, with the introduction of the "positive" method, would become a science. Fiction, said Zola, consciously paraphrasing, had been an art but would henceforth be an instrument for the scientific study of man and society. The mind could be studied as a "chemical" function of hereditary and environmental forces, and this positive approach to its working would ultimately makes its every aspect and activity *predictable*. A generation later the investigations of Freud and others had led to the discovery that the mind was more complicated than had ever before been imagined. Motives were hidden beneath layer upon layer of "censorship" and compensation. The hope of predicting was abandoned. Psychologists and writers were content to observe and record this fascinating complexity of mental phenomena, happy indeed if they could explain certain human reactions which had previously been attributed to original sin but not presuming to predict anything by the application of mechanistic formulas.

II

Thus the theory of naturalism is not single but several: it is moral, amoral, radical, conservative, optimistic, and pessimistic. When we consider what happens when a theory is embodied in a novel, we find that various considerations of another order complicate the problem and further confuse the deductions which one is tempted to make. A novel is an imitation of an action; its esthetic quality cannot be deduced from the philosophical beliefs of its writer. There is no anomaly in the fact that Zola's best novels are studies in degeneration and failure, whereas his attitude toward science was religious in its fervor—and it was this attitude which controlled the novels. Yet these facts appear impossibly confusing if one approaches them from the conviction that the character of a novel can be deduced from the writer's philosophical beliefs. It is not possible to deduce that a naturalistic novel will be optimistic or pessimistic merely because naturalistic theory as it appears in scientific and philosophical writings is optimistic or pessimistic. The question of whether a novel is optimistic or pessimistic is surely irrelevant. Yet this issue is central in most recent writing about the naturalistic novel.

Another bugaboo is free will. Naturalistic theories of man, nature, and society have not displaced the element of will from the novel. They may account for it in theory, perhaps by declaring it a fiction (as behaviorists define mind as "the functional integration of sensory and motor responses"), but they do not *therefore* eliminate it from the novel, which is why statements of the philosophical or social bearings of naturalistic theory do not account for what actually takes place in the "naturalistic" novel. The scientific student of man does not judge and condemn him for failure to obey moral absolutes. He seeks only to understand. But the citizen and the artist are used to dealing with their fellow men as if they were responsible for their actions.

The novelist, furthermore, is working in a genre which has traditionally employed the concept of free will or, rather, the active force of free will. Plots have, in the past, been built around conflicts between individuals who were assumed to be free to choose their courses of action. These individuals have been characterized in terms of ethical qualities (honesty, loyalty, selfishness, jealousy,

pride) which in themselves embody ethical judgments. To say a man is proud is to use the language of judgment. The novelist who undertakes to be a naturalist, then, is working against his own instinctive attitude and against the tradition of his art. He is hardly to be condemned if he fails to exclude moral judgment and the idea of ethical responsibility from his novel. The critic's problem is to describe the outcome of this tension between theory and practice in the works of the "naturalistic" novelists. A successful definition will be historical and descriptive, rather than a categorical formulation of certain rules which have never been perfectly embodied in a novel. The naturalist, in particular, should be pragmatic in his eagerness to see how his theory *works* in the solid body of a novel.

Finally, art is always an assertion of human freedom. Even while it denies man's freedom it asserts it, for it imposes plan and meaning and order on its materials. The act of writing a naturalistic novel, even one that purports to demonstrate man's utter helplessness, denies its own intent. All naturalistic novels have meanings and effects which are not even implied by the philosophical or scientific theories of naturalism. The following section will attempt to show how these remarks apply to a particular "naturalistic" novel.

III

Frank Norris' *Vandover and the Brute* was written for Professor Gates' composition class at Harvard in 1894–95. It was Norris' first long work and an attempt to imitate the method of the French naturalists with a particularly naturalistic subject—the destruction of an individual by a degenerative disease. *Vandover* has not the scope of *The Octopus* or the primordial violence of *McTeague*, but it contains some of Norris' most effective writing; it has, indeed, been considered his most memorable work. It stands at the opposite end of the scale of naturalistic motifs from novels dealing with the broad external workings of social and economic forces. Here the forces are internal and physiological; the book purports to be a "clinical" study of a disease.

The novelist's reason for dealing with a mental disease would seem to be his enthusiasm for science. He would, perhaps, be inspired by the experimental zeal which Zola described, the desire to show in detail how certain psychoneurotic manifestations could be clinically diagnosed and systematically presented— subjected to the clear light of knowledge so that man would know for at least one malady whether he had germs or "lesions" to cope with. This would, then, be a factual scientific report, rich with information vital to human welfare. Its interest would depend upon the new subject matter and the reader's aroused zeal for human betterment. This hypothetical description, with its implication that the facts of the case will be scientifically related and established, leaves no place for an unpredictable element like the free human will. A disease is strictly physical; it is a problem in material causes and effects. Spiritual values, morality, or personal struggle would not *seem* to be relevant to an understanding of it.

Vandover is the son of a prosperous San Francisco businessman. He is a painter, but he neglects his art. "Vandover was self-indulgent—he loved these sensuous pleasures, he loved to eat good things, he loved to be warm, he loved to sleep. He hated to be bored and worried—he liked to have a good time." His disintegration begins when a girl he has seduced commits suicide in terror at the prospect of having an illegitimate child.

Next his father, weakened by the shock of Vandover's deed, dies. When the reason for the girl's suicide becomes known, Vandover is socially ostracized and loses the love of Turner Mavis, a fine girl who had been a powerful influence for good in his life. After his father's death, his income is greatly curtailed. At this point Vandover resolves to reform, and throws himself into his painting with furious energy. But too late. The disease, lycanthropy, first appears in a terrifying scene when he finds that he can no longer paint, that his hand will not reproduce the image in his mind; and thereafter his descent is rapid and inexorable. The dead girl's father sues him for a large sum. One of his friends, on the pretext of "handling" the case out of court, cheats him of money and property. What is left from the sale of his father's house Vandover squanders in reckless gambling and debauchery, his unnatural life punctuated by attacks of lycanthropy, during which he creeps about naked on all fours, snarling and yapping like a wolf. Finally he is living from hand to mouth, dirty, unkempt, estranged from friends, sometimes near starvation—a hopeless wreck. The story ends with a pitiful scene in which Vandover is cleaning a filthy kitchen for the friend who had defrauded him.

An appearance of factual reality is created by the method Norris employs. The style and tone of *Vandover* suit the commonplace unromantic people and setting of the story admirably. Details of Vandover's life and activity are accumulated with meticulous and dispassionate thoroughness. This was a new note in American letters. The quantity and "meanness" of the detail, with the objective tone, give the effect of authentic "documentation" in the best naturalistic tradition. We are shown, step by step, how "In his idleness he grew to have small and petty ways. . . . It became a fad with him to do without matches, using as a substitute 'lights,' tapers of twisted paper to be ignited at the famous stove. He found amusement for two days in twisting and rolling these 'lights,' cutting frills in the larger ends with a pair of scissors, and stacking them afterward in a Chinese flower jar he had bought for the purpose and stood on top of the bookcases. The lights were admirably made and looked very pretty. When he had done he counted them. He had made two hundred exactly. What a coincidence!"

Structurally, the novel is not "well-made" or dramatic, in the sense of being organized around a conflict between free moral agents. Instead Norris has conformed his structure to the steady and "inevitable" disintegration of Vandover under a succession of blows from forces over which he has no control. In one passage Norris announces a deterministic philosophy very explicitly. It is when Vandover, after his first attack of the disease, prays for help:

There was no answer, nothing but the deaf silence, the blind darkness . . . there was nothing for him. Even that vast mysterious power to which he had cried *could* not help him now, could not help him, could not stay the inexorable law of nature, could not reverse that vast terrible engine with its myriad spinning wheels that was riding him down relentless, grinding him into the dust.[2]

There is no climactic choice in the story; it moves evenly on a chain of circumstances.

These elements of style, tone, documentation, structure, and explicit determinism constitute the naturalism of *Vandover and the Brute*. But they do not really account for the novel. In spite of its explicit determinism, the conflict

[2] 1914 edition, pp. 244–45.

in this novel *is* a thoroughly moral one. It is a conflict between Vandover's free and responsible spirit and a series of circumstantial influences (the disease is merely one of several) which win out over him largely because of his *culpable* moral weakness. Examination reveals (1) that Vandover is morally responsible for his downfall, (2) that the forces which thrust him down are circumstantial rather than inevitable, and (3) that the novel has the form and effect of a tragedy. It appears, also, that the tragic effect would have been stronger if Norris had not allowed so much moral condemnation to intrude; if, that is, he had held to a more rigorous determinism!

The tone of moral judgment appears in passages like the following, where Vandover broods on his decline:

And with the eyes of this better self he saw again . . . the eternal struggle between good and evil that had been going on within him since his very earliest years. He was sure that at the first the good had been the strongest. Little by little the brute had grown, and he . . . luxurious, self-indulgent . . . had shut his ears to the voices that shouted warnings of the danger, and had allowed the brute to thrive and to grow, its abominable famine gorged from the store of that in him which he felt to be the purest, the cleanest . . . [214–15].

Again:

It was gone—his art was gone, the one thing that could save him. That, too, like all the other good things of his life, he had destroyed [229].

And:

It was the punishment that he had brought upon himself, some fearful nervous disease, the result of his long indulgence in vice, his vile submission to the brute that was to destroy his reason . . . till he should have reached the last stages of idiocy [243].

Although these passages are presented as Vandover's thought, they come as auctorial comment also, for it is clear that Norris' attitude is represented in these and many other passages like them. One is reminded of Milton's

> But, when lust
> By unchaste looks, loose gestures, and foul talk,
> But most by lewd and lavish acts of sin,
> Lets in defilement to the inward parts,
> The soul grows clotted by contagion,
> Imbodies, and imbrutes, till she quite lose
> The divine property of her first being.

Far from illustrating the operation of determinism, Vandover's degradation is presented as the result of some internal failure which *allows* the brutish side to grow and thrust out the good. Vandover's moral responsibility depends on his being a person of intelligence and social position; regardless of the author's intention, the naturalistic approach is disrupted because the human being is more important, more intimately known, and therefore more credible than the forces which supposedly dominate him.

There is no established set of forces, either hereditary or environmental, which can bring about his degeneration in such a way that it appears to be inevitable. Vandover is not shown to inherit qualities from his parents that would make him subject to lycanthropy. He does not move in a society that is notable for the pressure it exerts upon its members. He is free from the sort of influences that obtain in industrial areas, or among the poorer classes anywhere. In all these respects he is free from the forces which can be shown, even in the contrived simplicity of the novel, to have shaped a character or bent it toward an unalterable end. Thus the bars which prevent the invasion of his beast must be withdrawn by Chance, that is, by pressures which

are not presented as an inescapable part of the milieu; and half of the book is devoted to the impact of various kinds of chance upon him. There is nothing typical, nothing that might contribute to the science of sociology in the course by which he is destroyed. At any time Vandover might take a turn for the better. The events which thrust him down are more coincidental than the acts of fate that destroy some of Hardy's characters. But nevertheless they are presented with such a wealth of convincing detail that the average reader accepts them as probable.

It appears, then, that the Beast—the disease—is an external and adventitious factor like the suicide of the girl or the swindle by the friend. The disease is not studied for its own sake. Vandover does not become a mere organism subjected to clinical examination. The shred of manhood, of free will, that he retains is always at the focal point of attention. The question is not what new form will the disease take, or what does one learn from the data about its growth and operation, but what is the last tiny bit of conscious individuality thinking and feeling and suffering as it approaches the moment of final extinction. The reader's attention is not fixed by the progress of the disease but by wonder and pity at the fact that the human spark continues so long to survive and so to suffer.

The conflict, then, is between a free but fallible individual and a fatal but indefinable enemy. We never see the operation of "That vast terrible engine with its myriad spinning wheels." What we see is a real young man with a well-developed personality and a whole set of convincing mannerisms, who succumbs because of the impact of circumstances upon him—and not the least of these circumstances is the disease lycanthropy, for it is not "scientifically" traced to a source or accounted for. Chance, of course, does not exist in the theory of naturalism. When it appears we know that another frame of reference has been introduced, whether intentionally or not.

There are two extreme points of view which produce inferior art. One extreme is the belief in pure mechanistic determinism. When this attitude is "pure," it is expressed in scientific reports dealing perhaps with pathological or physiological disturbances of the human organism. The "person" being described or examined does not, for the purposes of the report, exist. He is merely a certain amount of tissue, part of which is isolated as a breeding ground for germs or tumors. In pure science, this attitude may be essential for the study of diseases *per se*, although even scientists are not so sure as they were fifty years ago that a disease is anything *per se*, apart, that is, from the nature of the organism in which it lives. The same impersonal attitude is pure in statistical studies of social trends, and it is perhaps approximated in sociological reports. It is doubtful whether it can be anywhere near pure in a work of fiction. Employed by a very cynical writer who despised the human race and delighted to portray the helpless wrigglings of men impaled on the pins of Fate, it would in effect be an assertion of the writer's superiority and spiritual independence. If it were free of such ironic overtones, it would produce a dismal and boring novel with little or no feeling for the dignity of man.

At the other extreme, there is plenty of fiction which fatuously assumes that nature is benign and man is perfectly in tune with it and with himself. From this view come novels which present an easy universe where justice is always done, evil punished (but merely for the delight and beatitude of the Good), and ambitions fulfilled. It is the world of easy pleasure, happy people, and barren complacency. It is a moral world, constructed entirely for the protection of little men. Its perfect "artistic" expression is Hollywood's doctrine of the unique temptation, according to which one has to resist evil only once in order to be forever blessed. Because this sort of thinking cannot or will not acknowledge the power and unpredictability of nature, it can have no true sense of the dignity of man.

Between these extremes moves the tragic view, which underestimates neither man nor the forces against which he contends. The greatest men face the greatest oppositions and suffer most greatly; therein lies the grandeur of the Greek and Shakespearian tragedy—and all great tragic artists show man rising to greatness as he pits himself against forces over which he can never triumph. To acknowledge the might of these forces while not losing faith in the men who challenge them is to possess the tragic view of life.

Vandover and the Brute is in this tragic area. The hero, an ordinary attractive young man, is caught and crushed—not in the "vast terrible engine" that Norris describes, but by social and personal forces which twentieth-century man knows all too well. In so far as he *blames* Vandover for *moral* weakness, Norris moves toward the pole of fatuity, for by doing so he assumes that a moral man would avoid conflict with the moral order. In so far as he talks about the vast terrible engine, Norris moves toward the pole of inhuman mechanism. But in reality the effect of his novel is between these extremes, if only because the reader is pulled in both directions. Vandover is accepted for what he is—not judged—and the reader, I believe, identifies himself with the struggling spirit of the protagonist *as well as* with the social and personal evil which destroys him. The tragic conflict is within the individual and also between him and the society which is composed of the fallible wills of all individuals.

A bold and massive array of external forces demands a corresponding grandeur in the characters who struggle against them. This is Shakespeare's pattern, but it is not so descriptive of the modern dilemma. Instead of man against the cosmos, we now have society against man, which is to say, mankind against mankind. The tragic struggle in *An American Tragedy* and *Studs Lonigan* is similarly conceived. Clyde Griffiths and Studs are modern man, ruined in the milieu which modern man has made, and the reader participates in the tragic *agon*, aware of the dangerous forces within himself; yet in a manner somewhat different from that of the spectator of a Shakespearian tragedy, for the terrible forces against which Shakespeare's heroes contend are viewed with awe and wonder and fear; not only are they unconquerable, they are indeed beyond man's power of comprehension. The catharsis of pity and terror is to be reached *only* through art. The modern tragedy locates the opposing forces in society and the nature of man, where they are not quite so terrible. It is true that the "nature of man" could appear as mysterious and ungovernable as an unknowable Fate, but the fact is that social institutions do appear, in these novels of Dreiser and Farrell, to be subject, however tenuously, to the will and knowledge of man. Hence the conflict they present cannot be as grand as Shakespeare's. The idea of progress, the necessity for social action, creep into these modern tragedies and offer an alternative or added release for the emotions which Shakespeare purges through pity and terror alone. The modern tragedy thus unconsciously presents two orders of symbolic action: One shows man struggling with Fate and his own nature. The other "attacks" the social order as the embodiment of injustice and heedlessness.

Vandover and the Brute is a modern tragedy in a minor and imperfect key. If the book had been more exhaustively "naturalistic," it would have shown more fully the nature of the social (that is, human) forces that destroy the hero—and there would have been correspondingly less need to impose a Sunday school moral censure upon him. Thus the weakness of *Vandover* shows very clearly the potential strength of naturalism as a foundation for tragedy—so long as it is not carried to a point of diminishing returns in lifeless mechanism. In short, so long as it is essentially transcendental naturalism will give full recognition to the power and immensity of the physical world but will also assume a meaning in it that is akin to and ideally accessible to the mind of man; so that man achieves tragic dignity as he strives to penetrate and master his own nature and the physical universe which repeats the tension of actual and potential, real and ideal, fate and will, evil and good, and matter and spirit, that is in the nature of man. Seen in this light, naturalism is no revolutionary departure from the world view of Shakespearian tragedy. It is rather a mode of presenting in realistic "modern" terms the forces, microcosmic and macrocosmic, against which man has always tragically contended. Naturalism is the modern approach to Fate. It is more hopeful in that it suggests rational means of coping with Fate; if it is "pessimistic" it is so only because it has to accord less dignity to man. When it is confused it is so because the polar attractions of mechanism and social action draw it away, in one direction or the other, from the tragic center.

CHAPTER 9

Surrealism

FROM SURREALISM
Georges Lemaitre[*]

Surrealism, says Lemaitre, rejects chronological or rational sequence, conscious effort at organization, syntactical discipline; it accepts dreams, fantasies, or associational sequences—products of the subconscious with minimal contribution from the sensuous and objective world. Surrealistic literature, therefore, composed as it is, or as it should be, of "images from the subconscious," is an expression of these elements.

The attempt of André Breton to bring about a "Congrès de l'Esprit Moderne" [Congress of the Modern Spirit] had been to a large extent prompted by a peculiar discovery he had made almost by chance, and which was to affect in a decisive manner the whole course of contemporary literature and art.

As early as 1919—that is to say, in the very midst of the Dadaist turmoil—Breton had a most unusual personal experience. One evening, as he was about to fall asleep, he became aware that a sentence, grammatically correct, though preposterous from the standpoint of reason, was, according to his own expression, "knocking at the window-pane"[1] of his consciousness. The wording of that sentence, which he could not recall exactly afterwards, was something like this: "Il y eut un homme coupé en deux par une fenêtre"[2] [There was a man cut in two by a window]. At the same time he fancied that he saw, though very faintly, the image of a man walking erect, whose body was truncated at the waist by a large horizontal window. However surprised he must have been at the oddity of the sentence and the accompanying image, André Breton was too good a Dadaist

* The selection is reprinted by permission of the publishers from Georges Lemaitre, *From Cubism to Surrealism in French Literature*, Cambridge, Mass.: Harvard University Press, Copyright, 1941, by the President and Fellows of Harvard College.

[1] A. Breton, *Manifeste du Surréalisme* (Paris: S. Kra, 1929), p. 39.
[2] *Ibid.*

to reject either on account of their absurdity. He therefore made a point of retaining them in his consciousness. No sooner had they taken their place in the stream of his thoughts than they were followed by another sentence and another image, both apparently unconnected with the former and equally absurd. These, having been in their turn admitted by Breton, brought in their train a series of similar phrases all appearing spontaneously and all completely irrational.

It must be said that, when all this occurred, André Breton was so miserably poor that, as he informs us himself, "Je ne mangeais pas tous les jours à cette époque"[3] [I was not eating every day at that time], and it is quite possible that sheer starvation may have been the true cause of this curious brain storm. Whatever their origin, these incomprehensible sentences obsessed him so imperiously that he felt impelled to investigate thoroughly the mysterious message they might be meant to convey.

André Breton discussed at length with his friend Philippe Soupault the phases and aspects of his psychic experience. Both decided to try to place themselves, as an experiment, in conditions which would reproduce as closely as possible the circumstances of the original phenomenon. Sitting together in a quiet room, and excluding as best they could all definite and clear ideas from their intellect, as happens naturally when we are about to fall asleep, they jotted down on paper whatever rambling thoughts came to their passive minds. At the end of one day they had each covered approximately fifty pages of fairly close writing. They then compared the results obtained. Certain similarities between their "productions" were truly striking. In both cases the writer, reading over the pages he had composed, experienced the feeling of having a text completely foreign to his own personality. He discovered elements which did not seem to belong to the Ego that he knew, elements which, in fact, surprised him as if coming from a source entirely different from his normal conscious self. Further, throbbing between the lines, there seemed to be an emotion infinitely more intense and rich than that usually evoked by the individual sentences. Finally, these pages offered, in spite of their absurdity, a wealth of imagery which neither author would have been able to produce deliberately even at the cost of long and arduous effort.

After a close study of their texts, Breton and Soupault reached the conclusion that these revealed a number of hidden spiritual qualities and facts, less obvious than the properties of the material forms surrounding us, but existing really, objectively—as really and objectively as anything we can perceive. This subconscious "divulgation d'un certain nombre de propriétés et de faits non moins objectifs, en somme, que les autres"[4] [divulgation of a certain number of properties and facts not less objective, after all, than the others] is the very foundation of the movement known as Surrealism.

André Breton and Philippe Soupault had thought at first of calling "supernaturaliste"—after Gérard de Nerval—this new mode of investigation and expression. Subsequently, however, they decided to adopt the name "Surréalisme" as a homage to the memory of Guillaume Apollinaire.[5] Apollinaire had used the word "Surréaliste" in connection with the attempt—not infrequent among Cubist writers—to attain a higher reality through the medium of an unbridled verbalism; but Apollinaire does not seem to have

[3] *Manifeste du Surréalisme*, p. 40.

[4] *Manifeste du Surréalisme*, p. 44.
[5] *Ibid.*

considered this process as a regular method of research, and he never propounded a systematic theory of its legitimate use. André Breton and Philippe Soupault set out to formulate a comprehensive and coherent program of studies, taking as a basic principle the possibility of the revelation of a superior, "surrealist" truth, thanks to the automatic development of man's subconscious psychic powers.

Their first step was to pursue the work of automatic writing which they had practiced originally as an experiment. In 1921 they were able to publish under the title of *Les Champs magnétiques* a small volume presenting, without correction or improvement of any sort, a number of pages composed by themselves according to the new method, while their rational minds were in a state of more or less perfect vacuity. . . .

Like the Cubists of the pre-war period, many of the younger men belonging to the new generation were anxious to reach beyond the screen of our visible universe a higher truth of an ideal nature; like the Cubists, they believed that this could be achieved only through the systematic disintegration of conventional concepts. The Dadaists had added to this a note of angry violence. After them, the destruction of the conventional concepts could be viewed only in terms of aggressive and subversive absurdity.

It has been seen how at the close of the nineteenth century scientific discoveries had provoked a grave spiritual crisis by shaking the belief in the value of the forms of reality amidst which we live. Now the latest results of scientific investigation, revealed to the general public in the years following the first World War, definitively ruined what remained of the former confidence in the value of logical reasoning. The theories about relativity, devised mainly by Einstein, left aghast those who, in spite of everything, had obstinately trusted the evidence of common sense. . . .

Approximately at the same time the spread of the psychoanalytic doctrines of Freud and his associates brought about an almost complete revolution in the accepted ideas about the workings of the human mind. Certain widely known aspects of Freud's theories—for instance, those pertaining to the rôle of sex—have little to do with the development of Surrealism. Some of his clinical principles and therapeutic methods, however, exerted a decisive influence upon the elaboration of the program of the new school. André Breton himself was a physician specializing in nervous and mental diseases, and therefore thoroughly acquainted with the medical angle of the Freudian doctrines. As a rule, the Surrealists took from psychoanalysis the general notion that the subconscious constitutes the fundamental basis, the essential reality of our mental life. The subconscious *is* the truth, a truth most of the time too crude and too potent for our shy, convention-ridden selves to bear; so clear intelligence is constantly busy disguising that truth, suppressing our instinctive, obscure cravings or giving them a fallacious, sublimated expression through symbolical ideas or imaginings. The all-important subconscious can be reached and liberated only by some method capable of eliminating intelligence temporarily from the field of man's mental activity. . . .

According to the Surrealists, the liberation of our subconscious mind can best be effected through an attitude of deliberate censorship towards all the accepted forms of traditional thinking. In their view, the interpretation of the world offered by our intellect does not correspond to anything truly essential either in the deep constitution of man or in the fundamental nature of things. In truth, intellect may be compared to a screen interposed between our Ego and the radiant effulgence of the universe. Such a screen may be convenient for practical purposes, but it is decidedly an obstacle to our direct communication with the rest of the Cosmos. Therefore, all means are legitimate which might bring about its total and final disintegration. Irony, ridicule, sarcasm are our most efficient weapons in this struggle for our complete inward enfranchisement. Every fixed form of opinion or expression must be discarded as arbitrary and absurd. Every established law about aesthetics or morals must be ruthlessly swept away in order to leave room for absolute freedom....

One may well wonder, it is true, by what process a literary work, for instance, is capable of bringing to us such supernatural revelation. Since the time of Baudelaire, much attention has been paid to the inexplicable, miraculous power of certain words. Rimbaud showed conclusively that words possess, besides their obvious and usual signification, secret magic properties which can sometimes illumine with a sudden flash a mystic universe inaccessible to our senses. Mallarmé tried to find a rigorous method enabling the poet to make use of these properties with unerring precision. The Surrealists in their turn believe that the essential value of words lies not in their objective, trite, and worn-out meaning, but in the forces of subconscious poetical suggestion which are enclosed in the web of their syllables. How to release these forces constitutes for them the main technical literary problem. This problem they have approached with an emphatic earnestness. Only too often in the past the French have found entertainment in dexterously playing with curious vocables. According to the Surrealists, relations between words should be taken very seri-

ously. Their fortuitous association sometimes arouses in us unexpectedly intense feelings, and in certain cases their union proves fecund in truly momentous and abiding results. André Breton could indeed affirm: "Les mots ... ont fini de jouer. Les mots font l'amour."[6] [Words have finished playing. Words make love.] ...

A Surrealist writer is not supposed to make any effort to express and organize his sentiments or thoughts. He must be content to listen to the voice of his subconsciousness—"la voix surréaliste"—and to take down verbatim whatever that voice may fancy to dictate. In order to receive this faint, whispered dictation, he must shut out, as far as possible, all disturbing outside influences. Reducing the activity of his will power to a minimum, and putting, as it were, his faculties of critical judgment asleep, he will lapse insensibly into a semiconscious state; then he will record automatically with his pen absolutely every sentence that may present itself to his indifferent mind.

Complete automatism is the condition *sine qua non* of the successful recording of the Surrealist message. One word must draw another word without the solicitation of any external stimulus and without any interference on the part of discriminating intellect. Then a long train of phrases, all impregnated with the substance of the inner self, will flow irresistibly from the very depths of subconsciousness. The same automatism which provides the writer with an endless chain of associated vocables may offer to the painter an inexhaustible series of loosely jointed images. The artist has but to adopt an absolutely passive attitude of mind and let his brush run over the canvas without conscious control in order to obtain a juxtaposition of lines and

[6] "Les Mots sans rides," *Les Pas perdus*, p. 171.

shapes reflecting the authentic aspects of his personality. It is easy to conceive of the extension of this method to all the other forms of creative art—so much so that psychic automatism has come to be considered as the keystone of the whole structure of Surrealist method. André Breton himself has given the following celebrated definition of Surrealism: "Automatisme psychique pur par lequel on se propose d'exprimer soit verbalement, soit par écrit, soit de toute autre manière, le fonctionnement réel de la pensée. Dictée de la pensée, en l'absence de tout contrôle exercé par la raison, en dehors de toute préoccupation esthétique ou morale."[7] [A pure psychic automatism by which we propose to express either verbally, or in writing, or in any other way, the real functioning of thought. A dictation of thought, in the absence of any surveillance exerted by reason, outside of any moral or esthetic preoccupation.] ...

Nevertheless, even if uncontrolled automatism is accepted in theory as an efficient method of attaining the enigmatic *Surréel*, it must be admitted that in practice this process has only too often proved to be extremely disappointing. One may go over pages and pages of monotonous Surrealist writings and fail to discover in them—except for brief, occasional flashes—any feature of intense or compelling interest. The Surrealists themselves have become aware of this lack of human and artistic appeal in the majority of their works, and many of them have already given up the pure and simple presentation of the raw subconscious material which was considered around 1924 solely authentic and genuine. The prevailing tendency today is to allow intelligent will power a not inconsiderable measure of controlling influence. The author thus selects consciously a center of psychic resonance, and also controls undue divagations which might

[7] *Manifeste du Surréalisme*, p. 46.

develop too far from its original, fundamental note. Such interference on the part of clear consciousness could ultimately open the way to a return to discipline and common sense. Yet, up to now at least, so wide a scope has still been left to the irradiation of subliminal thought that the general principles of Surrealism cannot be considered as markedly affected by this slight alteration in the practical modalities of its applied technique. ...

Are we to believe, as certain adventurous minds fondly hope, that these phantasmagoric productions merely constitute prefigurations of more elaborate works of a similar kind that will develop magnificently in the years to come? Will their childish *naïveté* and all their other defects, which are so obvious at the present stage, be viewed by ulterior generations with the indulgent curiosity that we bestow now upon the "Primitifs" of past ages? Are they not, on the contrary, grave and disturbing symptoms of the moral confusion prevailing in our unbalanced epoch? In any case, it would be a mistake to consider modernistic theories either as a passing fashion or as the product of a few exceptional and pathological minds. The continuity of their development and their persistency under various forms throughout several anxious generations show conclusively that they correspond to something really deep and important in contemporary life. Starting essentially from France—though often elaborated by artists or writers of foreign origin—they have spread rapidly over the rest of Europe and America, adapting themselves here and there to the special conditions prevailing in each part of this extensive domain. In every case they have followed, as if on a parallel, the evolution of our social and political vicissitudes. Whatever their intrinsic worth, they express strikingly a genuinely pathetic reaction to the stress of our times.

FROM INTRODUCTION TO SURREALISM
Herbert Read[*]

While the "universal truths of classicism may be merely the temporal prejudices of an epoch, the universal truths of romanticism are coeval with the evolving consciousness of mankind. It is in this sense ... that Surrealism is a reaffirmation of the romantic principle." Although surrealism—superrealism—is the extension of that principle, it cannot really be called romanticism because its intentions and methods are not quite those of romanticism. The senses are regarded as interfering with the "inner eye" instead of providing a source of subjective extension and symbol as they do for the romantic.

June, 1936. After a winter long drawn out into bitterness and petulance, a month of torrid heat, of sudden efflorescence, of clarifying storms. In this same month the International Surrealist Exhibition broke over London, electrifying the dry intellectual atmosphere, stirring our sluggish minds to wonder, enchantment and derision. The press, unable to appreciate the significance of a movement of such unfamiliar features, prepared an armoury of mockery, sneers and insults. The duller desiccated weeklies, no less impelled to anticipate the event, commissioned their polyglot gossips, their blasé globe-trotters, their old-boy-scouts, to adopt their usual pose of I know all, don't be taken in, there's nothing new under the sun—a pose which merely reflects the general lack of intellectual curiosity in this country. But in the event they were all deceived; their taunts fell on deaf ears, and though for a time there was no lack of the laughing jackass—an animal extinct in most parts of the world and even in this country generally emerging only from beyond the pale of the ineffectual Cheviots—in the outcome people, and mostly young people, came in their hundreds and their thousands not to sneer, but to learn, to find enlightenment, to live. When the foam and froth of society and the press had subsided, we were left with a serious public of scientists, artists, philosophers and socialists, and it is for the sake of this public, and in the confident hope of extending its membership, that we have prepared this definitive manifesto.

From the moment of its birth Surrealism was an international phenomenon—the spontaneous generation of an international and fraternal *organism* in total contrast to the artificial manufacture of a collective *organisation* such as the League of Nations. It would therefore be contrary to the nature of the movement to present, as some have suggested, a specifically English edition of Surrealism. We who in England have announced our adherence to this movement have no other desire than to pool our resources in the general effort. Nevertheless, there is an English contribution to be made to this effort, and its strength and validity can only be shown by tracing its sources in the native tradition of our art and literature. The evidences on which we base the claims of Surrealism are scattered through the centuries, the partial and incoherent revelations of permanent human characteristics; and nowhere are these evidences so plentiful as in England. My main purpose in this Introduction will be to present this English evidence, to unite it with the general theory of Surrealism, and to reaffirm on this wider basis the truths which other writers, above all André Breton, have already declared.

In an Introduction which I contributed to the catalogue of the exhibition I asserted, in the cryptic and exiguous manner demanded by the occasion, that "superrealism in general is the romantic principle in art." It will be noted that I used a variation of the word "surrealism." When it first became essential to find an English equivalent for the original French word, I made an attempt to establish "superrealism." Pedantically, euphonically and logically I think I was right; "superrealism" is not only simple to say, but self-explanatory to the meanest intelligence ("super" is slang, "sur" is a purely grammatical affix). But I was defeated by that obscure instinct which determines word-formation in the life of a language, and for which I have the greatest respect. The very clarity of the term "superrealism" was against it; the public wanted a strange and not too intelligible word for a strange and not too intelligible thing; and I bow to that decree. But I do not propose to abandon the word "superrealism" altogether; I propose rather to make a distinction between superrealism in general and Surrealism in particular, employing the first word for the tentative and historical manifestations of what has now become a conscious and deliberate artistic principle. And those tentative and historical manifestations of superrealism I shall identify with some of the essential characteristics of romanticism—but of romanticism understood in a certain strict and not too comprehensive sense.

No critic of experience will return to a discussion of the terms "romanticism" and "classicism" with anything but extreme reluctance; no subject has provoked so much weary logomachy since the Scholastics argued themselves out on the question of nominalism. I only take up the discussion again (eating my own words in the process) because I think that Surrealism has settled it. So long as romanticism and classicism were considered as alternative attitudes, rival camps, professions of *faith*, an interminable struggle was in prospect, with the critics as profiteers. But what in effect Surrealism claims to do is to resolve the conflict—not, as I formerly hoped, by establishing a synthesis which I was prepared to call "reason" or "humanism" —but by liquidating classicism, by showing its complete irrelevance, its *anaesthetic* effect, its contradiction of the creative impulse. Classicism, let it be stated without further preface, represents for us now, and has always represented, the forces of oppression. Classicism is the intellectual counterpart of political tyranny. It was so in the ancient world and in the medieval empires; it was renewed to express the dictatorships of the Renaissance and has ever since been the official creed of capitalism. Wherever the blood of martyrs stains the ground, there you will find a doric column or perhaps a statue of Minerva.

Academic critics have not been unaware of this alignment, but have united, of course, to give living colours to the corpse they have embalmed. I have often praised Sir Herbert Grierson's clean handling of this problem; like Brunetière, whose main line of demarcation he follows, he is not altogether unsympathetic towards romanticism, but there is a question of values involved which must be challenged. A classical literature, he writes, "is the product of a nation and a generation which has consciously achieved a definite advance, moral, political, intellectual; and is filled with the belief that its view of life is more natural, human, universal and wise than that from which it has escaped. It has effected a synthesis which enables it to look round on life with a sense of its wholeness, its unity in variety; and the work of the artist is to give expression to that consciousness; hence the solidity of his work and hence too its definiteness, and in the hands of great artists its beauty. . . . The work of the classical artist is to give individual expression, the beauty of form, to a body of common sentiments and thoughts which he shares with his audience, thoughts and views which have for his generation the validity of universal truths.

"Classical and romantic—these are the systole and diastole of the human heart in history. They represent on the one hand our need of order, of synthesis, of a comprehensive yet definite, therefore *exclusive* as well as inclusive, ordering of thought and feeling and action; and on the other hand the inevitable finiteness of every human synthesis, the inevitable discovery that, in Carlyle's metaphor, our clothes no longer fit us, that the classical has become the conventional, that our spiritual aspirations are being starved, or that our secular impulses are 'cribb'd, cabin'd, and confined.' " . . .[1]

The particular danger of this argument

[1] *The Background of English Literature.* London, 1925. Pp. 266, 287–8.

is due to its false dialecticism. A certain type of society is regarded as a "synthesis," a natural order or balance of forces, a state of equilibrium; and any deviation from that standard is regarded as abnormal, degenerate or revolutionary. Actually such types of society merely represent the dominance of one particular class—the economic dominance and therefore the cultural dominance of that class. For the stability of such a society a certain uniformity of ideas and modes of expression is a fundamental necessity; and the less novelty these ideas and modes of expression show the better. This explains the constant return to the norms of classical art; for these norms (in architecture we call them the "orders") are the typical patterns of order, proportion, symmetry, equilibrium, harmony and of all static and inorganic qualities. They are intellectual concepts which control or repress the vital instincts on which growth and therefore change depend, and in no sense represent a freely determined preference, but merely an imposed ideal.

The fallacy we are discussing is logical in its origin. It is a sophism by means of which two terms are conceived as dialectical opposites whereas actually they represent types of action and reaction. This is a very important distinction, and its neglect is the cause of much confusion. In dialectics the thesis and the antithesis are both objective facts, and the necessity for a resolution or synthesis is due to the real existence of a contradiction. But "classic" and "romantic" do not represent such a contradiction. They correspond rather to the husk and the seed, the shell and the kernel. There is a principle of life, of creation, of liberation, and that is the romantic spirit; there is a principle of order, of control and of repression, and that is the classical spirit. Naturally there is some purpose in the latter principle—the instincts are curbed in the interest of some particular ideal or set of values; but on analysis it always resolves into the defence of some particular structure of society, the perpetuation of the rule of some particular class. To identify romanticism with revolt as Grierson does is true enough as an historical generalisation; but it merely distorts the values involved if such revolt is conceived in purely literary or academic terms. It would be much nearer the truth to identify romanticism with the artist and classicism with society; classicism being the political concept of art to which the artist is expected to conform.

It may be as well to forestall at once the criticism that on this showing the artist is merely the individualist in conflict with society. To a certain extent, as I have shown elsewhere,[2] this is true; the mental personality of the artist is originally determined by a failure in social adaptation. But his whole effort is directed towards a reconciliation with society, and what he offers to society is not a bagful of his own tricks, his idiosyncrasies, but rather some knowledge of the secrets to which he has had access, the secrets of the self which are buried in every man alike, but which only the sensibility of the artist can reveal to us in all their actuality. This "self" is not the personal possesion we imagine it to be; it is largely made up of elements from the unconscious, and the more we learn about the unconscious, the more collective it appears to be—in fact, "a body of common sentiments and thoughts . . . universal truths" such as Grierson assumes to be the exclusive concern of the classical artist. But whereas the universal truths of classicism may be merely the temporal prejudices of an epoch, the universal truths of romanticism are

[2] *Art and Society*, Chap. VI.

coeval with the evolving consciousness of mankind.

It is in this sense, then, that Surrealism is a reaffirmation of the romantic principle; and though poets and painters in all ages have clung to a belief in the inspirational and even the obsessional nature of their gifts, repudiating in deeds if not in words the rigid bonds of classical theory, it is only now, with the aid of modern dialectics and modern psychology, in the name of Marx and Freud, that they have found themselves in a position to put their beliefs and practices on a scientific basis, thereby initiating a continuous and deliberate creative activity whose only laws are the laws of its own dynamics.

Before passing on to a more precise examination of the romantic principle as actually manifested in English art and literature, there is one further interpretation of the classic-romantic antithesis which is worth referring to, especially as it finds its justification in modern psychology—I mean the theory that the two terms correspond to the general distinction between "extravert" and "introvert" types of personality. The comparison is valid enough if it has reference to the personalities involved; what is questionable is the very existence of such a type as an extravert *artist*. To the degree in which he becomes extravert the artist, we would say, ceases to be, in any essential sense of the word, an artist. Now admittedly there is much in the process of producing a work of art which involves, or may involve, an objective attitude towards the materials the artist is using; only the purely automatic text or drawing is purely subjective, and though the Surrealist insists on the significance of such automatic expression, he is far from asserting that all art must of necessity be produced under such conditions.

What he does assert, however, is the absolute impossibility of producing a work of art by the conscious exercise of talents. The notion that a work of art can be created by observing a set of rules is only to be compared with the notion that a human being can be produced in a test-tube.

"Verbal and graphic automatism," Breton has said, "only represents a *limit* towards which the poet or artist should tend." The opposed limit is represented by all those "arts of poetry," those academic discourses on painting, in which various ages have sought to codify for all time the laws of art. Between these limits we find the whole range of aesthetic expression, but it is towards the limit of automatism, and away from the limit of rational control, that we find the most enduring vitality, the words which live when the poet is dead, when even his name is forgotten.

A rose-red city half as old as time

—a single line surviving from the complete works of a poet, and surviving precisely by virtue of its irrationality. . . .

The philosophical justification of Surrealism is to be found, if anywhere in the past, in Hegel. But it is a Hegel deprived for the most part of those elements which he would have considered of the greatest importance. Just as Marx, for his purposes, turned Hegel upside down, "sloughed off" the mystical form of Hegel's dialectic, so the Surrealist, for his purposes, subjects the philosopher to the same indignity. If I am asked why, in this matter, we should return to Hegel rather than start our philosophy of art afresh, there are various answers to give —answers similar to those which have to be given in the field of political philosophy. One is that Hegel represents a convenient *crux* in philosophy: all previ-

ous philosophies seem to meet in him, to be sorted and smelted and reduced to the purest and least contradictory elements of human thought. Hegel is the great scavenger of philosophical systems; he cleans them up and leaves a tidy piece of ground on which we can build. More than that, he provides a scaffolding within which we can build—the scaffold of his dialectic.

This dreaded word *dialectic*—a word which the English-speaking public finds difficult to digest and which even our so-called socialists, with a few exceptions, would willingly forget—this word is actually the name of a very simple and very necessary process of thought. If we consider the natural world, we soon become aware that its most striking characteristic is not permanency, solidity or stability, but *continuous change* or development. Physicists now affirm that not merely the organic world, not merely this earth we live on, but the whole universe is undergoing a process of continuous change. Dialectics is nothing more than a logical explanation of how such a change takes place. It does not suffice to say that "it grows," or "it decays," "it runs down," "it expands"; these phrases are vague abstractions. The change must take place in a definite way. Between one phase and another of that development there must intervene an active principle, and Hegel suggested that this principle was actually one of opposition and interaction. That is to say, to produce any new situation (i.e., any departure from an existing condition of equilibrium) there must previously exist two elements so opposed to each other and yet so related to each other that a solution or resolution is demanded; such a solution being in effect a new phase of development (temporary state of equilibrium) which preserves some of the elements of the interacting phases, eliminates others, but is qualitatively different from the previously existing state of opposition.

Such is the dialectical logic, elaborated by Hegel for idealistic purposes and brilliantly adapted by Marx for materialistic purposes. As an instrument of thought it enabled Marx to explain the evolution of human society from primitive communism to feudalism and through the various stages of capitalism; it enabled him, moreover, to predict the self-extinction of capitalism and the coming of the socialist state. But that is by the way. What I wish to stress now is that Surrealism is an application of the same logical method to the realm of art. By the dialectical method we can explain the development of art in the past and justify a revolutionary art at the present time.

In dialectical terms we claim that there is a continual state of opposition and interaction between the world of objective fact—the sensational and social world of active and economic existence —and the world of subjective fantasy. This opposition creates a state of disquietude, a lack of spiritual equilibrium, which it is the business of the artist to resolve. He resolves the contradiction by creating a synthesis, a work of art which combines elements from both these worlds, eliminates others, but which for the moment gives us a qualitatively new experience—an experience on which we can dwell with equanimity. Superficial critics may pretend to be unable to distinguish such a qualitatively new state from an ordinary compromise, and it is to be feared that in practice most dialectical solutions are of this kind. But a true synthesis is never a reversion; it is always a progression.

That is the central core of the surrealist claim, and any attempt to discredit or criticise Surrealism must present an adequate philosophical alternative; just as any criticism of dialectical materialism as embodied in the socialism of Marx must present an adequate philosophical alternative. At present any alternatives worthy of our consideration are lacking.

To return for a moment to Hegel. He dealt with the subject of art at such length (in his *Aesthetik*) that one would expect to find there some approach to the dialectical interpretation of art which the Surrealist now advances. Actually we no more find that than, in his other works, we find an anticipation of Marx. Everything, in his philosophy, is sacrificed to the necessity of making "ideas," or states of self-consciousness, the supreme forces in creative development. As Marx observed in his Preface to the first edition of *Kapital*,

"My dialectic method is not only different from the Hegelian, but its direct opposite. To Hegel, the life-process of the human brain, i.e., the process of thinking, which, under the name of 'the Idea,' he even transforms into an independent subject, is the demiurgos of the real world, and the real world is only the external, phenomenal form of 'the Idea.' With me, on the contrary, the ideal is nothing else than the material world reflected by the human mind, and translated into forms of thought."

With the Surrealists, we might also say, the ideal is nothing else than the material world reflected by the human mind, and translated into images. But "reflection" and "translation" are not, for us today, such simple mechanical processes as perhaps Marx implies. For us the process is infinitely complicated: a passage through a series of distorting mirrors and underground labyrinths. . . .

Surrealism demands nothing less than . . . a revaluation of all aesthetic values. It has no respect for any academic tradition, least of all for the classical-capitalist tradition of the last four hundred years. It believes that as a general rule even men of genius during this period—and it has no difficulty in conceding genius where it is due—have been hampered and repressed by the conventions of their education and by their social environment. For poets like Dryden and Pope, for painters like Michelangelo and Poussin, and for many lesser artists, we can only have an angry and in no sense patronising pity. The spectacle of the immense genius of Michelangelo, for example, caught in the toils of the rational ideals of the Grand Manner, is a titanic tragedy. On the other hand the exaltation of conforming mediocrities in every age into a position of authority is a melancholy farce. It is true that only a small proportion of them survive the inevitable ridicule of posterity, but there still remain on every self-styled Parnassus stuffed corpses that should be thrown on the dunghill.

That such a revaluation would be in effect merely a rehabilitation of romanticism is true enough, if the definition of romanticism I have already given is borne in mind. I would suggest, merely as examples of the tasks awaiting us, and merely in the restricted field of English literature, the following:

1. A *fuller acknowledgment of the supreme poetic quality of our ballads and anonymous literature.* I do not refer to the actual work of recovering and editing the material; to that ghoulish activity it is time to cry halt. The ballads have become the happy hunting ground of academic competence; they must be rescued from such dead hands and be fully recognised as the most fundamental and authentic of all poetry. Ballads are partly collective (if not in origin, at least in development) and to some degree automatic, and illustrate the intrinsic nature

of surrealist poetry. I include in this category, not merely the familiar Border Ballads, but the popular ballads of more recent times (even Woolworth's Song Sheets) and the vast store of primitive poetry mostly still hidden in anthropological works.

2. *Driving home the inescapable significance of Shakespeare.* To claim Shakespeare as an ally will be treated as an act of impudence by academic critics, but to justify our claim it is only necessary to point to the history of Shakespearean criticism. The rehabilitation of Shakespeare's genius, after the class and classical denigration of the seventeenth and eighteenth centuries, has been the work of specifically romantic critics, beginning with Coleridge and ending, for the moment, with Middleton Murry. Other critics have tinkered with his text—usually to little purpose—or have elaborated the historical background. But the poetic status of Shakespeare—his relative position among the poets of England and of the world—that depends on the romantic theory of poetry. It is impossible —the very attempt is absurd—to establish the genius of Shakespeare on any classical basis. He breaks all the academic rules.

A critic who would not be described as romantic—Professor Dover Wilson— recently published a long book on a vexed question: the problem of Hamlet.[3] Most critics have been puzzled by the incoherency of this, the most famous of Shakespeare's plays—an incoherency which affects not only the action of the play, but also the character of the hero. Various solutions have been proposed, and Professor Wilson reviews them all and finds them wanting. He has great fun demolishing the clumsy or ingen-

[3] *What Happens in Hamlet.* By J. Dover Wilson. Cambridge, 1935.

ious attempts which have been made to explain the inexplicable; and ends where they might all have begun—by accepting the inexplicable at its face-value, its value as inexplicableness, as irrationality. The heart of the mystery proves to be the mystery itself:

"In fine, we were never intended to reach the heart of the mystery. That it has a heart is an illusion; the mystery itself is an illusion; Hamlet is an illusion. The secret that lies behind it all is not Hamlet's, but Shakespeare's; the technical devices he employed to create this supreme illusion of a great and mysterious character, who is at once mad and the sanest of geniuses, at once a procrastinator and a vigorous man of action, at once a miserable failure and the most adorable of heroes. The character of Hamlet, like the appearance of his successive impersonators on the stage, is a matter of 'make-up.' "

Not since Warton defended the irrational imagery of Milton has such light streamed into the dark cloisters of the academic mind! It is really a very significant event in the history of scholarship. Professor Wilson is not a stray wolf in academic robes—such do occasionally find their way into the fold. He is the authentic type, the adept of a modern apparatus of the most efficient kind. He moves his apparatus into position; sets it in motion to do its carding and sorting and tidy ordering and then discovers that it will not work. Abandoning his apparatus he approaches the work of genius with his naked eye, and is dazzled. Rest, rest, perturbed spirit.[4]

4 This critic's acknowledgment of the irrationality of Shakespeare's genius is not confined to this one instance. For example, what can he mean in saying that in *King Lear* Shakespeare "has fashioned a mirror of art in which, more successfully than any man before or since, he has caught the whole of life and focussed it to one intense and burning point of terror

3. *The exact relations between metaphysics and poetry.* This is a subject to which I have devoted a good deal of attention in the past, but I am by no means satisfied that I have exhausted its interest.

e il pensamento in sogno transmutai

[it is thought transmuted into vision]

—Dante's line is the perfect description of a process which has yet to be given a full psychological explanation. We think we know how one kind of poetry originates—in inspiration, directly from the sensational awareness of the objective world, or no less directly from the promptings of the unconscious. But we have to admit—it is the only justification of the poetic elements in classical verse—that poetry may be generated by discursive reasoning or metaphysical speculation. In an early essay I described metaphysical poetry as "felt thought," and I still think that no thought can become poetic unless it is apprehended in its mental configuration—we lack the equivalent of the more exact German word *Gestalt*. But what is still necessary is some explanation of why thoughts or ideas should evoke, not merely a metaphorical imagery, but a sensuous identification with visual images: thought transmuted into dream. Obviously it is some extension of the "association of ideas" upon which psychoanalysis relies; the poet passes from the idea to the image unconsciously, and for reasons which might be revealed in analysis. But from our present point of view it is only necessary to affirm and prove that even

and beauty"? (*The Essential Shakespeare.* Cambridge, 1932. Page 127.) It is not in such terms that the academic critic is wont to award his marks.

in its most intellectual forms poetry acquires its poetic quality by a process which brings it into line with the irrational sources of lyrical and romantic poetry.

This fact has not been generally acknowledged by critics in the past, but one who enjoys great respect in quarters where the Surrealists expect none had some inkling of the truth. "Although poets often have unusual powers of reflective thought," wrote A. C. Bradley, "the specific genius of a poet does not lie there, but in the imagination. Therefore his deepest and most original interpretation is likely to come by way of the imagination. And the specific way of imagination is not to clothe in imagery consciously held ideas; *it is to produce half-consciously a matter* from which, when produced, the reader may, if he chooses, extract ideas." ...

Hitherto poets and critics have shown singularly little curiosity about the actual mechanism of poetic inspiration. There are, of course, many disjointed statements which throw light on the subject, such as Wordsworth's quasi-psychological description of emotion recollected in tranquillity, and Keats and Rilke, as I have noted in *Form in Modern Poetry*, have observed themselves to some profit. Not long before his death A. E. Housman disconcerted his academic cronies by confessing that inspiration was most often induced in him by a pint of beer; that in any case it had physical symptoms. My own suggestion is that poetic inspiration has an exact parallel in dream-formation. In what respect the two processes differ can only be shown by the analysis of a particular case of inspiration, which is what I propose to undertake. But first I must make sure that the reader has a clear picture of the process of dream-formation as described by Freud.

In his latest "Revision of the Theory of Dreams" (*New Introductory Lectures*, 1933. Chapter 1) Freud gives the following schematic summary of the process:

"The introduction: the wish to sleep, the voluntary withdrawal from the outside world. Two things follow from this: firstly, the possibility for older and more primitive modes of activity to manifest themselves, i.e., regression; and secondly, the decrease of the repression-resistance which weighs on the unconscious. As a result of this latter feature an opportunity for dream-formation presents itself, which is seized upon by the factors which are the occasion of the dream; that is to say, the internal and external stimuli which are in activity. The dream which thus eventuates is already a compromise formation; it has a double function: it is on the one hand in conformity with the ego ('ego-syntonic'), since it subserves the wish to sleep by draining off the stimuli which would otherwise disturb it, while on the other hand it allows to a repressed impulse the satisfaction which is possible in these circumstances in the form of an hallucinatory wish-fulfilment. The whole process of dream-formation, which is permitted by the sleeping ego, is, however, under the control of the censorship, a control which is exercised by what is left of the forces of repression."

What is allowed to emerge as a dream —that is to say, what is remembered as a dream—Freud calls the dream-text or the *manifest* dream; but what the analyst suspects to lie beyond the dream, its motive force, these are the *latent* dream-thoughts. "Their dominating element is the repressed impulse, which has obtained some kind of expression, toned down and disguised though it may be, by associating itself with stimuli which happen to be there and by tacking itself on to the residue of the day before." The rest of Freud's description should be followed with close attention, because its bearing on the process of poetic inspiration is direct and immensely significant:

"Just like any other impulse this one presses forward towards satisfaction in action, but the path to motor discharge is closed to it on account of the physiological characteristics of the state of sleep, and so it is forced to travel in the retrograde direction to perception, and content itself with an hallucinatory satisfaction. The latent dream-thoughts are therefore turned into a collection of sensory images and visual scenes. As they are travelling in this direction something happens to them which seems to us new and bewildering. All the verbal apparatus by means of which the more subtle thought-relations are expressed, the conjunctions and prepositions, the variations of declension and conjugation, are lacking, because the means of portraying them are absent: just as in primitive grammarless speech, only the raw material of thought can be expressed, and *the abstract is merged again in the concrete from which it sprang*. What is left over may very well seem to lack coherence. It is as much the result of the archaic regression in the mental apparatus as of the demands of the censorship that so much use is made of the representation of certain objects and processes by means of symbols which have become strange to conscious thought. But of more far-reaching import are the other alterations to which the elements comprising the dream-thoughts are subjected. Such of them as have any point of contact are *condensed* into new unities. When the thoughts are translated into pictures those forms are indubitably preferred which allow of this kind of telescoping, or

condensation; it is as though a force were at work which subjected the material to a process of pressure or squeezing together. As a result of condensation one element in a manifest dream may correspond to a number of elements of the dream-thoughts; but conversely one of the elements from among the dream-thoughts may be represented by a number of pictures in the dream."

This spate of quotation is already too long, but there are two further refinements in the process of dream-formation which are still relevant. The first is *displacement* or transference of accent. The individual ideas which make up the dream-thoughts are not all of equal value; "they have various degrees of affective tone attached to them, and, corresponding to these, they are judged as more or less important, and more or less worthy of attention. In the dream-work these ideas are separated from their affects; the affects are treated separately. They may be transferred to something else, they may remain where they were, they may undergo transformation, or they may disappear from the dream entirely. *The importance of the ideas which have been shorn of their affect reappears in the dream in the form of the sensuous vividness of the dream-pictures*; but we notice that this accent, which should lie on important elements, has been transferred to unimportant ones, so that what seems to be pushed to the forefront in the dream, as the most important element in it, only plays a subsidiary role in the dream-thoughts, and conversely, what is important among the dream-thoughts obtains only incidental and rather indistinct representation in the dream."

The other refinement in the process is, from our point of view, perhaps the most important of all. "After these operations

on the dream-thoughts the dream is almost ready. There is still, however, a
more or less non-constant factor, the so-
called secondary elaboration, that makes
its appearance after the dream has come
into consciousness as an object of perception. When the dream has come into
consciousness, we treat it in exactly the
same way that we treat any content of
perception; we try to fill in the gaps,
we add connecting links, and often
enough we let ourselves in for serious
misunderstandings. But this, as it were,
rationalising activity, which at its best
provides the dream with a smooth façade,
such as cannot correspond to its real
content, may be altogether absent in
some cases, or only operate in a very
feeble way, in which case the dream displays to view all its gaps and inconsistencies. . . ."

To trace the parallel between dream-
formation and poem-formation it is necessary to analyse a particular poem, and of
necessity such a poem must be one of my
own (or otherwise I should have to conduct a long and searching analysis of
another poet). The poem I shall take is
actually based on a dream. On December
31, 1935, I was present at a family gather-
ing in Yorkshire, and at midnight we
celebrated the passing of the Old Year
and the birth of the New Year by drinking a rum-punch (I am, it will be seen,
about to confirm Housman's diagnosis).
I retired to bed and dreamt a vivid dream.
It was still vivid to me when next day I
travelled by train back to London, and
since, like several poets of my acquaintance, I have always found the rhythm of
a train journey conducive to poetic
composition, I began to transfer to paper
the haunting images of my dream. The
following poem was the result—I will
explain the significance of the italics
presently:

The narrow labyrinth has light
which casts our shadows on the wall
as in extremity of flight
I follow one whose face I have not seen.

The walls are white
and turn at intervals to make a screen
on which our racing shadows rise and fall
like waves against the bleached cliff.

Anxious to make my mentor turn
I lift my hands and make a pass
which casts upon the facing wall
a silhouette hovering like a baffled bird.

But on he leads unmoved
and fatally I follow till at last
we leave the labyrinth and I find myself
alone, upon a plinth.

The houses in the square below
stand newly built, brick-rough, bright
bathed in some *Castilian* light.
In the unpaved area a few children play.

This must be a foreign land, I say,
and gaze about with eager eyes.
Then suddenly know that it is *Heaven*
to which *Death* has led me in disguise.

What I described in this poem was,
of course, the *manifest* content of my
dream; the *latent* content could only be
elicited by analysis, and is of no immediate interest. But our poetic analysis of
the poem should begin by asking to what
extent I succeeded in conveying the manifest content. Is the poem efficient merely
as the narrative of an experience? As far
as the events of the poem are concerned,
I think it is only towards the end that I
myself am conscious of any failure. I
fancy that in the dream the identity of
the unknown figure was revealed to me,
and that immediately I awoke—in the
process of awaking—this identity slipped
from me and I was left with a sense of
being baffled. The notion of suddenly
finding myself in a Heaven was present
in the dream, but identifying the figure

with Death was a subsequent rationalisation; it did not, if I can trust my memory, occur to me until I began to write the poem.

Let us now examine the images in the poem. In the dream the labyrinth was real; an intricate maze always turning at right angles and full of an evenly diffused white light; the figure, clad rather like a harlequin in close-fitting tights, never turned. I made the pass by lifting my hands above my head and making a shadow on the wall in the manner of the shadow-game played by children; the image of the baffled bird—the fluttering shadow like a bird beating against a window-pane—*occurred to me in my dream.* In this it differs from the wave-image I have used to describe the shadows of our bodies on the walls of the labyrinth, which is a conscious image produced in the process of writing the poem; I would on that account call it a metaphor rather than an image. In a similar way the word "Castilian," used to describe the peculiar light which was diffused over the square, is an epithet derived from my conscious experience; the nearest equivalent in my memory being certain effects of sunlight in Spain. I have not conveyed exactly enough the vivid impression I have of the effect of this dream-light on the houses; I have a distinct sensuous image of the porous quality of the brick into which the light seemed to soak, as if absorbed. The children in the square (it was a new square, not yet paved or laid out in any way, rough and uneven) seemed to be self-centred, detached, in a different perspective to the rest of the scene; an effect which Salvador Dali often conveys in his paintings.

It will be observed that there are several rhymes, but no regular rhyme system; these rhymes were not sought by me, but came unconsciously in the act of writing the poem. If I had sought for rhymes I should inevitably have been compelled to distort my narrative and my imagery, and to that extent to be false to my inspiration. And such, indeed, has always been my practice in writing poetry. I neither seek rhymes nor avoid them, for either attitude would involve a too conscious control of my expression—would defeat the desirable automatism. But this does not prevent me from recognising that when there is no total inspiration—when a poet is writing line by line—the search for rhymes may lead to the discovery of surprising images. That is merely a different method of composition; a mosaic as opposed to a reflection. If a poet wishes to remain faithful to a myth—a myth presented to him integrally—he cannot afford to go off in pursuit of surface ornaments.

Perhaps the most important distinction which this analysis reveals is that between images and metaphors—a distinction which has already been made by Pierre Reverdy and which I have referred to before (Breton also quotes it in the First Surrealist Manifesto):

"L'image est une création pure de l'esprit.

"Elle ne peut naître d'une comparaison mais du rapprochement de deux réalités plus ou moins éloignées.

"Plus les rapports des deux réalités rapprochées seront lointains et justes, plus l'image sera forte—plus elle aura de puissance émotive et de réalité poétique...."

[The image is purely a creation of spirit. It is not born of comparison but of reconciliation of two realities more or less alien. The more remote and exact the affinities of the two reconciled realities, the stronger the image will be—the greater emotive power and poetic reality it will have.]

In my poem the metaphor of the waves

against the bleached cliff, though to my mind accurate enough as description, has not the same force as the image of the baffled bird; and actually, of course, the whole content of the poem—labyrinth, square, light, children—is a series of images, but of images whose counterpart is not manifest, and which therefore we call symbols.

The metaphor may have its associational significance within the psychological unity of the poem; if it is purely intellectual in origin it is apt to stick out of the poem like an irrelevant ornament.

This type of poem, then, we might describe, to adopt Freud's terminology, as the manifest content of a dream whose latent thoughts have been turned into sensory images or visual scenes; the abstract, that is to say, is merged again in the concrete form from which it sprang.[5] Certain of the dream-thoughts have been condensed into images or symbols, whose latent significance resists any analysis, but which nevertheless, *and perhaps precisely on that account*, have extreme poetic force. Then, to disguise any gaps or incoherency, the conscious mind of the poet has worked over the poem, and given it that smooth façade which is generally demanded by the literary conventions of an age, and which in any case makes for ease of communication.

It is not every poem that has the integral character of a dream, but every authentic image is conceived in the unconscious; that is to say, the two realities of which Reverdy speaks, though more or less distantly separated, cohere as an image and gain their emotive power from the presence in the unconscious of a hidden connecting link. There is no need, in any poetic analysis, to reveal that repressed connection; the poetic reality lies in the evident power of the image, and is no stronger—indeed, may be much weaker—if its latent meaning is made manifest. The whole irrationality of art, and the surrealist defence of irrationality, is explained by the Freudian theory of regression. An unconscious impulse creates the poem no less than the dream; it provides, that is to say, the mental energy required for its formation. That impulse seeks in the poem, no less and no otherwise than in the dream, its desired satisfaction. The latent ideas or thoughts are turned into visual images, are dramatised and illustrated, are finally liberated in the hallucinatory reality of the poem.

That the actual choice of words—the poet's language as distinct from his imagery—is formed by a similar process of unconscious association, would seem to be a fair deduction from the evidence of psychoanalysis. In the degree that they are poetic such words are automatic associations of an aural rather than a visual nature. It may be that some poets search the dictionary of their conscious memory for the apt epithet, and in that way display an inventive wit; but such a faculty —the faculty of a Pope or a Dryden— is not the essentially poetic gift. Poetry,

---

[5] Compare Vico's theory of poetry, especially the following passage: "[So for us] the whole art of Poetry reduces itself to this, that anyone who wishes to excel as a poet must unlearn all his native language, and return to the pristine beggary of words; by this necessity he will express the feelings of his mind by means of the most obvious and easily perceived aspects of things; he will, by the aid of the senses and the imagination, paint the most striking and lovely images of things, manners and feelings; and just as anyone who wishes to be a philosopher must first purge himself of the prejudices of children and common people, so anyone who would write a poem must feel and think entirely according to the childlike and common views of the world. In this way he will become really imaginative, and will compose at once sublimely and in accordance with the popular understanding." *De Constantia Philologiae.* (Trans. by H. S. Davies.)

to adapt a saying of Picasso's, is found, not sought. It emerges, perhaps not easily but at any rate directly, from the well of the unconscious. It may be elaborated or distorted by the exercise of conscious skill, but there is no evidence at all to show that as a result the poem ever gains in its specifically poetic power.

We are so uncertain of the limits of mental activity—its actual range and effectiveness—that even as materialists we must not exclude the possibility of hitherto unsuspected modes of operation. For example, psychoanalysis has already been compelled to admit the scientific possibility of thought-transference or telepathy. On the analogy of such "occult" phenomena, it is possible that the mind of the poet or painter, during the course of its ordinary activity, picks up and transmits "messages" in a wholly unconscious manner. I think it is possible that such "messages" are always in the form of "images"—that is to say, the ideas they deal with are not verbalised. In this way, for example, the "residues" of the day's activity, in their least unimportant and unobserved details, are taken up and "used" in the course of the dream activity. A pattern in a wall, a patch of lichen, or any abstract pattern which I have for a moment stared at, may in this way sink into my mind and determine the form of my unconscious images, which when called up in the activity of painting, emerge in this apparently inexplicable and illogical shape. That process is comparatively easy to understand; but in the contrary direction it is also possible that ideas, with which we have been obsessed during the activity of thought, may, when conscious thought is for the time being superseded by instinctive modes of expression, so guide such expression that it corresponds to the latent thought. Salvador Dali relates

how a splash of paint on his palette had assumed *unknown to his conscious mind* the shape of a distorted skull which he had consciously and vainly been trying to discover. It is another aspect of automatism; and all that is necessary to admit is the superreality, the something-more-than-conscious naturalism, which encompasses all our actions....

To close this essay without a personal note of explanation would be discreet, perhaps, but unnecessarily indefinite. I am often accused of contradictions, and do not doubt that these exist in my critical writings. But I must confess that I am not particularly uneasy about them. They are related to the contradictions of my personality, and, if I am then told that it is very wrong or weak of me to possess such a personality, the objection is meaningless to me. For I am conscious that, such as it is, my personality is integral, and I do not choose to present a falsely regular façade. I have a strong dislike for people with symmetrical faces; if not criminals (an attested fact), they are at any rate stupid or depraved. I do not necessarily glory in contradictions, but if they come as a natural consequence of a natural disposition I leave them to be reconciled in that synthetic judgment which is the last judgment.

In that judgment it will be seen that my main affiliations have always been romantic, in the sense in which I have interpreted romanticism in this essay. I have always had an instinctive preference for those poets and painters who have exceeded the limits of convention, which are the limits of moral experience; and in the history of criticism my interest quickens from the moment that romanticism begins to acquire a rational and scientific basis in psychology and philosophy: the line of development from Vico to Freud. That in the present desperate circumstances, when at any moment every poet and artist may be called upon to find his position *in the line*, that at such a time I should in spite of all my past pontifical detachment declare for Surrealism—that, I assert, should be regarded as merely an affirmation of all that is most real and active in my work. . . .

THE FUNCTIONS OF STREAM OF CONSCIOUSNESS
Robert Humphrey*

Stream-of-consciousness literature is "psychological literature" with the primary purpose of "revealing the psychic being of the characters," according to Humphrey. It is concerned with what lies beneath the surface, a literature influenced by psychological discoveries of the unconscious and preconscious levels of the mind. Humphrey points out that since unconscious thought processes are not "rationally controlled" or "logically ordered," the form of stream-of-consciousness literature is one which suggests such thought processes. Theoretically, the stream-of-consciousness device is a means of expressing an inner, prespeech realism and as such can be considered a kind of language of the surreal.

The discovery that memories, thoughts, and feelings exist outside the primary consciousness is the most important step forward that has occurred in psychology since I have been a student of that science.
—William James

Stream of consciousness is one of the delusive terms which writers and critics use. It is delusive because it sounds concrete and yet it is used as variously—and vaguely—as "romanticism," "symbolism," and "surrealism." We never know whether it is being used to designate the bird of technique or the beast of genre—and we are startled to find the creature designated is most often a mon-

strous combination of the two. The purpose of this study is to examine the term and its literary implications.

STREAM OF CONSCIOUSNESS DEFINED

Stream of consciousness is properly a phrase for psychologists. William James coined it.[1] The phrase is most clearly useful when it is applied to mental processes, for as a rhetorical locution it becomes doubly metaphorical; that is, the word "consciousness" as well as the word "stream" is figurative, hence, both are less precise and less stable. If, then, the term stream of consciousness (I shall use it since it is already established as a literary label) is reserved for indicating an approach to the presentation of

* The essay is reprinted from Chapter I of *Stream of Consciousness in the Modern Novel*, by Robert Humphrey, by permission of the University of California Press. Copyright 1954 by the University of California Press.

[1] In *The Principles of Psychology* (New York, Henry Holt, 1890), I, 239.

psychological aspects of character in fiction, it can be used with some precision. This reservation I shall make, and it is the basis from which the contradicting and often meaningless commentary on the stream-of-consciousness novel can be resolved.[2]

The stream-of-consciousness novel is identified most quickly by its subject matter. This, rather than its techniques, its purposes, or its themes, distinguishes it. Hence, the novels that are said to use the stream-of-consciousness *technique* to a considerable degree prove, upon analysis, to be novels which have as their essential subject matter the consciousness of one or more characters; that is, the depicted consciousness serves as a screen on which the material in these novels is presented.

"Consciousness" should not be confused with words which denote more restricted mental activities, such as "intelligence" or "memory." The justifiably irate comments of the psychology scholars deplore the layman's use of the term. One of these scholars writes: "It has been said that no philosophical term is at once so popular and so devoid of standard meaning as *consciousness*; and the layman's usage of the term has been credited with begging as many metaphysical questions as will probably be the privilege of any single word."[3] The area which we are to examine here is an important one in which this confusion has been amassed. Since our study will

concern persons who are laymen in psychology, it is necessary that we proceed with the "layman's usage." Naturally, the stream-of-consciousness writers have not defined their label. We readers who have stamped it on them must try to do it.

Consciousness indicates the entire area of mental attention, from preconsciousness on through the levels of the mind up to and including the highest one of rational, communicable awareness.[4] This last area is the one with which almost all psychological fiction is concerned. Stream-of-consciousness fiction differs from all other psychological fiction precisely in that it is concerned with those levels that are more inchoate than rational verbalization—those levels on the margin of attention.

So far as stream-of-consciousness fiction is concerned, it is pointless to try to make definite categories of the many levels of consciousness. Such attempts demand the answers to serious metaphysical questions, and they put serious questions about the stream-of-consciousness writers' concepts of psychology and their aesthetic intentions—questions which the epistemologists, the psychologists, and the literary historians have not yet answered satisfactorily. It is desirable for an analysis of stream-of-consciousness fiction to assume that there are levels of consciousness from the lowest one just above oblivion to the highest one which is represented by verbal (or other formal) communication. "Low" and "high" simply indicate degrees of the rationally

[2] At least two writers, Frederick Hoffman and Harry Levin, have recognized this loose use of "stream of consciousness." Levin employs in its place the French rhetorical term *monologue intérieur*. Although Levin uses even this term too loosely for any general discussion of that technique, it serves well for his special purposes. I am indebted to him for the basic distinction between the terms in question. See his book, *James Joyce: A Critical Introduction* (Norfolk, Conn., New Directions, 1941), p. 89.

[3] James Grier Miller, *Unconsciousness* (New York, J. Wiley and Sons, 1942), p. 18.

[4] See the dictionaries of philosophy, particularly *Philosophisches Wörterbuch*, ed. Heinrich Schmidt, 10th ed. (Stuttgart, A. Kröner, 1943), and *The Dictionary of Philosophy*, ed. D. D. Runes (New York, The Philosophical Library, 1942). See also Frederick J. Hoffman's classification of stream-of-consciousness techniques according to four levels of consciousness in *Freudianism and the Literary Mind* (Baton Rouge, La., Louisiana State University Press, 1945), pp. 126–129.

ordered. The adjectives "dim" and "bright" could be used just as well to indicate these degrees. There are, however, two levels of consciousness which can be rather simply distinguished: the "speech level" and the "prespeech level." There is a point at which they overlap, but otherwise the distinction is quite clear. The prespeech level, which is the concern of most of the literature under consideration in this study, involves no communicative basis as does the speech level (whether spoken or written). This is its salient distinguishing characteristic. In short, the prespeech levels of consciousness are not censored, rationally controlled, or logically ordered. By "consciousness," then, I shall mean the whole area of mental processes, including especially the prespeech levels. The term "psyche" I shall use as a synonym for "consciousness," and at times, even the word "mind" will serve as another synonym. These synonyms, although they are handicapped by the various evocative qualities they possess, are convenient to use because they lend themselves well to the forming of adjectives and adverbs.

Hence, "consciousness" must not be confused with "intelligence" or "memory" or any other such limiting term. Henry James has written novels which reveal psychological processes in which a single point of view is maintained so that the entire novel is presented through the intelligence of a character. But these, since they do not deal at all with prespeech levels of consciousness, are not what I have defined as stream-of-consciousness novels. Marcel Proust has written a modern classic which is often cited as an example of stream-of-consciousness fiction,[5] but A la recherche du temps perdu is concerned only with

the reminiscent aspect of consciousness. Proust was deliberately recapturing the past for the purposes of communication; hence he did not write a stream-of-consciousness novel. Let us think of consciousness as being in the form of an iceberg—the whole iceberg and not just the relatively small surface portion. Stream-of-consciousness fiction is, to follow this comparison, greatly concerned with what lies below the surface.

With such a concept of consciousness, we may define stream-of-consciousness fiction as a type of fiction in which the basic emphasis is placed on exploration of the prespeech levels of consciousness for the purpose, primarily, of revealing the psychic being of the characters.

When some of the novels which fall into this classification are considered, it becomes immediately apparent that the techniques by which the subjects are controlled and the characters are presented are palpably different from one novel to the next. Indeed, there is no stream-of-consciousness technique. Instead, there are several quite different techniques which are used to present stream of consciousness.

THE SELF-CONSCIOUS MIND

It is not an uncommon misconception that many modern novels, and particularly the ones that are generally labeled stream of consciousness, rely greatly upon private symbols to represent private confusions. The misconception comes primarily from considering whatever is "internal" or "subjective" in characterization as arrant fantasy, or, at best, as psychoanalytical.[6] Serious misreadings and unsound evaluations result from this

[5] For example: Edward Wagenknecht, Cavalcade of the English Novel from Elizabeth to George VI (New York, Henry Holt, 1943), p. 505.

[6] It is, of course, true that there are several attempts to represent character in fiction in psychoanalytical terms—notably in Conrad Aiken's novels, Blue Voyage and The Great Circle—but these attempts are for the most part curiosities, and they are finally insignifican̸

initial misunderstanding, particularly in discussion of major twentieth-century novels. I refer to such subjective fiction as *Ulysses, Mrs. Dalloway, To the Lighthouse,* and *The Sound and the Fury.* These novels may very well be within a category we can label stream of consciousness, so long as we know what we are talking about. The evidence reveals that we never do—or never have done so.

It is meaningless to label all of the novels stream of consciousness that are generally named as such, unless we mean by that phrase simply "inner awareness." The expression of this quality is what they have in common. It is, however, apparent that that is not what has been meant when they have been so labeled and forced to share the same categorical niche. It is not what William James meant when he coined the term. James was formulating psychological theory and he had discovered that "memories, thoughts, and feelings exist outside the primary consciousness" and, further, that they appear to one, not as a chain, but as a stream, a flow.[7] Whoever, then, first applied the phrase to the novel did so correctly only if he was thinking of a *method* of representing inner awareness. What has actually happened is that *monologue intérieur* was clumsily translated into English. But it is palpably true that the methods of the novels in which this device is used are different, and that there are dozens of other novels which use internal monologue which no one would seriously classify as stream of consciousness. Such are, for example, *Moby Dick, Les Faux-monnayeurs,* and *Of Time and the River.* Stream of consciousness, then, is not a synonym for *monologue intérieur.* It is not a term to name a particular

[7] *The Principles of Psychology,* I, 239.

method or technique; although it probably was used originally in literary criticism for that purpose. One can safely conjecture that such a loose and fanciful term was a radiant buoy to well-meaning critics who had lost their bearings. The natural, and historically accurate, association of the term with psychology, along with the overwhelming psychoanalytical trend of twentieth-century thought, has resulted in giving all novels that could be loosely associated with the loose phrase "stream of consciousness" a marked Viennese accent.

The word "stream" need not concern us immediately, for representation of the flow of consciousness is, provided one is convinced that consciousness flows, entirely a matter of technique. The approach to take is to consider the word "consciousness" and to attempt to formulate what, to the various writers, is the ultimate significance of what consciousness contains. It is, in short, a psychological and a philosophical question. Stream-of-consciousness literature is psychological literature, but it must be studied at the level on which psychology mingles with epistemology. Immediately the question confronts us: What does consciousness contain? Then, too, what does it contain so far as philosophy and psychology have investigated it *and* what does it contain so far as the novelists in question have represented it? These may be mutually exclusive questions; they are certainly different ones. But the concern here is not with psychological theory; it is with novelistic subject matter. The question for this study is a phenomenological one: What does consciousness contain in the sense of what has it contained so far as the consciousness of the novelists have experienced it? Any answer must respect the possible range of a creative writer's sensitivity and imagination. No answer needs proving beyond the gesture of saying: There it is in Virginia Woolf; there it is in James Joyce. It should be remembered that, first, we are attempting to clarify a literary term; and second, we are trying to determine how fictional art is enriched by the depiction of inner states.

The attempt to create human consciousness in fiction is a modern attempt to analyze human nature. Most of us will be convinced, now, that it can be the starting point of that most important of all intellectual functions. We have, for example, Henry James's word for it that "experience is never limited, and it is never complete." He continues in the same context to point to the "chamber of consciousness" as the chamber of experience.[8] Consciousness, then, is *where* we are aware of human experience. And this is enough for the novelist. He, collectively, leaves nothing out: sensations and memories, feelings and conceptions, fancies and imaginations—and those very unphilosophic, but consistently unavoidable phenomena we call intuitions, visions, and insights. These last terms, which usually embarrass the epistemologist, unlike the immediately preceding series, are not always included under the label "mental life." Precisely for this reason it is important to point them up here. Human "knowledge" which comes not from "mental" activity but from "spiritual" life is a concern of novelists, if not of psychologists. Knowledge, then, as a category of consciousness must include intuition, vision, and sometimes even the occult, so far as twentieth-century writers are concerned.

Thus, we may, on inductive grounds, conclude that the realm of life with which stream-of-consciousness literature is concerned is mental and spiritual ex-

perience—both the whatness and the howness of it. The whatness includes the categories of mental experiences: sensations, memories, imaginations, conceptions, and intuitions. The howness includes the symbolizations, the feelings, and the processes of association. It is often impossible to separate the what from the how. Is, for example, memory a part of mental content or is it a mental process? Such fine distinctions, of course, are not the concern of novelists as novelists. Their object, if they are writing stream of consciousness, is to enlarge fictional art by depicting the inner states of their characters.

The problem of character depiction is central to stream-of-consciousness fiction. The great advantage, and consequently the best justification of this type of novel, rests on its potentialities for presenting character more accurately and more realistically. There is the example of the *roman expérimental* behind James Joyce, Virginia Woolf, and Dorothy Richardson, and though a little farther removed, behind William Faulkner. But there is a difference, and it is a tremendous one, between Zola and Dreiser, say, two novelists who attempted a kind of laboratory method in fiction, and the stream-of-consciousness writers. It is indicated chiefly in the difference in subject matter —which is, for the earlier novelists, motive and action (external man) and for the later ones, psychic existence and functioning (internal man). The difference is also revealed in the psychological and philosophical thinking in back of this. Psychologically it is the distinction between behavioristic concepts and psychoanalytical ones; philosophically, it is that between a broad materialism and a generalized existentialism. Combined, it is the difference between being concerned about what one does and being concerned about what one is.

[8] "Art of Fiction," *Partial Portraits* (London, Macmillan, 1905), p. 388.

I do not offer a Freudian or Existential brief for stream-of-consciousness literature. All of its authors doubtless were familiar, more or less, with psychoanalytical theories and with the twentieth-century recrudescence of personalism and were directly or indirectly influenced by them. Even more certain can we be that these writers were influenced by the broader concepts of a "new psychology" and a "new philosophy"—a nebulous label for all postbehavioristic and non-positivistic thinking, including any philosophy or psychology which emphasized man's inner mental and emotional life (e.g., Gestalt psychology, psychoanalytical psychology, Bergsonian ideas of *durée* and the *élan vital*, religious mysticism, much symbolic logic, Christian existentialism, etc.). It is this background which led to the great difference between Zola's subject matter and Joyce's; between Balzac's and Dorothy Richardson's. Yet as novelists all of these writers were concerned with the problem of characterization. There is naturalism in character depiction found in the work of both the late and the early of the above novelists, but there is a contrast and it is determined by the difference in psychological focusing. In short, the stream-of-consciousness novelists were, like the naturalists, trying to depict life accurately; but unlike the naturalists, the life they were concerned with was the individual's psychic life.

In examining the chief stream-of-consciousness writers in order to discover their diverse evaluations of inner awareness, we need to keep in mind two important questions: What can be accomplished by presenting character as it exists psychically? How is fictional art enriched by the depiction of inner states? The direction of the following discussion will be toward answering these questions.

IMPRESSIONS AND VISIONS

Unlike most originators of artistic genres, the twentieth-century pioneer in stream of consciousness remains the least well-known of the important stream-of-consciousness writers. It is the price a writer pays, even an experimental writer, for engendering monotony. Readers may justifiably neglect Dorothy Richardson, but no one who would understand the development of twentieth-century fiction can. With a great debt to Henry James and Joseph Conrad, she invented the fictional depiction of the flow of consciousness. Sometimes she is brilliant; always she is sensitive to the subtleties of mental functioning; but finally, she becomes lost in the overflow —a formless, unending deluge of realistic detail.

It is difficult to grasp Dorothy Richardson's aims. She gives this account of them herself in the brilliant foreword to *Pilgrimage:*

...the present writer, proposing at this moment to write a novel and looking around for a contemporary pattern, was faced with the choice between following one of her regiments and attempting to produce a feminine equivalent of the current masculine realism. Choosing the latter alternative, she presently set aside, at the bidding of a dissatisfaction that revealed its nature without cause, a considerable mass of manuscript. Aware, as she wrote, of the gradual falling away of the preoccupations that for a while had dictated the briskly moving script, and of the substitution, for these inspiring preoccupations, *of a stranger in the form of contemplated reality having for the first time in her experience its own say, and apparently justifying those who acclaim writing as the surest means of discovering the truth about one's own thoughts* and beliefs, she had been at the same time increasingly tormented, not only by the failure, of this now so independently assertive reality, adequately to appear within the text, but by its revelation, whencesoever focused, of a hundred faces, any one of which, the moment it was entrapped within the close mesh of direct statement, summoned its fellows to disqualify it.[9]

The italics are mine and the words they emphasize reveal just what a reader gets from *Pilgrimage*. It is a psychical autobiography, which means that it is almost impossible for a reader to be empathic toward it or to understand the importance of its implications. It is difficult to see either a microcosm or an exemplum here. There is a certain amount of universal interest possible in looking in on how a fairly sensitive but greatly limited mind functions and in discovering how it classifies and rejects; and there is even an interest in discovering what a great amount of dullness a mind encounters in the world—but such an interest is not likely to last throughout twelve volumes. The one possibility left for Dorothy Richardson was to reveal some of the mysteries of psychic life, to depict it as an area from which something of the external world could be explained. But this she does not do. She does not investigate the world of consciousness on a level that is deep enough.

Two interpretations of *Pilgrimage* have suggested a thematic significance in the work: John Cowper Powys, Dorothy Richardson's most persuasive admirer, justifies her novel because it is a presentation of the feminine view of life, which he is convinced is a worth-while thing in itself, necessary to supplement the masculine picture of things.[10] Dorothy Richardson herself evidently believed this also. She says, we recall, that she began writing in order "to produce a feminine equivalent of the current masculine realism." Unfortunately, the dichotomy between the feminine and masculine viewpoints is too tenuous, if not wholly inadequate, for any degree of profundity. Granted a possible over-all difference between these two classes of attitudes, still the basic problems and situations of life (hence of art) are neither masculine nor feminine, but simply human. One might as well propose that Faulkner writes in order to present a psychotic equivalent of the current sane realism! Faulkner has, certainly, advantages, which we shall consider presently, in presenting life from an abnormal person's point of view—and likewise there are certain values inherent in the presentation of life from a feminine point of view—but these values cannot be realized in a vacuum. An adequate purpose is not found in presenting these viewpoints merely for the sake of novelty. It is hardly justified, at least, for important literature. Another critic, Joseph Warren Beach, thinks of *Pilgrimage* as a quest story. He believes the point of the novel lies in Miriam's continuous search for a symbolic "little coloured garden," and again that she is on a pilgrimage "to some elusive shrine, glimpsed here and there and lost to view." This theory is easily credible, and it gives an important justification to the novel; but as Beach intimates, how digressive, how vague, and how long![11]

Dorothy Richardson deserves more credit as a pioneer in novelistic method than as a successful creator of fiction. There are indications that the pioneering fever was the conscious impetus, for the

[9] *Pilgrimage*, 4 vols. (New York, Alfred A. Knopf, 1938), I, 10.

[10] In *Dorothy M. Richardson* (London, Joiner and Steele, 1931), pp. 8 ff.

[11] *The Twentieth Century Novel: Studies in Technique* (New York, D. Appleton–Century, 1932), pp. 393 ff.

opening chapters of *Pilgrimage* were "written to the accompaniment of a sense of being upon a fresh pathway, an adventure so searching and, sometimes, so joyous as to produce a longing for participation."[12] By "participation" Dorothy Richardson meant "readers"; but I suspect she will always be rather bland hors d'oeuvres for the reading public. However, another kind of participation came. Dorothy Richardson recognizes this, too, in her foreword: "The lonely track, meanwhile, had turned out to be a populous highway. Amongst those who had simultaneously entered it, two figures stood out. One a woman mounted upon a magnificently caparisoned charger, the other a man walking, with eyes devoutly closed, weaving as he went a rich garment of new words wherewith to clothe the antique dark material of his engrossment." The woman we take to be Virginia Woolf; the man, who is described more aptly, is certainly James Joyce. There is little difficulty in determining why either of these writers used stream-of-consciousness methods.

Virginia Woolf speaks eloquently as a critic herself, and the key to her purposes is in her critical writing. Less eloquently, though authoritatively, are her purposes spoken by a number of other critics, partly because she gives them the key and partly because she lucidly reveals in her novels what she is about. Since Virginia Woolf's accomplishments have been so thoroughly analyzed,[13] it is necessary here only to summarize in order to provide a direct answer to the question which is in front of us: For what purpose does this writer use stream of consciousness?

12 Foreword to *Pilgrimage*, p. 10.
13 I refer particularly to the following: David Daiches, *Virginia Woolf* (Norfolk, Conn., New Directions, 1942); Bernard Blackstone, *Virginia Woolf: A Commentary* (London, Hogarth Press, 1949); and E. M. Forster, *Virginia Woolf* (New York, Harcourt, Brace, 1942).

Let us answer the question at once and show afterward why we have come to the answer. Virginia Woolf wanted to formulate the possibilities and processes of inner realization of truth—a truth she reckoned to be inexpressible; hence only on a level of the mind that is not expressed could she find this process of realization functioning. At least this is true with her three stream-of-consciousness novels. The first two of these, *Mrs. Dalloway* and *To the Lighthouse*, can be considered together, since they illustrate in only slightly different ways the same achievement. *The Waves* marks a different approach.

Clarissa Dalloway, Mrs. Ramsay, and Lily Briscoe all have moments of vision. Not that they are disciplined mystics who have prepared themselves for this, but their creator believed that the important thing in human life is the search the individual constantly has for meaning and identification. The fulfillment of her characters is therefore achieved when Virginia Woolf feels they are ready to receive the vision. The novels are a record of their preparations for the final insight. The preparations are in the form of fleeting insights into other characters and syntheses of present and past private symbols.

We know from Virginia Woolf's essays that she believed the important thing for the artist to express is his private vision of reality, of what life, subjectively, is. She thought that the search for reality is not a matter of dramatic external action. "Examine an ordinary mind on an ordinary day," she says, and again: "Life is ... a luminous halo, a semi-transparent envelope surrounding us from the beginning of consciousness to the end. Is it not the task of the novelists to convey this varying, this unknown and uncircumscribed spirit . . . ?"[14] Thus the search, thought Virginia Woolf, is a psychic activity, and it is the preoccupation (it surrounds us) of most human beings. The only thing is that most human beings are not aware of this psychic activity, so deep down is it in their consciousness. This is one of the reasons Virginia Woolf chose characters who are extraordinarily sensitive, whose psyches would at least occasionally be occupied with this search. And it is, above all, the reason that she chose the stream-of-consciousness medium for her most mature presentation of this theme.

Analogically, we may call the Virginia Woolf of these two stream-of-consciousness novels a mystic. She is a mystic in that she is interested in the search her characters make for unification. The climax of *Mrs. Dalloway* suggests the mystic's search for cosmic identification. And what, in the novel, is more nearly the mystic's vision of light than Lily Briscoe's crucial attainment of vision in *To the Lighthouse*? It is because this novelist is building up to the moments of illumination that her method is one of presenting psychic impressions. She selects these impressions as stages toward arriving at a vision. It is not the undifferentiated trivia that impinge on consciousness which interest her; it is the illusive event that is meaningful and that carries the germ of the final insight.

The Waves is a different kind of accomplishment. In this novel there is no mystical quest after identity and subjective essence; it is a presentation of the

14 "Modern Fiction," *The Common Reader* (New York, Harcourt, Brace, 1925), p. 212. Other essays in which Virginia Woolf expresses her ideas of reality and the novel are: "How It Strikes a Contemporary," in *The Common Reader*; *Mr. Bennett and Mrs. Brown* (New York, Harcourt, Brace, 1924); and *A Room of One's Own* (New York, Harcourt, Brace, 1929).

purest psychological analysis in literature. Not, let it be noted, of psychoanalysis. Spontaneous psychic life is presented in this novel. The achievement is the tracing of the growth of psychic lives. The method is as much the presentation of uncensored observations by the characters of each other as it is of the characters' own psychological make-up. Indeed, the two are the same thing in this "X-ray of intuition," as Bernard Blackstone labels it.

The psychic anatomy here is not a bare analysis, however. It is full of the impressionist's sensitivity to color, sound, and shapes as Virginia Woolf's earlier novels are. The formal soliloquies are close to poetry in their concentrated quality, their dependence on rhythms, and their exact diction. This work is the most eloquent of this eloquent novelist's fiction. It is also the most uncommunicative, for here Virginia Woolf's private sense of the significant is confined to characters who remain only individuals and never compose into universal symbols. Reality is the aim and it is achieved, but the rich symbolic significance of the characters of the two earlier stream-of-consciousness novels is lacking. As much as we may admire and enjoy this work, we are almost bound to agree with David Daiches that it is overloaded with technique.

SATIRES AND IRONIES

A person much more often charged with such artistic trammeling is James Joyce. In creative productions the ends justify the means, and Joyce has contributed hugely to a revitalized fiction. What the ends of *Ulysses* finally are, I do not expect to determine. The many volumes which have been written to explain Joyce's purposes threaten the cursory appraisal; but I should like at least to suggest one important achievement of Joyce's in *Ulysses* which is central to his whole purpose and which is greatly dependent on stream-of-consciousness techniques. This is the marvelous degree of objectivity which he achieves. Joyce, more than any other novelist, gains what Joseph Warren Beach terms "dramatic immediacy." In *A Portrait of the Artist as a Young Man*, Joyce, in the guise of Stephen, states his theory of the evolution of artistic form when he maintains that "the personality of the artist, at first a cry or a cadence or a mood and then a fluid and lambent narrative, finally refines itself out of existence, impersonalizes itself, so to speak. The esthetic image in the dramatic form is life purified in and projected from the human imagination. The mystery of esthetic like that of material creation is accomplished. The artist, like the God of the creation, remains within or behind or beyond or above his handiwork, invisible, refined out of existence, indifferent, paring his fingernails."[15] The author is almost "refined out of existence" in *Ulysses*. Why does Joyce place such an important emphasis on ridding his work of signs of its author? As a feat in itself it would be nothing more than an interesting tour de force. The effect of this great accomplishment is to make the reader feel he is in direct contact with the life represented in the book. It is a method for doing what Joyce wanted to do, and that is to present life as it actually is, without prejudice or direct evaluations. It is, then, the goal of the realist and the naturalist. The thoughts and actions of the characters are there, as if they were created by an invisible, indifferent creator. We must accept them, because they exist.

If Joyce's accomplishment is, then, that of the most successful of realists,

[15] *Viking Portable Joyce* (New York, 1947), p. 481.

what is his aim? What view of life can he communicate by impersonalizing his creation through presenting the direct interior monologues of his characters? The answer is this—and it is from this basis that a future evaluation of *Ulysses* must start: for Joyce, existence is a comedy and man is to be satirized, gently not bitterly, for his incongruous and pitiful central role in it. The objective distance of the author, working as it chiefly does in *Ulysses* on the level of man's daydreams and mental delusions, shows the smallness of man, the great disparity between his ideals and his actualities, and the prosaicness of most of the things he considers special. Joyce's methods point to this: the *Odyssey* pattern is a means for equating the heroic and the ordinary, and the undifferentiated internal monologue is a means for equating the trivial and the profound. Life is depicted by Joyce so minutely that there is no room for any values to stand out. Joyce presents life with its shortcomings and its inherent contradictions, and the result is satire. Only within stream of consciousness could the necessary objectivity be attained for making it all convincingly realistic; for the pathos is in the fact that *man* thinks he is special and heroic, not that *Joyce* thinks he is pitiful.

Joyce is a writer of comedy and of satiric comedy at that. He is not a jokester or a funny man. The novel is not as a whole, in any sense, a hoax: the overtones are too far-reaching; there is too credible a concept of man's psychic life presented. It is obvious, however, that *Ulysses* is, fundamentally, a satirical comment on modern man's life. Joyce could never have shown this convincingly with any subject other than man's life on the level of consciousness, where the ideal can be reached for, even by the everyman Leopold Bloom, whose very next act or thought will show how far he actually is from it.[16]

The only other writer who utilizes effectively this natural advantage for satire in depiction of psyche is William Faulkner. But there is a difference. Faulkner, although he makes wide use of comic materials, is not a writer of comedy, not even of divine comedy. Faulkner's satires of circumstance are, like those of the Hardy of *Jude the Obscure* and the poems, irrevocably tragic. And they are more profound than Joyce's. One way to explain this is to consider Faulkner as a stream-of-consciousness writer who combines the views of life of Woolf with those of Joyce. Faulkner's views are not the same in either case; but the cast is similar in both. His characters search for insight, and their search is fundamentally ironic.

Since relatively little study has been published on Faulkner, it is necessary to consider his accomplishment more thoroughly than we have those of the other writers. It is tempting to go afield in doing this, but we shall try to focus on answering that question which underlies the present study: Why does Faulkner choose to deal with psychic processes in *The Sound and the Fury* and *As I Lay Dying*? One commentator has it that Faulkner, in the former novel, which we shall consider first, was trying to depict the Freudian idea of dream mechanism and consequently was dealing with unconscious manifestations of libido activity.[17] This certainly, if valid, would automatically put the novel in the stream-of-consciousness genre—if, that is, it could produce a work of art at all. An-

other writer decides that since the date of the Benjy episode is an Easter Sunday, Benjy is a Christ symbol, etc., which puts the novel I don't know where.[18] These interpretations may be discarded because they involve the heresies of dehumanization, which Faulkner must hate more than anything else. Three much more convincing and sensible critics agree on the basic proposition that all of Faulkner's work can be interpreted on a basis of broad myth and related symbolism. The principle of this interpretation is that Faulkner's entire work is a dramatization, in terms of myth, of the social conflict between the sense of ethical responsibilities in traditional humanism and the amorality of modern naturalism (animalism) in Faulkner, in the South, and by extension, I suppose, universally.[19]

If we begin with this principle as a basis for interpretation of *The Sound and the Fury*, we can understand that the novel is another chapter in the history of the collapse of the humanism of the Sartoris (here Compson) family in a world of the animalism of the Snopeses. The chief character symbol of the Sartoris-Compson code is Quentin III, who commits suicide; the symbol of the Snopes code is Jason IV (actually a Sartoris-Compson), who collapses most completely in that he embraces Snopesism. The other characters represent symbolically stages in degeneracy of, and escape

[16] Richard Kain, of the commentators on *Ulysses*, treats the satiric cast of the novel with the most understanding: *Fabulous Voyager* (Chicago, University of Chicago Press, 1947), chaps. i and xv.

[17] Ruel E. Foster, "Dream as Symbolic Act in Faulkner," *Perspective*, II (1949).

[18] Sumner C. Powell, "William Faulkner Celebrates Easter, 1928," *Perspective*, II (1949).

[19] George Marion O'Donnell in a remarkably seminal, if cursory, analysis of Faulkner's work ("Faulkner's Mythology," *Kenyon Review*, I, 1939) establishes this principle of interpretation. It is elaborated by Malcolm Cowley in the introduction to the *Viking Portable Faulkner* (New York, 1946). It is further modified by Robert Penn Warren in two essays that first appeared in *The New Republic* (1946); they are reprinted in *Forms of Modern Fiction*, ed. William Van O'Connor (Minneapolis, University of Minnesota Press, 1948).

from, the Sartoris-Compson code: Benjy by inherited idiocy; Candace by sexual promiscuity; Mr. Compson by rhetoric and liquor; Mrs. Compson by invalidism; Maury by liquor and laziness. The main conflict then is focused on Quentin and Jason, protagonists respectively of Sections II and III of the novel. But Section I has Benjy as the center of things. The reason for this is that Benjy, with an idiot's mind, is able to present the necessary exposition in not only its simplest tragic terms, but also in terms of symbols, which because they are from an idiot's mind are conveniently general in their meaning and are therefore flexible. It must be remembered, too, that Faulkner saw idiocy as a possible way for a Sartoris-Compson to escape the ethical rigor of a code that depends on exertion of intellect and will. Benjy's role, then, is both to reflect an aspect of Compson degeneracy and to introduce the terms of the main conflict with the simple, forceful symbols available to an idiot.

This conflict is centered on Quentin. Thus the central episode of the novel, which concerns him, is the crucial one. Quentin is determined to preserve the Sartoris-Compson traditions of humanism—in terms of the honor of the Compsons. His obsession is with his sister Candace, who has given in to Snopesism sexually; but Quentin must not accept the fact of her promiscuity, for to him, her honor is a symbol of the dying honor of the Compsons. He convinces himself that he is the violator of Candace's chastity. This conviction is finally without effect because no one else believes him. Eventually Quentin has to accept his defeat and recognition of the Compson defeat. Unable to stand this, he, too, escapes—by suicide.

Faulkner's method puts the struggle in terms of Quentin's psychic conflict, for it is on a prespeech level of mental life that

his actual defeat comes—his consciousness defeats him. He can escape everything (he goes to Harvard and he is a gentleman) except his knowledge of the truth. He even attempts to escape his consciousness of the factual world (he takes the hands off his watch; he attempts a substitute for his sister with the little Italian girl), but the only way to do this is by death. In an important sense, then, it is Quentin's consciousness that is his antagonist.

It is almost enough to submit that the advantages of the stream-of-consciousness method for this novel are explained by the central role consciousness itself plays in it. However, we might suggest here the advantages stream-of-consciousness fiction has in presenting symbols as substitutes for rationally formulated ideas. This can be illustrated in both the Benjy and Quentin sections of the novel. The two kinds of mental aberration represented reveal themselves naturally in terms of images and symbols. Because they are represented as coming directly from a premeditative stage of conscious activity, they carry a convincingness and a fuller impact than they otherwise would. The three symbols that signify everything for Benjy (firelight, the pasture, and Candace) are used so frequently that they come to dominate not only Benjy's consciousness, but the reader's also. Yet, such repetition has a naturalness about it because it comes from a mind as simple as Benjy's is. With Quentin, mental simplicity is not the thing; but obsession tends to give the same effect. Here the significance of the odor of honeysuckle image, the wedding announcement symbol, and all of the other symbol or image motifs grows in importance simply by the frequent repetition, which repetition is quite natural to an obsessed mind.

On a more immediate basis, the use of stream-of-consciousness techniques is appropriate in this novel because of the fundamental problem involved in describing an idiot or an obsessed person with any objectivity. Faulkner, among others, has done it out of a stream-of-consciousness context (in *The Hamlet*, *Wild Palms*, etc.), but never has he been able to get the objective distance necessary to prevent either a bizarre or farcical marring of it except in his stream-of-consciousness novels.

An additional effect Faulkner achieves is a contrast in *not* using stream-of-consciousness techniques in the last two episodes of the novel. It is in these sections that Jason's side of the story is presented. The techniques are soliloquy and conventional omniscient narration, with little attempt to present unspoken thoughts. The meaning this change of technique carries is that Jason's acceptance of the amoral Snopesian world is complete—it pervades his whole mental life; hence on the level of psychic life with which the novel had been dealing, there is no conflict for Jason. His conflicts are entirely in the material world of things and acts, not in the ideal one of thoughts.

So, it would seem on first consideration, are those of the characters in Faulkner's other stream-of-consciousness novel, *As I Lay Dying*. The poverty-stricken, ignorant, hill folk presented there are, however, not Snopeses, despite their Snopes-like qualities of hypocrisy, promiscuity, and avarice. The macabre pilgrimage to bury the dead, which is the central subject of the novel, is motivated by a sense of duty and honor as rigid as any the Sartoris-Compsons might have.

As I Lay Dying is, then, a marginal work in the Faulkner canon. It functions in relation to the whole Snopes-Sartoris drama as a device for repetition on a lighter scale—a minor parallel theme, so to speak. It deals with neither Snopeses nor Sartorises, but it does deal with the

question of ethical codes. The method of presentation involves showing the contrast of the Snopes-like external lives of the Bundrens (the selfishness of Anse, the promiscuity of Dewey Dell, etc.) with the Sartoris-like rigidity of their internal sense of form and moral obligation (the fortitude of Addie, the persistence in duty in Cash, the heroism and loyalty of Jewel, etc.). Through the use of soliloquy to present stream of consciousness, this inner aspect of these hill people is eloquently established. Their humanism is primitive and distorted, but it as rigid and moral as that of the Sartoris clan; and their animalism is as ugly and perverse as is that of the Snopeses—but there is ignorance, not amorality, at the base.

Stream-of-consciousness fiction is essentially a technical feat. Its successful working-out depended on technical resources exceeding those of any other type of fiction. Because this is so, any study of the genre must be essentially an examination of method. A study of devices and form becomes significant if we understand the achievement that justifies all of the virtuosity. Stream of consciousness is not technique for its own sake. It is based on a realization of the force of the drama that takes place in the minds of human beings.

One writer saw it as metaphysically significant, and her own predilections for the reality of visions led her to demonstrate the insight which the ordinary mind is capable of. For Virginia Woolf, the fleeting but vital visions of the human mind had to be expressed within the setting of that mind—and she was right; for she alone has been able to communicate precisely that sense of vision. Another writer saw it as high comedy, and he saw that it was pitiful too. Joyce's insight into man's mind was complemented by an equal insight into man's surface actions. The juxtaposition of the two was material for comedy, because the comparison between man's aspirations and his achievements was for Joyce the stuff of the comic: incongruity so great it could not produce tears, and if one were as faithless as Joyce was, it could not produce visions either. Faulkner saw one aspect of the drama as a tragedy of blood. (In other aspects he saw it as comedy, both high and low.) "The mind, mind has mountains" Faulkner might say; and he would have to add that the human being usually falls from the sheer cliffs to destruction. The tragedy of being conscious of a dying way of life, and the abortive attempts of the mind to lead the individual to isolation from the materials of a decaying reality gave Faulkner his themes. These come to the reader most forcibly in that writer's stream-of-consciousness novels, where the scene can be the one in which the tragedy actually takes place.

What these writers have contributed to fiction is broadly one thing: they have opened up for it a new area of life. They have added mental functioning and psychic existence to the already established domain of motive and action. They have created a fiction centered on the core of human experience, which if it has not been the usual domain of fiction, is not, they have proved, an improper one. Perhaps the most significant thing the stream-of-consciousness writers have demonstrated about the mind has been done obliquely: they have, through their contributions, proved that the human mind, especially the artist's, is too complex and wayward ever to be channeled into conventional patterns. . . .

CHAPTER 10

Symbolism, Allegory, and Myth

NATURALISM AND SYMBOLISM
Albert Cook*

Cook argues that all symbols, properly so called, whether "imaginative" or rationalistic, must start from actual facts and transcend them into meaning—the angels and devils of medieval literature, or Ibsen's wild duck. "How much the natural facts must change and combine does not determine the character of the fact in literature.... The angel of Dante and the wild duck of Ibsen belong in the same class as symbols; but the wild duck is as far removed from a barnyard duck of Zola as is the angel." Allegory, on the other hand, seeks the "physical representation of a *concept*."

These two great aesthetic movements of our time do not differ in rational basis from the classic–romantic antinomy. Naturalism, as selection of typical social events, equals classicism. Symbolism, like romanticism, can be either fanciful, as with the Surrealists, or imaginative, as with Mann, Kafka, Eliot. The difference is great, however, between the twentieth century and its predecessors. Ours is more willing to face the existence of evil, and is more pessimistic because the dichot-

omy between artist and society has become explicit, both financially and ideologically. How profoundly lonely and sour are these lines in *Bateau Ivre* [*The Drunken Boat*]:

Toute lune est atroce, et tout soleil amer.
L'âcre amour m'a gonflé de torpeurs enivrantes.
O! que ma quille éclate, O! que j'aille à la mer!

[Any moon is atrociously painful, and any sun bitter.
Acrid love has filled me with intoxicating torpors.

* The essay is reprinted from *The Dark Voyage and the Golden Mean*, by Albert Cook, by permission of the author. Copyright 1949 by Albert Cook.

335

Oh, let my keel split open, let me go to
the sea.]

To Rimbaud the wonderful of the moon-
richened night is only atrocious and the
probable of the glowing day only bitter.

All symbolism must start from actual
facts and symbolize them, rather than
combine them in merely logical patterns.
Dante said of his own symbolism that
the first level is the literal meaning. A
symbol that was not particularized in
some way would be either nonsymbol or
beyond symbol (God). For even the
three mystic rings in the last Canto of
the *Paradiso* are symbolic of the intuition
of God. They do not equal God though
they transcend His mere effects of light
and sound, however eternal and beautiful,
in the *primum mobile*.

A question of degree is at issue. To cite
two common symbols, the unicorn is further from natural fact than the fish; yet
the unicorn is a synthesis of several natural animals. Compare angels and devils
as symbols in medieval literature with
Ibsen's wild-duck symbol, where presumably the latter would be a "combination
of naturalism and symbolism." The angels and devils are imaginative syntheses
of known physiological facts (light, black-
ness, physical force, lovely eyes, wings);
the wild duck is a direct transformation
of a physical fact to the symbolic level.
Whole ducks exist in nature, as do the
separate physical facts that are synthe-
sized to create angel and devil symbols.
How much the natural facts must change
and combine does not determine the
character of the fact in literature. There
is either imaginative symbol or rationalist
type, depending on the practice of the
artist—assuming, as some do not, that

art can be merely rationalist. The angel
of Dante and the wild duck of Ibsen belong in the same class as symbols; but the
wild duck is as far removed from a barnyard duck of Zola as is the angel.

There is no such thing as "naturalism
and symbolism combined" in the foregoing sense of the terms, though symbolism
can include naturalism in transcending it.
Allegory is another matter. As John
Finley points out, allegory is the literary
method of the aesthetic rationalist; it is
generally embodied as a physical representation of a *concept* by one who
thinks probably and conceptually. Mr.
Worldly Wiseman is rationalist, allegorical; Dante's angel, whatever Dante may
have said rationally about him, is symbolic.

Joyce, then, does not achieve what has
been credited to him, a "combination of
naturalism and symbolism," not even
outside the terminology of our system,
although Dostoievsky or Shakespeare
might. His writing is not symbolistic, but
fourth-dimensional allegory. In *Ulysses*,
family patterns, father-son, Bloom-Ste-
phen, art-science, the events of the
Odyssey, the times of day, the geography
of Dublin, significant human events
(birth, death, adultery, marriage, job)
are analogically juxtaposed against one
another, but allegorically and rational-
istically. It is significant that both Joyce's
great books are probable, social, man-
nered.... To a conceptualist, this criticism of Joyce will appear a quibble. To
one who understands symbolism (which
Joyce half believed in, but was unable to
achieve), it is the basic question to ask
about the *attitude* of his art—scope being
wholly, and depth partly another matter.

FROM THE SYMBOLISM OF POETRY
William Butler Yeats*

All sounds, all colors, all forms, either because of their preordained
energies or because of long association, evoke indefinable yet precise responses which cannot be transcribed into prose. Yeats
distinguishes between emotional symbols (white, purple) and intellectual symbols (a cross, a crown of thorns), and between
symbolism as the essence of poetry and "descriptions of nature for
the sake of nature, of the moral law for the sake of the moral
law."

. . . In "Symbolism in Painting," I tried
to describe the element of symbolism
that is in pictures and sculpture, and described a little the symbolism in poetry,
but did not describe at all the continuous
indefinable symbolism which is the substance of all style.

There are no lines with more melancholy beauty than these by Burns—

The white moon is setting behind the white
    wave.
And Time is setting with me, O!

and these lines are perfectly symbolical.
Take from them the whiteness of the
moon and of the wave, whose relation to
the setting of Time is too subtle for the
intellect, and you take from them their
beauty. But, when all are together, moon
and wave and whiteness and setting Time
and the last melancholy cry, they evoke
an emotion which cannot be evoked by
any other arrangement of colours and
sounds and forms. We may call this
metaphorical writing, but it is better to
call it symbolical writing, because metaphors are not profound enough to be

* Reprinted with permission of The Macmillan Company from *Essays and Introduc-
tions* by William Butler Yeats. © Mrs. W. B.
Yeats, 1961.

moving, when they are not symbols, and
when they are symbols they are the most
perfect of all, because the most subtle,
outside of pure sound, and through them
one can the best find out what symbols
are. If one begins the reverie with any
beautiful lines that one can remember,
one finds they are like those of Burns.
Begin with this line by Blake—

The gay fishes on the wave when the moon
    sucks up the dew;

or these lines by Nash—

Queens have died young and fair,
Brightness falls from the air,
Dust hath closed Helen's eye;

or these lines by Shakespeare—

Timon hath made his everlasting mansion
Upon the beached verge of the salt flood;
Who once a day with his embossed froth
The turbulent surge shall cover;

or take some line that is quite simple,
that gets its beauty from its place in a
story, and see how it flickers with the
light of the many symbols that have
given the story its beauty, as a sword-

blade may flicker with the light of burning towers.

All sounds, all colours, all forms, either because of their preordained energies or because of long association, evoke indefinable and yet precise emotions, or, as I prefer to think, call down among us certain disembodied powers, whose footsteps over our hearts we call emotions; and when sound, and colour, and form are in a musical relation, a beautiful relation to one another, they become as it were one sound, one colour, one form, and evoke emotion that is made out of their distinct evocations and yet is one emotion. . . .

Besides emotional symbols, symbols that evoke emotions alone,—and in this sense all alluring or hateful things are symbols, although their relations with one another are too subtle to delight us fully, away from rhythm and pattern,—there are intellectual symbols, symbols that evoke ideas alone, or ideas mingled with emotions; and outside the very definite traditions of mysticism and the less definite criticism of certain modern poets, these alone are called symbols. Most things belong to one or another kind, according to the way we speak of them and the companions we give them, for symbols, associated with ideas that are more than fragments of the shadows thrown upon the intellect by the emotions they evoke, are the playthings of the allegorist or the pedant, and soon pass away. If I say "white" or "purple" in an ordinary line of poetry, they evoke emotions so exclusively that I cannot say why they move me; but if I bring them into the same sentence with such obvious intellectual symbols as a cross or a crown of thorns, I think of purity and sovereignty. Furthermore, innumerable meanings, which are held to "white" or to "purple" by bonds of subtle suggestion, and alike in the emotions and in the in-

tellect, move visibly through my mind, and more invisibly beyond the threshold of sleep, casting lights and shadows of an indefinable wisdom on what had seemed before, it may be, but sterility and noisy violence. It is the intellect that decides where the reader shall ponder over the procession of the symbols, and if the symbols are merely emotional, he gazes from amid the accidents and destinies of the world; but if the symbols are intellectual too, he becomes himself a part of pure intellect, and he is himself mingled with the procession. If I watch a rushy pool in the moonlight, my emotion at its beauty is mixed with memories of the man that I have seen ploughing by its margin, or of the lovers I saw there a night ago; but if I look at the moon herself and remember any of her ancient names and meanings, I move among divine people, and things that have shaken off our mortality, the tower of ivory, the queen of waters, the shining stag among enchanted woods, the white hare sitting upon the hilltop, the fool of faery with his shining cup full of dreams, and it may be "make a friend of one of these images of wonders," and "meet the Lord in the air." So, too, if one is moved by Shakespeare, who is content with emotional symbols that he may come the nearer to our sympathy, one is mixed with the whole spectacle of the world; while if one is moved by Dante, or by the myth of Demeter, one is mixed into the shadow of God or of a goddess. So too one is furthest from symbols when one is busy doing this or that, but the soul moves among symbols and unfolds in symbols when trance, or madness, or deep meditation has withdrawn it from every impulse but its own. "I then saw," wrote Gérard de Nerval of his madness, "vaguely drifting into form, plastic images of antiquity, which outlined themselves, became definite, and seemed to represent symbols of which I only seized the idea with difficulty." In an earlier time he would have been of that multitude, whose souls austerity withdrew, even more perfectly than madness could withdraw his soul, from hope and memory, from desire and regret, that they might reveal those processions of symbols that men bow to before altars, and woo with incense and offerings. But being of our time, he has been like Maeterlinck, like Villiers de l'Isle Adam in *Axël*, like all who are preoccupied with intellectual symbols in our time, a foreshadower of the new sacred book, of which all the arts, as somebody has said, are begging to dream. How can the arts overcome the slow dying of men's hearts that we call the progress of the world, and lay their hands upon men's heart-strings again, without becoming the garment of religion as in old times?

If people were to accept the theory that poetry moves us because of its symbolism, what change should one look for in the manner of our poetry? A return to the way of our fathers, a casting out of descriptions of nature for the sake of nature, of the moral law for the sake of the moral law, a casting out of all anecdotes and of that brooding over scientific opinion that so often extinguished the central flame in Tennyson, and of that vehemence that would make us do or not do certain things; or, in other words, we should come to understand that the beryl stone was enchanted by our fathers that it might unfold the pictures in its heart, and not to mirror our own excited faces, or the boughs waving outside the window. With this change of substance, this return to imagination, this understanding that the laws of art, which are the hidden laws of the world, can alone bind the imagination, would come a change of style, and we would cast out of serious poetry those energetic rhythms, as of a man running, which are the invention of the will with its eyes always on something to be done or undone; and we would seek out those wavering, meditative, organic rhythms, which are the embodiment of the imagination, that neither desires nor hates, because it has done with time, and only wishes to gaze upon some reality, some beauty; nor would it be any longer possible for anybody to deny the importance of form, in all its kinds, for although you can expound an opinion, or describe a thing when your words are not quite well chosen, you cannot give a body to something that moves beyond the senses, unless your words are as subtle, as complex, as full of mysterious life, as the body of a flower or of a woman. The form of sincere poetry, unlike the form of the popular poetry, may indeed be sometimes obscure, or ungrammatical as in some of the best of the Songs of Innocence and Experience, but it must have the perfections that escape analysis, the subtleties that have a new meaning every day, and it must have all this whether it be but a little song made out of a moment of dreamy indolence, or some great epic made out of the dreams of one poet and of a hundred generations whose hands were never weary of the sword.

SETTLING THE COLONEL'S HASH
Mary McCarthy*

Mary McCarthy attacks the current literary craze of symbolizing. She defines metaphor as part of our means of communication; then, turning to "literary symbolism," she claims that the meaning behind the symbol becomes confused in some vast fairyland of myth, a "dream forest" where "all symbols become arbitrary. . . . The Colonel's hash can be a Eucharist or a cannibal feast or the banquet of Atreus. . . ." She points out the uniqueness of a valid symbol, like the whale in *Moby Dick*, the train in *Anna Karenina*. These symbols derive their power from the work and in turn contribute an added dimension to the work. They do not necessarily relate to any system of meaning beyond the story itself. Symbols arise from the commonplace, not from some vast and ambiguous mythical system.

Seven years ago, when I taught in a progressive college, I had a pretty girl student in one of my classes who wanted to be a short-story writer. She was not studying writing with me, but she knew that I sometimes wrote short stories, and one day, breathless and glowing, she came up to me in the hall, to tell me that she had just written a story that her writing teacher, a Mr. Converse, was terribly excited about.

"He thinks it's wonderful," she said, "and he's going to help me fix it up for publication."

I asked what the story was about; the girl was a rather simple being who loved clothes and dates. Her answer had a deprecating tone. It was just about a girl (herself) and some sailors she had met on the train. But then her face, which had looked perturbed for a moment, gladdened.

"Mr. Converse is going over it with me and we're going to put in the symbols."

Another girl in the same college, when asked by us in her sophomore orals why she read novels (one of the pseudo-profound questions that ought never to be put) answered in a defensive flurry: "Well, *of course*, I don't read them to find out what happens to the hero."

At the time, I thought these notions were peculiar to progressive education: it was old-fashioned or regressive to read a novel to find out what happens to the hero or to have a mere experience empty of symbolic pointers. But I now discover that this attitude is quite general, and that readers and students all over the country are in a state of apprehension, lest they read a book or story literally and miss the presence of a symbol. And like everything in America, this search for meanings has become a socially competitive enterprise; the best reader is the one who detects the most symbols in a given stretch of prose. And the be-nighted reader who fails to find any symbols humbly assents when they are pointed out to him; he accepts his morti-fication.

I had no idea how far this process had gone until last spring, when I began to get responses to a story I had published in *Harper's*. I say "story" because that was what it was called by *Harper's*. I myself would not know quite what to call it; it was a fragment of autobiography—an account of my meeting with an anti-Semitic army Colonel. It began in the club car of a train going to St. Louis; I was wearing an apple-green shirtwaist and a dark-green skirt and pink earrings; we got into an argument about the Jews. The Colonel was a rather dapper, flashy kind of Irish-American with a worldly blue eye; he took me, he said, for a sculptress, which made me feel, to my horror, that I looked Bohemian and therefore rather suspect. He was full of the usual profound clichés that anti-Semites air, like original epigrams, about the Jews: that he could tell a Jew, that they were different from other people, that you couldn't trust them in business, that some of his best friends were Jews, that he distinguished between a Jew and a kike, and finally that, of course, he didn't agree with Hitler; Hitler went too far; the Jews were human beings.

All the time we talked, and I defended the Jews, he was trying to get my angle, as he called it; he thought it was ab-normal for anybody who wasn't Jewish not to feel as he did. As a matter of fact, I have a Jewish grandmother, but I de-cided to keep this news to myself: I did not want the Colonel to think that I had any interested reason for speaking on be-half of the Jews, that is, that I was preju-diced. In the end, though, I got my come-uppance. Just as we were parting, the Colonel asked me my married name,

which is Broadwater, and the whole mys-tery was cleared up for him, instantly; he supposed I was married to a Jew and that the name was spelled B-r-o-dwater. I did not try to enlighten him; I let him think what he wanted; in a certain sense, he was right; he had unearthed my Jewish grandmother or her equivalent. There were a few details that I must mention to make the next part clear: in my car, there were two nuns, whom I talked to as a distraction from the Colonel and the moral problems he raised. He and I finally had lunch together in the St. Louis rail-road station, where we continued the dis-cussion. It was a very hot day. I had a sandwich; he had roast-beef hash. We both had an old-fashioned.

The whole point of this "story" was that it really happened; it is written in the first person; I speak of myself in my own name, McCarthy; at the end, I mention my husband's name, Broadwater. When I was thinking about writing the story, I decided not to treat it fictionally; the chief interest, I felt, lay in the fact that it happened, in real life, last sum-mer, to the writer herself, who was a good deal at fault in the incident. I wanted to embarrass myself and, if possible, the reader too.

Yet, strangely enough, many of my readers preferred to think of this account as fiction. I still meet people who ask me confidentially, "That story of yours about the Colonel;—was it really true?" It seemed to them perfectly natural that I would write a fabrication, in which I figured under my own name, and sign it, though in my eyes this would be like perjuring yourself in court or forging checks. Shortly after the story was pub-lished, I got a kindly letter from a man in Mexico, in which he criticized the menu from an artistic point of view: he thought salads would be better for hot weather and it would be more in character for the narrator-heroine to have a martini. I did not answer the letter, though I was moved to, because I had the sense that he would not understand the distinction between what *ought* to have happened and what *did* happen.

Then in April I got another letter, from an English teacher in a small college in the Middle West, that reduced me to despair. I am going to cite it at length. "My students in freshmen English chose to analyze your story, 'Artists in Uniform,' from the March issue of *Harper's*. For a week I heard oral discussions on it and then the students wrote critical analyses. In so far as it is possible, I stayed out of their discussions, encouraging them to read the story closely with your intentions as a guide to their understanding. Although some of them insisted that the story has no other level than the realistic one, most of them decided it has symbolic overtones.

"The question is: how closely do you want the symbols labeled? They wrestled with the nuns, the author's two shades of green with pink accents, with the 'materialistic godlessness' of the Colonel.... A surprising number wanted exact symbols; for example, they searched for the significance of the Colonel's eating hash and the author eating a sandwich.... From my standpoint, the story was an entirely satisfactory springboard for understanding the various shades of prejudice, for seeing how much of the artist goes into his painting. If it is any satisfaction to you, our campus was alive with discussion about 'Artists in Uniform.' We liked the story and we thought it amazing that an author could succeed in making readers dislike the author—for a purpose, of course!"

I probably should have answered this letter, but I did not. The gulf seemed to me too wide. I could not applaud the backward students who insisted that the story has no other level than the realistic one without giving offense to their teacher, who was evidently a well-meaning person. But I shall try now to address a reply, not to this teacher and her unfortunate class, but to a whole school of misunderstanding. There were no symbols in this story; there was no deeper level. The nuns were in the story because they were on the train; the contrasting greens were the dress I happened to be wearing; the Colonel had hash because he had hash; materialistic godlessness meant just what it means when a priest thunders it from the pulpit—the phrase, for the first time, had meaning for me as I watched and listened to the Colonel.

But to clarify the misunderstanding, one must go a little further and try to see what a literary symbol is. Now in one sense, the Colonel's hash and my sandwich can be regarded as symbols; that is, they typify the Colonel's food tastes and mine. (The man in Mexico had different food tastes which he wished to interpose into our reality.) The hash and the sandwich might even be said to show something very obvious about our sexes; I was a woman, he was a man. And though on another day I might have ordered hash myself, that day I did not, because the Colonel and I, in our disagreement, were polarizing each other.

The hash and the sandwich, then, could be regarded as symbols of our disagreement, almost conscious symbols. And underneath our discussion of the Jews, there was a thin sexual current running, as there always is in such random encounters or pick-ups (for they have a strong suggestion of the illicit). The fact that I ordered something conventionally feminine and he ordered something conventionally masculine represented, no doubt, our awareness of a sexual possibility; even though I was not attracted to the Colonel, or he to me, the circumstances of our meeting made us define ourselves as a woman and a man.

The sandwich and the hash were our provisional, *ad hoc* symbols of ourselves. But in this sense all human actions are symbolic because they represent the person who does them. If the Colonel had ordered a fruit salad with whipped cream, this too would have represented him in some way; given his other traits, it would have pointed to a complexity in his character that the hash did not suggest.

In the same way, the contrasting greens of my dress were a symbol of my taste in clothes and hence representative of me—all too representative, I suddenly saw, in the club car, when I got an "artistic" image of myself flashed back at me from the men's eyes. I had no wish to stylize myself as an artist, that is, to parade about as a symbol of flamboyant unconventionality, but apparently I had done so unwittingly when I picked those colors off a rack, under the impression that they suited me or "expressed my personality" as salesladies say.

My dress, then, was a symbol of the perplexity I found myself in with the Colonel; I did not want to be categorized as a member of a peculiar minority—an artist or a Jew; but brute fate and the Colonel kept resolutely cramming me into both those uncomfortable pigeonholes. I wished to be regarded as ordinary or rather as universal, to be anybody and therefore everybody (that is, in one sense, I wanted to be on the Colonel's side, majestically above minorities); but every time the Colonel looked at my dress and me in it with my pink earrings I shrank to minority status, and felt the dress in the heat shriveling me, like the shirt of Nessus, the centaur, that consumed Hercules.

But this is not what the students meant when they wanted the symbols "labeled."

They were searching for a more recondite significance than that afforded by the trite symbolism of ordinary life, in which a dress is a social badge. They supposed that I was engaging in literary or artificial symbolism, which would lead the reader out of the confines of reality into the vast fairy tale of myth, in which the color green would have an emblematic meaning (or did the two greens signify for them what the teacher calls "shades" of prejudice), and the Colonel's hash, I imagine, would be some sort of Eucharistic mincemeat.

Apparently, the presence of the nuns assured them there were overtones of theology; it did not occur to them (a) that the nuns were there because pairs of nuns are a standardized feature of summer Pullman travel, like crying babies, and perspiring business men in the club car, and (b) that if I thought the nuns worth mentioning, it was also because of something very simple and directly relevant; the nuns and the Colonel and I all had something in common—we had all at one time been Catholics—and I was seeking common ground with the Colonel, from which to turn and attack his position.

In any account of reality, even a televised one, which comes closest to being a literal transcript or replay, some details are left out as irrelevant (though nothing is really irrelevant). The details that are not eliminated have to stand as symbols of the whole, like stenographic signs, and of course there is an art of selection, even in a newspaper account: the writer, if he has any ability, is looking for the revealing detail that will sum up the picture for the reader in a flash of recognition.

But the art of abridgment and condensation, which is familiar to anybody who tries to relate an anecdote or give a direction—the art of natural symbolism, which is at the basis of speech and all representation—has at bottom a centripetal intention. It hovers over an object, an event, or series of events and tries to declare what it is. Analogy (that is, comparison to other objects) is inevitably one of its methods. "The weather was soupy," *i.e.*, like soup. "He wedged his way in," *i.e.*, he had to enter, thin edge first, as a wedge enters, and so on. All this is obvious. But these metaphorical aids to communication are a far cry from literary symbolism, as taught in the schools and practiced by certain fashionable writers. Literary symbolism is centrifugal and flees from the object, the event, into the incorporeal distance, where concepts are taken for substance and floating ideas and archetypes assume a hieratic authority.

In this dream-forest, symbols become arbitrary; all counters are interchangeable; anything can stand for anything else. The Colonel's hash can be a Eucharist or a cannibal feast or the banquet of Atreus, or all three, so long as the actual dish set before the actual man is disparaged. What is depressing about this insistent symbolization is the fact that while it claims to lead to the infinite, it quickly reaches very finite limits—there are only so many myths on record, and once you have got through Bulfinch, the Scandinavian, and the Indian there is not much left. And if all stories reduce themselves to myth and symbol, qualitative differences vanish, and there is only a single, monotonous story.

American fiction of the symbolist school demonstrates this mournful truth, without precisely intending to. A few years ago, when the mode was at its height, chic novels and stories fell into three classes; those which had a Greek myth for their framework, which the reader was supposed to detect, like finding the faces in the clouds in old newspaper puzzle contests; those which had symbolic modern figures, dwarfs, her-maphrodites, and cripples, illustrating maiming and loneliness; and those which contained symbolic animals, cougars, wild cats, and monkeys. One young novelist, a product of the Princeton school of symbolism, had all three elements going at once, like the ringmaster of a three-ring circus, with the freaks, the animals, and the statues.

The quest for symbolic referents had, as its object, of course the deepening of the writer's subject and the reader's awareness. But the result was paradoxical. At the very moment when American writing was penetrated by the symbolic urge, it ceased to be able to create symbols of its own. Babbitt, I suppose, was the last important symbol to be created by an American writer; he gave his name to a type that henceforth would be recognizable to everybody. He passed into the language. The same thing could be said, perhaps though to a lesser degree, of Caldwell's Tobacco Road, Eliot's Prufrock, and possibly of Faulkner's Snopeses. The discovery of new symbols is not the only function of a writer, but the writer who cares about this must be fascinated by reality itself, as a butterfly collector is fascinated by the glimpse of a new specimen. Such a specimen was Mme. Bovary or M. Homais or M. de Charlus or Jupien; these specimens were precious to their discoverers, not because they repeated an age-old pattern but because their markings were new. Once the specimen has been described, the public instantly spots other examples of the kind, and the world seems suddenly full of Babbitts and Charlus, where none had been noted before.

A different matter was Joyce's Mr. Bloom. Mr. Bloom can be called a symbol of eternal recurrence—the wandering Jew, Ulysses the voyager—but he is a symbol thickly incarnate, fleshed out in a Dublin advertising-canvasser. He is not like Ulysses or vaguely suggestive of Ulysses; he is Ulysses, circa 1905. Joyce evidently believed in a cyclical theory of history, in which everything repeated itself; he also subscribed in youth to the doctrine of the Incarnation, which declares that the Host, a piece of bread, is also God's body and blood. How it can be both things at the same time, consubstantially, is a mystery, and Mr. Bloom is just such a mystery: Ulysses in the visible Appearance of a Dublin advertising-canvasser.

Mr. Bloom is not a symbol of Ulysses, but Ulysses-Bloom together, one and indivisible, symbolize or rather demonstrate eternal recurrence. I hope I make myself clear. The point is consubstantiation: Bloom and Ulysses are transfused into each other and neither reality is diminished. Both realities are locked together, like the protons and neutrons of an atom. *Finnegans Wake* is a still more ambitious attempt to create a fusion, this time a myriad fusion, and to exemplify the mystery of how a thing can be itself and at the same time be something else. The world is many and it is also one.

But the clarity and tension of Joyce's thought brought him closer in a way to the strictness of allegory than to the diffuse practices of latter-day symbolists. In Joyce, the equivalences and analogies are very sharp and distinct and the real world is almost querulously audible, like the voices of the washer-women on the Liffey that come into Earwicker's dream. But this is not true of Joyce's imitators or of the imitators of his imitators, for whom reality is only a shadowy pretext for the introduction of a whole *corps de ballet* of dancing symbols in mythic draperies and animal skins.

Let me make a distinction. There are some great writers, like Joyce or Melville, who have consciously introduced symbolic elements into their work; and there

are great writers who have written fables or allegories. In both cases, the writer makes it quite clear to the reader how he is to be read; only an idiot would take *Pilgrim's Progress* for a realistic story, and even a young boy, reading *Moby Dick*, realizes that there is something more than whale-fishing here, though he cannot be sure what it is. But the great body of fiction contains only what I have called natural symbolism, in which selected events represent or typify a problem, a kind of society or psychology, a philosophical theory, in the same way they do in real life. What happens to the hero becomes of the highest importance. This symbolism needs no abstruse interpretation and abstruse interpretation will only lead the reader away from the reality that the writer is trying to press on his attention.

I will give an example or two of what I mean by natural symbolism and I will begin with a rather florid one: Henry James's *The Golden Bowl*. This is the story of a rich American girl who collects European objects. One of these objects is a husband, a Prince Amerigo, who proves to be unfaithful. Early in the story, there is a visit to an antique shop in which the Prince picks out a gold bowl for his fiancée and finds, to his annoyance, that it is cracked. It is not hard to see that the cracked bowl is a symbol, both of the Prince himself, who is a valuable antique but a little flawed, morally, and also of the marriage, which represents an act of acquisition or purchase on the part of the heroine and her father. If the reader should fail to notice the analogy, James himself helps him out in the title.

I myself would not regard the introduction of this symbol as necessary to this particular history; it seems to me, rather, an ornament of the kind that was fashionable in the architecture and interior decoration of the period, like stylized sheaves of corn or wreaths on the façade of a house. Nevertheless, it is handsome and has an obvious appropriateness to the theme. It leads the reader into the gilded matter of the novel, rather than away from it. I think there is also a scriptural echo in the title that conveys the idea of punishment. But having seen and felt the weight of meaning that James put in this symbol, one must not be tempted to go further and look at the bowl as a female sex symbol, a chalice, the Holy Grail, and so on; a book is not a pious excuse for reciting a litany of associations.

My second example is from Tolstoy's *Anna Karenina*. At the beginning of the novel, Anna meets the man who will be her lover, Vronsky, on the Moscow-St. Petersburg express; as they meet, there has been an accident; a workman has been killed by the train coming in to the station. This is the beginning of Anna's doom, which is completed when she throws herself under a train and is killed; and the last we see of Vronsky is in a train, with a toothache; he is being seen off by a friend to the wars. The train is necessary to the plot of the novel, and I believe it is also symbolic, both of the iron forces of material progress that Tolstoy hated so and that played a part in Anna's moral destruction, and also of those iron laws of necessity and consequence that govern human action when it remains on the sensual level.

One can read the whole novel, however, without being aware that the train is a symbol; we do not have to "interpret" to feel the import of doom and loneliness conveyed by the train's whistle —the same import we ourselves can feel when we hear a train go by in the country, even today. Tolstoy was a greater artist than James, and one cannot be certain that the train was a conscious device with him. The appropriateness to Anna's history may have been only a *felt* appropriateness; everything in Tolstoy has such a supreme naturalness that one shrinks from attributing contrivance to him, as if it were a sort of fraud. Yet he worked very hard on his novels—I forget how many times the Countess Tolstoy copied out *War and Peace* by hand.

The impression one gets from his diaries is that he wrote by ear; he speaks repeatedly, even as an old man, of having to start a story over again because he has the wrong tone, and I suspect that he did not think of the train as a symbol but that it sounded "right" to him, because it was, in that day, an almost fearsome emblem of ruthless and impersonal force, not only to a writer of genius but to the poorest peasant who watched it pass through the fields. And in Tolstoy's case, I think it would be impossible, even for the most fanciful critic, to extricate the train from the novel and try to make it bear a meaning that the novel itself does not proclaim, explicitly and tacitly, on every page. Every detail in Tolstoy has an almost cruel and vise-like meaningfulness and truth to itself that makes it tautological to talk of symbolism; he was a moralist and to him the tiniest action, even the curiosities of physical appearance, Vronsky's bald spot, the small white hands of Prince Andrei, told a moral tale.

It is now considered very old-fashioned and tasteless to speak of an author's "philosophy of life" as something that can be harvested from his work. Actually, most of the great authors did have a philosophy of life which they were eager to communicate to the public; this was one of their motives for writing. And to disentangle a moral philosophy from a work that evidently contains one is far less damaging to the author's purpose and the integrity of his art than to violate his imagery by symbol-hunting, as though reading a novel were a sort of paper chase.

The images of a novel or a story belong, as it were, to a family, very closely knit and inseparable from each other; the parent "idea" of a story or a novel generates events and images all bearing a strong family resemblance. And to understand a story or a novel, you must look for the parent "idea" which is usually in plain view, if you read quite carefully and literally what the author says.

I will go back, for a moment, to my own story, to show how this can be done. Clearly, it is about the Jewish question, for that is what the people are talking about. It also seems to be about artists, since the title is "Artists in Uniform." Then there must be some relation between artists and Jews. What is it? They are both minorities that other people claim to be able to recognize by their appearance. But artists and Jews do not care for this categorization; they want to be universal, that is, like everybody else. But this aim is really hopeless, for life has formed them as Jews or artists, in a way that immediately betrays them to the majority they are trying to melt into. In my conversation with the Colonel, I was endeavoring to play a double game. I was trying to force him into a minority by treating anti-Semitism as an aberration, which, in fact, I believe it is. On his side, the Colonel resisted this attempt and tried to show that anti-Semitism was normal, and he was normal, while I was the queer one. He declined to be categorized as an anti-Semite; he regarded himself as an independent thinker, who by happy chance thought the same as everybody else.

I imagined I had a card up my sleeve; I had guessed that the Colonel was Irish (*i.e.*, that he belonged to a minority) and presumed that he was a Catholic. I did not see how he could possibly guess that

I, with my Irish name and Irish appearance, had a Jewish grandmother in the background. Therefore when I found I had not convinced him by reasoning, I played my last card; I told him that the Church, his Church, forbade anti-Semitism. I went even further; I implied that God forbade it, though I had no right to do this, since I did not believe in God, but was only using Him as a whip to crack over the Colonel, to make him feel humble and inferior, a raw Irish Catholic lad under discipline. But the Colonel, it turned out, did not believe in God, either, and I lost. And since, in a sense, I had been cheating all along in this game we were playing, I had to concede the Colonel a sort of moral victory in the end; I let him think that my husband was Jewish and that that "explained" everything satisfactorily.

Now there are a number of morals or meanings in this little tale, starting with the simple one: don't talk to strangers on a train. The chief moral or meaning (what I learned, in other words, from this experience) was this: you cannot be a universal unless you accept the fact that you are a singular, that is, a Jew or an artist or what-have-you. What the Colonel and I were discussing, and at the same time illustrating and enacting, was the definition of a human being. I was trying to be something better than a human being: I was trying to be the voice of pure reason; and pride went before a fall. The Colonel, without trying, was being something worse than a human being, and somehow we found ourselves on the same plane—facing each other, like mutually repellent twins. Or, put it another way: it is dangerous to be drawn into discussions of the Jews with anti-Semites: you delude yourself that you are spreading light, but you are really sinking into muck; if you endeavor to be dispassionate, you are really claiming for yourself a privileged position, a little mountain top, from which you look down, impartially, on both the Jews and the Colonel.

Anti-Semitism is a horrible disease from which nobody is immune, and it has a kind of evil fascination that makes an enlightened person draw near the source of infection, supposedly in a scientific spirit, but really to sniff the vapors and dally with the possibility. The enlightened person who lunches with the Colonel in order, as she tells herself, to improve him, is cheating herself, having her cake and eating it. This attempted cheat, on my part, was related to the question of the artist and the green dress; I wanted to be an artist but not to pay the price of looking like one, just as I was willing to have Jewish blood but not willing to show it, where it would cost me something—the loss of superiority in an argument.

These meanings are all there, quite patent, to anyone who consents to look *into* the story. They were *in* the experience itself, waiting to be found and considered. I did not perceive them all at the time the experience was happening; otherwise, it would not have taken place, in all probability—I should have given the Colonel a wide berth. But when I went back over the experience, in order to write it, I came upon these meanings, protruding at me, as it were, from the details of the occasion. I put in the green dress and my mortification over it because they were part of the truth, just as it had occurred, but I did not see how they were related to the general question of anti-Semitism and my grandmother until they *showed* me their relation in the course of writing.

Every short story, at least for me, is a little act of discovery. A cluster of details presents itself to my scrutiny, like a mystery that I will understand in the course of writing or sometimes not fully until

afterward, when, if I have been honest and listened to these details carefully, I will find that they are connected and that there is a coherent pattern. This pattern is *in* experience itself; you do not impose it from the outside and if you try to, you will find that the story is taking the wrong tack, dribbling away from you into artificiality or inconsequence. A story that you do not learn something from while you are writing it, that does not illuminate something for you, is dead, finished before you started it. The "idea" of a story is implicit in it, on the one hand; on the other hand, it is always ahead of the writer, like a form dimly discerned in the distance; he is working *toward* the "idea."

It can sometimes happen that you begin a story thinking that you know the "idea" of it and find, when you are finished, that you have said something quite different and utterly unexpected to you. Most writers have been haunted all their lives by the "idea" of a story or a novel that they think they want to write and see very clearly: Tolstoy always wanted to write a novel about the Decembrists and instead, almost against his will, wrote *War and Peace*; Henry James thought he wanted to write a novel about Napoleon. Probably these ideas for novels were too set in their creators' minds to inspire creative discovery.

In any work that is truly creative, I believe, the writer cannot be omniscient in advance about the effects that he proposes to produce. The suspense in a novel is not only in the reader, but in the novelist himself, who is intensely curious too about what will happen to the hero. Jane Austen may know in a general way that Emma will marry Mr. Knightley in the end (the reader knows this too, as a matter of fact); the suspense for the author lies in the how, in the twists and turns of circumstance, waiting but as yet unknown, that will bring the consummation about. Hence, I would say to the student of writing that outlines, patterns, arrangements of symbols may have a certain usefulness at the outset for some kinds of minds, but in the end they will have to be scrapped. If the story does not contradict the outline, overrun the pattern, break the symbols, like an insurrection against authority, it is surely a stillbirth. The natural symbolism of reality has more messages to communicate than the dry Morse code of the disengaged mind.

The tree of life, said Hegel, is greener than the tree of thought; I have quoted this before but I cannot forbear from citing it again in this context. This is not an incitement to mindlessness or an endorsement of realism in the short story (there are several kinds of reality, including interior reality); it means only that the writer must be, first of all, a listener and observer, who can pay attention to reality, like an obedient pupil, and who is willing, always, to be surprised by the messages reality is sending through to him. And if he gets the messages correctly he will not have to go back and put in the symbols; he will find that the symbols are there, staring at him significantly from the commonplace.

FROM SYMBOL AND MYTH
George Whalley*

An image becomes a symbol by losing its "opaqueness as a 'thing-in-itself'" and serving as a "lens through which the poet 'sees' a world of spirit" beyond reality, Whalley argues. "Myth is ... a grouping of symbols which brings them into resonance with each other to embody a comprehensive view of reality." Myth deteriorates, he goes on to say, when (1) in taking on narrative form it becomes *legend* ("a narrative which treats (or purports to treat) of historical events with some imaginative freedom"), (2) its symbolic coherence is submitted to "the alien coherence of logic," (3) it is lost in an unstable society amid a multitude of unrelated beliefs, or (4) it becomes crystallized into system.

... If an image is to become a symbol, an integral part of the reality which it renders intelligible, it must in experience serve a double function. It will assume a focal position as an object of contemplation (whether or not "actually" present): the poet's attention concentrates in a "fixed gaze," and an activity supervenes which is not that of observation but of

* The selection is reprinted from *Poetic Process*, by George Whalley, by permission of Routledge & Kegan Paul, Ltd. Copyright 1953 by Routledge & Kegan Paul, Ltd.

vision in the mystical sense. The object loses its distinct outline as "thing" and its opaqueness as a "thing-in-itself"; it becomes translucent, luminous, the focal point through which the complex energy of an event of reality flows in, the lens through which the poet "sees" a world of spirit beyond. This world he recognizes as his world of here-and-now transfigured. In this heightened mood of vision "images of memory flow in on the impulse of immediate perception," and in the developing event of reality the focal image, the symbol, sustains and concentrates the whole feeling of the event. If the feeling of the event is to be enucleated and bodied forth with its pristine power and with structural fidelity, the focal symbol alone cannot be a sufficient vehicle: the symbol may be there by accident, and in any case it cannot be a direct substitute for the event. When the process moves from contemplation into the purifying phase of embodiment, the focal symbols gather to themselves— from the perceived present and from the shaping well of memory—other images, thoughts, tunes. If the poet is faithfully to embody his moment of vision he requires not only distinct symbols but "a system of symbols." "All art is sensuous," Yeats admits; "but when a man puts only his contemplative nature and his more vague desires into his art, the sensuous images through which it speaks become broken, fleeting, uncertain, or are chosen for their distance from general experience, and all grows unsubstantial and fantastic. When imagination moves in a dim world . . . we go to it for delight indeed but in our weariness. If we are to sojourn there that world must grow consistent with itself, emotion must be related to emotion by a system of ordered images. . . . It must grow to be symbolic, that is, for the soul can only achieve a distinct separated life where many related objects at once distinguish and arouse its energies in its fullness." Symbols appear in clusters, in ordered patterns, harmoniously disposed. And when Coleridge shifts from a visual to a sonic term we are reminded again of the metaphorical resonance. . . .

A myth is a direct metaphysical statement beyond science. It embodies in an articulated structure of symbol or narrative a vision of reality. It is a condensed account of man's Being and attempts to represent reality with structural fidelity, to indicate at a single stroke the salient and fundamental relations which for a man constitute reality. A myth in this sense is primitive, communal, and religious in origin; and its only possible mode of expression is Poetic. Myth is not an obscure, oblique, or elaborate way of expressing reality—it is the *only* way. Myth has as its purpose, its source and end, revelation; myth is not make-believe but the most direct and positive assertion of belief that man can discover.[1] Myth is an indispensable principle of unity in individual lives and in the life of society.

"Make-believe is an enervating exercise of fancy not to be confused with imaginative growth. The saner and greater mythologies are not fancies; they are the utterance of the whole soul of man and, as such, inexhaustible to meditation. They are no amusement or diversion to be sought as a relaxation and an escape from the hard realities of life. They are these hard realities in projection, their symbolic recognition, co-ordination and acceptance. Through such mythologies our will is collected, our powers unified, our growth controlled. Through them the infinitely divergent strayings of our being are brought into 'balance and reconciliation.' "[2]

As with the word "symbol," this meaning of myth must be asserted as clearly as

---

[1] Jung supports this view in his recent contribution to an *Introduction to a Science of Mythology* (1951): "The primitive mentality does not invent myths, it *experiences* them. Myths are original revelations of the preconscious psyche, involuntary statements about unconscious psychic happenings, and anything but allegories of physical processes."

[2] I. A. Richards, *Coleridge on Imagination* (1934, 1951). Cf. Paul Valéry: "The image of this world is part of a family of images, an infinite group, all the elements of which we possess—but unconsciously—consciousness of possession is the secret of the inventors" (*Note and Digression*, 1919).

possible; for the "ordinary" meaning of myth has no bearing upon Poetic, or upon the attitude of mind from which myth springs. The *New English Dictionary* records only a meaning of 1830, defining myth as "A purely fictitious narrative usually involving supernatural persons, actions, or events, and embodying some popular idea concerning natural or historical phenomena. Often used vaguely to include any narrative having fictitious elements." And "mythical" is defined as "Having no foundation in fact." Despite the efforts of several critics and aestheticians in this century to restore an older meaning to the word, this is the way most people at present would define myth. And the dominant notion of myth —as fictitious, having no foundation in fact, embodying some "popular idea"— clearly indicates the dominance of the technical way of mind. Myth, as an articulated image of reality, has nothing to do with "fact" in the scientific sense; it reveals Being and Value, and is not primarily concerned to record a series of events as they "actually happened" in historical sequence. The myth becomes most translucent, it would seem, when a mythical narrative can also be shown to be "a true story"; that is one reason for the vitality and variety of the Christian myth. The primary requirements for vital myth are that it should spring from belief, and that it should embody the *quality* of spiritual events and not merely that it should establish the historicity of certain physical events. . . .

I have spoken so far as though a myth were a symbolical narrative; but this was only for convenience. It seems to me that narrative is an accidental and not an essential feature of myth. Myth is rather a grouping of symbols which brings them into resonance with each other to embody a comprehensive view of reality. The relations which induce the resonance

are not explicit and logical but dialectical and in the order of Poetic. Narrative order, on the other hand, is a logical order, even though the narrative take the loosely knit manner of epic—a string of episodes spun around a central heroic figure and related only through that figure. Whether or not "superatural" incidents are included does not affect the logicality of narrative structure. Once the myth has taken a narrative form it has started to fall from grace, to move in the direction of "legend"—a narrative which treats (or purports to treat) of historical events with some "imaginative" freedom.[3] It is the function of myth to hold symbols in resonance. . . .

A sane and stable society will supply itself with a coherent structure of symbols for the mythical expression of reality and Value. But a myth can never be a formula for directed action. Whenever myth is turned in a practical direction it decays by losing its inner Poetic coherence, by submitting to the alien coherence of logic. Symbols need constantly to be recreated and clarified if they are to preserve the inner vitality of myth. But myth, being religious, draws its vitality not from communal lip-service but from vivid personal creations and recreations. In an unstable or disintegrating society the communal myth has collapsed and been replaced with a multitude of unrelated superstitions. The artists, the myth-makers, are then deprived of the established structure of symbol and are obliged to rediscover and revive ancient symbols and even to create symbols and

[3] Legend as pseudo-history is a movement away from true myth towards the "ordinary" or vulgar view that the function of imagination is to lead one into what Keats called "the realms of gold." This movement is clearly to be seen in Ezra Pound's poem *The Flame,* in which he meditates nostalgically upon Provençal legend. The word "legend" is almost a late return to the original sense of *logos*—"what is said."

myths of their own.[4] Symbols, whether ancient and established or not, must constantly be discovered and rediscovered and made personal to the poet if they are not to degenerate into cyphers or emblems. The present disintegration of society presents only a special instance of a general problem for the poet. But the artist has in this century been so isolated from society that the artist's introspective preoccupation with his work has secreted a great deal of valuable detail about the way poetic symbols are created.

In a little angry verse Yeats celebrated his own departure from a tapestried archaeological manner:

> I made my song a coat
> Covered with embroideries
> Out of old mythologies
> From heel to throat;
> But the fools caught it,
> Wore it in the world's eyes
> As though they'd wrought it.
> Song, let them take it,
> For there's more enterprise
> In walking naked.

From an adaptation of historic symbols not his own, he turned to discover and shape to his personal vision personal symbols, no matter of what origin so long

as they were his own, grasped and set afire by his own experience. The stark, passionate, terrifying metaphysics of *Byzantium* and *The Second Coming* prove upon the pulse that Yeats succeeded in his quest for a personal symbolism. Without an extensive mythological gloss, without even the "vehiculatory gear and swim-bladders" of *Per Amica Silentia Lunae* and *A Vision*, his personal symbols—of pern and gyre, swan and heron and hawk, the winding stair, the tower, Byzantium—convey directly their charges of feeling, their "meaning" in Poetic.[5] If this were not so they would not be symbols. How this came about is more than hinted in his poem *On a Picture of a Black Centaur by Edmund Dulac*:

---

[4] This accounts for the private, fragmentary, and archaeological character of much twentieth-century art. In such conditions there is a very wide gulf between the best and second-best artists, because of the almost insuperable difficulty, when society has no eye or ear for symbolical expression, of raising personal vision to the level of vital symbol. Of contemporary esoteric writing Paul Valéry notes in *Note-Book B1910:* "An important part of modern literature is given to communicating—not the final state of impressions, the state of something seized, unravelled, organized, cleared up—but the initial state, that of having still to understand (the encounter still to be met), the problematical state, confused, sentimental, sensorial. Instead of writing formulas, it writes data in the form of implicit functions—somewhat as the modern definitions are made by independent postulates and no longer by one single sentence. Much the same as music."

[5] While this chapter was in final revision I have read with great profit T. R. Henn's *The Lonely Tower* (1950). From his book I have lifted an epigraph: for I have not read Albert Béguin's *L'Âme Romantique et Le Rêve.*

I do not suggest that Yeats's poems—or anybody else's—should be read one by one, out of the context of the whole corpus of his work. But the single poem must contain within itself the power which, if inscrutable, will send us in search of clarification. With Yeats the clarification can be found within his own work; with other poets this is not so. (See Rosamund Tuve, *A Reading of George Herbert* (1952), for the importance of knowing what a poet took for granted.) Yeats himself does not argue for unreflective impressionism. "Take some line that is quite simple, that gets its beauty from its place in a story, and see how it flickers with the light of the many symbols that have given the story its beauty, as a sword-blade may flicker with the light of burning towers." "A poetical passage cannot be understood without a rich memory, and like the older school of painting appeals to a tradition ... in rhythm, in vocabulary; for the ear must notice slight variations upon old cadences and customary words, all that high breeding of poetical style where there is nothing ostentatious, nothing crude, no breath of parvenu or journalist." "Day after day I have sat in my chair turning a symbol over in my mind, exploring all its details, defining and again defining its elements, testing my convictions and those of others by its unity, attempting to substitute particulars for an abstraction like that of algebra."

yet I, being driven half insane
Because of some green wing, gathered old
  mummy wheat
In the mad abstract dark and ground it
  grain by grain
And after baked it slowly in an oven; but
  now
I bring full-flavoured wine out of a barrel
  found
Where seven Ephesian topers slept and
  never knew
When Alexander's empire passed, they slept
  so sound.

The self-contained, self-evident force of
Yeats's mature metaphysical manner
might be regarded as an isolated psychological development, not typical of the
symbolic process in poetry. But the same
process is to be seen in the work of other
poets. And it can be clearly demonstrated,
where one would perhaps be least disposed to find it, in the work of Coleridge.
In *The Ancient Mariner* he had fashioned a myth in narrative form, weaving
it around a group of symbols, few of
which—and notably the albatross—were
consecrated by previous symbolic use.[6]
Beyond *The Ancient Mariner* and his
better-known poems he sustained, without conscious intent, a coherent structure
of personal symbols powerful enough to
animate many a passage of his intimate
prose as well as his poems. These symbols, some of which touch primordial
references, attained symbolic stature by
being taken up from direct observation
in actual events, made objects of contemplation and vehicles of the contemplative passion. ("When a man writes
any work of genius, or invents some
creative action, is it not," Yeats asks, "because some knowledge or power has come
into his mind from beyond his mind? It
is called up by an image, as I think; ...
but our images must be given to us, we
cannot choose them deliberately.") Coleridge's personal symbols—the moon, the
blue sky, the ocean, trees, fire, the candle
flame (if they are to be called by name)
—control the power of the Moon-gloss in
The Ancient Mariner: "In his loneliness
and fixedness he yearneth towards the
journeying Moon, and the stars that still
sojourn, yet still move onward; and everywhere the blue sky belongs to them, and
is their appointed rest and their native
country and their own natural homes,
which they enter unannounced, as lords
that are certainly expected, and yet there
is a silent joy at their arrival." ...

[6] I incline to the view that *Dejection: an
Ode* is not less impersonal and mythical than
The Ancient Mariner.

A NOTE ON ALLEGORY
George Whalley*

True allegory, like myth, is a "symbolic mode," but its achievement is so rare that the usual definition of allegory is based on a
decayed form, a kind of ciphering device in which the "luminous
identity" of the surface story and the implied allegorical meaning
is lost and the narrative sacrifices a life of its own in order to serve
simply as a code to some "criticism of social, political, and theological issues beneath an innocent surface."

* The selection is reprinted from *Poetic
Process*, by George Whalley, by permission of
Routledge & Kegan Paul, Ltd. Copyright 1953
by Routledge & Kegan Paul, Ltd.

Allegory is almost invariably represented as the antithesis of symbol—"a translation," as Coleridge says, "of abstract notions into a picture-language, which is itself nothing but an abstraction from objects of the senses." The effort to isolate the transcendent power of symbol has turned too often upon a comparison with the formulated allegory—allegory in decay. The same attitude is expressed by Yeats: "Symbolism said things which could not be said so perfectly in any other way, and needed but a right instinct for its understanding; while Allegory said things which could be said as well, or better, in another way, and needed a right knowledge for its understanding. The one thing gave dumb things voices, and bodiless things bodies; while the other read a meaning—which had never lacked its voice or its body—into something heard or seen, and loved less for the meaning than for its own sake."[1] C. S. Lewis's *Allegory of Love* (1936) on the other hand has clarified the nature of true allegory, but only at the expense of confusing the nature of symbol. I wish to advance the view that allegory in its full poetic development is a symbolic mode, and in its formulated state is a species of cyphering.

Allegory is a convention by which the inner drama of conscience and love may be revealed. Different features of the individual soul are personified and, within the conventional setting of a dream, the personifications take on individual identity and act out the inner drama in a discursive (usually epic) narrative. In allegory two levels of attention and action operate simultaneously. Lewis has scotched the standard view that a reader cannot sustain

[1] Elsewhere, he writes: "I find that though I love symbolism, which is often the only fitting speech for some mystery of disembodied life, I am for the most part bored by allegory, which is made, as Blake says, by the 'daughters of memory,' and coldly, with no wizard frenzy."

two levels of action at once. "It is a mischievous error to suppose that in an allegory the author is 'really' talking about the thing symbolized, and not at all about the thing that symbolizes; the very essence of the art is to talk about both."

Allegory in its full development is a highly specialized form of symbolic expression. But because the purpose of allegory is psychological revelation, it arises at best from a mixed poetic intension, and very easily becomes the vehicle for deliberate didacticism. Allegory reveals by dissection; it separates out prominent psychic elements and personifies them as dramatic "characters." And this substitution, which is cyphering or embleming and not symbolization, makes allegory extremely unstable; for it establishes an unpoetic coherence at variance with the integrity of consciousness. This unpoetic strain is further strengthened by two other demands for technical coherence: the narrative, as principal focus of interest, must at least be a coherent narrative; and if the narrative element is allowed to develop fully *as narrative* the personified psychic elements will tend to lose their distinct identity as cyphers by becoming more or less complex in response to the need for a "life-like" effect in the narrative. True allegory—allegory as a symbolic mode—is therefore a very rare achievement: the list would perhaps only include *The Romance of the Rose*, *Pilgrim's Progress* (with some reservations), and parts of *The Faerie Queene*. (Symbolical allegory occurs in limited passages of poems which do not attempt to sustain a full narrative allegory; but these too are rare.) In the symbolic allegory we find the characteristic symbolical resonance between the allegorical persons and the faculties of the soul, between the narrative and the inner drama; and the character of this resonance is precisely what Coleridge postulated for symbol. The most prominent feature of symbolic allegory is the distinct self-subsistence of both the "surface" story and the implied allegorical "meaning." As soon as the self-subsistence of the allegory at both levels of interpretation relaxes or ceases, symbolism has degenerated into cyphering.

Symbolical allegory can only appear at a particular phase of personal and social self-consciousness: a burning desire to understand and describe inner conflict must arise at a time when there is no satisfactory direct means of revealing "inner goings-on." Such a period will be of short duration; and while it lasts, allegory is the only symbolic means of psychological revelation. For symbolic writing is not an alternative or indirect or calligraphic way of saying something—it is at certain times the *only* way. As a method, allegory is cumbersome and inflexible, and doomed to give place to more direct and economical modes of expression; and this process is hastened by the inherently unsymbolic character of allegorical structure. In the Middle Ages —probably because it proved a powerful instrument for teaching religion and manners—allegory continued as a conventional mould, a debilitated formula long after the internal necessity for the method had disappeared. As soon as the luminous identity between the story and the allegorical meaning is lost, allegory degenerates into a cryptographic cyphering device for concealing a criticism of social, political, and theological issues beneath an innocent surface. Much the greatest quantity of allegory is of this sort; and so it comes about that the degenerate allegory has almost invariably been regarded as the type of allegory and the antithesis of symbol. Many sections of *The Faerie Queene*, though not all, are formulated allegory. And Swift's

Gulliver, though not strictly an allegory, is as much the degenerate offspring of true allegory as the morality play is.

The work of a perceptive and original writer, however, is not doomed to decline with an outworn mode. Chaucer, steeped in the tradition of symbolic allegory, recognized that allegory had ceased to be a necessary method of expressing his psychological insight. He suddenly breaks off in the middle of writing *Anelide and Arcite*, abandons the elaborate high manner of romance, and turns to write one of the greatest psychological poems ever written—*Troilus and Criseyde*. And this poem (as C. S. Lewis has shown) preserves some of the allegorical cypher-persons, but changed back into real persons. Pandarus is not *really* the Bialacoil of the allegory of love: he is a perplexed, well-meaning man-of-the-world, absent-mindedly vicious. And Criseyde is not a cypher for any quality or any group of qualities; she is not even an emblem of feminine fickleness and wilful infidelity. She is a person of "slyding corage," muddled, frightened almost to the point of paralysis, capable only of languid, despairing action—a person so credible, alive, and pitiful that Chaucer himself cannot pass judgment upon her even when he goes through the motions of drawing a moral to his tale.

If symbol and allegory, emblem and cypher, can be clearly discriminated, the nature of symbol emerges very clearly. The word "symbol" is most important as a central critical term and should if possible be protected from vague usage. There is a further consideration. There are signs—especially in the novels of James Joyce and Franz Kafka, to mention only two writers—that we are entering upon, or may even have entered, one of those small areas of history in which symbolical allegory is the only possible mode for original psychological revelation. Psychological theory in this century —in the general mind at any rate—has turned the *psyche* into such an unastonishing little machine that we probably require the refreshment of a stylized mode that will make beforehand few easy assumptions about what is to be revealed.

FROM YEATS: THE POET AS MYTH-MAKER
Cleanth Brooks[*]

Cleanth Brooks discusses Yeats' private myth, found in A *Vision*, and relates the richness of some of his poetic production to the background of the myth. Yeats turns from science to the fantasy world of his highly complex mythical system. But he does not discard science; rather, "he has preferred to write these elements in something of the manner in which they are fused in a religion." Like Eliot, he is searching for "the unification of sensibility."

William Butler Yeats has produced in his *Vision* one of the most remarkable books of the last hundred years. It is the most ambitious attempt made by any poet of our time to set up a "myth." The framework is elaborate and complex; the concrete detail constitutes some of the finest prose and poetry of our time. But the very act of boldly setting up a myth will be regarded by most critics as an impertinence, or, at the least, as a fantastic vagary. And the latter view will be reinforced by Yeats's account of how he received the system from the spirits through the mediumship of his wife.

The privately printed edition of A *Vision* appeared so long ago as 1925, but it has been almost completely ignored by the critics even though there has been,

* The selection is reprinted from *Modern Poetry and the Tradition*, by Cleanth Brooks, by permission of The University of North Carolina Press. Copyright 1939 by The University of North Carolina Press. "Sailing to Byzantium" is reprinted with the permission of the publisher from *Collected Poems* by William Butler Yeats. Copyright 1928 by the Macmillan Company. Renewed 1956 by Georgie Yeats.

since the publication of *The Tower* in 1928, a remarkable resurgence of interest in Yeats's poetry. Indeed, Edmund Wilson has been the only critic thus far to deal with A *Vision* in any detail. His treating it in any detail is all the more admirable in view of his general interpretation of the significance of Yeats's system. For Wilson, as we have already seen, considers the symbolist movement as a retreat from science and reality; and Yeats's system, with its unscientific paraphernalia, its gyres and cones, its strange psychology described in terms of Masks and Bodies of Fate, and most of all its frank acceptance of the supernatural, is enough to try the patience of any scientific modernist. A very real regard for the fineness of Yeats's later poetry has kept him from carrying too far the view of Yeats as an escapist. But to regard the magical system as merely a piece of romantic furniture is to miss completely the function which it has performed for Yeats.

The central matter is science, truly

enough, and Edmund Wilson is right in interpreting the symbolist movement as an antiscientific tendency. But the really important matter to determine is the grounds for Yeats's hostility to science. The refusal to accept the scientific account in matters where the scientific method is valid and relevant is unrealistic, but there is nothing "escapist" about a hostility to science which orders science off the premises as a trespasser when science has taken up a position where it has no business to be. For example, Victorian poetry will illustrate the illegitimate intrusion of science, and Yeats in his frequent reprehension of the "impurities" in such poetry—far from being a romantic escapist—is taking a thoroughly realistic position. The formulas which Edmund Wilson tends to take up —scientific, hard-headed, realistic; antiscientific-romantic, escapist—are far too simple.

We have argued in earlier chapters that all poetry since the middle of the seventeenth century has been characterized by the impingement of science upon the poet's world. Yeats, after a brief enthusiasm for natural science as a boy, came, he tells us, to hate science "with a monkish hate." "I am," Yeats tells us, "very religious, and deprived by Huxley and Tindall . . . of the simple-minded religion of my childhood, I had made a new religion, almost an infallible church of poetic tradition, of a fardel of stories, and of personages, and of emotions, inseparable from their first expression, passed on from generation to generation by poets and painters with some help from philosophers and theologians." Here is the beginning of Yeats's system.

It is easy, when one considers the system as expressed in A Vision to argue that Yeats's quarrel with science was largely that the system of science allowed no place for the supernatural—visions,

trances, and incredible happenings— which began to manifest itself to Yeats at a very early period in his life. Undoubtedly Yeats wished for an account of experience which would make room for such happenings. But if we insist on this aspect of the matter, as most critics have done, we neglect elements which are far more important. Granting that Yeats had never had a single supernatural manifestation, many of his objections to science would have remained. The account given by science is still abstract, unconcerned with values, and affording no interpretations. Yeats wished for an account of experience which would surmount such defects: as he once put it, a philosophy which was at once "logical and boundless." The phrase is an important one. Had Yeats merely been content to indulge himself in fairy tales and random superstitions, he would never, presumably, have bothered with a system of beliefs at all. A philosophy which was merely "boundless" would allow a person to live in a pleasant enough anarchy. The "logical" quality demands a systematization, though in Yeats's case one which would not violate and oversimplify experience.

The whole point is highly important. If Yeats had merely been anxious to indulge his fancy, not caring whether the superstition accepted for the moment had any relation to the world about him—had he been merely an escapist, no system would have been required at all. For the system is an attempt to make a coherent formulation of the natural and the supernatural. The very existence of the system set forth in A Vision therefore indicates that Yeats refused to run away from life.

But if he refused to run away from life he also refused to play the game with the counters of science. For the abstract, meaningless, valueless system of science, he proposed to substitute a concrete, meaningful system, substituting symbol for concept. As he states in the introduction to A Vision, "I wished for a system of thought that would leave my imagination free to create as it chose and yet make all it created, or could create, part of the one history, and that the soul's."[1] Or if we prefer Mr. Eliot's terms, Yeats set out to build a system of references which would allow for a unification of sensibility. Yeats wanted to give the authority of the intellect to attitudes and the intensity of emotion to judgments. The counsel of I. A. Richards is to break science and the emotions cleanly apart —to recognize the separate validity and relevance of "statements" (scientific propositions) on the one hand and of "pseudostatements" (unscientific but emotionally valid statements) on the other.

Yeats, on the contrary, instead of breaking science and poetry completely apart, has preferred to reunite these elements in something of the manner in which they are fused in a religion. His system has for him, consequently, the authority and meaning of a religion, combining intellect and emotion as they were combined before the great analytic and abstracting process of modern science broke them apart. In short, Yeats has created for himself a myth. He says so frankly in the closing paragraphs of A Vision (1925 edition): "A book of modern philosophy may prove to our logical capacity that there is a transcendental portion of our being that is timeless and spaceless ... and yet our imagination remains subjected to nature as before. ... It was not so with ancient philosophy because the ancient philoso-

[1] This statement occurs in the privately printed edition of A Vision which appeared in 1925. The new edition does not differ from the earlier fundamentally in the system that it sets forth, though it has many omissions and revisions of statement, and some extensions.

pher had something to reinforce his thought,—the Gods, the Sacred Dead, Egyptian Theurgy, the Priestess Diotime. ... I would restore to the philosopher his mythology."

It is because most of us misunderstand and distrust the myth and because we too often trust science even when it has been extended into contexts where it is no longer science that most of us misunderstand the function of Yeats's mythology. A further caution is in order. Yeats has called his system "magical," and the term may mislead us. Yeats even claims for the system a capacity for prediction. In 1917, in his "Anima Hominis," he wrote: "I do not doubt those heaving circles, those winding arcs, whether in one man's life or in that of an age, are mathematical, and that some in the world, or beyond the world, have foreknown the event and pricked upon the calendar the life-span of a Christ, a Buddha, a Napoleon"; and in the earlier edition of A Vision, there actually occurs a prophecy of the next two hundred years. But the system does not serve the ends of "vulgar magic." Yeats obviously does not propose to use his system to forecast the movements of the stock market, or to pick the winner of the Grand National. The relation of the system to science and the precise nature of Yeats's belief in it will be discussed later. For the present, the positive qualities of the myth may be best discussed by pointing out its relation to Yeats's poetry.

The system may be conveniently broken up into three parts: a picture of history, an account of human psychology, and an account of the life of the soul after death. The theory of history is the easiest aspect of the system. It bears a close resemblance to Spengler's cyclic theory. (Yeats takes notice of this, but he points out that his system was complete before he had read Spengler.) Civilizations run through cycles of two thousand-odd years, periods of growth, of maturity, and lastly, of decline; but instead of Spengler's metaphor of the seasons, spring-summer-autumn-winter, Yeats uses a symbolism drawn from the twenty-eight phases of the moon. For example, whereas Spengler speaks of the spring time of a culture. Yeats speaks of phases 1 to 8 (the first quarter of the moon). A civilization reaches its zenith at the full moon (phase 15) and then gradually declines, passing through phases 16 to 28 (the dark of the moon) again. Yeats further complicates his scheme by dividing his cycle into two subcycles of twenty-eight phases and of one thousand-odd years each. The phases 15 of these two subcycles which make up the two thousand years of Christian civilization are, for example, Byzantine civilization under Justinian and the Renaissance. Our own period is at phase 23 of the second subcycle; the moon is rapidly rounding toward the dark when the new civilization to dominate the next two thousand years will announce itself—"the Second Coming."

The full moon (phase 15) symbolizes pure subjectivity, the height of what Yeats calls the "antithetical" which predominates from phase 8 (the half moon of the first quarter) to the full moon and on to phase 22 (the half moon of the last quarter). The dark of the moon ("full sun") symbolizes pure objectivity, the height of what Yeats calls the "primary," which dominates from phase 22 to phase 8. The critical phases themselves, 8 and 22, since they represent equal mixtures of primary and antithetical, are periods of great stress and change. So much for the four cardinal phases. Each of the various twenty-eight phases, indeed, is assigned a special character in like manner.

An account of phase 23 will be sufficient illustration—all the more since this phase is the subject of several of Yeats's poems. Yeats regards phase 22 as always a period of abstraction. Synthesis is carried to its furthest lengths and there comes "synthesis for its own sake, organization where there is no masterful director, books where the author has disappeared, painting where some accomplished brush paints with an equal pleasure, or with a bored impartiality, the human form or an old bottle, dirty weather and clean sunshine" (A Vision). In the next phase, phase 23, which the present world has already entered upon (Yeats gives the year of transition as 1927) "in practical life one expects the same technical inspiration, the doing of this or that not because one would, or should, but because one can, consequent license, and with those 'out of phase' anarchic violence with no sanction in general principles."[2]

It is a vision of this period which Yeats gives us in what is perhaps the best known of his historical poems, "The Second Coming":

Turning and turning in the widening gyre
The falcon cannot hear the falconer;
Things fall apart; the center cannot hold;
Mere anarchy is loosed upon the world . . .

In "Meditations in Time of Civil War" Yeats gives another vision of the same period, one which employs again the symbol of the hawk but this time joined with the symbol of the darkening moon itself. In Section VII of this poem the poet has a vision of abstract rage, "The rage-driven . . . troop" crying out for vengeance for Jacques Molay, followed by a vision of perfect loveliness—ladies riding magical unicorns. But both visions fade out and

[2] From the earlier edition. The account of history in the 1938 edition breaks off after the discussion of phase 22.

Give place to an indifferent multitude, give
place
To brazen hawks. Nor self-delighting reverie,
Nor hate of what's to come, nor pity for
what's gone,
Nothing but grip of claw, and the eye's
complacency,
The innumerable clanging wings that have
put out the moon.

The moon is used as a symbol of the
imagination in its purity, of the completely subjective intellect. It has this
general meaning in many of Yeats's
poems—for example, in the poem,
"Blood and the Moon," where it is
played off against blood (which is comparable to the sun, or the dark of the
moon) as a symbol of active force—of
the objective, or the primary.

An examination of the various meanings of blood in this poem will indicate
how flexible and subtle the "meanings"
attached to one of Yeats's concrete
images can be. The symbol first occurs in
the phrase, "A bloody, arrogant power."
The tower on which the poet stands has
been built by such a force and the symbolic meaning of the term is partially
indicated by the characterization of the
power as "bloody," shedding blood. But
the meaning is extended and altered
somewhat in the reference to Swift's
heart: "in his blood-sodden breast" which
"dragged him down into mankind."
Blood here is associated with elemental
sympathy, though the reference to Swift's
particular quality of sympathy qualifies
it properly—a sympathy grounded in
one's elemental humanity which cannot
be escaped and which—from the standpoint of the pure intellect—may be said
to drag one down. The third reference to
blood occurs in the phrase, "blood and
state," and a third connection emerges—
the connection of blood with nobility
and tradition.

These references, it is important to
notice, do not so much define the meaning of the symbol as indicate the limits
within which the meaning (or manifold
of meanings) is to be located. That
meaning emerges fully only when we
reach the last two sections of the poem
where the symbols of blood and moon
enter into active contrast: action contrasted with contemplation, power with
wisdom, the youth of a civilization with
its age.

The purity of the unclouded moon
Has flung its arrowy shaft upon the floor.
Seven centuries have passed and it is pure,
The blood of innocence has left no stain.
There, on blood-saturated ground, have
stood
Soldier, assassin, executioner,
Whether for daily pittance or in blind fear
Or out of abstract hatred, and shed blood,
But could not cast a single jet thereon.
Odor of blood on the ancestral stair!
And we that have shed none must gather
there
And clamour in drunken frenzy for the
moon.

Upon the dusty, glittering windows cling,
And seem to cling upon the moonlit skies,
Tortoiseshell butterflies, peacock butterflies,
A couple of night-moths are on the wing.
Is every modern nation like the tower,
Half dead at the top? No matter what I
said,
For wisdom is the property of the dead,
A something incompatible with life; and
power,
Like everything that has the stain of blood,
A property of the living; but no stain
Can come upon the visage of the moon
When it has looked in glory from a cloud,

The development is very rich, and even
though the poet in the last stanza has
apparently reduced his meaning to abstract statement, the meaning is fuller
than the statement taken as mere statement. We must read the lines in their

full context to see how their meaning is made more complex, and, if one likes, more "precise" by the development of the symbols already made.

The tower itself, it is probably unnecessary to add, is the symbol of the poet's own old age and the old age of the civilization to which he belongs—

Is every modern nation like the tower,
Half dead at the top?

The poem itself is a very fine example of the unification of sensibility. As we have said, the poem refuses to be reduced to allegory—allegory which is perhaps the first attempt which man makes to unite the intellect and the emotions when they begin to fall apart—Spenser's *Faerie Queene*, for example. Moreover, the poet has repudiated that other refuge of a divided sensibility, moralization following on a piece of description—Tennyson's *Princess*, for instance. One can imagine how the poem would probably have been written by a Victorian: The old man standing upon the tower surveys from its vantage point the scene about him; then the poet, having disposed of the concrete detail, moralizes abstractly on the scene to the effect that wisdom and power are incompatibles. Instead, Yeats has confidence in his symbols; the concrete and the abstract, thought and feeling, coincide. The poet refuses to define the moralization except in terms of the specific symbols and the specific situation given. . . .

The relation of the artist to the souls of the dead is apparently a highly important one for Yeats, and two of Yeats's finest poems, the "Byzantium" poems, depend heavily upon a knowledge of this relationship.

Byzantium, as Mr. R. P. Blackmur has pointed out, is the heaven of man's mind. But more especially it is a symbol of the heaven of man's imagination, and pre-eminently of a particular kind of imagination, the nature of which Yeats suggests for us in the following passage from *A Vision*. "I think if I could be given a month of Antiquity and leave to spend it where I chose, I would spend it in Byzantium a little before Justinian opened St. Sophia and closed the Academy of Plato. I think I could find in some little wineshop some philosophical worker in mosaic who could answer all my questions, the supernatural descending nearer to him than to Plotinus even. . . .

"I think that in early Byzantium, maybe never before or since in recorded history, religious, aesthetic and practical life were one, that architect and artificers—though not, it may be, poets, for language had been the instrument of controversy and must have grown abstract—spoke to the multitude and the few alike. . . .

"[In Byzantium of this period . . . all about . . . is an incredible splendor like that which we see pass under our closed eyelids as we lie between sleep and waking, no representation of a living world but the dream of a somnambulist. Even the drilled pupil of the eye, when the drill is in the hand of some Byzantine worker in ivory, undergoes a somnambulistic change, for its deep shadow among the faint lines of the tablet, its mechanical circle, where all else is rhythmical and flowing, give to Saint or Angel a look of some great bird staring at miracle."

So much for the symbol of Byzantium itself. The poem "Sailing to Byzantium," as the less difficult of the two, may properly be considered first.

That is no country for old men. The young
In one another's arms, birds in the trees,
—Those dying generations—at their song,
The salmon-falls, the mackerel-crowded
    seas,

Fish, flesh, or fowl, commend all summer
    long
Whatever is begotten, born, and dies.
Caught in that sensual music all neglect
Monuments of unageing intellect.

An aged man is but a paltry thing,
A tattered coat upon a stick, unless
Soul clap its hands and sing, and louder
    sing
For every tatter in its mortal dress,
Nor is there singing school but studying
Monuments of its own magnificence;
And therefore I have sailed the seas and
    come
To the holy city of Byzantium.

The poet appeals to the

    . . . sages standing in God's holy fire
    As in the gold mosaic of a wall,

asking them to

Come from the holy fire, perne in a gyre,
And be the singing-masters of my soul.

A quotation from "Anima Mundi" is
illuminating at this point: "There are
two realities, the terrestrial and the condition of fire. All power is from the terrestrial condition, for there all opposites
meet and there only is the extreme of
choice possible, full freedom. And there
the heterogeneous is, and evil, for evil is
the strain one upon another of opposites;
but in the condition of fire is all music
and all rest. . . ." The dead whose souls
have gone through all the sequences, and
whose sequences have come to an end are
in the condition of fire: ". . . the soul
puts on the rhythmic or spiritual body
or luminous body and contemplates all
the events of its memory and every possible impulse in an eternal possession of
itself in one single moment."

There is a close connection between
the dead living in their passionate memories, and Yeats's theory of *Anima*

Mundi or the Great Memory. In the
same essay he tells us: "Before the mind's
eye, whether in sleep or waking, came
images that one was to discover presently
in some book one had never read, and
after looking in vain for explanation to
the current theory of forgotten personal
memory, I came to believe in a great
memory passing on from generation to
generation." From this great memory
come two influences: First, "that inflowing coming alike to men and to animals
is called natural." It is this, for example,
that teaches a bird to build her nest or
which shapes the child in the womb. But
the second inflowing "which is not natural but intellectual . . . is from the
fire. . . ." It is this inflow which the poet
wishes to come to him and to transform
him, shaping him to a "bodily form"
which is not taken

            from any natural thing,
But such a form as Grecian goldsmiths
    make
Of hammered gold and gold enamelling . . .

And if we inquire why the symbol of
this "unnatural" form is denoted by that
of a bird, though a bird of metal, we may
find the reason in reading further in
"Anima Mundi": "From tradition and
perception, one thought of one's own life
as symbolized by earth, the place of
heterogeneous things [compare "the terrestrial condition" *supra*], the images as
mirrored in water and the images themselves one could divine but as air; and
beyond it all there was, I felt confident,
certain aims and governing loves, the fire
that makes all simple. Yet the images
themselves were fourfold, and one judged
their meaning in part from the predominance of one out of the four elements,
or that of the fifth element, the veil hiding another four, a bird born out of the
fire."

The poem can be taken on a number of levels: as the transition from sensual art to intellectual art; as the poet's new and brilliant insight into the nature of the Byzantine imagination; as the poet's coming to terms with age and death. The foregoing account of the development of the symbols in the poet's personal experience will not in itself explain the fineness of the poem, or even indicate its aesthetic structure: it will not indicate, for example, the quality of self-irony in his characterization of himself as a "monument of unageing intellect" or as a "tattered coat upon a stick" or the play of wit achieved in such a phrase as "the artifice of eternity." The account given will, for that matter, do no more than indicate the series of contrasts and paradoxes on which the poem is founded—it will not assess their function in giving the poem its power. But it may indicate the source of the authority which dictates the tone of the poem. The real importance of the symbolic system is that it allows the poet a tremendous richness and coherency. . . .

So much for the general nature of Yeats's myth and for its relation to his own great poetry; and now, one further reference to the vexing question of Yeats's belief in his system. "The saner and greater mythologies," as Richards says, "are not fancies; they are the utterance of the whole soul of man and, as such, inexhaustible to meditation." The statement can be claimed for Yeats's myth. We have already uttered a warning against the use of the misleading term "magic" for Yeats's system. Magical in the sense that it proposes to use unscientific means to accomplish ends better accomplished by scientific means the system is not. Properly speaking it is a world-view or a philosophy—an "utterance of the whole soul of man" having for its object imaginative contemplation.

Yeats, as we have seen, apparently has no objection himself to referring to his system as a myth, but we are to remember that in calling it this, he is not admitting that it is trivial, or merely fanciful, or "untrue." And this is doubtless why Yeats, in answering the question of whether or not he believes in his system, can only reply with a counterquestion as to whether the word "belief," as the questioner will use it, belongs to our age. For the myth is not scientifically true, and yet though a fiction, though a symbolical representation, intermeshes with reality. It is imaginatively true, and if most people will take this to mean that it is after all trivial, this merely shows in what respect our age holds the imagination.

PART III

FORM

FORM AS an abstraction does, of course, exist, but to say anything meaningful about it as such is exceedingly difficult. Most critics faced with the problem of defining, describing, and discussing form-in-general are tempted to conclude that there is no such thing; that there are only forms—of infinite number, variety, and complexity; that the only element all of them have in common is a kind of ghostly Platonic idea almost impossible to analyze; that each work of art has its own unique form, which, however closely it may resemble the form of another, is nevertheless not the same; and that these singular forms, individually and comparatively, can be extensively talked about and are all that can be extensively talked about. Therefore, the problem of form is approached in this section through several analyses of the various forms of specific works of poetry, fiction, and drama.

CHAPTER 11

Form

THE PROBLEM OF ESTHETIC FORM
Dewitt H. Parker*

Dewitt Parker lists six principles of esthetic form: (1) the principle of organic unity or unity in variety, (2) the principle of the theme, (3) the principle of thematic variation, (4) balance, (5) the principle of hierarchy, and (6) evolution. *Organic unity* constitutes the wholeness of the work of art; *theme*, the dominant elements of a work of art; *thematic variation*, their elaboration and embroidery; *balance*, the disposition of elements; *hierarchy*, the disposition of elements in an ascending scale; *evolution*, progression. The principle of organic unity is the greatest of these and contains all the others.

I shall try to reduce the general characteristics of esthetic form to their simplest principles, hoping to provide the elements of what might be called a logic of esthetic form. These principles are, I think, very few; as few, indeed, as six: the principle of organic unity, or unity in variety, as it has been called; the principle of the theme; the principle of thematic variation; balance; the principle of hierarchy; and evolution. I do not assert that there are no more principles, but I at least have been unable to find any of

* The essay is reprinted from *The Analysis of Art*, by Dewitt Parker, by permission of Yale University Press. Copyright 1924 by Yale University Press.

equal generality. Others that have been suggested can be shown either to be identical with the six mentioned or to be special cases of them. I shall consider each at some length.

First, the long-established principle of organic unity. By this is meant the fact that each element in a work of art is necessary to its value, that it contains no elements that are not thus necessary, and that all that are needful are there. The beautiful object is organized all through, "baked all through like a cake." Since everything that is necessary is there, we are not led to go beyond it to seek something to complete it; and since there are no unnecessary elements, there is nothing present to disturb its value. Moreover, the value of the work as a whole depends upon the reciprocal relations of its elements: each needs, responds to, demands, every other element. For example, in the Young Woman with a Water Jug (by Johannes Vermeer: Metropolitan Museum), the cool green needs the warm yellow and both need the red; the casement demands the table, the map requires the dark shadow under the casement, to balance it. In a melody, each tone requires its successor to continue the trend that is being established. In short, the meaning of the whole is not something additional to the elements of the work of art, but their coöperative deed.

This principle cannot, however, be described in so external a fashion. For the unity of a work of art is the counterpart of a unity within the experience of the beholder. Since the work of art becomes an embodiment not only of the imagination of the artist, but of the imagination of the spectator as well, his own experience is, for the moment, concentrated there. He is potentially as completely absorbed in it as he is in a dream; it is for the moment, in fact, his dream. And he can and does remain in the dream because the artist has so fashioned his work that everything there tends to continue and deepen it, and nothing to disturb and interrupt it. Art is the expression of the whole man, because it momentarily makes of man a whole. The "isolation" of the esthetic experience of Hugo Münsterberg[1] and the "repose in the object" of Ethel Puffer[2] are descriptions of the fact to which I am calling attention. This does not mean, of course, that the work of art is not related to other things or that it is actually isolated; but only that its relations are irrelevant to its value,

and that it cuts itself off from the rest of the world during appreciation; and this it does, first, because it embodies my dream and, second, because it is so constructed as to make me dream on. The marble of which the statue is made comes from a certain quarry and has an interesting geological history there; it stands in a certain part of space, and hence is related to other parts of space; but all such facts are of no account to its beauty. By placing the statue on a pedestal, we indicate its isolation from the space of the room, as by putting a frame around a picture we isolate it, too, from everything else in the world. It is true that, in order to understand a work of art in its historical relations, I must connect it with the artist's personality, with other works of his, with the "moral temperature" of the age, with the development of artistic styles, and the full appreciation of its beauty depends upon acquaintance with its spiritual background. Who, for example, can appreciate the whole meaning of Signorelli's Pan without some knowledge of classical antiquity and the Italian Renaissance? Yet at the moment of appreciation, all such knowledge becomes focused in the work of art, gathered and contained there like rays in a prism, and does not divert us from it.

The ancient law of organic unity is the master principle of esthetic form; all the other principles serve it. First among them is what I would call the principle of the theme. This corresponds to the "dominant character" or idee mère of Taine.[3] In every complex work of art there is some one (or there may be several) preëminent shape, color, line, melodic pattern or meaning, in which is concentrated the characteristic value of the whole. It contains the work of art in little; represents it; provides the key to our appreciation and understanding of it.

[1] The Eternal Values, chap. IX.
[2] The Psychology of Beauty, chap. III.

[3] Philosophie de l'art, part I, p. 5.

Thus every good pattern is built up of one or more shapes, the disposition of which constitutes the design. When there is color as well as shape, there is some dominant color that appears again and again or in related degrees of saturation, or else there is a color chord that is similarly repeated or is analyzed. In architecture, each style has its characteristic shape, line, or volume, as the pointed arch of the Gothic, the round arch of the Roman, the ellipse of the baroque. In music, there are the one or more themes that express the essential significance of each composition. Likewise, every sculptor, every draughtsman, has his unique and inimitable line. In every poem, there is a peculiar inflection and a regnant idea which constitute the basis of the design. In the drama or the novel, there is some one, or there may be several persons, whose character and fate create the plot.

The third principle is thematic variation. It is not sufficient to state the theme of a work of art; it must be elaborated and embroidered. One of the prominent ways of doing this is to make it echo and reëcho in our minds. Usually, if the theme can be repeated once only we are better pleased than with a single appearance. Yet to find the same thing barely repeated is monotonous; hence what we want is the same, to be sure, but the same with a difference: thematic variation. The simplest type of thematic variation is recurrence of the theme, as in any pattern built upon a repeat. Here is the maximum of sameness with the minimum of difference: mere difference of spatial or temporal position. A slight acquaintance with primitive art is sufficient to convince one of the overwhelming importance of recurrence there. Yet it is needless to say that recurrence is not confined to primitive art. We find it in all civilized art: the recurrence of the same shape and proportions in archi-

tecture and sculpture; the recurrence of the theme in music; the recurrence of the same type of foot in meter; repetition of the same color in painting; recurrence of lines and directions of lines (parallelism) in painting and sculpture and architecture; the refrain in poetry; the reappearance of the hero in different scenes in the drama and novel. However, because of the monotony of mere repetition, recurrence gives place to what may be called, in a generalized sense, transposition of theme, as when a melody is transposed to another key or tempo; or when in a design the same shape appears in a different color, or a color appears in different degrees of saturation or brightness; or in architecture, where a shape occurs in different sizes or members—in doors, windows, gables, choirstalls, and the like. Still another kind of thematic variation is alternation, which requires, of course, more than one theme, or at least two different transpositions of the same theme. Of this, again, the illustrations are legion. Finally, there is inversion of theme, as when melody is inverted or, in painting or sculpture, a curve is reversed. These are not all the possible types of thematic variation, but they are, I think, the most important and usual.

Another principle of esthetic form is balance. Balance is equality of opposing or contrasting elements. Balance is one kind of esthetic unity, for despite the opposition of the elements in balance, each needs the other and together they create a whole. Thus the blue demands the gold and the gold the blue, and together they make a new whole, gold-and-blue. Opposition or contrast is never absent from balance, for even in symmetry, where the balancing elements are alike, the directions of these elements are opposed, right and left. But contrast is never by itself esthetically satisfactory, for the contrasting elements must offset each other, they must balance. In color, the warm offsets the cold; in a picture, the small object, properly placed, offsets the large one. Hence, just as only equal weights will balance in a scale pan, so only elements that are somehow equal in value, despite their opposition, will balance esthetically. Not every tint of blue will balance every shade of yellow; that depth of blue must reappear in a corresponding depth of yellow; a light, superficial blue would never balance a deep yellow. But the identity of the opposites is even greater than this. For, as has been remarked, the elements of a balanced unity demand each other; the blue demands the yellow; the line which falls in one direction demands the line that falls in the opposite direction. Now the demand which the color or line makes for its opposite is itself a foreshadowing of the latter; in its demand it already contains the prophecy of its opposite. And even when, as may occur in painting, there is balance between elements of unlike quality—balance, say, of brightness of color against distance or size— the attention value of each must be the same, though opposed in direction. The essential thing about balance is equality of opposed values, however unlike be the things that embody or carry the values.

The pervasiveness of the principle of balance is too generally recognized to need much illustration or argument. In painting we expect, with a reservation that I shall consider in a moment, a threefold balance: horizontal, perpendicular, and radial or diagonal—between the right and left sides, the upper and lower portions, and between what may roughly be called the corners. This last has not received the attention which it deserves; but in many pictures, as for example, Tintoretto's Mercury and the Three Graces, the diagonal axis is the main axis; and in all cases of circular composition, radial balance is fundamental. In architecture, we find balance between right and left, and often between upper and lower parts. In music, there is not seldom a balance between earlier and later parts of a composition, or between opposing themes. In sculpture, there is the balance characteristic of the human body made more perfect by the artist.

Pervasive as balance is, its universality has not stood unquestioned. Nevertheless, many apparent exceptions can be explained away, as is well known, as cases of disguised or subtle balance. The older interpretation of balance after the analogy of symmetry—the balance of like parts—is only a special kind of balance, and has to be supplemented by the wider conception of balance of unlike parts.[4] With this richer conception in mind, we can understand the balance —as in Bruegel's Harvesters—between prominent objects in the right-hand part and little except a vista on the left. Similarly, there is a balance—as in the same picture—between the upper and lower halves of a painting, even when the horizon line is high, and the upper part seems therefore to be relatively empty of masses; for the distance values in the sky balance the heavier lower part. No more difficult of explanation are some cases where asymmetry appears to be definitely sought, as when a girl will put a patch on one cheek but not on another, or will tie the lock of hair on the right with a ribbon, but not the lock on the left. For the piquancy of this procedure comes from the fact that there is a background of decisive symmetry, against which the asymmetrical element stands out. This is quite different from

[4] Compare Ethel Puffer, "Studies in Symmetry," Harvard Psychological Studies, vol. I, 1902.

absolute lack of balance. One finds similar eccentric elements in all complex patterns; but always with a background of emphatic balance. And if it is true that such elements disturb symmetry, it is equally true that they serve to emphasize it. The triangle of passion is another illustration; for there also a balanced relationship is the background against which the unbalanced derives its interest.

There are, however, more difficult cases to consider. Many works of art, of the temporal arts in particular, are superficially considered rhythmical rather than balanced, and rhythm may seem to be opposed to balance. Yet an analysis of rhythm shows it to be built upon the two fundamental esthetic forms, thematic repetition and balance. For what are the typical characteristics of rhythm? Every rhythm is a motion of waves, all of a relatively constant or lawfully varying shape and temporal and spatial span, with balancing crests and troughs. The crest may be an accent or the swing up of a line; the trough may be one or more unaccented syllables, a pause, or the swing back of a line in the opposite direction. The rhythm may begin with the trough, as in iambic meter. The swing up and the swing back may both be very complex, as in free verse, yet the fundamental pattern, as it has just been described, is maintained: in every case there is the recurrence of a certain type of wave form, and the opposition—and balance—between the rising and falling swings. The simplest repeat, if you take its elements in succession, is a rhythm. In the diaper pattern, for example, there is the recurrence of the rising and falling lines, and their opposition and balance, two by two. Or a colonnade, as you apprehend the columns in succession, is a rhythm of identical and balancing filled and empty spaces, the columns corresponding to the arsis, and the spatial interval to the thesis.

Hence when balance seems to be replaced by rhythm, balance is still present, only it is not the simple type of balance so easily recognized, but balance as an element in the complex structure we call rhythm. This more subtle type of balance exists oftentimes in pictorial composition—in "open" as opposed to "closed" forms—where the ordinary mode of balance is rejected. I remember one of Monet's Lily Ponds, in which I searched vainly for the usual type of balance with reference to some axis, only to find that the elements of the picture were arranged in a clear-cut rhythm. Rhythm often replaces right-and-left balance in wall paintings, as in those of Puvis de Chavannes. In the Metropolitan Museum he has two paintings, both decorative sketches, which illustrate this: Inter Artes et Naturam and The River. In the former, notice how we do not view the picture from a vertical central axis, but rather from left or right, taking each group of figures in turn as an element in a rhythmically disposed sequence of filled and empty spaces. In The River, the rhythmical arrangement is in deep space.

Another and last type of unity I call evolution. By this I mean the unity of a process when the earlier parts determine the later, and all together create a total meaning. For illustrations, one naturally turns first to the temporal arts. The course of a well-fashioned story is a good example, for each incident determines its follower and all the incidents determine the destiny of the characters involved. The drama offers similar illustrations: the form is the same, only transposed to theatrical presentation. In the older, orthodox story or play there were three stages in the development,

an initial one of introduction of characters, a second stage of complication,
ending in the climax, and then the
unraveling. But these stages may be compressed. The story may begin with the
complication already there; the play may
begin with the climax and proceed to the
unraveling, and go back, as in Ibsen, to
the preparation. But in every case, there
is a necessary relation between means
and consequences, causes and effects, and
a total resulting meaning. Illustrations of
this type of unity abound also in the
static arts. Any line which we appreciate
as having a beginning, middle, and end,
and any composition of figures where
we are led on from one figure or group
of figures to another, is an illustration;
for there, too, although the figures be
physically static, our appreciation of
them is a process in time, and through
the process the meaning of the whole
is evolved. Of all painters, I think El
Greco offers the best illustrations of
evolution, as in the Crucifixion (Prado
museum), where we follow an intensely
dramatic movement from the lower to
the upper part of the picture.

Is evolution a genuinely distinct type
of esthetic unity? Can it be reduced to
one or more of the preceding forms?
The most closely allied form is rhythm;
yet that evolution is distinct from
rhythm can easily be seen. For in
rhythm, unless combined with evolution,
there is no obvious development, no
tendency toward a goal. Rhythm is recurrence and balance of systole and
diastole, with no growth from one phase
to another. It is true that we sometimes
speak of any movement of growth as a
rhythm, as when we talk of the rhythm
of life, but in such cases rhythm exists in
combination with evolution. For there
is, of course, a rhythm in all life—birth
and death, sleep and waking, activity and
repose. And if life be taken generically

or historically, there are other equally
well-known rhythms, as in the history of
art, with the alternation of the opposed
directions from realism to romanticism.
In melody also, except in the most
eccentric types of music, harmonic evolution is joined with an accentual or
time rhythm. Moreover, even in the most
mechanical types of rhythm, like the
simple repeat, provided they be esthetic,
there is some felt growth of value through
the recurrence and balance of parts, and
some, however slight, looking forward
to the end term as a goal. Only in purely
natural rhythms, as of the tides, is there
no growth at all, but these, unless they
enter into the mind and emotion of man,
are not esthetic in character. Nevertheless, although there is always some evolution in every esthetic rhythm, evolution is
not itself necessarily rhythmical. In literature, the rhythm of prose and poetry
overlies a development of meanings
which does not itself have a quasi-
mechanical character of rhythm; the
rhythm of time and accent is united
with the melodic development of the
musical theme, but does not constitute
it. The essential character of evolution
is, as Bergson has shown, growth or accumulation of meaning, which need not
be rhythmical.

Two different types of evolutionary
unity must be discriminated, the dramatic and the non-dramatic. In the
dramatic type there is an element of
overshadowing importance, the climax
or goal; in the other type, this element
is lacking. To be sure, every process
must have an end, and the end has a
distinctive importance as such, but it is
not always true that the end has a
greater importance than some other element or elements. The consummation
of the meaning may occur through the
agency of all parts evenly, rather than
through a particular one. Many stories

are of this character; there is an unfolding, a working out of something, with
no obvious high points. Here and there
the meaning rises, but there is no place
where it becomes so central that we feel
that the whole story depends upon it.
And, if I mistake not, there is much
music of this character; there is a definite drift or unfolding, but no climax or
finale.

Closeness of connection, yet ultimate
difference, marks the relation between
evolution and the other types of esthetic
unity, balance and thematic variation.
The static character of balance is
opposed to the dynamic character of
evolution; indeed, all movement depends
upon the upsetting of an established
equilibrium. Yet seldom, even in the
static arts, is balance found without
movement; for there exists a tendency
to proceed from one to another of the
balanced elements. In a simple color
contrast, for example, there is ever so
slight a movement from the cold to the
warm color. And, on the other hand,
there is often a balance within evolution, between the complication and the
unraveling of the plot, or the earlier and
later parts of a musical theme. But the
union of evolution and balance does not
militate against the uniqueness of either.
There remains for comparison, thematic
variation. This form, too, might seem
at first sight to be opposed to evolution,
yet not so, for there is probably no case
of variation in which the evolutionary
element is not present. For the series of
variations is not fruitless; each contributes
something to a meaning which accumu-
lates and is complete when the variations are over. So many, and no more,
exist as are necessary to this end. In so
far as, in this way, a meaning is worked
out, evolution and thematic variation
approach and meet. Yet a difference
remains. For the mode of the creation

of the meaning is different. In the one
case, it occurs through the recurrence
of the central meaning in new shapes;
in the other, through the realization of
some single dominant idea, which extends over the entire work and is
expressed once and once only. In the
one case, we start with an idea already
given, and work it out by repetition; in
the other, we have no definite, but only
a very vague idea to start with, and construct it step by step. The one method
may be called analytic, the other synthetic. For example, we do not know
what a musical theme is like until we
have heard it entire; building it up is
one thing; then, having got it, it is another thing to modulate, invert, and vary
it. The same is true of a line.

Nevertheless, in the construction of a
theme, both thematic variation and balance may be employed. For example,
in building a melody, we may proceed from tone to tone consonant with
a given tone, thus repeating the fundamental psychophysical rhythm of the
two tones which is the basis of their
harmony; or we may proceed through
opposition by introducing dissonances.
Again, in constructing a linear theme,
it is possible to proceed either by repeating or continuing the curve with which
we start, or else by introducing opposing
and balancing lines. Or for the elucidation of a story it may be expedient to
place the persons in various situations,
in order that they may manifest their
characters—the method of thematic
variation—or to balance them against
unlike characters. Yet by themselves
neither mere variation of theme nor balance of opposites will create evolution.
Thematic variation, balance, and evolution remain, therefore, the fundamental
and irreducible types of esthetic unity.
I personally have been unable to find
other types. Types which seem to be

different, like rhythm or circular composition, can easily be shown to be species of one or another of these preëminent forms. The reduction of rhythm has already been effected. As for circular composition, it is evidently a case of evolution; for there is always a beginning and an end; but evolution is combined with repetition, for the beginning and the end are the same. A melody that begins and ends on the tonic is a simple illustration. I have shown that all three forms are intermingled; and most works of art contain all three; yet they remain, nevertheless, distinct.[5]

The principle of hierarchy is not so much a mode of organic unity, like thematic variation, balance, and evolution, as rather a species of organization of elements in each of these modes. Sometimes, although not always, there is some one element, or there may be more, of a complex work of art which occupies a position of commanding importance there. These elements always embody the theme in an emphatic way, and have a significance far greater than any of the other elements. Thus, in a portrait, the figure is more important than the background, and the face is more significant than anything else. In a novel or drama there may be a scene of unusual significance for the development of the plot, or in a musical composition a single passage, like the Liebestod in Tristan, which overshadows the remainder of the composition or is the climax of its movement. Every dramatic species of evolution illustrates this, as we have seen. In balance also, as again we have already observed, one or the other of the elements may dominate, though slightly. However, dominance is a relative matter, and an element, not itself of unusual importance in the whole, may nevertheless overshadow another element, relatively. Thus, in the Young Woman with a Water Jug of Vermeer, the pitcher is more prominent than the box. Any quality whatever—large size, unusual brightness, richness of elaboration, central position, fullness of meaning—that attracts the attention to itself more strongly than the attention is attracted to other elements, creates relative dominance. However, there may be no elements of outstanding importance in the whole, as is the case in many a landscape painting and in the non-dramatic types of evolution, but only varying degrees of importance among all the elements.

[5] I am reminded by my friend, Miss Shio Sakanishi, that in many forms of Japanese art symmetry and repetition are carefully avoided, yet balance is scrupulously observed.

TECHNIQUE AS DISCOVERY
Mark Schorer[*]

Mark Schorer holds that technique makes the difference between experience or content and *"achieved* content, the form of the work of art as a work of art." Through the form established by technique the artist not merely organizes given material, he actually discovers and defines its meaning.

* The essay is reprinted from *The Hudson Review*, Vol. I, No. 1 (Spring, 1948) by permission of the author and *The Hudson Review*. Copyright 1948 by The Hudson Review, Inc.

I

Modern criticism, through its exacting scrutiny of literary texts, has demonstrated with finality that in art beauty and truth are indivisible and one. The Keatsian overtones of these terms are mitigated and an old dilemma solved if for beauty we substitute form, and for truth, content. We may, without risk of loss, narrow them even more, and speak of technique and subject matter. Modern criticism has shown us that to speak of content as such is not to speak of art at all, but of experience; and that it is only when we speak of the *achieved* content, the form of the work of art as a work of art, that we speak as critics. The difference between content, or experience, and achieved content, or art, is technique.

When we speak of technique, then, we speak of nearly everything. For technique is the means by which the writer's experience, which is his subject matter, compels him to attend to it; technique is the only means he has of discovering, exploring, developing his subject, of conveying its meaning, and, finally, of evaluating it. And surely it follows that certain techniques are sharper tools than others, and will discover more; that the writer capable of the most exacting technical scrutiny of his subject matter, will produce works with the most satisfying content, works with thickness and resonance, works which reverberate, works with maximum meaning.

We are no longer able to regard as seriously intended criticism of poetry which does not assume these generalizations; but the case for fiction has not yet been established. The novel is still read as though its content has some value in itself, as though the subject matter of fiction has greater or lesser value in itself, and as though technique were not a primary but a supplementary element, capable perhaps of not unattractive embellishments upon the surface of the subject, but hardly of its essence. Or technique is thought of in blunter terms than those which one associates with poetry, as such relatively obvious matters as the arrangement of events to create plot; or, within plot, of suspense and climax; or as the means of revealing character motivation, relationship, and development; or as the use of point of view, but point of view as some nearly arbitrary device for the heightening of dramatic interest through the narrowing or broadening of perspective upon the material, rather than as a means toward the positive definition of theme. As for the resources of language, these, somehow, we almost never think of as a part of the technique of fiction—language as used to create a certain texture and tone which in themselves state and define themes and meanings; or language, the counters of our ordinary speech, as forced, through conscious manipulation, into all those larger meanings which our ordinary speech almost never intends. Technique in fiction, all this is a way of saying, we somehow continue to regard as merely a means to organizing material which is "given" rather than as the means of exploring and defining the values in an area of experience which, for the first time *then*, are being given.

Is fiction still regarded in this odd, divided way because it is really less tractable before the critical suppositions which now seem inevitable to poetry? Let us look at some examples: two well-known novels of the past, both by writers who may be described as "primitive," although their relative innocence of technique is of a different sort—Defoe's *Moll Flanders* and Emily Brontë's *Wuthering Heights;* and three well-known novels of

this century—*Tono-Bungay*, by a writer
who claimed to eschew technique; *Sons
and Lovers*, by a novelist who, because
his ideal of subject matter ("the poetry
of the immediate present") led him at
last into the fallacy of spontaneous and
unchangeable composition, in effect
eschewed technique; and *A Portrait of
the Artist as a Young Man*, by a novelist
whose practice made claims for the su-
premacy of technique beyond those made
by anyone in the past or by anyone else
in this century.

Technique in fiction is, of course, all
those obvious forms of it which are
usually taken to be the whole of it, and
many others; but for the present purposes, let it be thought of in two respects
particularly: the uses to which language,
as language, is put to express the quality
of the experience in question; and the
uses of point of view not only as a mode
of dramatic delimitation, but more particularly, of thematic definition. Technique is really what T. S. Eliot means by
"convention"—any selection, structure,
or distortion, any form or rhythm imposed upon the world of action; by
means of which—it should be added—
our apprehension of the world of action
is enriched or renewed. In this sense,
everything is technique which is not the
lump of experience itself, and one cannot properly say that a writer has no
technique or that he eschews technique,
for, being a writer, he cannot do so. We
can speak of good and bad technique, of
adequate and inadequate, of technique
which serves the novel's purpose, or dis-
serves.

II

In the prefatory remarks to *Moll Flanders*, Defoe tells us that he is not writing
fiction at all, but editing the journals of
a woman of notorious character, and
rather to instruct us in the necessities and
the joys of virtue than to please us. We
do not, of course, take these professions
seriously, since nothing in the conduct
of the narrative indicates that virtue is
either more necessary or more enjoyable
than vice. On the contrary, we discover
that Moll turns virtuous only after a life
of vice has enabled her to do so with
security; yet it is precisely for this reason
that Defoe's profession of didactic purpose has interest. For the actual morality
which the novel enforces is the morality
of any commercial culture, the belief that
virtue pays—in worldly goods. It is a
morality somewhat less than skin deep,
having no relation to motives arising
from a sense of good and evil, least of
all, of evil-*in*-good, but exclusively from
the presence or absence of food, drink,
linen, damask, silver, and time-pieces.
It is the morality of measurement, and
without in the least intending it, *Moll
Flanders* is our classic revelation of the
mercantile mind: the morality of measurement, which Defoe has completely
neglected to measure. He fails not only
to evaluate this material in his announced
way, but to evaluate it at all. His announced purpose is, we admit, a pious
humbug, and he meant us to read the
book as a series of scandalous events;
and thanks to his inexhaustible pleasure
in excess and exaggeration, this element
in the book continues to amuse us. Long
before the book has been finished, however, this element has also become an
absurdity; but not half the absurdity as
that which Defoe did not intend at all—
the notion that Moll could live a rich
and full life of crime, and yet, repenting,
emerge spotless in the end. The point is,
of course, that she has no moral being,
nor has the book any moral life. Every-

thing is external. Everything can be weighed, measured, handled, paid for in gold, or expiated by a prison term. To this, the whole texture of the novel testifies: the bolts of goods, the inventories, the itemized accounts, the landlady's bills, the lists, the ledgers: all this, which taken together comprises what we call Defoe's method of circumstantial realism.

He did not come upon that method by any deliberation: it represents precisely his own world of value, the importance of external circumstance to Defoe. The point of view of Moll is indistinguishable from the point of view of her creator. We discover the meaning of the novel (at unnecessary length, without economy, without emphasis, with almost none of the distortions or the advantages of art) in spite of Defoe, not because of him. Thus the book is not the true chronicle of a disreputable female, but the true allegory of an impoverished soul —the author's; not an anatomy of the criminal class, but of the middle class. And we read it as an unintended comic revelation of self and of a social mode. Because he had no adequate resources of technique to separate himself from his material, thereby to discover and to define the meanings of his material, his contribution is not to fiction but to the history of fiction, and to social history.

The situation in *Wuthering Heights* is at once somewhat the same and yet very different. Here, too, the whole novel turns upon itself, but this time to its estimable advantage; here, too, is a revelation of what is perhaps the author's secret world of value, but this time, through what may be an accident of technique, the revelation is meaningfully accomplished. Emily Brontë may merely have stumbled upon the perspectives which define the form and the theme of

her book. Whether she knew from the outset, or even at the end, what she was doing, we may doubt; but what she did and did superbly we can see.

We can assume, without at all becoming involved in the author's life but merely from the tone of somnambulistic excess which is generated by the writing itself, that this world of monstrous passion, of dark and gigantic emotional and nervous energy, is for the author, or was in the first place, a world of ideal value; and that the book sets out to persuade us of the moral magnificence of such unmoral passion. We are, I think, expected, in the first place, to take at their own valuation these demonic beings, Heathcliff and Cathy: as special creatures, set apart from the cloddish world about them by their heightened capacity for feeling, set apart, even, from the ordinary objects of human passion as, in their transcendental, sexless relationship, they identify themselves with an uncompromising landscape and cosmic force. Yet this is absurd, as much of the detail that surrounds it ("Other dogs lurked in other recesses") is absurd. The novelist Emily Brontë had to discover these absurdities to the girl Emily; her technique had to evaluate them for what they were, so that we are persuaded that it is not Emily who is mistaken in her estimate of her characters, but they who are mistaken in their estimate of themselves. The theme of the moral magnificence of unmoral passion is an impossible theme to sustain, and what interests us is that it was device—and this time, mere, mechanical device—which taught Emily Brontë that, the needs of her temperament to the contrary, all personal longing and reverie to the contrary, perhaps—that this was indeed not at all what her material must mean as art. Technique objectifies.

To lay before us the full character of

this passion, to show us how it first comes into being and then comes to dominate the world about it and the life that follows upon it, Emily Brontë gives her material a broad scope in time, lets it, in fact, cut across three generations. And to manage material which is so extensive, she must find a means of narration, points of view, which can encompass that material, and, in her somewhat crude concept of motive, justify its telling. So she chooses a foppish traveller who stumbles into this world of passionate violence, a traveller representing the thin and conventional emotional life of the far world of fashion, who wishes to hear the tale: and for her teller she chooses, almost inevitably, the old family retainer who knows everything, a character as conventional as the other, but this one representing not the conventions of fashion, but the conventions of the humblest moralism. What has happened is, first, that she has chosen as her narrative perspective those very elements, conventional emotion and conventional morality, which her hero and heroine are meant to transcend with such spectacular magnificence; and second, that she has permitted this perspective to operate throughout a long period of time. And these two elements compel the novelist to see what her unmoral passions come to. Moral magnificence? Not at all; rather, a devastating spectacle of human waste; ashes. For the time of the novel is carried on long enough to show Heathcliff at last an emptied man, burned out by his fever ragings, exhausted and will less, his passion meaningless at last. And it goes even a little further, to Lockwood, the fop, in the graveyard, sententiously contemplating headstones. Thus in the end the triumph is all on the side of the cloddish world, which survives.

Perhaps not all on that side. For, like Densher at the end of *The Wings of the Dove*, we say, and surely Hareton and the second Cathy say, "We shall never be again as we were!" But there is more point in observing that a certain body of materials, a girl's romantic daydreams, have, through the most conventional devices of fiction, been pushed beyond their inception in fancy to their meanings, their conception as a written book —that they, that is, are not at all as they were.

III

Technique alone objectifies the materials of art; hence technique alone evaluates those materials. This is the axiom which demonstrates itself so devastatingly whenever a writer declares, under the urgent sense of the importance of his materials (whether these are autobiography, or social ideas, or personal passions)—whenever such a writer declares that he cannot linger with technical refinements. That art will not tolerate such a writer H. G. Wells handsomely proves. His enormous literary energy included no respect for the techniques of his medium, and his medium takes its revenge upon his bumptiousness. "I have never taken any very great pains about writing. I am outside the hierarchy of conscious and deliberate writers altogether. I am the absolute antithesis of Mr. James Joyce. . . . Long ago, living in close conversational proximity to Henry James, Joseph Conrad, and Mr. Ford Madox Hueffer, I escaped from under their immense artistic preoccupations by calling myself a journalist."[1] Precisely. And he escaped—he disappeared—from literature into the annals of an era.

[1] H. G. Wells, "Introduction" to *H. G. Wells* by Geoffrey West (New York, 1930), pp. xvii–xviii.—Ed.

Yet what confidence! "Literature," Wells said, "is not jewelry, it has quite other aims than perfection, and the more one thinks of 'how it is done' the less one gets it done. These critical indulgences lead along a fatal path, away from every natural interest towards a preposterous emptiness of technical effort, a monstrous egotism of artistry, of which the later work of Henry James is the monumental warning. 'It,' the subject, the thing or the thought, has long since disappeared in these amazing works; nothing remains but the way it has been 'manipulated.' "[2] Seldom has a literary theorist been so totally wrong; for what we learn as James grows for us and Wells disappears, is that without what he calls "manipulation," there *is* no "it," no "subject" in art. There is again only social history.

The virtue of the modern novelist—from James and Conrad down—is not only that he pays so much attention to his medium, but that, when he pays most, he discovers through it a new subject matter, and a greater one. Under the "immense artistic preoccupations" of James and Conrad and Joyce, the form of the novel changed, and with the technical change, analogous changes took place in substance, in point of view, in the whole conception of fiction. And the final lesson of the modern novel is that technique is not the secondary thing that it seems to Wells, some external machination, a mechanical affair, but a deep and primary operation; not only that technique *contains* intellectual and moral implications, but that it *discovers* them. For a writer like Wells, who wished to give us the intellectual and the moral history of our times, the lesson is a hard one: it tells us that the order of intellect and the order of morality

do not exist at all, in art, except as they are organized in the order of art.

Wells's ambitions were very large. "Before we have done, we will have all life within the scope of the novel."[3] But that is where life already is, within the scope of the novel; where it needs to be brought is into novels. In Wells we have all the important topics in life, but no good novels. He was not asking too much of art, or asking that it include more than it happily can; he was not asking anything of it—as art, which is all that it can give, and that is everything.

A novel like *Tono-Bungay*, generally thought to be Wells's best, is therefore instructive. "I want to tell—*myself*," says George, the hero, "and my impressions of the thing as a whole"—the thing as a whole being the collapse of traditional British institutions in the twentieth century. George "tells himself" in terms of three stages in his life which have rough equivalents in modern British social history, and this is, to be sure, a plan, a framework; but it is the framework of Wells's abstract thinking, not of his craftsmanship, and the primary demand which one makes of such a book as this, that means be discovered whereby the dimensions of the hero contain the experiences he recounts, is never met. The novelist flounders through a series of literary imitations—from an early Dickensian episode, through a kind of Shavian interlude, through a Conradian episode, to a Jules Verne vision at the end. The significant failure is in that end, and in the way that it defeats not only the entire social analysis of the bulk of the novel, but Wells's own ends as a thinker. For at last George finds a purpose in science. "I decided that in power and knowledge lay the salvation of my life, the secret

---

[2] "A Footnote to Hueffer," *English Review* (August 1920).—Ed.

[3] *An Englishman Looks at the World* (London, 1914), p. 169.—Ed.

that would fill my need; that to these things I would give myself."

But science, power and knowledge, are summed up at last in a destroyer. As far as one can tell Wells intends no irony, although he may here have come upon the essence of the major irony in modern history. The novel ends in a kind of meditative rhapsody which denies every value that the book had been aiming toward. For of all the kinds of social waste which Wells has been describing, this is the most inclusive, the final waste. Thus he gives us in the end not a novel, but a hypothesis; not an individual destiny, but a theory of the future; and not his theory of the future, but a nihilistic vision quite opposite from everything that he meant to represent. With a minimum of attention to the virtues of technique, Wells might still not have written a good novel; but he would at any rate have established a point of view and a tone which would have told us what he meant.

To say what one means in art is never easy, and the more intimately one is implicated in one's material, the more difficult it is. If, besides, one commits fiction to a therapeutic function which is to be operative not on the audience but on the author, declaring, as D. H. Lawrence did, that "One sheds one's sicknesses in books, repeats and presents again one's emotions to be master of them,"[4] the difficulty is vast. It is an acceptable theory only with the qualification that technique, which objectifies, is under no other circumstances so impera tive. For merely to repeat one's emotions, merely to look into one's heart and write, is also merely to repeat the round of emotional bondage. If our books are to be exercises in self-analysis, then tech-

nique must—and alone can—take the place of the absent analyst.

Lawrence, in the relatively late Introduction to his *Collected Poems*, made that distinction of the amateur between his "real" poems and his "composed" poems, between the poems which expressed his demon directly and created their own form "willy-nilly," and the poems which, through the hocus pocus of technique, he spuriously put together and could, if necessary, revise.[5] His belief in a "poetry of the immediate present," poetry in which nothing is fixed, static, or final, where all is shimmeriness and impermanence and vitalistic essence, arose from this mistaken notion of technique. And from this notion, an unsympathetic critic like D. S. Savage can construct a case which shows Lawrence driven "concurrently to the dissolution of personality and the dissolution of art."[6] The argument suggests that Lawrence's early, crucial novel, *Sons and Lovers*, is another example of meanings confused by an impatience with technical resources.

The novel has two themes: the crippling effects of a mother's love on the emotional development of her son; and the "split" between kinds of love, physical and spiritual, which the son develops, the kinds represented by two young women, Clara and Miriam. The two themes should, of course, work together, the second being, actually, the result of the first: this "split" is the "crippling." So one would expect to see the novel developed, and so Lawrence, in his famous letter to Edward Garnett, where he says that Paul is left at the end with the "drift towards death," apparently thought he had developed it.[7] Yet in the

---

[4] *The Letters of D. H. Lawrence*, ed. Aldous Huxley (New York, 1923), p. 152.—Ed.

[5] (New York, 1929), I, 5–6.—Ed.

[6] *The Personal Principle* (London, 1944), p. 154.—Ed.

[7] *Letters*, ed. Huxley, pp. 78–80.—Ed.

last few sentences of the novel, Paul rejects his desire for extinction and turns towards "the faintly humming, glowing town," to life—as nothing in his previous history persuades us that he could unfalteringly do.

The discrepancy suggests that the book may reveal certain confusions between intention and performance.

The first of these is the contradiction between Lawrence's explicit characterizations of the mother and father and his tonal evaluations of them. It is a problem not only of style (of the contradiction between expressed moral epithets and the more general texture of the prose which applies to them) but of point of view. Morel and Lawrence are never separated, which is a way of saying that Lawrence maintains for himself in this book the confused attitude of his character. The mother is a "proud, *honorable* soul," but the father has a "small, *mean* head." This is the sustained contrast; the epithets are characteristic of the whole; and they represent half of Lawrence's feelings. But what is the other half? Which of these characters is given his real sympathy—the hard, self-righteous, aggressive, demanding mother who comes through to us, or the simple, direct, gentle, downright, fumbling, ruined father? There are two attitudes here. Lawrence (and Morel) loves his mother, but he also hates her for compelling his love; and he hates his father with the true Freudian jealousy, but he also loves him for what he is in himself, and he sympathizes more deeply with him because his wholeness has been destroyed by the mother's domination, just as his, Lawrence-Morel's, has been.

This is a psychological tension which disrupts the form of the novel and obscures its meaning, because neither the contradiction in style nor the confusion in point of view is made to right itself.

Lawrence is merely repeating his emotions, and he avoids an austerer technical scrutiny of his material because it would compel him to master them. He would not let the artist be stronger than the man.

The result is that, at the same time that the book condemns the mother, it justifies her; at the same time that it shows Paul's failure, it offers rationalizations which place the failure elsewhere. The handling of the girl, Miriam, if viewed closely, is pathetic in what it signifies for Lawrence, both as man and artist. For Miriam is made the mother's scape-goat, and in a different way from the way that she was in life. The central section of the novel is shot through with alternate statements as to the source of the difficulty: Paul is unable to love Miriam wholly, and Miriam can love only his spirit. The contradictions appear sometimes within single paragraphs, and the point of view is never adequately objectified and sustained to tell us which is true. The material is never seen as material; the writer is caught in it exactly as firmly as he was caught in his experience of it. "That's how women are with me," said Paul. "They want me like mad, but they don't want to belong to me." So he might have said, and believed it; but at the end of the novel, Lawrence is still saying that, and himself believing it.

For the full history of this technical failure, one must read *Sons and Lovers* carefully and then learn the history of the manuscript from the book called *D. H. Laurence: A Personal Record*, by one E. T., who was Miriam in life. The basic situation is clear enough. The first theme—the crippling effects of the mother's love—is developed right through to the end; and then suddenly, in the last few sentences, turns on itself, and Paul gives himself to life, not death.

But all the way through, the insidious rationalizations of the second theme have crept in to destroy the artistic coherence of the work. A "split" would occur in Paul; but as the split is treated, it is superimposed upon rather than developed in support of the first theme. It is a rationalization made from it. If Miriam is made to insist on spiritual love, the meaning and the power of theme one are reduced; yet Paul's weakness is disguised. Lawrence could not separate the investigating analyst, who must be objective, from Lawrence, the subject of the book; and the sickness was not healed, the emotion not mastered, the novel not perfected. All this, and the character of a whole career, would have been altered if Lawrence had allowed his technique to discover the fullest meaning of his subject.

A *Portrait of the Artist as a Young Man*, like *Tono-Bungay* and *Sons and Lovers*, is autobiographical, but unlike these it analyzes its material rigorously, and it defines the value and the quality of its experience not by appended comment or moral epithet, but by the texture of the style. The theme of *A Portrait*, a young artist's alienation from his environment, is explored and evaluated through three different styles and methods as Stephen Dedalus moves from childhood through boyhood into maturity. The opening pages are written in something like the stream of consciousness of *Ulysses*, as the environment impinges directly on the consciousness of the infant and the child, a strange, opening world which the mind does not yet subject to questioning, selection, or judgment. But this style changes very soon, as the boy begins to explore his surroundings, and as his sensuous experience of the world is enlarged, it takes on heavier and heavier rhythms and a fuller and fuller body of sensuous detail, until it

reaches a crescendo of romantic opulence in the emotional climaxes which mark Stephen's rejection of domestic and religious values. Then gradually the style subsides into the austerer intellectuality of the final sections, as he defines to himself the outlines of the artistic task which is to usurp his maturity.

A highly self-conscious use of style and method defines the quality of experience in each of these sections, and, it is worth pointing out in connection with the third and concluding section, the style and method evaluate the experience. What has happened to Stephen is, of course, a progressive alienation from the life around him as he progressed in his initiation into it, and by the end of the novel, the alienation is complete. The final portion of the novel, fascinating as it may be for the developing esthetic creed of Stephen-Joyce, is peculiarly bare. The life experience was not bare, as we know from *Stephen Hero*; but Joyce is forcing technique to comment. In essence, Stephen's alienation is a denial of the human environment; it is a loss; and the austere discourse of the final section, abstract and almost wholly without sensuous detail or strong rhythm, tells us of that loss. It is a loss so great that the texture of the notation-like prose here suggests that the end is really all an illusion, that when Stephen tells us and himself that he is going forth to forge in the smithy of his soul the uncreated conscience of his race, we are to infer from the very quality of the icy, abstract void he now inhabits, the implausibility of his aim. For *Ulysses* does not create the conscience of the race; it creates our consciousness.

In the very last two or three paragraphs of the novel, the style changes once more, reverts from the bare, notative kind to the romantic prose of Stephen's adolescence. "Away! Away!

The spell of arms and voices; the white arms of roads, their promise of close embraces and the black arms of tall ships that stand against the moon, their tale of distant nations. They are held out to say: We are alone—come." Might one not say that the austere ambition is founded on adolescent longing? That the excessive intellectual severity of one style is the counterpart of the excessive lyric relaxation of the other? And that the final passage of A *Portrait* punctuates the illusory nature of the whole ambition?

For *Ulysses* does not create a conscience. Stephen, in *Ulysses*, is a little older, and gripped now by guilt, but he is still the cold young man divorced from the human no less than the institutional environment. The environment of urban life finds a separate embodiment in the character of Bloom, and Bloom is as lost as Stephen, though touchingly groping for moorings. Each of the two is weakened by his inability to reach out, or to do more than reach out to the other. Here, then, is the theme again, more fully stated, as it were in counterpoint.

But if Stephen is not much older, Joyce is. He is older as an artist not only because he can create and lavish his Godlike pity on a Leopold Bloom, but also because he knows now what both Stephen and Bloom mean, and *how much*, through the most brilliant technical operation ever made in fiction, they can be made to mean. Thus *Ulysses*, through the imaginative force which its techniques direct, is like a pattern of concentric circles, with the immediate human situation at its center, this passing on and out to the whole dilemma of modern life, this passing on and out beyond that to a vision of the cosmos, and this to the mythical limits of our experience. If we read *Ulysses* with more satisfaction than any other novel of this century, it is because its author held an attitude toward technique and the technical scrutiny of subject matter which enabled him to order, within a single work and with superb coherence, the greatest amount of our experience.

IV

In the United States during the last twenty-five years, we have had many big novels but few good ones. A writer like James T. Farrell apparently assumes that by endless redundancy in the description of the surface of American Life, he will somehow write a book with the scope of *Ulysses*. Thomas Wolfe apparently assumed that by the mere disgorging of the raw material of his experience he would give us at last our epic. But except in a physical sense, these men have hardly written novels at all.

The books of Thomas Wolfe were, of course, journals, and the primary role of his publisher in transforming these journals into the semblance of novels is notorious. For the crucial act of the artist, the unique act which is composition, a sympathetic editorial blue pencil and scissors were substituted. The result has excited many people, especially the young, and the ostensibly critical have observed the prodigal talent with the wish that it might have been controlled. Talent there was, if one means by talent inexhaustible verbal energy, excessive response to personal experience, and a great capacity for auditory imitativeness, yet all of this has nothing to do with the novelistic quality of the written result; until the talent is controlled, the material organized, the content achieved, there is simply the man and his life. It remains to be demonstrated that Wolfe's conversations were any less interesting as novels than his books, which is to say that his books are without interest as novels. As with Lawrence, our response to the books is determined, not by their qualities as novels but by our response to him and his qualities as a temperament.

This is another way of saying that Thomas Wolfe never really knew what he was writing *about*. Of Time and the River is merely a euphemism for Of a Man and his Ego. It is possible that had his conception of himself and of art included an adequate respect for technique and the capacity to pursue it, Wolfe would have written a great novel on his true subject—the dilemma of romantic genius; it was his true subject, but it remains his undiscovered subject, it is the subject which *we* must dig out for him, because he himself had neither the lamp nor the pick to find it in and mine it out of the labyrinths of his experience. Like Emily Brontë, Wolfe needed a point of view beyond his own which would separate his material and its effect.

With Farrell, the situation is opposite. He knows quite well what his subject is and what he wishes to tell us about it, but he hardly needs the novel to do so. It is significant that in sheer clumsiness of style, no living writer exceeds him, for his prose is asked to perform no service beyond communication of the most rudimentary kind of fact. For his ambitions, the style of the newspaper and the lens of the documentary camera would be quite adequate, yet consider the diminution which Leopold Bloom, for example, would suffer, if he were to be viewed from these, the technical perspectives of James Farrell. Under the eye of this technique, the material does not yield up enough; indeed, it shrinks.

More and more writers in this century have felt that naturalism as a method imposes on them strictures which prevent them from exploring through all the resources of technique the full amplifications of their subjects, and that thus it seriously limits the possible breadth of aesthetic meaning and response. James Farrell is almost unique in the complacency with which he submits to the blunt techniques of naturalism; and his fiction is correspondingly repetitive and flat.

That naturalism had a sociological and disciplinary value in the nineteenth century is obvious; it enabled the novel to grasp materials and make analyses which had eluded it in the past, and to grasp them boldly; but even then it did not tell us enough of what, in Virginia Woolf's phrase, is "really real," nor did it provide the means to the maximum of reality coherently contained. Even the Flaubertian ideal of objectivity seems, today, an unnecessarily limited view of objectivity, for as almost every good writer of this century shows us, it is quite as possible to be objective about subjective states as it is to be objective about the circumstantial surfaces of life. Dublin, in *Ulysses*, is a moral setting: not only a city portrayed in the naturalistic fashion of Dickens's London, but also a map of the modern psyche with its oblique and baffled purposes. The second level of reality in no way invalidates the first, and a writer like Joyce shows us that, if the artist truly respects his medium, he can be objective about both at once. What we need in fiction is a devoted fidelity to every technique which will help us to discover and to evaluate our subject matter, and more than that, to discover the amplifications of meaning of which our subject matter is capable.

Most modern novelists have felt this demand upon them. André Gide allowed one of his artist-heroes to make an observation which considerably resembles an observation we have quoted from Wells. "My novel hasn't got a subject.... Let's say, if you prefer it, it hasn't got *one* subject.... 'A slice of life,' the naturalist school said. The great defect of that school is that it always cuts its slice in the same direction; in time, lengthwise. Why not in breadth? Or in depth? As for me I should like not to cut at all. Please understand; I should like to put everything in my novel."[8] Wells, with his equally large blob of potential material, did not know how to cut it to the novel's taste; Gide cut, of course—in every possible direction. Gide and others. And those "cuts" are all the new techniques which modern fiction has given us. None, perhaps, is more important than that inheritance from French symbolism which Huxley, in the glittering wake of Gide, called "the musicalization of fiction." Conrad anticipated both when he wrote that the novel "must strenuously aspire to the plasticity of sculpture, to the colour of painting, and to the magic suggestiveness of music—which is the art of arts,"[9] and when he said of that early but wonderful piece of symbolist fiction, *Heart of Darkness*, "It was like another art altogether. That sombre theme had to be given a sinister resonance, a tonality of its own, a continued vibration that, I hoped, would hang in the air and dwell on the ear after the last note had been struck."[10] The analogy with music, except as a metaphor, is inexact, and except as it points to techniques which fiction can employ as fiction, not very useful to our sense of craftsmanship. It has had an approximate exactness in only one work, Joyce's final effort, and an effort unique in literary history, *Finnegans Wake*, and here, of course, those readers willing to approach the "ideal" effort Joyce demands, discovering an inexhaustible wealth and scope, are most forcibly reminded of the primary importance of

[8] *The Counterfeiters* (New York, 1927), p. 172.—Ed.

[9] In his Preface to *The Nigger of the Narcissus*.—Ed.

[10] In his Preface to *Youth*.—Ed.

technique to subject, and of their indivisibility.

The techniques of naturalism inevitably curtail subject and often leave it in its original area, that of undefined social experience. Those of our writers who, stemming from this tradition, yet, at their best, achieve a novelistic definition of social experience—writers like the occasional Sherwood Anderson, William Carlos Williams, the occasional Erskine Caldwell, Nathanael West, and Ira Wolfert in *Tucker's People*, have done so by pressing naturalism far beyond itself, into positively gothic distortions. The structural machinations of Dos Passos and the lyrical interruptions of Steinbeck are the desperate maneuvers of men committed to a method of whose limitations they despair. They are our symbolists *manqués*, who end as allegorists.

Our most accomplished novels leave no such impression of desperate and intentional struggle, yet their precise technique and their determination to make their prose work in the service of their subjects have been the measure of their accomplishment. Hemingway's *The Sun Also Rises* and Wescott's *The Pilgrim Hawk* are works of art not because they may be measured by some external, neoclassic notion of form, but because their forms are so exactly equivalent with their subjects, and because the evaluation of their subjects exists in their styles.

Hemingway has recently said that his contribution to younger writers lay in a certain necessary purification of the language; but the claim has doubtful value. The contribution of his prose was to his subject, and the terseness of style for which his early work is justly celebrated is no more valuable, as an end in itself, than the baroque involutedness of Faulkner's prose, or the cold elegance of Wescott's. Hemingway's early subject, the exhaustion of value, was perfectly investigated and invested by his bare style, and in story after story, no meaning at all is to be inferred from the fiction except as the style itself suggests that there is no meaning in life. This style, more than that, was the perfect technical substitute for the conventional commentator; it expresses and it measures that peculiar morality of the stiff lip which Hemingway borrowed from athletes. It is an instructive lesson, furthermore, to observe how the style breaks down when Hemingway moves into the less congenial subject matter of social affirmation: how the style breaks down, the effect of verbal economy as mute suffering is lost, the personality of the writer, no longer protected by the objectification of an adequate technique, begins its offensive intrusion, and the entire structural integrity slackens. Inversely, in the stories and the early novels, the technique was the perfect embodiment of the subject and it gave that subject its astonishing largeness of effect and of meaning.

One should correct Buffon and say that style is the subject.[11] In Wescott's *Pilgrim Hawk*, a novel which bewildered its many friendly critics by the apparent absence of subject, the subject, the story, is again in the style itself. This novel, which is a triumph of the sustained point of view, is only bewildering if we try to make a story out of the narrator's observations upon others; but if we read his observations as oblique and unrecognized observations upon himself the story emerges with perfect coherence, and it reverberates with meaning is as suited to continuing reflection as the greatest lyrics.

The rewards of such respect for the medium as the early Hemingway and the

11 Buffon was the critic who said, in a famous speech given to the French Academy, "The style is the man himself" (1753).—Ed.

occasional Wescott have shown may be observed in every good writer we have. The involutions of Faulkner's style are the perfect equivalent of his involved structures, and the two together are the perfect representation of the moral labyrinths he explores, and of the ruined world which his novels repeatedly invoke and in which these labyrinths exist. The cultivated sensuosity of Katherine Anne Porter's style has charm in itself, of course, but no more than with these others does it have aesthetic value in itself; its values lie in the subtle means by which sensuous details become symbols, and in the way that the symbols provide a network which is the story, and which at the same time provides the writer and us with a refined moral insight by means of which to test it. When we put such writers against a writer like William Saroyan, whose respect is reserved for his own temperament, we are appalled by the stylistic irresponsibility we find in him, and by the almost total absence of theme, or defined subject matter, and the abundance of unwarranted feeling. Such a writer inevitably becomes a sentimentalist because he has no means by which to measure his emotion. Technique, at last, is measure.

These writers, from Defoe to Porter, are of unequal and very different talent, and technique and talent are, of course, after a point, two different things. What Joyce gives us in one direction, Lawrence, for all his imperfections as a technician, gives us in another, even though it is not usually the direction of art. Only in some of his stories and in a few of his poems, where the demands of technique are less sustained and the subject matter is not autobiographical, Lawrence, in a different way from Joyce, comes to the same aesthetic fulfilment. Emily Brontë, with what was perhaps her intuitive grasp of the need to establish a tension between her subject matter and her perspective upon it, achieves a similar fulfilment; and, curiously, in the same way and certainly by intuition alone, Hemingway's early work makes a moving splendor from nothingness.

And yet, whatever one must allow to talent and forgive in technique, one risks no generalization in saying that modern fiction at its best has been peculiarly conscious of itself and of its tools. The technique of modern fiction, at once greedy and fastidious, achieves as its subject matter not some singleness, some topic or thesis, but the whole of the modern consciousness. It discovers the complexity of the modern spirit, the difficulty of personal morality, and the fact of evil—all the untractable elements under the surface which a technique of the surface alone can not approach. It shows us—in Conrad's words, from *Victory*—that we all live in an "age in which we are camped like bewildered travellers in a garish, unrestful hotel," and while it puts its hard light on our environment, it penetrates, with its sharp weapons, the depths of our bewilderment. These are not two things, but only an adequate technique can show them as one. In a realist like Farrell, we have the environment only, which we know from the newspapers; in a subjectivist like Wolfe, we have the bewilderment only, which we record in our own diaries and letters. But the true novelist gives them to us together, and thereby increases the effect of each, and reveals each in its full significance.

Elizabeth Bowen, writing of Lawrence, said of modern fiction, "We want the naturalistic surface, but with a kind of internal burning. In Lawrence every bush burns."[12] But the bush burns brighter in some places than in others, and it burns brightest when a passionate private vision finds its objectification in exacting technical search. If the vision finds no such objectification, as in Wolfe and Saroyan, there is a burning without a bush. In our committed realists, who deny the resources of art for the sake of life, whose technique forgives both innocence and slovenliness—in Defoe and Wells and Farrell, there is a bush but it does not burn. There, at first glance, the bush is only a bush; and then, when we look again, we see that, really, the thing is dead.

[12] *Collected Impressions* (London, 1950), p. 159.—Ed.

FORM AND POINT OF VIEW
Percy Lubbock*

The point of view from which a story is told is a factor of its form. In his discussion of point of view, Percy Lubbock defines a range between the loosely conceived first person narrative and the completely objective form of the drama. His essay is primarily concerned with how point of view and form merge in the method of relating the story.

* The essay is reprinted from *The Craft of Fiction* by Percy Lubbock. All Rights Reserved.

Reprinted by permission of The Viking Press, Inc.

The whole intricate question of method, in the craft of fiction, I take to be governed by the question of the point of view—the question of the relation in which the narrator stands to the story. He tells it as *he* sees it, in the first place; the reader faces the story-teller and listens, and the story may be told so vivaciously that the presence of the minstrel is forgotten, and the scene becomes visible, peopled with the characters of the tale. It may be so, it very often is so for a time. But it is not so always, and the story-teller himself grows conscious of a misgiving. If the spell is weakened at any moment, the listener is recalled from the scene to the mere author before him, and the story rests only upon the author's direct assertion. Is it not possible, then, to introduce another point of view, to set up a fresh narrator to bear the brunt of the reader's scrutiny? If the story-teller is *in* the story himself, the author is dramatized; his assertions gain in weight, for they are backed by the presence of the narrator in the pictured scene. It is advantage scored; the author has shifted his responsibility, and it now falls where the reader can see and measure it; the arbitrary quality which may at any time be detected in the author's voice is disguised in the voice of his spokesman. Nothing is now imported into the story from without; it is self-contained, it has no associations with anyone beyond its circle.

Such is the first step towards dramatization, and in very many a story it may be enough. The spokesman is there, in recognizable relation with his matter, no question of his authority can arise. But now a difficulty may be started by the nature of the tale that he tells. If he has nothing to do but to relate what he has seen, what anyone might have seen in his position, his account will serve very well; there is no need for more. Let him unfold his chronicle as it appears in his memory. But if he is himself the subject of his story, if the story involves a searching exploration of his own consciousness, an account in his own words, after the fact, is not by any means the best imaginable. Far better it would be to see him while his mind is actually at work in the agitation, whatever it may be, which is to make the book. The matter would then be objective and visible to the reader, instead of reaching him in the form of a report at second hand. But how to manage this without falling back upon the author and *his* report, which has already been tried and for good reasons, as it seemed, abandoned? It is managed by a kind of repetition of the same stroke, a further shift of the point of view. The spectator, the listener, the reader, is now himself to be placed at the angle of vision; not an account or a report, more or less convincing, is to be offered him, but a direct sight of the matter itself, while it is passing. Nobody expounds or explains; the story is enacted by its look and behaviour at particular moments. By the first stroke the narrator was brought into the book and set before the reader; but the action appeared only in his narrative. Now the action is there, proceeding while the pages are turned; the narrator is forestalled, he is watched while the story is in the making. Such is the progress of the writer of fiction towards drama; such is his method of evading the drawbacks of a mere reporter and assuming the advantages, as far as possible, of a dramatist. How far he may choose to push the process in his book— that is a matter to be decided by the subject; it entirely depends upon the kind of effect that the theme demands. It may respond to all the dramatization it can get, it may give all that it has to give for less. The subject dictates the method.

And now let the process be reversed,

let us start with the purely dramatic sub-ject, the story that will tell itself in perfect rightness, unaided, to the eye of the reader. This story never deviates from a strictly scenic form; one occasion or episode follows another, with no inter-ruption for any reflective summary of events. Necessarily it must be so, for it is only while the episode is proceeding that no question of a narrator can arise; when the scene closes the play ceases till the opening of the next. To glance upon the story from a height and to give a gen-eral impression of its course—this is at once to remove the point of view from the reader and to set up a new one some-where else; the method is no longer con-sistent, no longer purely dramatic. And the dramatic story is not only scenic, it is also limited to so much as the ear can hear and the eye see. In rigid drama of this kind there is naturally no admission of the reader into the private mind of any of the characters; their thoughts and motives are transmuted into action. A subject wrought to this pitch of objec-tivity is no doubt given weight and com-pactness and authority in the highest degree; it is like a piece of modelling, standing in clear space, casting its shadow. It is the most finished form that fiction can take.

But evidently it is not a form to which fiction can aspire in general. It implies many sacrifices, and these will easily seem to be more than the subject can usefully make. It is out of the question, of course, wherever the main burden of the story lies within some particular consciousness, in the study of a soul, the growth of a character, the changing history of a tem-perament; there the subject would be needlessly crossed and strangled by dram-atization pushed to its limit. It is out of the question, again, wherever the story is too big, too comprehensive, too widely ranging, to be treated scenically, with no

opportunity for general and panoramic survey; it has been discovered, indeed, that even a story of this kind *may* fall into a long succession of definite scenes, under some hands, but it has also ap-peared that in doing so it incurs unneces-sary disabilities, and will likely suffer. These stories, therefore, which will not naturally accommodate themselves to the reader's point of view, and the reader's alone, we regard as rather pic-torial than dramatic—meaning that they call for some narrator, somebody who *knows*, to contemplate the facts and cre-ate an impression of them. Whether it is the omniscient author or a man in the book, he must gather up his experience, compose a vision of it as it exists in his mind, and lay *that* before the reader. It is the reflection of an experience; and though there may be all imaginable diver-sity of treatment within the limits of the reflection, such is its essential character. In a pictorial book the principle of the structure involves a point of view which is not the reader's.

It is open to the pictorial book, how-ever, to use a method in its picture-making that is really no other than the method of drama. It is somebody's ex-perience, we say, that is to be reported, the general effect that many things have left upon a certain mind; it is a fusion of innumerable elements, the deposit of a lapse of time. The straightforward way to render it would be for the narrator—the author or his selected creature—to view the past retrospectively and dis-course upon it, to recall and meditate and summarize. That is picture-making in its natural form, using its own method. But exactly as in drama the subject is dis-tributed among the characters and en-acted by them, so in picture the effect may be entrusted to the elements, the re-actions of the moment, and *performed* by these. The mind of the narrator becomes the stage, his voice is no longer heard. His voice *is* heard so long as there is narrative of any sort, whether he is speaking in person or is reported obliquely; his voice is heard, because in either case the language and the intonation are his, the direct expression of his experience. In the drama of his mind there is no personal voice, for there is no narrator; the point of view becomes the reader's once more. The shapes of thought in the man's mind tell their own story. And that is the art of picture-making when it uses the dramatic method.

But it cannot always do so. Constantly it must be necessary to offer the reader a summary of facts, an impression of a train of events, that can only be given as somebody's narration. Suppose it were required to render the general effect of a certain year in a man's life, a year that has filled his mind with a swarm of many memories. Looking into his consciousness after the year has gone, we might find much there that would indicate the nature of the year's events without any word on his part; the flickers and flashes of thought from moment to moment might indeed tell us much. But we shall need an account from him too, no doubt; too much has happened in a year to be wholly acted, as I call it, in the movement of the man's thought. He must narrate—he must make, that is to say, a picture of the events as he sees them, glancing back. Now if he speaks in the first person there can, of course, be no uncertainty in the point of view; he has his fixed position, he cannot leave it. His description will represent the face that the facts in their sequence turned towards *him*; the field of vision is defined with perfect distinctness, and his story cannot stray outside it. The reader, then, may be said to watch a reflection of the facts in a mirror of which the edge is nowhere in doubt; it is rounded by

the bounds of the narrator's own personal experience.

This limitation may have a convenience and a value in the story, it may contribute to the effect. But it need not be forfeited, it is clear, if the first person is changed to the third. The author may use the man's field of vision and keep as faithfully within it as though the man were speaking for himself. In that case he retains this advantage and adds to it another, one that is likely to be very much greater. For now, while the point of view is still fixed in space, still assigned to the man in the book, it is free in *time*; there no longer stretches, between the narrator and the events of which he speaks, a certain tract of time, across which the past must appear in a more or less distant perspective. All the variety obtainable by a shifting relation to the story in time is thus in the author's hand; the safe serenity of a far retrospect, the promising or threatening urgency of the present, every gradation between the two, can be drawn into the whole effect of the book, and all of it without any change of the seeing eye. It is a liberty that may help the story indefinitely, raising this matter into strong relief, throwing that other back into vaguer shade.

And next, still keeping mainly and ostensibly to the same point of view, the author has the chance of using a much greater latitude than he need appear to use. The seeing eye is with somebody in the book, but its vision is reinforced; the picture contains more, becomes richer and fuller, because it is the author's as well as his creature's, both at once. Nobody notices, but in fact there are now two brains behind that eye; and one of them is the author's, who adopts and shares the *position* of his creature, and at the same time supplements his wit. If you analyse the picture that is now presented, you find that it is not all the work of the personage whose vision the author has adopted. There are touches in it that go beyond any sensation of his, and indicate that some one else is looking over his shoulder—seeing things from the same angle, but seeing more, bringing another mind to bear upon the scene. It is an easy and natural extension of the personage's power of observation. The impression of the scene may be deepened as much as need be; it is not confined to the scope of one mind, and yet there is no blurring of the focus by a double point of view. And thus what I have called the sound of the narrator's voice (it is impossible to avoid this mixture of metaphors) is less insistent in oblique narration, even while it seems to be following the very same argument that it would in direct, because another voice is speedily mixed and blended with it.

So this is another resource upon which the author may draw according to his need; sometimes it will be indispensable, and generally, I suppose, it will be useful. It means that he keeps a certain hold upon the narrator *as an object*; the sentient character in the story, round whom it is grouped, is not utterly subjective, completely given over to the business of seeing and feeling on behalf of the reader. It is a considerable point; for it helps to meet one of the great difficulties in the story which is carefully aligned towards a single consciousness and consistently so viewed. In that story the man or woman who acts as the vessel of sensation is always in danger of seeming a light, uncertain weight compared with the other people in the book—simply because the other people are objective images, plainly outlined, while the seer in the midst is precluded from that advantage, and must see without being directly seen. He, who doubtless ought to bulk in the story more massively than

any one, tends to remain the least recognizable of the company, and even to dissolve in a kind of impalpable blur. By his method (which I am supposing to have been adopted in full strictness) the author is of course forbidden to look this central figure in the face, to describe and discuss him; the light cannot be turned upon him immediately. And very often we see the method becoming an embarrassment to the author in consequence, and the devices by which he tries to mitigate it, and to secure some reflected sight of the seer, may even be tiresomely obvious. But the resource of which I speak is of a finer sort.

It gives to the author the power of imperceptibly edging away from the seer, leaving his consciousness, ceasing to use his eyes—though still without substituting the eyes of another. To revert for a moment to the story told in the first person, it is plain that in that case the narrator has no such liberty; his own consciousness must always lie open; the part that he plays in the story can never appear in the same terms, on the same plane, as that of the other people. Though he is not visible in the story to the reader, as the others are, he is at every moment *nearer* than they, in his capacity of the seeing eye, the channel of vision; nor can he put off his function, he must continue steadily to see and to report. But when the author is reporting *him* there is a margin of freedom. The author has not so completely identified himself, as narrator, with his hero that he can give him no objective weight whatever. If necessary he can allow him something of the value of a detached and phenomenal personage, like the rest of the company in the story, and that without violating the principle of his method. He cannot make his hero actually visible—there the method is uncompromising; he cannot step forward, leaving the man's point of view, and picture him from without. But he can place the man at the same distance from the reader as the other people, he can almost lend him the same effect, he can make of him a dramatic actor upon the scene.

And how? Merely by closing (when it suits him) the open consciousness of the seer—which he can do without any look of awkwardness or violence, since it conflicts in no way with the rule of the method. That rule only required that the author, having decided to share the point of view of his character, should not proceed to set up another of his own; it did not debar him from allowing his hero's act of vision to lapse, his function as the sentient creature in the story to be intermitted. The hero (I call him so for convenience—he may, of course, be quite a subordinate onlooker in the story) can at any moment become impenetrable, a human being whose thought is sealed from us; and it may seem a small matter, but in fact it has the result that he drops into the plane of the people whom he has hitherto been seeing and judging. Hitherto subjective, communicative in solitude, he has been in a category apart from them; but now he may mingle with the rest, engage in talk with them, and his presence and his talk are no more to the fore than theirs. As soon as some description or discussion of them is required, then, of course, the seer must resume his part and unseal his mind; but meanwhile, though the reader gets no direct view of him, still he is there in the dialogue with the rest, his speech (like theirs) issues from a hidden mind and has the same dramatic value. It is enough, very likely, to harden our image of him, to give precision to his form, to save him from dissipation into that luminous blur of which I spoke just now. For the author it is a resource to be welcomed on that account, and not on that account alone.

For besides the greater definition that the seer acquires, thus detached from us at times and relegated to the plane of his companions, there is much benefit for the subject of the story. In the tale that is quite openly and nakedly somebody's narrative there is this inherent weakness, that a scene of true drama is impossible. In true drama nobody *reports* the scene; it *appears*, it is constituted by the aspect of the occasion and the talk and the conduct of the people. When one of the people who took part in it sets out to report the scene, there is at once a mixture and a confusion of effects; for his own contribution to the scene has a different quality from the rest, cannot have the same crispness and freshness, cannot strike in with a new or unexpected note. This weakness may be well disguised, and like everything else in the whole craft it may become a positive and right effect in a particular story, for a particular purpose; it is always there, however, and it means that the full and unmixed effect of drama is denied to the story that is rigidly told from the point of view of one of the actors. But when that point of view is held in the manner I have described, when it is open to the author to withdraw from it silently and to leave the actor to play his part, true drama—or something so like it that it passes for true drama—is always possible; all the figures of the scene are together in it, one no nearer than another. Nothing is wanting save only that direct, unequivocal sight of the hero which the method does indeed absolutely forbid.

Finally there is the old, immemorial, unguarded, unsuspicious way of telling a story, where the author entertains the reader, the minstrel draws his audience round him, the listeners rely upon his word. The voice is then confessedly and alone the author's; he imposes no limitation upon his freedom to tell what he pleases and to regard his matter from a point of view that is solely his own. And if there is anyone who can proceed in this fashion without appearing to lose the least of the advantages of a more cautious style, for him the minstrel's licence is proper and appropriate; there is no more to be said. But we have yet to discover him; and it is not very presumptuous in a critic, as things are, to declare that a story will never yield its best to a writer who takes the easiest way with it. He curtails his privileges and chooses a narrower method, and immediately the story responds; its better condition is too notable to be forgotten, when once it has caught the attention of a reader. The advantages that it gains are not nameless, indefinable graces, pleasing to a critic but impossible to fix in words; they are solid, we can describe and recount them. And I can only conclude that if the novel is still as full of energy as it seems to be, and is not a form of imaginative art that, having seen the best of its day, is preparing to give place to some other, the novelist will not be willing to miss the inexhaustible opportunity that lies in its treatment. The easy way is no way at all; the only way is that by which the most is made of the story to be told, and the most was never made of any story except by a choice and disciplined method.

PREFACE TO *THE AMBASSADORS*
Henry James*

"One's work should have composition, because composition alone is positive beauty." James' statement on the importance of form furnishes a basis for his discussion of his search for form in *The Ambassadors*. He is searching, he says, after intensity, which, once grasped, becomes the supreme beauty of any work of art. To achieve this intensity it is sometimes necessary to make various sacrifices of details that have a momentary attraction in themselves. He gains it in *The Ambassadors* by giving his protagonist, Lambert Strether, all the subjective "say," which requires and provides a tightness that cannot be obtained through the looseness and fluidity of a first person narrator.

Nothing is more easy than to state the subject of "The Ambassadors," which first appeared in twelve numbers of *The North American Review* (1903) and was published as a whole the same year. The

* Henry James's Preface to the New York Edition of *The Ambassadors* is reprinted with the permission of Charles Scribner's Sons. Copyright 1909 Charles Scribner's Sons; renewal copyright 1937 Henry James.

situation involved is gathered up betimes, that is in the second chapter of Book Fifth, for the reader's benefit, into as few words as possible—planted or "sunk," stiffly and saliently, in the centre of the current, almost perhaps to the obstruction of traffic. Never can a composition of this sort have sprung straighter from a dropped grain of suggestion, and never can that grain, developed, overgrown and smothered, have yet lurked more in the mass as an independent particle. The whole case, in fine, is in Lambert Strether's irrepressible outbreak to little Bilham on the Sunday afternoon in Gloriani's garden, the candour with which he yields, for his young friend's enlightenment, to the charming admonition of that crisis. The idea of the tale resides indeed in the very fact that an hour of such unprecedented ease should have been felt by him *as* a crisis, and he is at pains to express it for us as neatly as we could desire. The remarks to which he thus gives utterance contain the essence of "The Ambassadors," his fingers close, before he has done, round the stem of the full-blown flower; which, after that fashion, he continues officiously to present to us. "Live all you can; it's a mistake not to. It doesn't so much matter what you do in particular so long as you have your life. If you haven't had that what *have* you had? I'm too old—too old at any rate for what I see. What one loses one loses; make no mistake about that. Still, we have the illusion of freedom; therefore don't, like me to-day, be without the memory of that illusion. I was either, at the right time, too stupid or too intelligent to have it, and now I'm a case of reaction against the mistake. Do what you like so long as you don't make it. For it *was* a mistake. Live, live!" Such is the gist of Strether's appeal to the impressed youth, whom he likes and whom he desires to befriend; the word "mistake" occurs several times, it will be seen, in the course of his remarks—which gives the measure of the signal warning he feels attached to his case. He has accordingly missed too much, though perhaps after all constitutionally qualified for a better part, and he wakes up to it in conditions that press the spring of a terrible question. W*ould* there yet perhaps be time for

reparation?—reparation, that is, for the injury done his character; for the affront, he is quite ready to say, so stupidly put upon it and in which he has even himself had so clumsy a hand? The answer to which is that he now at all events *sees*; so that the business of my tale and the march of my action, not to say the precious moral of everything, is just my demonstration of this process of vision.

Nothing can exceed the closeness with which the whole fits again into its germ. That had been given me bodily, as usual, by the spoken word, for I was to take the image over exactly as I happened to have met it. A friend had repeated to me, with great appreciation, a thing or two said to him by a man of distinction, much his senior, and to which a sense akin to that of Strether's melancholy eloquence might be imputed—said as chance would have, and so easily might, in Paris, and in a charming old garden attached to a house of art, and on a Sunday afternoon of summer, many persons of great interest being present. The observation there listened to and gathered up had contained part of the "note" that I was to recognise on the spot as to my purpose—had contained in fact the greater part; the rest was in the place and the time and the scene they sketched: these constituents clustered and combined to give me further support, to give me what I may call the note absolute. There it stands, accordingly, full in the tideway; driven in, with hard taps, like some strong stake for the noose of a cable, the swirl of the current roundabout it. What amplified the hint to more than the bulk of hints in general was the gift with it of the old Paris garden, for in that token were sealed up values infinitely precious. There was of course the seal to break and each item of the packet to count over and handle and estimate; but somehow, in the light of the hint, all the elements of a situation of the sort most to my taste were there. I could even remember no occasion on which, so confronted, I had found it of a livelier interest to take stock, in this fashion, of suggested wealth. For I think, verily, that there are degrees of merit in subjects—in spite of the fact that to treat even one of the most ambiguous with due decency we must for the time, for the feverish and prejudiced hour, at least figure its merit and its dignity as *possibly* absolute. What it comes to, doubtless, is that even among the supremely good—since with such alone is it one's theory of one's honour to be concerned—there is an ideal *beauty* of goodness the invoked action of which is to raise the artistic faith to its maximum. Then truly, I hold, one's theme may be said to shine, and that of "The Ambassadors," I confess, wore this glow for me from beginning to end. Fortunately thus I am able to estimate this as, frankly, quite the best, "all round," of all my productions; any failure of that justification would have made such an extreme of complacency publicly fatuous.

I recall then in this connexion no moment of subjective intermittence, never one of those alarms as for a suspected hollow beneath one's feet, a felt ingratitude in the scheme adopted, under which confidence fails and opportunity seems but to mock. If the motive of "The Wings of the Dove," as I have noted, was to worry me at moments by a sealing-up of its face—though without prejudice to its again, of a sudden, fairly grimacing with expression—so in this other business I had absolute conviction and constant clearness to deal with; it had been a frank proposition, the whole bunch of data, installed on my premises like a monotony of fine weather. (The order of composition, in these things, I may mention, was reversed by the order of publication; the earlier written of the two books having

appeared as the later.) Even under the weight of my hero's years I could feel my postulate firm; even under the strain of the difference between those of Madame de Vionnet and those of Chad Newsome, a difference liable to be denounced as shocking, I could still feel it serene. Nothing resisted, nothing betrayed, I seem to make out, in this full and sound sense of the matter; it shed from any side I could turn it to the same golden glow. I rejoiced in the promise of a hero so mature, who would give me thereby the more to bite into—since it's only into thickened motive and accumulated character, I think, that the painter of life bites more than a little. My poor friend should have accumulated character, certainly; or rather would be quite naturally and handsomely possessed of it, in the sense that he would have, and would always have felt he had, imagination galore, and that this yet wouldn't have wrecked him. It was immeasurable, the opportunity to "do" a man of imagination, for if *there* mightn't be a chance to "bite," where in the world might it be? This personage of course, so enriched, wouldn't give me, for his type, imagination in *predominance* or as his prime faculty, nor should I, in view of other matters, have found that convenient. So particular a luxury—some occasion, that is, for study of the high gift in *supreme* command of a case or of a career—would still doubtless come on the day I should be ready to pay for it; and till then might, as from far back, remain hung up well in view and just out of reach. The comparative case meanwhile would serve— it was only on the minor scale that I had treated myself even to comparative cases.

I was to hasten to add however that, happy stopgaps as the minor scale had thus yielded, the instance in hand should enjoy the advantage of the full range of the major; since most immediately to the point was the question of that *supplement* of situation logically involved in our gentleman's impulse to deliver himself in the Paris garden on the Sunday afternoon —or if not involved by strict logic then all ideally and enchantingly implied in it. (I say "ideally," because I need scarce mention that for development, for expression of its maximum, my glimmering story was, at the earliest stage, to have nipped the thread of connexion with the possibilities of the actual reported speaker. *He* remains but the happiest of accidents; his actualities, all too definite, precluded any range of possibilities; it had only been his charming office to project upon that wide field of the artist's vision— which hangs there ever in place like the white sheet suspended for the figures of a child's magic-lantern—a more fantastic and more moveable shadow.) No privilege of the teller of tales and the handler of puppets is more delightful, or has more of the suspense and the thrill of a game of difficulty breathlessly played, than just this business of looking for the unseen and the occult, in a scheme half-grasped, by the light or, so to speak, by the clinging scent, of the gage already in hand. No dreadful old pursuit of the hidden slave with bloodhounds and the rag of association can ever, for "excitement," I judge, have bettered it at its best. For the dramatist always, by the very law of his genius, believes not only in a possible right issue from the rightly-conceived tight place; he does much more than this—he believes, irresistibly, in the necessary, the precious "tightness" of the place (whatever the issue) on the strength of any respectable hint. It being thus the respectable hint that I had with such avidity picked up, what would be the story to which it would most inevitably form the centre? It is part of the charm attendant on such questions that the "story," with the omens true,

as I say, puts on from this stage the authenticity of concrete existence. It then *is*, essentially—it begins to be, though it may more or less obscurely lurk; so that the point is not in the least what to make of it, but only, very delightfully and very damnably, where to put one's hand on it.

In which truth resides surely much of the interest of that admirable mixture for salutary application which we know as art. Art deals with what we see, it must first contribute full-handed that ingredient; it plucks its material, otherwise expressed, in the garden of life— which material elsewhere grown is stale and uneatable. But it has no sooner done this than it has to take account of a *process*—from which only when it's the basest of the servants of man, incurring ignominious dismissal with no "character," does it, and whether under some muddled pretext of morality or on any other, pusillanimously edge away. The process, that of the expression, the literal squeezing-out, of value is another affair—with which the happy luck of mere finding has little to do. The joys of finding, at this stage, are pretty well over; that quest of the subject as a whole by "matching," as the ladies say at the shops, the big piece with the snippet, having ended, we assume, with a capture. The subject is found, and if the problem is then transferred to the ground of what to do with it the field opens out for any amount of doing. This is precisely the infusion that, as I submit, completes the strong mixture. It is on the other hand the part of the business that can least be likened to the chase with horn and hound. It's all a sedentary part—involves as much ciphering, of sorts, as would merit the highest salary paid to a chief accountant. Not, however, that the chief accountant hasn't *his* gleams of bliss; for the felicity, or at least the equilibrium, of the artist's state dwells less, surely, in the further delightful complications he can smuggle in than in those he succeeds in keeping out. He sows his seed at the risk of too thick a crop; wherefore yet again, like the gentlemen who audit ledgers, he must keep his head at any price. In consequence of all which, for the interest of the matter, I might seem here to have my choice of narrating my "hunt" for Lambert Strether, of describing the capture of the shadow projected by my friend's anecdote, or of reporting on the occurrences subsequent to that triumph. But I had probably best attempt a little to glance in each direction; since it comes to me again and again, over this licentious record, that one's bag of adventures, conceived or conceivable, has been only half-emptied by the mere telling of one's story. It depends so on what one means by that equivocal quantity. There is the story of one's hero, and then, thanks to the intimate connexion of things, the story of one's story itself. I blush to confess it, but if one's a dramatist one's a dramatist, and the latter imbroglio is liable on occasion to strike me as really the more objective of the two.

The philosophy imputed to him in that beautiful outbreak, the hour there, amid such happy provision, striking for him, would have been then, on behalf of my man of imagination, to be logically and, as the artless craft of comedy has it, "led up" to; the probable course to such a goal, the goal of so conscious a perdicament, would have in short to be finely calculated. Where has he come from and why has he come, what is he doing (as we Anglo-Saxons, and we only, say, in our foredoomed clutch of exotic aids to expression) in that *galère?* To answer these questions plausibly, to answer them as under cross-examination in the witness-box by counsel for the prosecution, in other words satisfactorily to account for Strether and for his "pe-

culiar tone," was to possess myself of the entire fabric. At the same time the clue to its whereabouts would lie in a certain *principle* of probability: he wouldn't have indulged in his peculiar tone without a reason; it would take a felt predicament or a false position to give him so ironic an accent. One hadn't been noting "tones" all one's life without recognising when one heard it the voice of the false position. The dear man in the Paris garden was then admirably and unmistakeably *in* one—which was no small point gained; what next accordingly concerned us was the determination of *this* identity. One could only go by probabilities, but there was the advantage that the most general of the probabilities were virtual certainties. Possessed of our friend's nationality, to start with, there was a general probability in his narrower localism; which, for that matter, one had really but to keep under the lens for an hour to see it give up its secrets. He would have issued, our rueful worthy, from the very heart of New England—at the heels of which matter of course a perfect train of secrets tumbled for me into the light. They had to be sifted and sorted, and I shall not reproduce the detail of that process; but unmistakeably they were all there, and it was but a question, auspiciously, of picking among them. What the "position" would infallibly be, and why, on his hands, it had turned "false" —these inductive steps could only be as rapid as they were distinct. I accounted for everything—and "everything" had by this time become the most promising quantity—by the view that he had come to Paris in some state of mind which was literally undergoing, as a result of new and unexpected assaults and infusions, a change almost from hour to hour. He had come with a view that might have been figured by a clear green liquid, say, in a neat glass phial; and the liquid, once poured into the open cup of *application,* once exposed to the action of another air, had begun to turn from green to red, or whatever, and might, for all he knew, be on its way to purple, to black, to yellow. At the still wilder extremes represented perhaps, for all he could say to the contrary, by a variability so violent, he would at first, naturally, but have gazed in surprise and alarm; whereby the *situation* clearly would spring from the play of wildness and the development of extremes. I saw in a moment that, should this development proceed both with force and logic, my "story" would leave nothing to be desired. There is always, of course, for the story-teller, the irresistible determinant and the incalculable advantage of his interest in the story *as such;* it is ever, obviously, overwhelmingly, the prime and precious thing (as other than this I have never been able to see it); as to which what makes for it, with whatever headlong energy, may be said to pale before the energy with which it simply makes for itself. It rejoices, none the less, at its best, to seem to offer itself in a light, to seem to know, and with the very last knowledge, what it's about— liable as it yet is at moments to be caught by us with its tongue in its cheek and absolutely no warrant but its splendid impudence. Let us grant then that the impudence is always there—there, so to speak, for grace and effect and *allure;* there, above all, because the Story is just the spoiled child of art, and because, as we are always disappointed when the pampered don't "play up," we like it, to that extent, to look all its character. It probably does so, in truth, even when we most flatter ourselves that we negotiate with it by treaty.

All of which, again, is but to say that the *steps,* for my fable, placed themselves with a prompt and, as it were, functional assurance—an air quite as of readiness to have dispensed with logic had I been in fact too stupid for my clue. Never, positively, none the less, as the links multiplied, had I felt less stupid than for the determination of poor Strether's errand and for the apprehension of his issue. These things continued to fall together, as by the neat action of their own weight and form, even while their commentator scratched his head about them; he easily sees now that they were always well in advance of him. As the case completed itself he had in fact, from a good way behind, to catch up with them, breathless and a little flurried, as best he could. *The false position, for our belated man of the world*—belated because he had endeavoured so long to escape being one, and now at last had really to face his doom— the false position for him, I say, was obviously to have presented himself at the gate of that boundless menagerie primed with a moral scheme of the most approved pattern which was yet framed to break down on any approach to vivid facts; that is to any at all liberal appreciation of them. There would have been of course the case of Strether prepared, wherever presenting himself, only to judge and to feel meanly; but *he* would have moved for me, I confess, enveloped in no legend whatever. The actual man's note, from the first of our seeing it struck, is the note of discrimination, just as his drama is to become, under stress, the drama of discrimination. It would have been his blest imagination, we have seen, that had already helped him to discriminate; the element that was for so much of the pleasure of my cutting thick, as I have intimated, into his intellectual, into his moral substance. Yet here it was, at the same time, just here, that a shade for a moment fell across the scene.

There was the dreadful little old tradition, one of the platitudes of the human comedy, that people's moral scheme *does* break down in Paris; that nothing is more frequently observed; that hundreds of thousands of more or less hypocritical or more or less cynical persons annually visit the place for the sake of the probable catastrophe, and that I came late in the day to work myself up about it. There was in fine the *trivial* association, one of the vulgarest in the world; but which gave me pause no longer, I think, simply because its vulgarity is so advertised. The revolution performed by Strether under the influence of the most interesting of great cities was to have nothing to do with any *bêtise* of the imputably "tempted" state; he was to be thrown forward, rather, thrown quite with violence, upon his lifelong trick of intense reflexion: which friendly test indeed was to bring him out, through winding passages, through alternations of darkness and light, very much *in* Paris, but with the surrounding scene itself a minor matter, a mere symbol for more things than had been dreamt of in the philosophy of Woollett. Another surrounding scene would have done as well for our show could it have represented a place in which Strether's errand was likely to lie and his crisis to await him. The *likely* place had the great merit of sparing me preparations; there would have been too many involved—not at all impossibilities, only rather worrying and delaying difficulties —in positing elsewhere Chad Newsome's interesting relation, his so interesting complexity of relations. Strether's appointed stage, in fine, could be but Chad's most luckily selected one. The young man had gone in, as they say, for circumjacent charm; and where he would have found it, by the turn of his mind, most "authentic," was where his earnest friend's analysis would most find *him*; as well as where, for that matter, the former's whole analytic faculty would be led such a wonderful dance.

"The Ambassadors" had been, all conveniently, "arranged for"; its first appearance was from month to month, in *The North American Review* during 1903, and I had been open from far back to any pleasant provocation for ingenuity that might reside in one's actively adopting—so as to make it, in its way, a small compositional law—recurrent breaks and resumptions. I had made up my mind here regularly to exploit and enjoy these often rather rude jolts—having found, as I believed, an admirable way to it; yet every question of form and pressure, I easily remember, paled in the light of the major propriety, recognised as soon as really weighed; that of employing but one centre and keeping it all within my hero's compass. The thing was to be so much this worthy's intimate adventure that even the projection of his consciousness upon it from beginning to end without intermission or deviation would probably still leave a part of its value for him, and *a fortiori* for ourselves, unexpressed. I might, however, express every grain of it that there would be room for —on condition of contriving a splendid particular economy. Other persons in no small number were to people the scene, and each with his or her axe to grind, his or her situation to treat, his or her coherency not to fail of, his or her relation to my leading motive, in a word, to establish and carry on. But Strether's sense of these things, and Strether's only, should avail me for showing them; I should know them but through his more or less groping knowledge of them, since his very gropings would figure among his most interesting motions, and a full observance of the rich rigour I speak of would give me more of the effect I should be most "after" than all other possible observances together. It would give me a large unity, and that in turn would crown me with the grace to which the enlightened story-teller will at any time, for his interest, sacrifice if need be all other graces whatever. I refer of course to the grace of intensity, which there are ways of signally achieving and ways of signally missing—as we see it, all round us, helplessly and woefully missed. Not that it isn't, on the other hand, a virtue eminently subject to appreciation—there being no strict, no absolute measure of it; so that one may hear it acclaimed where it has quite escaped one's perception, and see it unnoticed where one has gratefully hailed it. After all of which I am not sure, either, that the immense amusement of the whole cluster of difficulties so arrayed may not operate, for the fond fabulist, when judicious not less than fond, as his best of determinants. That charming principle is always there, at all events, to keep interest fresh: it is a principle, we remember, essentially ravenous, without scruple and without mercy, appeased with no cheap nor easy nourishment. It enjoys the costly sacrifice and rejoices thereby in the very odour of difficulty—even as ogres, with their "Fee-faw-fum!" rejoice in the smell of the blood of Englishmen.

Thus it was, at all events, that the ultimate, though after all so speedy, definition of my gentleman's job—his coming out, all solemnly appointed and deputed, to "save" Chad, and his then finding the young man so disobligingly and, at first, so bewilderingly not lost that a new issue altogether, in the connexion, prodigiously faces them, which has to be dealt with in a new light—promised as many calls on ingenuity and on the higher branches of the compositional art as one could possibly desire. Again and yet again, as, from book to book, I proceed with my survey, I find no source of interest equal to this verification after the fact, as I may call it, and the more in detail the better, of the scheme of con-

sistency "gone in" for. As always—since the charm never fails—the retracing of the process from point to point brings back the old illusion. The old intentions bloom again and flower—in spite of all the blossoms they were to have dropped by the way. This is the charm, as I say, of adventure *transposed*—the thrilling ups and downs, the intricate ins and outs of the compositional problem, made after such a fashion admirably objective, becoming the question at issue and keeping the author's heart in his mouth. Such an element, for instance, as his intention that Mrs. Newsome, away off with her finger on the pulse of Massachusetts, should yet be no less intensely than circuitously present through the whole thing, should be no less felt as to be reckoned with than the most direct exhibition, the finest portrayal at first hand could make her, such a sign of artistic good faith, I say, once it's unmistakeably there, takes on again an actuality not too much impaired by the comparative dimness of the particular success. Cherished intention too inevitably acts and operates, in the book, about fifty times as little as I had fondly dreamt it might; but that scarce spoils for me the pleasure of recognizing the fifty ways in which I had sought to provide for it. The mere charm of seeing such an idea constituent, in its degree; the fineness of the measures taken—a real extension, if successful, of the very terms and possibilities of representation and figuration—such things alone were, after this fashion, inspiring, such things alone were a gage of the probable success of that dissimulated calculation with which the whole effort was to square. But oh the cares begotten, none the less, of that same "judicious" sacrifice to a particular form of interest! One's work should have composition, because composition alone is positive beauty; but all the while—apart from one's inevitable consciousness too of the dire paucity of readers ever recognising or ever missing positive beauty—how, as to the cheap and easy, at every turn, how, as to immediacy and facility, and even as to the commoner vivacity, positive beauty might have to be sweated for and paid for! Once achieved and installed it may always be trusted to make the poor seeker feel he would have blushed to the roots of his hair for failing of it; yet, how, as its virtue can be essentially but the virtue of the whole, the wayside traps set in the interest of muddlement and pleading but the cause of the moment, of the particular bit in itself, have to be kicked out of the path! All the sophistications in life, for example, might have appeared to muster on behalf of the menace—the menace to a bright variety—involved in Strether's having all the subjective "say," as it were, to himself.

Had I, meanwhile, made him at once hero and historian, endowed him with the romantic privilege of the "first person"—the darkest abyss of romance this, inveterately, when enjoyed on the grand scale—variety, and many other queer matters as well, might have been smuggled in by a back door. Suffice it, to be brief, that the first person, in the long piece, is a form foredoomed to looseness, and that looseness, never much my affair, had never been so little so as on this particular occasion. All of which reflexions flocked to the standard from the moment—a very early one—the question of how to keep my form amusing while sticking so close to my central figure and constantly taking its pattern from him had to be faced. He arrives (arrives at Chester) as for the dreadful purpose of giving his creator "no end" to tell about him—before which rigorous mission the serenest of creators might well have quailed. I was far from the serenest; I was more than agitated enough to reflect that, grimly deprived of one alternative or one substitute for "telling," I must address myself tooth and nail to another. I couldn't, save by implication, make other persons tell *each other* about him —blest resource, blest necessity, of the drama, which reaches its effects of unity, all remarkably, by paths absolutely opposite to the paths of the novel: with other persons, save as they were primarily *his* persons (not he primarily but one of theirs), I had simply nothing to do. I had relations for him none the less, by the mercy of Providence, quite as much as if my exhibition *was* to be a muddle; if I could only by implication and a show of consequence make other persons tell each other about him, I could at least make him tell *them* whatever in the world he must; and could so, by the same token—which was a further luxury thrown in—see straight into the deep differences between what that could do for me, or at all events for *him*, and the large ease of "autobiography." It may be asked why, if one so keeps to one's hero, one shouldn't make a single mouthful of "method," shouldn't throw the reins on his neck and, letting them flap there as free as in "Gil Blas" or in "David Copperfield," equip him with the double privilege of subject and object—a course that has at least the merit of brushing away questions at a sweep. The answer to which is, I think, that one makes that surrender only if one is prepared *not* to make certain precious discriminations.

The "first person" then, so employed, is addressed by the author directly to ourselves, his possible readers, whom he has to reckon with, at the best, by our English tradition, so loosely and vaguely after all, so little respectfully, on so scant a presumption of exposure to criticism. Strether, on the other hand, encaged and provided for as "The Ambassadors" encages and provides, has to keep in view proprieties much stiffer and more salutary than any our straight and credulous gape are likely to bring home to him, has exhibitional conditions to meet, in a word, that forbid the terrible *fluidity* of self-revelation. I may seem not to better the case for my discrimination if I say that, for my first care, I had thus inevitably to set him up a confidant or two, to wave away with energy the custom of the seated mass of explanation after the fact, the inserted block of merely referential narrative, which flourishes so, to the shame of the modern impatience, on the serried page of Balzac, but which seems simply to appal our actual, our general weaker, digestion. "Harking back to make up" took at any rate more doing, as the phrase is, not only than the reader of to-day demands, but than he will tolerate at any price any call upon him either to understand or remotely to measure; and for the beauty of the thing when done the current editorial mind in particular appears wholly without sense. It is not, however, primarily for either of these reasons, whatever their weight, that Strether's friend Waymarsh is so keenly clutched at, on the threshold of the book, or that no less a pounce is made on Maria Gostrey—without even the pretext, either, of *her* being, in essence, Strether's friend. She is the reader's friend much rather—in consequence of dispositions that make him so eminently require one; and she acts in that capacity, and *really* in that capacity alone, with exemplary devotion, from beginning to end of the book. She is an enrolled, a direct, and to lucidity, she is in fine, to tear off her mask, the most unmitigated and abandoned of *ficelles*. Half the dramatist's art, as we well know—since if we don't it's not the fault of the proofs that lie scattered about us—is in the use of *ficelles*; by which I mean in a deep dissimulation of his dependence on them.

Waymarsh only to a slighter degree belongs, in the whole business, less to my subject than to my treatment of it; the interesting proof, in these connexions, being that one has but to take one's subject for the stuff of drama to interweave with enthusiasm as many Gostreys as need be.

The material of "The Ambassadors," conforming in this respect exactly to that of "The Wings of the Dove," published just before it, is taken absolutely for the stuff of drama; so that, availing myself of the opportunity given me by this edition for some prefatory remarks on the latter work, I had mainly to make on its behalf the point of its scenic consistency. It disguises that virtue, in the oddest way in the world, by just *looking*, as we turn its pages, as little scenic as possible; but it sharply divides itself, just as the composition before us does, into the parts that prepare, that tend in fact to over-prepare, for scenes, and the parts, or otherwise into the scenes, that justify and crown the preparation. It may definitely be said, I think, that everything in it that is not scene (not, I of course mean, complete and functional scene, treating *all* the submitted matter, as by logical start, logical turn, and logical finish) is discriminated preparation, is the fusion and synthesis of picture. These alternations propose themselves all recogniseably, I think, from an early stage, as the very form and figure of "The Ambassadors"; so that, to repeat, such an agent as Miss Gostrey, pre-engaged at a high salary, but waits in the draughty wing with her shawl and her smelling-salts. Her function speaks at once for itself, and by the time she has dined with Strether in London and gone to a play with him her intervention as a *ficelle* is, I hold, expertly justified. Thanks to it we have treated scenically, and scenically alone, the whole lumpish question of Strether's "past," which has seen us more happily on the way than anything else could have done; we have strained to a high lucidity and vivacity (or at least we hope we have) certain indispensable facts; we have seen our two or three immediate friends all conveniently and profitably in "action"; to say nothing of our beginning to descry others, of a remoter intensity, getting into motion, even if a bit vaguely as yet, for our further enrichment. Let my first point be here that the scene in question, that in which the whole situation at Woollett and the complex forces that have propelled my hero to where this lively extractor of his value and distiller of his essence awaits him, is normal and entire, is really an excellent *standard* scene; copious, comprehensive, and accordingly never short, but with its office as definite as that of the hammer on the gong of the clock, the office of expressing *all that is in* the hour.

The *"ficelle"* character of the subordinate party is as artfully dissimulated, throughout, as may be, and to that extent that, with the seams or joints of Maria Gostrey's ostensible connectedness taken particular care of, duly smoothed over, that is, and anxiously kept from showing as "pieced on," this figure doubtless achieves, after a fashion, something of the dignity of a prime idea: which circumstance but shows us afresh how many quite incalculable but none the less clear sources of enjoyment for the infatuated artist, how many copious springs of our never-to-be-slighted "fun" for the reader and critic susceptible of contagion, may sound their incidental plash as soon as an artistic process begins to enjoy free development. Exquisite—in illustration of this —the mere interest and amusement of such at once "creative" and critical questions as how and where and why to make Miss Gostrey's false connexion carry itself, under a due high polish, as a real

one. Nowhere is it more of an artful expedient for mere consistency of form, to mention a case, than in the last "scene" of the book, where its function is to give or to add nothing whatever, but only to express as vividly as possible certain things quite other than itself and that are of the already fixed and appointed measure. Since, however, all art is *expression*, and is thereby vividness, one was to find the door open here to any amount of delightful dissimulation. These verily are the refinements and ecstasies of method—amid which, or certainly under the influence of any exhilarated demonstration of which, one must keep one's head and not lose one's way. To cultivate an adequate intelligence for them and to make that sense operative is positively to find a charm in any produced ambiguity of appearance that is not by the same stroke, and all helplessly, an ambiguity of sense. To project imaginatively, for my hero, a relation that has nothing to do with the matter (the matter of my subject) but has everything to do with the manner (the manner of my presentation of the same) and yet to treat it, at close quarters and for fully economic expression's possible sake, as if it were important and essential—to do that sort of thing and yet muddle nothing may easily become, as one goes, a signally attaching proposition; even though it all remains but part and parcel, I hasten to recognise, of the merely general and related question of expressional curiosity and expressional decency.

I am moved to add after so much insistence on the scenic side of my labour that I have found the steps of re-perusal almost as much waylaid here by quite another style of effort in the same signal interest—or have in other words not failed to note how, even so associated and so discriminated, the finest properties and charms of the non-scenic may, under the right hand for them, still keep their intelligibility and assert their office. Infinitely suggestive such an observation as this last on the whole delightful head, where representation is concerned, of possible variety, of effective expressional change and contrast. One would like, at such an hour as this, for critical licence, to go into the matter of the noted inevitable deviation (from too fond an original vision) that the exquisite treachery even of the straightest execution may ever be trusted to inflict even on the most mature plan—the case being that, though one's last reconsidered production always seems to bristle with that particular evidence, "The Ambassadors" would place a flood of such light at my service. I must attach to my final remark here a different import; noting in the other connexion I just glanced at that such passages as that of my hero's first encounter with Chad Newsome, absolute attestations of the non-scenic form though they be, yet lay the firmest hand too—so far at least as intention goes—on representational effect. To report at all closely and completely of what "passes" on a given occasion is inevitably to become more or less scenic; and yet in the instance I allude to, *with* the conveyance, expressional curiosity and expressional decency are sought and arrived at under quite another law. The true inwardness of this may be at bottom but that one of the suffered treacheries has consisted precisely, for Chad's whole figure and presence, of a direct presentability diminished and compromised—despoiled, that

is, of its *proportional* advantage; so that, in a word, the whole economy of his author's relation to him has at important points to be redetermined. The book, however, critically viewed, is touchingly full of these disguised and repaired losses, these insidious recoveries, these intensely redemptive consistencies. The pages in which Mamie Pocock gives her appointed and, I can't but think, duly felt lift to the whole action by the so inscrutably-applied side-stroke or short-cut of our just watching, and as quite at an angle of vision as yet untried, her single hour of suspense in the hotel salon, in our partaking of her concentrated study of the sense of matters bearing on her own case, all the bright warm Paris afternoon, from the balcony that overlooks the Tuileries garden—these are as marked an example of the representational virtue that insists here and there on being, for the charm of opposition and renewal, other than the scenic. It wouldn't take much to make me further argue that from an equal play of such oppositions the book gathers an intensity that fairly adds to the dramatic—though the latter is supposed to be the sum of all intensities; or that has at any rate nothing to fear from juxtaposition with it. I consciously fail to shrink in fact from that extravagance—I risk it, rather, for the sake of the moral involved; which is not that the particular production before us exhausts the interesting questions it raises, but that the Novel remains still, under the right persuasion, the most independent, most elastic, most prodigious of literary forms.

FROM PATTERN AND RHYTHM
E. M. Forster[*]

> Forster finds the esthetic beauty of the novel in pattern, which is
> closely related to the geometrical shape of the plot. He discusses
> three novels that best exemplify such a pattern: Anatole France's
> *Thais* (hourglass), Percy Lubbock's *Roman Pictures* (grand
> chain), and Henry James' *The Ambassadors* (hourglass). How-
> ever, the presence of such a pattern in a novel, while giving a
> certain technical beauty, exerts a tyranny which eliminates much
> of the "immense richness of material which life provides." The
> solution, hinted at by Forster at the conclusion of the essay, is
> the substitution of rhythm for pattern, a rhythm that is vaguely
> analagous to the beat in music and that can exert the necessary
> control of form without too rigidly restricting the type of material
> to be included in the novel.

... Before I discuss what pattern en-
tails, and what qualities a reader must
bring to its appreciation, I will give two
examples of books with patterns so definite that a pictorial image sums them
up: a book the shape of an hour-glass
and a book the shape of a grand chain in
that old-time dance, the Lancers.

Thais, by Anatole France, is the shape
of an hour-glass.

There are two chief characters, Paphnuce the ascetic, Thais the courtesan.
Paphnuce lives in the desert, he is saved
and happy when the book starts. Thais
leads a life of sin in Alexandria, and it is
his duty to save her. In the central scene
of the book they approach, he succeeds;
she goes into a monastery and gains salvation, because she has met him, but he,
because he has met her, is damned. The
two characters converge, cross, and recede
with mathematical precision, and part of

the pleasure we get from the book is due
to this. Such is the pattern of *Thais*—so
simple that it makes a good starting-point
for a difficult survey. It is the same as the
story of *Thais*, when events unroll in their
time-sequence, and the same as the plot
of *Thais*, when we see the two characters
bound by their previous actions and taking fatal steps whose consequence they
do not see. But whereas the story appeals
to our curiosity and the plot to our intelligence, the pattern appeals to our
aesthetic sense, it causes us to see the
book as a whole. We do not see it as an
hour-glass—that is the hard jargon of
the lecture room which must never be
taken literally at this advanced stage of
our enquiry. We just have a pleasure
without knowing why, and when the
pleasure is past, as it is now, and our
minds are left free to explain it, a geometrical simile such as an hour-glass will
be found helpful. If it was not for this
hour-glass story, the plot, and the characters of Thais and Paphnuce would none
of them exert their full force, they would

none of them breathe as they do. "Pattern," which seems so rigid, is connected with atmosphere, which seems so fluid.

Now for the book that is shaped like the grand chain: *Roman Pictures* by Percy Lubbock.

Roman Pictures is a social comedy. The narrator is a tourist in Rome; he there meets a kindly and shoddy friend of his, Deering, who rebukes him superciliously for staring at churches and sets him out to explore society. This he does, demurely obedient; one person hands him on to another; café, studio, Vatican and Quirinal purlieus are all reached, until finally, at the extreme end of his career he thinks, in a most aristocratic and dilapidated palazzo, whom should he meet but the second-rate Deering; Deering is his hostess's nephew, but had concealed it owing to some backfire of snobbery. The circle is complete, the original partners have rejoined, and greet one another with mutual confusion which turns to mild laughter.

What is so good in *Roman Pictures* is not the presence of the "grand chain" pattern—any one can organize a grand chain—but the suitability of the pattern to the author's mood. Lubbock works all through by administering a series of little shocks, and by extending to his characters an elaborate charity which causes them to appear in a rather worse light than if no charity was wasted on them at all. It is the comic atmosphere, but sub-acid, meticulously benign. And at the end we discover to our delight that the atmosphere has been externalized, and that the partners, as they click together in the marchesa's drawing-room, have done the exact thing which the book requires, which it required from the start, and have bound the scattered incidents together with a thread woven out of their own substance.

Thais and *Roman Pictures* provide easy examples of pattern; it is not often that one can compare a book to a pictorial object with any accuracy, though curves, etc., are freely spoken of by critics who do not quite know what they want to say. We can only say (so far) that pattern is an aesthetic aspect of the novel, and that though it may be nourished by anything in the novel—any character, scene, word —it draws most of its nourishment from the plot. We noted, when discussing the plot, that it added to itself the quality of beauty; beauty a little surprised at her own arrival: that upon its neat carpentry there could be seen, by those who cared to see, the figure of the Muse; that Logic, at the moment of finishing its own house, laid the foundation of a new one. Here, here is the point where the aspect called pattern is most closely in touch with its material; here is our starting point. It springs mainly from the plot, accompanies it like a light in the clouds, and remains visible after it has departed. Beauty is sometimes the shape of the book, the book as a whole, the unity, and our examination would be easier if it was always this. But sometimes it is not. When it is not I shall call it rhythm. For the moment we are concerned with pattern only.

Let us examine at some length another book of the rigid type, a book with a unity, and in this sense an easy book, although it is by Henry James. We shall see in it pattern triumphant, and we shall also be able to see the sacrifices an author must make if he wants his pattern and nothing else to triumph.

The Ambassadors, like *Thais*, is the shape of an hour-glass. Strether and Chad, like Paphnuce and Thais, change places, and it is the realization of this that makes the book so satisfying at the close. The plot is elaborate and subtle, and proceeds by action or conversation or meditation through every paragraph.

Everything is planned, everything fits; none of the minor characters are just decorative like the talkative Alexandrians at Nicias's banquet; they elaborate on the main theme, they work. The final effect is pre-arranged, dawns gradually on the reader, and is completely successful when it comes. Details of intrigue, of the various missions from America, may be forgotten, but the symmetry they have created is enduring.

Let us trace the growth of this symmetry.[1]

Strether, a sensitive middle-aged American, is commissioned by his old friend, Mrs. Newsome, whom he hopes to marry, to go to Paris and rescue her son Chad, who has gone to the bad in that appropriate city. The Newsomes are sound commercial people, who have made money over manufacturing a small article of domestic utility. Henry James never tells us what the small article is, and in a moment we shall understand why. Wells spits it out in *Tono-Bungay*, Meredith reels it out in *Evan Harrington*, Trollope prescribes it freely for Miss Dunstable, but for James to indicate how his characters made their pile—it would not do. The article is somewhat ignoble and ludicrous—that is enough. If you choose to be coarse and daring and visualize it for yourself as, say, a button-hook, you can, but you do so at your own risk: the author remains uninvolved.

Well, whatever it is, Chad Newsome ought to come back and help make it, and Strether undertakes to fetch him. He has to be rescued from a life which is both immoral and unremunerative.

Strether is a typical James character— he recurs in nearly all the books and is an essential part of their construction. He is the observer who tries to influence the action, and who through his failure to do so gains extra opportunities for observation. And the other characters are such as an observer like Strether is capable of observing—through lenses procured from a rather too first-class oculist. Everything is adjusted to his vision, yet he is not a quietist—no, that is the strength of the device; he takes us along with him, we move as well as look on.

When he lands in England (and a landing is an exalted and enduring experience for James, it is as vital as Newgate for Defoe; poetry and life crowd round a landing): when Strether lands, though it is only old England, he begins to have doubts of his mission, which increase when he gets to Paris. For Chad Newsome, far from going to the bad, has improved; he is distinguished, he is so sure of himself that he can be kind and cordial to the man who has orders to fetch him away; his friends are exquisite, and as for "women in the case" whom his mother anticipated, there is no sign of them whatever. It is Paris that has enlarged and redeemed him—and how well Strether himself understands this!

His greatest uneasiness seemed to peep at him out of the possible impression that almost any acceptance of Paris might give one's authority away. It hung before him this morning, the vast bright Babylon, like some huge iridescent object, a jewel brilliant and hard, in which parts were not to be discriminated nor differences comfortably marked. It twinkled and trembled and melted together; and what seemed all surface one moment seemed all depth the next. It was a place of which, unmistakably, Chad was fond; wherefore, if he, Strether, should like it too much, what on earth, with such a bond, would become of either of them?

Thus, exquisitely and firmly, James sets his atmosphere—Paris irradiates the

[1] There is a masterly analysis of *The Ambassadors* from another standpoint in *The Craft of Fiction* [by Percy Lubbock].

book from end to end, it is an actor though always unembodied, it is a scale by which human sensibility can be measured, and when we have finished the novel and allow its incidents to blur that we may see the pattern plainer, it is Paris that gleams at the centre of the hour-glass shape—Paris—nothing so crude as good or evil. Strether sees this soon, and sees that Chad realizes it better than he himself can; and when he has reached this stage of initiation the novel takes a turn: there is, after all, a woman in the case; behind Paris, interpreting it for Chad, is the adorable and exalted figure of Mme. de Vionnet. It is now impossible for Strether to proceed. All that is noble and refined in life concentrates in Mme. de Vionnet and is reinforced by her pathos. She asks him not to take Chad away. He promises—without reluctance, for his own heart has already shown him as much—and he remains in Paris not to fight it but to fight for it.

For the second batch of ambassadors now arrives from the New World. Mrs. Newsome, incensed and puzzled by the unseemly delay, has despatched Chad's sister, his brother-in-law, and Mamie, the girl whom he is supposed to marry. The novel now becomes, within its ordained limits, most amusing. There is a superb set-to between Chad's sister and Mme. de Vionnet, while as for Mamie—here is disastrous Mamie, seen as we see all things, through Strether's eyes.

As a child, as a "bud," and then again as a flower of expansion, Mamie had bloomed for him, freely, in the almost incessantly open doorways of home; where he remembered her at first very forward, as then very backward—for he had carried on at one period, in Mrs. Newsome's parlours, a course of English literature reinforced by exams and teas—and once more, finally, as very much in advance. But he had kept no

great sense of points of contact; it not being in the nature of things at Woollett that the freshest of the buds should find herself in the same basket with the most withered of the winter apples. . . . He none the less felt now, as he sat with the charming girl, the signal growth of a confidence. For she *was* charming, when all was said, and none the less so for the visible habit and practice of freedom and fluency. She was charming, he was aware, in spite of the fact that if he hadn't found her so he would have found her something he should have been in peril of expressing as "funny." Yes, she was funny, wonderful Mamie, and without dreaming it; she was bland, she was bridal—with never, that he could make out as yet, a bridegroom to support it; she was handsome and portly, and easy and chatty, soft and sweet and almost disconcertingly reassuring. She was dressed, if we might so far discriminate, less as a young lady than as an old one—had an old one been supposable to Strether as so committed to vanity; the complexities of her hair missed moreover also the looseness of youth; and she had a mature manner of bending a little, as to encourage and reward, while she held neatly in front of her a pair of strikingly polished hands: the combination of all of which kept up about her the glamour of her "receiving," placed her again perpetually between the windows and within sound of the ice cream plates, suggested the enumeration of all the names, gregarious specimens of a single type, she was happy to "meet."

Mamie! She is another Henry James type; nearly every novel contains a Mamie —Mrs. Gereth in *The Spoils of Poynton* for instance, or Henrietta Stackpole in *The Portrait of a Lady*. He is so good at indicating instantaneously and constantly that a character is second rate, deficient in sensitiveness, abounding in the wrong sort of worldliness; he gives such a character so much vitality that its absurdity is delightful.

So Strether changes sides and loses all

hopes of marrying Mrs. Newsome. Paris is winning—and then he catches sight of something new. Is not Chad, as regards any fineness in him, played out? Is not Chad's Paris after all just a place for a spree? This fear is confirmed. He goes for a solitary country walk, and at the end of the day he comes across Chad and Mme. de Vionnet. They are in a boat, they pretend not to see him, because their relation is at bottom an ordinary liaison, and they are ashamed. They were hoping for a secret week-end at an inn while their passion survived; for it will not survive, Chad will tire of the exquisite Frenchwoman, she is part of his fling; he will go back to his mother and make the little domestic article and marry Mamie. They know all this, and it is revealed to Strether though they try to hide it; they lie, they are vulgar—even Mme. de Vionnet, even her pathos, once so exquisite, is stained with commonness.

It was like a chill in the air to him, it was almost appalling, that a creature so find could be, by mysterious forces, a creature so exploited. For, at the end of all things, they *were* mysterious; she had but made Chad what he was—so why could she think she had made him infinite? She had made him better, she had made him best, she had made him anything one would; but it came to our friend with supreme queerness that he was none the less only Chad. The work, however admirable, was nevertheless of the strict human order, and in short it was marvellous that the companion of mere earthly joys, of comforts, aberrations—however one classed them—within the common experience, should be so transcendently prized. She was older for him tonight, visibly less exempt from the touch of time; but she was as much as ever the finest and subtlest creature, the happiest apparition, it had been given him, in all his years, to meet; and yet he could see her there as vulgarly troubled, in very truth, as a maidservant

crying for a young man. The only thing was that she judged herself as the maidservant wouldn't; the weakness of which wisdom too, the dishonour of which judgment, seemed but to sink her lower.

So Strether loses them too. As he says: "I have lost everything—it is my only logic." It is not that they have gone back. It is that he has gone on. The Paris they revealed to him—he could reveal it to them now, if they had eyes to see, for it is something finer than they could ever notice for themselves, and his imagination has more spiritual value than their youth. The pattern of the hour-glass is complete; he and Chad have changed places, with more subtle steps than Thais and Paphnuce, and the light in the clouds proceeds not from the well-lit Alexandria, but from the jewel which "twinkled and trembled and melted together, and what seemed all surface one moment seemed all depth the next."

The beauty that suffuses *The Ambassadors* is the reward due to a fine artist for hard work. James knew exactly what he wanted, he pursued the narrow path of aesthetic duty, and success to the full extent of his possibilities has crowned him. The pattern has woven itself with modulation and reservations Anatole France will never attain. Woven itself wonderfully. But at what sacrifice!

So enormous is the sacrifice that many readers cannot get interested in James, although they can follow what he says (his difficulty has been much exaggerated), and can appreciate his effects. They cannot grant his premise, which is that most of human life has to disappear before he can do us a novel.

He has, in the first place, a very short list of characters. I have already mentioned two—the observer who tries to influence the action, and the second-rate outsider (to whom, for example, all the brilliant opening of *What Maisie Knew* is entrusted). Then there is the sympathetic foil—very lively and frequently female—in *The Ambassadors*. Maria Gostrey plays this part; there is the wonderful rare heroine, whom Mme. de Vionnet approached and who is consummated by Milly in *The Wings of the Dove*; there is sometimes a villain, sometimes a young artist with generous impulses; and that is about all. For so fine a novelist it is a poor show.

In the second place, the characters, beside being few in number, are constructed on very stingy lines. They are incapable of fun, of rapid motion, of carnality, and of nine-tenths of heroism. Their clothes will not take off, the diseases that ravage them are anonymous, like the sources of their income, their servants are noiseless or resemble themselves, no social explanation of the world we know is possible for them, for there are no stupid people in their world, no barriers of language, and no poor. Even their sensations are limited. They can land in Europe and look at works of art and at each other, but that is all. Maimed creatures can alone breathe in Henry James's pages—maimed yet specialized. They remind one of the exquisite deformities who haunted Egyptian art in the reign of Akhenaton—huge heads and tiny legs, but nevertheless charming. In the following reign they disappear.

Now this drastic curtailment, both of the numbers of human beings and of their attributes, is in the interests of the pattern. The longer James worked, the more convinced he grew that a novel should be a whole—not necessarily geometric like *The Ambassadors*, but it should accrete round a single topic, situation, gesture, which should occupy the characters and provide a plot, and should also fasten up the novel on the outside— catch its scattered statements in a net, make them cohere like a planet, and

swing through the skies of memory. A pattern must emerge, and anything that emerged from the pattern must be pruned off as wanton distraction. Who so wanton as human beings? Put Tom Jones or Emma or even Mr. Casaubon into a Henry James book, and the book will burn to ashes, whereas we could put them into one another's books and only cause local inflammation. Only a Henry James character will suit, and though they are not dead—certain selected recesses of experience he explores very well—they are gutted of the common stuff that fills characters in other books, and ourselves. And this castrating is not in the interests of the Kingdom of Heaven, there is no philosophy in the novels, no religion (except an occasional touch of superstition), no prophecy, no benefit for the superhuman at all. It is for the sake of a particular aesthetic effect which is certainly gained, but at this heavy price.

H. G. Wells has been amusing on this point, and perhaps profound. In *Boon*— one of his liveliest works—he had Henry James much upon his mind, and wrote a superb parody of him.

James begins by taking it for granted that a novel is a work of art that must be judged by its oneness. Some one gave him that idea in the beginning of things and he has never found it out. He doesn't find things out. He doesn't even seem to want to find things out. He accepts very readily and then—elaborates. . . . The only living human motives left in his novels are a certain avidity and an entirely superficial curiosity. . . . His people nose out suspicions, hint by hint, link by link. Have you ever known living human beings do that? The thing his novel is *about* is always there. It is like a church lit but with no congregation to distract you, with every light and line focussed on the high altar. And on the altar, very reverently placed, intensely there, is a dead kitten, an egg shell, a piece of string. . . . Like his *Altar of the Dead* with nothing to the dead at all. . . . For if there was, they couldn't all be candles, and the effect would vanish.

Wells sent *Boon* as a present to James, apparently thinking the master would be as much pleased by such heartiness and honesty as was he himself. The master was far from pleased, and a most interesting correspondence ensued.[2] Each of the eminent men becomes more and more himself as it proceeds. James is polite, reminiscent, bewildered, and exceedingly formidable: he admits that the parody has not "filled him with a fond elation," and regrets in conclusion that he can sign himself "only yours faithfully, Henry James." Wells is bewildered too, but in a different way; he cannot understand why the man should be upset. And, beyond the personal comedy, there is the great literary importance of the issue. It is this question of the rigid pattern: hour-glass or grand chain or converging lines of the cathedral or diverging lines of the Catherine wheel, or bed of Procrustes—whatever image you like as long as it implies unity. Can it be combined with the immense richness of material which life provides? Wells and James would agree it cannot, Wells would go on to say that life should be given the preference, and must not be whittled or distended for a pattern's sake. My own prejudices are with Wells. The James novels are a unique possession and the reader who cannot accept his premises misses some valuable and exquisite sensations. But I do not want more of his novels, especially when they are written by some one else, just as I do not want the art of Akhenaton to extend into the reign of Tutankhamen.

That then is the disadvantage of a rigid pattern. It may externalize the atmosphere, spring naturally from the plot, but it shuts the doors on life and leaves the novelist doing exercises, generally in the drawing-room. Beauty has arrived, but in too tyrannous a guise. In plays— the plays of Racine, for instance—she may be justified because beauty can be a great empress on the stage, and reconcile us to the loss of the men we knew. But in the novel, her tyranny as it grows powerful grows petty, and generates regrets which sometimes take the form of books like *Boon*. To put it in other words, the novel is not capable of as much artistic development as the drama: its humanity or the grossness of its material hinder it (use whichever phrase you like). To most readers of fiction the sensation from a pattern is not intense enough to justify the sacrifices that made it, and their verdict is "Beautifully done, but not worth doing."

Still this is not the end of our quest. We will not give up the hope of beauty yet. Cannot it be introduced into fiction by some other method than the pattern? Let us edge rather nervously towards the idea of "rhythm."

Rhythm is sometimes quite easy. Beethoven's Fifth Symphony, for instance, starts with the rhythm "diddidy dum," which we can all hear and tap to. But the symphony as a whole has also a rhythm—due mainly to the relation between its movements—which some people can hear but no one can tap to. This second sort of rhythm is difficult, and whether it is substantially the same as the first sort only a musician could tell us. What a literary man wants to say though is that the first kind of rhythm, the diddidy dum, can be found in certain novels and may give them beauty. And the other rhythm, the difficult one—the rhythm of the Fifth Symphony as a whole—I cannot quote you any parallels for that in fiction, yet it may be present. . . .

[2] See the *Letters of H. James*, Vol. II.

FROM *TRADITION AND*
POETIC STRUCTURE
J. V. Cunningham*

> Cunningham sees in Marvell's *To His Coy Mistress* a lyric whose apparent and general structure is in the logical form of the syllogism, which acts "as a kind of expandable filing system" for "elements of a different order: in this case, ... conceits and erotic propositions in the tradition of Jonson and Herrick."

... May the poem be not merely subject to logical analysis but logical in form? May ... the subject and structure of a poem be conceived and expressed syllogistically? Anyone at all acquainted with modern criticism and the poems that are currently in fashion will think in this connection of Marvell's *To His Coy Mistress.* The apparent structure of that poem is an argumentative syllogism, explicitly stated. "Had we but world enough and time," the poet says,

This coyness, lady, were no crime ...

But at my back I always hear
Time's winged chariot hurrying near ...

Now, therefore ...
... let us sport us while we may ...

If we had all the time and space in the world we could delay consummation. But we do not. Therefore. The structure is formal. The poet offers to the lady a practical syllogism, and if she assents to it the appropriate consequence, he hopes, will follow:

Had we but world enough, and time,
This coyness, Lady, were no crime;

* The selection is reprinted from *Tradition and Poetic Structure*, by J. V. Cunningham, by permission of the publisher, Alan Swallow. Copyright 1951, 1960, by J. V. Cunningham.

We would sit down and think which way
To walk and pass our long love's day.
Thou by the Indian Ganges side
Shouldst rubies find: I by the tide
Of Humber would complain. I would
Love you ten years before the Flood,
And you should, if you please, refuse
Till the conversion of the Jews.
My vegetable love should grow
Vaster than empires, and more slow;
An hundred years should go to praise
Thine eyes and on thy forehead gaze;
Two hundred to adore each breast;
But thirty thousand to the rest;
An age at least to every part,
And the last age should show your heart;
For, Lady, you deserve this state,
Nor would I love at lower rate.

But at my back I always hear
Time's winged chariot hurrying near;
And yonder all before us lie
Deserts of vast eternity.
Thy beauty shall no more be found,
Nor in thy marble vault shall sound
My echoing song: then worms shall try
That long preserved virginity,
And your quaint honor turn to dust,
And into ashes all my lust:
The grave's a fine and private place,
But none, I think, do there embrace.

Now, therefore, while the youthful hue
Sits on thy skin like morning lew,
And while thy willing soul transpires
At every pore with instant fires,
Now let us sport us while we may,

And now, like amorous birds of prey,
Rather at once our time devour
Than languish in his slow-chapt power.
Let us roll all our strength and all
Our sweetness up into one ball,
And tear our pleasures with rough strife
Thorough the iron gates of life:
Thus, though we cannot make our sun
Stand still, yet we will make him run.[1]

The logical nature of the argument here has been generally recognised, though often with a certain timidity. Mr. Eliot hazards: "the three strophes of Marvell's poem have something like a syllogistic relation to each other." And in a recent scholarly work we read: "The dialectic of the poem lies not only or chiefly in the formal demonstration explicit in its three stanzas, but in all the contrasts evoked by its images and in the play between the immediately sensed and the intellectually apprehended."[2] That is, the logic is recognised, but minimized, and our attention is quickly distracted to something more reputable in a poem, the images or the characteristic tension of metaphysical poetry. For Mr. Eliot the more important element in this case is a principle of order common in modern poetry and often employed in his own poems. He points out that the theme of Marvell's poem is "one of the great traditional commonplaces of European literature . . . the theme of . . . *Gather ye rosebuds*, of *Go, lovely rose*." "Where the wit of Marvell," he continues, "renews the theme is in the variety and order of the images." The dominant principle of order in the poem, then, is an implicit one rather than the explicit

[1] H. M. Margouliouth, ed., *The Poems and Letters* (Oxford, 1927), II.
[2] T. S. Eliot, *Selected Essays* (new ed., New York, 1950), p. 254; Helen C. White, Ruth C. Wallerstein, and Ricardo Quintana, edd., *Seventeenth Century Verse and Prose* (New York, 1951), I, 454.

principle of the syllogism, and implicit in the succession of images.

Mr. Eliot explains the implicit principle of order in this fashion:

In the first of the three paragraphs Marvell plays with a fancy that begins by pleasing and leads to astonishment. . . . We notice the high speed, the succession of concentrated images, each magnifying the original fancy. When this process has been carried to the end and summed up, the poem turns suddenly with that surprise which has been one of the most important means of poetic effect since Homer:

But at my back I always hear
Time's winged chariot hurrying near,
And yonder all before us lie
Deserts of vast eternity.

A whole civilization resides in these lines:

Pallida Mors aequo pulsat pede pauperum
    tabernas
Regumque turres . . .

A modern poet, had he reached the height, would very likely have closed on this moral reflection.

What is meant by this last observation becomes clear a little later where it is said that the wit of the poem "forms the crescendo and diminuendo of a scale of great imaginative power." The structure of the poem, then, is this: it consists of a succession of images increasing in imaginative power to the sudden turn and surprise of the image of time, and then decreasing to the conclusion. But is there any sudden turn and surprise in the image of time? and does the poem consist of a succession of images?

This talk of images is a little odd since there seem to be relatively few in the poem if one means by image what people usually do—a descriptive phrase that invites the reader to project a sensory construction. The looming imminence of Time's winged chariot is, no doubt, an image, though not a full-blown one since there is nothing in the phrasing that properly invites any elaboration of sensory detail. But when Mr. Eliot refers to "successive images" and cites "my *vegetable* love," with *vegetable* italicised, and "Till the conversion of the Jews," one suspects that he is provoking images where they do not textually exist. There is about as much of an image in "Till the conversion of the Jews" as there would be in "till the cows come home," and it would be a psychiatrically sensitive reader who would immediately visualize the lowing herd winding slowly o'er the lea. But "my *vegetable* love" will make the point. I have no doubt that Mr. Eliot and subsequent readers do find an image here. They envisage some monstrous and expanding cabbage, but they do so in mere ignorance. V*egetable* is no vegetable but an abstract and philosophical term, known as such to every educated man of Marvell's day. Its context is the doctrine of the three souls: the rational, which in man subsumes the other two; the sensitive, which men and animals have in common and which is the principle of motion and perception; and, finally, the lowest of the three, the vegetable soul, which is the only one that plants possess, and which is the principle of generation and corruption, of augmentation and decay. Marvell says, then, my love, denied the exercise of sense, but possessing the power of augmentation, will increase "vaster than empires." It is an intellectual image, and hence no image at all but a conceit. For if one calls any sort of particularity or detail in a poem an image, the use of the wrong word will invite the reader to misconstrue his experience in terms of images, to invent sensory constructions and to project them on the poem.

A conceit is not an image. It is a piece of wit. It is in the tradition in which Marvell was writing, among other possibilities, the discovery of a proposition referring to one field of experience in terms of an intellectual structure derived from another field, and often enough a field of learning, as is the case in "my vegetable love." This tradition, though it goes back to the poetry of John Donne, and years before that, was current in Marvell's day. The fashionable poetry at the time he was writing this poem, the poetry comparable to that of Eliot or of Auden in the past two decades, was the poetry of John Cleveland, and the fashionable manner was generally known as Clevelandising. It consisted in the invention of a series of witty hyperbolical conceits, sometimes interspersed with images, and containing a certain amount of roughage in the form of conventional erotic statements:

> Thy beauty shall no more be found,
> Nor in thy marble vault shall sound
> My echoing song . . .

It was commonly expressed in the octosyllabic couplet. Cleveland, for example, writes *Upon Phillis Walking in a Morning before Sun-rising*:

> The trees, like yeomen of the guard,
> Serving her more for pomp than ward . . .

The comparison here does not invite visualization. It would be inappropriate to summon up the colors and serried ranks of the guard. The comparison is made solely with respect to the idea: the trees like the guard serve more for pomp than ward. Again:

> The flowers, called out of their beds,
> Start and raise up their drowsy heads,
> And he that for their color seeks
> May see it vaulting to her cheeks,

Where roses mix—no civil war
 Divides her York and Lancaster.[3]

One does not here picture in panorama
the Wars of the Roses. One sees rather
the aptness and the wit of York and Lancaster, the white rose and the red, reconciled in her cheeks, or one rejects it as
forced and far-fetched. This is a matter
of taste.

But if the poem is not a succession of
images, does it exhibit that other principle which Mr. Eliot ascribes to it, the
turn and surprise which he finds in the
abrupt introduction of time's chariot and
which forms a sort of fulcrum on which
the poem turns. Subsequent critics have
certainly felt that it has. In a current textbook we read:

The poem begins as a conventional love
poem in which the lover tries to persuade
his mistress to give in to his entreaties.
But with the introduction of the image of
the chariot in l. 21, the poet becomes
obsessed by the terrible onrush of time, and
the love theme becomes scarcely more than
an illustration of the effect which time has
upon human life.

And the leading scholar in the field, a
man who is generally quite unhappy with
Mr. Eliot's criticism, nevertheless says:

the poet sees the whole world of space and
time as the setting for two lovers. But wit
cannot sustain the pretence that youth and
beauty and love are immortal, and with a
quick change of tone—like Catullus' *nobis
cum semel occidit brevis lux* or Horace's
sed Timor et Minae—the theme of time
and death is developed with serious and
soaring directness. . . .[4]

[3] John M. Berdan, ed., *The Poems* (New
Haven, 1911), pp. 80–1.
[4] Wright Thomas and Stuart Gerry Brown,
edd., *Reading Poems* (New York, 1941), p.
702; Douglas Bush, *English Literature in the
Earlier Seventeenth Century* (Oxford, 1945),
p. 163.

These, I believe, are not so much accounts of the poem as accounts of Mr.
Eliot's reading of the poem. Let us
question the fact. Does the idea of
time and death come as any surprise
in this context? The poem began, "Had
we but world enough and time." That
is, it began with an explicit condition
contrary to fact, which by all grammatical rules amounts to the assertion
that we do not have world enough and
time. There is no surprise whatever when
the proposition is explicitly made in line
21. It would rather have been surprising
if it had not been made. Indeed, the only
question we have in this respect, after we
have read the first line, is, How many
couplets will the poet expend on the
ornamental re-iteration of the initial
proposition before he comes to the expected *but?* The only turn in the poem is
the turn which the structure of the syllogism had led us to await.

Mr. Eliot compares the turn and surprise which he finds in this poem to a
similar turn in an ode of Horace's, and
the scholars seem to corroborate the comparison. This is the fourth ode of the first
book:

Solvitur acris hiems grata vice veris et
 Favoni, trahuntque siccas machinae
 carinas . . .

The poem begins with a picture of spring
and proceeds by a succession of images,
images of the external world and mythological images:

Sharp winter relaxes with the welcome
change to Spring and the west wind, and
the cables haul the dry keels of ships. The
herd no longer takes pleasure in its stalls
or the farmer in his fire, and the pastures
no longer whiten with hoar frost. Cytherean
Venus leads her dancers beneath the over-
hanging moon, and the beautiful graces
and nymphs strike the ground with alternate foot, while blazing Vulcan visits the

grim forges of the Cyclops. Now is the time to wind your bright hair with green myrtle or with the flowers that the thawed earth yields. Now is the time to sacrifice to Faunus in the shadowed woods, whether it be a lamb he asks or a kid:

Pallida mors aequo pulsat pede pauperum
    tabernas regumque turres.

Pallid death with indifferent foot strikes the poor man's hut and the palaces of kings. Now, fortunate Sestius, the brief sum of life forbids our opening a long account with hope. Night will soon hem you in, and the fabled ghosts, and Pluto's meagre house.[5]

Death occurs in this poem with that suddenness and lack of preparation with which it sometimes occurs in life. The structure of the poem is an imitation of the structure of such experiences in life. And as we draw from such experiences often a generalization, so Horace from the sudden realization of the abruptness and impartiality of death, reflects

vitae summa brevis spem nos vetat incohare
    longam.

The brief sum of life forbids our opening a
    long account with hope.

But the proposition is subsequent to the experience; it does not rule and direct the poem from the outset. And the experience in Horace *is* surprising and furnishes the fulcrum on which the poem turns. It has, in fact, the characteristics which are ascribed to Marvell's poem but which

[5] My translation, except for "the brief sum of life forbids our opening a long account with hope," which is Gildersleeve's; see Paul Shorey, ed., Shorey and Gordon J. Lang, *Odes and Epodes* (rev. ed.; Chicago, 1910), *ad loc.*

Marvell's poem does not have. The two are two distinct kinds of poetry, located in distinct and almost antithetical traditions; both are valuable and valid methods, but one is not to be construed in terms of the other.

In brief, the general structure of Marvell's poem is syllogistic, and it is located in the Renaissance tradition of formal logic and of rhetoric. The structure exists in its own right and as a kind of expandable filing system. It is a way of disposing of, of making a place for, elements of a different order: in this case, Clevelandizing conceits and erotic propositions in the tradition of Jonson and Herrick. These re-iterate the propositions of the syllogism. They do not develop the syllogism, and they are not required by the syllogism; they are free and extra. There could be more or less of them since there is nothing in the structure that determines the number of interpolated couplets. It is a matter of tact, and a matter of the appetite of the writer and the reader.

The notion of a structure as a kind of expandable filing system may deserve a few sentences. The narative structure of a Shakespearean play can be regarded as a structure of this order. It exists in its own right, of course, but it is also a method for disposing various kinds of material or other orders, a set speech or passion here, an interpolated comic routine in another place. The structure offers a series of hooks upon which different things can be hung. Whether the totality will then form a whole, a unity, is a question of interpretation and a question of value. It is a question, for example, of what sort of unity is demanded, and whether there are various sorts....

FROM SPATIAL FORM IN MODERN LITERATURE
Joseph Frank*

By *spatial form*, Frank means a form of literature in which no consecutive sequence of parts can be perceived. With Pound's definition of image as "that which presents an intellectual and emotional complex in an instant of time," poetry began to be viewed as an organic unity in which one part might not follow another in logical sequence, but in which the parts taken all together constitute a unity. In the modern novel, techniques such as stream of consciousness are employed to give a similar spatial totality. The "reader must continually fit fragments together and keep allusions in mind until, by reflexive reference, he can link them to their complements."

Modern Anglo-American poetry received its initial impetus from the Imagist movement of the years directly preceding and following the first World War. Imagism was important not for any actual poetry written by Imagist poets— no one knew quite what an Imagist poet was—but rather because it opened the way for later developments by its clean break with sentimental Victorian verbiage. The critical writings of Ezra Pound, the leading theoretician of Imagism, are an astonishing farrago of keen esthetic perceptions thrown in among a series of boyishly naughty remarks, whose chief purpose, it would seem, is to *épater le bourgeois*—to startle the stuffed shirts. But Pound's definition of the image, perhaps the keenest of his perceptions, is of fundamental importance for any discussion of modern literary form.

"An image" Pound wrote, "is that which presents an intellectual and emo-

tional complex in an instant of time." The implications of his definition should be noted—an image is defined not as a pictorial reproduction, but as unification of disparate ideas and emotions into a complex presented spatially in an instant of time. Such a complex is not to proceed discursively, according to the laws of language, but is rather to strike the reader's sensibility with an instantaneous impact. Pound stresses this aspect by adding, in a later passage, that only the instantaneous presentation of such complexes gives "that sense of sudden liberation; that sense of freedom from time limits and space limits; that sense of sudden growth, which we experience in the presence of the greatest works of art."[1]

At the very outset, therefore, modern poetry advocates a poetic method in direct contradiction to Lessing's analysis of language. And if we compare Pound's definition of the image with Eliot's description of the psychology of the poetic

* The selection is reprinted from *The Widening Gyre*, by Joseph Frank, by permission of Rutgers University Press. Copyright 1963 by Rutgers University Press.

[1] Ezra Pound, *Make It New* (London: Faber and Faber, 1934), p. 336.

process, we can see clearly how profoundly this conception has influenced our modern idea of the nature of poetry. For Eliot, the distinctive quality of a poetic sensibility is its capacity to form new wholes, to fuse seemingly disparate experiences into an organic unity. The ordinary man, Eliot writes, "falls in love, or reads Spinoza, and these two experiences have nothing to do with each other, or with the noise of the typewriter or the smell of cooking; in the mind of the poet these experiences are always forming new wholes."[2] Pound had attempted to define the image in terms of its esthetic attributes; Eliot, in this passage, is describing its psychological origin; but the result in a poem would be the same in both cases.

Such a view of the nature of poetry immediately gave rise to numerous problems. How was more than one image to be included in a poem? If the chief value of an image was its capacity to present an intellectual and emotional complex simultaneously, linking up images in a sequence would clearly destroy most of their efficacy. Or was the poem itself one vast image, whose individual components were to be apprehended as a unity? But then it would be necessary to undermine the inherent consecutiveness of language, frustrating the reader's normal expectation of a sequence and forcing him to perceive the elements of the poem juxtaposed in space rather than unrolling in time.

This is precisely what Eliot and Pound attempted in their major works. Both poets, in their earlier work, still retained some elements of conventional structure. Their poems were looked upon as daring and revolutionary chiefly because of technical matters, like the loosening of metrical pattern and the handling of subjects

[2] T. S. Eliot, *Selected Essays* (New York: Harcourt, Brace), p. 247.

ordinarily considered nonpoetic. Perhaps this is less true of Eliot than of Pound, especially the Eliot of the more complex early works like *Prufrock*, *Gerontion* and *Portrait of a Lady*; but even here, although the sections of the poem are not governed by syntactical logic, the skeleton of an implied narrative structure is always present. The reader of *Prufrock* is swept up in a narrative movement from the very first lines:

> Let us go then, you and I,
> When the evening . . .

And the reader, accompanying Prufrock, finally arrives at their mutual destination:

> In the room the women come and go
> Talking of Michelangelo.

At this point the poem becomes a series of more or less isolated fragments, each stating some aspect of Prufrock's emotional dilemma. But the fragments are now localized and focused on a specific set of circumstances, and the reader can organize them by referring to the implied situation. The same method is employed in *Portrait of a Lady*, while in *Gerontion* the reader is specifically told that he has been reading the "thoughts of a dry brain in a dry season"—the stream-of-consciousness of "an old man in a dry month, being read to by a boy, waiting for the rain." In both poems there is a perceptible framework, around which the seemingly disconnected passages of the poem can be organized.

This was one reason why Pound's *Mauberly* and Eliot's early work were first regarded, not as forerunners of a new poetic form, but as latter-day *vers de société*—witty, disillusioned, with a somewhat brittle charm, but lacking that quality of "high seriousness" which Matthew Arnold had brandished as the touchstone of poetic excellence. These poems were considered unusual mainly because *vers de société* had long fallen out of fashion, but there was little difficulty in accepting them as an entertaining departure from the grand style of the nineteenth century.

In the *Cantos* and *The Waste Land*, however, it should have been clear that a radical transformation was taking place in aesthetic structure; but this transformation has been touched on only peripherally by modern critics. R. P. Blackmur comes closest to the central problem while analyzing what he calls Pound's "anecdotal" method. The special form of the *Cantos*, Blackmur explains, "is that of the anecdote begun in one place, taken up in one or more other places, and finished, if at all, in still another. This deliberate disconnectedness, this art of a thing continually alluding to itself, continually breaking off short, is the method by which the *Cantos* tie themselves together. So soon as the reader's mind is concerted with the material of the poem, Mr. Pound deliberately disconcerts it, either by introducing fresh and disjunct material or by reverting to old and, apparently, equally disjunct material."[3]

Blackmur's remarks apply equally well to *The Waste Land*, where syntactical sequence is given up for a structure depending on the perception of relationships between disconnected word-groups. To be properly understood, these word-groups must be juxtaposed with one another and perceived simultaneously. Only when this is done can they be adequately grasped; for, while they follow one another in time, their meaning does not depend on this temporal relationship. The one difficulty of these poems, which no amount of textual exegesis can wholly overcome,

[3] R. P. Blackmur, *The Double Agent* (New York: Arrow Editions, 1935), p. 49.

is the internal conflict between the time-logic of language and the space-logic implicit in the modern conception of the nature of poetry.

Aesthetic form in modern poetry, then, is based on a space-logic that demands a complete re-orientation in the reader's attitude towards language. Since the primary reference of any word-group is to something inside the poem itself, language in modern poetry is really reflexive. The meaning-relationship is completed only by the simultaneous perception in space of word-groups that have no comprehensible relation to each other when read consecutively in time. Instead of the instinctive and immediate reference of words and word-groups to the objects or events they symbolize and the construction of meaning from the sequence of these references, modern poetry asks its readers to suspend the process of individual reference temporarily until the entire pattern of internal references can be apprehended as a unity. . . .

For a study of aesthetic form in the modern novel, Flaubert's famous county fair scene in *Madame Bovary* is a convenient point of departure. This scene has been justly praised for its mordant caricature of bourgeois pomposity, its portrayal—unusually sympathetic for Flaubert—of the bewildered old servant, and its burlesque of the pseudo-romantic rhetoric by which Rodolphe woos the sentimental Emma. At present, however, it is enough to notice the method by which Flaubert handles the scene—a method we might as well call cinematographic since this analogy comes immediately to mind.

As Flaubert sets the scene, there is action going on simultaneously at three levels, and the physical position of each level is a fair index to its spiritual significance. On the lowest plane, there is the surging, jostling mob in the street, mingling with the livestock brought to the exhibitions. Raised slightly above the street by a platform are the speech-making officials, bombastically reeling off platitudes to the attentive multitudes. And on the highest level of all, from a window overlooking the spectacle, Rodolphe and Emma are watching the proceedings and carrying on their amorous conversation in phrases as stilted as those regaling the crowds. Albert Thibaudet has compared this scene to the medieval mystery play, in which various related actions occur simultaneously on different stage levels;[4] but this acute comparison refers to Flaubert's intention rather than to his method. *"Everything should sound simultaneously,"* Flaubert later wrote, in commenting on this scene; "one should hear the bellowing of the cattle, the whisperings of the lovers and the rhetoric of the officials all at the same time."[5]

But since language proceeds in time, it is impossible to approach this simultaneity of perception except by breaking up temporal sequence. And this is exactly what Flaubert does. He dissolves sequence by cutting back and forth between the various levels of action in a slowly-rising crescendo until—at the climax of the scene—Rodolphe's Chateaubriandesque phrases are read at almost the same moment as the names of prize winners for raising the best pigs. Flaubert takes care to underline this satiric similarity by description, as well as by juxtaposition, as if he were afraid the reflexive relations of the two actions might not be grasped: "From magnetism, by slow degrees, Rodolphe had arrived at affinities, and while M. le Président was citing Cincinnatus at his plow, Diocle-

tian planting his cabbages and the emperors of China ushering in the new year with sowing-festivals, the young man was explaining to the young woman that these irresistible attractions sprang from some anterior existence."

This scene illustrates, on a small scale, what we mean by the spatialization of form in a novel. For the duration of the scene, at least, the time-flow of the narrative is halted, attention is fixed on the interplay of relationships within immobilized time-area. These relationships are juxtaposed independently of the progress of the narrative, and the full significance of the scene is given only by the reflexive relations among the units of meaning. In Flaubert's scene, however, the unit of meaning is not, as in modern poetry, a word-group or a fragment of an anecdote; it is the totality of each level of action taken as an integer. The unit is so large that the scene can be read with an illusion of complete understanding, yet with a total unawareness of what Thibaudet calls the "dialectic of platitude" interweaving all levels and finally linking them together with devastating irony.

In other words, the adoption of spatial form in Pound and Eliot resulted in the disappearance of coherent sequence after a few lines; but the novel, with its larger unit of meaning, can preserve coherent sequence within the unit of meaning and break up only the time-flow of narrative. Because of this difference readers of modern poetry are practically forced to read reflexively to get any literal sense, while readers of a novel like *Nightwood*, for example, are led to expect narrative sequence by the deceptive normality of language sequence within the unit of meaning. But this does not affect the parallel between aesthetic form in modern poetry and the form of Flaubert's scene. Both can be properly understood only when their units of meaning are ap-

[4] Albert Thibaudet, *Gustave Flaubert* (Paris: Gallimard, 1935), p. 105.

[5] Gustave Flaubert, "Correspondence," Vol. III (1852–1854), p. 75, *Oeuvres Complètes* (Paris: Louis Conard, 1947).

prehended reflexively in an instant of time.

Flaubert's scene, although interesting in itself, is of minor importance to his novel as a whole and is skillfully blended back into the main narrative structure after fulfilling its satiric function. But Flaubert's method was taken over by James Joyce and applied on a gigantic scale in the composition of *Ulysses*. Joyce composed his novel of an infinite number of references and cross references which relate to one another independently of the time-sequence of the narrative. These references must be connected by the reader and viewed as a whole before the book fits together into any meaningful pattern. Ultimately, if we are to believe Stuart Gilbert, these systems of reference form a complete picture of practically everything under the sun, from the stages of man's life and the organs of the human body to the colors of the spectrum; but these structures are far more important for Joyce, as Harry Levin has remarked, than they could ever possibly be for the reader.[6] And while students of Joyce, fascinated by his erudition, have usually applied themselves to exegesis, our problem is to inquire into the perceptual form of his novel.

Joyce's most obvious intention in *Ulysses* is to give the reader a picture of Dublin seen as a whole—to re-create the sights and sounds, the people and places, of a typical Dublin day, much as Flaubert had re-created his *comice agricole*. And like Flaubert, Joyce aimed at attaining the same unified impact, the same sense of simultaneous activity occurring in different places. As a matter of fact, Joyce frequently makes use of the same method as Flaubert (cutting back and forth between different actions occurring at the same time) and he usually does so to obtain the same ironic effect. But Joyce had the problem of creating this impression of simultaneity for the life of a whole teeming city, and of maintaining it—or rather of strengthening it—through hundreds of pages that must be read as a sequence. To meet this problem Joyce was forced to go far beyond what Flaubert had done. Flaubert had still maintained a clear-cut narrative line except in the county fair scene; but Joyce breaks up his narrative and transforms the very structure of his novel into an instrument of his aesthetic intention.

Joyce conceived *Ulysses* as a modern epic. And in the epic, as Stephen Dedalus tells us in *The Portrait of the Artist as a Young Man*, "the personality of the artist, at first sight a cry or a cadence and then a fluid and lambent narrative, finally refines itself out of existence, impersonalizes itself, so to speak ... the artist, like the God of creation, remains within or beyond or above his handiwork, invisible, refined out of existence, indifferent, paring his fingernails." The epic is thus synonymous for Joyce with the complete self-effacement of the author; and, with his usual uncompromising rigor Joyce carries this implication further than anyone had previously dared.

For Joyce assumes—what is obviously not true—that his readers are Dubliners, intimately acquainted with Dublin life and the personal history of his characters. This allows him to refrain from giving any direct information about his characters and thus betraying the presence of an omniscient author. What Joyce does, instead, is to present the elements of his narrative—the relations between Stephen and his family, between Bloom and his wife, between Stephen and Bloom and the Dedalus family—in fragments, as they are thrown out unexplained in the

[6] Stuart Gilbert, *James Joyce's Ulysses* (New York: Alfred Knopf, 1952); Harry Levin, *James Joyce* (Norfolk, Conn.: New Directions, 1941), p. 75.

course of casual conversation, or as they lie embedded in the various strata of symbolic reference. The same is true of all the allusions to Dublin life, history, and the external events of the twenty-four hours during which the novel takes place. All the factual background summarized for the reader in an ordinary novel must here be reconstructed from fragments, sometimes hundreds of pages apart, scattered through the book. As a result, the reader is forced to read *Ulysses* in exactly the same manner as he reads modern poetry, that is, by continually fitting fragments together and keeping allusions in mind until, by reflexive reference, he can link them to their complements.

Joyce desired in this way to build up in the reader's mind a sense of Dublin as a totality, including all the relations of the characters to one another and all the events which enter their consciousness. The reader is intended to acquire this sense as he progresses through the novel, connecting allusions and references spatially and gradually becoming aware of the pattern of relationships. At the conclusion it might almost be said that Joyce literally wanted the reader to become a Dubliner. For this is what Joyce demands: that the reader have at hand the same instinctive knowledge of Dublin life, the same sense of Dublin as a huge, surrounding organism, which the Dubliner possesses as a birthright. It is this birthright that, at any one moment of time, gives the native a knowledge of Dublin's past and present as a whole; and it is only such knowledge that would enable the reader, like the characters, to place all the references in their proper context. This, it should be realized, is the equivalent of saying that Joyce cannot be read—he can only be reread. A knowledge of the whole is essential to an understanding of any part; but unless one is

a Dubliner such knowledge can be obtained only after the book has been read, when all the references are fitted into their proper place and grasped as a unity. The burdens placed on the reader by this method of composition may well seem insuperable. But the fact remains that Joyce, in his unbelievably laborious fragmentation of narrative structure, proceeded on the assumption that a unified spatial apprehension of his work would ultimately be possible.

In a far more subtle manner than in either Joyce or Flaubert, the same principle of composition is at work in Marcel Proust. Since Proust himself tells us that his novel will have imprinted on it "a form which usually remains invisible, the form of Time," it may seem strange to speak of Proust in connection with spatial form. He has almost invariably been considered the novelist of time *par excellence*: the literary interpreter of that Bergsonian "real time" intuited by the sensibility, as distinguished from the abstract, chronological time of the conceptual intelligence. To stop at this point, however, is to miss what Proust himself considered the deepest significance of his work.

Obsessed and oppressed by a sense of the ineluctability of time, Proust was suddenly, he tells us, visited by certain quasi-mystical experiences (described in detail in the last volume of his work, *Le Temps Retrouvé*). These experiences provided him with a spiritual technique for transcending time, and thus enabled him to escape time's domination. Proust believed that these transcendent extratemporal moments contained a clue to the ultimate secrets of reality; and he wished to translate these moments to the level of aesthetic form by writing a novel. But no ordinary narrative, which tried to convey their meaning indirectly through exposition and description, could really do them justice. For Proust desired, through the medium of his novel, to communicate to his reader the full impact of these moments as he had felt them himself.

To define the method by which this is accomplished, one must first understand clearly the precise nature of the Proustian revelation. Each such experience was marked by a feeling that "the permanent essence of things, usually concealed, is set free and our true self, which had long seemed dead but was not dead in other ways, awakes, takes on fresh life as it receives the celestial nourishment brought to it." This celestial nourishment consists of some sound, or odor, or other sensory stimulus, "sensed anew, simultaneously in the present and the past."

But why should these moments seem so overwhelmingly valuable that Proust calls them celestial? Because, Proust observes, his imagination could only operate on the past; the material presented to his imagination thus lacks any sensuous immediacy. At certain moments, however, the physical sensations of the past came flooding back to fuse with the present; and Proust believed that in these moments he grasped a reality "real without being of the present moment, ideal but not abstract." Only in these moments did he attain his most cherished ambition—"to seize, isolate, immobilize for the duration of a lightning flash" what otherwise he could not apprehend, "namely: a fragment of time in its pure state." For a person experiencing this moment, Proust adds, the word "death" no longer has meaning. "Situated outside the scope of time, what could he fear from the future?"

The significance of this experience, though obscurely hinted at throughout the book, is made explicit only in the concluding pages which describe the final appearance of the narrator at the reception of the Princesse de Guermantes. And the narrator decides to dedicate the remainder of his life to re-creating these experiences in a work of art. This work will differ essentially from all others because, at its root, will be a vision of reality that has been refracted through an extratemporal perspective. . . .

The prototype of this method, like the analysis of the revelatory moment, occurs during the reception at the Princesse de Guermantes. The narrator has spent years in a sanatorium and has lost touch almost completely with the fashionable world of the earlier volumes; now he comes out of seclusion to attend the reception. Accordingly, he finds himself bewildered by the changes in social position, and the even more striking changes in character and personality among his former friends. No doubt these pages paint a striking picture of the invasion of French aristocratic society by the upper bourgeoisie, and the gradual breakdown of all social and moral standards caused by the first World War; but, as the narrator takes great pains to tell us, it is far from being the most important theme of this section of the book. Much more crucial is that, almost with the force of a blow, these changes jolt the narrator into a consciousness of the passage of time. He tries painfully to recognize old friends under the masks that, he feels, the years have welded to them. And when a young man addresses him respectfully instead of familiarly, he realizes suddenly that, without being aware of it, he too has assumed a mask—the mask of an elderly gentleman. The narrator now begins to understand that in order to become conscious of time it has been necessary for him to absent himself from his accustomed environment (in other words, from the stream of time acting on that environment) and then to plunge back into the stream after a lapse of years. In so doing he finds himself presented with two images—the world as he had formerly known it and the world, transformed by time, that he now sees before him. When these two images become juxtaposed, the narrator discovers, the passage of time may suddenly be experienced through its visible effects.

Habit is a universal soporific which ordinarily conceals the passage of time from those who have gone their accustomed ways. At any one moment of time the changes are so minute as to be imperceptible. "Other people," Proust writes, "never cease to change places in relation to ourselves. In the imperceptible, but eternal march of the world, we regard them as motionless in a moment of vision, too short for us to perceive the motion that is sweeping them on. But we have only to select in our memory two pictures taken of them at different moments, close enough together however for them not to have altered in themselves—perceptibly, that is to say—and the difference between the two pictures is a measure of the displacement that they have undergone in relation to us." By comparing these two images in a moment of time, the passage of time can be experienced concretely, in the impact of its visible effects on the sensibility. And this discovery provides the narrator with a method that, in T. S. Eliot's phrase, is an "objective correlative" to the visionary apprehension of the fragment of "pure time" intuited in the revelatory moment.

When the narrator discovers this method of communicating his experience of the revelatory moment, he decides, as we have already observed, to incorporate it in a novel. But the novel the narrator undertakes to write has just been finished by the reader; and its form is controlled by the method that the narrator has outlined in its concluding pages. In other words, the reader is substituted for the narrator, and is placed by the author throughout the book in the same position as that occupied by the narrator before his own experience at the reception of the Princesse de Guermantes. This is done by the discontinuous presentation of character—a simple device which nonetheless is the clue to the form of Proust's vast structure.

Every reader soon notices that Proust does not follow any of his characters continuously through the whole course of his novel. Instead, they appear and reappear in various stages of their lives. Hundreds of pages sometimes go by between the time they are last seen and the time they reappear; and when they do turn up again, the passage of time has invariably changed them in some decisive way. Rather than being submerged in the stream of time and intuiting a character progressively, in a continuous line of development, the reader is confronted with various snapshots of the characters "motionless in a moment of vision" taken at different stages in their lives; and in juxtaposing these images he experiences the effects of the passage of time exactly as the narrator had done. As Proust has promised, therefore, he does stamp his novel indelibly with the form of time; but we are now in a position to understand exactly what he meant by this engagement.

To experience the passage of time, Proust learned, it was necessary to rise above it and to grasp both past and present simultaneously in a moment of what he called "pure time." But "pure time," obviously, is not time at all—it is perception in a moment of time, that is to say, space. And, by the discontinuous presentation of character Proust forces the reader to juxtapose disparate images spatially, in a moment of time, so that the experience of time's passage is communicated directly to his sensibility. . . .

There is a striking analogy here between Proust's method and that of his beloved Impressionist painters; but this analogy goes far deeper than the usual comments about the "impressionism" of Proust's style. The Impressionist painters juxtaposed pure tones on the canvas, instead of mixing them on the palette, in order to leave the blending of colors to the eye of the spectator. Similarly, Proust gives us what might be called pure views of his characters—views of them "motionless in a moment of vision" in various phases of their lives—and allows the sensibility of the reader to fuse these views into a unity. Each view must be apprehended by the reader as a unit; and Proust's purpose is achieved only when these units of meaning are referred to each other reflexively in a moment of time. As with Joyce and the modern poets, we see that spatial form is also the structural scaffolding of Proust's labyrinthine masterpiece.

PSYCHOLOGY AND FORM

Kenneth Burke*

The form that the artist gives to a work of art is often based upon the psychological mechanism of the audience. Such form is designed, Burke explains, for creating an "appetite" in the audience or reader and for the "adequate satisfying of that appetite."

It is not until the fourth scene of the first act that Hamlet confronts the ghost of his father. As soon as the situation has been made clear, the audience has been, consciously or unconsciously, waiting for his ghost to appear, while in the fourth scene this moment has been definitely promised. For earlier in the play Hamlet had arranged to come to the platform at night with Horatio to meet the ghost, and it is now night, he is with Horatio and Marcellus, and they are standing on the platform. Hamlet asks Horatio the hour.

Hor: I think it lacks of twelve.
Mar: No, it is struck.
Hor: Indeed? I heard it not: then it draws near the season
Wherein the spirit held his wont to walk.

Promptly hereafter there is a sound off-stage. "A flourish of trumpets, and ordnance shot off within." Hamlet's friends have established the hour as twelve. It is time for the ghost. Sounds off-stage, and of course it is not the ghost. It is, rather, the sound of the king's carousal, for the king "keeps wassail." A tricky and useful detail. We have been waiting for a ghost, and get, startlingly, a blare of trumpets. And, once the trumpets are silent, we feel how desolate are these three men waiting for a ghost, on a bare "platform," feel it by this sudden juxtaposition of an imagined scene of lights and merriment. But the trumpets announcing a carousal have suggested a

* The essay is reprinted from *Counter-Statement*, by Kenneth Burke, revised and augmented edition, Hermes Publications, Los Altos, California, 1953. Reprinted by permission of the author.

subject of conversation. In the darkness Hamlet discusses the excessive drinking of his countrymen. He points out that it tends to harm their reputation abroad, since, he argues, this one showy vice makes their virtues "in the general censure take corruption." And for this reason, although he himself is a native of this place, he does not approve of the custom. Indeed, there in the gloom he is talking very intelligently on these matters, and Horatio answers, "Look, my Lord, it comes." All this time we had been waiting for a ghost, and it comes at the one moment which was not pointing towards it. This ghost, so assiduously prepared for, is yet a surprise. And now that the ghost has come, we are waiting for something further. Program: a speech from Hamlet. Hamlet must confront the ghost. Here again Shakespeare can feed well upon the use of contrast for his effects. Hamlet has just been talking in a sober, rather argumentative manner—but now the floodgates are unloosed:

Angels and ministers of grace defend us!
Be thou a spirit of health or goblin damn'd.
Bring with thee airs from heaven or blasts
    from hell . . .

and the transition from the matter-of-fact to the grandiose, the full-throated and full-voweled, is a second burst of trumpets, perhaps more effective than the first, since it is the rich fulfillment of a promise. Yet this satisfaction in turn becomes an allurement, an itch for further developments. At first desiring solely to see Hamlet confront the ghost, we now want Hamlet to learn from the ghost the details of the murder—which are, however, with shrewdness and husbandry, reserved for "Scene V—Another part of the Platform."

I have gone into this scene at some length, since it illustrates so perfectly the relationship between psychology and form, and so aptly indicates how the one is to be defined in terms of the other. That is, the psychology here is not the psychology of the *hero*, but the psychology of the *audience*. And by that distinction, form would be the psychology of the audience. Or, seen from another angle, form is the creation of an appetite in the mind of the auditor, and the adequate satisfying of that appetite. This satisfaction—so complicated is the human mechanism—at times involves a temporary set of frustrations, but in the end these frustrations prove to be simply a more involved kind of satisfaction, and furthermore serve to make the satisfaction of fulfillment more intense. If, in a work of art, the poet says something, let us say, about a meeting, writes in such a way that we desire to observe that meeting, and then, if he places that meeting before us—that is form. While obviously, that is also the psychology of the audience, since it involves desires and their appeasements.

The seeming breach between form and subject-matter, between technique and psychology, which has taken place in the last century is the result, it seems to me, of scientific criteria being unconsciously introduced into matters of purely esthetic judgment. The flourishing of science has been so vigorous that we have not yet had time to make a spiritual readjustment adequate to the changes in our resources of material and knowledge. There are disorders of the social system which are caused solely by our undigested wealth (the basic disorder being, perhaps, the phenomenon of overproduction: to remedy this, instead of having all workers employed on half time, we have half working full time and the other half idle, so that whereas overproduction could be the greatest reward of applied science, it has been, up to now, the most menacing condition our modern civilization has had to face). It would be absurd to suppose that such social disorders would not be paralleled by disorders of culture and taste, especially since science is so pronouncedly a spiritual factor. So that we are, owing to the sudden wealth science has thrown upon us, all *nouveaux-riches* in matters of culture, and most poignantly in that field where lack of native firmness is most readily exposed, in matters of esthetic judgment.

One of the most striking derangements of taste which science has temporarily thrown upon us involves the understanding of psychology in art. Psychology has become a body of information (which is precisely what psychology in science should be, or must be). And similarly, in art, we tend to look for psychology as the purveying of information. Thus, a contemporary writer has objected to Joyce's *Ulysses* on the ground that there are more psychoanalytic data available in Freud. (How much more drastically he might, by the same system, have destroyed Homer's *Odyssey!*) To his objection it was answered that one might, similarly, denounce Cézanne's trees in favor of state forestry bulletins. Yet are not Cézanne's landscapes themselves tainted with the psychology of information? Has he not, by perception, *pointed out* how one object lies against another, *indicated* what takes place between two colors (which is the psychology of science, and is less successful in the medium of art than in that of science, since in art such processes are at best implicit, whereas in science they are so readily made explicit)? Is Cézanne not, to that extent, a state forestry bulletin, except that he tells what goes on in the eye instead of on the tree? And do not the true values

of his work lie elsewhere—and precisely in what I distinguish as the psychology of form?

Thus, the great influx of information has led the artist also to lay his emphasis on the giving of information—with the result that art tends more and more to substitute the psychology of the hero (the subject) for the psychology of the audience. Under such an attitude, when form is preserved it is preserved as an annex, a luxury, or, as some feel, a downright affectation. It remains, though sluggish, like the human appendix, for occasional demands are still made upon it; but its true vigor is gone, since it is no longer organically required. Proposition: The hypertrophy of the psychology of information is accompanied by the corresponding atrophy of the psychology of form.

In information, the matter is intrinsically interesting. And by intrinsically interesting I do not necessarily mean intrinsically valuable, as witness the intrinsic interest of backyard gossip or the most casual newspaper items. In art, at least the art of the great ages (Aeschylus, Shakespeare, Racine), the matter is interesting by means of an extrinsic use, a function. Consider, for instance, the speech of Mark Antony, the "Brutus is an honourable man." Imagine in the same place a very competently developed thesis on human conduct, with statistics, intelligence tests, definitions; imagine it as the finest thing of the sort ever written, and as really being at the roots of an understanding of Brutus. Obviously, the play would simply stop until Antony had finished. For in the case of Antony's speech, the value lies in the fact that his words are shaping the future of the audience's desires, not the desires of the Roman populace, but the desires of the pit. This is the psychology of form as distinguished from the psychology of information.

The distinction is, of course, absolutely true only in its nonexistent extremes. Hamlet's advice to the players, for instance, has little of the quality which distinguishes Antony's speech. It is, rather, intrinsically interesting, although one could very easily prove how the play would benefit by some such delay at this point, and that anything which made this delay possible without violating the consistency of the subject would have, in this, its formal justification. It would, furthermore, be absurd to rule intrinsic interest out of literature. I wish simply to have it restored to its properly minor position, seen as merely one out of many possible elements of style. Goethe's prose, often poorly imagined or neutral in its line-for-line texture, especially in the treatment of romantic episode—perhaps he felt that the romantic episode in itself was enough?—is strengthened into a style possessing affirmative virtues by his rich use of aphorism. But this is, after all, but one of many possible facets of appeal. In some places, notably in *Wilhelm Meisters Lehrjahre* when Wilhelm's friends disclose the documents they have been collecting about his life unbeknown to him, the aphorisms are almost rousing in their efficacy, since they involve the story. But as a rule the appeal of aphorism is intrinsic: that is, it satisfies without being functionally related to the context.[1] Also, to return to the matter

---

[1] Similarly, the epigram of Racine is "pure art," because it usually serves to formulate or clarify some situation within the play itself. In Goethe the epigram is most often of independent validity, as in *Die Wahlverwandtschaften*, where the ideas of Ottilie's diary are obviously carried over boldly from the author's notebook. In Shakespeare we have the union of extrinsic and intrinsic epigram, the epigram growing out of its context and yet valuable independent of its context.

of Hamlet, it must be observed that the style in this passage is no mere "information-giving" style; in its alacrity, its development, it really makes this one fragment into a kind of miniature plot.

One reason why music can stand repetition so much more sturdily than correspondingly good prose is because music, of all the arts, is by its nature least suited to the psychology of information, and has remained closer to the psychology of form. Here form cannot atrophy. Every dissonant chord cries for its solution, and whether the musician resolves or refuses to resolve this dissonance into the chord which the body cries for, he is dealing in human appetites. Correspondingly good prose, however, more prone to the temptations of pure information, cannot so much bear repetition since the esthetic value of information is lost once that information is imparted. If one returns to such a work again it is purely because, in the chaos of modern life, he has been able to forget it. With a desire, on the other hand, its recovery is as agreeable as its discovery. One can memorize the dialogue between Hamlet and Guildenstern, where Hamlet gives Guildenstern the pipe to play on. For, once the speech is known, its repetition adds a new element to compensate for the loss of novelty. We cannot take a recurrent pleasure in the new (in information) but we can in the natural (in form). Already, at the moment when Hamlet is holding out the pipe to Guildenstern and asking him to play upon it, we "gloat over" Hamlet's triumphal descent upon Guildenstern, when, after Guildenstern has, under increasing embarrassment, protested three times that he cannot play the instrument, Hamlet launches the retort for which all this was preparation:

Why, look you now, how unworthy a thing you make of me. You would play upon me, you would seem to know my stops; you would pluck out the heart of my mystery; you would sound me from my lowest note to the top of my compass; and there is much music, excellent voice, in this little organ, yet cannot you make it speak. 'Sblood, do you think I am easier to be played on than a pipe? Call me what instrument you will, though you can fret me, you cannot play upon me.[2]

In the opening lines we hear the promise of the close, and thus feel the emotional curve even more keenly than at first reading. Whereas in most modern art this element is underemphasized. It gives us the gossip of a plot, a plot which too often has for its value the mere fact that we do not know its outcome.[3]

Music, then, fitted less than any other art for imparting information, deals minutely in frustrations and fulfillments of desire,[4] and for that reason more often gives us those curves of emotion which, because they are natural, can bear repetition without loss. It is for this reason that music, like folk tales, is most capable of lulling us to sleep. A lullaby is a melody which comes quickly to rest, where the obstacles are easily overcome —and this is precisely the parallel to those waking dreams of struggle and conquest which (especially during childhood) we permit ourselves when falling asleep or when trying to induce sleep. Folk tales are just such waking dreams. Thus it is right that art should be called a "waking dream." The only difficulty with this definition (indicated by Charles Baudouin in his *Psychoanalysis and Aesthetics*, a very valuable study of Verhaeren) is that today we understand it to mean art as a waking dream for the artist. Modern criticism, and psychoanalysis in particular, is too prone to define the essence of art in terms of the artist's weaknesses. It is, rather, the audience which dreams, while the artist oversees the conditions which determine this dream. He is the manipulator of blood, brains, heart, and bowels which, while we sleep, dictate the mold of our desires. This is, of course, the real meaning of artistic felicity—an exaltation at the correctness of the procedure, so that we enjoy the steady march of doom in a Racinian tragedy with exactly the same equipment as that which produces our delight with Benedick's "Peace! I'll stop your mouth. (*Kisses her*)" which terminates the imbroglio of *Much Ado About Nothing*.

The methods of maintaining interest which are most natural to the psychology of information (as it is applied to works of pure art) are surprise and suspense. The method most natural to the psychology of form is eloquence. For this reason the great ages of Aeschylus, Shakespeare, and Racine, dealing as they did with material which was more or less a matter of common knowledge so that the broad outlines of the plot were known in advance (while it is the broad outlines which are usually exploited to secure surprise and suspense), developed

[2] One might indicate still further appropriateness here. As Hamlet finishes his speech, Polonius enters, and Hamlet turns to him, "God bless you, sir!" Thus, the plot is continued (for Polonius is always the promise of action) and a full stop is avoided: the embarrassment laid upon Rosencrantz and Guildenstern is not laid upon the audience.

[3] Yet modern music has gone far in the attempt to renounce this aspect of itself. Its dissonances become static, demanding no particular resolution. And whereas an unfinished modulation by a classic musician occasions positive dissatisfaction, the refusal to resolve a dissonance in modern music does not dissatisfy us, but irritates or stimulates. Thus, "energy" takes the place of style.

[4] Suspense is the least complex kind of anticipation, as surprise is the least complex kind of fulfillment.

formal excellence, or eloquence, as the basis of appeal in their work.

Not that there is any difference in kind between the classic method and the method of the cheapest contemporary melodrama. The drama, more than any other form, must never lose sight of its audience: here the failure to satisfy the proper requirements is most disastrous. And since certain contemporary work is successful, it follows that rudimentary laws of composition are being complied with. The distinction is one of intensity rather than of kind. The contemporary audience hears the lines of a play or novel with the same equipment as it brings to reading the lines of its daily paper. It is content to have facts placed before it in some more or less adequate sequence. Eloquence is the minimizing of this interest in fact, *per se*, so that the "more or less adequate sequence" of their presentation must be relied on to a much greater extent. Thus, those elements of surprise and suspense are subtilized, carried down into the writing of a line or a sentence, until in all its smallest details the work bristles with disclosures, contrasts, restatements with a difference, ellipses, images, aphorism, volume, sound-values, in short all that complex wealth of minutiae which in their line-for-line aspect we call style and in their broader outlines we call form.

As a striking instance of a modern play with potentialities in which the intensity of eloquence is missing, I might cite a recent success, Capek's *R. U. R.* Here, in a melodrama which was often astonishing in the rightness of its technical procedure, when the author was finished he had written nothing but the scenario for a play by Shakespeare. It was a play in which the author produced time and again the opportunity, the demand, for eloquence, only to move on. (At other times, the most successful

moments, he utilized the modern discovery of silence, writing moments wherein words could not possibly serve but to detract from the effect: this we might call the "flowering" of information.) The Adam and Eve scene of the last act, a "commission" which the Shakespeare of the comedies would have loved to fill, was in the verbal barrenness of Capek's play something shameless to the point of blushing. The Robot, turned human, prompted by the dawn of love to see his first sunrise, or hear the first bird-call, and forced merely to say, "Oh, see the sunrise," or, "Hear the pretty birds"—here one could do nothing but wring his hands at the absence of that esthetic mold which produced the overslung "speeches" of *Romeo and Juliet*.

Suspense is the concern over the possible outcome of some specific detail of plot rather than for general qualities. Thus, "Will A marry B or C?" is suspense. In *Macbeth*, the turn from the murder scene to the porter scene is a much less literal channel of development. Here the presence of one quality calls forth the demand for another, rather than one tangible incident of plot awaking an interest in some other possible tangible incident of plot. To illustrate more fully, if an author managed over a certain number of his pages to produce a feeling of sultriness, or oppression, in the reader, this would unconsciously awaken in the reader the desire for a cold, fresh north wind—and thus some aspect of a north wind would be effective if called forth by some aspect of stuffiness. A good example of this is to be found in a contemporary poem, T. S. Eliot's *The Waste Land*, where the vulgar, oppressively trivial conversation in the public house calls forth in the poet a memory of a line from Shakespeare. These slobs in a public house, after a desolately low-visioned conversation, are now forced by closing time to leave the saloon. They say good-night. And suddenly the poet, feeling his release, drops into another good-night, a good-night with *désinvolture*, a good-night out of what was, within the conditions of the poem at least, a graceful and irrecoverable past.

"Well that Sunday Albert was home, they
    had a hot gammon,
And they asked me in to dinner, to get
    the beauty of it hot"—
[at this point the bartender interrupts:
    it is closing time]
"Goonight Bill. Goonight Lou. Goo-
    night May. Goonight. Ta ta. Goo-
    night. Goonight.
Good-night, ladies, good-night, sweet
    ladies, good-night, good-night."

There is much more to be said on these lines, which I have shortened somewhat in quotation to make my issue clearer. But I simply wish to point out here that this transition is a bold juxtaposition of one quality created by another, an association in ideas which, if not logical, is nevertheless emotionally natural. In the case of *Macbeth*, similarly, it would be absurd to say that the audience, after the murder scene, wants a porter scene. But the audience does want the quality which this porter particularizes. The dramatist might, conceivably, have introduced some entirely different character or event in this place, provided only that the event produced the same quality of relationship and contrast (grotesque seriousness followed by grotesque buffoonery). One of the most beautiful and satisfactory "forms" of this sort is to be found in Baudelaire's "Femmes Damnées," where the poet, after describing the business of a Lesbian seduction, turns to the full oratory of his apostrophe:

Descendez, descendez, lamentables vic-
    times,
Descendez le chemin de l'enfer éternel ...

while the stylistic efficacy of this transition contains a richness which transcends all moral (or unmoral) sophistication: the efficacy of appropriateness, of exactly the natural curve in treatment. Here is morality even for the godless, since it is a morality of art, being justified, if for no other reason, by its paralleling of that staleness, that disquieting loss of purpose, which must have followed the procedure of the two characters, the *femmes damnées* themselves, a remorse which, perhaps only physical in its origin, nevertheless becomes psychic.[5]

But to return, we have made three terms synonymous: form, psychology, and eloquence. And eloquence thereby becomes the essence of art, while pity, tragedy, sweetness, humor, in short all the emotions which we experience in life proper, as non-artists, are simply the material on which eloquence may feed. The arousing of pity, for instance, is not the central purpose of art, although it may be an adjunct of artistic effectiveness. One can feel pity much more keenly at the sight of some actual misfortune—and it would be a great mistake to see art merely as a weak representation of some actual experience.[6] That artists today are content to write under such an esthetic accounts in part for the inferior position which art holds in the community. Art, at least

[5] As another aspect of the same subject, I could cite many examples from the fairy tale. Consider, for instance, when the hero is to spend the night in a bewitched castle. Obviously, as darkness descends, weird adventures must befall him. His bed rides him through the castle; two halves of a man challenge him to a game of nine-pins played with thigh bones and skulls. Or entirely different incidents may serve instead of these. The quality comes first, the particularization follows.

[6] Could not the Greek public's resistance to Euripides be accounted for in the fact that he, of the three great writers of Greek tragedy, betrayed his art, was guilty of esthetic impiety, in that he paid more attention to the arousing of emotion *per se* than to the sublimation of emotion into eloquence?

in the great periods when it has flowered, was the conversion, or transcendence, of emotion into eloquence, and was thus a factor added to life. I am reminded of St. Augustine's caricature of the theatre: that whereas we do not dare to wish people unhappy, we do want to feel sorry for them, and therefore turn to plays so that we can feel sorry although no real misery is involved. One might apply the parallel interpretation to the modern delight in happy endings, and say that we turn to art to indulge our humanitarianism in a well-wishing which we do not permit ourselves towards our actual neighbors. Surely the catharsis of art is more complicated than this, and more reputable.

Eloquence itself, as I hope to have established in the instance from *Hamlet* which I have analyzed, is no mere plaster added to a framework of more stable qualities. Eloquence is simply the end of art, and is thus its essence. Even the poorest is eloquent, but in a poor way, with less intensity, until this aspect is obscured by others fattening upon its leanness. Eloquence is not showiness; it is, rather, the result of that desire in the artist to make a work perfect by adapting it in every minute detail to the racial appetites.

The distinction between the psychology of information and the psychology of form involves a definition of esthetic truth. It is here precisely, to combat the deflection which the strength of science has caused to our tastes, that we must examine the essential breach between scientific and artistic truth. Truth in art is not the discovery of facts, not an addition to human knowledge in the scientific sense of the word.[7] It is, rather,

the exercise of human propriety, the formulation of symbols which rigidify our sense of poise and rhythm. Artistic truth is the externalization of taste.[8] I sometimes wonder, for instance, whether the "artificial" speech of John Lyly might perhaps be "truer" than the revelations of Dostoevsky. Certainly at its best, in its feeling for a statement which returns upon itself, which attempts the systole to a diastole, it *could* be much truer than Dostoevsky.[9] And if it is not, it fails not through a mistake of Lyly's esthetic, but because Lyly was a man poor in character whereas Dostoevsky was rich and

---

[7] One of the most striking examples of the encroachment of scientific truth into art is the doctrine of "truth by distortion," whereby one aspect of an object is suppressed the better to emphasize some other aspect; this is, obviously, an attempt to *indicate* by art some fact of knowledge, to make some implicit aspect of an object as explicit as one can by means of the comparatively dumb method of art (dumb, that is, as compared to the perfect ease with which science can indicate its discoveries). Yet science has already made discoveries in the realm of this "factual truth," this "truth by distortion" which must put to shame any artist who relies on such matter for his effects. Consider, for instance, the motion-picture of a man vaulting. By photographing this process very rapidly, and running the reel very slowly, one has upon the screen the most striking set of factual truths to aid in our understanding of an athlete vaulting. Here, at our leisure, we can observe the contortions of four legs, a head, and a butt. This squirming thing we saw upon the screen showed us an infinity of factual truths anent the balances of an athlete vaulting. We can, from this, observe the marvelous system of balancing which the body provides for itself in the adjustments of moving. Yet, so far as the esthetic truth is concerned, this on the screen was not an athlete, but a squirming thing, a horror, displaying every fact of vaulting except the exhilaration of the act itself.

[8] The procedure of science involves the elimination of taste, employing as a substitute the corrective norm of a pragmatic test, the empirical experiment, which is entirely intellectual. Those who oppose the "Intellectualism" of critics like Matthew Arnold are involved in an hilarious blunder, for Arnold's entire approach to the appreciation of art is through delicacies of taste intensified to the extent almost of squeamishness.

[9] As for instance, the "conceit" of Endymion's awakening, when he forgets his own name, yet recalls that of his beloved.

complex. When Swift, making the women of Brobdingnag enormous, deduces from this discrepancy between their size and Gulliver's that Gulliver could sit astride their nipples, he has written something which is esthetically true, which is, if I may be pardoned, profoundly "proper," as correct in its Euclidean deduction as any corollary in geometry. Given the companions of Ulysses in the cave of Polyphemus, it is true that they would escape clinging to the bellies of the herd let out to pasture. St. Ambrose, detailing the habits of God's creatures, and drawing from them moral maxims for the good of mankind, St. Ambrose in his limping natural history rich in scientific inaccuracies that are at the very heart of emotional rightness, St. Ambrose writes "Of night-birds, especially the nightingale which hatches her eggs by song; of the owl, the bat, and the cock at cock-crow; in what these may apply to the guidance of our habits,"

and in the sheer rightness of that program there is the truth of art. In introducing this talk of night-birds, after many pages devoted to other of God's creatures, he says:

What now! While we have been talking, you will notice how the birds of night have already started fluttering about you, and, in this same fact of warning us to leave off with our discussion, suggest thereby a further topic—

and this seems to me to contain the best wisdom of which the human frame is capable, an address, a discourse, which can make our material life seem blatant almost to the point of despair. And when the cock crows, and the thief abandons his traps, and the sun lights up, and we are in every way called back to God by the well-meaning admonition of this bird, here the very blindnesses of religion become the deepest truths of art.

PART IV

CRITICAL APPROACHES
AND METHODS

IT IS always possible to multiply distinctions in the kinds of approaches and methods that can be adopted for the criticism of literature. But most of these—most, at least, that are worthwhile—will fall under one or another of the four divisions following. The once fashionable approach known as "explication of text," for instance, in which the critic builds his interpretation almost exclusively on what is given in the text itself, may be subsumed under "Philological Focus." As a cautionary observation, it might be pointed out that there are other terms for the categories employed here, and also that most acts of criticism make use of—and need to make use of—more than one of the approaches and methods, of which the essays on *Hamlet* in this section are singularly pure examples.

CHAPTER 12

Historical Focus

TOWARD AN
INSTITUTIONAL METHOD
Harry Levin*

Levin contends that literature, "instead of reflecting life, refracts it. This is to say that while it may and does add to, subtract from, or distort the environment in which it grows, it is at all times an intrinsic part of it, 'a particular function of the whole social organism.'" Even the most personal and original writers reveal a "collective consciousness," so that social and historical analysis must take its place with other critical methods.

This provisional conclusion would explain why literary historians, under the influence of realism, have slighted literary form. In their impatience to lay bare the so-called content of a work, they have missed a more revealing characteristic: the way the artist handles the appropriate conventions. Whether it is possible, or even desirable, to eliminate artifice from art—that is one of the largest questions that criticism must face. But realistic novelists who declare their

* The essay was part of an essay entitled "Literature As An Institution," *Accent*, Vol. VI (1946). Reprinted in a slightly altered version from *The Gates of Horn* by Harry Levin. Copyright © 1963 by Harry Levin. Reprinted by permission of Oxford University Press, Inc.

intentions of transcribing life have an obvious advantage over realistic critics who expect every book to be a literal transcript. Stendhal, when he declares that "a novel is a mirror riding along a highway," is in a position to fulfil his picaresque intention. When Taine echoes this precept, defining the novel as "a kind of portable mirror which can be conveyed everywhere, and which is most convenient for reflecting all aspects of nature and life," he puts the mirror before the horse. He is then embarrassed to discover so few reflections of the *ancien régime* in French novels of the eighteenth century. His revulsion from neo-classical generalities and his pref-

437

erence for descriptive details carry him back across the channel, from Marmontel and Crébillon *fils* to Fielding and Smollett. Some mirrors, Taine finally discovered, are less reliable than others.

The metaphor of the mirror held up to nature, the idea that literature reflects life, was mentioned by Plato only to be rejected. By the time of Cicero it was already a commonplace of criticism. It was applied by the ancients to comedy, the original vehicle of realism; later it became a byword for artistic didacticism, for the medieval zeal to see vice exposed and virtue emulated. When Shakespeare invoked it, he had a definite purpose which those who quote him commonly ignore. Hamlet is not merely describing a play, he is exhorting the players. His advice is a critique of bad acting as well as an apology for the theater, a protest against unnatural conventions as well as a plea for realism. Like modern critics who derive their metaphors from photography, he implies a further comparison with more conventionalized modes of art—particularly with painting. To hold up a photograph or a mirror, as it were, is to compare the "abstract and brief chronicles of the time" with the distorted journeywork that "imitated humanity so abominably." Art should be a reflection of life, we are advised, not a distortion —as it has all too frequently been. Criticism, in assuming that art invariably reflects and forgetting that it frequently distorts, wafts us through the looking-glass into a sphere of its own, where everything is clear and cool, logical and literal, and more surrealistic than real.

In questioning the attempts of scholars to utilize Shakespeare as the mirror of his time, Professor Stoll has reminded them that their business is to separate historical fact from literary illusion, to distinguish the object from its reflected image. Literature, instead of reflecting life, refracts

it. Our task, in any given case, is to determine the angle of refraction. Since the angle depends upon the density of the medium, it is always shifting, and the task is never easy. We are aided today, however, by a more flexible and accurate kind of critical apparatus than Taine was able to employ. An acquaintance with artistic conventions, which can best be acquired through comparative studies in technique, should complement an awareness of social backgrounds. "Literature is complementary to life." This formula of Lanson's is broad enough to include the important proviso that there is room in the world of art for ideals and projects, fantasies and anxieties, which do not ordinarily find a habitation in the world of reality. But, in recognizing that literature adds something to life or that it subtracts something from life, we must not overlook the most important consideration of all— that literature is at all times an intrinsic part of life. It is, if we can work out the implications of Leslie Stephen's phrase, "a particular function of the whole social organism."

The organic character of this relationship has been most explicitly formulated by a statesman and historian, Prosper de Barante. Writing of the ideas behind the French revolution while they were still fresh in men's minds, his comprehension of their political interplay was broader than Taine's. "In the absence of regular institutions," wrote Barante, "literature became one." The truth, though it has long been obscured by a welter of personalities and technicalities, is that literature has always been an institution. Like other institutions, the church or the law, it cherishes a unique phase of human experience and controls a special body of precedents and devices; it tends to incorporate a self-perpetuating discipline, while responding to the main currents of each succeeding period; it is continually accessible to all the impulses of life at large, but it must translate them into its own terms and adapt them to its peculiar forms. Once we have grasped this fact, we begin to perceive how art may belong to society and yet be autonomous within its own limits, and are no longer puzzled by the apparent polarity of social and formal criticism. These, in the last analysis, are complementary frames of reference whereby we may discriminate the complexities of a work of art. In multiplying these discriminations between external impulses and internal peculiarities—in other words, between the effects of environment and convention—our ultimate justification is to understand the vital process to which they are both indispensable.

To consider the novel as an institution, then, imposes no dogma, exacts no sacrifice, and excludes none of the critical methods that have proved illuminating in the past. If it tends to subordinate the writer's personality to his achievement, it requires no further apology, for criticism has long been unduly subordinated to biography. The tendency of the romanticists to live their writings and write their lives, and the consequent success of their critics as biographers, did much to justify this subordination; but even Sainte-Beuve's "natural history of souls," though it unified and clarified an author's works by fitting them into the pattern of his career, was too ready to dismiss their purely artistic qualities as "rhetoric." More recently the doctrines of Freud, while imposing a topheavy vocabulary upon the discussion of art, have been used to corroborate and systematize the sporadic intuitions of artists; but the psychologists, like the sociologists, have been more interested in utilizing books for documentary purposes than in exploring their intrinsic nature. Mean-

while, on the popular level, the confusion between a novelist and his novels has been consciously exploited. A series of novelized biographies, calling itself *Le Roman des grandes existences*, invites the common reader to proceed from "the prodigious life of Balzac" through "the mournful life of Baudelaire" to "the wise and merry life of Montaigne."

If fiction has seldom been discussed on a plane commensurate with its achievements, it is because we are too often sidetracked by personalities. If, with Henry James, we recognize the novelist's intention as a figure in a carpet, we must recognize that he is guided by his material, his training, his commission, by the size and shape of his loom, and by his imagination to the extent that it accepts and masters those elements. Psychology—illuminating as it has been—has treated literature too often as a record of personal idiosyncrasies, too seldom as the basis of a collective consciousness. Yet it is on that basis that the greatest writers have functioned. Their originality has been an ability to "seize on the public mind," in Bagehot's opinion; conventions have changed and styles have developed as lesser writers caught "the traditional rhythm of an age." The irreducible element of individual talent would seem to play the same role in the evolution of *genres* that natural selection plays in the origin of species. Amid the mutations of modern individualism, we may very conceivably have overstressed the private aspects of writing. One convenience of the institutional method is that it gives due credit to the never-ending collaboration between writer and public. It sees no reason to ignore what is relevant in the psychological prepossessions of the craftsman, and it knows that he is ultimately to be judged by the technical resources of his craftsmanship; but it attains its clearest and most comprehensive scope by centering on his craft—on his social status and his historical function as participant in a skilled group and a living tradition.

When Edgar Quinet announced a course at the Collège de France in *La Littérature et les institutions comparées de l'Europe méridionelle,* he was requested by Guizot's ministry to omit the word "institutions" and to limit himself to purely literary discussion. When he replied that this would be impossible, his course was suspended, and his further efforts went directly into those reform agitations which culminated in the democratic revolution of the following year, 1848. Thereby proceeding from sociological to social criticism, he demonstrated anew what French critics and novelists have understood particularly well—the dynamic interaction between ideas and events. In a time which has

seen that demonstration repeated on so vast a scale, the institutional forces that impinge upon literature are self-evident. The responsibilities that literature owes to itself, and the special allegiance it exacts from us, should also become apparent when we conceive it as an institution in its own right. The misleading dichotomy between substance and form, which permits literary historians, like Parrington, to dismiss "belletristic philandering," and esthetic impressionists, like Mr. R. P. Blackmur, to dispose of "separable content," should disappear as soon as abstract categories are dropped and concrete relations are taken up. And the jurisdictional conflict between truth and beauty should dissolve when esthetics discovers the truth about beauty; when criticism becomes—as Bacon intended, and Renan and Sainte-Beuve remembered, and all too many other critics have forgotten—the science of art.

HAMLET . . .
Theodore Spencer*

Spencer demonstrates that a good understanding of *Hamlet* must rest on a knowledge of the two conflicting views of man's nature which were characteristic of the age in which Shakespeare lived.

I

At the beginning of the seventeenth century, Shakespeare had behind him ten years of successful play-writing. He had proved himself a master of comedy, of the chronicle play, of a certain kind of tragedy, and he had proved himself a master of plot-construction, of character and blank verse. He had brilliantly

developed the dramatic conventions given him by his time and he had admirably used the traditional sixteenth-century beliefs about man's nature as a mine for metaphor, as a means of describing character, and as a means of defining values by which character and action could be understood.

Toward the end of this period, as many students of Shakespeare have pointed out, there are indications of increasing seriousness, an anticipatory

* The essay is reprinted with permission of the publisher from *Shakespeare and the Nature of Man,* by Theodore Spencer. Copyright 1942, 1949 by The Macmillan Company.

clouding over of Shakespeare's view of the human situation. His half-satiric, half-sympathetic portrayal of the melancholy Jaques in *As You Like It*, a tone of something alien to comedy in *Twelfth Night*, the seriousness which he gives to the character of Brutus in *Julius Caesar*, all appear to foreshadow the presentation of evil which is the basis of the later tragedies.[1] In *Hamlet* evil appears fullfledged, and we have a very different kind of tragedy from anything that Shakespeare had previously written. For with *Hamlet* we feel as if Shakespeare had had a new vision of what a play could contain, and in this play, as in the other tragedies that follow it, the characters and events become larger than the characters of the 1590's; they make more reverberations in our minds; they take on a symbolic and universal meaning.

To describe how this is accomplished is one of the central problems in Shakespearean criticism: I suggest that we can understand it best by realizing that in *Hamlet* Shakespeare for the first time used to the full the conflict between the two views of man's nature which was so deeply felt in his age. On one side was the picture of man as he should be—it was bright, orderly and optimistic. On the other was the picture of man as he is—it was full of darkness and chaos. Shakespeare puts an awareness of this contrast into the character of Hamlet, and his having done so is one of the main reasons for *Hamlet's* greatness.

[1] Brutus, incidentally, makes excellent metaphorical use of the familiar parallel between the body and the state in his famous lines:

Between the acting of a dreadful thing
And the first motion, all the interim is
Like a phantasma, or a hideous dream:
The genius and the mortal instruments
Are then in council; and the state of man,
Like to a little kingdom, suffers then
The nature of an insurrection.

(ii, 1, 63)

Previously Shakespeare had used the traditional beliefs *descriptively* as part of the background—the sun is compared to the king, the human body is compared to the state—and there is no question as to whether the beliefs are true. But in *Hamlet* they are not in the background, they are an essential part of the hero's consciousness, and his discovery that they are not true, his awareness of the conflict between what theory taught and what experience proves, wrecks him. Shakespeare had used the difference between appearance and reality as a dramatic device many times before, but never like this, and never in such close relation to the thought and feeling of his time.

For Hamlet, before his mother's second marriage, had been, as Shakespeare is careful to point out, the ideal Renaissance nobleman; according to Ophelia, he had a "noble mind," "the courtier's, soldier's, scholar's, eye, tongue, sword." He was

The expectancy and rose of the fair state,
The glass of fashion and the mould of form;

he had, to use Bradley's somewhat romantic expression, "an unbounded delight and faith in everything good and beautiful." He was conceived by Shakespeare, in other words, as a young man who had been trained to believe, and by temperament was inclined to believe, in the traditional optimistic view of the nature of man. But the discovery of his mother's lust and the fact that the kingdom is in the hands of a man he considers unworthy—these shatter his belief into ruins, and the world, the state and the individual are to him suddenly corrupt. There is no better illustration than *Hamlet* of the fact that in Shakespeare's day the three spheres were so closely related that to destroy one was to destroy the others as well. Nor is there any better illustration of the sixteenth-century dramatic convention which invariably placed individual action against the background of a universal truth. In *Hamlet* the two traditions, the tradition of belief and the tradition of dramatic practice, are magnificently fused in the creation of the most absorbing character the stage has ever known.

There are two related aspects of Hamlet's thought which Shakespeare deliberately emphasizes in first presenting him to the audience. Hamlet is preoccupied with the difference between appearance and reality, and he extends his feelings about his particular situation to cover his feelings about the world as a whole.

> *King:* But now, my cousin Hamlet, and my son,—
> *Hamlet:* (*Aside.*) A little more than kin, and less than kind.
> *King:* How is it that the clouds still hang on you?
> *Hamlet:* Not so, my lord; I am too much i' the sun.

Again, when the queen asks him why the death of his father seems so particular with him, he answers,

> Seems, madam! Nay, it is; I know not "seems,"

and he discourses, roused for the first time, on the contrast between the outer trappings of grief, and the feeling within "which passeth show."

So much he can say in public, but when he is left alone, we see that his whole view of life is turned upside down. It is characteristic of Shakespeare's conception of Hamlet's universalizing mind that he should make Hamlet think first of the general rottenness; to him *all* the uses of the world are weary, stale, flat

and unprofitable; things rank and gross in nature possess it completely. From this he passes to the king, the head of the state, bitterly comparing his god-like father to his satyrlike uncle, and he finally dwells at length on individual perversion, the lustfulness of his mother, who has violated natural law by the brevity of her grief and the haste of her marriage.

> O God! a beast, that wants discourse of reason,
> Would have mourned longer.

Hamlet's thought, like that of so many men of the time, involves the world, the state and the individual, and one reason this first soliloquy is so broken, its rhythms so panting, is that it reflects Hamlet's disillusionment about all three spheres at once.

Hamlet's generalizing mind is everywhere emphasized; his thought invariably leaps out to embrace the world as a whole, he talks of infinite space, his rhetoric includes the stars. It is characteristic of him that when he approaches Laertes after Laertes has jumped into Ophelia's grave, he should ask who it is who

> Conjures the wandering stars, and makes them stand
> Like wonder-wounded hearers,

when, as a matter of fact, Laertes had not mentioned the stars at all. It is as if Hamlet were attributing to Laertes a thought that would be natural to him, but not to Laertes. Again, the first thing that Hamlet exclaims after the ghost has given his message is "O all you host of heaven!"; and in his mother's closet, when he upbraids her with her marriage, he describes it not merely as violating human contracts, but as affecting the world as a whole:

heaven's face doth glow,
Yea this solidity and compound mass,
With tristful visage, as against the doom,
Is thought-sick at the act.

But the occasion on which Hamlet speaks at greatest length of the heavens is, of course, when he describes his state of mind to Rosencrantz and Guildenstern in the second act. The situation is a critical one for Hamlet. He knows that his former fellow-students are spies of the king, and he obviously cannot tell them the real cause of his distemper. What explanation can he give them? He gives them just the kind of explanation that would be most clearly understood by young intellectuals, particularly young intellectuals who were familiar with his own generalizing type of mind and who might be expected to have shared his previous acceptance of the optimistic view of the world. All three young men had been taught that the surest way to comprehend man's place in the universe and to realize the magnificence of God's creation, was to contemplate the glory of the superior heavens which surrounded the earth, those heavens of which Spenser had so glowingly written in his "Hymn of Heavenly Beauty," and which Thomas Digges, in his *Perfect Description of the Celestial Orbs* (1576) described more scientifically, but with equal enthusiasm.[2] La Primaudaye and countless other Renaissance writers had written in the same way, and had inevitably

turned, as Hamlet turns, from the contemplation of the stars to the contemplation of man, for whom all this splendor had been made. But Hamlet reverses the application, and the clearest way he can explain his melancholy to his fellow-students is to tell them that he sees in the heavens, as well as in the world around him, the reality of evil underneath the appearance of good. Nothing could be more plausible, for everyone knew that such were the opinions of the man afflicted with melancholy. For example in 1599, just before Shakespeare wrote *Hamlet*, there appeared an English translation of a French medical work called *Of the Diseases of Melancholy* by a certain Dr. Du Laurens. Like the other sixteenth-century writers on melancholy, Du Laurens describes a state of mind very similar to Hamlet's. He begins with the usual exaltation of man: "Coming to extol man unto the highest degree and step of his glory, behold him I pray thee the best furnished and most perfect of all other living creatures, having... in his soul the image of God, and in his body the model of the whole world."[3] But the melancholy man is a very different object, he is "the most caitiff and miserable creature that is in the world, spoiled of all his graces, deprived of judgment, reason

---

[2] Digges wrote of the motionless heaven of fixed stars according to the Copernican system, and in his case, as in others, the acceptance of Copernicus did not mean that the universe was not beautiful. "This orb of stars," he says, "fixed infinitely up extendeth himself in altitude spherically and therefore immoveable, the palace of felicity garnished with perpetually shining glorious lights innumerable, far excelling our sun in quantity and quality, the very court of celestial angels, devoid of grief and replenished with perfect endless joy, the habitacle for the elect." See Francis R. Johnson, *Astronom-*

ical Thought in Renaissance England, Baltimore, 1937, p. 166. Digges' tract is published in *The Huntington Library Bulletin*, No. 5, April, 1934, by F. R. Johnson and S. V. Larkey. Perhaps Shakespeare knew of his description; Digges was a kind of sixteenth century Eddington or Jeans, his book went through six editions before 1600, Shakespeare could have found these words merely by looking at the title page where they are inscribed in a diagram, and Hamlet's description of the heavens sounds more like the motionless outer sphere of Copernicus than the revolving heavens of Ptolemy.

[3] *A Discourse of the Preservation of the Sight*, etc., trans. Richard Surphlet, *Shakespeare Association Facsimiles*, No. 15, London, 1938, p. 80.

and counsel, enemy of men and of the Sun, straying and wandering in solitary places; to be brief, so altered and changed, as that he is no more a man, as not retaining anything more than the very name."[4]

Hamlet, of course, enlarges this concept, as he enlarges everything, but the conventional views of man, both general and specialized, gave him an excellent groundwork to build on, and both his two interlocutors and the audience

[4] Many other symptoms of the melancholy man, as Du Laurens (among other specialists) describes him, are shared by Hamlet: the melancholy man has "dreadful dreams" (p. 82), he is "witty" and "excels others" (p. 86); "sadness doth never forsake him, suspicion doth secretly gall him, sighings, watchings, fearful dreams, silence, solitariness . . . and the abhorring of the sun, are as it were unseparable accidents of this miserable passion" (p. 89). Melancholy men "conceive of death as a terrible thing, and notwithstanding (which is strange) they often times desire it, yea so eagerly, as that they will not let to destroy themselves" (p. 92). Hamlet says (ii, 2, 635):

> The spirit that I have seen
> May be the devil: and the devil hath power
> To assume a pleasing shape; yea and perhaps
> Out of my weakness and my melancholy—
> As he is very potent with such spirits—
> Abuses me to damn me.

Du Laurens tells us that the imaginations of melancholic persons are troubled in three ways; "by nature, that is to say, by the constitution of the body; by the mind, that is to say, by some violent passion, whereunto they had given themselves; and by the intercourse or meddling of evil angels, which cause them often-times to foretell and forge very strange things in their imaginations" (p. 100). I am indebted to Dr. John Floyd for calling my attention to Du Laurens' treatise. Parallels between *Hamlet* and another contemporary medical work, Timothy Bright's A *Treatise of Melancholy* (1586), have been pointed out by Miss Mary Isobelle Sullivan, "Hamlet and Dr. Timothy Bright," *P.M.L.A.*, XLI (1926), 667–79. Miss Sullivan thinks that Hamlet's character was moulded directly from Bright's description. But, apparently unaware of Du Laurens or the other contemporary descriptions of melancholy, she overstates her case: we cannot say that Shakespeare relied on any one text; he merely used the ideas which were part of the common knowledge of his time.

would have understood Hamlet's magnificent generalizations more richly than we do, since they had been trained in the same beliefs as his own:

I have of late,—but wherefore I know not,—lost all my mirth, forgone all custom of exercises; and indeed it goes so heavily with my disposition that this goodly frame, the earth, seems to me a sterile promontory; this most excellent canopy, the air, look you, this brave o'erhanging firmament, this majestical roof fretted with golden fire, why, it appears no other thing to me but a foul and pestilent congregation of vapours.

And from this consideration of the macrocosm he passes at once to the microcosm; the sequence of thought was, in his time, almost automatic; and again he uses the familiar vocabulary of his age, describing the natural hierarchy in the technical language he could count on his school-fellows to understand:

What a piece of work is a man; how noble in reason, how infinite in faculties; in form and moving, how express and admirable in action; how like an angel in apprehension; how like a god! the beauty of the world; the paragon of animals. And yet to me, what is this quintessence of dust? Man delights not me.[5]

This use of generalization, which is one of the most important and attractive sides of Hamlet's character, is also a further example of how Shakespeare weaves into the texture of his play a standard of value or a point of view so that the particular action can stand out more clearly. It is a device which the dramatic tradition gave him, and which he had used many times before, notably in *Henry V*, but it had never before been made so important a part of char-

[5] My punctuation is based on that of the second quarto and of J. Dover Wilson, which alone makes sense in terms of Elizabethan psychology. . . .

acter. A further example can be seen in what Hamlet has to say about reason, the specific virtue of a human being (which Montaigne had so ingeniously labored to minimize). Horatio speaks (i, 4, 73) of the "sovereignty of reason," as does Ophelia, but Hamlet himself, as is appropriate in a play where the conflict is so deeply psychological, is the one who describes the traditional view most fully (iv, 4, 33):

> What is a man,
> If his chief good and market of his time
> Be but to sleep and feed? a beast, no more.
> Sure he that made us with such large discourse,
> Looking before and after, gave us not
> That capability and god-like reason
> To fust in us unus'd.

It is worth observing in what terms Shakespeare speaks of reason in important passages throughout the play. Reason, the specific function of man in the order of Nature, is twice referred to as "noble," an adjective, like "sovereign" (also applied to reason), that has connotations in the political order, and, in the passage I have just quoted, it is described as "god-like," an adjective that, to an Elizabethan, would have cosmological connotations as well. It may not be fantastic to see in this adjectival microcosm an image of the macrocosm we have been trying to define.

At all events, the standard which Hamlet's soliloquy describes is not only the standard which his own lack of action so agonizingly seems to violate, it is also the standard which was violated by Gertrude in mourning so briefly for her first husband, and in unnaturally yielding to her lust, so that her reason, in Hamlet's words, has become a pander to her will (her fleshly desire), thus disgustingly reversing the natural order. Hamlet's own standards are high. "Give me that man," he says to Horatio

> That is not passion's slave, and I will wear him
> In my heart's core, ay, in my heart of heart,
> As I do thee.

And it is because he has this high standard that he is so torn apart by discovering that the traditional order in which reason should be in control of passion is only an appearance, and that the reality of his mother's action proves human beings to be only beasts, their specific function gone.

II

Shakespeare uses the traditional views of kingship in the same way that he uses cosmology and psychology. Throughout *Hamlet* there is an emphasis on the importance of the king as the center of the state. Rosencrantz and Guildenstern describe the accepted ideal most fully (iii, 3, 8):

> *Guild.*: Most holy and religious fear it is
> To keep those many many bodies safe
> That live and feed upon your majesty.
>   *Ros.*: The single and peculiar life is bound
> With all the strength and armour of the mind
> To keep itself from noyance; but much more
> That spirit upon whose weal depend and rest
> The lives of many. The cease of majesty
> Dies not alone, but, like a gulf doth draw
> What's near it with it; it is a massy wheel,
> Fix'd on the summit of the highest mount,
> To whose huge spokes ten thousand lesser things
> Are mortis'd and adjoin'd; which, when it falls,

Each small annexment, petty consequence,
Attends the boisterous ruin. Never alone
Did the king sigh, but with a general groan.

Hamlet himself is described by Laertes at the beginning in the same terms in which Rosencrantz describes Claudius. Laertes tells Ophelia that Hamlet

          may not, as unvalu'd persons do
Carve for himself, for on his choice depends
The safety and the health of the whole state;
And therefore must his choice be circumscrib'd
Unto the voice and yielding of that body
Whereof he is the head.

                (i, 3, 19)

Once more we have the kingdom compared to the human frame, and once more we have an illustration of how careful Shakespeare is, from the very beginning of the play, to emphasize the political side of the action. Much state business is transacted before the king, in the second scene of the first act, finally turns to the particular problem of Hamlet's melancholy; Shakespeare deliberately puts Hamlet's situation in a political environment. This not only increases the scope of the play, it also emphasizes the dramatic conflict. For from whatever side we regard the action there is something politically wrong. From Claudius' point of view it is bad for the state to have a disaffected heir, particularly since he is so much loved by the multitude. From Hamlet's point of view it is abominable to have an unworthy and lustful king. And the appearance of the ghost emphasizes in more general terms our sense of uneasiness about the condition of the state. It bodes, says Horatio, "some strange eruption to our state," Hamlet dwells on the fact that the ghost is armed, and the armor implies that the ghost has more than a private purpose in showing himself. No wonder Marcellus says that there is something rotten in the *state* of Denmark. He, and the king, and the ghost, reinforce Hamlet's feelings about the situation, and the speeches of Rosencrantz and Laertes on kingship apply not only to an immediate necessity but also to the importance of kingship itself, and hence they emphasize the enormity of Claudius' previous action in murdering his kingly brother. Again it is worth remembering the strength of Hamlet's feeling about his uncle's unworthiness as a king—a feeling that shocks, as Hamlet means it to do, the conventional Guildenstern (iv, 2, 30):

> *Hamlet*: The king is a thing—
> *Guild*.: A thing, my lord!

Hamlet's description of the king is much stronger elsewhere: he is the "bloat king" —a "king of shreds and patches"—and Hamlet's tendency to generalization surrounds the notion of kingship as it surrounds all his thoughts:

Imperious Caesar, dead and turned to clay,
Might stop a hole to keep the wind away.

A king may go a progress through the guts of a beggar; the illusion of kingly power is not the reality; nothing is but thinking makes it so. What is true of the king, of the queen, is true of the whole "drossy age," where the orders of society have broken down, and "the age is grown so picked, that the toe of the peasant comes so near the heel of the courtier that he galls his kibe." "To be honest, as this world goes, is to be one man picked out of ten thousand." "I am very proud, revengeful, ambitious; with more offenses at my back than I have thought to put them in, imagination to give them shape, or time to act them in. What should such fellows as I do crawling between heaven and earth? We are arrant knaves all." The discovery of individual evil, and the inevitable generalizations, once granted Shakespeare's conception of Hamlet's character, that follow upon it, almost crack his comprehension: cruelty to the innocent Ophelia, again expressed in generalization, is one of the consequences.

In fact the way Hamlet treats Ophelia, like the way he treats love in general, is a further striking example of Shakespeare's handling of the contrast between appearance and truth. For here too there is an ideal in the background against which the present reality seems coarse and vile. The relation between Hamlet's mother and father had been perfect; he was as fine a husband as he had been a king, his

> love was of that dignity
> That it went hand in hand even with that
> vow
> (He) made to her in marriage;
>
> (i, 5, 48)

he was, says Hamlet,

> so loving to my mother
> That he might not beteem the winds of
> heaven
> Visit her face too roughly.
>
> (i, 2, 140)

But this ideal, an ideal as deeply embedded in the sixteenth-century mind as the ideal of kingship and of human reason, is violated by Gertrude's marriage to Claudius, which he calls "incestuous," as according to the law of Nature, it actually was.[6] Hamlet through-

out the play can think of the relations between the sexes only in the coarsest terms; he tortures both Ophelia and himself by doing so, attributing to her in his usual generalizing way the faults of her sex as a whole which his mother's behavior had revealed. And the innocent Ophelia herself, in delirium, sings songs at which her maidenly sanity would have blushed.

This sense of the reality of evil—in the cosmos, in the state, and in man— this enlargement of dramatic dimension by significant generalization, this dramatic use of one of the essential conflicts of the age, is what helps to make *Hamlet* so large an organism, and to give it, as the expression of a universal situation, so profound a meaning. Hamlet's disillusionment is a partial expression of a general predicament; the emotions he gives voice to were shared in his own time and have been shared ever since by many people less miraculously articulate than himself. His discovery of the difference between appearance and reality, which produced in his mind an effect so disillusioning that it paralysed the sources of deliberate action, was a symptom that the Renaissance in general had brought with it a new set of problems, had opened new psychological vistas, which the earlier views of man had not so completely explored. As we look back on the period, it appears that the contrast between outward seeming and inner truth had begun, at the beginning of the seventeenth century, to seem the most easily available example of a more portentous awareness, which could by no other means be so readily described. It is one of the keys to an understanding of Shakespearean tragedy, to that stretching into hitherto

---

[6] See J. Dover Wilson's edition of *Hamlet*, Cambridge (England), 1936, p. 152. Miss Victoria Schrager has suggested to me that Shakespeare's audience would remember that Henry VIII's marriage to Catherine of Aragon

was proved illegal because it violated the law of Nature: it was incestuous because he had married, like Claudius, his brother's wife.

inarticulate reaches of experience, which is one of the chief emotional legacies of the Renaissance.[7]

III

But we can find, if we return to the play itself, more in Shakespeare's conception of Hamlet's character than an embodiment, however profound, of the difference between appearance and reality. Shakespeare had made several earlier experiments with the development of character; in portraying Romeo and Prince Hal, among others, he had shown his ability to make a hero change as the result of the play's action. But just as *Hamlet* illustrates both a more expanded and a more fused control of dramatic convention and traditional belief than the earlier plays, so it shows a greater mastery of how to describe the growth, inside dramatic limits, of a hero. This can be clearly seen if we examine, in order, Hamlet's great soliloquies. When we first see Hamlet alone, he is emotionally in pieces, and the chaos of his thought and feeling is reflected in the grammatical chaos of his utterances; before he can finish a sentence some new agonizing disruptive thought explodes to distract his mind.[8] The order of the world, of the state, and of the individual are all in pieces, and the chaotic grammar reflects the universal chaos of his thought. The same is true of his second great soliloquy, the one beginning,

[7] The difference between appearance and reality is continually referred to throughout the play by other people besides Hamlet himself; Polonius, the ghost, the king, all mention it in one way or another; the frequency with which images of painting, of covering up hidden diseases, are used is another illustration of its prevalence; and it is the central idea of Hamlet's meditations in the graveyard.

[8] J. Dover Wilson quite rightly uses the very light punctuation of Q2 to illustrate Shakespeare's apparent intention in this matter.

O, what a rogue and peasant slave am I!

in which he bursts into violent self-deprecation as he thinks of the difference between stage-playing and real action. But even in this speech, at the end, he pulls himself together and orders his thought to plan the testing of the king. Planned action takes the place, as it had not before, of emotional desperation.

In the soliloquy that follows (as far as the audience is concerned, about three minutes later), the "To be or not to be" soliloquy, we see a Hamlet who is able to generalize on a new level. No longer is there a grammatical torrent, and no longer is Hamlet thinking about existence as opposed to non-existence only in relation to himself; he has grown, psychologically and philosophically, so that he can think of the problem more universally. In the first soliloquy it was "*This* too too solid flesh"—Hamlet's own —about which he was concerned. Now, as the play reaches its center, it is no longer "I," but "we"—all humanity— that he reflects upon: "When *we* have shuffled off this mortal coil" . . .

And makes *us* rather bear those ills *we* have
Than fly to others that *we* know not of.
Thus conscience doth make cowards of *us all.* . . .

Even the soliloquy in the fourth act— "How all occasions do inform against me" —when Hamlet compares his behavior to that of Fortinbras, combining, as usual personal and general reflection—even this agonized soliloquy has much more order, both logically and grammatically, than the first two violent outbursts. In fact there can be little doubt that Shakespeare thought of Hamlet as growing much older, emotionally, intellectually and even physically, during the course of the play, than the literal time covered by the action could possibly justify.[9] At the beginning Hamlet is fresh from the university; he is about twenty. In the graveyard scene he is unmistakably described as thirty. Shakespeare was in the habit of using concrete numerical details to make a particular scene vivid, regardless of previous data, and this is an obvious example of how his view of his hero had changed, perhaps unconsciously, at the end of the play. Throughout the fifth act, Hamlet is a very different man from the distracted undergraduate he was at the beginning. At the beginning there was a horrible split between his view of the world as it should be and the world as it is. At the end he is reconciled; and his reconciliation has both matured and ennobled him. He sees himself no longer in relation to a lustful mother and a vicious king; the immediate is replaced by the universal:

> and that should learn us
> There's a divinity that shapes our ends
> Rough-hew them how we will.[10]

[9] It has long been noticed that there are "two series of times" in *Hamlet*, as in many Elizabethan plays, "the one suggestive and illusory, the other visible and explicitly stated." See Furness, *Variorum Hamlet*, Philadelphia, 1877, I, pp. xv–xvii. "At the close," says Furness, "as though to smooth away any discrepancy between his mind and his years, or between the execution of his task and his years, a chance allusion by the Grave-digger is thrown out, which, if we are quick enough to catch, we can apply to Hamlet's age, and we have before us Hamlet in his full maturity."

[10] See Hardin Craig, "Hamlet's Book," *Huntington Library Bulletin*, Nov., 1934, for an interesting analogy between Hamlet's ideas and those expressed by Cardan, in his widely read *Comfort*. In this article Professor Craig, as elsewhere, gives a most illuminating picture of the

He is no longer *in* the tumult, but above it; he is no longer "passion's slave," but a man who sees himself as a part of the order of things, even though his final view of that order, exhausted, resigned, and in a way exalted, is very different from the youthful rosy picture his Renaissance theoretical education had given him.

If it be now, 'tis not to come; if it be not to come, it will be now; if it be not now, yet it will come: the readiness is all.

The thought may be a neo-stoic Renaissance commonplace, but Hamlet's expression of it, through his incomparable control of rhythm, enlarges our feeling about Hamlet's character. To be resigned, as Hamlet is resigned, is to be made, by experience instead of by theory, once more aware of the world's order. The last time we know Hamlet emotionally, he has transcended his own situation; he is no longer a victim of it. That is why we feel so moved, so in a way glorified, by the inevitability of his death. We have seen the purgation of a soul, and when Fortinbras enters at the end to be the king that Hamlet might have been, we know in another way and on another level—a more practical level that brings us back to the world in which we live— that we have also seen, with the accomplishment of Hamlet's revenge, the purgation of a state. . . .

relation between Shakespeare and the intellectual life of his time. See especially *The Enchanted Glass*, New York, 1936.

CHAPTER 13

Psychological Focus

FREUD AND LITERATURE
Lionel Trilling*

Trilling examines the influence of literature on the theories of
Freud and the reciprocal influence of those theories upon literature.
He attacks Freud's specific discussions of literature as "illusion"
and "narcotic" but illustrates how certain of Freud's investigations
helpfully connect the methods of poetry with the methods of the
unconscious mind.

I

The Freudian psychology is the only
systematic account of the human mind
which, in point of subtlety and complexity, of interest and tragic power, deserves
to stand beside the chaotic mass of psychological insights which literature has
accumulated through the centuries. To
pass from the reading of a great literary
work to a treatise of academic psychology
is to pass from one order of perception to
another, but the human nature of the
Freudian psychology is exactly the stuff
upon which the poet has always exercised
his art. It is therefore not surprising that

* The essay is reprinted from *The Liberal
Imagination: Essays on Literature and Society*
by Lionel Trilling. Copyright 1940, 1947, 1950
by Lionel Trilling. Reprinted by permission of
The Viking Press, Inc.

the psychoanalytical theory has had a
great effect upon literature. Yet the relationship is reciprocal, and the effect of
Freud upon literature has been no greater
than the effect of literature upon Freud.
When, on the occasion of the celebration
of his seventieth birthday, Freud was
greeted as the "discoverer of the unconscious," he corrected the speaker and
disclaimed the title. "The poets and
philosophers before me discovered the
unconscious," he said. "What I discovered was the scientific method by
which the unconscious can be studied."

A lack of specific evidence prevents us
from considering the particular literary
"influences" upon the founder of psychoanalysis; and, besides, when we think of
the men who so clearly anticipated many

of Freud's own ideas—Schopenhauer and Nietzsche, for example—and then learn that he did not read their works until after he had formulated his own theories, we must see that particular influences cannot be in question here but that what we must deal with is nothing less than a whole *Zeitgeist*, a direction of thought. For psychoanalysis is one of the culminations of the Romanticist literature of the nineteenth century. If there is perhaps a contradiction in the idea of a science standing upon the shoulders of a literature which avows itself inimical to science in so many ways, the contradiction will be resolved if we remember that this literature, despite its avowals, was itself scientific in at least the sense of being passionately devoted to a research into the self.

In showing the connection between Freud and this Romanticist tradition, it is difficult to know where to begin, but there might be a certain aptness in starting even back of the tradition, as far back as 1762 with Diderot's *Rameau's Nephew*. At any rate, certain men at the heart of the nineteenth-century thought were agreed in finding a peculiar importance in this brilliant little work: Goethe translated it, Marx admired it, Hegel—as Marx reminded Engels in the letter which announced that he was sending the book as a gift—praised and expounded it at length, Shaw was impressed by it, and Freud himself, as we know from a quotation in his *Introductory Lectures*, read it with the pleasure of agreement.

The dialogue takes place between Diderot himself and a nephew of the famous composer. The protagonist, the younger Rameau, is a despised, outcast, shameless fellow; Hegel calls him the "disintegrated consciousness" and credits him with great wit, for it is he who breaks down all the normal social values and makes new combinations with the pieces. As for Diderot, the deuteragonist, he is what Hegel calls the "honest consciousness," and Hegel considers him reasonable, decent, and dull. It is quite clear that the author does not despise his Rameau and does not mean us to. Rameau is lustful and greedy, arrogant yet self-abasing, perceptive yet "wrong," like a child. Still, Diderot seems actually to be giving the fellow a kind of superiority over himself, as though Rameau represents the elements which, dangerous but wholly necessary, lie beneath the reasonable decorum of social life. It would perhaps be pressing too far to find in Rameau Freud's id and in Diderot Freud's ego; yet the connection does suggest itself; and at least we have here the perception which is to be the common characteristic of both Freud and Romanticism, the perception of the hidden element of human nature and of the opposition between the hidden and the visible. We have too the bold perception of just what lies hidden: "If the little savage [i.e., the child] were left to himself, if he preserved all his foolishness and combined the violent passions of a man of thirty with the lack of reason of a child in the cradle, he'd wring his father's neck and go to bed with his mother."

From the self-exposure of Rameau to Rousseau's account of his own childhood is no great step; society might ignore or reject the idea of the "immorality" which lies concealed in the beginning of the career of the "good" man, just as it might turn away from Blake struggling to expound a psychology which would include the forces beneath the propriety of social man in general, but the idea of the hidden thing went forward to become one of the dominant notions of the age. The hidden element takes many forms and it is not necessarily "dark" and "bad"; for Blake the "bad" was the good, while for Wordsworth and Burke what was hidden and unconscious was wisdom and power, which work in despite of the conscious intellect.

The mind has become far less simple; the devotion to the various forms of autobiography—itself an important fact in the tradition—provides abundant examples of the change that has taken place. Poets, making poetry by what seems to them almost a freshly discovered faculty, find that this new power may be conspired against by other agencies of the mind and even deprived of its freedom; the names of Wordsworth, Coleridge, and Arnold at once occur to us again, and Freud quotes Schiller on the danger to the poet that lies in the merely analytical reason. And it is not only the poets who are threatened; educated and sensitive people throughout Europe become aware of the depredations that reason might make upon the affective life, as in the classic instance of John Stuart Mill.

We must also take into account the preoccupation—it began in the eighteenth century, or even in the seventeenth—with children, women, peasants, and savages, whose mental life, it is felt, is less overlaid than that of the educated adult male by the proprieties of social habit. With this preoccupation goes a concern with education and personal development, so consonant with the historical and evolutionary bias of the time. And we must certainly note the revolution in morals which took place at the instance (we might almost say) of the *Bildungsroman*, for in the novels fathered by *Wilhelm Meister* we get the almost complete identification of author and hero and of the reader with both, and this identification almost inevitably suggests a leniency of moral judgment. The autobiographical novel has a further in-

fluence upon the moral sensibility by its exploitation of all the modulations of motive and by its hinting that we may not judge a man by any single moment in his life without taking into account the determining past and the expiating and fulfilling future.

It is difficult to know how to go on, for the further we look the more literary affinities to Freud we find, and even if we limit ourselves to bibliography we can at best be incomplete. Yet we must mention the sexual revolution that was being demanded—by Shelley, for example, by the Schlegel of *Lucinde*, by George Sand, and later and more critically by Ibsen; the belief in the sexual origin of art, baldly stated by Tieck, more subtly by Schopenhauer; the investigation of sexual maladjustment by Stendhal, whose observations on erotic feeling seem to us distinctly Freudian. Again and again we see the effective, utilitarian ego being relegated to an inferior position and a plea being made on behalf of the anarchic and self-indulgent id. We find the energetic exploitation of the idea of the mind as a divisible thing, one part of which can contemplate and mock the other. It is not a far remove from this to Dostoevski's brilliant instances of ambivalent feeling. Novalis brings in the preoccupation with the death wish, and this is linked on the one hand with sleep and on the other hand with the perception of the perverse, self-destroying impulses, which in turn leads us to that fascination by the horrible which we find in Shelley, Poe, and Baudelaire. And always there is the profound interest in the dream—"Our dreams," said Gerard de Nerval, "are a second life"—and in the nature of metaphor, which reaches its climax in Rimbaud and the later Symbolists, metaphor becoming less and less communicative as it approaches the relative autonomy of the dream life.

But perhaps we must stop to ask, since these are the components of the *Zeitgeist* from which Freud himself developed, whether it can be said that Freud did indeed produce a wide literary effect. What is it that Freud added that the tendency of literature itself would not have developed without him? If we were looking for a writer who showed the Freudian influence, Proust would perhaps come to mind as readily as anyone else; the very title of his novel, in French more than in English, suggests an enterprise of psychoanalysis and scarcely less so does his method—the investigation of sleep, of sexual deviation, of the way of association, the almost obsessive interest in metaphor; at these and at many other points the "influence" might be shown. Yet I believe it is true that Proust did not read Freud. Or again, exegesis of *The Waste Land* often reads remarkably like the psychoanalytic interpretation of a dream, yet we know that Eliot's methods were prepared for him not by Freud but by other poets.

Nevertheless, it is of course true that Freud's influence on literature has been very great. Much of it is so pervasive that its extent is scarcely to be determined; in one form or another, frequently in perversions or absurd simplifications, it has been infused into our life and become a component of our culture of which it is now hard to be specifically aware. In biography its first effect was sensational but not fortunate. The early Freudian biographers were for the most part Guildensterns who seemed to know the pipes but could not pluck out the heart of the mystery, and the same condemnation applies to the early Freudian critics. But in recent years, with the acclimatization of psychoanalysis and the increased sense of its refinements and complexity, criticism has derived from the Freudian system much that is of great value, most notably

the license and the injunction to read the work of literature with a lively sense of its latent and ambiguous meanings, as if it were, as indeed it is, a being no less alive and contradictory than the man who created it. And this new response to the literary work has had a corrective effect upon our conception of literary biography. The literary critic or biographer who makes use of the Freudian theory is no less threatened by the dangers of theoretical systematization than he was in the early days, but he is likely to be more aware of these dangers; and I think it is true to say that now the motive of his interpretation is not that of exposing the secret shame of the writer and limiting the meaning of his work, but, on the contrary, that of finding grounds for sympathy with the writer and for increasing the possible significances of the work.

The names of the creative writers who have been more or less Freudian in tone or assumption would of course be legion. Only a relatively small number, however, have made serious use of the Freudian ideas. Freud himself seems to have thought this was as it should be: he is said to have expected very little of the works that were sent to him by writers with inscriptions of gratitude for all they had learned from him. The Surrealists have, with a certain inconsistency, depended upon Freud for the "scientific" sanction of their program. Kafka, with an apparent awareness of what he was doing, has explored the Freudian conceptions of guilt and punishment, of the dream, and of the fear of the father. Thomas Mann, whose tendency, as he himself says, was always in the direction of Freud's interests, has been most susceptible to the Freudian anthropology, finding a special charm in the theories of myths and magical practices. James Joyce, with his interest in the numerous states of receding consciousness, with his use of words as things and of words which point to more than one thing, with his pervading sense of the interrelation and interpenetration of all things, and, not least important, his treatment of familial themes, has perhaps most thoroughly and consciously exploited Freud's ideas.

II

It will be clear enough how much of Freud's thought has significant affinity with the anti-rationalist element of the Romanticist tradition. But we must see with no less distinctness how much of his system is militantly rationalistic. Thomas Mann is at fault when, in his first essay on Freud, he makes it seem that the "Apollonian," the rationalistic, side of psychoanalysis is, while certainly important and wholly admirable, somehow secondary and even accidental. He gives us a Freud who is committed to the "night side" of life. Not at all: the rationalistic element of Freud is foremost; before everything else he is positivistic. If the interpreter of dreams came to medical science through Goethe, as he tells us he did, he entered not by way of the *Walpurgisnacht* but by the essay which played so important a part in the lives of so many scientists of the nineteenth century, the famous disquisition on Nature.

This correction is needed not only for accuracy but also for any understanding of Freud's attitude to art. And for that understanding we must see how intense is the passion with which Freud believes that positivistic rationalism, in its golden-age pre-Revolutionary purity, is the very form and pattern of intellectual virtue. The aim of psychoanalysis, he says, is the control of the night side of life. It is "to strengthen the ego, to make it more independent of the super-ego, to widen its

field of vision, and so to extend the organization of the id." "Where id was,"—that is, where all the irrational, non-logical, pleasure-seeking dark forces were —"there shall ego be,"—that is, intelligence and control. "It is," he concludes, with a reminiscence of Faust, "reclamation work, like the draining of the Zuyder Zee." This passage is quoted by Mann when, in taking up the subject of Freud a second time, he does indeed speak of Freud's positivistic program; but even here the bias induced by Mann's artistic interest in the "night side" prevents him from giving the other aspect of Freud its due emphasis. Freud would never have accepted the role which Mann seems to give him as the legitimizer of the myth and the dark irrational ways of the mind. If Freud discovered the darkness for science he never endorsed it. On the contrary, his rationalism supports all the ideas of the Enlightenment that deny validity to myth or religion; he holds to a simple materialism, to a simple determinism, to a rather limited sort of epistemology. No great scientist of our day has thundered so articulately and so fiercely against all those who would sophisticate with metaphysics the scientific principles that were good enough for the nineteenth century. Conceptualism or pragmatism is anathema to him through the greater part of his intellectual career, and this, when we consider the nature of his own brilliant scientific methods, has surely an element of paradox in it.

From his rationalistic positivism comes much of Freud's strength and what weakness he has. The strength is the fine, clear tenacity of his positive aims, the goal of therapy, the desire to bring to men a decent measure of earthly happiness. But upon the rationalism must also be placed the blame for the often naïve scientific principles which characterize his early thought—they are later much modified—and which consist largely of claiming for his theories a perfect correspondence with an external reality, a position which, for those who admire Freud and especially for those who take seriously his views on art, is troublesome in the extreme.

Now Freud has, I believe, much to tell us about art, but whatever is suggestive in him is not likely to be found in those of his works in which he deals expressly with art itself. Freud is not insensitive to art—on the contrary—nor does he ever intend to speak of it with contempt. Indeed, he speaks of it with a real tenderness and counts it one of the true charms of the good life. Of artists, especially of writers, he speaks with admiration and even a kind of awe, though perhaps what he most appreciates in literature are specific emotional insights and observations; as we have noted, he speaks of literary men, because they have understood the part played in life by the hidden motives, as the precursors and coadjutors of his own science.

And yet eventually Freud speaks of art with what we must indeed call contempt. Art, he tells us, is a "substitute gratification," and as such is "an illusion in contrast to reality." Unlike most illusions, however, art is "almost always harmless and beneficent" for the reason that "it does not seek to be anything but an illusion. Save in the case of a few people who are, one might say, obsessed by Art, it never dares make any attack on the realm of reality." One of its chief functions is to serve as a "narcotic." It shares the characteristics of the dream, whose element of distortion Freud calls a "sort of inner dishonesty." As for the artist, he is virtually in the same category with the neurotic. "By such separation of imagination and intellectual capacity," Freud says of the hero of a novel, "he is destined to be a poet or a neurotic, and he

belongs to that race of beings whose realm is not of this world."

Now there is nothing in the logic of psychoanalytical thought which requires Freud to have these opinions. But there is a great deal in the practice of the psychoanalytical therapy which makes it understandable that Freud, unprotected by an adequate philosophy, should be tempted to take the line he does. The analytical therapy deals with illusion. The patient comes to the physician to be cured, let us say, of a fear of walking in the street. The fear is real enough, there is no illusion on that score, and it produces all the physical symptoms of a more rational fear, the sweating palms, pounding heart, and shortened breath. But the patient knows that there is no cause for the fear, or rather that there is, as he says, no "real cause": there are no machine guns, man traps, or tigers in the street. The physician knows, however, that there is indeed a "real" cause for the fear, though it has nothing at all to do with what is or what is not in the street; the cause is within the patient, and the process of the therapy will be to discover, by gradual steps, what this real cause is and so free the patient from its effects.

Now the patient in coming to the physician, and the physician in accepting the patient, make a tacit compact about reality; for their purpose they agree to the limited reality by which we get our living, win our loves, catch our trains and our colds. The therapy will undertake to train the patient in proper ways of coping with this reality. The patient, of course, has been dealing with this reality all along, but in the wrong way. For Freud there are two ways of dealing with external reality. One is practical, effective, positive; this is the way of the conscious self, of the ego which must be made independent of the super-ego and extend its organization over the id, and it is the right way. The antithetical way may be called, for our purpose now, the "fictional" way. Instead of doing something about, or to, external reality, the individual who uses this way does something to, or about, his affective states. The most common and "normal" example of this is daydreaming, in which we give ourselves a certain pleasure by imagining our difficulties solved or our desires gratified. Then, too, as Freud discovered, sleeping dreams are, in much more complicated ways, and even though quite unpleasant, at the service of this same "fictional" activity. And in ways yet more complicated and yet more unpleasant, the actual neurosis from which our patient suffers deals with an external reality which the mind considers still more unpleasant than the painful neurosis itself.

For Freud as psychoanalytic practitioner there are, we may say, the polar extremes of reality and illusion. Reality is an honorific word, and it means what is *there*; illusion is a pejorative word, and it means a response to what is *not there*. The didactic nature of a course of psychoanalysis no doubt requires a certain firm crudeness in making the distinction; it is after all aimed not at theoretical refinement but at practical effectiveness. The polar extremes are practical reality and neurotic illusion, the latter judged by the former. This, no doubt, is as it should be; the patient is not being trained in metaphysics and epistemology.

This practical assumption is not Freud's only view of the mind in its relation to reality. Indeed what may be called the essentially Freudian view assumes that the mind, for good as well as bad, helps create its reality by selection and evaluation. In this view, reality is malleable and subject to creation; it is not static but is rather a series of situations which are dealt with in their own terms. But beside this conception of the mind stands the conception which arises from Freud's

therapeutic-practical assumptions; in this view, the mind deals with a reality which is quite fixed and static, a reality that is wholly "given" and not (to use a phrase of Dewey's) "taken." In his epistemological utterances, Freud insists on this second view, although it is not easy to see why he should do so. For the reality to which he wishes to reconcile the neurotic patient is, after all, a "taken" and not a "given" reality. It is the reality of social life and of value, conceived and maintained by the human mind and will. Love, morality, honor, esteem—these are the components of a created reality. If we are to call art an illusion then we must call most of the activities and satisfactions of the ego illusions; Freud, of course, has no desire to call them that.

What, then, is the difference between, on the one hand, the dream and the neurosis, and, on the other hand, art? That they have certain common elements is of course clear; that unconscious processes are at work in both would be denied by no poet or critic; they share too, though in different degrees, the element of fantasy. But there is a vital difference between them which Charles Lamb saw so clearly in his defense of the sanity of true genius: "The ... poet dreams being awake. He is not possessed by his subject but he has dominion over it."

That is the whole difference: the poet is in command of his fantasy, while it is exactly the mark of the neurotic that he is possessed by his fantasy. And there is a further difference which Lamb states; speaking of the poet's relation to reality (he calls it Nature), he says, "He is beautifully loyal to that sovereign directress, even when he appears most to betray her"; the illusions of art are made to serve the purpose of a closer and truer relation with reality. Jacques Barzun, in an acute and sympathetic discussion of Freud, puts the matter well: "A good analogy between art and *dreaming* has led him to a false one between art and *sleeping*. But the difference between a work of art and a dream is precisely this, that the work of art *leads us back to the outer reality by taking account of it.*" Freud's assumption of the almost exclusively hedonistic nature and purpose of art bar him from the perception of this.

Of the distinction that must be made between the artist and the neurotic Freud is of course aware; he tells us that the artist is not like the neurotic in that he knows how to find a way back from the world of imagination and "once more get a firm foothold in reality." This however seems to mean no more than that reality is to be dealt with when the artist suspends the practice of his art; and at least once when Freud speaks of art dealing with reality he actually means the rewards that a successful artist can win. He does not deny to art its function and its usefulness; it has a therapeutic effect in releasing mental tension; it serves the cultural purpose of acting as a "substitute gratification" to reconcile men to the sacrifices they have made for culture's sake; it promotes the social sharing of highly valued emotional experiences; and it recalls men to their cultural ideals. This is not everything that some of us would find that art does, yet even this is a good deal for a "narcotic" to do.

III

I started by saying that Freud's ideas could tell us something about art, but so far I have done little more than try to show that Freud's very conception of art is inadequate. Perhaps, then, the suggestiveness lies in the application of the analytic method to specific works of art or to the artist himself? I do not think so, and it is only fair to say that Freud himself was aware both of the limits and

the limitations of psychoanalysis in art, even though he does not always in practice submit to the former or admit the latter.

Freud has, for example, no desire to encroach upon the artist's autonomy; he does not wish us to read his monograph on Leonardo and then say of the "Madonna of the Rocks" that it is a fine example of homosexual, autoerotic painting. If he asserts that in investigation the "psychiatrist cannot yield to the author," he immediately insists that the "author cannot yield to the psychiatrist," and he warns the latter not to "coarsen everything" by using for all human manifestations the "substantially useless and awkward terms" of clinical procedure. He admits, even while asserting that the sense of beauty probably derives from sexual feeling, that psychoanalysis "has less to say about beauty than about most other things." He confesses to a theoretical indifference to the form of art and restricts himself to its content. Tone, feeling, style, and the modification that part makes upon part he does not consider. "The layman," he says, "may expect perhaps too much from analysis ... for it must be admitted that it throws no light upon the two problems which probably interest him the most. It can do nothing toward elucidating the nature of the artistic gift, nor can it explain the means by which the artist works—artistic technique."

What, then, does Freud believe that the analytical method can do? Two things: explain the "inner meanings" of the work of art and explain the temperament of the artist as man.

A famous example of the method is the attempt to solve the "problem" of *Hamlet* as suggested by Freud and as carried out by Dr. Ernest Jones, his early and distinguished follower. Dr. Jones's monograph is a work of painstaking scholarship and of really masterly ingenuity.

The research undertakes not only the clearing up of the mystery of Hamlet's character, but also the discovery of "the clue to much of the deeper workings of Shakespeare's mind." Part of the mystery in question is of course why Hamlet, after he had so definitely resolved to do so, did not avenge upon his hated uncle his father's death. But there is another mystery to the play—what Freud calls "the mystery of its effect," its magical appeal that draws so much interest toward it. Recalling the many failures to solve the riddle of the play's charm, he wonders if we are to be driven to the conclusion "that its magical appeal rests solely upon the impressive thoughts in it and the splendor of its language." Freud believes that we can find a source of power beyond this.

We remember that Freud has told us that the meaning of a dream is its intention, and we may assume that the meaning of a drama is its intention, too. The Jones research undertakes to discover what it was that Shakespeare intended to say about Hamlet. It finds that the intention was wrapped by the author in a dreamlike obscurity because it touched so deeply both his personal life and the moral life of the world; what Shakespeare intended to say is that Hamlet cannot act because he is incapacitated by the guilt he feels at his unconscious attachment to his mother. There is, I think, nothing to be quarreled with in the statement that there is an Oedipus situation in *Hamlet*; and if psychoanalysis has indeed added a new point of interest to the play, that is to its credit.[1] And, just so, there

is no reason to quarrel with Freud's conclusion when he undertakes to give us the meaning of *King Lear* by a tortuous tracing of the mythological implications of the theme of the three caskets, of the relation of the caskets to the Norns, the Fates, and the Graces, of the connection of these triadic females with Lear's daughters, of the transmogrification of the death goddess into the love goddess and the identification of Cordelia with both, all to the conclusion that the meaning of *King Lear* is to be found in the tragic refusal of an old man to "renounce love, choose death, and make friends with the necessity of dying." There is something both beautiful and suggestive in this, but it is not *the* meaning of *King Lear* any more than the Oedipus motive is *the* meaning of *Hamlet*.

It is not here a question of the validity of the evidence, though that is of course important. We must rather object to the conclusions of Freud and Dr. Jones on the ground that their proponents do not have an adequate conception of what an artistc meaning is. There is no single meaning to any work of art; this is true not merely because it is better that it should be true, that is, because it makes art a richer thing, but because historical and personal experience show it to be true. Changes in historical context and in personal mood change the meaning of a work and indicate to us that artistic understanding is not a question of fact but of value. Even if the author's intention were, as it cannot be, precisely determinable, the meaning of a work cannot lie in the author's intention alone. It must also lie in its effect. We can say of a volcanic eruption on an inhabited

---

[1] However, A. C. Bradley, in his discussion of Hamlet (*Shakespearean Tragedy*), states clearly the intense sexual disgust which Hamlet feels and which, for Bradley, helps account for his uncertain purpose; and Bradley was anticipated in this view by Löning. It is well known, and Dover Wilson has lately emphasized the point, that to an Elizabethan audience Hamlet's

mother was not merely tasteless, as to a modern audience she seems, in hurrying to marry Claudius, but actually adulterous in marrying him at all because he was, as her brother-in-law, within the forbidden degrees.

island that it "means terrible suffering," but if the island is uninhabited or easily evacuated it means something else. In short, the audience partly determines the meaning of the work. But although Freud sees something of this when he says that in addition to the author's intention we must take into account the mystery of *Hamlet*'s effect, he nevertheless goes on to speak as if, historically, *Hamlet*'s effect had been single and brought about solely by the "magical" power of the Oedipus motive to which, unconsciously, we so violently respond. Yet there was, we know, a period when *Hamlet* was relatively in eclipse, and it has always been scandalously true of the French, a people not without filial feeling, that they have been somewhat indifferent to the "magical appeal" of *Hamlet*.

I do not think anything I have said about the inadequacies of the Freudian method of interpretation limits the number of ways we can deal with a work of art. Bacon remarked that experiment may twist nature on the rack to wring out its secrets, and criticism may use any instruments upon a work of art to find its meanings. The elements of art are not limited to the world of art. They reach into life, and whatever extraneous knowledge of them we gain—for example, by research into the historical context of the work—may quicken our feelings for the work itself and even enter legitimately into those feelings. Then, too, anything we may learn about the artist himself may be enriching and legitimate. But one research into the mind of the artist is simply not practicable, however legitimate it may theoretically be. That is, the investigation of his unconscious intention as it exists apart from the work itself. Criticism understands that the artist's statement of his conscious intention, though it is sometimes useful, cannot finally determine meaning. How much

less can we know from his unconscious intention considered as something apart from the whole work? Surely very little that can be called conclusive or scientific. For, as Freud himself points out, we are not in a position to question the artist; we must apply the technique of dream analysis to his symbols, but, as Freud says with some heat, those people do not understand his theory who think that a dream may be interpreted without the dreamer's free association with the multitudinous details of his dream.

We have so far ignored the aspect of the method which finds the solution to the "mystery" of such a play as *Hamlet* in the temperament of Shakespeare himself and then illuminates the mystery of Shakespeare's temperament by means of the solved mystery of the play. Here it will be amusing to remember that by 1935 Freud had become converted to the theory that it was not Shakespeare of Stratford but the Earl of Oxford who wrote the plays, thus invalidating the important bit of evidence that Shakespeare's father died shortly before the composition of *Hamlet*. This is destructive enough to Dr. Jones's argument, but the evidence from which Dr. Jones draws conclusions about literature fails on grounds more relevant to literature itself. For when Dr. Jones, by means of his analysis of *Hamlet*, takes us into "the deeper workings of Shakespeare's mind," he does so with a perfect confidence that he knows what *Hamlet* is and what its relation to Shakespeare is. It is, he tells us, Shakepeare's "chief masterpiece," so far superior to all his other works that it may be placed on "an entirely separate level." And then, having established his ground on an entirely subjective literary judgment, Dr. Jones goes on to tell us that *Hamlet* "probably expresses the core of Shakespeare's philosophy and outlook as no other work of his does." That is, all the contradictory or complicating or modifying testimony of the other plays is dismissed on the basis of Dr. Jones's acceptance of the peculiar position which, he believes, *Hamlet* occupies in the Shakespeare canon. And it is upon this quite inadmissible judgment that Dr. Jones bases his argument: "It may be expected *therefore* that anything which will give us the key to the inner meaning of the play will *necessarily* give us the clue to much of the deeper workings of Shakespeare's mind." (The italics are mine.)

I should be sorry if it appeared that I am trying to say that psychoanalysis can have nothing to do with literature. I am sure that the opposite is so. For example, the whole notion of rich ambiguity in literature, of the interplay between the apparent meaning and the latent—not "hidden"—meaning, has been reinforced by the Freudian concepts, perhaps even received its first impetus from them. Of late years, the more perceptive psychoanalysts have surrendered the early pretensions of their teachers to deal "scientifically" with literature. That is all to the good, and when a study as modest and precise as Dr. Franz Alexander's essay on *Henry IV* comes along, an essay which pretends not to "solve" but only to illuminate the subject, we have something worth having. Dr. Alexander undertakes nothing more than to say that in the development of Prince Hal we see the classic struggle of the ego to come to normal adjustment, beginning with the rebellion against the father, going on to the conquest of the super-ego (Hotspur, with his rigid notions of honor and glory), then to the conquests of the *id* (Falstaff, with his anarchic self-indulgence), then to the identification with the father (the crown scene) and the assumption of mature responsibility. An analysis of this sort is not momentous and not exclusive of other meanings; per-

haps it does no more than point up and formulate what we all have already seen. It has the tact to *accept* the play and does not, like Dr. Jones's study of *Hamlet*, search for a "hidden motive" and a "deeper working," which implies that there is a reality to which the play stands in the relation that a dream stands to the wish that generates it and from which it is separable; it is this reality, this "deeper working," which, according to Dr. Jones, produced the play. But *Hamlet* is not merely the product of Shakespeare's thought, it is the very instrument of his thought, and if meaning is intention, Shakespeare did not intend the Oedipus motive or anything less than *Hamlet*; if meaning is effect then it is *Hamlet* which affects us, not the Oedipus motive. *Coriolanus* also deals, and very terribly, with the Oedipus motive, but the effect of the one drama is very different from the effect of the other.

IV

If, then, we can accept neither Freud's conception of the place of art in life nor his application of the analytical method, what is it that he contributes to our understanding of art or to its practice? In my opinion, what he contributes outweighs his errors; it is of the greatest importance, and it lies in no specific statement that he makes about art but is, rather, implicit in his whole conception of the mind.

For, of all mental systems, the Freudian psychology is the one which makes poetry indigenous to the very constitution of the mind. Indeed, the mind, as Freud sees it, is in the greater part of its tendency exactly a poetry-making organ. This puts the case too strongly, no doubt, for it seems to make the working of the unconscious mind equivalent to poetry itself, forgetting that between the unconscious mind and the finished poem there supervene the social intention and the formal control of the conscious mind. Yet the statement has at least the virtue of counterbalancing the belief, so commonly expressed or implied, that the very opposite is true, and that poetry is a kind of beneficent aberration of the mind's right course.

Freud has not merely naturalized poetry; he has discovered its status as a pioneer settler, and he sees it as a method of thought. Often enough he tries to show how, as a method of thought, it is unreliable and ineffective for conquering reality; yet he himself is forced to use it in the very shaping of his own science, as when he speaks of the topography of the mind and tells us with a kind of defiant apology that the metaphors of space relationship which he is using are really most inexact since the mind is not a thing of space at all, but that there is no other way of conceiving the difficult idea except by metaphor. In the eighteenth century Vico spoke of the metaphorical, imagistic language of the early stages of culture; it was left to Freud to discover how, in a scientific age, we still feel and think in figurative formations, and to create, what psychoanalysis is, a science of tropes, of metaphor and its variants, synecdoche and metonomy.

Freud showed, too, how the mind, in one of its parts, could work without logic, yet not without that directing purpose, that control of intent from which, perhaps it might be said, logic springs. For the unconscious mind works without the syntactical conjunctions which are logic's essence. It recognizes no *because*, no *therefore*, no *but*; such ideas as similarity, agreement, and community are expressed in dreams imagistically by compressing the elements into a unity. The unconscious mind in its struggle with the conscious always turns from the general to the concrete and finds the tangible trifle more congenial than the large abstraction. Freud discovered in the very organization of the mind those mechanisms by which art makes its effects, such devices as the condensations of meanings and the displacement of accent.

All this is perhaps obvious enough and, though I should like to develop it in proportion both to its importance and to the space I have given to disagreement with Freud, I will not press it further. For there are two other elements in Freud's thought which, in conclusion, I should like to introduce as of great weight in their bearing on art.

Of these, one is a specific idea which, in the middle of his career (1920), Freud put forward in his essay *Beyond the Pleasure Principle*. The essay itself is a speculative attempt to solve a perplexing problem in clinical analysis, but its relevance to literature is inescapable, as Freud sees well enough, even though his perception of its critical importance is not sufficiently strong to make him revise his earlier views of the nature and function of art. The idea is one which stands beside Aristotle's notion of the catharsis, in part to supplement, in part to modify it.

Freud has come upon certain facts which are not to be reconciled with his earlier theory of the dream. According to this theory, all dreams, even the unpleasant ones, could be understood upon analysis to have the intention of fulfilling the dreamer's wishes. They are in the service of what Freud calls the pleasure principle, which is opposed to the reality principle. It is, of course, this explanation of the dream which had so largely conditioned Freud's theory of art. But now there is thrust upon him the necessity for reconsidering the theory of the dream, for it was found that in cases of war neurosis—what we once called shell-shock—the patient, with the utmost anguish, recurred in his dreams to the very situation, distressing as it was, which had precipitated his neurosis. It seemed impossible to interpret these dreams by any assumption of a hedonistic intent. Nor did there seem to be the usual amount of distortion in them: the patient recurred to the terrible initiatory situation with great literalness. And the same pattern of psychic behavior could be observed in the play of children; there were some games which, far from fulfilling wishes, seemed to concentrate upon the representation of those aspects of the child's life which were most unpleasant and threatening to his happiness.

To explain such mental activities Freud evolved a theory for which he at first refused to claim much but to which, with the years, he attached an increasing importance. He first makes the assumption that there is indeed in the psychic life a repetition-compulsion which goes beyond the pleasure principle. Such a compulsion cannot be meaningless, it must have an intent. And that intent, Freud comes to believe, is exactly and literally the developing of fear. "These dreams," he says, "are attempts at restoring control of the stimuli by developing apprehension, the pretermission of which caused the traumatic neurosis." The dream, that is, is the effort to reconstruct the bad situation in order that the failure to meet it may be recouped; in these dreams there is no obscured intent to evade but only an attempt to meet the situation, to make a new effort of control. And in the play of children it seems to be that "the child repeats even the unpleasant experiences because through his own activity he gains a far more thorough mastery of the strong impression than

was possible by mere passive experience."

Freud, at this point, can scarcely help being put in mind of tragic drama; nevertheless, he does not wish to believe that this effort to come to mental grips with a situation is involved in the attraction of tragedy. He is, we might say, under the influence of the Aristotelian tragic theory which emphasizes a qualified hedonism through suffering. But the pleasure involved in tragedy is perhaps an ambiguous one; and sometimes we must feel that the famous sense of cathartic resolution is perhaps the result of glossing over terror with beautiful language rather than an evacuation of it. And sometimes the terror even bursts through the language to stand stark and isolated from the play, as does Oedipus's sightless and bleeding face. At any rate, the Aristotelian theory does not deny another function for tragedy (and for comedy, too) which is suggested by Freud's theory of the traumatic neurosis—what might be called the mithridatic function, by which tragedy is used as the homeopathic administration of pain to inure ourselves to the greater pain which life will force upon us. There is in the cathartic theory of tragedy, as it is usually understood, a conception of tragedy's function which is too negative and which inadequately suggests the sense of active mastery which tragedy can give.

In the same essay in which he sets forth the conception of the mind embracing its own pain for some vital purpose, Freud also expresses a provisional assent to the idea (earlier stated, as he reminds us, by Schopenhauer) that there is perhaps a human drive which makes of death the final and desired goal. The death instinct is a conception that is rejected by many of even the most thoroughgoing Freudian theorists (as, in his last book, Freud mildly noted); the late Otto Fenichel in his authoritative work on the neurosis argues cogently against it. Yet even if we reject the theory as not fitting the facts in any operatively useful way, we still cannot miss its grandeur, its ultimate tragic courage in acquiescence to fate. The idea of the reality principle and the idea of the death instinct form the crown of Freud's broader speculation on the life of man. Their quality of grim poetry is characteristic of Freud's system and the ideas it generates for him.

And as much as anything else that Freud gives to literature, this quality of his thought is important. Although the artist is never finally determined in his work by the intellectual systems about him, he cannot avoid their influence; and it can be said of various competing systems that some hold more promise for the artist than others. When, for example, we think of the simple humanitarian optimism which, for two decades, has been so pervasive, we must see that not only has it been politically and philosophically inadequate, but also that it implies, by the smallness of its view of the varieties of human possibility, a kind of check on the creative faculties. In Freud's view of life no such limitation is implied. To be sure, certain elements of his system seem hostile to the usual notions of man's dignity. Like every great critic of human nature—and Freud is that—he finds in human pride the ultimate cause of human wretchedness, and he takes pleasure in knowing that his ideas stand with those of Copernicus and Darwin in making pride more difficult to maintain. Yet the Freudian man is, I venture to think, a creature of far more dignity and far more interest than the man which any other modern system has been able to conceive. Despite popular belief to the contrary, man, as Freud conceives him, is not to be understood by any simple formula (such as sex) but is rather an inextricable tangle of culture and biology. And not being simple, he is not simply good; he has, as Freud says somewhere, a kind of hell within him from which rise everlastingly the impulses which threaten his civilization. He has the faculty of imagining for himself more in the way of pleasure and satisfaction than he can possibly achieve. Everything that he gains he pays for in more than equal coin; compromise and the compounding with defeat constitute his best way of getting through the world. His best qualities are the result of a struggle whose outcome is tragic. Yet he is a creature of love; it is Freud's sharpest criticism of the Adlerian psychology that to aggression it gives everything and to love nothing at all.

One is always aware in reading Freud how little cynicism there is in his thought. His desire for man is only that he should be human, and to this end his science is devoted. No view of life to which the artist responds can insure the quality of his work, but the poetic qualities of Freud's own principles, which are so clearly in the line of the classic tragic realism, suggest that this is a view which does not narrow and simplify the human world for the artist but on the contrary opens and complicates it.

THE PROBLEM OF HAMLET AND
THE OEDIPUS-COMPLEX
Ernest Jones*

Jones uses Freudian concepts and psychoanalytic techniques to examine Hamlet's conduct in the play and to explain, among other things, his delay in executing his revenge.

It has been found that with poetic creations the critical procedure cannot halt at the work of art itself; to isolate this from its creator is to impose artificial limits to our understanding of it. A work of art is too often regarded as a finished thing-in-itself, something almost independent of the creator's personality, so that little would be learned about the one or the other by connecting the two studies. Informed criticism, however, shews that a correlated study of the two sheds light in both directions, on the inner nature of the composition and on the mentality of its author. The two can be separated only at the expense of diminished appreciation, whereas to increase our knowledge of either automatically deepens our understanding of the other. Masson well says: "What a man shall or can imagine, equally with what he shall or can desire, depends ultimately on his own nature, and so even on his acquisitions and experiences.... Imagination is not, after all, creation out of nothing, but only re-combination, at the bidding of moods and of conscious purposes, out of the materials furnished by memory, reading and experience; which materials vary with the individual cases." In asserting this deterministic

point of view, one characteristic also of modern clinical psychology, Masson gives us a hint of one of the difficulties that psychological analysis has to overcome— namely the preference for the belief that poetic ideas arise in their finished form, perhaps from one quasi-divine source, rather than as elaborations of simple and familiar elements devoid in themselves of glamour or aesthetic beauty.

This attitude becomes still more comprehensible when one realises that the deeper, unconscious mind, which is doubtless the actual source of such ideas, as of all abstract ideas, is comprised of mental material discarded or rejected by the conscious mind as being incompatible with its standards: material which has to be extensively transformed and purified before it can be presented to consciousness. The attitude, in short, is one more illustration of the constant resistance that man displays against any danger he may be in of apprehending his inner nature. The artist himself has always avoided a closely analytic attitude towards his work, evidently for the same reason as the ordinary man. He usually dissociates the impelling motive force from his conscious will, and sometimes ascribes it to an actual external agency, divine or demonic. D'Annunzio, for example, in his *Flame of Life* makes his artist-hero think of "the extraordinary moments in which

* The essay is reprinted from the Introduction to *Hamlet*, by Ernest Jones, by permission of Vision Press, Ltd., London. Copyright 1947 by Vision Press, Ltd.

his hand had written an immortal verse that had seemed to him not born of his brain, but dictated by an impetuous deity to which his unconscious organ had obeyed like a blind instrument." Nowhere is the irresistible impetuosity of artistic creation more perfectly portrayed than in the memorable passage in *Ecce Homo* where Nietzsche describes the birth of *Thus Spake Zarathustra*, and its involuntary character has been plainly indicated by most great writers, from Socrates to Goethe.

The particular problem of Hamlet, with which we are here concerned, is intimately related to some of the most frequently recurring problems that are presented in the course of psycho-analytic work, and it has thus seemed possible to secure a fresh point of view from which an answer might be proffered to questions that have baffled attempts made along purely literary and non-analytical lines. Some of the most competent literary authorities have freely acknowledged the inadequacy of all the solutions of the problem that have hithterto been suggested, and when judged by psychological standards their inadequacy is still more evident. The problem presented by the tragedy of *Hamlet* is one of peculiar interest in at least two respects. In the first place, the play is almost universally considered to be the chief masterpiece of one of the greatest minds the world has known. It probably expresses the core of Shakespeare's psychical personality and outlook on life as no other work of his does. It may be expected, therefore, that anything which will give us the key to the inner meaning of the play will necessarily provide a clue to much of the deeper workings of Shakespeare's mind. In the second place, the intrinsic interest of the play itself is exceedingly great. The central mystery in it—namely, the cause of Hamlet's hesitancy in seeking to obtain revenge for his father's murder—has well been called the Sphinx of modern Literature.

The cause of Hamlet's vacillation lies in some special feature of the task which renders it peculiarly difficult or repugnant to him. He suffers from an inhibition of the power to will in the particular direction of avenging his father's death. This conclusion, that Hamlet at heart does not want to carry out the task, seems so obvious that it is hard to see how any open-minded reader of the play could avoid making it. The whole picture presented by Hamlet, his deep depression, the hopeless note in his attitude towards the world and towards the value of life, his dread of death that is a dread of the unresolved and seething darkness within, his fear of dying into eternal conflict because, not conscious of what constitutes the burden of his repression, he can never reach redemption either in life or in the grave, his repeated reference to bad dreams, his self-accusations, his desperate efforts to get away from the thoughts of his duty, and his vain attempts to find an excuse for his procrastination; all this unequivocally points to a tortured conscience, to some hidden ground for shirking his task, a ground which he dare not or cannot avow to himself. We have, therefore, to seek for some evidence that may serve to bring to light the hidden counter-motive.

The extensive experience of the psychoanalytic researches carried out by Freud has amply demonstrated that certain kinds of mental processes shew a greater tendency to be inaccessible to consciousness, to be "repressed," than others. In order therefore to gain a proper perspective it is necessary briefly to inquire into the relative frequency with which various sets of mental processes are repressed. Experience shews that this can be correlated with the relation between these various sets and their degree of compatibility with the ideals and standards accepted by the conscious ego; the less compatible they are with these the more likely are they to be repressed. As the standards acceptable to consciousness are in a considerable measure derived from the immediate environment, one may formulate the following generalisation: those processes are most likely to be repressed by the individual which are most disapproved of by the particular circle of society to whose influence he has chiefly been subjected during the period when his character was being formed. Biologically stated, this law would run: "That which is unacceptable to the herd becomes unacceptable to the individual member," it being understood that the term herd is intended here in the sense of the particular circle defined above, which is by no means necessarily the community at large. It is for this reason that moral, social, ethical or religious tendencies are hardly ever repressed, for, since the individual originally received them from his herd, they can hardly ever come into conflict with the dicta of the latter. By the term "repression" we denote an active dynamic process. Thoughts that are repressed are actively kept from consciousness by a definite force and with the expenditure of more or less mental effort, though the person concerned is seldom aware of this. Further, what is thus kept from consciousness typically possesses an energy of its own. A little consideration of the genetic aspects of the matter will make it comprehensible that the trends most likely to be repressed are those belonging to what are called the natural instincts. As the herd unquestionably selects from the natural instincts the sexual one on which to lay its heaviest ban, so it is the various psycho-sexual trends that are most often repressed by the individual. We have here the explanation of the clinical experience that the more intense and the more ob-

scure is a given case of deep mental conflict the more certainly will it be found on adequate analysis to centre about some sexual problem. On the surface, of course, this does not appear so, since, by means of various psychological defensive mechanisms, the depression, doubt, despair and other manifestations of the conflict are transferred on to more tolerable and permissible topics, such as anxiety about worldly success or failure, about immortality and the salvation of the soul, philosophical considerations about the value of life, the future of the world, and so on.

Bearing these considerations in mind, let us return to Hamlet. It should now be evident that the conflict hypotheses which see Hamlet's conscious impulse towards revenge inhibited by an unconscious misgiving of a highly ethical kind, are based on ignorance of what actually happens in real life, for misgivings of this order belong in fact to the more conscious layers of the mind rather than to the deeper, unconscious ones. Hamlet's intense self-study would speedily have made him aware of any such misgivings and, although he might subsequently have ignored them, it would almost certainly have been by the aid of some process of rationalisation which would have enabled him to deceive himself into believing that they were ill-founded; he would in any case have remained conscious of the nature of them. We have therefore to invert these hypotheses and realise that the positive striving for vengeance, the pious task laid on him by his father, was to him the moral and social one, the one approved by his consciousness, and that the repressed inhibiting striving against the act of vengeance arose in some hidden source connected with his more personal, instinctive life. The former striving is manifest in every speech in which Hamlet debates the matter; the second is, from its nature, more obscure and has to be investigated. This is perhaps most easily done by inquiring more intently into Hamlet's precise attitude towards the object of his vengeance, Claudius, and towards the crimes that have to be avenged. These are two: Claudius' incest with the Queen, and the murder of his brother. It is of great importance to note the profound difference in Hamlet's attitude towards both these crimes. Intellectually of course he abhors both, but there can be no question about which arouses in him the deeper loathing. Whereas the murder of his father evokes in him indignation and a plain recognition of his obvious duty to avenge it, his mother's guilty conduct awakes in him the intensest horror. Now, in trying to define Hamlet's attitude towards his uncle we have to guard against assuming off-hand that this is a simple one of mere execration, for there is a possibility of complexity arising in the following way: The uncle has not merely committed *each* crime, he has committed *both* crimes, a distinction of considerable importance, for the *combination* of crimes allows the admittance of a new factor, produced by the possible inter-relation of the two, which prevents the result from being simply one of summation. In addition it has to be borne in mind that the perpetrator of the crimes is a relative, and an exceedingly near relative. The possible inter-relationship of the crimes, and the fact that the author of them is an actual member of the family, gives scope for a confusion in their influence on Hamlet's mind which may be the cause of the very obscurity we are seeking to clarify.

Let us first pursue further the effect on Hamlet of his mother's misconduct. Before he even knows that his father has been murdered he is in deepest depression, and evidently on account of this misconduct. The connection between the two is unmistakable in the monologue in Act 1, Scene 2, in reference to which Furnivall writes: "One must insist on this, that before any revelation of his father's murder is made to Hamlet, before any burden of revenging that murder is laid upon him, he thinks of suicide as a welcome means of escape from this fair world of God's, made abominable to his diseased and weak imagination by his mother's lust and the dishonour done by her to his father's memory." But we can rest satisfied with this seemingly adequate explanation of Hamlet's weariness of life only if we accept unquestioningly the conventional standards of the causes of deep emotion. Many years ago Connolly, a well-known psychiatrist, pointed out the disproportion here existing between cause and effect and gave as his opinion that Hamlet's reaction to his mother's marriage indicated in itself a mental instability, "a predisposition to actual unsoundness"; he writes: "The circumstances are not such as would at once turn a healthy mind to the contemplation of suicide, the last resource of those whose reason has been overwhelmed by calamity and despair." We have unveiled, therefore, only the exciting cause, not the predisposing cause. The very fact that Hamlet is content with the explanation arouses our grave suspicions, since, as will presently be expounded, from the very nature of the emotion he cannot be aware of the true cause of it. If we ask, not what ought to produce such soul-paralysing grief and distaste for life, but what in actual fact does produce it, we are compelled to go beyond this explanation and seek for some deeper cause. In real life speedy second marriages occur commonly enough without leading to any such result as is here depicted, and when we see them followed by this result we invariably find that there is some other and more hidden reason why the event is followed by this inordinately great effect. The reason always is that the event has awakened to increased activity mental processes that have been repressed from the subject's consciousness. The person's mind has been specially prepared for the catastrophe by previous mental processes with which those directly resulting from the event have entered into association. This is perhaps what Furnivall means when he speaks of the world being made abominable to Hamlet's "diseased imagination." In short, the special nature of the reaction presupposes some special feature in the mental predisposition. Analysis of such states always reveals the operative activity of some buried group of mental processes. Hamlet's state of mind, as Freud has pointed out, corresponds with that characteristic of a certain form of hysteria. Therefore if Hamlet has been plunged into this abnormal state by the news of his mother's second marriage it must be because the news has awakened into activity some slumbering memory of an associated kind, which is so painful that it may not become conscious. For some deep-seated reason, which is to him unacceptable, Hamlet is plunged into anguish at the thought of his father being replaced in his mother's affections by someone else. It is as though his devotion to his mother had made him so jealous for her affection that he had found it hard enough to share this even with his father and could not endure to share it with still another man. Against this thought, however, suggestive as it is, may be urged three objections. First, if it were in itself a full statement of the matter, Hamlet would have been aware of the jealousy, whereas we have concluded that the mental process we are seeking is hidden from him. Secondly, we see in it no evidence of the arousing of an old and forgotten memory. And,

thirdly, Hamlet is being deprived by Claudius of no greater share in the Queen's affection than he had been by his own father, for the two brothers made exactly similar claims in this respect—namely, those of a loved husband. The last-named objection, however, leads us to the heart of the situation. How if, in fact, Hamlet had in years gone by, as a child, bitterly resented having had to share his mother's affection even with his own father, had regarded him as a rival, and had secretly wished him out of the way so that he might enjoy undisputed and undisturbed the monopoly of that affection? If such thoughts had been present in his mind in childhood days they evidently would have been repressed, and all traces of them obliterated by filial piety and other educative influences. The actual realisation of his early wish in the death of his father at the hands of a jealous rival would have produced, in the form of depression and aggression, guilt and sadism, an obscure aftermath of his childhood's conflict. Furthermore, it is typical that the feelings of tenderness are directed only towards the dead father, the father who is no longer a rival, and are totally withheld from the uncle, the living father-imago. This is at all events the mechanism of the Oedipus-complex that is actually found in the real Hamlets who are investigated psychologically.

In order that the point of view put forward above may be better apprehended I feel constrained to interpolate a few considerations on two matters that are not at all commonly appreciated at their true importance—namely a child's feeling of jealousy and his ideas on the subject of death. It was reserved for the genetic studies of psycho-analytic research to demonstrate the lasting and profound influence that infantile jealousies may have upon later character reactions and upon the whole course of a person's life.

The close relation between adult jealousy and the desire for the removal of the rival by the most effective means, that of death, and also the common process of suppression of such feelings, is clearly illustrated in a remark of Stanley Hall's to the effect that "Many a noble and even great man has confessed that mingled with profound grief for the death and misfortune of their best friends, they were often appalled to find a vein of secret joy and satisfaction, as if their own sphere were larger or better." He has doubtless in mind such passages as the following from La Rochefoucauld: "Dans l'adversité de nos meilleurs amis, il y a quelque chose qui ne nous déplaît pas" [In the misfortune of our better friends there is something that does not displease us]. A similar thought is more openly expressed by Bernard Shaw when he makes Don Juan, in the Hell Scene, remark: "You may remember that on earth—though of course we never confessed it—the death of any one we knew, even those we liked best, was always mingled with a certain satisfaction at being finally done with them." Such cynicism in the adult is exceeded to an incomparable extent by that of the child, with its notorious, and to the parents often heartbreaking, egotism, with its undeveloped social instincts, and with its ignorance of the dread significance of death. A child very often unreasoningly interprets the various encroachments on its privileges, and the obstacles interposed to the immediate gratification of its desires, as meaningless cruelty, and the more imperative is the desire that has been thwarted the more pronounced is the hostility towards the agent of this supposed cruelty, most often of course a parent. The most important encroachment, and the most frequent, is that made on the child's desire for affection.

The resulting hostility is very often seen on the occasion of the birth of a subsequent child, and is usually regarded with amusement as an added contribution to the general gaiety called forth by the happy event. When a child, on being told that the doctor has brought him another playfellow, responds with the cry "Tell him to take it away again," he intends this, however, not, as is commonly believed, as a joke for the entertainment of his elders, but as an earnest expression of his intuition that in future he will have to renounce his previously unquestioned pre-eminence in the family circle, a matter that to him is serious enough.

The second point, on which there is also much misunderstanding, is that of the child's attitude toward the subject of death, it being commonly assumed that this is necessarily the same as that of an adult. When a child first hears of anyone's death, the only part of its meaning that he realises is that the person is *no longer there*, a consummation which time and again he has fervently desired when being interfered with by the persons around him. It is only gradually that the grimmer implications of the phenomenon are borne in upon him. When, therefore, a child expresses the wish that a given person, even a near relative, would die, our feelings would not be so shocked as they sometimes are, were we to interpret the wish from the point of view of the child. The same remark applies to the dreams of adults in which the death of a near and dear relative takes place, dreams in which the underlying repressed wish is usually concealed by an emotion of grief. But on the other hand the significance of these death-wishes is not to be under-estimated, either, for the later conflicts they may give rise to can be of the utmost importance for the person's mental welfare, and this in spite of the fact that in the vast majority of cases they remain merely wishes. Not that they always remain wishes, even in children. The recent case in which a group of schoolboys sought to murder their headmaster (the father-imago) comes at once to mind.

Of the infantile jealousies the most important, and the one with which we are here occupied, is that experienced by a boy towards his father. The precise form of early relationship between child and father is in general a matter of vast importance in both sexes and plays a predominating part in the future development of the child's character. The only aspect that at present concerns us is the resentment felt by a boy towards his father when the latter disturbs, as he necessarily must, his enjoyment of his mother's exclusive affection. This feeling is the deepest source of the world-old conflict between father and son, between the younger and the older generation, the favourite theme of so many poets and writers, the central *motif* of most mythologies and religions. The fundamental importance that this conflict, and the accompanying breaking away of the child from the authority of his parents, has both for the individual and for society is clearly stated in the following passage of Freud's: "The detachment of the growing individual from the authority of the parents is one of the most necessary, but also one of the most painful, achievements of development. It is absolutely necessary for it to be carried out, and we may assume that every normal human being has to a certain extent managed to achieve it. Indeed, the progress of society depends in general on this opposition of the two generations."

It was Freud who first demonstrated, when dealing with the subject of the earliest manifestations of the sexual instinct in children, that the conflict rests in the last resort on sexual grounds. He has shewn that this instinct does not, as is generally supposed, differ from other biological functions by suddenly leaping into being at the age of puberty in all its full and developed activity, but that like other functions it undergoes a gradual evolution and only slowly attains the particular form in which we know it in the adult.

It must be mentioned how frequently these earliest dim awakenings are evoked by the intimate physical relations existing between the child and the persons of his immediate environment, above all, therefore, his mother. There is a considerable variability in both the date and the intensity of these early sexual impressions, this depending partly on the boy's constitution and partly on the mother's. When the attraction exercised by the mother is excessive it may exert a controlling influence over the boy's later destiny; a mass of evidence in demonstration of this, too extensive to refer to in detail, has been published in the psycho-analytical literature. Of the various results that may be caused by the complicated interaction between this influence and others only one or two need be mentioned. If the awakened passion undergoes an insufficient repression—an event most frequent when the mother is a widow—then the boy may remain throughout life abnormally attached to his mother and unable to love any other woman, a not uncommon cause of bachelorhood. He may be gradually weaned from the attachment if it is less strong, though it often happens that the weaning is incomplete so that he is able to fall in love only with women who in some way resemble the mother; the latter occurrence is a frequent cause of marriage between relatives, as has been interestingly pointed out by Abraham. The maternal influence may also manifest itself by imparting a strikingly tender feminine side to the later character. The trait in Hamlet's character has often been the subject of comment. Vining even suggests that Hamlet really was a woman. That the same trait was a prominent one of Shakespeare's himself is well known, a fact which the appellation of "Gentle Will" sufficiently recalls; Harris even writes: "Whenever we get under the skin, it is Shakespeare's femininity which startles us." The relationship with Ophelia never flowers because Hamlet's unconscious only partly desires her; in part Ophelia is felt to be a permitted substitute for the desired relationship with Laertes.

When the aroused feeling is intensely repressed and associated with shame, guilt, and similar reactions the submergence may be so complete as to render the person incapable of experiencing any feeling at all of attraction for the opposite sex; to him all women are as forbidden as his mother. This may declare itself in pronounced misogyny or even, when combined with other factors, in actual homosexuality.

The attitude towards the successful rival, namely the father, also varies with —among other factors—the extent to which the aroused feelings have been repressed. If this is only slight, then the natural resentment against the father may be more or less openly manifested later on, a rebellion which occurs commonly enough, though the true meaning of it is not recognised. To this source many social revolutionaries—perhaps all —owe the original impetus of their rebelliousness against authority, as can often be plainly traced—for instance, with Shelley and Mirabeau. The unimpeded train of thought in the unconscious logically culminates in the idea, or rather the wish, that the father (or his substitute) may disappear from the scene, i.e., that he may die. Shakespeare himself provides a good example of this (King Henry IV, Part II) in the scene between the dying king and his son:

Prince Henry: I never thought to hear you speak again.
King Henry: Thy wish was father, Harry, to that thought.

If, on the other hand, the repression is considerable, then the hostility towards the father will be correspondingly concealed from consciousness; this is often accompanied by the development of the opposite sentiment, namely of an exaggerated regard and respect for him, identification with his temperament and social aims, and a morbid solicitude for his welfare, which completely cover the underlying attitude. The complete expression of the repressed wish is not only that the father should die, but that the son, taking over the sexual role of the father, should then espouse the mother. The son, who so often inherits the character-formation of the father, is merely a repressed father-image. As soon as the father is out of the way the repressed identification with him returns to the surface and the son endeavours to outdo the father in the practising of fatherhood. Hamlet has all the makings of as great a criminal as was Claudius. The desire to espouse the mother was openly expressed by Diderot in speaking of boys: "If we were left to ourselves and if our bodily strength only came up to that of our phantasy we would wring our fathers' necks and sleep with our mothers." The attitude of son to parents is so transpicuously illustrated in the Oedipus legend, as developed for instance in Sophocles' tragedy, that the group of mental processes in question is generally known under the name of the Oedipus-complex.

We are now in a position to expand

and complete the suggestions offered above in connection with the Hamlet problem. Here, as throughout, I closely follow Freud's interpretation given in a footnote to his *The Interpretation of Dreams*. He there points out the inadequacy of the earlier explanations, deals with Hamlet's feelings towards his mother, father, and uncle, and mentions two other matters, the significance of Hamlet's reaction against Ophelia and of the probability that the play was written immediately after the death of Shakespeare's own father. The story thus interpreted would run somewhat as follows. As a child Hamlet had experienced the warmest affection for his mother, and this, as is always so, had contained elements of a disguised erotic quality. The polsence of two traits in the Queen's character go to corroborate this assumption, namely her markedly sensual nature and her passionate fondness for her son. The former is indicated in too many places in the play to need specific reference, and is generally recognised. The latter is also manifest; Claudius says, for instance (Act IV, Sc. 7), "The Queen his mother lives almost by his looks." Nevertheless Hamlet seems to have with more or less success weaned himself from her and to have fallen in love with Ophelia. The precise nature of his original feeling for Ophelia is a little obscure. We may assume that at least in part it was composed of a normal love for a prospective bride, though the extravagance of the language used (the passionate need for absolute certainty, etc.) suggests a somewhat morbid frame of mind. There are indications that even here the influence of the old attraction for the mother is still exerting itself. Although some writers, following Goethe, see in Ophelia many traits of resemblance to the Queen, surely more striking are the traits contrasting with those of the Queen. Whatever truth there may be in the many German conceptions of Ophelia as a sensual wanton—misconceptions that have been confuted by Loening and others—still the very fact that it needed what Goethe happily called the "innocence of insanity" to reveal the presence of any such libidinous thoughts demonstrates in itself the modesty and chasteness of her habitual demeanour. Her naive piety, her obedient resignation and her unreflecting simplicity, sharply contrast with the Queen's character, and seem to indicate that Hamlet by a characteristic reaction towards the opposite extreme had unknowingly been impelled to choose a woman who should least remind him of his mother. A case might even be made out for the view that part of his courtship originated not so much in direct attraction for Ophelia as in an unconscious desire to play her off against his mother, just as a disappointed and piqued lover so often has resort to the arms of a more willing rival. It would be hard otherwise to understand the readiness with which he later throws himself into this part. When, for instance, in the play scene he replies to his mother's request to sit by her with the words "No, good mother, here's metal more attractive" and proceeds to lie at Ophelia's feet, we seem to have a direct indication of this attitude; and his coarse familiarity and bandying of ambiguous jests with the woman he has recently so ruthlessly jilted are hardly intelligible unless we bear in mind that they were carried out under the heedful gaze of the Queen. It is as though his unconscious were trying to convey to her the following thought: "You give yourself to other men whom you prefer to me. Let me assure you that I can dispense with your favours and even prefer those of a woman whom I no longer love." His extraordinary outburst of bawdiness on this occasion, so unexpected in a man of obviously fine feeling, points unequivocally to the sexual nature of the underlying turmoil.

Now comes the father's death and the mother's second marriage. The association of the idea of sexuality with his mother, buried since infancy, can no longer be concealed from his consciousness. As Bradley well says: "Her son was forced to see in her action not only an astounding shallowness of feeling, but an eruption of coarse sensuality, 'rank and gross,' speeding post-haste to its horrible delight." Feelings which once, in the infancy of long ago, were pleasurable desires can now, because of his repressions, only fill him with repulsion. The long repressed desire to take his father's place in his mother's affection is stimulated to unconscious activity by the sight of someone usurping this place exactly as he himself had once longed to do. More, this someone was a member of the same family, so that the actual usurpation further resembled the imaginary one in being incestuous. Without his being in the least aware of it these ancient desires are ringing in his mind, are once more struggling to find conscious expression, and need such an expenditure of energy again to repress them that he is reduced to the deplorable mental state he himself so vividly depicts.

There follows the Ghost's announcement that the father's death was a willed one, was due to murder. Hamlet, having at the moment his mind filled with natural indignation at the news, answers normally enough with the cry (Act I, Sc. 5):

Haste me to know't, that I, with wings as swift
As meditation or the thoughts of love,
May sweep to my revenge.

The momentous words follow revealing who was the guilty person, namely a relative who had committed the deed at the bidding of lust. It is not maintained that this was by any means Claudius' whole motive, but it was evidently a powerful one and the one that most impressed Hamlet. Hamlet's second guilty wish had thus also been realised by his uncle, namely to procure the fulfilment of the first—the possession of the mother—by a personal deed, in fact by murder of the father. The two recent events, the father's death and the mother's second marriage, seemed to the world to have no inner causal relation to each other, but they represented ideas which in Hamlet's unconscious fantasy had for many years been closely associated. These ideas now in a moment forced their way to conscious recognition in spite of all repressing forces, and found immediate expression in his almost reflex cry: "O my prophetic soul! My uncle?" The frightful truth his unconscious had already intuitively divined his consciousness had now to assimilate, as best it could. For the rest of the interview Hamlet is stunned by the effect of the internal conflict thus re-awakened, which from now on never ceases, and into the essential nature of which he never penetrates.

One of the first manifestations of the awakening of the old conflict in Hamlet's mind is his reaction against Ophelia. This is doubly conditioned, by the two opposing attitudes in his own mind. In the first place, there is a complex reaction in regard to his mother. As was explained above, the being forced to connect the thought of his mother with sensuality leads to an intense sexual revulsion, one that is only temporarily broken down by the coarse outburst discussed above. Combined with this is a fierce jealousy, unconscious because of its forbidden origin, at the sight of her giving herself to another man, a man whom he had no reason whatever either to love or to respect. Consciously this is allowed to express itself, for instance after the prayer scene, only in the form of extreme resentment and bitter reproaches against her. His resentment against women is still further inflamed by the hypocritical prudishness with which Ophelia follows her father and brother in seeing evil in his natural affection, an attitude which poisons his love in exactly the same way that the love of his childhood, like that of all children, must have been poisoned. He can forgive a woman neither her rejection of his sexual advances nor, still less, her alliance with another man. Most intolerable of all to him, as Bradley well remarks, is the sight of sensuality in a quarter from which he had trained himself ever since infancy rigorously to exclude it. The total reaction culminates in the bitter misogyny of his outburst against Ophelia, who is devastated at having to bear a reaction so wholly out of proportion to her own offence and has no idea that in reviling her Hamlet is really expressing his bitter resentment against his mother. The identification is further demonstrated in the course of the play by Hamlet's killing the men who stand between him and his mother and Ophelia (Claudius and Polonius). On only one occasion does he for a moment escape from the sordid implication with which his love has been impregnated and achieve a healthier attitude toward Ophelia, namely at the open grave when in remorse he breaks out at Laertes for presuming to pretend that his feeling for her could ever equal that of her lover.

The intensity of Hamlet's repulsion against woman in general, and Ophelia in particular, is a measure of the powerful repression to which his sexual feelings are being subjected. The outlet for those feelings in the direction of his mother has always been firmly dammed, and now that the narrower channel in Ophelia's direction has also been closed the increase in the original direction consequent on the awakening of early memories tasks all his energy to maintain the repression. His pent up feelings find a partial vent in other directions. The petulant irascibility and explosive outbursts called forth by his vexation at the hands of Guildenstern and Rosencrantz, and especially of Polonius, are evidently to be interpreted in this way, as also is in part the burning nature of his reproaches to his mother. Indeed towards the end of his interview with his mother the thought of her misconduct expresses itself in that almost physical disgust which is so characteristic a manifestation of intensely repressed sexual feeling.

Let the bloat king tempt you again to bed;
Pinch wanton on your cheek; call you his
  mouse;
And let him, for a pair of reechy kisses,
Or paddling in your neck with his damn'd
  fingers,
Make you to ravel all this matter out,
                            (Act III, Sc. 4)

Hamlet's attitude towards Polonius is highly instructive. Here the absence of family tie and of other similar influences enables him to indulge to a relatively unrestrained extent his hostility towards the prating and sententious dotard. The analogy he effects between Polonius and Jephthah is in this connection especially pointed. It is here that we see his fundamental attitude towards moralising elders who use their power to thwart the happiness of the young, and not in the over-drawn and melodramatic portrait in which he delineates his father: A "combination and a form indeed, where every god did seem to set his seal to give the world assurance of a man."

It will be seen from the foregoing that Hamlet's attitude towards his uncle-father is far more complex than is generally supposed. He of course detests him, but it is the jealous detestation of one evil-doer towards his successful fellow. Much as he hates him, he can never denounce him with the ardent indignation that boils straight from his blood when he reproaches his mother, for the more vigorously he denounces his uncle the more powerfully does he stimulate to activity his own unconscious and repressed complexes. He is therefore in a dilemma between on the one hand allowing his natural detestation of his uncle to have free play, a consummation which would stir still further his own horrible wishes, and on the other hand ignoring the imperative call for the vengeance that his obvious duty demands. His own evil prevents him from completely denouncing his uncle's, and in continuing to repress the former he must strive to ignore, to condone, and if possible even to forget the latter; *his moral fate is bound up with his uncle's for good or ill.* In reality his uncle incorporates the deepest and most buried part of his own personality, so that he cannot kill him without also killing himself. This solution, one closely akin to what Freud has shewn to be the motive of suicide in melancholia, is actually the one that Hamlet finally adopts. The course of alternate action and inaction that he embarks on, and the provocations he gives to his suspicious uncle, can lead to no other end than to his own ruin and, incidentally, to that of his uncle. Only when he has made the final sacrifice and brought himself to the door of death is he free to fulfil his duty, to avenge his father, and to slay his other self—his uncle.

Having identified himself with his uncle's erotic life he must, as a consequence of his incestuous sexual guilt, turn the death wish against his uncle (the father-imago) against himself according to the law with which all neurotics ultimately direct against themselves death wishes relating to others. In the last analysis Hamlet deals himself the punishment of death because death represents the most absolute form of castration.

There is a second reason why the call of duty to kill his step-father cannot be obeyed, and that is because it links itself with the unconscious call of his nature to kill his mother's husband, whether this is the first or the second; the absolute repression of the former impulse involves the inner prohibition of the latter also. It is no chance that Hamlet says of himself that he is prompted to his revenge "by heaven and hell."

In this discussion of the motives that move or restrain Hamlet we have purposely depreciated the subsidiary ones, which also play a part, so as to bring out in greater relief the deeper and effective ones that are of preponderating importance. These, as we have seen, spring from sources of which he is quite unaware, and we might summarise the internal conflict of which he is the victim as consisting in a struggle of the repressed mental processes to become conscious. The call of duty, which automatically arouses to activity these unconscious processes, conflicts with the necessity of repressing them still more strongly; for the more urgent is the need for external action the greater is the effort demanded of the repressing forces. Action is paralysed at its very inception, and there is thus produced the picture of apparently causeless inhibition which is so inexplicable both to Hamlet and to readers of the play. This paralysis arises, however, not from physical or moral cowardice, but from that intellectual cowardice, that reluctance to dare the exploration of his inner soul, which Hamlet shares with the rest of the human race. "Thus conscience does make cowards of us all."

Finally, in order to amplify the psychological interpretation given above, we shall examine certain aspects of the original Hamlet saga. Dealing with earlier versions of the play Storfer writes: "When we compare the earlier versions of the Hamlet theme with Shakespeare's tragedy, Shakespeare's great psychological intuition becomes evident. The earlier versions turned on a political action relating to the state: the heir to the throne wreaks vengeance on the usurper for the murder of the king. In Shakespeare the family tragedy is placed in the foreground. The origin of all revolutions is the revolution in the family. Shakespeare's Hamlet is too philosophical a man, too much given to introspection, not to feel the personal and family motive behind the general political undertaking. Laertes, on the other hand, is blind and deaf to this etymology of feeling, to the unconscious mind; his response to his father Polonius' murder is a political revolt. The behaviour of the two men whose fathers had been murdered well characterises the conscious and the unconscious mind in the psychology of the revolutionary and of the political criminal."

Here may be mentioned a matter which on account of its general psychological interest has provoked endless discussion, namely Hamlet's so-called "simulation of madness." There is of course no question of insanity in the proper sense of the word; Hamlet's behaviour is that of a psycho-neurotic and as such naturally aroused the thought on the part of those surrounding him that he was suffering from some inner affliction. The traits in Hamlet's behaviour that are commonly called "feigning madness" are brought to expression by Shakespeare in such a refined and subtle manner as to be not very transpicuous unless one compares them with the corresponding part of the original saga. The fine irony exhibited by Hamlet in the play, which enables him to express contempt and hostility in an indirect and disguised form—beautifully illustrated, for instance, in his conversations with Polonius—is a transmutation of the still more concealed mode of expression adopted in the saga, where the hero's audience commonly fails to apprehend his meaning. He here combines a veiled form of speech, full of obvious equivocations and intent to deceive, with a curiously punctilious insistence on verbal truthfulness. Saxo gives many examples of this and adds: "He was loth to be thought prone to lying about any matter, and wished to be held a stranger to falsehood; and accordingly he mingled craft and candour in such wise that, though his words did not lack truth, yet there was nothing to betoken the truth and betray how far his keenness went." Even in the saga, however, we read that "some people, therefore, declared that his mind was quick enough, and fancied that he only played the simpleton in order to hide his understanding, and veiled some deep purpose under a cunning feint." The king and his friends applied all sorts of tests to him to determine this truth, tests which of course the hero successfully withstands. It is made plain that Amleth deliberately adopts this curious behaviour in order to further his scheme of revenge, to which—thus differing from Hamlet—he had whole-heartedly devoted himself. The actual mode of operation of his simulation here is very instructive to observe, since it gives us the clue to a deeper psychological interpretation of the process. His conduct in this respect has three characteristics, first the obscure and disguised manner of speech just referred to, secondly a demeanour of indolent inertia and general purposelessness, and thirdly conduct of childish and at times quite imbecillic foolishness (*Dummstellen*); the third of these is well exemplified by the way in which he rides into the palace seated backwards on a donkey, imitates a cock crowing and flapping its wings, rolling on the floor, and similar asininities. His motive in so acting was, by playing the part of a harmless fool, to deceive the king and court concerning his projects of revenge, and unobserved to get to know their plans and intentions; in this he admirably succeeded. Belleforest adds the interesting touch that Amleth, being a Latin scholar, had adopted this device in imitation of the younger Brutus: both names signify "doltish," "stupid"; the derived Norwegian word "amlod" is still a colloquialism for "fool." Belleforest evidently did not know how usual it was for famous young heroes to exhibit this trait; similar stories of "simulated foolishness" are narrated of David, Moses, Cyros, Kaikhosrav, William Tell, Parsifal, and many others besides Hamlet and Brutus.

The behaviour assumed by Amleth in the saga is not that of any form of insanity. It is a form of syndrome well-known to occur in hysteria. The complete syndrome comprises the following features: foolish, witless behaviour, an inane, inept kind of funniness and silliness, and childishness. Now, in reading the numerous examples of Amleth's "foolish" behaviour as narrated by Saxo one cannot help being impressed by the *childish* characteristics manifested throughout in them. His peculiar riddling sayings, obviously aping the innocence of childhood, his predilection for dirt and for smearing himself with filth, his general shiftlessness, and above all the highly characteristic combination of fondness for deception as a thing in itself (apart from the cases where there is a definite motive)

with a punctilious regard for verbal truth, are unmistakably childish traits. The whole syndrome is an exaggeration of a certain type of demeanour displayed at one time or another by most children, and psycho-analysis of it has demonstrated beyond any doubt that their motive in behaving so is to simulate innocence and often extreme childishness, even "foolishness," in order to delude their elders into regarding them as being "too young to understand" or even into altogether disregarding their presence. The purpose of the artifice is that by these means children can view and overhear various private things which they are not supposed to. It need hardly be said that the curiosity thus indulged in is in most cases concerned with matters of a directly sexual nature; even marital embraces are in this way investigated by quite young children far oftener than is generally suspected or thought possible. The core of Amleth's attitude is secrecy and spying: secrecy concerning his own thoughts, knowledge, and plans; spying as regards those of his enemy, his step-father. These two character traits are certainly derived from forbidden curiosity about secret, i.e. sexual matters in early childhood. So is the love of deception for its own sake, a trait which sometimes amounts to what is called pathological lying; it is a defiant reaction to the lies almost always told to the child, and always detected by him. In so behaving the child is really caricaturing the adult's behaviour to himself, as also in the punctiliousness about verbal truth that is sometimes combined with the tendency to deceive; he is pretending to tell the truth as the parent pretended to tell it to him, deceiving going on all the while in both cases. That the theme of the Amleth *motif* is derived from an infantile and sexual source can easily be shewn from the material provided in the saga itself.

The main test applied to him by Feng in order to discover whether he was really stupid or only pretending to be so was to get a young girl (the prototype of Ophelia) to seduce him away to a lonely part of the woods and then send retainers to spy on them and find out whether he knew how to perform the sexual act or not. Then follows a long story of how Amleth is warned of the plot and manages to outwit the spies and also to attain his sexual goal. This passage, so obviously inappropriate if taken literally as applying to a man of Amleth's age and previous intelligence, can only be understood by correlating it with the unconscious source of the theme, and this always emanates from the impulses of childhood. "Knowledge" is often felt to be synonymous with "sexual knowledge," the two terms being in many contexts interchangeable: for instance, the legal expression "to have knowledge of a girl," the Biblical one "and Adam knew Eve his wife" (after eating of the tree of knowledge), and so on. If a child has mastered the great secret he feels that he knows what matters in life; if he hasn't he is in the dark. And, as in the Amleth saga, to prove that someone is ignorant of this fundamental matter is the supreme test of his stupidity and "innocence."

Spying and overhearing play such a constant part in the Amleth saga as to exclude the possibility of their being unconnected with the central theme of the story. After the plot just mentioned had failed, Feng's counsellor, the prototype of Polonius, devises another in which Amleth is to be spied on when talking to his mother in her bedroom. During the voyage to England the king's retainers enter Amleth's bedroom to listen to his conversation. Before this Amleth had spied on his companions and replaced their letter by one of his own. In the later part of the saga, not utilised by

Shakespeare, two other instances of spying occur. In "Hamlet" Shakespeare has retained those scenes and added one other. The first time is when the interview between Hamlet and Ophelia, doubtless taken from the test described above, is overlooked by the king and Polonius; the second when Hamlet's interview with his mother is spied on by Polonius, who thereby loses his life; and the third when the same interview is watched by the Ghost. It is appropriate to the underlying theme of sexual curiosity that two out of these should take place in the mother's bedchamber, the original scene of such curiosity; on both occasions the father-substitute comes *between* Hamlet and his mother, as though to separate them, the reversal of a theme common in primitive cosmogonies. The most striking example in "Hamlet" of a spying scene is the famous "play within a play," for in a very neat analysis Rank has shewn that this play scene is a disguised representation of the infantile curiosity theme discussed above.

From this point of view we can specify more nearly the precise aspect of the father that is represented by the "decomposed" figure Polonius. It is clearly the spying, watching, "all-knowing" father, who is appropriately outwitted by the cunning youth.

Amleth's feigned stupidity in the saga is very crudely depicted and its meaning is quite evident. The use Shakespeare made of this unpromising material, and the way in which he made it serve his aim of completely transforming the old story, is one of the master-strokes of the drama. Amleth's gross acting, for a quite deliberate purpose, is converted into a delicately drawn character trait. Merciless satire, caustic irony, ruthless penetration together with the old habit of speaking in riddles: all these betray not simply the caution of a man who has to keep his secret from those around him, as with Amleth, but the poignant sufferings of a man who is being torn and tortured within his own mind, who is struggling to escape from knowing the horrors of his own heart. With Amleth the feigned stupidity was the weapon used by a single-hearted man in his fight against external difficulties and deliberate foes; with Hamlet it—or rather what corresponds to it, his peculiar behaviour—was the agent by which the secret of a man torn by suffering was betrayed to a previously unsuspecting foe and increasing difficulties were created in his path where none before existed. In the issue Amleth triumphed; Hamlet was destroyed. The different use made of this feature in the story symbolises more finely than anything else the transformation effected by Shakespeare. An inertia pretended for reasons of expediency becomes an inertia unavoidably forced on the hero from the depths of his nature. In this he shews that the tragedy of man is within himself, that, as the ancient saying goes: Character is Fate. It is the essential difference between pre-historic and civilised man with his highly developed sense of guilt arising out of the ceaseless conflict between ego and the personal and social super-ego; the difficulties with which the former had to contend came from without, those with which the latter have to contend really come from within. This inner conflict modern psychologists know as neurosis, and it is only by study of neurosis that one can learn the fundamental motives and instincts that move men. Here, as in so many other aspects, Shakespeare was the first modern.

It is highly instructive now to review the respects in which the plot of "Hamlet" deviates from that of the original saga. We are here, of course, not concerned with the poetic and literary rep-

resentation, which not merely revivified an old story, but created an entirely new work of genius. The changes effected were mainly two and it can be said that Shakespeare was only very slightly indebted to others for them. The first is as follows: In the saga Feng (Claudius) had murdered his brother in public, so that the deed was generally known, and further had with lies and false witnesses sought to justify the deed by pretending it was done to save the Queen from the cruel threats of her husband. Those acquainted with psycho-analytic work will have no difficulty in discerning the infantile sadistic origin of this pretext. Young children commonly interpret an overheard coitus as an act of violence imposed on the mother and they are in any case apt to come to this conclusion whichever way they are enlightened on the facts of sex. The view in question is certainly an aggravating cause of the unconscious hostility against the father. This point again confirms our conclusion that Claudius partly incorporates Hamlet's repressed wishes, for we see in the saga that he not only kills the father-king but also gives as an excuse for it just the reason that the typical son feels. This view of the matter he successfully imposed on the nation, so that, as Belleforest has it, "son péché trouva excuse à l'endroit du peuple et fut reputé comme justice envers la noblesse—et qu'au reste, en lieu de la poursuyvre comme parricide et incestueux, chacun des courtisans luy applaudissoit et le flattoit en sa fortune prospere" [his sin found excuse in regard for the people and was looked upon as justice toward the nobility—and as for the rest, in place of prosecuting it as parricide and incest, each of the courtiers rejoiced and congratulated himself on his propitious fortune]. Now was the change from this to a secret murder effected by Shakespeare or by Kyd? It is

of course to be correlated with the introduction of the Ghost, of whom there is
no trace in either Saxo or Belleforest.
This must have been done early in the
history of the Elizabethan "Hamlet," for
it is referred to by Lodge in 1596 and is
also found in "Der bestrafte Bruder-
mord," though neither of these reasons
is decisive for excluding Shakespeare's
hand. But purely literary considerations
make it likely enough, as Robertson has
pointed out, that the change was introduced by Kyd, who seems to have had a
partiality for Ghost scenes. In the saga
there was delayed action due to the external difficulties of penetrating through
the king's watchful guard. Kyd seems to
have retained these external difficulties
as an explanation for the delay, though
his introduction of the Ghost episode
for reasons of his own—probably first in
the form of a prologue—somewhat weakened them as a justification, since to
have the Ghost episode the murder had
to be a secret one—otherwise there would
be nothing for the Ghost to reveal and
no reason for his appearance. But his
Hamlet, as in the saga, had a quite single-
hearted attitude towards the matter of
revenge; he at once confided in Horatio,
secured his help, and devoted himself
entirely to his aim. There was no self-
reproaching, no doubting, and no psychological problem. Shakespeare, however,
saw the obvious advantages of the
change in the plot—if he did not introduce it himself—for his intention of
transforming the play from an external
struggle into an internal tragedy. The
change minimises the external difficulties
of Hamlet's task, for plainly it is harder
to rouse a nation to condemn a crime
and assist the avenger when it has been
openly explained and universally forgiven
than when it has been guiltily concealed.
If the original plot had been retained
there would be more excuse for the Klein-
Werder hypothesis, though it is to be
observed that even in the saga Hamlet
successfully executed his task, herculean
as it was. The present rendering makes
still more conspicuous Hamlet's recal-
citrancy, for it disposes of the only justi-
fiable plea for delay. That Shakespeare
saw the value of the change thus unwittingly and ununderstandingly introduced by Kyd is proved by the fact that
later on he took steps to remove the last
traces of even a relative publicity concerning the murder. In the first Quarto Hamlet secures his mother's promise to help
him in his plans of revenge, and later
Horatio in an interview with the Queen
speaks with knowledge of Hamlet's plans
of revenge and learns from the Queen
that she sympathises with them. Both
these passages were omitted in the second
Quarto. The omission unmistakably indicates Shakespeare's intention to depict
Hamlet not as a man dismayed by external difficulties and naturally securing
the cooperation of those he could trust,
but as a man who could not bring himself to speak to his best friend about his
quite legitimate desire for revenge, simply
because his own mind was in dire conflict
on the matter.

The second and all-important respect
in which Shakespeare, and he alone,
changed the story and thus revolution-
ised the tragedy is the vacillation and
hesitancy he introduced into Hamlet's
attitude towards his task, with the consequent paralysis of his action. In all the
previous versions Hamlet was throughout a man of rapid decision and action
whenever possible, not—as with Shakespeare's version—in everything except in
the one task of vengeance. He had, as
Shakespeare's Hamlet felt he should
have, swept to his revenge unimpeded
by any doubts or scruples and had never
flinched from the straightforward path of
duty. With him duty and natural inclina-

tion went hand in hand; from his heart he wanted to do that which he believed he ought to do, and thus was harmoniously impelled by both the summons of his conscience and the cry of his blood. There was none of the deep-reaching conflict that was so disastrous to Shakespeare's Hamlet. It is as if Shakespeare, on reading the story, had realised that had *he* been placed in a similar situation he would not have found the path of action so obvious as was supposed, but would on the contrary have been torn in a conflict which was all the more intense for the fact that he could not explain its nature. Bradley might well say that this was the only tragic situation to which Shakespeare himself would not have been equal, and we now know the reason must have been that his penetration had unconsciously revealed to his feeling, though not to his conscious intelligence, the fundamental meaning of the story. His own Oedipus-complex was too strong for him to be able to repudiate it as readily as Amleth and Laertes had done, and he could only create a hero who was unable to escape from its toils.

In this transformation Shakespeare exactly reversed the plot of the tragedy. Whereas in the saga this consisted in the overcoming of external difficulties and dangers by a single-hearted hero, in the play these are removed and the plot lies in the fateful unrolling of the consequences that result from an internal conflict in the hero's soul. From the struggles of the hero issue dangers which at first did not exist, but which, as the effect of his untoward essays, loom increasingly portentous until at the end they close and involve him in final destruction. More than this, every action he so reluctantly engages in for the fulfilment of his obvious task seems half-wittingly to be disposed in such a way as to provoke destiny, in that, by arousing the suspicion and hostility of his enemy, it defeats its own purpose and helps to encompass his own ruin. The conflict in his soul is to him insoluble and the only steps he can make are those which inexorably draw him nearer and nearer to his doom. In him, as in every victim of a powerful unconscious conflict, the Will to Death is fundamentally stronger than the Will to Life, and his struggle is at heart one long despairing fight against suicide, the least intolerable solution of the problem. Being unable to free himself from the ascendency of his past he is necessarily impelled by Fate along the only path he can travel—to Death. In thus vividly exhibiting the desperate but unavailing struggle of a strong man against Fate Shakespeare achieved the very essence of the Greek conception of tragedy, but he went beyond this and shewed that the real nature of man's Fate is inherent in his own soul.

There is thus reason to believe that the new life which Shakespeare poured into the old story was the outcome of inspirations that took their origin in the deepest and darkest regions of his mind. He responded to the peculiar appeal of the story by projecting into it his profoundest thoughts and emotions in a way that has ever since wrung wonder from all who have heard or read the tragedy. It is only fitting that the greatest work of the world-poet should have had to do with the deepest problem and the intensest conflict that have occupied the mind of man since the beginning of time —the revolt of youth and of the impulse to love against the restraint imposed by the jealous eld.

CHAPTER 14

Philological Focus

A CRITIC'S JOB OF WORK
R. P. Blackmur*

Blackmur warns against psychological, sociological, and philosophical dogma and methodology in criticism. Scholarship is the basis of criticism in that of all critical approaches its findings are least debatable. Next in line is Blackmur's own approach, which he calls *technical*—that is, "an approach to literary criticism . . . primarily through the technique, in the widest sense of that word, of the examples handled." Its advantages are that it invites and incorporates other approaches and exceeds them "in its capacity of reduction to literary fact." What Blackmur means by *technical* in the widest sense has been elsewhere defined as *philological*—ascertaining the intention, meaning, and spirit of a work of literature through its mode of expression.

Criticism, I take it, is the formal discourse of an amateur. When there is enough love and enough knowledge represented in the discourse it is a self-sufficient but by no means an isolated art. It witnesses constantly in its own life its interdependence with the other arts. It lays out the terms and parallels of appreciation from the outside in order to convict itself of internal intimacy; it names and arranges what it knows and loves, and searches endlessly with every fresh impulse or impression for better names and more orderly arrangements. It is only in this sense that poetry (or some other art) is a criticism of life; poetry names and arranges, and thus arrests and transfixes its subject in a form which has a life of its own forever separate but springing from the life which confronts it. Poetry is life at the remove of form and meaning; not life lived but life framed and identified. So the criticism of poetry is bound to be

* The essay is reprinted from *Language As Gesture*, copyright, 1952, by Richard P. Blackmur. Reprinted by permission of Harcourt, Brace & World, Inc.

occupied at once with the terms and modes by which the remove was made and with the relation between—in the ambiguous stock phrase—content and form; which is to say with the establishment and appreciation of human or moral value. It will be the underlying effort of this essay to indicate approaches to criticism wherein these two problems —of form and value—will appear inextricable but not confused—like the stones in an arch or the timbers in a building.

These approaches—these we wish to eulogize—are not the only ones, nor the only good ones, nor are they complete. No approach opens on anything except from its own point of view and in terms of its own prepossessions. Let us set against each other for a time the facts of various approaches to see whether there is a residue, not of fact but of principle.

The approaches to—or the escapes from—the central work of criticism are as various as the heresies of the Christian church, and like them testify to occasional needs, fanatic emphasis, special interest, or intellectual pride, all flowing from and even the worst of them enlightening the same body of insight. Every critic like every theologian and every philosopher is a casuist in spite of himself. To escape or surmount the discontinuity of knowledge, each resorts to a particular heresy and makes it predominant and even omnivorous.[1]

For most minds, once doctrine is sighted and is held to be the completion of insight, the doctrinal mode of thinking seems the only one possible. When doctrine totters it seems it can fall only into the gulf of bewilderment; few minds risk the fall; most seize the remnants and swear the edifice remains, when doctrine

becomes intolerable dogma.[2] All fall notwithstanding; for as knowledge itself is a fall from the paradise of undifferentiated sensation, so equally every formula of knowledge must fall the moment too much weight is laid upon it—the moment it becomes omnivorous and pretends to be omnipotent—the moment, in short, it is taken literally. Literal knowledge is dead knowledge; and the worst bewilderment—which is always only comparative—is better than death. Yet no form, no formula, of knowledge ought to be surrendered merely because it runs the risk in bad or desperate hands of being used literally; and similarly, in our own thinking, whether it is carried to the point of formal discourse or not, we cannot only afford, we ought scrupulously to risk the use of any concept that seems propitious or helpful in getting over gaps. Only the use should be consciously provisional, speculative, and dramatic. The end-virtue of humility comes only after a long train of humiliations; and the chief labor of humbling is the constant, resourceful restoration of ignorance.

The classic contemporary example of use and misuse is attached to the name of Freud. Freud himself has constantly emphasized the provisional, dramatic character of his speculations: they are employed as imaginative illumination, to be relied on no more and no less than the sailor relies upon his buoys and beacons.[3] But the impetus of Freud was so great that a school of literalists arose

[1] The rashest heresy of our day and climate is that exemplified by T. S. Eliot when he postulates an orthodoxy which exists whether anyone knows it or not.

[2] Baudelaire's sonnet "Le Gouffre" dramatizes this sentiment at once as he saw it surmounted in Pascal and as it occurred insurmountably in himself.

[3] Santayana's essay "A Long Way Round to Nirvana" (in Some Turns of Thought in Modern Philosophy) illustrates the poetic-philosophic character of Freud's insight into death by setting up its analogue in Indian philosophy; and by his comparison only adds to the stimulus of Freud.

with all the mad consequence of schism and heresy and fundamentalism which have no more honorable place in the scientific than the artistic imagination. Elsewhere, from one point of view, Caesarism in Rome and Berlin is only the literalist conception of the need for a positive state. So, too, the economic insights of Marxism, merely by being taken literally in their own field, are held to affect the subject and value of the arts, where actually they offer only a limited field of interest and enliven an irrelevant purpose. It is an amusing exercise—as it refreshes the terms of bewilderment and provides a common clue to the secrets of all the modes of thinking—to restore the insights of Freud and Fascism and Marxism to the terms of the Church; when the sexual drama in Freud becomes the drama of original sin, and the politics of Hitler and Lenin becomes the politics of the City of God in the sense that theology provides both the sanctions of economics and the values of culture. Controversy is in terms absolutely held, when the problems argued are falsely conceived because necessarily abstracted from "real" experience. The vital or fatal nexus is in interest and emotion and is established when the terms can be represented dramatically, almost, as it were, for their own sakes alone and with only a pious or ritualistic regard for the doctrines in which they are clothed. The simple, and fatal, example is in the glory men attach to war, the vital, but precarious example, is in the intermittent conception of free institutions and the persistent reformulation of the myth of reason. Then the doctrines do not matter, since they are taken only for what they are worth (whatever rhetorical pretensions to the contrary) as guides and props, as aids to navigation. What does matter is experience, the life represented and the value discovered, and both dram-

atized or enacted under the banner of doctrine. All banners are wrong-headed, but they make rallying points, free the impulse to cry out, and give meaning to the cry itself simply by making it seem appropriate.

It is on some analogue or parallel to these remarks alone that we understand and use the thought and art of those whose doctrines differ from our own. We either discount, absorb, or dominate the doctrine for the sake of the life that goes with it, for the sake of what is *formed* in the progressive act of thinking. When we do more—when we refine or elaborate the abstracted notion of form —we play a different game, which has merit of its own like chess, but which applied to the world we live in produces false dilemmas like solipsism and infant damnation. There is, taking solipsism for example, a fundamental distinction. Because of the logical doctrine prepared to support it, technical philosophers employ years[4] to get around the impasse in which it leaves them; whereas men of poetic imagination merely use it for the dramatic insight it contains—as Eliot uses it in the last section of *The Waste Land;* or as, say, everyone uses the residual mythology of the Greek religion— which its priests nevertheless used as literal sanction for blood and power.

Fortunately, there exist archetypes of unindoctrinated thinking. Let us incline our minds like reflectors to catch the light of the early Plato and the whole Montaigne. Is not the inexhaustible stimulus and fertility of the *Dialogues* and the *Essays* due as much as anything to the absence of positive doctrine? Is it not that the early Plato always holds conflicting ideas in shifting balance, present-

---

[4] Santayana found it necessary to resort to his only sustained labor of dialectic, *Scepticism and Animal Faith,* which, though a beautiful monument of intellectual play, is ultimately valuable for its *incidental* moral wisdom.

ing them in contest and evolution, with victory only the last shift? Is it not that Montaigne is always making room for another idea, and implying always a third for provisional adjudicating irony? Are not the forms of both men themselves ironic, betraying in its most intimate recesses the duplicity of every thought, pointing out, so to speak, in the act of self-incrimination, and showing it not paled on a pin but in the buff life? ... Such an approach, such an attempt at vivid questing, borrowed and no doubt adulterated by our own needs, is the only rational approach to the multiplication of doctrine and arrogant technologies which fills out the body of critical thinking. Anything else is a succumbing, not an approach; and it is surely the commonest of ironies to observe a man altogether out of his depth do his cause fatal harm merely because, having once succumbed to an idea, he thinks it necessary to stick to it. Thought is a beacon not a life-raft, and to confuse the functions is tragic. The tragic character of thought—as any perspective will show—is that it takes a rigid mold too soon; chooses destiny like a Calvinist, in infancy, instead of waiting slowly for old age, and hence for the most part works against the world, good sense, and its own object: as anyone may see by taking a perspective of any given idea of democracy, of justice, or the nature of the creative act.

Imaginative skepticism and dramatic irony—the modes of Montaigne and Plato—keep the mind athletic and the spirit on the stretch. Hence the juvenescence of *The Tempest* and hence, too, perhaps, the air almost of precocity in *Back to Methuselah*. Hence, at any rate, the sustaining power of such varied works as *The Brothers Karamazoff, Cousine Bette,* and *The Magic Mountain*. Dante, whom the faithful might take to the contrary, is yet "the chief imagination of Christendom"; he took his doctrine once and for all from the Church and from St. Thomas and used it as a foil (in the painter's sense) to give recessiveness, background, and contrast. Virgil and Aristotle, Beatrice and Bertrans de Born have in their way as much importance as St. Thomas and the Church. It was this security of reference that made Dante so much more a free spirit than were, say, Swift and Laurence Sterne. Dante had a habit (not a theory) of imagination which enabled him to dramatize with equal ardor and effect what his doctrine blessed, what it assailed, and what, at heart, it was indifferent to. Doctrine was the seed and structure of vision, and for his poems (at least to us) never more. *The Divine Comedy* no less than the *Dialogues* and the *Essays* is a true *Speculum Mentis*.

With lesser thinkers and lesser artists —and in the defective works of the greater—we have in reading, in criticising, to supply the skepticism and the irony, or, as may be, the imagination and the drama, to the degree, which cannot be complete since then we should have had no prompts, that they are lacking. We have to rub the looking-glass clear. With Hamlet, for example, we have to struggle and guess to bring the motive out of obscurity: a struggle which, aiming at the wrong end, the psychoanalysts have darkened with counsel. With Shelley we have to flesh out the Platonic Ideas, as with Blake we have to cut away, since it cannot be dramatized, all the excrescence of doctrine. With Baudelaire we have sometimes to struggle with and sometimes to suppress the problem of belief, working out the irony implicit in either attitude. Similarly, with a writer like Pascal, in order to get the most out of him, in order to compose an artistic judgment, we must consider such an idea as that of the necessity of the wager, not solemnly as Pascal took it, but as a dramatized possibility, a savage, but provisional irony; and we need to show that the skepticisms of Montaigne and Pascal are not at all the same thing—that where one produced serenity the other produced excruciation.

Again, speaking of André Gide, we should remind ourselves not that he has been the apologist of homosexuality, not that he has become a communist, but that he is *par excellence* the French puritan chastened by the wisdom of the body, and that he has thus an acutely scrupulous ethical sensibility. It is by acknowledging the sensibility that we feel the impact of the apologetics and the political conversion. Another necessity in the apprehension of Gide might be put as the recognition of similarity in difference of the precocious small boys in Dostoievski and Gide, *e.g.*, Kolya in *Karamazoff* and young George in *The Counterfeiters*: they are small, cruel engines, all naked sensibility and no scruple, demoniacally possessed, and used to keep things going. And these in turn may remind us of another writer who had a predilection for presenting the *terrible* quality of the young intelligence: of Henry James, of the children in *The Turn of the Screw*, of *Maisie*, and all the rest, all beautifully efficient agents of dramatic judgment and action, in that they take all things seriously for themselves, with the least prejudice of preparation, candidly, with an intelligence life has not yet violated.

Such feats of agility and attention as these remarks illustrate seem facile and even commonplace, and from facile points of view there is no need to take them otherwise. Taken superficially they provide escape from the whole labor of specific understanding; or, worse, they provide an easy vault from casual interpretation to an omnivorous world-view. We might take solemnly and as of universal application the two notions of demonic possession and inviolate intelligence of Gide, Dostoievski, and James, and on that frail nexus build an unassailable theory of the sources of art, wisdom, and value; unassailable because affording only a stereotyped vision, like that of conservative capitalism, without reference in the real world. The maturity of Shakespeare and of Gertrude Stein would then be found on the same childish level.

But we need not go so far in order to draw back. The modes of Montaigne and Plato contain their own safety. Any single insight is good only at and up to a certain point of development and not beyond, which is to say that it is a provisional and tentative and highly selective approach to its field. Furthermore, no observation, no collection of observations, ever tells the whole story; there is always room for more, and at the hypothetical limit of attention and interest there will always remain, quite untouched, the thing itself. Thus the complex character—I say nothing of the value—of the remarks above reveals itself. They flow from a dramatic combination of all the skills and conventions of the thinking mind. They are commonplace only as a criticism—as an end-product or function. Like walking, criticism is a pretty nearly universal art; both require a constant intricate shifting and catching of balance; neither can be questioned much in process; and few perform either really well. For either a new terrain is fatiguing and awkward, and in our day most men prefer paved walks or some form of rapid transit—some easy theory or outmastering dogma. A good critic keeps his criticism from becoming either instinctive or vicarious, and the labor of his understanding is always specific, like the art which he examines; and he knows that the sum of his best work comes only to the pedagogy of elucidation and appreciation. He observes facts and he delights in discriminations. The object remains, and should remain, itself, only made more available and seen in a clearer light. The imagination of Dante is for us only equal to what we can know of it at a given time.

Which brings us to what, as T. S. Eliot would say,[5] I have been leading up to all the time, and what has indeed been said several times by the way. Any rational approach is valid to literature and may be properly called critical which fastens at any point upon the work itself. The utility of a given approach depends partly upon the strength of the mind making it and partly upon the recognition of the limits appropriate to it. Limits may be of scope, degree, or relevance, and may be either plainly laid out by the critic himself, or may be determined by his readers; and it is, by our argument, the latter case that commonly falls, since an active mind tends to overestimate the scope of its tools and to take as necessary those doctrinal considerations which habit has made seem instinctive. No critic is required to limit himself to a single approach, nor is he likely to be able to do so; facts cannot be exhibited without comment, and comment involves the generality of the mind. Furthermore, a consciously complex approach like that of Kenneth Burke or T. S. Eliot, by setting up

---

[5] ...that when "morals cease to be a matter of tradition and orthodoxy—that is, of the habits of the community formulated, corrected, and elevated by the continuous thought and direction of the Church—and when each man is to elaborate his own, then *personality* becomes a thing of alarming importance." (*After Strange Gods.*) Thus Mr. Eliot becomes one of those viewers-with-alarm whose next step is the very hysteria of disorder they wish to escape. The hysteria of institutions is more dreadful than that of individuals.

parallels of reference, affords a more flexible, more available, more stimulating standard of judgment—though of course at a greater risk of prejudice—than a single approach. What produces the evil of stultification and the malice of controversy is the confused approach, when the limits are not seen because they tend to cancel each other out, and the driving power becomes emotional.

The worse evil of fanatic falsification —of arrogant irrationality and barbarism in all its forms—arises when a body of criticism is governed by an *idée fixe*, a really exaggerated heresy, when a notion of genuine but small scope is taken literally as of universal application. This is the body of tendentious criticism where, since something is assumed proved before the evidence is in, distortion, vitiation, and absolute assertion become supreme virtues. I cannot help feeling that such writers as Maritain and Massis —no less than Nordau before them— are tendentious in this sense. But even here, in this worst order of criticism, there is a taint of legitimacy. Once we reduce, in a man like Irving Babbitt, the magnitude of application of such notions as the inner check and the higher will, which were for Babbitt paramount—that is, when we determine the limits within which he really worked—then the massive erudition and acute observation with which his work is packed become permanently available.

And there is no good to be got in objecting to and disallowing those orders of criticism which have an ulterior purpose. *Ulterior* is not in itself a pejorative, but only so when applied to an enemy. Since criticism is not autonomous—not a light but a process of elucidation—it cannot avoid discovering constantly within itself a purpose or purposes ulterior in the good sense. The danger is in not knowing what is ulterior and what is not, which is much the same as the cognate danger in the arts themselves. The arts serve purposes beyond themselves; the purposes of what they dramatize or represent at that remove from the flux which gives them order and meaning and value; and to deny those purposes is like asserting that the function of a handsaw is to hang above a bench and that to cut wood is to belittle it. But the purposes are varied and so bound in his subject that the artist cannot always design for them. The critic, if that is his bent, may concern himself with those purposes or with some one among them which obsess him; but he must be certain to distinguish between what is genuinely ulterior to the works he examines and what is merely irrelevant; and he must further not assume except within the realm of his special argument that other purposes either do not exist or are negligible or that the works may not be profitably discussed apart from ulterior purposes and as examples of dramatic possibility alone.

II

Three examples of contemporary criticism primarily concerned with the ulterior purposes of literature should, set side by side, exhibit both the defects and the unchastened virtues of that approach; though they must do so only tentatively and somewhat invidiously—with an exaggeration for effect. Each work is assumed to be a representative ornament of its kind, carrying within it the seeds of its own death and multiplication. Let us take then, with an eye sharpened by the dangers involved, Santayana's essay on Lucretius (in *Three Philosophical Poets*), Van Wyck Brooks' *Pilgrimage of Henry James*, and Granville Hicks' *The Great Tradition*.

Though that of the third is more obvious in our predicament, the urgency in the approach is equal in all three.

Santayana's essay represents a conversion or transvaluation of an actually poetic ordering of nature to the terms of a moral philosophy which, whatever its own responsibilities, is free of the special responsibility of poetry. So ably and so persuasively is it composed, his picture seems complete and to contain so much of what was important in Lucretius that *De Rerum Natura* itself can be left behind. The philosophical nature of the insight, its moral scope and defect, the influence upon it of the Democritan atom, once grasped intellectually as Santayana shows us how to grasp them, seem a good substitute for the poem and far more available. But, what Santayana remembers but does not here emphasize since it was beyond his immediate interest, there is no vicar for poetry on earth. Poetry is idiom, a special and fresh saying, and cannot for its life be said otherwise; and there is, finally, as much difference between words used about a poem and the poem as there is between words used about a painting and the painting. The gap is absolute. Yet I do not mean to suggest that Santayana's essay—that any philosophical criticism—is beside the point. It is true that the essay may be taken as a venture in philosophy for its own sake, but it is also true that it reveals a body of facts about an ulterior purpose in Lucretius' poem—doubtless the very purpose Lucretius himself would have chosen to see enhanced. If we return to the poem it will be warmer as the facts come alive in the verse. The re-conversion comes naturally in this instance in that, through idioms differently construed but equally imaginative, philosophy and poetry both buttress and express moral value. The one enacts or represents in the flesh what the other reduces to principle or raises to the ideal. The only precaution the critic of poetry need take is negative: that neither poetry nor philosophy can ever fully satisfy the other's purposes, though each may seem to do so if taken in an ulterior fashion. The relationship is mutual but not equivalent.

When we turn deliberately from Santayana on Lucretius to Van Wyck Brooks on Henry James, we turn from the consideration of the rational ulterior purposes of art to the consideration of the irrational underlying predicament of the artist himself, not only as it predicts his art and is reflected in it, but also, and in effect predominantly, as it represents the conditioning of nineteenth-century American culture. The consideration is sociological, the method of approach that of literary psychology, and the burden obsessive. The conversion is from literary to biographical values. Art is taken not as the objectification or mirroring of social experience but as a personal expression and escape-fantasy of the artist's personal life in dramatic extension. The point for emphasis is that the cultural situation of Henry James' America stultified the expression and made every escape ineffectual—even that of Europe. This theme—the private tragedy of the unsuccessful artist—was one of Henry James' own; but James saw it as typical or universal—as a characteristic tragedy of the human spirit—illustrated, as it happened for him, against the Anglo-American background. Brooks, taking the same theme, raises it to an obsession, an omnivorous concept, under which all other themes can be subsumed. Applied to American cultural history, such obsessive thinking is suggestive in the very exaggeration of its terms, and applied to the private predicament of Henry James the man it dramatically emphasizes—

uses for all and more than it is worth —an obvious conflict that tormented him. As history or as biography the book is a persuasive imaginative picture, although clearly not the only one to be seen. Used as a nexus between James the man and the novels themselves, the book has only possible relevance and cannot be held as material. *Hamlet,* by a similar argument, could be shown to be an unsuccessful expression of Shakespeare's personaltiy. To remain useful in the field of literary criticism, Brooks' notions ought to be kept parallel to James' novels but never allowed to merge with them. The corrective, the proof of the gap, is perhaps in the great air of freedom and sway of mastery that pervades the "Prefaces" James wrote to his collected edition. For James art was enough because it molded and mirrored and valued all the life he knew. What Brooks' parallel strictures can do is to help us decide from another point of view whether to choose the values James dramatized. They cannot affect or elucidate but rather—if the gap is closed by will—obfuscate the values themselves.

In short, the order of criticism of which Brooks is a masterly exponent, and which we may call the psycho-sociological order, is primarily and in the end concerned less with the purposes, ulterior or not, of the arts than with some of the ulterior *uses* to which the arts can be appropriately put. Only what is said in the meantime, by the way—and does not depend upon the essence of argument but only accompanies it—can be applied to the arts themselves. There is nothing, it should be added, in Brooks' writings to show that he believes otherwise or would claim more; he is content with that scope and degree of value to which his method and the strength of his mind limit him; and his value is the greater and more urgent for that.

Such tacit humility, such implicit admission of contingency, are not immediate characteristics of Granville Hicks' *The Great Tradition*, though they may, so serious is his purpose, be merely virtues of which he deliberately, for the time being and in order to gain his point, deprives himself of the benefit. If this is so, however expedient his tactics may seem on the short view they will defeat him on the long. But let us examine the book on the ground of our present concern alone. Like Brooks, Hicks presents an interpretation of American literature since the Civil War, dealing with the whole body rather than single figures. Like Brooks he has a touchstone in an obsessive idea, but where we may say that Brooks *uses* his idea—as we think for more than it is worth—we must say that Hicks is victimized by his idea to the point where the travail of judgment is suspended and becomes the mere reiteration of formula. He judges literature as it expressed or failed to express the economic conflict of classes sharpened by the industrial revolution, and he judges individual writers as they used or did not use an ideology resembling the Marxist analysis as prime clue to the clear representation of social drama. Thus Howells comes off better than Henry James, and Frank Norris better than Mark Twain, and, in our own day, Dos Passos is stuck on a thin eminence that must alarm him.

Controversy is not here a profitable exercise, but it may be said for the sake of the record that although every period of history presents a class struggle, some far more acute than our own, the themes of great art have seldom lent themselves to propaganda for an economic insight, finding, as it happened, religious, moral or psychological—that is to say, interpretative—insights more appropriate impulses. If *Piers Plowman* dealt with the class struggle, *The Canterbury Tales* did not, and Hicks would be hard put, if he looked sharp, to make out a better case of social implication in Dostoievski than in Henry James.

What vitiates *The Great Tradition* is its tendentiousness. Nothing could be more exciting, nothing more vital, than a book by Hicks which discovered and examined the facts of a literature whose major theme hung on an honest dramatic view of the class struggle—and there is indeed such a literature now emerging from the depression. And on the other hand it would be worth while to have Hicks sharpen his teeth on all the fraudulent or pseudo-art which actually slanders the terms of the class and every other struggle.

The book with which he presents us performs a very different operation. There is an initial hortatory assumption that American literature ought to represent the class struggle from a Marxist viewpoint, and that it ought thus to be the spur and guide to political action. Proceeding, the point is either proved or the literature dismissed and its authors slandered. Hicks is not disengaging for emphasis and contemporary need an ulterior purpose; he is not writing criticism at all; he is writing a fanatic's history and a casuist's polemic, with the probable result—which is what was meant by suggesting above that he had misconceived his tactics—that he will convert no one who retains the least love of literature or the least knowledge of the themes which engage the most of life. It should be emphasized that there is no more quarrel with Hicks' economic insight as such than there was with the insights of Santayana and Van Wyck Brooks. The quarrel is deeper. While it is true and good that the arts may be used to illustrate social propaganda—though it is not a great use— you can no more use an economic insight as your chief critical tool than you can make much out of the Mass by submitting the doctrine of transubstantiation to chemical analysis.

These three writers have one great formal fact in common, which they illustrate as differently as may be. They are concerned with the separable content of literature, with what may be said without consideration of its specific setting and apparition in a form; which is why, perhaps, all three leave literature so soon behind. The quantity of what can be said directly about the content alone of a given work of art is seldom great, but the least saying may be the innervation of an infinite intellectual structure, which, however valuable in itself, has for the most part only an asserted relation with the works from which it springs. The sense of continuous relationship, of sustained contact, with the works nominally in hand is rare and when found uncommonly exhilarating; it is the fine object of criticism; as it seems to put us in direct possession of the principles whereby the works move without injuring or disintegrating the body of the works themselves. This sense of intimacy by inner contact cannot arise from methods of approach which hinge on seized separable content. We have constantly—if our interest is really in literature—to prod ourselves back, to remind ourselves that there was a poem, a play, or a novel of some initial and we hope terminal concern, or we have to falsify and set up fictions[6] to the effect that no matter what we are saying we

[6] Such a fiction, if not consciously so contrived, is the fiction of the organic continuity of all literature as expounded by T. S. Eliot in his essay, "Tradition and the Individual Talent." The locus is famous and represents that each new work of art slightly alters the relationships among the whole order of existing works. The notion has truth, but it is a mathematical truth and has little relevance to the arts. Used as Eliot uses it, it is an experimental conceit and pushes the mind forward. Taken seriously it is bad constitutional law, in the sense that it would provoke numberless artificial and insoluble problems.

are really talking about art after all. The question must often be whether the prodding and reminding is worth the labor, whether we might not better assign the works that require it to a different category than that of criticism.

III

Similar strictures and identical precautions are necessary in thinking of other, quite different approaches to criticism, where if there are no ulterior purposes to allow for there are other no less limiting features—there are certainly such, for example, for me in thinking of my own. The ulterior motive, or the limiting feature, whichever it is, is a variable constant. One does not always know what it is, nor what nor how much work it does; but one always knows it is there—for strength or weakness. It may be only the strength of emphasis—which is necessarily distortion; or it may be the worse strength of a simplifying formula, which skeletonizes and transforms what we want to recognize in the flesh. It may be only the weakness of what is unfinished, undeveloped, or unseen— the weakness that follows on emphasis; or it may be the weakness that shows when pertinent things are deliberately dismissed or ignored, which is the corresponding weakness of the mind strong in formula. No mind can avoid distortion and formula altogether, nor would wish to; but minds rush to the defense of qualities they think cannot be avoided, and that, in itself, is an ulterior motive, a limiting feature of the mind that rushes. I say nothing of one's personal prepossessions, of the damage of one's private experience, of the malice and false tolerance they inculcate into judgment. I know that my own essays suffer variously, but I cannot bring myself to specify the indulgences I would ask; mostly, I hope, that general indulgence which consists in the task of bringing my distortions and emphases and opinions into balance with other distortions, other emphases and better opinions.

But rather than myself, let us examine briefly, because of their differences from each other and from the three critics already handled, the modes of approach to the act of criticism and habits of critical work of I. A. Richards, Kenneth Burke, and S. Foster Damon. It is to characterize them and to judge the *character* of their work—its typical scope and value—that we want to examine them. With the objective validity of their varying theories we are not much here concerned. Objective standards of criticism, as we hope them to exist at all, must have an existence anterior and superior to the practice of particular critics. The personal element in a given critic—what he happens to know and happens to be able to understand—is strong or obstinate enough to reach into his esthetic theories; and as most critics do not have the coherence of philosophers it seems doubtful if any outsider could ever reach the same conclusions as the critic did by adopting his esthetics. Esthetics sometimes seems only as implicit in the practice of criticism as the atomic physics is present in sunlight when you feel it.

But some critics deliberately expand the theoretic phase of every practical problem. There is a tendency to urge the scientific principle and the statistical method, and in doing so to bring in the whole assorted world of thought. That Mr. Richards, who is an admirable critic and whose love and knowledge of poetry are incontestable, is a victim of the expansiveness of his mind in these directions, is what characterizes, and reduces, the scope of his work as literary criticism. It is possible that he ought not to be called a literary critic at all. If we list the titles of his books we are in a quandary: *The Foundations of Aesthetics, The Meaning of Meaning* (these with C. K. Ogden), *The Principles of Literary Criticism, Science and Poetry, Practical Criticism, Mencius on the Mind,* and *Coleridge on Imagination.* The apparatus is so vast, so labyrinthine, so inclusive— and the amount of actual literary criticism is so small that it seems almost a by-product instead of the central target. The slightest volume, physically, *Science and Poetry,* contains proportionally the most literary criticism, and contains, curiously, his one obvious failure in appreciation—since amply redressed—his misjudgment of the nature of Yeats' poetry. His work is for the most part *about* a department of the mind which includes the pedagogy of sensibility and the practice of literary criticism. The matters he investigates are the problems of belief, of meaning, of communication, of the nature of controversy, and of poetic language as the supreme mode of imagination. The discussion of these problems is made to focus for the most part on poetry because poetry provides the only great monuments of imagination available to verbal imagination. His bottom contention might, I think, be put as this: that words have a synergical power, in the realms of feeling, emotion, and value, to create a reality, or the sense of it, not contained in the words separately; and that the power and the reality as experienced in great poetry make the chief source of meaning and value for the life we live. This contention I share; except that I should wish to put on the same level, as sources of meaning and value, modes of imagination that have no medium in words—though words may call on them—and are not susceptible of verbal reformulation: the modes of great acting, architecture, music and painting.

Thus I can assent to Mr. Richards' positive statement of the task of criticism, because I can add to it positive tasks in analogous fields: "To recall that poetry is the supreme use of language, man's chief co-ordinating instrument, in the service of the most integral purposes of life; and to explore, with thoroughness, the intricacies of the modes of language as working modes of the mind." But I want this criticism, engaged in this task, constantly to be confronted with examples of poetry, and I want it so for the very practical purpose of assisting in pretty immediate appreciation of the use, meaning, and value of the language in that particular poetry. I want it to assist in doing for me what it actually assists Mr. Richards in doing, whatever that is, when he is reading poetry for its own sake.

Mr. Richards wants it to do that, too, but he wants it to do a great deal else first. Before it gets to actual poetry (from which it is said to spring) he wants literary criticism to become something else and much more: he wants it to become, indeed, the master department of the mind. As we become aware of the scope of poetry, we see, according to Mr. Richards that the

... study of the modes of language becomes, as it attempts to be thorough, the most fundamental and extensive of all inquiries. It is no preliminary or preparation for other profounder studies. . . . The very formation of the objects which these studies propose to examine takes place through the processes (of which imagination and fancy are modes) by which the words they use acquire their meanings. Criticism is the science of these meanings. . . . Critics in the future must have a theoretical equipment which has not been felt to be necessary in the past. . . . But the critical equipment will not be *primarily* philosophical.

It will be rather a command *of the methods of general linguistic analysis.*[7]

I think we may take it that *Mencius on the Mind* is an example of the kind of excursion on which Mr. Richards would lead us. It is an excursion into multiple definition, and it is a good one if that is where you want to go and are in no hurry to come back: you learn the enormous variety and complexity of the operations possible in the process of verbally describing and defining brief passages of imaginative language and the equal variety and complexity of the result; you learn the practical impossibility of verbally ascertaining what an author means—and you hear nothing of the other ways of apprehending meaning at all. The instance is in the translation of Mencius, because Mr. Richards happens to be interested in Mencius, and because it is easy to see the difficulties of translating Chinese; but the principles and method of application would work as well on passages from Milton or Rudyard Kipling. The real point of Mr. Richards' book is the impossibility of understanding, short of a lifetime's analysis and compensation, the mechanism of meaning in even a small body of work. There is no question of the exemplary value and stimulus of Mr. Richards' work; but there is no question either that few would care to emulate him for any purpose of literary criticism. In the first place it would take too long, and in the second he does not answer the questions literary criticism would put. The literal adoption of Mr. Richards' approach to literary criticism would stultify the very power it was aimed to enhance—the power of imaginative apprehension, of imaginative co-ordination of varied and separate elements. Mr. Richards' work

[7] All quoted material is from the last four pages of *Coleridge on Imagination.*

is something to be aware of, but deep awareness is the limit of use. It is notable that in his admirable incidental criticism of such poets as Eliot, Lawrence, Yeats and Hopkins, Mr. Richards does not himself find it necessary to be more than aware of his own doctrines of linguistic analysis. As philosophy from Descartes to Bradley transformed itself into a study of the modes of knowing, Mr. Richards would transform literary criticism into the science of linguistics. Epistemology is a great subject, and so is linguistics; but they come neither in first nor final places; the one is only a fragment of wisdom and the other only a fraction of the means of understanding. Literary criticism is not a science—though it may be the object of one; and to try to make it one is to turn it upside down. Right side up, Mr. Richards' contribution shrinks in weight and dominion but remains intact and preserves its importance. We may conclude that it was the newness of his view that led him to exaggerate it, and we ought to add the probability that had he not exaggerated it we should never have seen either that it was new or valuable at all.

From another point of view than that of literary criticism, and as a contribution to a psychological theory of knowledge, Mr. Richards' work is not heretical, but is integral and integrating, and especially when it incorporates poetry into its procedure; but from our point of view the heresy is profound—and is far more distorting than the heresies of Santayana, Brooks, and Hicks, which carry with them obviously the impetus for their correction. Because it is possible to apply scientific methods to the language of poetry, and because scientific methods engross their subject matter, Mr. Richards places the whole burden of criticism in the application of a scientific approach, and asserts it to be an implement

for the judgment of poetry. Actually, it can handle only the language and its words and cannot touch—except by assertion—the imaginative product of the words which is poetry: which is the object revealed or elucidated by criticism. Criticism must be concerned, first and last—whatever comes between—with the poem as it is read and as what it represents is felt. As no amount of physics and physiology can explain the *feeling* of things seen as green or even certify their existence, so no amount of linguistic analysis can explain the *feeling* or existence of a poem. Yet the physics in the one case and the linguistics in the other may be useful both to the poet and the reader. It may be useful, for example, in extracting facts of meaning from a poem, to show that, whether the poet was aware of it or not, the semantic history of a word was so and so; but only if the semantics can be resolved into the ambiguities and precisions created by the poem. Similarly with any branch of linguistics; and similarly with the applications of psychology—Mr. Richards' other emphasis. No statistical description can either explain or demean a poem unless the description is translated back to the imaginative apprehension or feeling which must have taken place without it. The light of science is parallel or in the background where feeling or meaning is concerned. The Oedipus complex does not explain *Oedipus Rex*; not that Mr. Richards would think it did. Otherwise he could not believe that "poetry is the supreme use of language" and more, could not convey in his comments on T. S. Eliot's *Ash Wednesday* the actuality of his belief that poetry is the supreme use.

It is the interest and fascination of Mr. Richards' work in reference to different levels of sensibility, including the poetic, that has given him both a wide and a penetrating influence. No literary critic can escape his influence; an influence that stimulates the mind as much as anything by showing the sheer excitement as well as profundity of the problems of language—many of which he has himself made genuine problems, at least for the readers of poetry: an influence, obviously, worth deliberately incorporating by reducing it to one's own size and needs. In T. S. Eliot the influence is conspicuous if slight. Mr. Kenneth Burke is considerably indebted, partly directly to Mr. Richards, partly to the influences which acted upon Mr. Richards (as Bentham's theory of Fictions) and partly to the frame of mind which helped mold them both. But Mr. Burke is clearly a different person—and different from anyone writing today; and the virtues, the defects, and the élan of his criticism are his own.

Some years ago, when Mr. Burke was an animating influence on the staff of *The Dial,* Miss Marianne Moore published a poem in that magazine called "Picking and Choosing" which contained the following lines:

> and Burke is a
> psychologist—of acute and racoon-
> like curiosity. *Summa diligentia*
> to the humbug, whose name is so amusing—very young
> and ve-
> ry rushed, Caesar crossed the Alps on the "top of a
> *diligence.*" We are not daft about the meaning but this familiarity
> with wrong meanings puzzles one.

In the index of Miss Moore's *Observations,* we find under Burke that the reference is to Edmund, but it is really to Kenneth just the same. There is no acuter curiosity than Mr. Burke's engaged in associating the meanings, right and wrong, of the business of literature with the business of life and vice versa. No one has a greater awareness—not even Mr. Richards—of the important part wrong meanings play in establishing the consistency of right ones. The writer of whom he reminds us, for the buoyancy and sheer remarkableness of his speculations, is Charles Santiago Saunders Peirce; one is enlivened by them without any *necessary* reference to their truth; hence they have truth for their own purposes, that it, for their own uses. Into what these purposes or uses are it is our present business to inquire.

As Mr. Richards in fact uses literature as a springboard or source for scientific method of a philosophy of value, Mr. Burke uses literature, not only as a springboard but also as a resort or home, for philosophy or psychology of moral possibility. Literature is the hold-all and the persuasive form for the patterns of possibility. In literature we see unique possibilities enacted, actualized, and in the moral and psychological philosophies we see the types of possibility generalized, see their abstracted, convertible forms. In some literature, and in some aspects of most literature of either great magnitude or great possibility, we see, so to speak, the enactment or dramatic representation of the type or patterns. Thus Mr. Burke can make a thrilling intellectual pursuit of the subintelligent writing of Erskine Caldwell: where he shows that Caldwell gains a great effect of humanity by putting in *none himself*, appealing to the reader's common stock: *i.e.*, what is called for so desperately by the pattern of the story must needs be generously supplied. Exactly as thrilling is his demonstration of the great emotional rôle of the outsider as played in the supremely intelligent works of Thomas Mann and André Gide. His common illustrations of the pervasive spread of symbolic pattern are drawn from Shakespeare and from the type of the popular or pulp press. I think that on the whole his method could be applied with equal fruitfulness to Shakespeare, Dashiell Hammett, or Marie Corelli; as indeed he does apply it with equal force both to the field of anarchic private morals and to the outline of a secular conversion to Communism—as in, respectively, *Toward a Better Life* and *Permanence and Change*.

The real harvest that we barn from Mr. Burke's writings is his presentation of the types of ways the mind works in the written word. He is more interested in the psychological means of the meaning, and how it might mean (and often really does) something else, than in the meaning itself. Like Mr. Richards, but for another purpose, he is engaged largely in the meaning of meaning, and is therefore much bound up with considerations of language, but on the plane of emotional and intellectual patterns rather than on the emotional plane; which is why his essays deal with literature (or other writings) as it dramatizes or unfolds character (a character is a pattern of emotions and notions) rather than with lyric or meditative poetry which is Mr. Richards' field. So we find language containing felt character as well as felt co-ordination. The representation of character, and of aspiration and symbol, must always be rhetorical; and therefore we find that for Mr. Burke the rightly rhetorical is the profoundly hortatory. Thus literature may be seen as an inexhaustible reservoir of moral or character philosophies in action.

It is the technique of such philosophies that Mr. Burke explores, as he pursues it through curiosities of development and conversion and duplicity; it is the technique of the notions that may be put into or taken out of literature, but it is only a part of the technique of literature itself. The final reference is to the psychological and moral possibilities of the mind, and these certainly do not exhaust the technique or the reality of literature. The reality in literature is an object of contemplation and of feeling, like the reality of a picture or a cathedral, not a route of speculation. If we remember this and make the appropriate reductions here as elsewhere, Mr. Burke's essays become as pertinent to literary criticism as they are to the general ethical play of the mind. Otherwise they become too much a methodology for its own sake on the one hand, and too much a philosophy at one remove on the other. A man writes as he can; but those who use his writings have the further reponsibility of redefining their scope, an operation (of which Mr. Burke is a master) which alone uses them to the full.

It is in relation to these examples which I have so unjustly held up of the philosophical, the sociological, or psychological approaches to criticism that I wish to examine an example of what composes, after all, the great bulk of serious writings about literature: a work of literary scholarship. Upon scholarship all other forms of literary criticism depend, so long as they are criticism, in much the same way that architecture depends on engineering. The great editors of the last century—men such as Dyce and Skeat and Gifford and Furness

—performed work as valuable to the use of literature, and with far less complement of harm, as men like Hazlitt and Arnold and Pater. Scholarship, being bent on the collection, arrangement, and scrutiny of facts, has the positive advantage over other forms of criticism that it is a co-operative labor, and may be completed and corrected by subsequent scholars; and it has the negative advantage that it is not bound to investigate the mysteries of meaning or to connect literature with other departments of life—it has only to furnish the factual materials for such investigations and connections. It is not surprising to find that the great scholars are sometimes good critics, though usually in restricted fields; and it is a fact, on the other hand, that the great critics are themselves either good scholars or know how to take great advantage of scholarship. Perhaps we may put it that for the most part dead critics remain alive in us to the extent that they form part of our scholarship. It is Dr. Johnson's statements of fact that we preserve of him as a critic; his opinions have long since become a part of that imaginative structure, his personality. A last fact about scholarship is this, that so far as its conclusions are sound they are subject to use and digestion not debate by those outside the fold. And of bad scholarship as of bad criticism we have only to find means to minimize what we cannot destroy.

It is difficult to find an example of scholarship pure and simple, of high character, which can be made to seem relevant to the discussion in hand. What I want is to bring into the discussion the omnipresence of scholarship as a background and its immediate and necessary availability to every other mode of approach. What I want is almost anonymous. Failing that, I choose S. Foster

Damon's *William Blake* (as I might have taken J. L. Lowes' *Road to Xanadu*) which, because of its special subject matter, brings its scholarship a little nearer the terms of discussion than a Shakespeare commentary would have done. The scholar's major problem with Blake happened to be one which many scholars could not handle, some refused to see, and some fumbled. A great part of Blake's meaning is not open to ordinarily well-instructed readers, but must be brought out by the detailed solution of something very like an enormous and enormously complicated acrostic puzzle. Not only earnest scrutiny of the poems as printed, but also a study of Blake's reading, a reconstruction of habits of thought, and an industrious piecing together into a consistent key of thousands of clues throughout the work, were necessary before many even of the simplest appearing poems could be explained. It is one thing to explain a mystical poet, like Crashaw, who was attached to a recognized church, and difficult enough; but it is a far more difficult thing to explain a mystical poet like Blake, who was so much an eclectic in his sources that his mystery as well as his apprehension of it was practically his own. All Mr. Damon had to go on besides the texts, and the small body of previous scholarship that was pertinent, were the general outlines of insight to which all mystics apparently adhere. The only explanation would be in the facts of what Blake meant to mean when he habitually said one thing in order to hide and enhance another; and in order to be convincing—poetry being what it is—the facts adduced had to be self-evident. It is not a question here whether the mystery enlightened was worth it. The result for emphasis is that Mr. Damon made Blake exactly what he seemed least to be, perhaps the most intellectually consistent of the greater poets in English. Since the chief weapons used are the extended facts of scholarship, the picture Mr. Damon produced cannot be destroyed even though later and other scholarship modifies, re-arranges, or adds to it with different or other facts. The only suspicion that might attach is that the picture is too consistent and that the facts are made to tell too much, and direct, but instructed, apprehension not enough.

My point about Mr. Damon's work is typical and double. First, that the same sort of work, the adduction of ultimately self-evident facts, can be done and must be done in other kinds of poetry than Blake's. Blake is merely an extreme and obvious example of an unusually difficult poet who hid his facts on purpose. The work must be done to the appropriate degree of digging out the facts in all orders of poetry—and especially perhaps in contemporary poetry, where we tend to let the work go either because it seems too easy or because it seems supererogatory. Self-evident facts are paradoxically the hardest to come by; they are not evident till they are seen; yet the meaning of a poem—the part of it which is intellectually formulable—must invariably depend on this order of facts, the facts about the meanings of the elements aside from their final meaning in combination. The rest of the poem, what it is, what it shows, its final value as a created emotion, its meanings, if you like, *as* a poem, cannot in the more serious orders of poetry develop itself to the full without this factual or intellectual meaning to show the way. The other point is already made, and has been made before in this essay, but it may still be emphasized. Although the scholarly account is indispensable it does not tell the whole story. It is only the basis and perhaps

ultimately the residue of all the other stories. But it must be seen to first.

My own approach, such as it is, and if it can be named, does not tell the whole story either; the reader is conscientiously left with the poem, with the real work yet to do; and I wish to advance it—as indeed I have been advancing it *seriatim* —only in connection with the reduced and compensated approaches I have laid out; and I expect, too, that if my approach is used at all it will require its own reduction as well as its compensations. Which is why this essay has taken its present form, preferring for once, in the realm of theory and apologetics, the implicit to the explicit statement. It is, I suppose, an approach to literary criticism—to the discourse of an amateur— primarily through the technique, in the widest sense of that word, of the examples handled; technique on the plane of words and even of linguistics in Mr. Richards' sense, but also technique on the plane of intellectual and emotional patterns in Mr. Burke's sense, and technique, too, in that there is a technique of securing and arranging and representing a fundamental view of life. The advantage of the technical approach is I think double. It readily admits other approaches and is anxious to be complemented by them. Furthermore, in a sense, it is able to incorporate the technical aspect, which always exists, of what is secured by other approaches—as I have argued elsewhere that so unpromising a matter as T. S. Eliot's religious convictions may be profitably considered as a dominant element in his technique of revealing the actual. The second advantage of the technical approach is a consequence of the first; it treats of nothing in literature except in its capacity of reduction to literary fact, which is where it resembles scholarship, only passing beyond it in that its facts are usually further into the heart of the literature than the facts of most scholarship. Aristotle, curiously, is here the type and master; as the *Poetics* is nothing but a collection and explanation of the facts of Greek poetry, it is the factual aspect that is invariably produced. The rest of the labor is in the effort to find understandable terms to fit the composition of the facts. After all, it is only the facts about a poem, a play, a novel, that can be reduced to tractable form, talked about, and examined; the rest is the product of the facts, from the technical point of view, and not a product but the thing itself from its own point of view. The rest, whatever it is, can only be known, not talked about.

But facts are not simple or easy to come at; not all the facts will appear to one mind, and the same facts appear differently in the light of different minds. No attention is undivided, no single approach sufficient, no predilection guaranteed, when facts or what their arrangements create are in question. In short, for the arts, *mere* technical scrutiny of any order is not enough without the direct apprehension—which may come first or last—to which all scrutinies that show facts contribute.

It may be that there are principles that cover both the direct apprehension and the labor of providing modes for the understanding of the expressive arts. If so, they are Socratic and found within, and subject to the fundamental skepticism as in Montaigne. There must be seeds, let us say—seeds, germs, beginning forms upon which I can rely and to which I resort. When I use a word, an image, a notion, there must be in its small nodular apparent form, as in the peas I am testing on my desk, at least prophetically, the whole future growth, the whole harvested life; and not rhetorically, nor in a formula, but stubbornly, pervasively, heart-hidden,

materially, in both the anterior and the eventual prospect as well as in the small handled form of the nub. What is it, what are they, these seeds of understanding? And if I know, are they logical? Do they take the processional form of the words I use? Or do they take a form like that of the silver backing a glass, a dark that enholds all brightness? Is every metaphor—and the assertion of understanding is our great metaphor—mixed by the necessity of its intention? What is the mixture of a word, an image, a notion?

The mixture, if I may start a hare so late, the mixture, even in the fresh use of an old word, is made in the preconscious, and is by hypothesis unascertainable. But let us not use hypotheses, let us not desire to ascertain. By intuition we adventure in the pre-conscious; and there, where the adventure is, there is no need or suspicion of certainty or meaning; there is the living, expanding, *prescient* substance without the tags and handles of conscious form. Art is the looking-glass of the pre-conscious, and when it is deepest seems to participate in it sensibly. Or, better, for purposes of criticism, our sensibility resumes the division of the senses and faculties at the same time that it preens itself into conscious form. Criticism may have as an object the establishment and evaluation (comparison and analysis) of the modes of making the pre-conscious *consciously* available.

But this emphasis upon the pre-conscious need not be insisted on; once recognized it may be tacitly assumed, and the effort of the mind will be, as it were, restored to its own plane—only a little sensitive to the tap-roots below. On its own plane—that is, the plane where almost everything is taken for granted in order to assume adequate implementation in handling what is taken for granted by others; where because you can list the items of your bewilderment and can move from one to another you assert that the achievement of motion is the experience of order; where, therefore, you must adopt always an attitude of provisional skepticism; where, imperatively, you must scrutinize and scrutinize until you have revealed, if it is there, the inscrutable divination, or, if it is not, the void of personal ambition; where, finally, you must stop short only when you have, with all the facts you can muster, indicated, surrounded, detached, somehow found the way demonstrably to get at, in pretty conscious terms which others may use, the substance of your chosen case.

THE WORLD OF HAMLET
Maynard Mack*

In an example (and model) of technical or philological criticism, Maynard Mack traces the "mysteriousness" of *Hamlet* through dialogue and patterns of imagery. He connects this quality of mysteriousness with the theme of "seeming"—the difference between appearance and reality—and relates it to the images of disease and madness.

My subject is the world of *Hamlet*. I do not of course mean Denmark, except as Denmark is given a body by the play; and I do not mean Elizabethan England, though this is necessarily close behind the scenes. I mean simply the imaginative environment that the play asks us to enter when we read it or go to see it.

Great plays, as we know, do present us with something that can be called a world, a microcosm—a world like our own in being made of people, actions, situations, thoughts, feelings and much more, but unlike our own in being perfectly, or almost perfectly, significant and coherent. In a play's world, each part implies the other parts, and each lives, each means, with the life and meaning of the rest.

This is the reason, as we also know, that the worlds of great plays greatly

* The essay is reprinted from *The Yale Review*, XLI (1952), by permission of *The Yale Review*. Copyright 1952 by Yale University Press.

differ. Othello in Hamlet's position, we sometimes say, would have no problem; but what we are really saying is that Othello in Hamlet's position would not exist. The conception we have of Othello is a function of the characters who help define him, Desdemona, honest Iago, Cassio, and the rest; of his history of travel and war; of a great storm that divides his ship from Cassio's, and a handkerchief; of a quiet night in Venice broken by cries about an old black ram; of a quiet night in Cyprus broken by sword-play; of a quiet bedroom where a woman goes to bed in her wedding sheets and a man comes in with a light to put out the light; and above all, of a language, a language with many voices in it, gentle, rasping, querulous, or foul, but all counterpointing the one great voice:

Put up your bright swords, for the dew will
   rust them.

O thou weed
Who art so lovely fair and smell'st so sweet
That the sense aches at thee. . . .

       Yet I'll not shed her blood
Nor scar that whiter skin of hers than
   snow,
And smooth as monumental alabaster.

       I pray you in your letters.
When you shall these unlucky deeds relate.
Speak of me as I am; nothing extenuate.
Nor set down aught in malice; then must
   you speak
Of one that loved not wisely but too well;
Of one not easily jealous, but being
   wrought,
Perplex'd in th' extreme; of one whose
   hand.
Like the base Indian, threw a pearl away
Richer than all his tribe. . . .

Without his particular world of voices, persons, events, the world that both expresses and contains him, Othello is unimaginable. And so, I think, are Antony, King Lear, Macbeth—and Hamlet. We come back then to Hamlet's world, of all the tragic worlds that Shakespeare made, easily the most various and brilliant, the most elusive. It is with no thought of doing justice to it that I have singled out three of its attributes for comment. I know too well, if I may echo a sentiment of Mr. E. M. W. Tillyard's, that no one is likely to accept another man's reading of *Hamlet*, that anyone who tries to throw light on one part of the play usually throws the rest into deeper shadow, and that what I have to say leaves out many problems— to mention only one, the knotty problem of the text. All I would say in defense of the materials I have chosen is that they seem to me interesting, close to the root of the matter even if we continue to differ about what the root of the matter is, and explanatory, in a modest way, of this play's peculiar hold on everyone's

imagination, its almost mythic status, one might say, as a paradigm of the life of man.

The first attribute that impresses us, I think, is mysteriousness. We often hear it said, perhaps with truth, that every great work of art has a mystery at the heart; but the mystery of *Hamlet* is something else. We feel its presence in the numberless explanations that have been brought forward for Hamlet's delay, his madness, his ghost, his treatment of Polonius, or Ophelia, or his mother; and in the controversies that still go on about whether the play is "undoubtedly a failure" (Eliot's phrase) or one of the greatest artistic triumphs; whether, if it is a triumph, it belongs to the highest order of tragedy; whether, if it is such a tragedy, its hero is to be taken as a man of exquisite moral sensibility (Bradley's view) or an egomaniac (Madariaga's view).

Doubtless there have been more of these controversies and explanations than the play requires; for in Hamlet, to paraphrase a remark of Falstaff's, we have a character who is not only mad in himself but a cause that madness is in the rest of us. Still, the very existence of so many theories and counter-theories, many of them formulated by sober heads, gives food for thought. *Hamlet* seems to lie closer to the illogical logic of life than Shakespeare's other tragedies. And while the causes of this situation may be sought by saying that Shakespeare revised the play so often that eventually the motivations were smudged over, or that the original old play has been here or there imperfectly digested, or that the problems of Hamlet lay so close to Shakespeare's heart that he could not quite distance them in the formal terms of art, we have still as critics to deal with effects, not causes. If I may quote again from Mr. Tillyard, the play's very lack of a rigorous type of causal logic seems to be a part of its point.

Moreover, the matter goes deeper than this. Hamlet's world is preëminently in the interrogative mood. It reverberates with questions, anguished, meditative, alarmed. There are questions that in this play, to an extent I think unparalleled in any other, mark the phases and even the nuances of the action, helping to establish its peculiar baffled tone. There are other questions whose interrogations, innocent at first glance, are subsequently seen to have reached beyond their contexts and to point towards some pervasive inscrutability in Hamlet's world as a whole. Such is that tense series of challenges with which the tragedy begins: Bernardo's of Francisco, "Who's there?" Francisco's of Horatio and Marcellus, "Who is there?" Horatio's of the ghost, "What art thou . . . ?" And then there are the famous questions. In them the interrogations seem to point not only beyond the context but beyond the play, out of Hamlet's predicaments into everyone's: "What a piece of work is a man! . . . And yet to me what is this quintessence of dust?" "To be, or not to be, that is the question." "Get thee to a nunnery. Why wouldst thou be a breeder of sinners?" "I am very proud, revengeful, ambitious, with more offences at my beck than I have thoughts to put them in, imagination to give them shape, or time to act them in. What should such fellows as I do crawling between earth and heaven?" "Dost thou think Alexander look'd o' this fashion i' th' earth? . . . And smelt so?"

Further, Hamlet's world is a world of riddles. The hero's own language is often riddling, as the critics have pointed out. When he puns, his puns have receding depths in them, like the one which constitutes his first speech: "A little more than kin, and less than kind." His ut-

terances in madness, even if wild and whirling, are simultaneously, as Polonius discovers, pregnant: "Do you know me, my lord?" "Excellent well. You are a fishmonger." Even the madness itself is riddling: How much is real? How much is feigned? What does it mean? Sane or mad, Hamlet's mind plays restlessly about his world, turning up one riddle upon another. The riddle of character, for example, and how it is that in a man whose virtues else are "pure as grace," some vicious mole of nature, some "dram of eale," can "all the noble substance oft adulter." Or the riddle of the player's art, and how a man can so project himself into a fiction, a dream of passion, that he can weep for Hecuba. Or the riddle of action: how we may think too little—"What to ourselves in passion we propose," says the player-king, "The passion ending, doth the purpose lose"; and again, how we may think too much: "Thus conscience does make cowards of us all, And thus the native hue of resolution Is sicklied o'er with the pale cast of thought."

There are also more immediate riddles. His mother—how could she "on this fair mountain leave to feed, And batten on this moor?" The ghost—which may be a devil, for "the de'il hath power T' assume a pleasing shape." Ophelia—what does her behavior to him mean? Surprising her in her closet, he falls to such perusal of her face as he would draw it. Even the king at his prayers is a riddle. Will a revenge that takes him in the purging of his soul be vengeance, or hire and salary? As for himself, Hamlet realizes, he is the greatest riddle of all— a mystery, he warns Rosencrantz and Guildenstern, from which he will not have the heart plucked out. He cannot tell why he has of late lost all his mirth, forgone all custom of exercises. Still less can he tell why he delays: "I do not know Why yet I live to say, 'This thing's to do,' Sith I have cause and will and strength and means To do 't."

Thus the mysteriousness of Hamlet's world is of a piece. It is not simply a matter of missing motivations, to be expunged if only we could find the perfect clue. It is built in. It is evidently an important part of what the play wishes to say to us. And it is certainly an element that the play thrusts upon us from the opening word. Everyone, I think, recalls the mysteriousness of that first scene. The cold middle of the night on the castle platform, the muffled sentries, the uneasy atmosphere of apprehension, the challenges leaping out of the dark, the questions that follow the challenges, feeling out the darkness, searching for identities, for relations, for assurance. "Bernardo?" "Have you had quiet guard?" "Who hath reliev'd you?" "What, is Horatio there?" "What, has this thing appear'd again tonight?" "Looks 'a not like the king?" "How now, Horatio! . . . Is not this something more than fantasy? What think you on 't?" "Is it not like the king?" "Why this same strict and most observant watch. . . ?" "Shall I strike at it with my partisan?" "Do you consent we shall acquaint [young Hamlet] with it?"

We need not be surprised that critics and playgoers alike have been tempted to see in this an evocation not simply of Hamlet's world but of their own. Man in his aspect of bafflement, moving in darkness on a rampart between two worlds, unable to reject, or quite accept, the one that, when he faces it, "to-shakes" his disposition with thoughts beyond the reaches of his soul—comforting himself with hints and guesses. We hear these hints and guesses whispering through the darkness as the several watchers speak. "At least, the whisper goes so," says one. "I think it be no other but e'en so," says

another. "I have heard" that on the crowing of the cock "Th' extravagant and erring spirit hies To his confine," says a third. "Some say" at Christmas time "this bird of dawning" sings all night, "And then, they say, no spirit dare stir abroad." "So have I heard," says the first, "and do in part believe it." However we choose to take the scene, it is clear that it creates a world where uncertainties are of the essence.

Meantime, such is Shakespeare's economy, a second attribute of Hamlet's world has been put before us. This is the problematic nature of reality and the relation of reality to appearance. The play begins with an appearance, an "apparition," to use Marcellus's term—the ghost. And the ghost is somehow real, indeed the vehicle of realities. Through its revelation, the glittering surface of Claudius's court is pierced, and Hamlet comes to know, and we do, that the king is not only hateful to him but the murderer of his father, that his mother is guilty of adultery as well as incest. Yet there is a dilemma in the revelation. For possibly the apparition *is* an apparition, a devil who has assumed his father's shape.

This dilemma, once established, recurs on every hand. From the court's point of view, there is Hamlet's madness. Polonius investigates and gets some strange advice about his daughter: "Conception is a blessing, but as your daughter may conceive, friend, look to 't." Rosencrantz and Guildenstern investigate and get the strange confidence that "Man delights not me; no, nor woman neither." Ophelia is "loosed" to Hamlet (Polonius's vulgar word), while Polonius and the king hide behind the arras; and what they hear is a strange indictment of human nature, and a riddling threat: "Those that are married already, all but one, shall live."

On the other hand, from Hamlet's

point of view, there is Ophelia. Kneeling here at her prayers, she seems the image of innocence and devotion. Yet she is of the sex for whom he has already found the name Frailty, and she is also, as he seems either madly or sanely to divine, a decoy in a trick. The famous cry—"Get thee to a nunnery"—shows the anguish of his uncertainty. If Ophelia is what she seems, this dirty-minded world of murder, incest, lust, adultery, is no place for her. Were she "as chaste as ice, as pure as snow," she could not escape its calumny. And if she is not what she seems, then a nunnery in its other sense of brothel is relevant to her. In the scene that follows he treats her as if she were indeed an inmate of a brothel.

Likewise, from Hamlet's point of view, there is the enigma of the king. If the ghost is *only* an appearance, then possibly the king's appearance is reality. He must try it further. By means of a second and different kind of "apparition," the play within the play, he does so. But then, immediately after, he stumbles on the king at prayer. This appearance has a relish of salvation in it. If the king dies now, his soul may yet be saved. Yet actually, as we know, the king's efforts to come to terms with heaven have been unavailing; his words fly up, his thoughts remain below. If Hamlet means the conventional revenger's reasons that he gives for sparing Claudius, it was the perfect moment not to spare him—when the sinner was acknowledging his guilt, yet unrepentant. The perfect moment, but it was hidden, like so much else in the play, behind an arras.

There are two arrases in his mother's room. Hamlet thrusts his sword through one of them. Now at last he has got to the heart of the evil, or so he thinks. But now it is the wrong man; now he himself is a murderer. The other arras he stabs through with his words—like dag-

gers, says the queen. He makes her shrink under the contrast he points between her present husband and his father. But as the play now stands (matters are somewhat clearer in the bad Quarto), it is hard to be sure how far the queen grasps the fact that her second husband is the murderer of her first. And it is hard to say what may be signified by her inability to see the ghost, who now for the last time appears. In one sense at least, the ghost is the supreme reality, representative of the hidden ultimate power, in Bradley's terms—witnessing from beyond the grave against this hollow world. Yet the man who is capable of seeing through to this reality, the queen thinks is mad. "To whom do you speak this?" she cries to her son. "Do you see nothing there?" he asks, incredulous. And she replies: "Nothing at all; yet all that is I see." Here certainly we have the imperturbable self-confidence of the worldly world, its layers on layers of habituation, so that when the reality is before its very eyes it cannot detect its presence.

Like mystery, this problem of reality is central to the play and written deep into its idiom. Shakespeare's favorite terms in *Hamlet* are words of ordinary usage that pose the question of appearances in a fundamental form. "Apparition" I have already mentioned. Another term is "seems." When we say, as Ophelia says of Hamlet leaving her closet, "He seem'd to find his way without his eyes," we mean one thing. When we say, as Hamlet says to his mother in the first court-scene, "Seems, Madam! . . . I know not 'seems,'" we mean another. And when we say, as Hamlet says to Horatio before the play within the play, "And after, we will both our judgments join In censure of his seeming," we mean both at once. The ambiguities of "seem" coil and uncoil throughout this play, and over against them is set the idea of "seeing."

So Hamlet challenges the king in his triumphant letter announcing his return to Denmark: "Tomorrow shall I beg leave to see your kingly eyes." Yet "seeing" itself can be ambiguous, as we recognize from Hamlet's uncertainty about the ghost; or from that statement of his mother's already quoted: "Nothing at all; yet all that is I see."

Another term of like importance is "assume." What we assume may be what we are not: "The de'il hath power T' assume a pleasing shape." But it may be what we are: "If it assume my noble father's person, I'll speak to it." And it may be what we are not yet, but would become; thus Hamlet advises his mother, "Assume a virtue, if you have it not." The perplexity in the word points to a real perplexity in Hamlet's and our own experience. We assume our habits—and habits are like costumes, as the word implies: "My father in his habit as he liv'd!" Yet these habits become ourselves in time: "That monster, custom, who all sense doth eat Of habits evil, is angel yet in this, That to the use of actions fair and good He likewise gives a frock or livery That aptly is put on."

Two other terms I wish to instance are "put on" and "shape." The shape of something is the form under which we are accustomed to apprehend it: "Do you see yonder cloud that's almost in shape of a camel?" But a shape may also be a disguise—even, in Shakespeare's time, an actor's costume or an actor's role. This is the meaning when the king says to Laertes as they lay the plot against Hamlet's life: "Weigh what convenience both of time and means May fit us to our shape." "Put on" supplies an analogous ambiguity. Shakespeare's mind seems to worry this phrase in the play much as Hamlet's mind worries the problem of acting in a world of surfaces, or the king's mind worries the meaning of Hamlet's

transformation. Hamlet has put an antic disposition on, that the king knows. But what does "put on" mean? A mask, or a frock or livery—our "habit"? The king is left guessing, and so are we.

What is found in the play's key terms is also found in its imagery. Miss Spurgeon has called attention to a pattern of disease images in *Hamlet,* to which I shall return. But the play has other patterns equally striking. One of these, as my earlier quotations hint, is based on clothes. In the world of surfaces to which Shakespeare exposes us in *Hamlet,* clothes are naturally a factor of importance. "The apparel oft proclaims the man," Polonius assures Laertes, cataloguing maxims in the young man's ear as he is about to leave for Paris. Oft, but not always. And so he sends his man Reynaldo to look into Laertes' life there —even, if need be, to put a false dress of accusation upon his son ("What forgeries you please"), the better by indirections to find directions out. On the same grounds, he takes Hamlet's vows to Ophelia as false apparel. They are bawds, he tells her—or if we do not like Theobald's emendation, they are bonds —in masquerade, "Not of that dye which their investments show, But mere implorators of unholy suits."

This breach between the outer and the inner stirs no special emotion in Polonius, because he is always either behind an arras or prying into one, but it shakes Hamlet to the core. Here so recently was his mother in her widow's weeds, the tears still flushing in her galled eyes; yet now within a month, a little month, before even her funeral shoes are old, she has married with his uncle. Her mourning was all clothes. Not so his own, he bitterly replies, when she asks him to cast his "nighted color off." "'Tis not alone my inky cloak, good mother"—and not alone, he adds, the sighs, the tears, the dejected havior of the visage—"that can denote me truly."

> These indeed seem,
> For they are actions that a man might play;
> But I have that within which passes show;
> These but the trappings and the suits of woe.

What we must not overlook here is Hamlet's visible attire, giving the verbal imagery a theatrical extension. Hamlet's apparel now is his inky cloak, mark of his grief for his father, mark also of his character as a man of melancholy, mark possibly too of his being one in whom appearance and reality are attuned. Later, in his madness, with his mind disordered, he will wear his costume in a corresponding disarray, the disarray that Ophelia describes so vividly to Polonius and that producers of the play rarely give sufficient heed to: "Lord Hamlet with his doublet all unbrac'd, No hat upon his head; his stockings foul'd, Ungarter'd, and down-gyved to his ankle." Here the only question will be, as with the madness itself, how much is studied, how much is real. Still later, by a third costume, the simple traveler's garb in which we find him new come from shipboard, Shakespeare will show us that we have a third aspect of the man.

A second pattern of imagery springs from terms of painting: the paints, the colorings, the varnishes that may either conceal, or, as in the painter's art, reveal. Art in Claudius conceals. "The harlot's cheek," he tells us in his one aside, "beautied with plastering art, Is not more ugly to the thing that helps it Than is my deed to my most painted word." Art in Ophelia, loosed to Hamlet in the episode already noticed to which this speech of the king's is prelude, is more complex. She looks so beautiful—"the celestial, and my soul's idol, the most beautified

Ophelia," Hamlet has called her in his love letter. But now, what does beautified mean? Perfected with all the innocent beauties of a lovely woman? Or "beautified" like the harlot's cheek? "I have heard of your paintings too, well enough. God hath given you one face, and you make yourselves another."

Yet art, differently used, may serve the truth. By using an "image" (his own word) of a murder done in Vienna, Hamlet cuts through to the king's guilt; holds "as 'twere, the mirror up to nature," shows "virtue her own feature, scorn her own image, and the very age and body of the time"—which is out of joint—"his form and pressure." Something similar he does again in his mother's bedroom, painting for her in words "the rank sweat of an enseamed bed," making her recoil in horror from his "counterfeit presentment of two brothers," and holding, if we may trust a stage tradition, his father's picture beside his uncle's. Here again the verbal imagery is realized visually on the stage.

The most pervasive of Shakespeare's image patterns in this play, however, is the pattern evolved around the three words, show, act, play. "Show" seems to be Shakespeare's unifying image in Hamlet. Through it he pulls together and exhibits in a single focus much of the diverse material in his play. The ideas of seeming, assuming, and putting on; the images of clothing, painting, mirroring; the episode of the dumb show and the play within the play; the characters of Polonius, Laertes, Ophelia, Claudius, Gertrude, Rosencrantz and Guildenstern, Hamlet himself—all these at one time or another, and usually more than once, are drawn into the range of implications flung round the play by "show."

"Act," on the other hand, I take to be the play's radical metaphor. It distills the various perplexities about the character of reality into a residual perplexity about the character of an act. What, this play asks again and again, is an act? What is its relation to the inner act, the intent? "If I drown myself wittingly," says the clown in the graveyard, "it argues an act, and an act hath three branches; it is to act, to do, to perform." Or again, the play asks, how does action relate to passion, that "laps'd in time and passion" I can let "go by Th' important acting of your dread command"; and to thought, which can so sickly o'er the native hue of resolution that "enterprises of great pitch and moment With this regard their currents turn awry, And lose the name of action"; and to words, which are not acts, and so we dare not be content to unpack our hearts with them, and yet are acts of a sort, for we may speak daggers though we use none. Or still again, how does an act (a deed) relate to an act (a pretense)? For an action may be nothing but pretense. So Polonius readying Ophelia for the interview with Hamlet, with "pious action," as he phrases it, "sugar[s] o'er The devil himself." Or it may not be a pretense, yet not what it appears. So Hamlet spares the king, finding him in an act that has some "relish of salvation in 't." Or it may be a pretense that is also the first foothold of a new reality, as when we assume a virtue though we have it not. Or it may be a pretense that is actually a mirroring of reality, like the play within the play, or the tragedy of *Hamlet*.

To this network of implications, the third term, play, adds an additional dimension. "Play" is a more precise word, in Elizabethan parlance at least, for all the elements in *Hamlet* that pertain to the art of the theatre; and it extends their field of reference till we see that every major personage in the tragedy is a player in some sense, and every major episode a play. The court plays, Hamlet

plays, the players play, Rosencrantz and Guildenstern try to play on Hamlet, though they cannot play on his recorders —here we have an extension to a musical sense. And the final duel, by a further extension, becomes itself a play, in which everyone but Claudius and Laertes plays his role in ignorance: "The queen desires you to show some gentle entertainment to Laertes before you fall to play." "I . . . will this brother's wager frankly play." "Give him the cup."—"I'll play this bout first."

The full extension of this theme is best evidenced in the play within the play itself. Here, in the bodily presence of these traveling players, bringing with them the latest playhouse gossip out of London, we have suddenly a situation that tends to dissolve the normal barriers between the fictive and the real. For here on the stage before us is a play of false appearances in which an actor called the player-king is playing. But there is also on the stage, Claudius, another player-king, who is a spectator of this player. And there is on the stage, besides, a prince who is a spectator of both these player-kings and who plays with great intensity a player's role himself. And around these kings and that prince is a group of courtly spectators—Gertrude, Rosencrantz, Guildenstern, Polonius, and the rest—and they, as we have come to know, are players too. And lastly there are ourselves, an audience watching all these audiences who are also players. Where, it may suddenly occur to us to ask, does the playing end? Which *are* the guilty creatures sitting at a play? When is an act not an "act"?

The mysteriousness of Hamlet's world, while it pervades the tragedy, finds its point of greatest dramatic concentration in the first act, and its symbol in the first scene. The problems of appearance and reality also pervade the play as a whole, but come to a climax in Acts II and III, and possibly their best symbol is the play within the play. Our third attribute, though again it is one that crops out everywhere, reaches its full development in Acts IV and V. It is not easy to find an appropriate name for this attribute, but perhaps "mortality" will serve, if we remember to mean by mortality the heartache and the thousand natural shocks that flesh is heir to, not simply death.

The powerful sense of mortality in *Hamlet* is conveyed to us, I think, in three ways. First, there is the play's emphasis on human weakness, the instability of human purpose, the subjection of humanity to fortune—all that we might call the aspect of failure in man. Hamlet opens this theme in Act I, when he describes how from that single blemish, perhaps not even the victim's fault, a man's whole character may take corruption. Claudius dwells on it again, to an extent that goes far beyond the needs of the occasion, while engaged in seducing Laertes to step behind the arras of a seemer's world and dispose of Hamlet by a trick. Time qualifies everything, Claudius says, including love, including purpose. As for love—it has a "plurisy" in it and dies of its own too much. As for purpose—"That we would do, We should do when we would, for this 'would' changes, And hath abatements and delays as many As there are tongues, are hands, are accidents; And then this 'should' is like a spendthrift's sigh, That hurts by easing." The player-king, in his long speeches to his queen in the play within the play, sets the matter in a still darker light. She means these protestations of undying love, he knows, but our purposes depend on our memory, and our memory fades fast. Or else, he suggests, we propose something to ourselves in a condi-

tion of strong feeling, but then the feeling goes, and with it the resolve. Or else our fortunes change, he adds, and with these our loves: "The great man down, you mark his favorite flies." The subjection of human aims to fortune is a reiterated theme in *Hamlet*, as subsequently in *Lear*. Fortune is the harlot goddess in whose secret parts men like Rosencrantz and Guildenstern live and thrive; the strumpet who threw down Troy and Hecuba and Priam; the outrageous foe whose slings and arrows a man of principle must suffer or seek release in suicide. Horatio suffers them with composure: he is one of the blessed few "Whose blood and judgment are so well co-mingled. That they are not a pipe for fortune's finger To sound what stop she please." For Hamlet the task is of a greater difficulty.

Next, and intimately related to this matter of infirmity, is the emphasis on infection—the ulcer, the hidden abscess, "th' imposthume of much wealth and peace That inward breaks and shows no cause without Why the man dies." Miss Spurgeon, who was the first to call attention to this aspect of the play, has well remarked that so far as Shakespeare's pictorial imagination is concerned, the problem in *Hamlet* is not a problem of the will and reason, "of a mind too philosophical or a nature temperamentally unfitted to act quickly," nor even a problem of an individual at all. Rather, it is a condition—"a condition for which the individual himself is apparently not responsible, any more than the sick man is to blame for the infection which strikes and devours him, but which, nevertheless, in its course and development, impartially and relentlessly, annihilates him and others, innocent and guilty alike." "That," she adds, "is the tragedy of *Hamlet*, as it is perhaps the chief tragic mystery of life." This is a perceptive comment, for it reminds us that Hamlet's situation is mainly not of his own manufacture, as are the situations of Shakespeare's other tragic heroes. He has inherited it; he is "born to set it right."

We must not, however, neglect to add to this what another student of Shakespeare's imagery has noticed—that the infection in Denmark is presented alternatively as poison. Here, of course, responsibility is implied, for the poisoner of the play is Claudius. The juice he pours into the ear of the elder Hamlet is a combined poison and disease, a "leperous distilment" that curds "the thin and wholesome blood." From this fatal center, unwholesomeness spreads out till there is something rotten in all Denmark. Hamlet tells us that his "wit's diseased," the queen speaks of her "sick soul," the king is troubled by "the hectic" in his blood, Laertes meditates revenge to warm "the sickness in my heart," the people of the kingdom grow "muddied, Thick and unwholesome in their thoughts"; and even Ophelia's madness is said to be "the poison of deep grief." In the end, all save Ophelia die of that poison in a literal as well as figurative sense.

But the chief form in which the theme of mortality reaches us, it seems to me, is as a profound consciousness of loss. Hamlet's father expresses something of the kind when he tells Hamlet how his "[most] seeming-virtuous queen," betraying a love which "was of that dignity That it went hand in hand even with the vow I made to her in marriage," had chosen to "decline Upon a wretch whose natural gifts were poor To those of mine." "O Hamlet, what a falling off was there!" Ophelia expresses it again, on hearing Hamlet's denunciation of love and woman in the nunnery scene, which she takes to be the product of a disordered brain:

O what a noble mind is here o'erthrown!
The courtier's, soldier's, scholar's, eye, tongue, sword;
Th' expectancy and rose of the fair state,
The glass of fashion and the mould of form,
Th' observ'd of all observers, quite, quite down!

The passage invites us to remember that we have never actually seen such a Hamlet—that his mother's marriage has brought a falling off in him before we meet him. And then there is that further falling off, if I may call it so, when Ophelia too goes mad—"Divided from herself and her fair judgment, Without the which we are pictures, or mere beasts."

Time was, the play keeps reminding us, when Denmark was a different place. That was before Hamlet's mother took off "the rose From the fair forehead of an innocent love" and set a blister there. Hamlet then was still "Th' expectancy and rose of the fair state"; Ophelia, the "rose of May." For Denmark was a garden then, when his father ruled. There had been something heroic about his father—a king who met the threats to Denmark in open battle, fought with Norway, smote the sledded Polacks on the ice, slew the elder Fortinbras in an honorable trial of strength. There had been something godlike about his father too: "Hyperion's curls, the front of Jove himself, An eye like Mars . . . , A station like the herald Mercury." But, the ghost reveals, a serpent was in the garden, and "the serpent that did sting thy father's life Now wears his crown." The martial virtues are put by now. The threats to Denmark are attended to by policy, by agents working deviously for and through an uncle. The moral virtues are put by too. Hyperion's throne is occupied by "a vice of kings," "a king of shreds and patches"; Hyperion's bed, by a satyr, a paddock, a bat, a gib, a bloat king with reechy kisses. The garden is unweeded now, and "grows to seed; things rank and gross in nature Possess it merely." Even in himself he feels the taint, the taint of being his mother's son; and that other taint, from an earlier garden, of which he admonishes Ophelia: "Our virtue cannot so inoculate our old stock but we shall relish of it." "Why wouldst thou be a breeder of sinners?" "What should such fellows as I do crawling between earth and heaven?"

"Hamlet is painfully aware," says Professor Tillyard, "of the baffling human predicament between the angels and the beasts, between the glory of having been made in God's image and the incrimination of being descended from fallen Adam." To this we may add, I think, that Hamlet is more than aware of it; he exemplifies it; and it is for this reason that his problem appeals to us so powerfully as an image of our own.

Hamlet's problem, in its crudest form, is simply the problem of the avenger: he must carry out the injunction of the ghost and kill the king. But this problem, as I ventured to suggest at the outset, is presented in terms of a certain kind of world. The ghost's injunction to act becomes so inextricably bound up for Hamlet with the character of the world in which the action must be taken—its mysteriousness, its baffling appearances, its deep consciousness of infection, frailty, and loss—that he cannot come to terms with either without coming to terms with both.

When we first see him in the play, he is clearly a very young man, sensitive and idealistic, suffering the first shock of growing up. He has taken the garden at face value, we might say, supposing mankind to be only a little lower than the angels. Now in his mother's hasty and incestuous marriage, he discovers evidence of something else, something bestial—though even a beast, he thinks, would have mourned longer. Then comes the revelation of the ghost, bringing a second shock. Not so much because he now knows that his serpent-uncle killed his father; his prophetic soul had almost suspected this. Not entirely, even, because he knows now how far below the angels humanity has fallen in his mother, and how lust—these were the ghost's words—"though to a radiant angel link'd Will sate itself in a celestial bed, And prey on garbage." Rather, because he now sees everywhere, but especially in his own nature, the general taint, taking from life its meaning, from woman her integrity, from the will its strength, turning reason into madness. "Why wouldst thou be a breeder of sinners?" "What should such fellows as I do crawling between earth and heaven?" Hamlet is not the first young man to have felt the heavy and the weary weight of all this unintelligible world; and, like the others, he must come to terms with it.

The ghost's injunction to revenge unfolds a different facet of his problem. The young man growing up is not to be allowed simply to endure a rotten world, he must also act in it. Yet how to begin, among so many enigmatic surfaces? Even Claudius, whom he now knows to be the core of the ulcer, has a plausible exterior. And around Claudius, swathing the evil out of sight, he encounters all those other exteriors, as we have seen. Some of them already deeply infected beneath, like his mother. Some noble, but marked for infection, like Laertes. Some not particularly corrupt but infinitely corruptible, like Rosencrantz and Guildenstern; some mostly weak and foolish like Polonius and Osric. Some, like Ophelia, innocent, yet in their innocence still serving to "skin and film the ulcerous place."

And this is not all. The act required of

him, though retributive justice, is one that necessarily involves the doer in the general guilt. Not only because it involves a killing; but because to get at the world of seeming one sometimes has to use its weapons. He himself, before he finishes, has become a player, has put an antic disposition on, has killed a man—the wrong man—has helped drive Ophelia mad, and has sent two friends of his youth to death, mining below their mines, and hoisting the engineer with his own petard. He had never meant to dirty himself with these things, but from the moment of the ghost's challenge to act, this dirtying was inevitable. It is the condition of living at all in such a world. To quote Polonius, who knew that world so well, men become "a little soil'd i' th' working." Here is another matter with which Hamlet has to come to terms.

Human infirmity—all that I have discussed with reference to instability, infection, loss—supplies the problem with its third phase. Hamlet has not only to accept the mystery of man's condition between the angels and the brutes, and not only to act in a perplexing and soiling world. He has also to act within the human limits—"with shabby equipment always deteriorating," if I may adapt some phrases from Eliot's *East Coker*, "In the general mess of imprecision of feeling, Undisciplined squads of emotion." Hamlet is aware of that fine poise of body and mind, feeling and thought, that suits the action to the word, the word to the action; that acquires and begets a temperance in the very torrent, tempest, and whirlwind of passion; but he cannot at first achieve it in himself. He vacillates between undisciplined squads of emotion and thinking too precisely on the event. He learns to his cost how easily action can be lost in "acting," and loses it there for a time himself. But these again are only the terms of every man's life. As Anatole France reminds us in a now famous apostrophe to Hamlet: "What one of us thinks without contradiction and acts without incoherence? What one of us is not mad? What one of us does not say with a mixture of pity, comradeship, admiration, and horror, Goodnight, sweet Prince!"

In the last act of the play (or so it seems to me, for I know there can be differences on this point), Hamlet accepts his world and we discover a different man. Shakespeare does not outline for us the process of acceptance any more than he had done with Romeo or was to do with Othello. But he leads us strongly to expect an altered Hamlet, and then, in my opinion, provides him. We must recall that at this point Hamlet has been absent from the stage during several scenes, and that such absences in Shakespearean tragedy usually warn us to be on the watch for a new phase in the development of the character. It is so when we leave King Lear in Gloucester's farmhouse and find him again in Dover fields. It is so when we leave Macbeth at the witches' cave and rejoin him at Dunsinane, hearing of the armies that beset it. Furthermore, and this is an important matter in the theatre—especially important in a play in which the symbolism of clothing has figured largely—Hamlet now looks different. He is wearing a different dress—probably, as Granville-Barker thinks, his "seagown scarf'd" about him, but in any case no longer the disordered costume of his antic disposition. The effect is not entirely dissimilar to that in *Lear*, when the old king wakes out of his madness to find fresh garments on him.

Still more important, Hamlet displays a considerable change of mood. This is not a matter of the way we take the passage about defying augury, as Mr. Tillyard among others seems to think. It is a matter of Hamlet's whole deportment, in which I feel we may legitimately see the deportment of a man who has been "illuminated" in the tragic sense. Bradley's term for it is fatalism, but if this is what we wish to call it, we must at least acknowledge that it is fatalism of a very distinctive kind—a kind that Shakespeare has been willing to touch with the associations of the saying in St. Matthew about the fall of a sparrow, and with Hamlet's recognition that a divinity shapes our ends. The point is not that Hamlet has suddenly become religious; he has been religious all through the play. The point is that he has now learned, and accepted, the boundaries in which human action, human judgment, are enclosed.

Till his return from the voyage he had been trying to act beyond these, had been encroaching on the role of providence, if I may exaggerate to make a vital point. He had been too quick to take the burden of the whole world and its condition upon his limited and finite self. Faced with a task of sufficient difficulty in its own right, he had dilated it into a cosmic problem—as indeed every task is, but if we think about this too precisely we cannot act at all. The whole time is out of joint, he feels, and in his young man's egocentricity, he will set it right. Hence he misjudges Ophelia, seeing in her only a breeder of sinners. Hence he misjudges himself, seeing himself a vermin crawling between earth and heaven. Hence he takes it upon himself to be his mother's conscience, though the ghost has warned that this is no fit task for him, and returns to repeat the warning: "Leave her to heaven, And to those thorns that in her bosom lodge." Even with the king, Hamlet has sought to play at God. *He* it must be who decides the issue of Claudius's salvation, saving him for a more damnable occasion. Now, he

has learned that there are limits to the before and after that human reason can comprehend. Rashness, even, is sometimes good. Through rashness he has saved his life from the commission for his death, "and prais'd be rashness for it." This happy circumstance and the unexpected arrival of the pirate ship make it plain that the roles of life are not entirely self-assigned. "There is a divinity that shapes our ends. Roughhew them how we will." Hamlet is ready now for what may happen, seeking neither to foreknow it nor avoid it. "If it be now, 'tis not to come; if it be not to come, it will be now; if it be not now, yet it will come: the readiness is all."

The crucial evidence of Hamlet's new frame of mind, as I understand it, is the graveyard scene. Here, in its ultimate symbol, he confronts, recognizes, and accepts the condition of being man. It is not simply that he now accepts death, though Shakespeare shows him accepting it in ever more poignant forms: first, in the imagined persons of the politician, the courtier, and the lawyer, who laid their little schemes "to circumvent God," as Hamlet puts it, but now lie here; then in Yorick, whom he knew and played with as a child; and then in Ophelia. This last death tears from him a final cry of passion, but the striking contrast between his behavior and Laertes's reveals how deeply he has changed.

Still, it is not the fact of death that invests this scene with its peculiar power. It is instead the haunting mystery of life itself that Hamlet's speeches point to, holding in its inscrutable folds those other mysteries that he has wrestled with so long. These he now knows for what they are, and lays them by. The mystery of evil is present here—for this is after all the universal graveyard, where, as the clown says humorously, he holds up

Adam's profession; where the scheming politician, the hollow courtier, the tricky lawyer, the emperor and the clown and the beautiful young maiden, all come together in an emblem of the world; where even, Hamlet murmurs, one might expect to stumble on "Cain's jawbone, that did the first murther." The mystery of reality is here too—for death puts the question, "What is real?" in its irreducible form, and in the end uncovers all appearances: "Is this the fine of his fines and the recovery of his recoveries, to have his fine pate full of fine dirt?" "Now get you to my lady's chamber, and tell her, let her paint an inch thick, to this favor she must come." Or if we need more evidence of this mystery, there is the anger of Laertes at the lack of ceremonial trappings, and the ambiguous character of Ophelia's own death. "Is she to be buried in Christian burial when she wilfully seeks her own salvation?" asks the gravedigger. And last of all, but most pervasive of all, there is the mystery of human limitation. The grotesque nature of man's little joys, his big ambitions. The fact that the man who used to bear us on his back is now a skull that smells; that the noble dust of Alexander somewhere plugs a bunghole; that "Imperious Caesar, dead and turn'd to clay, Might stop a hole to keep the wind away." Above all, the fact that a pit of clay is "meet" for such a guest as man, as the gravedigger tells us in his song, and yet that, despite all frailties and limitations. "That skull had a tongue in it and could sing once."

After the graveyard and what it indicates has come to pass in him, we know that Hamlet is ready for the final contest of mighty opposites. He accepts the world as it is, the world as a duel, in which, whether we know it or not, evil holds the poisoned rapier and the poisoned chalice waits; and in which, if we win at all, it costs not less than everything. I think we understand by the close of Shakespeare's *Hamlet* why it is that unlike the other tragic heroes he is given a soldier's rites upon the stage. For as William Butler Yeats once said, "Why should we honor those who die on the field of battle? A man may show as reckless a courage in entering into the abyss of himself."

CHAPTER 15

Philosophical Focus

CRITICISM AS PURE SPECULATION
John Crowe Ransom*

Ransom's thesis is that "the authority of criticism depends on its coming to terms with esthetics." In doing so, it functions on a rationale different from those rationales which are "psychologistic," or moralistic, or argumentative, or scientific. In examining a work of art, criticism must deal not merely with "logical structure" or "functional context," but with "local texture," a kind of poetic "increment." Criticism is a "speculative exercise" that is ontological in that its intent goes beyond what poetry or fiction says, to what it, of itself, is.

I

I will testify to the weight of responsibility felt by the critic who enters a serial discussion with such other lecturers as Mr. Wilson, Mr. Auden, and Mr. Foerster; and delivers his opinion to an audience at Princeton, where live at least two eminent critics, in Mr. Tate and Mr. Blackmur, und one eminent esthetician, in Mr. Greene.

Indeed, Mr. Blackmur and Mr. Greene have recently published books which

bear on this discussion.[1] Mr. Blackmur's essays are probably all that can be expected of a critic who has not explicitly submitted them to the discipline of general esthetics; but with that limitation the best critic in the world might expose himself to review and reproach. Mr. Greene's esthetic studies, in turn, may have wonderful cogency as philosophical discourse, but if throughout them he should fail to maintain intimate contact with the actual works of art he would invite damaging attentions from the lit-

* The essay is reprinted from *The Intent of the Critic*, edited by D. A. Stauffer, by permission of Princeton University Press. Copyright 1941 by Princeton University Press.

[1] *The Expense of Greatness*, by R. P. Blackmur, Arrow Editions, 1940; *The Arts and the Art of Criticism*, by Theodore Meyer Greene, Princeton University Press, 1940.

514

erary critics. I am far from suggesting such proceedings against them. Mr. Blackmur has his native philosophical sense to keep his critical foundations from sliding into the sea. Mr. Greene is in a very strong position: recognizing the usual weakness of formal esthetics, he tries a device to secure his own studies against it; for when he needs them he uses reports from reputable actual critics upon the practices in the several arts. A chasm, perhaps an abyss, separates the critic and the esthetician ordinarily, if the books in the library are evidence. But the authority of criticism depends on its coming to terms with esthetics, and the authority of literary esthetics depends on its coming to terms with criticism. Mr. Greene is an esthetician, and his department is philosophy, but he has subscribed in effect to this thesis. I am a sort of critic, and my department is English poetry, so that I am very much in Mr. Blackmur's position; and I subscribe to the thesis, and am altogether disposed to solicit Mr. Greene's philosophical services.

When we inquire into the "intent of the critic," we mean: the intent of the generalized critic, or critic as such. We will concede that any professional critic is familiar with the technical practices of poets so long as these are conventional, and is expert in judging when they perform them brilliantly, and when only fairly, or badly. We expect a critical discourse to cover that much, but we know that more is required. The most famous poets of our own time, for example, make wide departures from conventional practices: how are they to be judged? Innovations in poetry, or even conventions when pressed to their logical limits, cause the ordinary critic to despair. They cause the good critic to review his esthetic principles; perhaps to re-formulate his esthetic principles. He tries the poem

against his best philosophical conception of the peculiar character that a poem should have.

Mr. T. S. Eliot is an extraordinarily sensitive critic. But when he discusses the so-called "metaphysical" poetry, he surprises us by refusing to study the so-called "conceit" which is its reputed basis; he observes instead that the metaphysical poets of the seventeenth century are more like their immediate predecessors than the latter are like the eighteenth and nineteenth century poets, and then he goes into a very broad philosophical comparison between two whole "periods" or types of poetry. I think it has come to be understood that his comparison is unsound; it has not proved workable enough to assist critics who have otherwise borrowed liberally from his critical principles. (It contains the famous dictum about the "sensibility" of the earlier poets, it imputes to them a remarkable ability to "feel their thought," and to have a kind of "experience" in which the feeling cannot be differentiated from the thinking.) Now there is scarcely another critic equal to Eliot at distinguishing the practices of two poets who are closely related. He is supreme as a comparative critic when the relation in question is delicate and subtle; that is, when it is a matter of close perception and not a radical difference in kind. But this line of criticism never goes far enough. In Eliot's own range of criticism the line does not always answer. He is forced by discontinuities in the poetic tradition into sweeping theories that have to do with esthetics, the philosophy of poetry; and his own philosophy probably seems to us insufficient, the philosophy of the literary man.

The intent of the critic may well be, then, first to read his poem sensitively, and make comparative judgments about its technical practice, or, as we might say, to emulate Eliot. Beyond that, it is to read and remark the poem knowingly; that is, with an esthetician's understanding of what a poem generically "is."

Before I venture, with inadequate argument, to describe what I take to be the correct understanding of poetry, I would like to describe two other understandings which, though widely professed, seem to me misunderstandings. First, there is a smart and bellettristic theory of poetry which may be called "psychologistic." Then there is an altogether staid and commonplace theory which is moralistic. Of these in their order.

II

It could easily be argued about either of these untenable conceptions of poetry that it is an act of despair to which critics resort who cannot find for the discourse of poetry any precise differentia to remove it from the category of science. Psychologistic critics hold that poetry is addressed primarily to the feelings and motor impulses; they remind us frequently of its contrast with the coldness, the unemotionality, of science, which is supposed to address itself to the pure cognitive mind. Mr. Richards came out spectacularly for the doctrine, and furnished it with detail of the greatest ingenuity. He very nearly severed the dependence of poetic effect upon any standard of objective knowledge or belief. But the feelings and impulses which he represented as gratified by the poem were too tiny and numerous to be named. He never identified them; they seemed not so much psychological as intra-psychological. His was an esoteric poetic: it could not be disproved. But neither could it be proved, and I think it is safe at this distance to say that eventually his readers, and Richards himself, lost interest in it as being an improvisation,

much too unrelated to the public sense of a poetic experience.

With other critics psychologism of some sort is an old story, and one that will probably never cease to be told. For, now that all of us know about psychology, there must always be persons on hand precisely conditioned to declare that poetry is an emotional discourse indulged in resentment and compensation for science, the bleak cognitive discourse in its purity. It becomes less a form of knowledge than a form of "expression." The critics are willing to surrender the honor of objectivity to science if they may have the luxury of subjectivity for poetry. Science will scarcely object. But one or two things have to be said about that. In every experience, even in science, there is feeling. No discourse can sustain itself without interest, which is feeling. The interest, or the feeling, is like an automatic index to the human value of the proceeding—which would not otherwise proceed. Mr. Eliseo Vivas is an esthetician who might be thought to reside in the camp of the enemy, for his affiliations are positivist; yet in a recent essay he writes about the "passion" which sustains the heroic labors of the scientist as one bigger and more intense than is given to most men.

I do not mean to differ with that judgment at all in remarking that we might very well let the passions and the feelings take care of themselves; it is precisely what we do in our pursuit of science. The thing to attend to is the object to which they attach. As between two similar musical phrases, or between two similar lines of poetry, we may often defy the most proficient psychologist to distinguish the one feeling-response from the other; unless we permit him to say at long last that one is the kind of response that would be made to the first line, and the other is the kind of response that would be made to the second line. But that is to do, after much wasted motion, what I have just suggested: to attend to the poetic object and let the feelings take care of themselves. It is their business to "respond." There may be a feeling correlative with the minutest alteration in an object, and adequate to it, but we shall hardly know. What we do know is that the feelings are grossly inarticulate if we try to abstract them and take their testimony in their own language. Since it is not the intent of the critic to be inarticulate, his discriminations must be among the objects. We understand this so well intuitively that the critic seems to us in possession of some esoteric knowledge, some magical insight, if he appears to be intelligent elsewhere and yet refers confidently to the "tone" or "quality" or "value" of the feeling he discovers in a given line. Probably he is bluffing. The distinctness resides in the cognitive or "semantical" objects denoted by the words. When Richards bewilders us by reporting affective and motor disturbances that are too tiny for definition, and other critics by reporting disturbances that are too massive and gross, we cannot fail to grow suspicious of this whole way of insight as incompetent.

Eliot has a special version of psychologistic theory which looks extremely fertile, though it is broad and nebulous as his psychologistic terms require it to be. He likes to regard the poem as a structure of emotion and feeling. But the emotion is singular, there being only one emotion per poem, or at least per passage: it is the central emotion or big emotion which attaches to the main theme or situation. The feeling is plural. The emotion combines with many feelings; these are our little responses to the single words and phrases, and he does not think of them as being parts of the central emotion or even related to it. The terminology is greatly at fault, or we should recognize at once, I think, a principle that might prove very valuable. I would not answer for the conduct of a technical philosopher in assessing this theory; he might throw it away, out of patience with its jargon. But a lay philosopher who respects his Eliot and reads with all his sympathy might salvage a good thing from it, though I have not heard of anyone doing so. He would try to escape from the affective terms, and translate Eliot into more intelligible language. Eliot would be saying in effect that a poem has a central logic or situation or "paraphrasable core" to which an appropriate interest doubtless attaches, and that in this respect the poem is like a discourse of science behind which lies the sufficient passion. But he would be saying at the same time, and this is the important thing, that the poem has also a context of lively local details to which other and independent interests attach; and that in this respect it is unlike the discourse of science. For the detail of scientific discourse intends never to be independent of the thesis (either objectively or affectively) but always functional, and subordinate to the realization of the thesis. To say that is to approach to a structural understanding of poetry, and to the kind of understanding that I wish presently to urge.

III

As for the moralistic understanding of poetry, it is sometimes the specific moralists, men with moral axes to grind, and incidentally men of unassailable public position, who cherish that; they have a "use" for poetry. But not exclusively, for we may find it held also by critics who are more spontaneous and innocent: apparently they fall back upon it because it attributes some special character to poetry, which otherwise refuses to yield up to them a character. The moral interest is so much more frequent in poetry than in science that they decide to offer its moralism as a differentia.

This conception of poetry is of the greatest antiquity—it antedates the evolution of close esthetic philosophy, and persists beside it too. Plato sometimes spoke of poetry in this light—perhaps because it was recommended to him in this light—but nearly always scornfully. In the *Gorgias*, and other dialogues, he represents the poets as moralizing, and that is only what he, in the person of Socrates, is doing at the very moment, and given to doing; but he considers the moralizing of poets as mere "rhetoric," or popular philosophy, and unworthy of the accomplished moralist who is the real or technical philosopher. Plato understood very well that the poet does not conduct a technical or an original discourse like that of the scientist—and the term includes here the moral philosopher— and that close and effective moralizing is scarcely to be had from him. It is not within the poet's power to offer that if his intention is to offer poetry; for the poetry and the morality are so far from being identical that they interfere a little with each other.

Few famous estheticians in the history of philosophy have cared to bother with the moralistic conception; many critics have, in all periods. Just now we have at least two schools of moralistic critics contending for the official possession of poetry. One is the Neo-Humanist, and Mr. Foerster has identified himself with that. The other is the Marxist, and I believe it is represented in some degree and shade by Mr. Wilson, possibly by Mr. Auden. I have myself taken profit from the discussions by both schools, but recently I have taken more—I suppose this is because I was brought up in a scholastic discipline rather like the Neo-Humanist—from the writings of the Marxist critics. One of the differences is that the Neo-Humanists believe in the "respectable" virtues, but the Marxists believe that respectability is the greatest of vices, and equate respectable with "genteel." That is a very striking difference, and I think it is also profound.

But I do not wish to be impertinent; I can respect both these moralities, and appropriate moral values from both. The thing I wish to argue is not the comparative merits of the different moralities by which poetry is judged, but their equal inadequacy to the reading of the poet's intention. The moralistic critics wish to isolate and discuss the "ideology" or theme or paraphrase of the poem and not the poem itself. But even to the practitioners themselves, if they are sophisticated, comes sometimes the apprehension that this is moral rather than literary criticism. I have not seen the papers of my colleagues in this discussion, for that was against the rules, but it is reported to me that both Mr. Wilson and Mr. Foerster concede in explicit words that criticism has both the moral and the esthetic branches; Mr. Wilson may call them the "social" and esthetic branches. And they would hold the critical profession responsible for both branches. Under these circumstances the critics cease to be mere moralists and become dualists; that is better. My feeling about such a position would be that the moral criticism we shall have with us always, and have had always, and that it is easy—comparatively speaking—and that what is hard, and needed, and indeed more and more urgent after all the failures of poetic understanding, is a better esthetic criticism. This is the branch which is all but invariably neglected by the wise but morally zealous critics; they tend to forget their dual responsibility. I think I should go so far as to think that, in strictness, the business of the literary critic is exclusively with an esthetic criticism. The business of the moralist will naturally, and properly, be with something else.

If we have the patience to read for a little while in the anthology, paying some respect to the varieties of substance actually in the poems, we cannot logically attribute ethical character by definition to poetry; for that character is not universal in the poems. And if we have any faith in a community of character among the several arts, we are stopped quickly from risking such a definition for art at large. To claim a moral content for most of sculpture, painting, music, or architecture, is to plan something dialectically very roundabout and subtle, or else to be so arbitrary as to invite instant exposure. I should think the former alternative is impractical, and the latter, if it is not stupid, is masochistic.

The moralistic critics are likely to retort upon their accusers by accusing them in turn of the vapid doctrine known as Art for Art's Sake. And with frequent justice; but again we are likely to receive the impression that it is just because Art for Art's Sake, the historic doctrine, proved empty, and availed them so little esthetically, like all the other doctrines that came into default, that they have fled to their moralism. Moralism does at least impute to poetry a positive substance, as Art for Art's Sake does not. It asserts an autonomy for art, which is excellent; but autonomy to do what? Only to be itself, and to reduce its interpreters to a tautology? With its English adherents in the 'nineties the doctrine seemed to make only a negative requirement of art, that is, that it should be anti-Victorian as we should say today, a little bit naughty and immoral perhaps, otherwise at least nonmoral, or carefully squeezed dry of moral

substance. An excellent example of how two doctrines, inadequate equally but in opposite senses, may keep themselves alive by abhorring each other's errors.

It is highly probable that the poem considers an ethical situation, and there is no reason why it should repel this from its consideration. But, if I may say so without being accused of verbal trifling, the poetic consideration of the ethical situation is not the same as the ethical consideration of it. The straight ethical consideration would be prose; it would be an act of interested science, or an act of practical will. The poetic consideration, according to Schopenhauer, is the objectification of this act of will; that is, it is our contemplation and not our exercise of will, and therefore qualitatively a very different experience; knowledge without desire. That doctrine also seems too negative and indeterminate. I will put the point as I see it in another way. It should be a comfort to the moralist that there is ordinarily a moral composure in the poem, as if the poet had long known good and evil, and made his moral choice between them once and for all. Art is post-ethical rather than unethical. In the poem there is an increment of meaning which is neither the ethical content nor opposed to the ethical content. The poetic experience would have to stop for the poet who is developing it, or for the reader who is following it, if the situation which is being poetically treated should turn back into a situation to be morally determined; if, for example, the situation were not a familiar one, and one to which we had habituated our moral wills; for it would rouse the moral will again to action, and make the poetic treatment impossible under its heat. Art is more cool than hot, and a moral fervor is as disastrous to it as a burst of passion itself. We have seen Marxists recently so revolted by Shakespeare's addiction to royal or noble *personae* that they cannot obtain esthetic experience from the plays; all they get is moral agitation. In another art, we know, and doubtless we approve, the scruple of the college authorities in not permitting the "department of fine arts" to direct the collegians in painting in the nude. Doctor Hanns Sachs, successor to Freud, in a recent number of his *American Imago*, gives a story from a French author as follows:

"He tells that one evening strolling along the streets of Paris he noticed a row of slot machines which for a small coin showed pictures of women in full or partial undress. He observed the leering interest with which men of all kind and description, well dressed and shabby, boys and old men, enjoyed the peep show. He remarked that they all avoided one of these machines, and wondering what uninteresting pictures it might show, he put his penny in the slot. To his great astonishment the generally shunned picture turned out to be the Venus of Medici. Now he begins to ponder: Why does nobody get excited about her? She is decidedly feminine and not less naked than the others which hold such strong fascination for everybody. Finally he finds a satisfactory answer: They fight shy of her because she is beautiful."

And Doctor Sachs, though in his own variety of jargon, makes a number of wise observations about the psychic conditions precedent to the difficult apprehension of beauty. The experience called beauty is beyond the powerful ethical will precisely as it is beyond the animal passion, and indeed these last two are competitive, and coordinate. Under the urgency of either we are incapable of appreciating the statue or understanding the poem.

IV

The ostensible substance of the poem may be anything at all which words may signify: an ethical situation, a passion, a train of thought, a flower or landscape, a thing. This substance receives its poetic increment. It might be safer to say it receives some subtle and mysterious alteration under poetic treatment, but I will risk the cruder formula: the ostensible substance is increased by an x, which is an increment. The poem actually continues to contain its ostensible substance, which is not fatally diminished from its prose state: that is its logical core, or paraphrase. The rest of the poem is x, which we are to find.

We feel the working of this simple formula when we approach a poetry with our strictest logic, provided we can find deliverance from certain inhibiting philosophical prepossessions into which we have been conditioned by the critics we have had to read. Here is Lady Macbeth planning a murder with her husband:

When Duncan is asleep—
Whereto the rather shall his hard day's
    journey
Soundly invite him—his two chamberlains
Will I with wine and wassail so convince,
That memory, the warder of the brain,
Shall be a fume, and the receipt of reason
A limbec only; when in swinish sleep
Their drenched natures lie as in a death,
What cannot you and I perform upon
The unguarded Duncan? what not put
    upon
His spongy officers, who shall bear the guilt
Of our great quell?

It is easy to produce the prose argument or paraphrase of this speech; it has one upon which we shall all agree. But the passage is more than its argument. Any detail, with this speaker, seems capable of being expanded in some direction which is not that of the argument. For example, Lady Macbeth says she will make the chamberlains drunk so that they will not remember their charge, nor keep their wits about them. But it is indifferent to this argument whether memory according to the old psychology is located at the gateway to the brain, whether it is to be disintegrated into fume as of alcohol, and whether the whole receptacle of the mind is to be turned into a still. These are additions to the argument both energetic and irrelevant—though they do not quite stop or obscure the argument. From the point of view of the philosopher they are excursions into particularity. They give, in spite of the argument, which would seem to be perfectly self-sufficient, a sense of the real density and contingency of the world in which arguments and plans have to be pursued. They bring out the private character which the items of an argument can really assume if we look at them. This character spreads out in planes at right angles to the course of the argument, and in effect gives to the discourse another dimension, not present in a perfectly logical prose. We are expected to have sufficient judgment not to let this local character take us too far or keep us too long from the argument.

All this would seem commonplace remark, I am convinced, but for those philosophically timid critics who are afraid to think that the poetic increment is local and irrelevant, and that poetry cannot achieve its own virtue and keep undiminished the virtues of prose at the same time. But I will go a little further in the hope of removing the sense of strangeness in the analysis. I will offer a figurative definition of a poem.

A poem is, so to speak, a democratic state, whereas a prose discourse—mathematical, scientific, ethical, or practical and vernacular—is a totalitarian state. The intention of a democratic state is to perform the work of state as effectively as it can perform it, subject to one reservation of conscience: that it will not despoil its members, the citizens, of the free exercise of their own private and independent characters. But the totalitarian state is interested solely in being effective, and regards the citizens as no citizens at all; that is, regards them as functional members whose existence is totally defined by their allotted contributions to its ends; it has no use for their private characters, and therefore no provision for them. I indicate of course the extreme or polar opposition between two polities, without denying that a polity may come to us rather mixed up.

In this trope the operation of the state as a whole represents of course the logical paraphrase or argument of the poem. The private character of the citizens represents the particularity asserted by the parts in the poem. And this last is our x.

For many years I had seen—as what serious observer has not—that a poem as a discourse differentiated itself from prose by its particularity, yet not to the point of sacrificing its logical cogency or universality. But I could get no further. I could not see how real particularity could get into a universal. The object of esthetic studies became for me a kind of discourse, or a kind of natural configuration, which like any other discourse or configuration claimed universality, but which consisted actually, and notoriously, of particularity. The poem was concrete, yet universal, and in spite of Hegel I could not see how the two properties could be identified as forming in a single unit the "concrete universal." It is usual, I believe, for persons at this stage to assert that somehow the apparent diffuseness or particularity in the poem gets itself taken up or "assimilated" into the logic, to produce a marvellous kind of unity called a "higher unity," to which ordinary discourse is not eligible. The belief is that the "idea" or theme proves itself in poetry to be even more dominating than in prose by overcoming much more energetic resistance than usual on the part of the materials, and the resistance, as attested in the local development of detail, is therefore set not to the debit but to the credit of the unifying power of the poetic spirit. A unity of that kind is one which philosophers less audacious and more factual than Hegel would be loath to claim. Critics incline to call it, rather esoterically, an "imaginative" rather than a logical unity, but one supposes they mean a mystical, an ineffable, unity. I for one could neither grasp it nor deny it. I believe that is not an uncommon situation for poetic analysts to find themselves in.

It occurred to me at last that the solution might be very easy if looked for without what the positivists call "metaphysical prepossessions." Suppose the logical substance remained there all the time, and was in no way specially remarkable, while the particularity came in by accretion, so that the poem turned out partly universal, and partly particular, but with respect to different parts. I began to remark the dimensions of a poem, or other work of art. The poem was not a mere moment in time, nor a mere point in space. It was sizeable, like a house. Apparently it had a "plan," or a central frame of logic, but it had also a huge wealth of local detail, which sometimes fitted the plan functionally or served it, and sometimes only subsisted comfortably under it; in either case the house stood up. But it was the political way of thinking which gave me the first analogy which seemed valid. The

poem was like a democratic state, in action, and observed both macroscopically and microscopically.

The house occurred also, and provided what seems to be a more negotiable trope under which to construe the poem. A poem is a *logical structure* having a *local texture*. These terms have been actually though not systematically employed in literary criticism. To my imagination they are architectural. The walls of my room are obviously structural; the beams and boards have a function; so does the plaster, which is the visible aspect of the final wall. The plaster might have remained naked, aspiring to no character, and purely functional. But actually it has been painted, receiving color; or it has been papered, receiving color and design, though these have no structural value; and perhaps it has been hung with tapestry, or with paintings, for "decoration." The paint, the paper, the tapestry are texture. It is logically unrelated to structure. But I indicate only a few of the textural possibilities in architecture. There are not fewer of them in poetry.

The intent of the good critic becomes therefore to examine and define the poem with respect to its structure and its texture. If he has nothing to say about its texture he has nothing to say about it specifically as a poem, but is treating it only insofar as it is prose.

I do not mean to say that the good critic will necessarily employ my terms.

V

Many critics today are writing analytically and with close intelligence, in whatever terms, about the logical substance or structure of the poem, and its increment of irrelevant local substance or texture. I believe that the understanding of the ideal critic has to go even further than that. The final desideratum is an ontological insight, nothing less. I am committed by my title to a representation of criticism as, in the last resort, a speculative exercise. But my secret committal was to speculative in the complete sense of—ontological.

There is nothing especially speculative or ontological in reciting, or even appraising, the logical substance of the poem. This is its prose core—its science perhaps, or its ethics if it seems to have an ideology. Speculative interest asserts itself principally when we ask why we want the logical substance to be compounded with the local substance, the good lean structure with a great volume of texture that does not function. It is the same thing as asking why we want the poem to be what it is.

It has been a rule, having the fewest exceptions, for estheticians and great philosophers to direct their speculations by the way of overstating and overvaluing the logical substance. They are impressed by the apparent obedience of material nature, whether in fact or in art, to definable form or "law" imposed upon it. They like to suppose that in poetry, as in chemistry, everything that figures in the discourse means to be functional, and that the poem is imperfect in the degree that it contains items, whether by accident or intention, which manifest a private independence. It is a bias with which we are entirely familiar, and reflects the extent to which our philosophy hitherto has been impressed by the successes of science in formulating laws which would "govern" their objects. Probably I am here reading the state of mind of yesterday rather than of today. Nevertheless we know it. The world-view which ultimately forms itself in the mind so biassed is that of a world which is rational and intelligible. The view is sanguine, and naïve. Hegel's world-view, I think it is agreed, was a subtle version

of this, and if so, it was what determined his view of art. He seemed to make the handsomest concession to realism by offering to knowledge a kind of universal which was not restricted to the usual abstracted aspects of the material, but included all aspects, and was a concrete universal. The concreteness in Hegel's handling was not honestly, or at any rate not fairly, defended. It was always represented as being in process of pointing up and helping out the universality. He could look at a work of art and report all its substance as almost assimilated to a ruling "idea." But at least Hegel seemed to distingush what looked like two ultimate sorts of substance there, and stated the central esthetic problem as the problem of relating them. And his writings about art are speculative in the sense that he regarded the work of art not as of great intrinsic value necessarily, but as an object-lesson or discipline in the understanding of the world-process, and as its symbol.

I think of two ways of construing poetry with respect to its ultimate purpose; of which the one is not very handsome nor speculatively interesting, and the other will appear somewhat severe.

The first construction would picture the poet as a sort of epicure, and the poem as something on the order of a Christmas pudding, stuffed with what dainties it will hold. The pastry alone, or it may be the cake, will not serve; the stuffing is wanted too. The values of the poem would be intrinsic, or immediate, and they would include not only the value of the structure but also the incidental values to be found in the texture. If we exchange the pudding for a house, they would include not only the value of the house itself but also the value of the furnishings. In saying intrinsic or immediate, I mean that the poet is fond of the precise objects denoted by the words, and writes the poem for the reason that he likes to dwell upon them. In talking about the main value and the incidental values I mean to recognize the fact that the latter engage the affections just as truly as the former. Poetic discourse therefore would be more agreeable than prose to the epicure or the literally acquisitive man; for prose has but a single value, being about one thing only; its parts have no values of their own, but only instrumental values, which might be reckoned as fractions of the single value proportionate to their contributions to it. The prose is one-valued and the poem is many-valued. Indeed, there will certainly be poems whose texture contains many precious objects, and aggregates a greater value than the structure.

So there would be a comfortable and apparently eligible view that poetry improves on prose because it is a richer diet. It causes five or six pleasures to appear, five or six good things, where one had been before; an alluring consideration for robustious, full-blooded, bourgeois souls. The view will account for much of the poem, if necessary. But it does not account for all of it, and sometimes it accounts for less than at other times.

The most impressive reason for the bolder view of art, the speculative one, is the existence of the "pure," or "abstractionist," or non-representational works of art; though these will probably occur to us in other arts than poetry. There is at least one art, music, whose works are all of this sort. Tones are not words, they have no direct semantical function, and by themselves they mean nothing. But they combine to make brilliant phrases, harmonies, and compositions. In these compositions it is probable that the distinction between structure or functional content, on the

one hand, and texture or local variation and departure, on the other, is even more determinate than in an impure art like poetry. The world of tones seems perfectly inhuman and impracticable; there is no specific field of experience "about which" music is telling us. Yet we know that music is powerfully affective. I take my own musical feelings, and those attested by other audients, as the sufficient index to some overwhelming human importance which the musical object has for us. At the same time it would be useless to ask the feelings precisely what they felt; we must ask the critic. The safest policy is to take the simplest construction, and try to improvise as little fiction as possible. Music is not music, I think, until we grasp its effects both in structure and in texture. As we grow in musical understanding the structures become always more elaborate and sustained, and the texture which interrupts them and sometimes imperils them becomes more bold and unpredictable. We can agree in saying about the works of music that these are musical structures, and they are richly textured; we can identify these elements, and perhaps precisely. To what then do our feelings respond? To music as structural composition itself; to music as manifesting the structural principles of the world; to modes of structure which we feel to be ontologically possible, or even probable. Schopenhauer construed music very much in that sense. Probably it will occur to us that musical compositions bear close analogy therefore to operations in pure mathematics. The mathematicians confess that their constructions are "non-existential"; meaning, as I take it, that the constructions testify with assurance only to the structural principles, in the light of which they are possible but may not be actual, or if they are actual may not be useful. This would define the mathematical operations as speculative: as motivated by an interest so generalized and so elemental that no word short of ontological will describe it.

But if music and mathematics have this much in common, they differ sharply in their respective world-views or ontological biasses. That of music, with its prodigious display of texture, seems the better informed about the nature of the world, the more realistic, the less naive. Perhaps the difference is between two ontological educations. But I should be inclined to imagine it as rising back of that point: in two ontological temperaments.

There are also, operating a little less successfully so far as the indexical evidences would indicate, the abstractionist paintings, of many schools, and perhaps also works of sculpture; and there is architecture. These arts have tried to abandon direct representational intention almost as heroically as music. They exist in their own materials and indicate no other specific materials; structures of color, light, space, stone—the cheapest of materials. They too can symbolize nothing of value unless it is structure or composition itself. But that is precisely the act which denotes will and intelligence; which becomes the act of fuller intelligence if it carefully accompanies its structures with their material textures; for then it understands better the ontological nature of materials.

Returning to the poetry. It is not all poems, and not even all "powerful" poems, having high index-ratings, whose semantical meanings contain situations important in themselves or objects precious in themselves. There may be little correlation between the single value of the poem and the aggregate value of its contents—just as there is no such correlation whatever in music. The "effect" of the poem may be astonishingly disproportionate to our interest in its materials. It is true, of course, that there is no art employing materials of equal richness with poetry, and that it is beyond the capacity of poetry to employ indifferent materials. The words used in poetry are the words the race has already formed, and naturally they call attention to things and events that have been thought to be worth attending to. But I suggest that any poetry which is "technically" notable is in part a work of abstractionist art, concentrating upon the structure and the texture, and the structure-texture relation, out of a pure speculative interest.

At the end of *Love's Labour's Lost* occurs a little diversion which seems proportionately far more effective than that laborious play as a whole. The play is over, but Armado stops the principals before they disperse to offer them a show:

Arm.: But, most esteemed greatness, will you hear the dialogue that the two learned men have compiled in praise of the owl and the cuckoo? It should have followed in the end of our show.

King: Call them forth quickly; we will do so.

Arm.: Holla! approach. (*Re-enter, Holofernes, etc.*) This side is Hiems, Winter, this Ver, the Spring; the one maintained by the owl, the other by the cuckoo. Ver, begin.

THE SONG

Spring: When daisies pied and violets blue
And lady-smocks all silver-white
And cuckoo-buds of yellow hue
Do paint the meadows with delight,
The cuckoo then, on every tree,
Mocks married men; for thus sings he,
    Cuckoo;
Cuckoo, cuckoo: O word of fear,
Unpleasing to a married ear!

When shepherds pipe on oaten straws,
And merry larks are ploughmen's clocks,
When turtles tread, and rooks, and daws,
And maidens bleach their summer smocks,
The cuckoo then, on every tree,
Mocks married men; for thus sings he,
      Cuckoo;
Cuckoo, cuckoo: O word of fear,
Unpleasing to a married ear!

Winter: When icicles hang by the wall,
And Dick the shepherd blows his nail,
And Tom bears logs into the hall,
And milk comes frozen home in pail,
When blood is nipp'd and ways be foul,
Then nightly sings the staring owl,
      Tu-who;
Tu-whit, tu-who, a merry note,
While greasy Joan doth keel the pot.

When all aloud the wind doth blow,
And coughing drowns the parson's saw,
And birds sit brooding in the snow,
And Marian's nose looks red and raw,
When roasted crabs hiss in the bowl,
Then nightly sings the staring owl,
      Tu-who;
Tu-whit, tu-who, a merry note,
While greasy Joan doth keel the pot.

Arm.: The words of Mercury are harsh
after the songs of Apollo. You that way,—
we this way. (*Exeunt.*)

The feeling-index registers such strong
approval of this episode that a critic with
ambition is obliged to account for it.
He can scarcely account for it in terms
of the weight of its contents severally.

At first glance Shakespeare has provided only a pleasant little caricature of
the old-fashioned (to us, medieval) debate between personified characters. It
is easygoing, like nonsense; no labor is
lost here. Each party speaks two stanzas
and concludes both stanzas with the refrain about his bird, the cuckoo or the
owl. There is next to no generalized
argument, or dialectic proper. Each
argues by citing his characteristic exhibits. In the first stanza Spring cites

some flowers; in the second stanza, some
business by country persons, with interpolation of some birds that make love.
Winter in both his stanzas cites the
country business of the season. In the
refrain the cuckoo, Spring's symbol, is
used to refer the love-making to more
than the birds; and this repeats itself,
though it is naughty. The owl is only a
nominal symbol for Winter, an "emblem" that is not very emblematic, but
the refrain manages another reference to
the kitchen, and repeats itself, as if
Winter's pleasures focussed in the
kitchen.

In this poem texture is not very brilliant, but it eclipses structure. The argument, we would say in academic
language, is concerned with "the relative
advantages of Spring and Winter." The
only logical determinateness this structure has is the good coordination of the
items cited by Spring as being really
items peculiar to Spring, and of the
Winter items as peculiar to Winter. The
symbolic refrains look like summary or
master items, but they seem to be a little
more than summary and in fact to mean
a little more than they say. The argument is trifling on the whole, and the
texture from the point of view of felt
human importance lacks decided energy;
both which observations are to be made,
and most precisely, of how many famous
lyrics, especially those before that earnest
and self-conscious nineteenth century!
The value of the poem is greater than
the value of its parts: that is what the
critic is up against.

Unquestionably it is possible to as-
semble very fine structures out of ordinary materials. The good critic will study
the poet's technique, in confidence that
here the structural principles will be
discovered at home. In this study he
will find as much range for his activities
as he desires.

Especially must he study the metrics, and their implications for structural composition. In this poem I think the critic ought to make good capital of the contrast between the amateurishness of the pleasant discourse as meaning and the hard determinate form of it phonetically. The meter on the whole is out of relation to the meaning of the poem, or to anything else specifically; it is a musical material of low grade, but plastic and only slightly resistant material, and its presence in every poem is that of an abstractionist element that belongs to the art.

And here I will suggest another analogy, this one between Shakespeare's poem and some ordinary specimen of painting. It does not matter how old-fashioned or representational the painting is, we shall all, if we are instructed in the tradition of this art, require it to exhibit along with its represented object an abstract design in terms of pure physical balance or symmetry. We sense rather than measure the success of this design, but it is as if we had drawn a horizontal axis and a vertical axis through the center of the picture, and required the painted masses to balance with respect to each of these two axes. This is an over-simple statement of a structural requirement by which the same details function in two worlds that are different, and that do not correlate with each other. If the painting is of the Holy Family, we might say that this object has a drama, or an economy, of its own; but that the physical masses which compose it must enter also into another economy, that of abstract design; and that the value of any unit mass for the one economy bears no relation to its value for the other. The painting is of great ontological interest because it embodies this special dimension of abstract form. And turning to the poem, we should find that its represented "meaning" is analogous to the represented object in the painting, while its meter is analogous to the pure design.

A number of fascinating speculative considerations must follow upon this discovery. They will have to do with the most fundamental laws of this world's structure. They will be profoundly ontological, though I do not mean that they must be ontological in some recondite sense; ontological in such a homely and compelling sense that perhaps a child might intuit the principles which the critic will arrive at analytically, and with much labor.

I must stop at this point, since I am desired not so much to anticipate the critic as to present him. In conclusion I will remark that the critic will doubtless work empirically, and set up his philosophy only as the drift of his findings will compel him. But ultimately he will be compelled. He will have to subscribe to an ontology. If he is a sound critic his ontology will be that of his poets; and what is that? I suggest that the poetic world-view is Aristotelian and "realistic" rather than Platonic and "idealistic." He cannot follow the poets and still conceive himself as inhabiting the rational or "tidy" universe that is supposed by the scientists.

FROM HAMLET

H. D. F. Kitto[*]

What Ransom has called ontological speculation upon the relationship between local texture and logical structure is exemplified by this essay in which Kitto speculates upon what *Hamlet* of itself is that other similarly constructed tragedies are not.

This examination of *Hamlet* has been based on the same assumptions as our examination of certain Greek plays: that the dramatist said exactly what he meant, through the medium of his art, and means therefore exactly what he has said. We have tried therefore to observe what in fact he has said, considering every scene and every considerable passage (as one would in analysing a picture, for example, or a piece of music), not passing over this or that because it did not happen to interest us, or illustrate our point; nor being too ready to disregard a passage on the grounds that it was put there for some extraneous reason; remembering too that a dramatist can "say" things by means other than words. I do not so flatter myself as to suppose that anything new has been brought to light. Nevertheless, if this general account of the play is acceptable, if its structure has been made to appear purposeful, in details big and small, such that the interpretation (blunders excepted) carries some measure of authority, then the critical method and the assumptions on which it is based may be held to be sound. It seems to me that this may be true.

As we said at the outset, the first thing that strikes us, or should strike us, when

* The selection is reprinted from *Form and Meaning in Drama*, by H. D. F. Kitto, by permission of Methuen & Co. Ltd. Copyright 1956 by Methuen & Co. Ltd.

we contemplate the play is that it ends in the complete destruction of the two houses that are concerned. The character of Hamlet and the inner experience that he undergoes are indeed drawn at length and with great subtlety, and we must not overlook the fact; nevertheless, the architectonic pattern just indicated is so vast as to suggest at once that what we are dealing with is no individual tragedy of character, however profound, but something more like religious drama; and this means that unless we are ready, at every step, to relate the dramatic situation to its religious or philosophical background—in other words, to look at the play from a point of view to which more recent drama has not accustomed us—then we may not see either the structure or the meaning of the play as Shakespeare thought them.

Why do Rosencrantz and Guildenstern die, and Ophelia, and Laertes? Are these disasters casual by-products of "the tragedy of a man who could not make up his mind"? Or are they necessary parts of a firm structure? Each of these disasters we can refer to something that Hamlet has done or failed to do, and we can say that each reveals something more of Hamlet's character; but if we see no more than this we are shortsighted, and are neglecting Shakespeare's plain directions in favour of our own. We are told much more than this when we hear Horatio, and then Laertes, cry "Why, what a King is this!", "The King, the King's to blame"; also when Guildenstern says, with a deep and unconscious irony "We here give up ourselves . . . ," and when Laertes talks of "contagious blastments." Shakespeare puts before us a group of young people, friends or lovers, none of them wicked, one of them at least entirely virtuous, all surrounded by the poisonous air of Denmark (which also Shakespeare brings frequently and vividly before our minds), all of them brought to death because of its evil influences. Time after time, either in some significant patterning or with some phrase pregnant with irony, he makes us see that these people are partners in disaster, all of them borne down on the "massy wheel" to "boisterous ruin."

In this, the natural working-out of sin, there is nothing mechanical. That is the philosophic reason why character and situation must be drawn vividly. Neither here nor in Greek drama have we anything to do with characters who are puppets in the hands of Fate. In both, we see something of the power of the gods, or the designs of Providence; but these no more override or reduce to unimportance the natural working of individual character than the existence, in the physical world, of universal laws overrides the natural behaviour of natural bodies. It is indeed precisely in the natural behaviour of men, and its natural results, in given circumstances, that the operation of the divine laws can be discerned. In *Hamlet*, Shakespeare draws a complete character, not for the comparatively barren purpose of "creating" a Hamlet for our admiration, but in order to show how he, like the others, is inevitably engulfed by the evil that has been set in motion, and how he himself becomes the cause of further ruin.

The conception which unites these eight persons in one coherent catastrophe may be said to be this: evil, once started on its course, will so work as to attack and overthrow impartially the good and the bad; and if the dramatist makes us feel, as he does, that a Providence is ordinant in all this, that, as with the Greeks, is his way of universalising the particular event.

Claudius, the arch-villain, driven by crime into further crime, meets at last what is manifestly divine justice. "If his fitness speaks . . ." says Hamlet; the "fitness" of Claudius has been speaking for a long time. At the opposite pole stands Ophelia, exposed to corruption though uncorrupted, but pitifully destroyed as the chain of evil uncoils itself. Then Gertrude, one of Shakespeare's most tragic characters: she is the first, as Laertes is the last, to be tainted by Claudius; but while he dies in forgiveness and reconciliation, no such gentle influence alleviates her end. In the bedchamber scene Hamlet had pointed out to her the hard road to amendment; has she tried to follow it? On this, Shakespeare is silent; but her last grim experience of life is to find that "O my dear Hamlet, the drink, the drink! I am poisoned"—poisoned, as she must realise, by the cup that her new husband had prepared for the son whom she loved so tenderly. After her own sin, and as a direct consequence of it, everything that she holds dear is blasted. Her part in this tragedy is indeed a frightening one. She is no Claudius, recklessly given to crime, devoid of any pure or disinterested motive. Her love for her son shines through every line she speaks; this, and her affection for Ophelia, show us the Gertrude that might have been, if a mad passion had not swept her into the arms of Claudius. By this one sin she condemned herself to endure, and, still worse, to understand, all its devastating consequences: her son driven "mad," killing Polonius, denouncing herself and her crime in cruel terms that she cannot rebut, Ophelia driven out of her senses and into her grave—nearly a criminal's grave; all her hopes irretrievably ruined. One tragic little detail, just before the end, shows how deeply Shakespeare must have pondered on his Gertrude. We know that she has seen the wild struggle in the graveyard between Laertes and Hamlet. When the Lord enters, to invite Hamlet to the fencing-match, he says: "The Queen desires you to use some gentle entertainment to Laertes before you fall to play." "She well instructs me," says Hamlet. What can this mean, except that she has vague fears of Laertes' anger, and a pathetic hope that Hamlet might appease it, by talk more courteous than he had used in the grave-yard? It recalls her equally pathetic wish that Ophelia's beauty and virtue might "bring him to his wonted ways again." The mischief is always much greater than her worst fears. We soon see how Hamlet's gentle entertainment is received by Laertes; and she, in the blinding flash in which she dies, learns how great a treachery had been prepared against her Hamlet.

We cannot think of Gertrude's death, and the manner of it, without recalling what the Ghost had said: Leave her to Heaven. But if we are to see the hand of Providence—whatever that may signify—in her death, can we do other with the death of Polonius? A "casual slaughter"? A "rash and bloody deed"? Certainly; and let us by all means blame Hamlet for it, as also for the callousness with which he sends Rosencrantz and Guildenstern to their doom; but if we suppose that Shakespeare contrived these things only to show us what Hamlet was like, we shall be treating as secular

drama what Shakespeare designed as something bigger. In fact, Hamlet was *not* like this, any more than he was, by nature, hesitant or dilatory; any more than Ophelia was habitually mad. This is what he has become. The dramatist does indeed direct us to regard the killing of Polonius in two aspects at once: it is a sudden, unpremeditated attack made by Hamlet, "mad," on one who he hopes will prove to be Claudius; and at the same time it is the will of Heaven:

> For this same lord
> I do repent; but Heaven hath pleased it so
> To punish me with this and this with me,
> That I must be their scourge and minister.

Surely this is exactly the same dramaturgy that we meet in Sophocles' *Electra*. When Orestes comes out from killing his mother, Electra asks him how things are. "In the *palace*,"[1] he says, "all is well—if Apollo's oracle was well." Perhaps it was a "rash and bloody deed"; it seems to bring Orestes little joy. We may think of it what we like; Sophocles does not invite us to approve, and if we suppose that he does, we have not understood his play, or his gods. Apollo approves, and Orestes, though he acts for his own reasons, is the gods' "scourge and minister." Polonius, no unworthy Counsellor of this King, a mean and crafty man whose soul is mirrored in his language no less than in his acts, meets a violent death while spying; and that such a man should so be killed is, in a large sense, right. Hamlet may "repent"; Orestes may feel remorse at a dreadful act, but in each case Heaven was ordinant.

The death of Laertes too is a coherent part of this same pattern. To this friend of Hamlet's we can attribute one fault;

---

[1] I italicise this word in order to represent Sophocles' untranslateable μέν, which suggests a coming antithesis that in fact is not expressed.

nor are we taken by surprise when we meet it, for Shakespeare has made his preparations. Laertes is a noble and generous youth, but his sense of honour has no very secure foundations—and Polonius' farewell speech to him makes the fact easy to understand. His natural and unguarded virtue, assailed at once by his anger, his incomplete understanding of the facts, and the evil suggestions of Claudius, gives way; he falls into treachery, and through it, as he comes to see, he is "most justly killed."

Of Rosencrantz and Guildenstern, two agreeable though undistinguished young men, flattered and suborned and cruelly destroyed, there is no more to be said; but there remains Hamlet, last and greatest of the eight. Why must he be destroyed? It would be true to say that he is destroyed simply because he has failed to destroy Claudius first; but this is "truth" as it is understood between police-inspectors, on duty. The dramatic truth must be something which, taking this in its stride, goes much deeper; and we are justified in saying "must be" since this catastrophe too is presented as being directed by Providence, and therefore inevitable and "right." If "there is a special providence in the fall of a sparrow," there surely is in the fall of a Hamlet.

Of the eight victims, we have placed Claudius at one pole and Ophelia at the other; Hamlet, plainly, stands near Ophelia. In both Hamlet and Ophelia we can no doubt detect faults: she ought to have been able to see through Polonius, and he should not have hesitated. But to think like this is to behave like a judge, one who must stand outside the drama and sum up from a neutral point of view; the critic who tries to do this would be better employed in a police-court than in criticism. We must remain within the play, not try to peer at the characters through a window of our own constructing. If we do remain within the play, we observe that what Shakespeare puts before us, all the time, is not faults that we can attribute to Ophelia and Hamlet, but their virtues; and when he does make Hamlet do things deserving of blame, he also makes it evident on whom the blame should be laid. The impression with which he leaves us is not the tragedy that one so fine as Hamlet should be ruined by one fault; it is the tragedy that one so fine should be drawn down into the gulf; and, beyond this, that the poison let loose in Denmark should destroy indiscriminately the good, the bad and the indifferent. Good and bad, Hamlet and Claudius, are coupled in the one sentence "If his fitness speaks, mine is ready." That Claudius is "fit and seasoned for his passage" is plain enough; is it not just as plain that Hamlet is equally "ready"? What has he been telling us, throughout the play, but that life can henceforth have no meaning or value to him? Confronted by what he sees in Denmark, he, the man of action, has been reduced to impotence; the man of reason has gone "mad"; the man of religion has been dragged down to "knavery," and has felt the contagions of Hell. There is room, though not very much, for subtle and judicious appraisal of his character and conduct; the core of his tragedy is not here, but in the fact that such surpassing excellence is, like the beauty and virtue of Ophelia, brought to nothing by evil. Through all the members of these two doomed houses the evil goes on working, in a concatenation

Of carnal, bloody and unnatural acts,
Of accidental judgments, casual slaughters,
Of deaths put on by cunning and forced
   cause,

until none are left, and the slate is wiped clean.

The structure of *Hamlet*, then, suggests that we should treat it as religious drama, and when we do, it certainly does not lose either in significance or in artistic integrity. As we have seen more than once, it has fundamental things in common with Greek religious drama— yet in other respects it is very different, being so complex in form and texture. It may be worth while to enquire, briefly, why this should be so.

One naturally compares it with the two Greek revengetragedies, the *Choephori* and Sophocles' *Electra*, but whether we do this, or extend the comparison to other Greek religious tragedies like the *Agamemnon* or *Oedipus Tyrannus* or *Antigone*, we find one difference which is obviously pertinent to our enquiry: in the Greek plays the sin, crime or error which is the mainspring of the action is specific, while in Hamlet it is something more general, a quality rather than a single act. Thus, although there are crimes enough in the *Oresteia*, what we are really concerned with, throughout the trilogy, is the problem of avenging or punishing crime. The *Agamemnon* is full of hybris, blind folly, blood-lust, adultery, treachery; but what humanity is suffering from, in the play, is not these sins in themselves, but a primitive conception of Justice, one which uses, and can be made to justify, these crimes, and leads to chaos; and the trilogy ends not in any form of reconciliation or forgiveness among those who have injured each other, nor in any purging of sin, or acceptance of punishment, but in the resolution of the dilemma.

Hamlet resembles the *Choephori* in this, that the murder of a King, and adultery, or something like it, are the crimes which have to be avenged; also that these can be avenged only through

another crime, though perhaps a sinless one; but the differences are deep and far-reaching. They are not merely that Orestes kills, and Hamlet shrinks from killing. We may say that both in the Greek trilogy and in Shakespeare's play the Tragic Hero, ultimately, is humanity itself; and what humanity is suffering from, in *Hamlet*, is not a specific evil, but Evil itself. The murder is only the chief of many manifestations of it, the particular case which is the mainspring of the tragic action.

This seems to be typical. In the *Antigone* a whole house is brought down in ruin, and, again, the cause is quite a specific one. It is nothing like the comprehensive wickedness of Iago, or the devouring ambition of Macbeth, or the consuming and all-excluding love of Antony and Cleopatra. It is, quite precisely, that Creon makes, and repeats, a certain error of judgment, ἁμαρτία; and I use the phrase "error of judgment" meaning not that it is venial, nor that it is purely intellectual, but that it is specific. It is not a trivial nor a purely intellectual mistake if a man, in certain circumstances, rejects the promptings of humanity, and thinks that the gods will approve; but this is what Creon does, and the tragedy springs from this and from nothing else. He is not a wicked man—not lecherous or envious or ambitious or vindictive. All this is irrelevant. He is simply the man to make and maintain this one specific and disastrous error.

This contrast between the specific and the general obviously has a close connexion with the contrast between the singleness of the normal Greek tragic structure and the complexity of *Hamlet*. In the first place, since Shakespeare's real theme is not the moral or theological or social problem of crime and vengeance, still less its effect on a single mind and soul, but the corroding power of sin, he will present it not as a single "error of judgment" but as a hydra with many heads. We have shown, let us hope, how this explains, or helps to explain, such features of the play as, so to speak, the simultaneous presentation of three Creons: Claudius, Gertrude and Polonius, each of them, in his own degree, an embodiment of the general evil. Hence too the richer character-drawing. Claudius is a drunkard, and the fact makes its own contribution to the complete structure; if Sophocles had made Creon a drunkard, it would have been an excrescence on the play. Hence too the frequent changes of scene in the first part of the play; also the style of speech invented for Polonius and Osric. The general enemy is the rottenness that pervades Denmark; therefore it is shown in many persons and many guises.

Then, not only are the sources of the corruption diverse, but so are its ramifications too. We are to see how it spreads, whether from Claudius or from Gertrude or from Polonius, and how it involves one after another, destroying as it goes. To be sure, Greek tragedy shows us something similar—but it is not the same. For example, the condemnation of Antigone leads to the death of Haemon, and that to the death of Eurydice; in the *Oresteia* too there is a long succession of crime. In fact, we remarked above that Claudius recalls the *Agamemnon* and its πρώταρχος ἄτη, the crime that sets crime in motion. So he does; but there is a big difference. Both in *Hamlet* and in the Greek plays crime leads to crime, or disaster to disaster, in this linear fashion, but in *Hamlet* it spreads in another way too, one which is not Greek: it spreads from soul to soul, as a contagion, as when Laertes is tempted by Claudius, or, most notably, when, by his mother's example and Polonius' basely inspired interference, Hamlet's love is corrupted into lewdness, or when he turns against his two compromised friends and pitilessly sends them to death.

Extension of evil in this fashion is, I think, foreign to Greek tragedy. Clearly, it involves a dramatic form which is complexive, not linear and single, like the Greek. Of his successive victims, Sophocles does not even mention Haemon until the middle of the play, and Eurydice not until the end; and the effect is most dramatic. In *Hamlet* there are eight victims, all of whom we have to watch, from time to time, as they become more and more deeply involved.

Further, not only are more people involved at the same time in this more generalised Tragic Flaw, but they are involved more intimately, which again makes for a richer dramatic texture. We may compare Hamlet with Orestes. Externally, they are in a similar position. But when Aeschylus has shown us that Orestes is an avenger pure in heart, and that his dilemma is from every point of view an intolerable one, it is not far wrong to say that his interest in Orestes, as a character, is exhausted; anything more would be unnecessary. Hamlet exists in a different kind of tragedy, one which requires that we should see how the contagion gradually spreads over his whole spirit and all his conduct....

PART V

VALUE

THE PROBLEM of value is twofold. There is the general question of ascertaining where and how the value of literature, or, for that matter, of all art, stands with reference to other human values and to the aims and needs of the human race. Then there is the specific question of strictly literary judgment —what are the criteria used in determining whether a poem, a play, or a novel is to be considered good or great in relation to other poems, plays, and novels or to some ideal standard, or to both. In illustrations of such literary judgment, the section below offers four essays on Milton's *Lycidas*, by different critics, judging at different intervals according to different preferences, tenets, and qualifications. Evaluation is particularly ticklish where the testing process of time has not taken place, and for this reason the concluding essay in the collection is one that states the problem of judging contemporary writing.

CHAPTER 16

Literature and the Human Weal

THE POET AND THE STATE
Plato[*]

Plato, in his *Republic* (c. 373 B.C.), excludes the poet from the ideal state because he is merely an imitator, thrice removed from reality since he only reproduces appearances. Moreover, insofar as his authority derives from inspiration, he is dangerous because he might inspire neglect of rationality, the ennobling faculty of man.

Of the many excellences which I perceive in the order of our State, there is none which upon reflection pleases me better than the rule about poetry.

To what do you refer?

To the rejection of imitative poetry, which certainly ought not to be received; as I see far more clearly now that the parts of the soul have been distinguished.

What do you mean?

Speaking in confidence, for I should not like to have my words repeated to the tragedians and the rest of the imitative tribe—but I do not mind saying to you, that all poetical imitations are ruinous to the understanding of the hearers, and that the knowledge of their true nature is the only antidote to them.

Explain the purport of your remark.

Well, I will tell you, although I have always from my earliest youth had an awe and love of Homer, which even now makes the words falter on my lips, for he is the great captain and teacher of the whole of that charming tragic company; but a man is not to be reverenced more than the truth, and therefore I will speak out.

Very good, he said.

Listen to me then, or rather, answer me.

Put your question.

Can you tell me what imitation is? for I really do not know.

A likely thing, then, that I should know.

* The selection is reprinted from *The Dialogues of Plato*, translated by Benjamin Jowett, Oxford University Press, 1892.

537

Why not? for the duller eye may often see a thing sooner than the keener.

Very true, he said; but in your presence, even if I had any faint notion, I could not muster courage to utter it. Will you enquire yourself?

Well then, shall we begin the enquiry in our usual manner: Whenever a number of individuals have a common name, we assume them to have also a corresponding idea or form. Do you understand me?

I do.

Let us take any common instance; there are beds and tables in the world —plenty of them, are there not?

Yes.

But there are only two ideas or forms of them—one the idea of a bed, the other of a table.

True.

And the maker of either of them makes a bed or he makes a table for our use, in accordance with the idea—that is our way of speaking in this and similar instances—but no artificer makes the ideas themselves: how could he?

Impossible.

And there is another artist,—I should like to know what you would say of him.

Who is he?

One who is the maker of all the works of all other workmen.

What an extraordinary man!

Wait a little, and there will be more reason for your saying so. For this is he who is able to make not only vessels of every kind, but plants and animals, himself and all other things—the earth and heaven, and the things which are in heaven or under the earth; he makes the gods also.

He must be a wizard and no mistake.

Oh! you are incredulous, are you? Do you mean that there is no such maker or creator, or that in one sense there might be a maker of all these things but in another not? Do you see that there is a way in which you could make them all yourself?

What way?

An easy way enough; or rather, there are many ways in which the feat might be quickly and easily accomplished, none quicker than that of turning a mirror round and round—you would soon enough make the sun and the heavens, and the earth and yourself, and other animals and plants, and all the other things of which we were just now speaking, in the mirror.

Yes, he said; but they would be appearances only.

Very good, I said, you are coming to the point now. And the painter too is, as I conceive, just such another—a creator of appearances, is he not?

Of course.

But then I suppose you will say that what he creates is untrue. And yet there is a sense in which the painter also creates a bed?

Yes, he said, but not a real bed.

And what of the maker of the bed? Were you not saying that he too makes, not the idea which, according to our view, is the essence of the bed, but only a particular bed?

Yes, I did.

Then if he does not make that which exists he cannot make true existence, but only some semblance of existence; and if any one were to say that the work of the maker of the bed, or of any other workman, has real existence, he could hardly be supposed to be speaking the truth.

At any rate, he replied, philosophers would say that he was not speaking the truth.

No wonder, then, that his work too is an indistinct expression of truth.

No wonder.

Suppose now that by the light of the examples just offered we enquire who this imitator is?

If you please.

Well then, here are three beds: one existing in nature, which is made by God, as I think that we may say—for no one else can be the maker?

No.

There is another which is the work of the carpenter?

Yes.

And the work of the painter is a third?

Yes.

Beds, then, are of three kinds, and there are three artists who superintend them: God, the maker of the bed, and the painter?

Yes, there are three of them.

God, whether from choice or from necessity, made one bed in nature and one only; two or more such ideal beds neither ever have been nor ever will be made by God.

Why is that?

Because even if He had made but two, a third would still appear behind them which both of them would have for their idea, and that would be the ideal bed and not the two others.

Very true, he said.

God knew this, and He desired to be the real maker of a real bed, not a particular maker of a particular bed, and therefore He created a bed which is essentially and by nature one only.

So we believe.

Shall we, then, speak of Him as the natural author or maker of the bed?

Yes, he replied; inasmuch as by the natural process of creation He is the author of this and of all other things.

And what shall we say of the carpenter —is not he also the maker of the bed?

Yes.

But would you call the painter a creator and maker?

Certainly not.

Yet if he is not the maker, what is he in relation to the bed?

I think, he said, that we may fairly designate him as the imitator of that which the others make.

Good, I said; then you call him who is third in the descent from nature an imitator?

Certainly, he said.

And the tragic poet is an imitator, and therefore, like all other imitators, he is thrice removed from the king and from the truth?

That appears to be so.

Then about the imitator we are agreed. And what about the painter?—I would like to know whether he may be thought to imitate that which originally exists in nature, or only the creations of artists?

The latter.

As they are or as they appear? You have still to determine this.

What do you mean?

I mean, that you may look at a bed from different points of view, obliquely or directly or from any other point of view, and the bed will appear different, but there is no difference in reality. And the same of all things.

Yes, he said, the difference is only apparent.

Now let me ask you another question: Which is the art of painting designed to be—an imitation of things as they are, or as they appear—of appearance or of reality?

Of appearance.

Then the imitator, I said, is a long way off the truth, and can do all things because he lightly touches on a small part of them, and that part an image. For example: A painter will paint a cobbler, carpenter, or any other artist, though he knows nothing of their arts; and, if he is a good artist, he may deceive children or simple persons, when he shows them his picture of a carpenter from a distance, and they will fancy that they are looking at a real carpenter.

Certainly.

And whenever any one informs us that he has found a man who knows all the arts, and all things else that anybody knows, and every single thing with a higher degree of accuracy than any other man—whoever tells us this, I think that we can only imagine him to be a simple creature who is likely to have been deceived by some wizard or actor whom he met, and whom he thought all-knowing, because he himself was unable to analyze the nature of knowledge and ignorance and imitation.

Most true.

And so, when we hear persons saying that the tragedians, and Homer, who is at their head, know all the arts and all things human, virtue as well as vice, and divine things too, for that the good poet cannot compose well unless he knows his subject, and that he who has not this knowledge can never be a poet, we ought to consider whether here also there may not be a similar illusion. Perhaps they may have come across imitators and been deceived by them; they may not have remembered when they saw their works that these were but imitations thrice removed from the truth, and could easily be made without any knowledge of the truth, because they are appearances only and not realities? Or, after all, they may be in the right, and poets do really know the things about which they seem to the many to speak so well?

The question, he said, should by all means be considered.

Now do you suppose that if a person were able to make the original as well as the image, he would seriously devote himself to the image-making branch? Would he allow imitation to be the ruling principle of his life, as if he had nothing higher in him?

I should say not.

The real artist, who knew what he was imitating, would be interested in realities and not in imitations; and would desire to leave as memorials of himself works many and fair; and, instead of being the author of encomiums, he would prefer to be the theme of them.

Yes, he said, that would be to him a source of much greater honour and profit.

Then, I said, we must put a question to Homer; not about medicine, or any of the arts to which his poems only incidentally refer: we are not going to ask him, or any other poet, whether he has cured patients like Asclepius, or left behind him a school of medicine such as the Asclepiads were, or whether he only talks about medicine and other arts at second hand; but we have a right to know respecting military tactics, politics, education, which are the chiefest and noblest subjects of his poems, and we may fairly ask him about them. "Friend Homer," then we say to him, "if you are only in the second remove from truth in what you say of virtue, and not in the third—not an image maker or imitator—and if you are able to discern what pursuits make men better or worse in private or public life, tell us what State was ever better governed by your help? The good order of Lacedaemon is due to Lycurgus, and many other cities great and small have been similarly benefited by others; but who says that you have been a good legislator to them and have done them any good? Italy and Sicily boast of Charondas, and there is Solon who is renowned among us; but what city has anything to say about you?" Is there any city which he might name?

I think not, said Glaucon; not even

the Homerids themselves pretend that he was a legislator.

Well, but is there any war on record which was carried on successfully by him, or aided by his counsels, when he was alive?

There is not.

Or is there any invention of his, applicable to the arts or to human life, such as Thales the Milesian or Anacharsis the Scythian, and other ingenious men have conceived, which is attributed to him?

There is absolutely nothing of the kind.

But, if Homer never did any public service, was he privately a guide or teacher of any? Had he in his lifetime friends who loved to associate with him, and who handed down to posterity an Homeric way of life, such as was established by Pythagoras who was so greatly beloved for his wisdom, and whose followers are to this day quite celebrated for the order which was named after him?

Nothing of the kind is recorded of him. For surely, Socrates, Creophylus, the companion of Homer, that child of flesh, whose name always makes us laugh, might be more justly ridiculed for his stupidity, if, as is said, Homer was greatly neglected by him and others in his own day when he was alive?

Yes, I replied, that is the tradition. But can you imagine, Glaucon, that if Homer had really been able to educate and improve mankind—if he had possessed knowledge and not been a mere imitator—can you imagine, I say, that he would not have had many followers, and been honoured and loved by them? Protagoras of Abdera, and Prodicus of Ceos, and a host of others, have only to whisper to their contemporaries: "You will never be able to manage either your own house or your own State until you appoint us to be your ministers of education"— and this ingenious device of theirs has such an effect in making men love them that their companions all but carry them about on their shoulders. And is it conceivable that the contemporaries of Homer, or again of Hesiod, would have allowed either of them to go about as rhapsodists, if they had really been able to make mankind virtuous? Would they not have been as unwilling to part with them as with gold, and have compelled them to stay at home with them? Or, if the master would not stay, then the disciples would have followed him about everywhere, until they had got education enough?

Yes, Socrates, that, I think, is quite true.

Then must we not infer that all these poetical individuals, beginning with Homer, are only imitators; they copy images of virtue and the like, but the truth they never reach? The poet is like a painter who, as we have already observed, will make a likeness of a cobbler though he understands nothing of cobbling; and his picture is good enough for those who know no more than he does, and judge only by colours and figures.

Quite so.

In like manner the poet with his words and phrases[1] may be said to lay on the colours of the several arts, himself understanding their nature only enough to imitate them; and other people, who are as ignorant as he is, and judge only from his words, imagine that if he speaks of cobbling, or of military tactics, or of anything else, in metre and harmony and rhythm, he speaks very well—such is the sweet influence which melody and rhythm by nature have. And I think that you must have observed again and again what a poor appearance the tales of poets make when stripped of the colours which music puts upon them, and recited in simple prose.

[1] Or, "with his nouns and verbs."

Yes, he said.

They are like faces which were never really beautiful, but only blooming; and now the bloom of youth has passed away from them?

Exactly.

Here is another point: The imitator or maker of the image knows nothing of true existence; he knows appearances only. Am I not right?

Yes.

Then let us have a clear understanding, and not be satisfied with half an explanation.

Proceed.

Of the painter we say that he will paint reins, and he will paint a bit?

Yes.

And the worker in leather and brass will make them?

Certainly.

But does the painter know the right form of the bit and reins? Nay, hardly even the workers in brass and leather who make them; only the horseman who knows how to use them—he knows their right form.

Most true.

And may we not say the same of all things?

What?

That there are three arts which are concerned with all things: one which uses, another which makes, a third which imitates them?

Yes.

And the excellence or beauty or truth of every structure, animate or inanimate, and of every action of man, is relative to the use for which nature or the artist has intended them.

True.

Then the user of them must have the greatest experience of them, and he must indicate to the maker the good or bad qualities which develop themselves in use; for example, the flute-player will tell the flute-maker which of his flutes is satisfactory to the performer; he will tell him how he ought to make them, and the other will attend to his instructions?

Of course.

The one knows and therefore speaks with authority about the goodness and badness of flutes, while the other, confiding in him, will do what he is told by him?

True.

The instrument is the same, but about the excellence or badness of it the maker will only attain to a correct belief; and this he will gain from him who knows, by talking to him and being compelled to hear what he has to say, whereas the user will have knowledge?

True.

But will the imitator have either? Will he know from use whether or no his drawing is correct or beautiful? Or will he have right opinion from being compelled to associate with another who knows and gives him instructions about what he should draw?

Neither.

Then he will no more have true opinion than he will have knowledge about the goodness or badness of his imitations?

I suppose not.

The imitative artist will be in a brilliant state of intelligence about his own creations?

Nay, very much the reverse.

And still he will go on imitating without knowing what makes a thing good or bad, and may be expected therefore to imitate only that which appears to be good to the ignorant multitude?

Just so.

Thus far then we are pretty well agreed that the imitator has no knowledge worth mentioning of what he imitates. Imitation is only a kind of play or sport, and the tragic poets, whether they write in Iambic or in Heroic verse, are imitators in the highest degree?

Very true.

And now tell me, I conjure you, has not imitation been shown by us to be concerned with that which is thrice removed from the truth?

Certainly.

And what is the faculty in man to which imitation is addressed?

What do you mean?

I will explain: The body which is large when seen near, appears small when seen at a distance?

True.

And the same object appears straight when looked at out of the water, and crooked when in the water; and the concave becomes convex, owing to the illusion about colours to which the sight is liable. Thus every sort of confusion is revealed within us; and this is that weakness of the human mind on which the art of conjuring and of deceiving by light and shadow and other ingenious devices imposes, having an effect upon us like magic.

True.

And the arts of measuring and numbering and weighing come to the rescue of the human understanding—there is the beauty of them—and the apparent greater or less, or more or heavier, no longer have the mastery over us, but give way before calculation and measure and weight?

Most true.

And this, surely, must be the work of the calculating and rational principle in the soul?

To be sure.

And when this principle measures and certifies that some things are equal, or that some are greater or less than others, there occurs an apparent contradiction?

True.

But were we not saying that such a contradiction is impossible—the same

faculty cannot have contrary opinions at the same time about the same thing?

Very true.

Then that part of the soul which has an opinion contrary to measure is not the same with that which has an opinion in accordance with measure?

True.

And the better part of the soul is likely to be that which trusts to measure and calculation?

Certainly.

And that which is opposed to them is one of the inferior principles of the soul?

No doubt.

This was the conclusion at which I was seeking to arrive when I said that painting or drawing, and imitation in general, when doing their own proper work, are far removed from truth, and the companions and friends and associates of a principle within us which is equally removed from reason, and that they have no true or healthy aim.

Exactly.

The imitative art is an inferior who marries an inferior, and has inferior offspring.

Very true.

And is this confined to the sight only, or does it extend to the hearing also, relating in fact to what we term poetry?

Probably the same would be true of poetry.

Do not rely, I said, on a probability derived from the analogy of painting; but let us examine further and see whether the faculty with which poetical imitation is concerned is good or bad.

By all means.

We may state the question thus:— Imitation imitates the actions of men, whether voluntary or involuntary, on which, as they imagine, a good or bad result has ensued, and they rejoice or sorrow accordingly. Is there anything more?

No, there is nothing else.

But in all this variety of circumstances is the man at unity with himself—or rather, as in the instance of sight there was confusion and opposition in his opinions about the same things, so here also is there not strife and inconsistency in his life? Though I need hardly raise the question again, for I remember that all this has been already admitted; and the soul has been acknowledged by us to be full of these and ten thousand similar oppositions occurring at the same moment?

And we were right, he said.

Yes, I said, thus far we were right; but there was an omission which must now be supplied.

What was the omission?

Were we not saying that a good man, who has the misfortune to lose his son or anything else which is most dear to him, will bear the loss with more equanimity than another?

Yes.

But will he have no sorrow, or shall we say that although he cannot help sorrowing, he will moderate his sorrow?

The latter, he said, is the truer statement.

Tell me: will he be more likely to struggle and hold out against his sorrow when he is seen by his equals, or when he is alone?

It will make a great difference whether he is seen or not.

When he is by himself he will not mind saying or doing many things which he would be ashamed of any one hearing or seeing him do?

True.

There is a principle of law and reason in him which bids him resist, as well as a feeling of his misfortune which is forcing him to indulge his sorrow?

True.

But when a man is drawn in two op-posite directions, to and from the same object, this, as we affirm, necessarily implies two distinct principles in him?

Certainly.

One of them is ready to follow the guidance of the law?

How do you mean?

The law would say that to be patient under suffering is best, and that we should not give way to impatience, as there is no knowing whether such things are good or evil; and nothing is gained by impatience; also, because no human thing is of serious importance, and grief stands in the way of that which at the moment is most required.

What is most required? he asked.

That we should take counsel about what has happened, and when the dice have been thrown order our affairs in the way which reason deems best; not, like children who have had a fall, keeping hold of the part struck and wasting time in setting up a howl, but always accustoming the soul forthwith to apply a remedy, raising up that which is sickly and fallen, banishing the cry of sorrow by the healing art.

Yes, he said, that is the true way of meeting the attacks of fortune.

Yes, I said; and the higher principle is ready to follow this suggestion of reason?

Clearly.

And the other principle, which inclines us to recollection of our troubles and to lamentation, and can never have enough of them, we may call irrational, useless, and cowardly?

Indeed, we may.

And does not the latter—I mean the rebellious principle—furnish a great variety of materials for imitation? Whereas the wise and calm temperament, being always nearly equable, is not easy to imitate or to appreciate when imitated, especially at a public festival when a promiscuous crowd is assembled in a theatre. For the feeling represented is one to which they are strangers.

Certainly.

Then the imitative poet who aims at being popular is not by nature made, nor is his art intended, to please or to affect the rational principle in the soul; but he will prefer the passionate and fitful temper, which is easily imitated?

Clearly.

And now we may fairly take him and place him by the side of the painter, for he is like him in two ways: first, inasmuch as his creations have an inferior degree of truth—in this, I say, he is like him; and he is also like him in being concerned with an inferior part of the soul; and therefore we shall be right in refusing to admit him into a well-ordered State, because he awakens and nourishes and strengthens the feelings and impairs the reason. As in a city when the evil are permitted to have authority and the good are put out of the way, so in the soul of man, as we maintain, the imitative poet implants an evil constitution, for he indulges the irrational nature which has no discernment of greater and less, but thinks the same thing at one time great and at another small—he is a manufacturer of images and is very far removed from the truth.

Exactly.

But we have not yet brought forward the heaviest count in our accusation: —the power which poetry has of harming even the good (and there are very few who are not harmed), is surely an awful thing?

Yes, certainly, if the effect is what you say.

Hear and judge: The best of us, as I conceive, when we listen to a passage of Homer, or one of the tragedians, in which he represents some pitiful hero who is drawling out his sorrows in a long oration, of weeping, and smiting his breast—the best of us, you know, delight in giving way to sympathy, and are in raptures at the excellence of the poet who stirs our feelings most.

Yes, of course I know.

But when any sorrow of our own happens to us, then you may observe that we pride ourselves on the opposite quality —we would fain be quiet and patient; this is the manly part, and the other which delighted us in the recitation is now deemed to be the part of a woman.

Very true, he said.

Now can we be right in praising and admiring another who is doing that which any one of us would abominate and be ashamed of in his own person?

No, he said, that is certainly not reasonable.

Nay, I said, quite reasonable from one point of view.

What point of view?

If you consider, I said, that when in misfortune we feel a natural hunger and desire to relieve our sorrow by weeping and lamentation, and that this feeling which is kept under control in our own calamities is satisfied and delighted by the poets;—the better nature in each of us, not having been sufficiently trained by reason or habit, allows the sympathetic element to break loose because the sorrow is another's; and the spectator fancies that there can be no disgrace to himself in praising and pitying any one who comes telling him what a good man he is, and making a fuss about his troubles; he thinks that the pleasure is a gain, and why should he be supercilious and lose this and the poem too? Few persons ever reflect, as I should imagine, that from the evil of other men something of evil is communicated to themselves. And so the feeling of sorrow which has gathered strength at the sight of the misfortunes of others is with difficulty repressed in our own.

How very true!

And does not the same hold also of the ridiculous? There are jests which you would be ashamed to make yourself, and yet on the comic stage, or indeed in private, when you hear them, you are greatly amused by them, and are not at all disgusted at their unseemliness;—the case of pity is repeated;—there is a principle in human nature which is disposed to raise a laugh, and this which you once restrained by reason, because you were afraid of being thought a buffoon, is now let out again; and having stimulated the risible faculty at the theatre, you are betrayed unconsciously to yourself into playing the comic poet at home.

Quite true, he said.

And the same may be said of lust and anger and all the other affections, of desire and pain and pleasure, which are held to be inseparable from every action—in all of them poetry feeds and waters the passions instead of drying them up; she lets them rule, although they ought to be controlled, if mankind are ever to increase in happiness and virtue.

I cannot deny it.

Therefore, Glaucon, I said, whenever you meet with any of the eulogists of Homer declaring that he has been the educator of Hellas, and that he is profitable for education and for the ordering of human things, and that you should take him up again and again and get to know him and regulate your whole life according to him, we may love and honour those who say these things—they are excellent people, as far as their lights extend; and we are ready to acknowledge that Homer is the greatest of poets and first of tragedy writers; but we must remain firm in our conviction that hymns to the gods and praises of famous men are the only poetry which ought to be admitted into our State. For if you go beyond this and allow the honeyed muse to enter, either in epic or lyric verse, not law and the reason of mankind, which by common consent have ever been deemed best, but pleasure and pain will be the rulers in our State.

That is most true, he said.

And now since we have reverted to the subject of poetry, let this our defence serve to show the reasonableness of our former judgment in sending away out of our State an art having the tendencies which we have described; for reason constrained us. But that she may not impute to us any harshness or want of politeness, let us tell her that there is an ancient quarrel between philosophy and poetry; of which there are many proofs, such as the saying of "the yelping hound howling at her lord," or of one "mighty in the vain talk of fools," and "the mob of sages circumventing Zeus," and the "subtle thinkers who are beggars after all"; and there are innumerable other signs of ancient enmity between them. Notwithstanding this, let us assure our sweet friend and the sister arts of imitation that if she will only prove her title to exist in a well-ordered State we shall be delighted to receive her—we are very conscious of her charms; but we may not on that account betray the truth. I dare say, Glaucon, that you are as much charmed by her as I am, especially when she appears in Homer?

Yes, indeed, I am greatly charmed.

Shall I propose, then, that she be allowed to return from exile, but upon this condition only—that she make a defence of herself in lyrical or some other metre?

Certainly.

And we may further grant to those of her defenders who are lovers of poetry and yet not poets the permission to speak in prose on her behalf: let them show not only that she is pleasant but also useful to States and to human life, and we will listen in a kindly spirit; for if this can be proved we shall surely be the gainers—I mean, if there is a use in poetry as well as a delight?

Certainly, he said, we shall be the gainers.

If her defence fails, then, my dear friend, like other persons who are enamoured of something, but put a restraint upon themselves when they think their desires are opposed to their interests, so too must we after the manner of lovers give her up, though not without a struggle. We too are inspired by that love of poetry which the education of noble States has implanted in us, and therefore we would have her appear at her best and truest; but so long as she is unable to make good her defence, this argument of ours shall be a charm to us, which we will repeat to ourselves while

we listen to her strains; that we may not fall away into the childish love of her which captivates the many. At all events we are well aware that poetry being such as we have described is not to be regarded seriously as attaining to the truth; and he who listens to her, fearing for the safety of the city which is within him, should be on his guard against her seductions and make our words his law.

Yes, he said, I quite agree with you.

Yes, I said, my dear Glaucon, for great is the issue at stake, greater than appears, whether a man is to be good or bad. And what will any one be profited if under the influence of honour or money or power, aye, or under the excitement of poetry, he neglect justice and virtue?

Yes, he said; I have been convinced by the argument, as I believe that any one else would have been.

PREFACE TO *THE PICTURE OF DORIAN GRAY*
Oscar Wilde

Wilde's series of critical epigrams prefixed to his novel is famous as a manifesto of estheticism—Art-for-Art's-Sake, a doctrine of the late nineteenth century that insisted on the purely intrinsic value of art and rejected all criticism based on its pertinence and usefulness, moral or otherwise, to society.

The artist is the creator of beautiful things.

To reveal art and conceal the artist is art's aim.

The critic is he who can translate into another manner or a new material his impression of beautiful things.

The highest, as the lowest, form of criticism is a mode of autobiography. Those who find ugly meanings in beautiful things are corrupt without being charming. This is a fault.

Those who find beautiful meanings in beautiful things are the cultivated. For these there is hope. They are the elect to whom beautiful things mean only Beauty.

There is no such thing as a moral or an immoral book. Books are well written, or badly written. That is all. The nineteenth century dislike of Realism is the rage of Caliban seeing his own face in a glass.

The nineteenth century dislike of

Romanticism is the rage of Caliban not seeing his own face in a glass.

The moral life of man forms part of the subject-manner of the artist, but the morality of art consists in the perfect use of an imperfect medium. No artist desires to prove anything. Even things that are true can be proved.

No artist has ethical sympathies. An ethical sympathy in an artist is an unpardonable mannerism of style.

No artist is ever morbid. The artist can express everything.

Thought and language are to the artist instruments of an art.

Vice and virtue are to the artist materials for an art.

From the point of view of form, the type of all the arts is the art of the musician. From the point of view of feeling, the actor's craft is the type.

All art is at once surface and symbol.

Those who go beneath the surface do so at their peril.

Those who read the symbol do so at their peril.

It is the spectator, and not life, that art really mirrors.

Diversity of opinion about a work of art shows that the work is new, complex, and vital.

When critics disagree the artist is in accord with himself.

We can forgive a man for making a useful thing as long as he does not admire it. The only excuse for making a useless thing is that one admires it intensely.

All art is quite useless.

POETRY AND BELIEFS
I. A. Richards[*]

The dominant change in the world picture of our time, according to Richards, "may be described as the *Neutralization of Nature*," the transference from a magical view of the universe, from a belief in "a world of Spirits and Powers" that is congenial to man's emotional make-up, to the scientific outlook. The latter does not provide what literature gives us—experience, the ordering of our "responses to the world." "Experience is its own justification," Richards claims, and in it, rather than in specific beliefs, lies the ultimate humanistic value.

The business of the poet, as we have seen, is to give order and coherence, and so freedom, to a body of experience. To do so through words which act as its skeleton, as a structure by which the impulses which make up the experience are adjusted to one another and act together. The means by which words do this are many and varied. To work them out is a problem for psychology. A beginning has been indicated above, but only a beginning. What little can be done shows already that most critical dogmas of the past are either false or nonsense. A little

* The essay is reprinted from Chapter VI of *Science and Poetry*, by I. A. Richards, W. W. Norton and Company, Inc., 1926, by permission of the author.

knowledge is not here a danger, but clears the air in a remarkable way.

Roughly and inadequately, even in the light of our present knowledge, we can say that words work in the poem in two main fashions. As sensory stimuli and as (in the *widest* sense) symbols. We must refrain from considering the sensory side of the poem, remarking only that it is *not* in the least independent of the other side, and that it has for definite reasons prior importance in most poetry. We must confine ourselves to the other function of words in the poem, or rather, omitting much that is of secondary relevance, to one form of that function, let me call it *pseudo-statement*.

It will be admitted—by those who distinguish between scientific statement, where truth is ultimately a matter of verification as this is understood in the laboratory, and emotive utterance, where "truth" is primarily acceptability *by* some attitude, and more remotely is the acceptability *of* this attitude itself—that it is *not* the poet's business to make true statements. Yet poetry has constantly the air of making statements, and important ones; which is one reason why some mathematicians cannot read it. They find the alleged statements to be *false*. It will be agreed that their approach to poetry and their expectations from it are mistaken. But what exactly is the other, the right, the poetic, approach and how does it differ from the mathematical?

The poetic approach evidently limits the framework of possible consequences into which the pseudo-statement is taken. For the scientific approach this framework is unlimited. Any and every consequence is relevant. If any of the consequences of a statement conflicts with acknowledged fact then so much the worse for the statement. Not so with the pseudo-statement when poetically approached. The problem is—just how does the limitation work? The usual account is in terms of a supposed universe of discourse, a world of make-believe, of imagination, of recognised fictions common to the poet and his readers. A pseudo-statement which fits into this system of assumptions would be regarded as "poetically true"; one which does not, as "poetically false." This attempt to treat "poetic truth" on the model of general "coherence theories" is very natural for certain schools of logicians; but is inadequate, on the wrong lines from the outset. To mention two objections out of many; there is no means of discovering what the "universe of discourse" is on any occasion, and the kind of coherence which must hold within it, supposing it to be discoverable, is not an affair of logical relations. Attempt to define the system of propositions into which

O Rose, thou art sick!

must fit, and the logical relations which must hold between them if it is to be "poetically true"; the absurdity of the theory becomes evident.

We must look further. In the poetic approach the relevant consequences are not logical or to be arrived at by a partial relaxation of logic. Except occasionally and by accident logic does not enter at all. They are the consequences which arise through our emotional organisation. The acceptance which a pseudo-statement receives is entirely governed by its effects upon our feelings and attitudes. Logic only comes in, if at all, in subordination, as a servant to our emotional response. It is an unruly servant, however, as poets and readers are constantly discovering. A pseudo-statement is "true" if it suits and serves some attitude or links together attitudes which on other grounds are desirable. This kind of truth is so opposed to scientific truth that it is a pity to use so similar a word, but at present it is difficult to avoid the malpractice.[1]

This brief analysis may be sufficient to indicate the fundamental disparity and opposition between pseudo-statements as they occur in poetry and statements as they occur in science. A pseudo-statement is a form of words which is justified entirely by its effect in releasing or organising our impulses and attitudes (due regard being had for the better or worse organisations of these *inter se*); a statement, on the other hand, is justified by its truth, *i.e.*, its correspondence, in a highly technical sense, with the fact to which it points.

Statements true and false alike do of course constantly touch off attitudes and action. Our daily practical existence is largely guided by them. On the whole true statements are of more service to us than false ones. None the less we do not and, at present, cannot order our emotions and attitudes by true statements alone. Nor is there any probability that we ever shall contrive to do so. This is one of the great new dangers to which civilisation is exposed. Countless pseudo-statements—about God, about the universe, about human nature, the relations of mind to mind, about the soul, its rank and destiny—pseudo-statements which are pivotal points in the organisation of the mind, vital to its well-being, have suddenly become, for sincere, honest and informal minds, impossible to believe. For centuries they have been believed; now they are gone, irrecoverably; and the knowledge which has killed them is not of a kind upon which an equally

[1] For an account of the various senses of truth and of the ways in which they may be distinguished in discussion cf. *The Meaning of Meaning*, by C. K. Ogden and the author, Chapters VII and X.

fine organisation of the mind can be based.

This is the contemporary situation. The remedy, since there is no prospect of our gaining adequate knowledge, and since indeed it is fairly clear that genuine knowledge cannot serve us here and can only increase our practical control of Nature, is to cut our pseudo-statements free from belief, and yet retain them, in this released state, as the main instruments by which we order our attitudes to one another and to the world. Not so desperate a remedy as may appear, for poetry conclusively shows that even the most important among our attitudes can be aroused and maintained without any belief entering in at all. Those of Tragedy, for example. We need no beliefs, and indeed we must have none, if we are to read *King Lear*. Pseudo-statements to which we attach no belief and statements proper such as science provides cannot conflict. It is only when we introduce illicit beliefs into poetry that danger arises. To do so is from this point of view a profanation of poetry.

Yet an important branch of criticism which has attracted the best talents from prehistoric times until to-day consists of the endeavour to persuade men that the functions of science and poetry are identical, or that the one is a "higher form" of the other, or that they conflict and we must choose between them.

The root of this persistent endeavour has still to be mentioned; it is the same as that from which the Magical View of the world arose. If we give to a pseudo-statement the kind of unqualified acceptance which belongs by right only to certified scientific statements, if we can contrive to do this, the impulses and attitudes with which we respond to it gain a notable stability and vigour. Briefly, if we can contrive to believe poetry, then the world *seems*, while we do so, to be transfigured. It used to be comparatively easy to do this, and the habit has become well established. With the extension of science and the neutralisation of nature it has become difficult as well as dangerous. Yet it is still alluring; it has many analogies with drug-taking. Hence the endeavours of the critics referred to. Various subterfuges have been devised along the lines of regarding Poetic Truth as figurative, symbolic; or as more immediate, as a truth of Intuition, not of reason; or as a higher form of the same truth as reason yields. Such attempts to use poetry as a denial or as a corrective of science are very common. One point can be made against them all: they are never worked out in detail. There is no equivalent to Mill's *Logic* expounding any such view. The language in which they are framed is usually a blend of obsolete psychology and emotive exclamations.

The long-established and much-encouraged habit of giving to emotive utterances—whether pseudo-statements simple, or looser and larger wholes taken as saying something figuratively—the kind of assent which we give to established facts, has for most people debilitated a wide range of their responses. A few scientists, caught young and brought up in the laboratory, are free from it; but then, as a rule, they pay no *serious* attention to poetry. For most men the recognition of the neutrality of nature brings about—through this habit—a divorce from poetry. They are so used to having their responses propped up by beliefs, however vague, that when these shadowy supports are removed they are no longer able to respond. Their attitudes to so many things have been forced in the past, over-encouraged. And when the world-picture ceases to assist there is a collapse. Over whole tracts of natural emotional response we are to-day like a bed of dahlias whose sticks have been

removed. And this effect of the neutralisation of nature is only in its beginnings. Consider the probable effects upon love-poetry in the near future of the kind of enquiry into basic human constitution exemplified by psycho-analysis.

A sense of desolation, of uncertainty, of futility, of the groundlessness of aspirations, of the vanity of endeavour, and a thirst for a life-giving water which seems suddenly to have failed, are the signs in consciousness of this necessary reorganisation of our lives.[2] Our attitudes and impulses are being compelled to become self-supporting; they are being driven back upon their biological justification, made once again sufficient to themselves. And the only impulses which seem strong enough to continue unflagging are commonly so crude that, to more finely developed individuals, they hardly seem worth having. Such people cannot live by warmth, food, fighting, drink, and sex alone. Those who are least affected by the change are those who are emotionally least removed from the animals. As we shall see at the close of this essay, even a considerable poet may attempt to find relief by a reversion to primitive mentality.

It is important to diagnose the disease correctly and to put the blame in the right quarter. Usually it is some alleged "materialism" of science which is denounced. This mistake is due partly to clumsy thinking, but chiefly to relics of

[2] To those familiar with Mr. Eliot's *The Waste Land*, my indebtedness to it at this point will be evident. He seems to me by this poem, to have performed two considerable services for this generation. He has given a perfect emotive description of a state of mind which is probably inevitable for a while to all meditative people. Secondly, by effecting a complete severance between his poetry and *all* beliefs, and this without any weakening of the poetry, he has realised what might otherwise have remained largely a speculative possibility, and has shown the way to the only solution of these difficulties. "In the destructive element immerse. That is the way."

the Magical View. For even if the Universe were "spiritual" all through (whatever that assertion might mean; all such assertions are probably nonsense), that would not make it any more accordant to human attitudes. It is not what the universe is made of but how it works, the law it follows, which makes knowledge of it incapable of spurring on our emotional responses, and further the nature of knowledge itself makes it inadequate. The contact with things which we therein establish is too sketchy and indirect to help us. We are beginning to know too much about the bond which unites the mind to its object in knowledge for that old dream of a perfect knowledge which would guarantee perfect life to retain its sanction. What was thought to be pure knowledge, we see now to have been shot through with hope and desire with fear and wonder, and these intrusive elements indeed gave it all its power to support our lives. In knowledge, in the "How?" of events, we can find hints by which to take advantage of circumstances in our favour and avoid mischances. But we cannot get from it a *raison d'être* or a justification of more than a relatively lowly kind of life.

The justification, or the reverse, of any attitude lies, not in the object, but in itself, in its serviceableness to the whole personality. Upon its place in the whole system of attitudes, which is the personality, all its worth depends. This is true equally for the subtle, finely compounded attitudes of the civilised individual as for the simpler attitudes of the child.

In brief, experience is its own justification; and this fact must be faced, although sometimes—by a lover, for example—it may be very difficult to accept. Once it is faced, it is apparent that all the attitudes to other human beings and to the world in all its aspects, which have been serviceable to humanity, remain as they were, as valuable as ever. Hesitation felt in admitting this is a measure of the strength of the evil habit we have described. But many of these attitudes, valuable as ever, are, now that they are being set free, more difficult to maintain, because we still hunger after a basis in belief.

RELIGION AND LITERATURE
T. S. Eliot[*]

Eliot advances the proposition that the *greatness* of literature "cannot be determined solely by literary standards," that literary criticism "should be completed by criticism from a definite ethical and theological standpoint." Because literature affects not merely our esthetic sensibilities but our "moral and religious existence," we must criticize it according to principles and beliefs and not with the liberal secularism that embraces any and all experience for its own sake.

[*] The essay is reprinted from *Selected Essays of T. S. Eliot*, copyright, 1932, 1936, 1950, by Harcourt, Brace & World, Inc., © 1960, 1964, by T. S. Eliot. Reprinted by permission of the publishers.

What I have to say is largely in support of the following propositions: Literary criticism should be completed by criticism from a definite ethical and theological standpoint. In so far as in any age there is common agreement on ethical and theological matters, so far can literary criticism be substantive. In ages like our own, in which there is no such common agreement, it is the more necessary for Christian readers to scrutinize their reading, especially of works of imagination, with explicit ethical and theological standards. The "greatness" of literature cannot be determined solely by literary standards; though we must remember that whether it is literature or not can be determined only by literary standards.[1]

We have tacitly assumed, for some centuries past, that there is *no* relation between literature and theology. This is not to deny that literature—I mean, again, primarily works of imagination—has been, is, and probably always will be judged by some moral standards. But moral judgments of literary works are made only according to the moral code accepted by each generation, whether it lives according to that code or not. In any age which accepts some precise Christian theology, the common code may be fairly orthodox: though even in such periods the common code may exalt such concepts as "honour," "glory" or "revenge" to a position quite intolerable to Christianity. The dramatic ethics of the Elizabethan Age offers an interesting study. But when the common code is detached from its theological background, and is consequently more and more merely a matter of habit, it is exposed both to prejudice and to change. At such times morals are open to being altered

by literature; so that we find in practice that what is "objectionable" in literature is merely what the present generation is not used to. It is a commonplace that what shocks one generation is accepted quite calmly by the next. This adaptability to change of moral standards is sometimes greeted with satisfaction as an evidence of human perfectibility: whereas it is only evidence of what unsubstantial foundations people's moral judgments have.

I am not concerned here with religious literature but with the application of our religion to the criticism of any literature. It may be as well, however, to distinguish first what I consider to be the three senses in which we can speak of "religious literature." The first is that of which we say that it is religious "literature" in the same way that we speak of "historical literature" or of "scientific literature." I mean that we can treat the Authorized translation of the Bible, or the works of Jeremy Taylor, as literature, in the same way that we treat the historical writing of Clarendon or of Gibbon—our two great English historians—as literature; or Bradley's *Logic*, or Buffon's *Natural History*. All of these writers were men who, incidentally to their religious, or historical, or philosophic purpose, had a gift of language which makes them delightful to read to all those who can enjoy language well written, even if they are unconcerned with the objects which the writers had in view. And I would add that though a scientific, or historical, or theological, or philosophic work which is also "literature," may become superannuated as anything but literature, yet it is not likely to be "literature" unless it had its scientific or other value for its own time. While I acknowledge the legitimacy of this enjoyment, I am more acutely aware of its abuse. The persons who enjoy these

---

[1] As an example of literary criticism given greater significance by theological interests, I would call attention to Theodor Haecker: *Virgil* (Sheed and Ward).

writings *solely* because of their literary merit are essentially parasites; and we know that parasites, when they become too numerous, are pests. I could easily fulminate for a whole hour against the men of letters who have gone into ecstasies over "the Bible as literature," the Bible as "the noblest monument of English prose." Those who talk of the Bible as a "monument of English prose" are merely admiring it as a monument over the grave of Christianity. I must try to avoid the by-paths of my discourse: it is enough to suggest that just as the work of Clarendon, or Gibbon, or Buffon, or Bradley would be of inferior literary value if it were insignificant as history, science, and philosophy respectively, so the Bible has had a *literary* influence upon English literature *not* because it has been considered as literature, but because it has been considered as the report of the Word of God. And the fact that men of letters now discuss it as "literature" probably indicates the *end* of its "literary" influence.

The second kind of relation of religion to literature is that which is found in what is called "religious" or "devotional" poetry. Now what is the usual attitude of the lover of poetry—and I mean the person who is a genuine and first-hand enjoyer and appreciator of poetry, not the person who follows the admirations of others—towards this department of poetry? I believe, all that may be implied in his calling it a *department*. He believes, not always explicitly, that when you qualify poetry as "religious" you are indicating very clear limitations. For the great majority of people who love poetry, "*religious* poetry" is a variety of *minor* poetry: the religious poet is not a poet who is treating the whole subject matter of poetry in a religious spirit, but a poet who is dealing with a confined part of this subject matter: who is leaving out

what men consider their major passions, and thereby confessing his ignorance of them. I think that this is the real attitude of most poetry lovers towards such poets as Vaughan, or Southwell, or Crashaw, or George Herbert, or Gerard Hopkins.

But what is more, I am ready to admit that up to a point these critics are right. For there is a kind of poetry, such as most of the work of the authors I have mentioned, which is the product of a special religious awareness, which may exist without the general awareness which we expect of the major poet. In some poets, or in some of their works, this general awareness may have existed; but the preliminary steps which represent it may have been suppressed, and only the end-product presented. Between these, and those in which the religious or devotional genius represents the *special* and limited awareness, it may be very difficult to discriminate. I do not pretend to offer Vaughan, or Southwell, or George Herbert, or Hopkins as major poets: I feel sure that the first three, at least, are poets of this limited awareness. They are not great religious poets in the sense in which Dante, or Corneille, or Racine, even in those of their plays which do not touch upon Christian themes, are great Christian religious poets. Or even in the sense in which Villon and Baudelaire, with all their imperfections and delinquencies, are Christian poets. Since the time of Chaucer, Christian poetry (in the sense in which I shall mean it) has been limited in England almost exclusively to minor poetry.

I repeat that when I am considering Religion and Literature, I speak of these things only to make clear that I am not concerned primarily with Religious Literature. I am concerned with what should be the relation between Religion and all Literature. Therefore the third type of "religious literature" may be more quickly passed over. I mean the literary works of men who are sincerely desirous of forwarding the cause of religion: that which may come under the heading of Propaganda. I am thinking, of course, of such delightful fiction as Mr. Chesterton's *Man Who Was Thursday*, or his *Father Brown*. No one admires and enjoys these things more than I do; I would only remark that when the same effect is aimed at by zealous persons of less talent than Mr. Chesterton the effect is negative. But my point is that such writings do not enter into any serious consideration of the relation of Religion and Literature: because they are conscious operations in a world in which it is assumed that Religion and Literature are not related. It is a conscious and limited relating. What I want is a literature which should be *un*consciously, rather than deliberately and defiantly, Christian: because the work of Mr. Chesterton has its point from appearing in a world which is definitely not Christian.

I am convinced that we fail to realize how completely, and yet how irrationally, we separate our literary from our religious judgments. If there could be a complete separation, perhaps it might not matter: but the separation is not, and never can be, complete. If we exemplify literature by the novel—for the novel is the form in which literature affects the greatest number—we may remark this gradual secularization of literature during at least the last three hundred years. Bunyan, and to some extent Defoe, had moral purposes: the former is beyond suspicion, the latter may be suspect. But since Defoe the secularization of the novel has been continuous. There have been three chief phases. In the first, the novel took the Faith, in its contemporary version, for granted, and omitted it from its picture of life. Fielding, Dickens, and Thackeray belong to this phase. In the

second, it doubted, worried about, or contested the Faith. To this phase belong George Eliot, George Meredith, and Thomas Hardy. To the third phase, in which we are living, belong nearly all contemporary novelists except Mr. James Joyce. It is the phase of those who have never heard the Christian Faith spoken of as anything but an anachronism.

Now, do people in general hold a definite opinion, that is to say religious or anti-religious; and do they read novels, or poetry for that matter, with a separate compartment of their minds? The common ground between religion and fiction is behaviour. Our religion imposes our ethics, our judgment and criticism of ourselves, and our behaviour toward our fellow men. The fiction that we read affects our behaviour towards our fellow men, affects our patterns of ourselves. When we read of human beings behaving in certain ways, with the approval of the author, who gives his benediction to this behaviour by his attitude toward the result of the behaviour arranged by himself, we can be influenced towards behaving in the same way.[2] When the contemporary novelist is an individual thinking for himself in isolation, he may have something important to offer to those who are able to receive it. He who is alone may speak to the individual. But the majority of novelists are persons drifting in the stream, only a little faster. They have some sensitiveness, but little intellect.

We are expected to be broadminded about literature, to put aside prejudice or conviction, and to look at fiction as fiction and at drama as drama. With what is inaccurately called "censorship" in this country—with what is much more difficult to cope with than an official cen-

[2] Here and later I am indebted to Montgomery Belgion. *The Human Parrot* (chapter on "The Irresponsible Propagandist").

sorship, because it represents the opinions of individuals in an irresponsible democracy, I have very little sympathy; partly because it so often suppresses the wrong books, and partly because it is little more effective than Prohibition of Liquor; partly because it is one manifestation of the desire that state control should take the place of decent domestic influence; and wholly because it acts only from custom and habit, not from decided theological and moral principles. Incidentally, it gives people a false sense of security in leading them to believe that books which are *not* suppressed are harmless. Whether there *is* such a thing as a harmless book I am not sure: but there very likely are books so utterly unreadable as to be incapable of injuring anybody. But it is certain that a book is not harmless merely because no one is consciously offended by it. And if we, as readers, keep our religious and moral convictions in one compartment, and take our reading merely for entertainment, or on a higher plane, for aesthetic pleasure, I would point out that the author, whatever his conscious intentions in writing, in practice recognizes no such distinctions. The author of a work of imagination is trying to affect us wholly, as human beings, whether he knows it or not; and we are affected by it, as human beings, whether we intend to be or not. I suppose that everything we eat has some other effect upon us than merely the pleasure of taste and mastication; it affects us during the process of assimilation and digestion; and I believe that exactly the same is true of anything we read.

The fact that what we read does not concern merely something called our *literary taste*, but that it affects directly, though only amongst many other influences, the whole of what we are, is best elicited, I think, by a conscientious examination of the history of our individual literary education. Consider the adolescent reading of any person with some literary sensibility. Everyone, I believe, who is at all sensible to the seductions of poetry, can remember some moment in youth when he or she was completely carried away by the work of one poet. Very likely he was carried away by several poets, one after the other. The reason for this passing infatuation is not merely that our sensibility to poetry is keener in adolescence than in maturity. What happens is a kind of inundation, of invasion of the undeveloped personality, the empty (swept and garnished) room, by the stronger personality of the poet. The same thing may happen at a later age to persons who have not done much reading. One author takes complete possession of us for a time; then another; and finally they begin to affect each other in our mind. We weigh one against another; we see that each has qualities absent from others, and qualities incompatible with the qualities of others: we begin to be, in fact, critical; and it is our growing critical power which protects us from excessive possession by any one literary personality. The good critic—and we should all try to be critics, and not leave criticism to the fellows who write reviews in the papers—is the man who, to a keen and abiding sensibility, joins wide and increasingly discriminating reading. Wide reading is not valuable as a kind of hoarding, an accumulation of knowledge, or what sometimes is meant by the term "a well-stocked mind." It is valuable because in the process of being affected by one powerful personality after another, we cease to be dominated by any one, or by any small number. The very different views of life, cohabiting in our minds, affect each other, and our own personality asserts itself and gives each a place in some arrangement peculiar to ourself.

It is simply not true that works of fiction, prose or verse, that is to say works depicting the actions, thoughts and words and passions of imaginary human beings, *directly* extend our knowledge of life. Direct knowledge of life is knowledge directly in relation to ourselves, it is our knowledge of *how* people behave in general, of *what* they are like in general, in so far as that part of life in which we ourselves have participated gives us material for generalization. Knowledge of life obtained through fiction is only possible by another stage of self-consciousness. That is to say, it can only be a knowledge of other people's knowledge of life, not of life itself. So far as we are taken up with the happenings in any novel in the same way in which we are taken up with what happens under our eyes, we are acquiring at least as much falsehood as truth. But when we are developed enough to say: "This is the view of life of a person who was a good observer within his limits, Dickens, or Thackeray, or George Eliot, or Balzac; but he looked at it in a different way from me, because he was a different man; he even selected rather different things to look at, or the same things in a different order of importance, because he was a different man; so what I am looking at is the world as seen by a particular mind"—then we are in a position to gain something from reading fiction. We are learning *something* about life from these authors direct, just as we learn something from the reading of history direct; but these authors are only really helping us when we can see, and allow for, their differences from ourselves.

Now what we get, as we gradually grow up and read more and more, and read a greater diversity of authors, is a variety of views of life. But what people commonly assume, I suspect, is that we gain this experience of other men's views of life only by "improving reading." This, it is supposed, is a reward we get by applying ourselves to Shakespeare, and Dante, and Goethe, and Emerson, and Carlyle, and dozens of other respectable writers. The rest of our reading for amusement is merely killing time. But I incline to come to the alarming conclusion that it is just the literature that we read for "amusement," or "purely for pleasure" that may have the greatest, and least suspected influence upon us. It is the literature which we read with the least effort that can have the easiest and most insidious influence upon us. Hence it is that the influence of popular novelists, and of popular plays of contemporary life, requires to be scrutinized most closely. And it is chiefly *contemporary* literature that the majority of people ever read in this attitude of "purely for pleasure," of pure passivity.

The relation of what I have been saying to the subject announced for my discourse should now be a little more apparent. Though we may read literature merely for pleasure of "entertainment" or of "aesthetic enjoyment," this reading never affects simply a sort of special sense: it affects us as entire human beings; it affects our moral and religious existence. And I say that while individual modern writers of eminence can be improving, contemporary literature as a whole tends to be degrading. And that even the effect of the better writers, in an age like ours, may be degrading to some readers; for we must remember that what a writer does to people is not necessarily what he intends to do. It may be only what people are capable of having done to them. People exercise an unconscious selection, in being influenced. A writer like D. H. Lawrence may be in his effect either beneficial or pernicious.

I am not even sure that I have not had some pernicious influence myself.

At this point I anticipate a rejoinder from the liberal-minded, from all those who are convinced that if everybody says what he thinks, and does what he likes, things will somehow, by some automatic compensation and adjustment, come right in the end. "Let everything be tried," they say, "and if it is a mistake, then we shall learn by experience." This argument might have some value, if we were always the same generation upon earth; or if, as we know to be not the case, people ever learned much from the experience of their elders. These liberals are convinced that only by what is called unrestrained individualism, will truth ever emerge. Ideas, views of life, they think, issue distinct from independent heads, and in consequence of their knocking violently against each other, the fittest survive, and truth rises triumphant. Anyone who dissents from this view must be either a mediaevalist, wishful only to set back the clock, or else a fascist, and probably both.

If the mass of contemporary authors were really individualists, every one of them inspired Blakes, each with his separate vision, and if the mass of the contemporary public were really a mass of *individuals* there might be something to be said for this attitude. But this is not, and never has been, and never will be. It is not only that the reading individual to-day (or at any day) is not enough an individual to be able to absorb all the "views of life" of all the authors pressed upon us by the publishers' advertisements and reviewers, and to be able to arrive at wisdom by considering one against another. It is that the contemporary authors are not individuals enough either. It is not that the world of separate individuals of the liberal democrat is undesirable; it is simply that this world does not exist.

For the reader of contemporary literature is not, like the reader of the established great literature of all time, exposing himself to the influence of divers and contradictory personalities; he is exposing himself to a mass movement of writers who, each of them, think that they have something individually to offer, but are really all working together in the same direction. And there never was a time, I believe, when the reading public was so large, or so helplessly exposed to the influences of its own time. There never was a time, I believe, when those who read at all, read so many more books by living authors than books by dead authors; there never was a time so completely parochial, so shut off from the past. There may be too many publishers; there are certainly too many books published; and the journals ever incite the reader to "keep up" with what is being published. Individualistic democracy has come to high tide: and it is more difficult to-day to be an individual than it ever was before.

Within itself, modern literature has perfectly valid distinctions of good and bad, better and worse; and I do not wish to suggest that I confound Mr. Bernard Shaw with Mr. Noel Coward, Mrs. Woolf with Miss Mannin. On the other hand, I should like it to be clear that I am not defending a "high"-brow against a "low"-brow literature. What I do wish to affirm is that the whole of modern literature is corrupted by what I call Secularism, that it is simply unaware of, simply cannot understand the meaning of, the primacy of the supernatural over the natural life: of something which I assume to be our primary concern.

I do not want to give the impression that I have delivered a mere fretful jeremiad against contemporary literature. Assuming a common attitude between you, or some of you, and myself, the question is not so much, what is to be done about it? as, how should we behave towards it?

I have suggested that the liberal attitude towards literature will not work. Even if the writers who make their attempt to impose their "view of life" upon us were really distinct individuals, even if we as readers were distinct individuals, what would be the result? It would be, surely, that each reader would be impressed, in his reading, merely by what he was previously prepared to be impressed by; he would follow the "line of least resistance," and there would be no assurance that he would be made a better man. For literary judgment we need to be acutely aware of two things at once: of "what we like," and of "what we *ought* to like." Few people are honest enough to know either. The first means knowing what we really feel: very few know that. The second involves understanding our shortcomings; for we do not really know what we ought to like unless we also know why we ought to like it, which involves knowing why we don't yet like it. It is not enough to understand what we ought to be, unless we know what we are; and we do not understand what we are, unless we know what we ought to be. The two forms of self-consciousness, knowing what we are and what we ought to be, must go together.

It is our business, as readers of literature, to know what we like. It is our business, as Christians, *as well as* readers of literature, to know what we ought to like. It is our business as honest men not to assume that whatever we like is what we ought to like; and it is our business as honest Christians not to assume that we do like what we ought to like. And the last thing I would wish for would be the existence of two literatures, one for Christian consumption and the other for the pagan world. What I believe to be incumbent upon all Christians is the duty of maintaining consciously certain standards and criteria of criticism over and above those applied by the rest of the world; and that by these criteria and standards everything that we read must be tested. We must remember that the greater part of our current reading matter is written for us by people who have no real belief in a supernatural order, though some of it may be written by people with individual notions of a supernatural order which are not ours. And the greater part of our reading matter is coming to be written by people who not only have no such belief, but are even ignorant of the fact that there are still people in the world so "backward" or so "eccentric" as to continue to believe. So long as we are conscious of the gulf fixed between ourselves and the greater part of contemporary literature, we are more or less protected from being harmed by it, and are in a position to extract from it what good it has to offer us.

There are a very large number of people in the world to-day who believe that all ills are fundamentally economic. Some believe that various specific economic changes alone would be enough to set the world right; others demand more or less drastic changes in the social as well, changes chiefly of two opposed types. These changes demanded, and in some places carried out, are alike in one respect, that they hold the assumptions of what I call Secularism: they concern themselves only with changes of a temporal, material, and external nature; they concern themselves with morals only of a collective nature. In an exposition of one such new faith I read the following words:

> In our morality the one single test of any moral question is whether it impedes or destroys in any way the power of the individual to serve the State. [The individual]

must answer the questions: "Does this action injure the nation? Does it injure other members of the nation? Does it injure my ability to serve the nation?" And if the answer is clear on all those questions, the individual has absolute liberty to do as he will.

Now I do not deny that this is a kind of morality, and that it is capable of great good within limits; but I think that we should all repudiate a morality which had no higher ideal to set before us than that. It represents, of course, one of the violent reactions we are witnessing, against the view that the community is solely for the benefit of the individual; but it is equally a gospel of this world, and of this world alone. My complaint against modern literature is of the same kind. It is not that modern literature is in the ordinary sense

"immoral" or even "amoral"; and in any case to prefer that charge would not be enough. It is simply that it repudiates, or is wholly ignorant of, our most fundamental and important beliefs; and that in consequence its tendency is to encourage its readers to get what they can out of life while it lasts, to miss no "experience" that presents itself, and to sacrifice themselves, if they make any sacrifice at all, only for the sake of tangible benefits to others in this world either now or in the future. We shall certainly continue to read the best of its kind, of what our time provides; but we must tirelessly criticize it according to our own principles, and not merely according to the principles admitted by the writers and by the critics who discuss it in the public press.

FROM IN SEARCH OF FUNDAMENTAL VALUES
L. C. Knights*

Knights sees literature's fundamental value in its ability to "affect the quality of our relations with the world" by "energizing" the mind, by "strengthening the imagination," which is "the central creative drive . . . and the organ of all knowledge in which the individual is involved as more than a detached observer."

. . . There are many general statements that one could make: for example, literature increases our range of understanding of ourselves, of other people, of our world. But this and similar formulations of the function of literature belong to Coleridge's class of "truths . . . considered as *so* true, that they lose all the life and

* The selection is reprinted from *The Critical Moment: Essays from the Times Literary Supplement.* Copyright 1963. McGraw-Hill Book Company. Used by permission.

efficiency of truth"; they are likely to get no more than a perfunctory nod of recognition. When I cast around for the fundamental value of literature, recognizable in the smallest instance where delight announces its presence and from which all else springs, the point on which the edifice of "criticism" is raised, I find it in the energy of mind and imagination released by the creative use of words. Wordsworth's "Sonnet Composed upon

Westminster Bridge" will serve for an example:

Earth has not anything to show more fair;
Dull would he be of soul who could pass by
A sight so touching in its majesty ...

The peculiar pleasure of that last line —though the pleasure is independent of conscious recognition of the source— comes from the movement of mind by which we bring together in one apprehension "touching" and "majesty"; feelings and attitudes springing from our experience of what is young and vulnerable, that we should like to protect, fuse with our sense of things towards which we feel awe, in respect of which it is we who are young, inexperienced or powerless. That is London as Wordsworth saw it on an early autumn morning in 1803 and (to adapt his own words on another occasion) "planted, for immortality, ... in the celestial soil of the imagination." The whole poem grows from a similar fusion of opposites: the buildings momentarily appear as right—as proportioned, inviting and composed—as nature's valleys and hills; the old and shackled city ("Near where the charter'd Thames does flow") is as new as the morning. There is no self-deception: beauty that is "like a garment" can, we know, be put off; the "smokeless air" will soon be smoke-filled; and the supreme quiet contains the pulse of life about to resume its course. It is simply that paradox and hyperbole, recognizing themselves for what they are, so activate the mind that, as we read this most beautiful poem, new powers of vision and apprehension come into being.

I am not putting forward the view that paradox is the essential characteristic of poetry: I am simply pointing towards that energizing of the mind that poetry can achieve in an infinity of ways. The exact descriptive word; the surprising figure of speech that levers new recognitions ("Like a green thought ..."); naked simplicity ("How fast has brother followed brother, From sunshine to the sunless land!"); the alignment of a few objects or events so that the presented experience comes to stand for something as wide as human life itself (Blake's "Echoing Green" or Frost's "The Pasture"); slight shifts of tone (as in the last two lines of Frost's "Come in")— these are only random examples of the ways in which the poet can enlist that active collaboration of the reader through which a specific experience is realized.

I have referred so far to lyric poetry because that is easier to speak of in a short space than prose literature and the longer forms. But whether we read a short lyric, a play, or a novel—supposing each to be good of its kind—the same principles are at work: in varied ways the mind's energies are evoked and directed in a single "realizing intuition." In the larger works, of course, the scope is wider and the perceptions are likely to be related in more complex ways. In *King Lear* we not only respond with delight to the ever-changing local realizations—"Strike flat the thick rotundity of the world" (the reverberations of thunder in a blank verse line); "women's weapons, water drops" (a range of mistaken assumptions compressed into a phrase)— we bring together the varied and even contradictory meanings of "need," "justice," "folly," and so on, as imagery and action enforce. In this way routine notions and attitudes are broken down, and a new direction of consciousness emerges from the interplay of meanings: not meanings, so to speak, "out there," as though we were trying to understand a legal document, but meanings in which the reader or spectator is involved as a person, simply because movements of sympathy or antipathy, of assent or dissent—in short, of judgment from a personal centre—are a necessary part of them. A simple example is Lear's assumption that punishment is an essential function of justice:

Tremble, thou wretch
That hast within thee undivulged crimes,
Unwhipp'd of justice . . .

The way we take this is finally determined by our reaction to such things as the picture of the social outcast who is "whipp'd from tithing to tithing, and stock-punish'd, and imprison'd," and of the "rascal beadle," society's representative, lashing the whore with her blood on his hands. When the mind really attends to what Shakespeare says or implies about legal justice in *King Lear* it is forced to make strides across the convenient areas of obscurity in which our ignorance and hypocrisy habitually take refuge; it is compelled to make connexions, and its thinking about "justice," about man's relation to justice, is correspondingly enriched. It is the same with all the other central themes (those who dislike the word are at liberty to use another) of which *King Lear* is composed. Different aspects of experience are held together in what is virtually a single act of attention, and a new direction of thought emerges from the resulting tensions. But because the thinking is in terms of images, not abstract concepts, it is in the fullest possible relation to the intimate personal life of the reader or spectator; the knowledge gained is, as we say, brought home to him—in Keat's phrase, it is "proved on the pulses."

The philosopher may raise an eyebrow at the use of "knowledge" in this context, and indeed there is much defining that even an unphilosophic critic needs to do. I can only say briefly and parenthetically what seem to me the main features of response to literature considered as an activity of knowing. First, what is known is not an object existing independently of the reader: he is himself directly involved in the creative process, and without that involvement there would be no knowledge. In the experience of poetry there is, therefore, a paradoxical union of particularity (we submit to the discipline of what is "so, and not otherwise") with a spread of meanings that will vary with each individual; for what we have to deal with is not a cut and dried experience, but one that lives and, as it were, reverberates in the receiving mind. That is why literature can so powerfully affect the quality of our relations with the world. Secondly, the knowledge in question can never be completely conceptualized: partly because of the subtle intricacy of the texture of the work (even in a "classical" work, deliberately avoiding vagueness, there is bound to be a more or less large area of connotation); partly—and more important—because there are, it seems, matters of great concern that can only be known with the cooperation of mental powers below the level of full consciousness. Eliot, like Valéry, has testified that a poem "may tend to realize itself first as a particular rhythm before it reaches expression in words," and it may be assumed that unless the reader, in turn, is responsive to effects of rhythm that are ultimately unanalysable—as to other non-discursive elements of meaning such as poetic symbols—he will not fully enter into the presented experience. Knowledge of poetry—the knowledge that comes through poetry—demands not only an active but a relaxed and receptive mind.

Attention, collaboration, realization—these are the three basic activities (or, rather, phases or aspects of the same activity) that make up the critical, the fully engaged, response to literature. It is this realizing activity that often makes one want to speak of literature in terms of the depth and presentness of some given object (a person, an action, a landscape), and in a sense one is right to do so: after reading Keats's Ode we do know autumn as never before. But of course there is no object except the poem itself, which, as Susanne Langer insists, offers not ordinary experience but a virtual experience, a symbolic structure of meanings held in the mind. The contradiction, however, is only apparent. When we have undergone the experience of great poetry, of great literature, the world *is* present because the mind, the imagination, is present to the world. It is in this sense that the poet, as Edwin Muir says, releases us from the language—and therefore the world—of the third person and the onlooker, the world of generalities, and continually brings us back to direct confrontation with the particular. The importance of this at a time when, as Muir also points out in his book, *The Estate of Poetry*, so many agencies tempt us to a merely generalized apprehension of life—this needs no stressing. But perhaps it should be added that the sphere of unrealized experience is also the sphere of corrupting fantasy. Literature is a great cleanser, simply because, through language, it energizes the mind. As Coleridge said of Shakespeare's *Venus and Adonis*: "The reader is forced into too much action to sympathize with the merely passive of our nature." It was of course also Coleridge who spoke of "the beneficial after-effects of verbal precision in the preclusion of fanaticism, which masters the feelings more especially by indistinct watch-words."

It is, then, simply in the growth and strengthening of the imagination that the value of literature resides. Imagination, as I have used the term, is simultaneously the central creative drive of each human being and the organ of all knowledge in which the individual is involved as more than a detached observer. It is an active, relating, realizing power, through which the limited self, with its unlimited desires and its abysmal ignorance of everything that cannot be used or manipulated, grows into a person, freely moving in a world of values and relationships. It is the mediator between the unknown depths within and the so little-known world without. ("Every symbol is two-edged," says Tillich; "it opens up reality and it opens up the soul.") As a unifying power it simultaneously works towards the integrity and wholeness of the person and the creation of a cosmos from the world of mere experience which, without it, would remain fragmentary and deceptive. The importance of literature is therefore that indicated by Martin Foss when he speaks of "the work of art . . . giving to everybody and releasing in everybody the power of a creative spiritual life." But as Foss also reminds us, "what art brings to the surface is everywhere at work where men think and feel." Imaginative literature is simply one of the ways through which life comes to consciousness; and the claim that the teacher of literature may justifiably make for his vocation is only possible because what underlies and justifies his activities is what underlies and justifies all the arts and humane studies. To be sure, those who profess other "subjects" could often, one feels, profit from the insights that a familiarity with literature brings: there is clear profit for the psychologist in Shakespeare and Blake as well as in George Eliot and Henry James; and theologians could perhaps learn something from the symbolic language of great poetry. But then the critic and teacher of literature, in his turn, needs to know something of other ways of eliciting meanings from the world. The study of literature cannot remain self-enclosed. Indeed it is my own conviction ... that there is important work waiting to be done "on the frontiers," where the study of literature joins hands with the study of history, philosophy, theology, &c. But it will need to be done by those who really know what literature is, not by specialists in other subjects were merely look to literature for documentation. . . .

CHAPTER 17

Valuative Criticism

ORDERS OF
EVALUATIVE ASSUMPTIONS
Wayne Shumaker[*]

Shumaker makes the points that there is a staggering variety of assumptions on the basis of which the value, both esthetic and nonesthetic, of any work of literature may be determined, and that these assumptions are not discrete and self-contained but inextricably interwoven. In general, literature may be judged on the basis of one of two assumptions: (1) as art responsible only to the esthetic, or (2) as art and something else responsible "also to truth or morality, or both." Following this essay are four critical evaluations of Milton's *Lycidas*. It will be to the advantage of the reader to work out which of Shumaker's assumptions each exemplifies.

In its details, the establishment of a definition of literary value is the responsibility of the individual critic, who can feel certainties denied to the more impartial theorist. For every man some ideas are absolutely valid, some principles so necessary for the meaningfulness of experience that when they are admitted to fall into doubt the universe becomes

* The essay is reprinted from Chapter 10 of *Elements of Critical Theory*, by Wayne Shumaker, by permission of the University of California Press. Copyright 1952 by the University of California Press.

chaos. The general theorist, however, is bound by the logical aspects of things; and since it has already become clear that every definition of value is in some degree alogical he cannot give an unqualified preference to any single definition. The most he can do is to describe some of the large orders of assumptions and comment briefly on their differences. In metaphorical terms, he can merely try to find one or more natural boundaries dividing the speculative area and characterize as helpfully as possible the sections into which the area appears to fall.

The boundaries that the literary theorist will discover are not those that would seem most significant to the philosopher. The philosopher's eye is alert for a different order of phenomena—geological, so to speak, not botanical. The questions for which the literary critic wishes answers are relatively specific. He is not likely to ask, In what terms can the general concept "value" best be construed? What is the locus of value—the object, the human percipient, or a situation including both? Are value judgments propositions or emotive ejaculations? These and similar problems, which have importance for the philosopher, will probably be dismissed by the practical critic as outside his province. I shall be much mistaken if the practical critic does not wish chiefly to know what kinds of evaluative assumptions can be made intelligently. Once he has been informed about the kinds, he can choose, or abstain from choosing, among them on whatever grounds he is accustomed to use in making speculative decisions.

Since the attitude of the philosopher toward the ultimate problems of value is more serious than that of the critic, in the long run the philosopher will no doubt reach sounder conclusions. Any definition of literary value offered now is liable to modification in the comparatively near future in the light of new discoveries by value theorists. No useful purpose, however, would be served by confronting the deeper issues here. In the absence of substantial agreement about how the issues are to be resolved, the discussion would ramify formidably. It will be best to make a single dichotomous division of a kind suited to clarify fundamental preferences and then to develop each of the rival views as adequately as space permits. After all, the critic must cut off his examination of theory at some

point so as to return to his proper activities. With relation to the general theory of value, he is in the position of the farmer who, instead of performing his own experiments in poultry breeding, must await the publication of a definitive pamphlet by the Department of Agriculture, and in the meantime must set his hens in accordance with theories not yet known to be unsound.

The most helpful dichotomy is that between aesthetic and not wholly aesthetic definitions. Literature may be judged as art and nothing but art, or it may be considered as partly art and partly something else. That is to say, it may be assumed that good writing has a responsibility only to beauty, or that it has a responsibility also to truth or morality, or both.

The divergencies of critical opinion resulting from different choices between the alternatives are immense and probably unbridgeable in terms of particulars. For example, how can a man whose reaction to Proust's À la Recherche du temps perdu is, "What beautiful composition!" communicate with a man whose reaction is, "How morally diseased!" No amount of discussion can bring the two to agree on an evaluation as long as they confine their remarks to the literary work itself. Each could admit the validity of the other's comment without feeling in the least constrained to depart from his own evaluative judgment. There is no common ground, hence no real issue, except, of course, that the first man probably believes himself to have said "How good!" and the second "How bad!" Both have stated appraisals in what they thought were appropriate terms, but the two universes of discourse overlap only enough to make discussion confusing. The first critic has assumed literature to have a responsibility only to art, whereas the second has assumed it to have a responsibility also to morality.

The former of the two views derives from a feeling that the essence of literature is not touched by discussion of it as anything but art. At the present time, says David Daiches,

[criticism] is serving several functions—psychological, sociological, political, ethical, even metaphysical—and in so far as it serves these functions adequately it is valuable, but when criticism fulfilling any or all of these functions masquerades indiscriminately as "literary" the resulting confusion is overwhelming. The sociologist will find a value in Dickens, the psychologist, a value in Shakespeare, the feminist a value in Meredith, and other specialists will find other values in the same writers. But literary worth is distinct—even if, as some hold, it is composite.[1]

Again, in a later work, "to judge fiction as fiction is very difficult, while to judge it as history, sociology, or rhetoric is fairly easy. We all tend to take the line of least resistance."[2]

A great many students of literature must have had similar reflections. Scott's novels have considerable historical accuracy—but what bearing has that fact on my complete coldness to them? Ezra Pound is a fascist; very well, but some of his short poems are delightful. After much perplexity about the essential meaninglessness of many discoveries about literature that *seem* important, one may conclude that the discoveries are irrelevant because they are extraliterary. What, then, is literature? The reply may come finally, "It is a form of art, like music and painting; therefore criticism must discuss it as art." A consequence of this

[1] David Daiches, *New Literary Values: Studies in Modern Literature* (Edinburgh and London, Oliver and Boyd, 1936), p. 116.
[2] David Daiches, *A Study of Literature for Readers and Critics* (Ithaca, N.Y., Cornell University Press, 1948), p. 58.

decision is that critical methodology becomes aesthetic.

Unfortunately, the science of aesthetics is harder to pin down than such a science as physics or zoölogy. The characterization of a beautiful sonnet in half a dozen textbooks of elementary aesthetics would probably vary in a way not paralleled by a characterization of frogs or dogfish in half a dozen textbooks of elementary zoölogy. The reason is that in aesthetics there is as yet no complete agreement, as for a long time there has been in zoölogy, about the point of view an investigator must take. Every aesthetician has a choice of preliminary assumptions, and thence proceeds along whatever course seems to him dialectically soundest to whatever conclusions most commend themselves to his reason and emotions.

The absence of a body of formulated and generally accepted data makes it very difficult to summarize the implications for criticism of an aesthetic definition of literary value. It is impossible to discuss *the* aesthetic standard for literature, since none has strong predominance. The only feasible course of action is to offer a brief explanation of major emphases.

The most sharply drawn analysis of current emphases (we may disregard those of merely historical importance) seems to be that of Stephen Pepper, who, in *The Basis of Criticism in the Arts*, analyzes the aesthetic systems appropriate to four living philosophies which appear to give about equally adequate explanations of the universe of experience. I shall lean heavily on this analysis, supplying, however, my own explanations of the systems and introducing a secondary classification of which Professor Pepper might not approve.

Aesthetic definitions of literary value usually stress either the formal properties of art or the ability of art works to evoke sensations. Definitions of the former kind are suitable to organistic and formistic philosophies; definitions of the latter, to mechanistic and contextualistic philosophies.[3]

The classic statement of the organistic view is Bosanquet's *Three Lectures on Aesthetic*. This view requires of beauty an organic unity similar to that believed by organicists to obtain in the universe as a whole. Every detail in the perfect art work calls for the presence of every other; nothing is lacking, nothing is unnecessary; everything coalesces into the whole, the supremely neat and workmanlike whole. In criticizing fiction, writes Percy Lubbock, we have nothing to say until the author announces his subject.

But from that moment he is accessible, his privilege is shared; and the delight of treating the subject is acute and perennial. From point to point we follow the writer, always looking back to the subject itself in order to understand the logic of the course he pursues. We find that we are creating a design, large or small, simple or intricate, as the chapter finished is fitted into its place; or again there is a flaw and a break in the development, the author takes a turn that appears to contradict or to disregard the subject, and the critical question, strictly so called, begins. . . . So it goes, till the book is ended and we look back at the whole design.[4]

A "good" work, then, is one in which the design is adequate to the subject and completely harmonious with itself; a "bad" work has disharmonies, unresolved contradictions, materials lacking or in surplus. The difference between art and nonart, the beautiful and the not-beauti-ful, praiseworthy literature and literature which lacks merit, is to be sought in the details of construction.

The structural expectations of the formist differ from those of the organicist in permitting a narrower range of variation. The organicist's eye is always on completeness, roundness, reciprocation; to his mind the achievement of fused unity justifies any choice of techniques. The formist, on the other hand, insists on a certain deference to the usual ways of doing things, not necessarily because he is intellectually timid but because he sees value in normality, which tends to receive the approval of many judges. To the formist, traditional structures seem better than idiosyncratic ones because experience has proved them to have a natural fitness for the representation of normal human experience. In a manner of speaking, literature wants to be written in forms sanctioned by the community and resents being twisted into forms congenial only to individual talents. The straining of art toward norms is explained as consequent on the fact that nature is not continuous but discontinuous. Like the table of chemical elements (I borrow the illustration from Pepper), nature contains stable resting places separated by gaps which only unstable organizations can occupy. Authors ought to seek out and use the stable literary forms precisely as a man who must mount a ladder ought to feel for the rungs and not put his feet in the interstices. Thus the sonnet, once invented, proved to be the ideal medium for the expression of a certain range of poetic emotions. Moreover, the laws of each of the stable structures can be established rather accurately by induction (*vide* the method of Aristotle's *Poetics*, the most celebrated of formistic documents). The sonnet, for example, usually falls into two parts, the general and the specific; two rhyme

---

[3] This is the secondary classification mentioned in the text.

[4] Percy Lubbock, *The Craft of Fiction* (New York, Jonathan Cape, Ltd., and Harrison Smith, 1931), pp. 23–24.

schemes predominate in English; there are often rhythmical breaks at certain points; the tone is regularly confessional; and so on. The formist's appraisals, accordingly, turn on such ideas as those of genre, mimesis, and universality.

The aesthetics of sensation or feeling differs from that of structure in stressing the relationship between the art object and a percipient subject (and therefore is particularly liable to the problems of subjectivity). It has already been observed that for the mechanist there may be value in an undifferentiated texture—let us say that of a piece of velvet cloth not sewed into any pattern and therefore virtually without form. The taste of a pear or a slice of cold beef may seem to him aesthetically enjoyable, whereas the organicist ought properly to believe that such unconstructed tastes lie outside the aesthetic field. The point at issue is whether the artist's craftsmanship or the perceiver's feeling response is primary in aesthetic judgment. The answer returned to the question by the mechanist and contextualist requires that their definitions of aesthetic value be distinguished rather sharply from those of the organicist and the formist.

The motive behind the stressing of response becomes apparent if we remember the possibility of giving intellectual approval to works of literary (or other) art toward which we feel emotionally indifferent. "Yes, that's good," we may say, recognizing craftsmanship of an indubitably high order; but only compulsion could make us turn to the work a second time. The mechanist resolves this ambiguity of attitude by urging that the function of art is to give pleasure. Formal qualities are important to him only so far as they conduce to enjoyment, and whatever gives enjoyment without analyzable form has aesthetic value notwithstanding. A tantalizing perfume, the exhilarating bite of sea air, the murmur of wind among leaves, although not art, by stimulating the senses agreeably falls within the range of aesthetics; and human constructs like literature are aesthetically "good" in proportion as they evoke pleasurable sensations. "Not the fruit of experience," wrote Walter Pater in the famous conclusion to his *Renaissance*, "but experience itself, is the end. A counted number of pulses only is given to us of a variegated, dramatic life." Art is important because it can help us to "be present always at the focus where the greatest number of vital forces unite in their purest energy."

The contextualist also prizes sensory vividness, but is less insistent than the mechanist that the vividness be immediately pleasurable. To the contextualist, preëminently, art appears to be a form of knowledge, a mode of sensory cognition, a way of apprehending experience directly instead of through the medium of the discursive reason. Accordingly he feels that it is perceptions of quality, the feel of situations, which art is peculiarly fitted to communicate. The quality of a thundershower can be expressed more vividly by a poem than by a meteorological report; the quality of a marital quarrel, by a short story than by a syllogistic analysis; the quality of a war, by a novel than by a compilation of communiqués and logistics records. As sentient human beings we are quite as much concerned with the surface of experience as with the "factual" realities, physical, chemical, structural, and statistical, which underlie the surface. Water is a taste, a spectacle, a tactual sensation, and sometimes a sound, as well as a combination of hydrogen and oxygen in the proportion of two to one; and for consciousness the sensory qualities are quite as important as the chemical. The function of art is to do what other modes of expression do less effectively: to communicate sensory knowledge. The contextualistic measure of literary value has therefore been said to be the vividness and breadth of the perceptual experience initiated in the reader.[5]

The aesthetic emphases we have been considering have relevance to criticism only so far as literature is art. For several pages we have been assuming it to be wholly art; and certainly a fairly large number of contemporary critics seem to imply that it is nothing else. Excellent arguments can be offered in justification of their practice. For example, as what, if not as art, do we enjoy Aeschylus' *The Eumenides,* Virgil's description of Hades, or, perhaps, even Bunyan's *Pilgrim's Progress?* "No crash of systems," wrote William Vaughan Moody of *Paradise Lost* in his edition of Milton's poetry, "can drown its noble music." The music of literature, its sound, its imagery, its contagious feeling, its form, can continue to give satisfaction when the ideas that are partly responsible for its coherence seem quaint and perhaps despicable. Nevertheless, there has never been, possibly never will be, agreement among critics that literature ought always to be discussed in purely aesthetic terms.

The resistance to exclusively aesthetic standards of judgment can be explained by the fact that syntactical combinations of words can rarely avoid altogether the expression of ideas, and ideas can be criticized in their own right as valid or invalid formulations or evaluations of experience. A sonata or vase can approach pure form to a degree that even the purest lyric poem cannot. Something is usually said or implied by literature about the universe of everyday life—something that can be considered apart from the manner of the saying, something that can be appraised independently. More technically, literature may be thought insufficiently congruent with the other arts to fall entirely within the scope of general aesthetics. Certain aspects of it may be thought to fall outside the aesthetic field —aspects which can be disregarded only at the expense of forfeiting the claim to total appraisal.

This position has been argued recently with regard to poetry, in the *Journal of Aesthetics and Art Criticism;*[6] but the current tendency to discuss art in terms merely of form, texture, and sensation is opposed to a philosophical tradition of long standing. Samuel Alexander spoke in the tradition when he said, "The greater art is concerned more extensively, more profoundly and more subtly with the main tendencies in human nature and in things." For Alexander, adequate form and design sufficed only to place an object within the class of beautiful (aesthetic) objects; its rank within the class depended on subject matter or content.[7] The direct application to literature of a similar principle was made by the French literary theorist Ricardou in the very work in which he urged that scientific

[5] It is evident that this discussion has been fragmentary and superficial. Persons who wish to supplement it are advised to go first to Stephen C. Pepper, *The Basis of Criticism in the Arts* (Cambridge, Mass., Harvard University Press, 1945), which I have already cited as the source for the structure, and in part the content, of my summary, and then to the volumes mentioned by Pepper as classic treatments of the four types of aesthetic theory: Bernard Bosanquet's *Three Lectures on Aesthetic,* Aristotle's *Poetics,* George Santayana's *The Sense of Beauty,* and John Dewey's *Art as Experience.* To these may be added Pepper's *Aesthetic Quality* (New York, Charles Scribner's Sons, 1938), which deserves to stand beside the others as an excellent statement of one of the four points of view (the contextualist).

[6] The positive argument is by W. K. Wimsatt, the negative by Theodore M. Green. *Journal of Aesthetics and Art Criticism,* Vol. VIII, No. 4 (June, 1950), pp. 213–220, 221–228.

[7] Samuel Alexander, *Beauty and Other Forms of Value* (London, Macmillan and Co., Ltd., 1933), pp. 148, 137–138.

criticism ought to be aesthetic and not historical. "A literary work," he said in one of several formulations of his own evaluative criterion, "is more beautiful in proportion as it expresses more truth and morality in a more impressive form."[8] Literature overlaps the three speculative areas of the good, the true, and the beautiful and is fractured when discussed in terms of form and texture only. Henry Osborn Taylor declared that "The function of art . . . is to give utterance and form to the content of human life—thought, action, conviction, feeling, emotion—and to the setting, the natural environment, in which humanity acts and thinks and feels."[9] Critics with more modest philosophical pretensions have also many times stated analogous opinions. Thus Daiches, a professor of literature, argues—it seems to me—more cogently on this side of the aesthetic-nonaesthetic dichotomy than on the other:

> The critic must see literature as one of numerous activities, otherwise what function has he at all? . . . The critic is the link between the work of art and the world, and his duty is to determine their relation. The nature of literary value is dependent on the nature of the relation of art to the whole of life, and to attempt to pass judgment on literature without having come to some conclusion regarding this relation can have no useful result, because it means assessing value on an undetermined criterion.[10]

J. M. Murry, a journalistic critic, points out that many things besides art have been required of poetry: "Delight, music, subtlety of thought, a world of the heart's desire, fidelity to comprehensible experience, a glimpse through magic casements, profound wisdom."[11] The ordinary periodical reviewer rarely discusses literature solely as art; and the man in the street, whose reading is limited to an occasional novel or biography, would perhaps be astonished to learn of the possibility that literature might be so discussed.

From the most sophisticated levels of thought to the least sophisticated, from the most abstract to the most concrete, the view that a "good" literary work must have more than an adequate form and texture finds support. This does not mean that the view is necessarily "correct." I dwell on its intellectual respectability only because in recent years there has been a growing tendency, especially among "new" critics, to regard as stupid and tiresome any criticism which refuses to grant an author his right to hold even the wildest opinions about life and the universe.

To judge from their writings, some nonaesthetic critics go so far as to deny any importance whatever to literary artistry. Marxist critics have often been accused of following a party line, of judging literature solely with reference to political and sociological implications. The charge is probably false; nevertheless, such a work as Upton Sinclair's *Mammonart*—if it is Marxist—gives some color to the accusation. Jeremy Collier's *A Short View of the Profaneness and Immorality of the English Stage*, an influential document of the late seventeenth century, is concerned chiefly with the morality of stage situations. A psychological critic may speak of a novel in glowing terms because it illustrates the possibility of adjusting to apparently intolerable social circum-

---

[8] "Une œuvre littéraire est d'autant plus belle qu'elle exprime plus de vérité et de moralité en une forme plus puissante." A. Ricardou, *La Critique littéraire* (Paris, 1896), p. 270.

[9] Henry Osborn Taylor, *Human Values and Verities* (London, Macmillan and Co., Ltd., 1928), pp. 208–209.

[10] Daiches, *New Literary Values*, p. 8.

[11] J. M. Murry, *Aspects of Literature* (New York, Knopf, 1920), p. 176.

stances. Businessmen engaged in merchandising and clergymen who preach a doctrine of confident living seem to approve of any work which says, like the title of Betty MacDonald's recent book, *Anybody Can Do Anything*. It is probable, however, that all critics whose writings have much meaning for the readers of these pages would admit, if pressed, that literature has aesthetic responsibilities. The purpose of arguing a limited nonaesthetic thesis (as that Coleridge was a pious hypocrite) is not meant to imply a total condemnation (that none of Coleridge's poetry or prose has aesthetic value). At most, the denial of a specific nonliterary virtue to a work is intended to refute the work's claim to a particular kind of essential goodness. For this reason I have distinguished between criticism which is wholly aesthetic and that which is only partly so, instead of making a triadic division among aesthetic, partly aesthetic, and nonaesthetic criticism. Except in the preceding sentence, indeed, the word "nonaesthetic" has been used here as equivalent to "not wholly aesthetic." Few persons whose interest in literature is not wholly derivative from an interest in something else will believe that literature has none of the properties of art and hence can be judged solely with reference to standards drawn from politics, ethics, or sociology.

If, then, literature is granted to have nonaesthetic as well as aesthetic responsibilities, how is it possible to arrive at a definition of literary value which will permit the characterization of individual works as "good" or "bad"?

The question is complex—so complex that an attempt to reply to it in other than the most abstract terms would ramify beyond control. An adequate answer would require, first, the division of the whole realm of logical discourse into a number of distinct areas; next, the specification of areas into which literature

projects; and finally, the determination of exactly what properties or qualities discoverable in each area a literary work must possess in order to fulfill all its responsibilities. If it were decided that "good" literature must be at once moral and true and beautiful, the appraisal of a given work as good would require the preliminary establishment of definitions of morality and truth as well as beauty. But how are such definitions to be established? By a repetition of the processes through which we have gone in considering possible definitions of aesthetic value. Every ethical system—to follow out only one-half of the illustrative hypothesis—is adequate only from a particular point of view, with relation only to one configuration of extra-ethical thought. Evidently a determination to define ethical value would force us a second time to examine a whole series of alternative theories, organistic, formistic, mechanistic, and contextualistic. A similar process would then have to be repeated a third time in order to establish a criterion of truth. It is very likely, however, that the Platonic triad of speculative fields is not suited to modern thought. If it is not, some other schematization of knowledge than the traditional one of the good, the true, and the beautiful would have to be worked out, the connection of literary value with each area somehow decided, and an inclusive definition of all the value properties essential to good literature formulated.

The task may well appear monstrous. If the critic decides, in desperation, to fall back on the first and apparently simpler line of analysis, he will learn that the attempt to separate nonaesthetic experience from aesthetic is an almost equally exhausting discipline. One ought not to say, "Only this kind of experience is aesthetic," without first taking pains to learn how great is the range of possible experience and how all nonaesthetic experiences can best be categorized. The pains will lead the responsible aesthetician far afield before he reaches his conclusions. The truth is that on every vital world hypothesis except the formistic the entire universe of experience is one closely woven texture. Life is not a carved Indian ball of separately revolving spheres, but rather an incredibly huge and tangled skein of yarn. If we pull long enough on any strand we will come at last to all the others; and no piece can be torn free without some injury both to it and to the remainder. . . .

LYCIDAS
Samuel Johnson

. . . One of the poems on which much praise has been bestowed is "Lycidas"; of which the diction is harsh, the rhymes uncertain, and the numbers unpleasing. What beauty there is, we must therefore seek in the sentiments and images. It is not to be considered as the effusion of real passion, for passion runs not after remote allusions and obscure opinions. Passion plucks no berries from the myrtle and ivy, nor calls upon Arethuse and Mincius, nor tells of "rough satyrs and fauns with cloven heel." Where there is leisure for fiction there is little grief.

In this poem there is no nature, for there is no truth; there is no art, for there is nothing new. Its form is that of a pastoral, easy, vulgar, and therefore disgusting; whatever images it can supply are long ago exhausted, and its inherent improbability always forces dissatisfaction on the mind. When Cowley tells of Hervey[1] that they studied together, it is easy to suppose how much he must miss the companion of his labors and the partner of his discoveries; but what image of tenderness can be excited by these lines!

We drove afield, and both together heard
What time the grey-fly winds her sultry horn,

[1] *Cowley . . . Hervey:* Abraham Cowley, "On the Death of Mr. William Hervey," in *Miscellanies* (1656).

Battening our flocks with the fresh dews of night.

We know that they never drove afield, and that they had no flocks to batten; and though it be allowed that the representation may be allegorical, the true meaning is so uncertain and remote that it is never sought because it cannot be known when it is found.

Among the flocks and copses and flowers appear the heathen deities, Jove and Phoebus, Neptune and Aeolus, with a long train of mythological imagery, such as a college easily supplies. Nothing can less display knowledge or less exercise invention than to tell how a shepherd has lost his companion and must now feed his flocks alone, without any judge of his skill in piping; and how one god asks another god what is become of Lycidas, and how neither god can tell. He who thus grieves will excite no sympathy; he who thus praises will confer no honor.

This poem has yet a grosser fault. With these trifling fictions are mingled the most awful and sacred truths, such as ought never to be polluted with such irreverent combinations. The shepherd likewise is now a feeder of sheep, and afterwards an ecclesiastical pastor, a superintendent of a Christian flock. Such equivocations are always unskillful, but here they are indecent, and at least approach to impiety, of which, however, I believe the writer not to have been conscious.

Such is the power of reputation justly acquired that its blaze drives away the eye from nice examination. Surely no man could have fancied that he read "Lycidas" with pleasure had he not known its author. . . .

. . . AND *LYCIDAS*
E. M. W. Tillyard*

. . . *Lycidas* is the last and greatest English poem of Milton's youth. Though shorter, it is greater than *Comus*, written with newly-won but complete mastery and expressing a mental experience both valuable and profound.

Most criticism of *Lycidas* is off the mark, because it fails to distinguish between the nominal and the real subject, what the poem professes to be about and what it is about. It assumes that Edward King is the real, whereas he is but the nominal subject. Fundamentally *Lycidas* concerns Milton himself;[1] King is but the excuse for one of Milton's most personal poems. This cannot be proved: it can only be deduced from the impression the poem leaves. Most readers agree that Milton was not deeply grieved at King's death, as they agree that the poem is great. If it is great, it must contain deep feeling of some sort. What then is this deep feeling all about?

From the circumstances in which *Lycidas* was written and from the two obviously personal passages the question can be answered. When Milton wrote

Lycidas in 1637 he was twenty-nine years of age, and early in the next year he set out for Italy with perhaps the intention of going on to Greece. Whether the last line of the poem,

To morrow to fresh Woods, and Pastures new,

refers to this intended journey is doubtful; it may well do so. Anyhow at the time of writing *Lycidas* Milton must have had the Italian and possibly the Greek journey in his mind. When he heard of King's death, and still more when consenting to write the elegy he had to make his mind dwell on it, he cannot but have felt the analogy between King and himself. Milton and King had been at the same college in the same University. Their careers and interests had been similar there. Milton was a poet, King had written verse too. King had made a voyage on the sea, Milton was about to make voyages. How could Milton have missed the idea that *he* might make the analogy complete by getting drowned, like King, also? At a time when, through plagues and what not, life was less secure than in modern times of peace, Milton, having sacrificed so much to his great ambition, must anyhow, as the time of preparation drew to an end, have dwelt on the thought that it might be all for nothing. Not that he

---

* This essay is reprinted from *Milton*, by E. M. W. Tillyard, by permission of Chatto & Windus Ltd. Copyright 1930 by Chatto & Windus Ltd.

1 "Ce n'est pas King qu'il faut y chercher, c'est Milton lui-même" [It is not King who must be looked for there, it is Milton himself]. E. Legouis, in Legouis et Cazamian, *Histoire de la Littérature anglaise*, 567.

was a coward: but the fear that his ambitions might be ruined at the last moment must have been at times difficult to endure. Those who had experience of the late war must have known the miserable anxiety suffered immediately before going on leave. It was not that people feared to die more then than at other times, but the thought of being baulked by death of their desire for home was peculiarly harrowing. Milton's state of mind must at times have been somewhat similar, and in considering King's fate his fears must have come crowding on him. That he was at least partly thinking of his own possible fate is made clear by the reference in the first paragraph to his own destined urn and sable shroud. As a reason for his singing of Lycidas he writes:

So may som gentle Muse
With lucky words favour my destin'd Urn,
And as he passes turn,
And bid fair peace be to my sable shrowd,
For we were nurst upon the self-same hill,
Fed the same flock, by fountain, shade, and
    rill.[2]

In other words, "If I die, some one will requite me with a requiem, for in other ways the analogy between us was complete." And much more agonisingly does the thought of premature death start in his mind when he writes of poetic fame and "the blind *Fury* with th' abhorred shears." Why should he have submitted himself to rigorous self-denial, if to no end?

But his fears of premature death, though part of the subject, are not the whole. The real subject is the resolving of those fears (and of his bitter scorn of the clergy) into an exalted state of mental calm. The apotheosis of Lycidas

[2] For a note on the paragraphing of this passage—paragraphing here affects the connotations—see Appendix E, p. 385. [Here omitted.]

in the penultimate paragraph has a deeper meaning: it symbolises Milton's own balanced state of mind to which he won after the torments he had been through. This is the secret of the strength of *Lycidas* and the reason why it is a greater poem than *Comus*: in the one calm after struggle, in the other calm of a kind but without the preliminary struggle. To prove that the deepest and most satisfying calm is that which follows on mental struggle one has only to point to the greatest tragedies.

If the above idea is accepted, it is possible to see in *Lycidas* a unity of purpose which cannot be seen in it if the death of King is taken as the real subject of the poem. In particular the outburst against the clergy, usually regarded as a glorious excrescence, will be found perfectly in keeping with the profounder and less elegiac significance of the whole. Let me try to explain this harmony by describing how the purpose of the poem develops.

Milton begins with characteristic egotism. His first lines do not concern King but his own reluctance to write a poem before he is mature. But he must write, for Lycidas died prematurely—"*Young Lycidas*"—and for a premature death he must be willing to risk premature poetry. Moreover, if he writes an elegy for Lycidas, some other poet may reward him when he dies with an elegy too. The introduction, lines 1 to 24, thus ends on Milton's possible death.

The first section, beginning "Together both, ere the high Lawns appear'd," consists of lines 25 to 84. It contains a lament for the death of Lycidas, regret that the Muse could not protect her son, and leads up to the first great cause of pain in Milton's own mind: the risk of death before his great work is completed. What has been the use of all his laborious preparation, his careful chastity (for doubtless he means this by his references to Amaryllis and Neaera), if fame, for whose sake he has denied himself, is to escape him, anticipated by death? Earthly fame, he replies to himself in the person of Phoebus, has nothing to do with heavenly fame: it depends on deeds, not on what those deeds effect. So he argues, but one does not get the impression of emotional conviction yet: the final impression of the first section is that it would be a cruel shame and a wicked waste, if he were to die. It should be noted with what consummate skill Milton in this section works the subject from King to its climax in himself.

In the second section, lines 85 to 131, beginning "O Fountain *Arethuse*," he does exactly the same thing. In the elegiac tradition various persons come to visit the body. It is perfectly natural that St. Peter should come to visit a priest, and equally natural that he should proceed from lamenting the death of a good priest to denouncing the bad. But this denunciation reveals the second great cause of mental pain in Milton: his quarrel with contemporary England, typified by the rottenness of the clergy. Thus St. Peter's outburst is not an excrescence but strictly parallel with Milton's earlier outburst about the blind Fury. One can even see a close connection of ideas between the two grievances. One grievance is that "the hungry Sheep look up and are not fed"; England has bad or useless teachers: the other is that he, Milton, whose ambition was to teach by writing a great epic, to feed the hungry sheep of England, may easily be cut off before it can be realised. It should be noted too that the second grievance, like the first, is answered at the end of the second movement. Punishment is waiting; the two-handed engine stands ready to smite. But even less than at the end of the first section has mental calm been attained. The

end of the second section marks the climax of the poem. Milton has stated his quarrel with life: we await the conclusion.

Of the third section, lines 132 to 164, beginning "Return *Alpheus*," it is more difficult to describe the function. Some quieter interlude is clearly necessary between St. Peter's bitter outburst and the heavenly triumph of the final movement. But it is more than an interlude, it has value as a transition too. The sudden change from the terror of the two-handed engine to the incredible beauty of the description of the flowers contains an implication that somehow the "Dorique delicacy," of which the description of the flowers is the highest example in Milton, is not irreconcilable with the sterner mood, and hence is able to insinuate some comfort. So too from the dallying with a false surmise, the escape into a region of pure romance

Where the great vision of the Guarded
   Mount
Looks   toward   *Namancos*   and   *Bayona's*
   hold,

some comfort is allowed. But these sources of comfort are but minor, leading up to the greater solution.

The fourth section purports to describe the resurrection of Lycidas and his entry into heaven. More truly it solves the whole poem by describing the resurrection into a new kind of life of Milton's hopes, should they be ruined by premature death or by the moral collapse of his country. The loss or possible loss of human fame is made good by fame in heaven, the corrupt clergy are balanced by

all the Saints above
In solemn troops and sweet Societies,

and the harsh forebodings of Peter, the pilot of the Galilean lake, are forgotten

Through the dear might of him who walk'd the waves.

But above all the fourth section describes the renunciation of earthly fame, the abnegation of self by the great egotist, and the spiritual purgation of gaining one's life after losing it.

Some people might call *Lycidas* a religious poem, for Milton appears to found his comfort on his hopes of heaven: others might object that his grounds of comfort are extraordinarily flimsy and that the pessimism of *Paradise Lost* is truer to the facts of life than the optimism of *Lycidas*. But the question

of beliefs is unimportant; what matters and what makes *Lycidas* one of the greatest poems in English is that it expresses with success a state of mind whose high value can hardly be limited to a particular religious creed. Milton by ridding himself of his inhibiting fears, by subordinating the disturbing ambition to have done a thing to the serene intention of doing it as well as possible, had proved his mettle and issued from the ordeal a great man. *Lycidas* expresses a mind of the keenest sensibility and most powerful grasp acutely aware of a number of most moving sensations, but controlling these sensations so that they do not conflict but rather by contrast reinforce one another: a mind calm after struggle but keyed up to perform heroic deeds, should they need to be done.

HOW TO READ *LYCIDAS*
Paul Elmer More[*]

After passing, as I might say, through the valley of the shadow of death, after months of physical prostration when reading of any sort was beyond the strength of a depleted brain, the poet to whom I turned instinctively with the first renewal of health was Milton. And so I have been reading Milton again and books about him, with the old zest I had as a boy, and with an added joy of almost tremulous excitement such as a miser might feel at the rediscovery of a treasure of gold stolen from him and long buried out of sight. But with this delight have been mingled certain scruples which vexed me a little more than they did in the old days. Again, as many times be-

[*] The essay is reprinted from *On Being Human*, by Paul Elmer More, by permission of Princeton University Press. Copyright 1936 by Princeton University Press.

fore, on laying down one of the poems the familiar words of Tennyson would come unbidden to my mind:

O mighty-mouth'd inventor of harmonies,
O skill'd to sing of Time or Eternity,
    God-gifted organ-voice of England,
        Milton, a name to resound for ages.

Of the mighty harmonies there would be no doubt; God-gifted voice certainly, organ-voice certainly, for those who have ears to hear. If any one in English, Milton had the divine craft of words, the mastery of sonorous speech. His is not Shakespeare's incalculable gift; it lacks the element of magic that captures us in Shakespeare; it is, or soon after his earliest experiments it was, an art that came by reflection, and as we read him we

imagine that we might by equal deliberation attain the same perfection—only
we never do attain it. And something of
this distinction Milton himself seems to
have felt when he wrote of Shakespeare:

For whil'st to th' shame of slow-endeavor-
ing Art
Thy easie numbers flow.

The same distinction, I think, was
present to Irving Babbitt when he spoke,
as I have heard him do more than once,
of his experience in quoting. It was Babbitt's custom in the first draught of his
essays to cite from memory, and then,
before printing, to verify the quotation
by reference to the text. He would find
occasionally that even his retentive memory had slipped and that he had substituted a word of his own for the poet's.
And sometimes, he would say, he could
not see that the substitution was inferior
to the original—except in the case of
Shakespeare. He never made a change in
Shakespeare's language but some force or
charm was lost. That was not so even
with Milton.—Such a difference exists
between the seemingly careless spontaneity and the elaborated art of our two supreme masters of poetical diction; and he
would be a rash judge who should say
that the advantage was all on one side
or the other.

But to return to the question that
vexed my mood of acquiescent joy. God-
gifted organ-voice Milton possessed in
full measure—but "voice of England"?
Does he speak for the whole of England,
or, that being scarcely possible, does he
speak from the heart of England, giving
articulate expression to that central quality which has made England what we
know and love? And by his influence did
he maintain that balance and moderation, that sense of law enveloping the
individual, which made of Falkland a

true type of the Englishman that was to
be? Here the question begins with style,
but extends beyond mere style to psychology and to principles of government
and life.

Now, if there be any hesitation with
me to accept Milton's style as the norm
of good English, it is certainly not on the
ground of that "dissociation of sensibility" which draws a school of modern
critics and poets to repudiate what may
be called the Miltonic line of development and to seek their parentage in
Shakespeare and Donne and the "Meta-
physicals." If I understand what the
leader of that Choir means by this rather
obscure phrase, it is that Milton by conscious choice and judgment dissociated
his mind from one whole range of perceptions, refusing to respond to them
emotionally as foreign to his fixed theory
of values, and by the same deliberate act
of selection created a more or less artificial language; whereas the poets proceeding from Donne held their sensibility
open to any and every perception and
employed words to convey the sharp immediate impression of each fact of sense
and experience without discrimination.
The distinction is valid, and it is interesting; for the "modernist" in poetry it is
of vital significance. But I am not sure
that the "dissociation of sensibility," so
taken, has been the source of dead monotony and of verbal unreality in our
literature; and I am sure that if Milton
failed in national leadership it was not
for this reason. Rather I should say that
his influence in this respect has made for
sanity and form and for limitations which
are characteristically English. Rather I
should maintain that Milton's failure, so
far as he failed, was owing to something
essentially un-English, or only partially
English, to something belonging to his
individual temperament, which passed
into his philosophy of life and diverted

a noble love of liberty into a morbid and isolating passion. Here too Milton was clear-headed in his application of the law to others, but curiously perverse when his own interests were affected. In the second of the sonnets on the book called *Tetrachordon*, he berates his fellow countrymen as "Owles and Cuckoos, Asses, Apes and Doggs" for the very reason that they have lost the true meaning of liberty, while they

> bawle for freedom in this sense-
> less mood,
> And still revolt when truth would set them
> free.
> Licence they mean when they cry libertie;
> For who loves that, must first be wise and
> good;
> But from that mark, how far they roave we
> see
> For all this wast of wealth, and loss of
> blood.

That is sound doctrine, but—alas to say it!—Milton did not see how apt would be the retort, *de te fabula*; how easy the reply: License he meant when he cried liberty.

This book called *Tetrachordon*, written by Milton himself, was the second of his treatises on divorce, and is a bitter invective against those who, by opposing the facile freedom of marital separation, enslave the soul under man-made laws, forgetting that which "makes us holiest and likest to God's immortal image," and who, for the law of liberty, set up "that which makes us most conformable and captive to civil and subordinate precepts: ... although indeed no ordinance, human or from heaven, can bind against the good of man." By "the good of man," as Mr. Tillyard observes in his comment on the passage, Milton means what elsewhere he calls "nature" —damnable word, I add, into which have been distilled all the fallacies of

human wit through thousands of years. If you track the word down through its many ambiguities, you will discover that in the end it signifies that which a man temperamentally and personally desires as distinguished from that which is prescribed for him by human rule or divine precept. So it was that Milton, fretted and humiliated because his wife, finding existence with him intolerable, left him and ran away home,—so it was that incontinently he rebelled against the human and divine laws of marriage, and wrote his pleas for freedom of divorce as complying with natural law and the good of man. If ever there was a case of liberty becoming license, it was here. However they may have differed in other respects, in this quality Milton resembled Shelley: they both identified what they desired at any moment with the natural good of man; they both made self-righteousness the law of right.

That was the beginning of Milton's public career and of his prose writings, and it was typical of what ensued. If the bishops in any way interfered with his personal idea of worship, then down with episcopacy and away with the Church; if the monarchical form of government hampered his political independence, then down with monarchy and away with the Constitution. There is no more painful reading in English literature than these apologies for free divorce and regicide which occupied the greatest genius of the age between *Lycidas* and *Paradise Lost*, and the style in which they are written is as heavy and un-English as their spirit is perverse. There are purple patches scattered through these treatises, which are all that most readers know of Milton's prose and which would give the impression that he is as magnificent here as in his verse; but if these passages are examined it will be found that, taken apart from their context, they are expressions of personal ambition, legitimate in itself and magnificent in its devotion to the aim of a poet, while all about them floats and rages a sea of rebellious discontent. I will not endorse Hilaire Belloc's sweeping condemnation of the prose works, but in the mass they do certainly form a repellent body of reading. Following the ideas of the tractates through the surging verbiage, one is reminded of the monsters in the account of creation, "wallowing unweildie" in

the vast immeasurable Abyss
Outrageous as a Sea, dark, wasteful, wilde,
Up from the bottom turn'd by furious windes.

There is something disconcerting in the spectacle of a supreme artist, as Milton was in his verse, so losing his craftsmanship in another medium; what I would insist on is that the very style of his prose has a close relation to the fact that when he passes from imagination to theory his voice is not that of his people but of an exasperated individual. The seventeenth century, with all its greatness, is an age of frustration, filled with fine promises that, except in the field of science, came to no fruition, replete with noble utterance that somehow failed to convince. In the Church, in the State, in society, the one thing needed and not found was a commanding genius that should have been indeed the voice of England. It is the tragedy of the time that he who had the genius so to speak should have wasted his energies in querulous complaints against what was, and in the future was to show itself, the true spirit of the land. In a word that spirit may be described precisely as liberty, not license, as centrality, not dissent.

But I am not concerned to pass judgment on Milton's character and its effect upon his work as a whole; that is a longer theme than I care now to discuss. What I started out to do was to consider one small piece of his output, the *Lycidas*, and to ask myself how it should be read. To this question, at least in its acuter form, I was moved by chancing to take up at the same time Mr. Tillyard's estimation of the poem and Dr. Johnson's. As a whole I should regard Mr. Tillyard's *Milton* as about the best book we have on the man and the poet, a study admirable for its scholarship and discrimination, and particularly notable for its treatment of the philosophical problems raised by *Paradise Lost*, such as Milton's conception of the nature of evil and the cause of man's fall. Now to Mr. Tillyard "*Lycidas* is the last and greatest English poem of Milton's youth; though shorter, it is greater than *Comus*, written with newly won but complete mastery and expressing a mental experience both valuable and profound." That is a sentiment with which my own judgment is in perfect accord; indeed, I should go further and hold it to be the greatest short poem of any author in English, the very criterion and touchstone of poetical taste. Yet with that opinion I have felt bound to remember the sweeping condemnation of Johnson, to whom "the diction" of the poem "is harsh, the rhymes uncertain, and the numbers unpleasing." It is without passion and without art. In part no doubt Johnson's lack of appreciation can be set down to his known deficiency in the higher faculty of imagination. His comment on the diction and rhythm does nothing more than indicate a certain insensitiveness to the finer and more delicate effects of poetry in general. But one cannot read the whole essay without perceiving that his hostile criticism of the art of *Lycidas* sprang not so much from his miscomprehension and aesthetic obtuseness as from hostility to the poet and to all that Milton as a man stood for. Touching Milton's plea for looser laws of divorce, the neglect of which by the ruling Presbyterians turned him against that sect, Johnson observes, and justly: "He that changes his party by his humour is not more virtuous than he that changes it by his interest; he loves himself rather than truth." As for the political tirades, Johnson in his attack ran true to form: "Milton's republicanism was ... founded in an envious hatred of greatness, and a sullen desire of independence.... He hated monarchs in the State, and prelates in the Church; for he hated all whom he was required to obey.... He felt not so much the love of liberty as repugnance to authority." Now for myself I do not like Belloc's summary and contemptuous dismissal of Milton as "a man rotten with the two worst vices: falsehood and pride"; for somehow one shrinks from using such language of a very great poet. To Johnson's charge, on the contrary, I can subscribe without reservation (indeed I have already said much the same thing in weaker language), and I do not see how the charge, in substance, can be countered by any impartial student of Milton's life. But to Johnson the faults of the man were ruinous to the earlier work of the poet, and he denounced *Lycidas* because he read into it the author's ecclesiastical and political heresies; whereas I must reject the maker whilst admiring what he has made. And there the difficulty lies—or has lain for me: how can one so combine detestation and love? how can one make so complete a separation between Milton the destroyer of Church and State, and Milton the artist? how is one to read *Lycidas?*

That particular difficulty, it will be observed, opens up into one of the major problems of criticism in general: the re-

lation between the content of a poem and the art of a poem independent of its content. In the beginning, when that distinction first presented itself to the Greek mind, it took a very simple form and indeed was scarcely a question at all: the *Iliad* and the *Odyssey* were valued primarily, not for their charm and interest, but because in them the statesman, the soldier, the athlete, the man who desired to live honourably, could find the wisest precepts and the best models. For later times, and for us of the West, the principle involved was formulated by Horace in his famous saying that the most successful poet was he who knew how to mix the *utile* and the *dulce*. What Horace meant by the *dulce* is clear enough; it is just that in a poem which gives pleasure to the reader. And what he meant by the *utile* is equally clear; it is that in a poem from which we draw instruction. So in one of the *Epistles* he tells a friend, held in Rome by the practice of declaiming, no doubt about the schools of philosophy, that he is in the country reading Homer, who is a better teacher than all the philosophers:

Qui, quid sit pulchrum, quid turpe, quid utile, quid non,
Plenius ac melius Chrysippo et Crantore dicit.

[Who tells us what is beautiful, what is disgraceful, what is useful, and what is not, more fully and better than Chrysippus and Crantor.]

In exactly that form the question reached the renaissance critics, with the emphasis still heavily on the *utile*. So Puttenham, to name a single example, thinks it necessary to preface his treatise on *The Arte of English Poesie* with a long apology, wherein is shown how "poets were the first priests, the first prophets, the first legislators and politicians in the world," as seen in Homer, Orpheus, Amphion, and the rest. You are back a thousand years and more, and might be reading one of the ancient Greek commentators. But a change came with the advent of the romantic movement. The *utile* and the *dulce* took on new significance, and the old division was sharpened to something like an absolute contrast between two irreconcilable criteria of excellence. The *utile* was broadened so as to embrace the whole substance of a poem whether instructive or not, its sense or meaning. The *dulce* on the other side was refined to a conception of pure poetry, the quintessence of art, as a sort of abstract entity which could be felt and judged somehow apart from any articulate thought or story conveyed; indeed the ideal poem would be a succession of beautiful words with no meaning at all. Such a thesis, baldly stated, is manifestly bare nonsense; but practically the early romantics applied it to criticism by taking *Kubla Khan* as the ideal poem, because, while the content was no more than the shimmering matter of a dream, it reeked of that mysterious entity called pure poetry. And it was not so long ago that the theory flared up again in France under the impulse of the Abbé Bremond's monograph on *La Poésie pure*. The discussion that ensued was confused by the Abbé's association of aesthetic rapture with a mystical view of the function of prayer. More illuminating, to me at least, is T. S. Eliot's pursuit and final rejection of the same ideal of absolute poetry. In his earlier essays, particularly those on Seneca, Shakespeare, and Dante, you will see him eagerly pursuing this *ignis fatuus* as the ultimate standard of value. In the first of those studies he ranks Shakespeare and Dante together as the supreme poets of the world, and the two are equally great though the Italian has taken up

into the *Commedia* the profoundest wisdom of human experience as expounded in the Thomistic theology, whereas the Englishman has no interpretation of life's riddle beyond the stale platitudes of Seneca. "Perhaps it was Shakespeare's special rôle in history to have effected this peculiar union—perhaps it is a part of his special eminence to have expressed an inferior philosophy in the greatest poetry." It is true that Mr. Eliot has his reservations in supporting this romantic dream of pure poetry which came to him from certain early and, as I think, unfortunate associations. It is more important to note that in his latest enunciation he has worked himself quite clear of the disturbing inheritance. There lies before me now his recently published volume of *Essays Ancient and Modern*, and in the opening paragraph of one of the "modern" (that is, hitherto unprinted) essays I am held by this sentence: "The 'greatness' of literature cannot be determined solely by literary standards; though one must remember that whether it is literature or not can be determined only by literary standards." That I take to be a complete truth perfectly expressed; and the whole essay on "Religion and Literature" is a masterly application of this sentence to modern currents in verse and fiction. It is the critic come to full maturity after years of probation.

And so, to apply this canon of taste to *Lycidas*, it may be possible for a young man, enamoured of the sheer beauty of words and untroubled as yet by the graver issues of life, to enjoy the marvellous art of the poem with no throught of what the poem means if connected with the poet's place in the world of ideas and action. But such a rupture between the form and the substance of literature cannot long be maintained with the ripening of experience. Sooner or later we are bound to make up our account with that law of taste so ably formulated: "The 'greatness' of literature cannot be determined solely by literary standards; though one must remember that whether it is literature or not can be determined only by literary standards." That *Lycidas* is literature, poetry and not mere verse, depends on the language, the images, the form, on that mysterious working of the imagination which we can feel but cannot ultimately analyse or adequately describe; that it is great literature must depend on the junction of such qualities with nobility of content. And such nobility is there, in full measure.

The poem is an elegy prompted by the drowning of a college friend of the author. It has been the complaint of more than one critic that the expression of grief has little of that warmth which might be expected from such a subject. Dr. Johnson can find no "effusion of real passion, for passion runs not after remote allusions and obscure opinions." Against this charge of frigidity Mr. Tillyard contends with great acumen that the true theme of the poem is not the death of Edward King at all, but the possible death of the poet himself. Milton was writing just before he set out on his voyage to Italy, when such an adventure was more or less perilous and the chance of shipwreck and drowning might very well have occupied his mind. So taken, the charge of coldness towards a friend might be changed to one of cowardice or egotism. But Milton was no coward and, however he may have shown himself elsewhere, the note of egotism is relieved by the artful, though doubtless unconscious transference of anxiety for himself to sorrow for another. And it was not the mere termination of life that made him anxious, but the fear that his one all-absorbing passion might so be left unfulfilled. To understand his state of mind

and the emotion that was impelling him to write, the elegy should be read in the light of those passages of self-dedication scattered through his prose works. These purple patches laid upon the coarse cloth of controversy are too well known to need repeating here. The keynote is given by the words inserted in the gross *Apology for Smectymnuus:*

He who would not be frustrate of his hope to write well hereafter in laudable things, ought himself to be a true poem; that is, a composition and pattern of the best and honourablest things; not presuming to sing high praises of heroic men, or famous cities, unless he have in himself the experience and the practice of all that which is praiseworthy.

And joined with this personal ambition was the conviction that no loftier or purer service could be rendered to one's country and to the world than such a work as he was preparing himself to produce. Under the spell of a great heroic poem the mind of the people would respond in efforts towards great and heroic living. That was Milton's faith. It was the spirit of the reformer engrafted upon the temperament of the artist. In such a profession, wherein personal glory is identified with public welfare, pride with humility, there lurks, let us admit, a subtle danger; to fall short of brilliant success must leave the professor a monument of ridicule, like the mountains in labour that brought forth only a mouse. But, on the other hand, such a purpose, if carried through valiantly to a successful issue, makes the ordinary ambition of the artist and poet to appear in comparison no more than a cheap display of vanity. And Milton had the courage of conviction and the genius to succeed. In the history of English letters there is nothing like this determination carried through from youth to age, except the solemn dedication of Wordsworth to a similar purpose. All this must be read into *Lycidas*. Under the pretext of grief for the loss of a comrade in hope the poem is in reality as it were the quintessence of those prose passages through which there speaks a self-confidence as sublime as it was justified.

It is in the light of this life-long ambition that we should read the savage attack on the abuses in Church and State which raises the note of elegy to the "higher mood" of righteous indignation:

Last came and last did go,
The Pilot of the *Galilean* lake. . . .
He shook his Miter'd locks, and stern be-
    spake,
How well could I have spar'd for thee,
    young swain,
Anow of such as for their bellies sake,
Creep and intrude, and climb into the
    fold? . . .
But that two-handed engine at the door,
Stands ready to smite once, and smite no
    more.

And apart from any theory of episcopacy and royalty the abuses were there and cried out for remedy. Laud knew them as well as did Baxter, Charles as well as Cromwell; but none but Milton possessed the "dread voice" which—alas, but for defects of temper!—might have done so much to set them right.

In this light also we should interpret the allegorical symbolism of the poem:

The hungry Sheep look up, and are not fed.

To Dr. Johnson all this masquerade of sheep and shepherds is "easy, vulgar, and therefore disgusting," a cheap device of images without passion and without art. Johnson had good reason to be suspicious of a *genre* that has invited so many weak poets to indulge in flim-flam. But he should not have forgotten how all through the Old Testament, from the call that came to Amos, "who was among the herdmen of Tekoa," and all through the New Testament, from the angelic vision that broke upon the shepherds who were "abiding in the field" about Bethlehem to the parable that Jesus spake to his disciples, "I am the good shepherd and know my sheep,"—how all through the Bible this pastoral allegory of the Church runs like the very music of religion.

These were the thoughts that haunted the memory of the poet when he linked himself with his friend as shepherds:

Together both, ere the high Lawns appear'd
Under the opening eye-lids of the morn,
We drove a field.

Together they were practising their "rural ditties" in preparation for the louder chant that was to stir the nation from its ignoble lethargy, when one of the twain was washed away by the sounding sea, and his voice forever silenced. And what if a like fate awaited the other, who also was about to start on a voyage? "What boots it with incessant care . . . to meditate the thankless Muse," of what avail to "live laborious dayes," when, just as we

    think to burst out into sudden blaze,
Comes the blind *Fury* with th' abhorred
    shears,
And slits the thin spun life!

"But not the praise," he exclaims; the reward and the outcome are not confined to this world nor are they measured by success "on mortal soil," but in heaven before the "witness of all judging *Jove*." I do not know how others are affected, but I can never peruse the climax of the poem without a thrill such as scarcely any other verses of the language excite.

Weep no more, woful Shepherds weep no
    more,
For *Lycidas* your sorrow is not dead,
Sunk though he be beneath the watry floar,
So sinks the day-star in the Ocean bed,
And yet anon repairs his drooping head,
And tricks his beams, and with new
    spangled Ore,
Flames in the forehead of the morning sky:
So *Lycidas* sunk low, but mounted high,
Through the dear might of him that walk'd
    the waves
Where other groves, and other streams
    along,
With *Nectar* pure his oozy Lock's he laves,
And hears the unexpressive nuptiall Song,
In the blest Kingdoms meek of joy and
    love.
There entertain him all the Saints above,
In solemn troops, and sweet Societies
That sing, and singing in their glory move,
And wipe the tears for ever from his eyes.

Milton always rang true when he wrote of the world to come, but never before nor after did he attain quite this elevation, or achieve so realistic an expression of the invisible mysteries wrapt in the future. A few of his contemporaries possessed this power of giving substance to the hopes of eternity—notably Vaughan—but none of them approaches the master. And in later times the art was simply lost. Choose the best of the moderns, Newman for instance in *The Dream of Gerontius*, and they will appear cold and unconvincing beside Milton. Nor did any of the great poets of the earlier ages of faith quite equal him in this field. I would not compare the few lines of an elegy with the mighty structure of Dante's *Paradiso,* but for myself at least there is no single incident in Dante's voyage through the celestial spheres that touches me with the shock

of actuality like that which I feel when I read *Lycidas.* I am not competent to explain by what devices, by what choice of words, Milton obtains his sublime effect. It would be easy of course, if it seemed worth while, to point to the rich manipulation of vowel sounds in this or that verse, to note the startling obviousness of the allusion to the might of him that walked the waves, but the final alchemy of art escapes such an analysis; indeed I question whether any skill of criticism can penetrate to the heart of that mystery of the word which we call inspiration, and leave at that. But one phase of Milton's method impresses me: the fact that his images are borrowed from the simplest commonplaces of faith,—the return of dawn after the sinking of the sun in the ocean stream, the tears wiped away, the heavenly choiring of the blest. A comparison of Newman's attempt to translate the subtler speculations of theology into a poetic account of the soul's awakening after death shows how inevitably right was Milton's choice. There are regions of spiritual experience where the untutored imagination of the people goes deeper into reality than all the groping wisdom of philosophy.

One thing in the end is certain, the "greatness" of *Lycidas* is determined by an intimate marriage of form and matter, expression and substance. He who would read the poem worthily must see this, and must be equally sensitive to the delicacy of its art and to the sublimity of its ideas. This does not mean that he will forget or slur over the disagreeable traits of the poet's character or the repulsiveness of his ecclesiastical and political theories. But for our good fortune what repels us in the man and roused Johnson to a fury of protest is reserved for his prose and is excluded from his poetry—not completely indeed, for, not to mention the more outrageous sonnets, occasionally the bitterness of his disappointed soul breaks out in his later works, yet to such an extent that it is not impossible to keep the poet and the controversialist apart as two almost separate powers. That divorce has its unhappy aspect; for one thing it debars Milton, in his total effect, from being accepted as the voice of England. But it leaves to him the high credit of having raised in *Paradise Lost,* to the honour of his native land, the one monumentally successful product of that humanistic culture of the Renaissance in which originality of genius and faithfulness to the classical tradition are combined in perfect union. And for *Lycidas* there is this further apology, that the elegy was composed before Milton's splendid spirit of liberty was exacerbated by opposition into petulant license, when his personal pride flamed with a yet undiverted zeal to make of his own life a true poem and so to train himself for creating such a work of art as would lift his people from the ugly slough of faction and greed, where they were grovelling, into the finer atmosphere where pure religion and the love of beauty might flourish together.

A POEM NEARLY ANONYMOUS
John Crowe Ransom*

It was published in 1638, in the darkness preceding our incomparable modernity. Its origins were about as unlikely as they could be, for it was only one of the exhibits in a memorial garland, a common academic sort of volume. It appeared there without a title and signed only by a pair of initials, though now we know it both by a name and by an author. Often we choose to think of it as the work of a famous poet, which it was not; done by an apprentice of nearly thirty, who was still purifying his taste upon an astonishingly arduous diet of literary exercises; the fame which was to shine backwards upon this poem, and to be not very different from the fame which he steadily intended being as distant as it was great. Unfortunately it is one of the poems which we think we know best. Upon it is imposed the weight of many perfect glosses, respecting its occasion, literary sources, classical and contemporary allusions, exhausting us certainly and exhausting, for a good many persons, the poem. But I am bound to consider that any triteness which comes to mind with mention of the poem is a property of our own registration, and does not affect its freshness, which is perennial. The poem is young, brilliant, insubordinate. In it is an artist who wrestles with an almost insuperable problem, and is kinsman to some tortured modern artists. It has something in common with, for example, *The Waste Land.* In short, the poem is *Lycidas.*

A symbol is a great convenience in discussion, and therefore I will find one in the half-way anonymity of the poem; symbolic of the poet's admirable understanding of his art, and symbolic of the tradition that governed the art on the whole in one of its flourishing periods. Anonymity, of some real if not literal sort, is a condition of poetry. A good poem, even if it is signed with a full and well-known name, intends as a work of art to lose the identity of the author; that is, it means to represent him not actualized, like an eye-witness testifying in court and held strictly by zealous counsel to the point at issue, but freed from his juridical or prose self and taking an ideal or fictitious personality; otherwise his evidence amounts the less to poetry. Poets may go to universities and, if they take to education, increase greatly the stock of ideal selves into which they may pass for the purpose of being poetical. If on the other hand they insist too narrowly on their own identity and their own story, inspired by a simple but mistaken theory of art, they find their little poetic fountains drying up within them. Milton set out to write a poem mourning a friend and poet who had died; in order to do it he became a Greek shepherd, mourning another one. It was not that authority attached particularly to the discourse of a Greek shepherd; the Greek shepherd in his own person would have been hopeless; but Milton as a Greek shepherd was delivered from being Milton the scrivener's son, the Master of Arts from Cambridge, the handsome and finicky young man, and that was the point. In proceeding to his Master's degree he had made studies which gave him dramatic insight into many parts foreign to his own personal experience; which was precisely the technical resource he had required the moment he determined to be a poet. Such a training was almost the regular and unremarked procedure with the poets of his time. Today young men and women, as noble as Milton, those in university circles as much as those out of them, try to become poets on another plan, and with rather less success. They write their autobiographies, following perhaps the example of Words-worth, which on the whole may have been unfortunate for the prosperity of the art; or they write some of their intenser experiences, their loves, pities, griefs, and religious ecstasies; but too literally, faithfully, piously, ingenuously. They seem to want to do without wit and playfulness, dramatic sense, detachment, and it cuts them off from the practice of an art.

Briefly, it was Milton's intention to be always anonymous as a poet, rarely as a writer of prose. The poet must suppress the man, or the man would suppress the poet. What he wanted to say for himself, or for his principles, became eligible for poetry only when it became what the poet, the *dramatis persona* so to speak, might want to say for himself. The poet could not be directed to express faithfully and pointedly the man; nor was it for the sake of "expression" that the man abdicated in favor of the poet.

Strictly speaking, this may be a half-truth. But if we regard with a reformer's eye the decay, in our time, of poetry, it becomes almost the whole truth we are called to utter. I do not mind putting it flatly; nor drawing the conclusion that poetry appeared to the apprentice Milton, before it could appear anything else, and before it could come into proper existence at all, as a sort of exercise, very difficult, and at first sight rather beside the point. It was of course an exercise in pure linguistic technique, or metrics; it was also an exercise in the technique of what our critics of fiction refer to as "point of view." And probably we shall never find a better locus than *Lycidas* for exhibiting at once the poet and the man, the technique and the personal interest, bound up tightly and contending all but equally; the strain of contraries, the not quite resolvable dualism, that is art.

For we must begin with a remark quite unsuitable for those moderns to whom "expression" seems the essential quality of poetry. *Lycidas* is a literary exercise; and so is almost any other poem earlier than the eighteenth century; the craftsmanship, the formal quality which is written on it, is meant to have high visibility. Take elegy, for example. According to the gentle and extremely masculine tradition which once governed these matters, performance is not rated by the rending of garments, heartbreak, verisimilitude of desolation. After all, an artist is standing before the public, and bears the character of a qualified spokesman, and a male. Let him somewhat loudly sweep the strings, even the tender human ones, but not without being almost military and superficial in his restraint; like the pomp at the funeral of the king, whom everybody mourns publicly and nobody privately. Milton made a great point of observing the proprieties of verse. He had told Diodati, as plainly as Latin elegiacs allowed, that "expression" was not one of the satisfactions which they permitted to the poet: "You want to know in verse how much I love and cherish you; believe me that you will scarcely discover this in verse, for love like ours is not contained within cold measures, it does not come to hobbled feet." As for memorial verse, he had already written, in English or Latin, for the University beadle, the University carrier, the Vice-Chancellor, his niece the Fair Infant Dying of a Cough, the Marchioness of Winchester, the Bishop of Winchester, the Bishop of Ely; he was yet to write for his Diodati, and for Mrs. Katharine Thomason. All these poems are exercises, and some are very playful indeed. There is no great raw grief apparent ever, and sometimes, very likely, no great grief. For Lycidas he mourns with a very technical piety.

Let us go directly to the poem's metre —though this feature may seem a bristling technicality, and the sort of thing the tender reader may think he ought to be spared. I do not wish to be brutal, but I am afraid that metre is fundamental in the problem posed to the artist as poet. During the long apprenticeship Milton was the experimentalist, trying nearly everything. He does not ordinarily, in the Minor Poems, repeat himself metrically; another poem means another metre, and the new metre will scarcely satisfy him any better than the last one did. Evidently Milton never found the metre in which as a highly individual poet he could feel easy, and to which he was prepared to entrust his serious work, until he had taken the ragged blank verse of contemporary drama and had done something to it; tightening it up into a medium which was hard enough to exhibit form, and plastic enough to give him freedom. In other words, it defined the poet as somebody with a clipped, sonorous, figurative manner of speaking; but it also gave a possible if indirect utterance to the natural man. Here let us ask the question always in order against a Milton poem: What was the historic metrical pattern already before him, and what are the liberties he takes with it? For he does not cut patterns out of the whole cloth, but always takes an existing pattern; stretches it dangerously close to the limits that the pattern will permit without ceasing to be a pattern; and never brings himself to the point of defying that restraint which patterns inflict upon him, and composing something altogether unpatterned. That is to say, he tends habitually towards the formlessness which is modern, without quite caring to arrive at that destination. It is the principle we are interested in, not the literal answer to the question, which I will try to get over briefly.

The answer given by the Milton scholars, those who know their Italian, might well be that in this poem he made a very free adaptation of the canzone. This was a stanza of indeterminate length, running it might be to twenty lines or so, marked by some intricate rhyming scheme, and by a small number of six-syllable lines inserted among the ten-syllable lines which constituted the staple. The poet was free to make up his own stanza but, once that was given, had to keep it uniform throughout the poem. Milton employs it with almost destructive freedom, as we shall see. Yet, on the other hand, the correct stanza materials are there, and we can at least say that any one of the stanzas or paragraphs might make a passable canzone. And lest his irregularities be imputed to incompetence, we must observe the loving exactitude of his line-structure, that fundamental unit of any prosody, within the stanzas. He counts his syllables, he takes no liberties there: consisting with our rather fixed impression that he scarcely knew how in all his poetry to admit an imperfect line.

The Milton scholars know their Italian, and have me at a disadvantage. Milton knew his Italian. But he also knew his Spenser, and knowing that, it seems unnecessary to inquire whether he knew his Italian too; for he had only to adapt a famous Spenserian stanza, and his acquaintance with the canzone becomes really immaterial. I imagine this point has a slight importance. It would have something to do with the problem of the English poet who wants to employ an English technique in addressing himself to an English public which can be expected to know its English formal tradition. Spenser anticipated Milton by employing the canzone effectively in at least two considerable poems; they were not elegies, but at least they were marriage hymns. In 1596 he published his *Prothalamion*, upon the occasion of a noble alliance; the stanzas are exactly uniform, and they compose an admirable exercise in Italian canzoni. But he had published in 1595 his *Epithalamion*, upon the occasion of his own wedding, which is much more to Milton's purpose, and ours. Here are ten eighteen-line stanzas, but here are also twelve nineteen-line stanzas, and one of seventeen lines; and one of the eighteen-line stanzas does not agree in pattern with the others. If these details escape the modern reader, it is not at all certain that they were missed by Spenser's public. I should like to think that the poetical consciousness of the aristocratic literati of that age was a state of mind having metrical form in its foreground, and Spenser intended frankly to make use of the situation. Perhaps he calculated that if they would go to the trouble to analyze a poem composed of intricate but regular canzoni, they might go to still greater pains to analyze a poem whose canzoni were subtly irregular. I suppose this was something of a miscalculation, like other of his plans. But if it were a just calculation: then the advantage to be reaped by their going to such pains—it was their advantage as much as his—was the sort of addition to total effect which a labor of love can furnish. A public like Spenser's, if we are to construe it at its best, participates in the poem as does the author, and it is unfortunate if there lives today some modern Spenser who does not hope for such a reward to his efforts. But probably the sad truth is that a subtle art is unlikely in the first place, whose artist does not reckon upon the background of a severe technical tradition, and the prospect of a substantial public body of appreciation.

The enterprising Spenser prepared the way for the daring Milton, who remarks the liberties which his celebrated exemplar has taken and carries his own liberties further, to a point just this side of anarchy. The eleven stanzas of *Lycidas* occupy 193 lines, but are grossly unequal and unlike. Such stanzas are not in strictness stanzas at all; Milton has all but scrapped the stanza in its proper sense as a formal and binding element. But there is perhaps an even more startling lapse. Within the poem are ten lines which do not rhyme at all, and which technically do not belong therefore in any stanza, nor in the poem.

Now we may well imagine that the unrhymed lines did not escape Milton's notice, and also that he did not mean nor hope that they should escape ours. The opening line of the poem is unrhymed, which is fair warning. The ten unrhymed lines should be conspicuous among the 183 rhymed ones, like so many bachelors at a picnic of fast-mated families. Let us ask what readers of *Lycidas* have detected them, and we shall see what readers are equipped with the right sensibility for an effect in form. And if the effect in this case is an effect of prose formlessness, and if nevertheless it is deliberate, we had better ask ourselves what Milton wanted with it.

It is tempting to the imperious individualism of the modern reader, especially if he has heard somewhere about the enormous egoism of John Milton, to say that the "expression" in these lines must have seemed to their author "inevitable," and superior to any obligation to the law of the form. Just as we find them, they had leapt out of the tense creative fury of the poet, notable, possibly prophetic; and what higher considerations were there anywhere requiring him in cold blood to alter them? But that does not make sense as an account of the poetic processes of a Milton. The ten lines, as it happens, look at them hard as we like, do not seem more important than ten others, and are not the lines by which he could have set special store. As a matter of fact, he might have altered them easily, tinkering with them as long as necessary in order to bring them within the metre, and they would scarcely have been, by whatever standard, any the worse. So great is the suggestibility of the poet's mind, the associability of ideas, the margin in the meaning of words. It is the inexperienced artist who attributes sanctity to some detail of his inspiration. You may ask him to write a poem which will make sense and make metre at the same time, but in the performance he will sacrifice one or the other; the consequence will be good sense and lame metre, or good metre and nonsense; if he is a man of interests and convictions, the former. But the competent artist is as sure of his second thoughts as of his first ones. In fact, surer, if anything; second thoughts tend to be the richer, for in order to get them he has to break up the obvious train of association and explore more widely. Milton was not enamored of the ten lines, and they stand out from their context by no peculiar quality of their own but only because they do not belong to it metrically. Therefore I would say that they constitute the gesture of his rebellion against the formalism of his art, but not the rebellion itself. They are defiances, showing the man unwilling to give way to the poet; they are not based upon a special issue but upon surliness, and general principles. It is a fateful moment. At this critical stage in the poet's career, when he has come to the end of the period of Minor Poems, and is turning over in his head the grand subjects out of which he will produce great poems, he is uneasy, sceptical, about the whole foundation of poetry as an art. He has a lordly contempt for its tedious formalities, and is determined to show what he can do with only half trying to attend to them. Or he thinks they are definitely bad, and proposes to see if it is not better to shove them aside.

In this uncertainty he is a modern poet. In the irregular stanzas and the rhymeless lines is registered the ravage of his modernity; it has bit into him as it never did into Spenser. And we imagine him thinking to himself, precisely like some modern poets we know, that he could no longer endure the look of perfect regimentation which sat upon the poor ideas objectified before him upon the page of poetry, as if that carried with it a reflection upon their sincerity. I will go further. It is not merely easy for a technician to write in smooth metres; it is perhaps easier than to write in rough ones, after he has once started; but when he has written smoothly, and contemplates his work, he is capable actually, if he is a modern poet, of going over it laboriously and roughening it. I venture to think that just such a practice, speaking very broadly, obtained in the composition of *Lycidas*; that it was written smooth and rewritten rough; which was treason.

I will make a summary statement which is true to the best of my knowledge. There did not at the time anywhere exist in English, among the poems done by competent technical poets, another poem so wilful and illegal in form as this one.

An art never possesses the "sincerity" that consists in speaking one's mind, that is, in expressing one's first impression before it has time to grow cold. This sincerity is spontaneity, the most characteristic quality in modern poetry. Art is long, and time is fleeting, and we

have grown too impatient to relish more than the first motions towards poetic effect. The English and American Imagists exploited and consolidated this temper, which was no longer hospitable to a finished art. In their defence it may be said with justice that the writing of formal poetry, which they interrupted, was becoming a tedious parlor performance in which the poet made much ado about saying nothing of importance, while the man behind him quite escaped acquaintance through sheer lack of force. The verslibrists were determined to be bright, and fresh, and innocent of deep and ulterior designs; but their prose art was an anomaly. It wore out, and strict artistic economy has had a certain recovery; nothing like a complete one, for they left their mark upon our poetry, and I shall certainly not be so dogmatic as to say it has been entirely unfortunate.

It depends ultimately on taste whether we prefer prose to poetry, or prefer even a mixture of prose and poetry. Let us suppose two gentlemen talking a little wildly over their cups, until Mr. A insults Mr. B. Now if B is a modern man, he immediately strikes A down, with his knife if it happens to be in his hand, or his stick, or his fist. He has acted spontaneously, with a right and quick instinct, and he is admired for it. (I do not mean to raise any moral issues with my analogy.) But if the time is about a century or two earlier, B steps back and says drily: "My seconds will wait upon you, Sir." The next dawn A and B repair to the grove, attended by their respective partisans, draw their rapiers, and with great ceremony set in to kill each other. Or apparently they do; but if they are not really prepared to be hurt, nor to hurt each other, but are only passing the time until they are informed that their honors are satisfied, it is a bogus and ineffective action and the serious spectators feel cheated; that represents the sort of art against which the free versifiers revolted. If they fight till A puts his steel through the vitals of B, or *vice versa*, the spectators are well rewarded, and the ceremonial has justified itself, though it took time; that stands for the true art. But if they lose their tempers on the field and begin to curse, and kick, and throw stones and clods at each other, they are behaving too spontaneously for a formal occasion. Why were they not spontaneous yesterday if that was their intention? They will have to be recalled to the occasion and come to a conclusion under the terms nominated; and here we have the mixed affair of poetry and prose, a problem in taste; here, I am afraid, we have *Lycidas*.

At any rate Milton thought something of the kind. For he never repeated his bold experiment; and he felt at the time that it was not an altogether successful experiment. The last stanzas become much more patterned, and in the postscript Milton refers to the whole monody as the song of an "uncouth Swain," who has been "with eager thought warbling his *Dorick* lay." That is descriptive and deprecatory.

There is another possibility. Milton had much of the modern poet's awareness of his public; in this case the awareness of a public not quite capable of his own sustained artistic detachment. What sort of poem would it like? Too perfect an art might look cold and dead; and though an elegy had to be about the dead, it did not want itself to look dead, but to display incessant energy. So he read the formal poem he had written, and deformed it; or he had read other formal poems, like the *Epithalamion*, and remarked that the public, an increasingly mixed lot, thought them a little dull, and he now, as he composed his own poem, remembered to write into

it plenty of formlessness. "The formalism," he was thinking, "if unrelieved, will dull the perceptions of my reader, and unprepare him for my surprises, and my tireless fertility. Therefore let him sense an exciting combat between the artist and the man, and let the man interrupt with his prose (comparative prose) the pretty passages of the artist." In that case the artist was only pretending to give way to the man, calculating with the cunning of a psychologist, perhaps of a dramatist, and violating the law of his art entirely for its public effect; a Jesuit of an artist. But the Jesuit, according to the Protestant tradition which reaches me, and which I will trust to the extent of this argument, has an excessive respect for the depravity of the humanity he ministers to, and he needs beyond other priests to be firmly grounded in his principles, lest from fighting the devil with fire he change his own element insensibly, become himself a fallen angel, and bear the reputation of one. The best thing to say for Milton is that his principles were strong, and he did not again so flagrantly betray them.

But if the poem is a literary exercise, it does not consist only in a game of metrical hide-and-seek, played between the long lines and short lines, the rhymed and unrhymed. It is also a poem in a certain literary "type," with conventions of subject-matter and style. Milton set out to make it a pastoral elegy, and felt honor-bound to use the conventions which had developed in the pastoral elegies of the Greeks, of Virgil, of the Italians, of Spenser; possibly of the French. The course of the poem in outline therefore is not highly "creative," but rather commonplace and in order, when the dead shepherd is remembered and his virtues published; when nature is made to lament him, and the streams to dry up in sympathy; when the guardian nymphs are asked why they have not saved him; when the untimeliness of his doom is moralized; when the corrupt church is reproached; when the flowers are gathered for the hearse; and finally when it appears to the mourners that they must cease, since he is not dead, but translated into a higher region, where he lives in bliss of a not definitive sort. In the pastoral elegy at large one of my friends distinguishes eleven different topics of discourse, and points out that Milton, for doubtless the first time in this literature, manages to "drag them all into one poem"; a distinction for him, though perhaps a doubtful one. But in doing so he simply fills up the poem; there are no other topics in it. And where is Milton the individualist, whose metrical departures would seem to have advertised a performance which in some to-be-unfolded manner will be revolutionary?

When we attempt to define the poetic "quality" of this poet's performances, we are forced to confess that it consists largely in pure eclecticism; here is a poet who can simply lay more of his predecessors under tribute than another. This is not to deny that he does a good job of it. He assimilates what he receives, and adapts it infallibly to the business in hand, where scraps fuse into integer, and the awkward articulations cannot be detected. His second-hand effects are not as good as new but better; the features of pastoral elegy are not as pretty in *Lycidas* as they were in Moschus, or Virgil, or Spenser, but prettier; though generically, and even in considerable detail, the same features. We remember after all that Milton intended his effects; and among others, this one of indebtedness to models. He expected that the reader should observe his eclecticism, he was scarcely alarmed lest it be mistaken for plagiarism. It is because of something mean in our modernism, or at least in that of

our critics, that we, if we had composed the poem, would have found such an expectancy tainted with such an alarm. Like all the artists of the Renaissance, Milton hankered honestly after "Fame"; but he was not infected with our gross modern concept of "originality." The aesthetic of this point is perfectly rational. If a whole series of artists in turn develop the same subject, it is to the last one's advantage that he may absorb the others, in addition to being in whatever pointed or subtle manner his own specific self. His work becomes the climax of a tradition, and is better than the work of an earlier artist in the series. Unfortunately, there will come perhaps the day when there is no artist prepared to carry on the tradition; or, more simply, when the tradition has gone far enough and is not worth carrying further; that is, when it is worn out as a "heuristic" principle, and confines more than it frees the spirit. (Very few pastoral elegies can have been written since *Lycidas* in our language; very few critics can have deplored this.) On that day the art will need its revolutionist, to start another tradition. It is a bold step for the artist to take, and Milton did not think it needful to take it here. The revolutionist who does not succeed must descend to the rating, for history, of rebel; the fool of a wrong political intuition.

But revolutions, for all that, little and private ones if not big and general ones, come frequently into a healthy literary history, in which variety is a matter of course. The poet may do better with a make-believe of his own than with a time-honored one. There is no theoretical limit upon the variety of literary types, and each good type permits of many explorers, but tends at last to be exhausted. The point of view of Greek shepherds, as romantic innocents and rustics, is excellent, and offers a wide range of poetic discourse concerning friendship, love, nature, and even, a startling innovation of the Italian pastoralists, the "ruin of the clergy." The point of view of the amorous cavalier presenting his compliments and reproaches to his lady is also a good one; it ran through many hundreds of lyrics in the sixteenth and seventeenth centuries, and is still better than no point of view at all, which we find in some very young poet speaking in his own person to his own love. The studied "conceit" of the seventeenth century offered another field of discourse in which poetic exercises took place; logical and academic, but having rich possibilities, and eligible even for religious experiences. The sonnet is primarily a metrical form, but behind it there is an ideal and rather formidable speaker, far from actual, who must get what he has to say into a very small space and, according to the rules, into a very concise style of utterance. The ballad offers a point of view quite alien to the ordinary cultivated poet, because speaking in that form he must divest himself of the impedimenta of learning and go primitive. All these forms lend themselves to individual variations and innovations; call for them, in fact, in the course of time, when the poet can find no fresh experience within the usual thing. It is entirely according to the aesthetic of this art if a poet wants to enter the book of literature with a series of Choctaw incantations, provided he is steeped in Choctaw experience and able to make a substantial exhibit; or with a set of poems from the character of a mere Shropshire lad; or from that of a dry New England countryman. It is important mostly that the poet know his part and speak it fluently.

Of Milton's "style," in the sense of beauty of sound, imagery, syntax and dystax, idiom, I am quite unprepared to be very analytic. It is a grand style; which is to say, I suppose, that it is *the* grand style, or as much a grand style as English poets have known: the style produced out of the poet's remembrance of his classical models, chiefly Virgil. Milton has not been the only English poet to learn from Virgil, but he is doubtless the one who learned the most. Until the nineteenth century Virgil was perhaps the greatest external influence upon English literature. Dryden venerated but could not translate him:

. . . must confess to my shame, that I have not been able to Translate any part of him so well, as to make him appear wholly like himself. For where the Original is close, no Version can reach it in the same compass. Hannibal Caro's, in the Italian, is the nearest, the most Poetical, and the most Sonorous of any Translation of the Æneid's; yet, though he takes the advantage of blank Verse, he commonly allows two lines for one of Virgil, and does not always hit his sence. . . . Virgil, therefore, being so very sparing of his words, and leaving so much to be imagined by the Reader, can never be translated as he ought, in any modern Tongue. To make him Copious, is to alter his Character; and to translate him Line for Line is impossible; because the Latin is naturally a more succinct Language than either the Italian, Spanish, French, or even than the English (which, by reason of its Monosyllables, is far the most compendious of them). Virgil is much the closest of any Roman Poet, and the Latin Hexameter has more Feet than the English Heroick.

But in spite of the unfitness of an uninflected language like English, poets have occasionally managed a Virgilian style in it. We think at once of Marlowe. Naturally, it was not entirely beyond Shakespeare's powers; but Shakespeare at his highest pitch likes to rely on fury and hyperbole rather than the "smoothness" and "majesty" which Dryden commends in Virgil. Shakespeare writes:

Rumble thy bellyful! Spit, fire! Spout, rain!

and

You sulphurous and thought-executing fires,
Vaunt-couriers of oak-cleaving thunderbolts,
Singe my white head!

which is in a sublime style but not, if we care to be precise, the grand style. But Milton very nearly commanded this style. And with reason; for he had written Minor Poems in Latin as well as Minor Poems in English, and they were perhaps the more important item in his apprenticeship. This is one of the consequences:

But now my Oate proceeds,
And listens to the Herald of the Sea,
That came in *Neptune's* plea,
He ask'd the Waves, and ask'd the Fellon winds,
What hard mishap hath doom'd this gentle swain?
And question'd every gust of rugged wings
That blows from off each beaked Promontory,
They knew not of his story,
And sage *Hippotades* their answer brings,
That not a blast was from his dungeon stray'd,
The Ayr was calm, and on the level brine,
Sleek *Panope* with all her sisters play'd.
It was that fatall and perfidious Bark
Built in th'eclipse, and rigg'd with curses dark,
That sunk so low that sacred head of thine.

It is probable that no other English poet has this mastery of the Virgilian effect; it is much more Virgilian, too, than the later effect which Milton has in the lines of the *Paradise Lost*, where the great departure from the epical substance of the Virgil makes it needful to depart from the poetic tone. But Milton

proves here that he had fairly mastered it. He had simply learned to know it in the Latin—learning by the long way of performance as well as by the short one of observation—and then transferred it to his native English; where it becomes a heightened effect, because this language is not accustomed at once to ease and condensation like this, and there is little competition. The great repute of the Miltonic style—or styles, variants of a style—in our literature is a consequence of the scarcity of Miltons; that is, of poets who have mastered the technique of Latin poetry before they have turned to their own.

But the author of *Lycidas*, attended into his project by so much of the baggage of tradition, cannot, by a universal way of thinking, have felt, exactly, free. I shall risk saying that he was not free. Little chance there for him to express the interests, the causes, which he personally and powerfully was developing; the poem too occasional and too formal for that. Of course the occasion was a fundamental one, it was no less than Death; and there is nobody so aggressive and self-assured but he must come to terms with that occasion. But a philosophy of death seems mostly to nullify, with its irony, the philosophy of life. Milton was yet very much alive, and in fact he regarded himself as having scarcely begun to live. The poem is almost wasted if we are seeking to determine to what extent it permitted Milton to unburden his heart.

But not quite. The passage on mortality is tense; Professor Tillyard finds the man in it. It goes into a passage on the immortality of the just man's Fame, which gives Milton's Platonic version of the ends of Puritanism. More important perhaps is the kind of expressiveness which appears in the speech of Peter. The freedom with which Milton abuses the false shepherds surpasses anything which his predecessors in this vein had indulged. He drops his Latinity for plain speech, where he can express a Milton who is angry, violent, and perhaps a little bit vulgar. It is the first time in his career that we have seen in him a taste for writing at this level. With modern readers it may be greatly to his credit as a natural man that he can feel strongly and hit hard. Later, in the period of his controversial prose, we get more of it, until we have had quite enough of this natural man. In the *Paradise Lost* we will get some "strong" passages again, but they are not Milton's response to his own immediate situation, they are dramatically appropriate, and the persons and scenes of the drama are probably remote enough to bring the passages under the precise head of artistic effect. This may be thought to hold for *Lycidas*, since it is Peter speaking in a pastoral part, and Peter still represents his villains as shepherds; but I feel that Peter sounds like another Puritan zealot, and less than apostolic.

Before I offer some generalizations about the poet and his art, I wish to refer, finally, to a feature of *Lycidas* which critics have rarely mentioned, and which most readers of my acquaintance, I believe, have never noticed, but which is technically astonishing all the same, and ought to initiate an important speculation upon the intentions of this poet. Pastoral elegies are dramatic monologues, giving the words of a single shepherd upon a single occasion; or they are dialogues giving, like so much printed drama, the speeches of several shepherds in a single scene. They may have prologues, perhaps so denominated in the text, and printed in italics, or in a body separate from the elegy proper; and likewise epilogues; the prologues and epilogues being the author's envelope of narrative within

which is inserted the elegy. The composition is straightforward and explicitly logical.

Milton's elegy is otherwise. It begins without preamble as a monologue, and continues so through the former and bitterer half of the passage on Fame:

But the fair Guerdon when we hope to find,
And think to burst out into sudden blaze,
Comes the blind *Fury* with th'abhorred
   shears,
And slits the thin spun life. . . .

At this point comes an incredible interpolation:

      . . . But not the praise,
Phœbus repli'd, and touch'd my trembling
   ears . . .

And Phœbus concludes the stanza; after which the shepherd apologizes to his pastoral Muses for the interruption and proceeds with his monologue. But dramatic monologue has turned for a moment into narrative. The narrative breaks the monologue several times more, presenting action sometimes in the present tense, sometimes in the past. And the final stanza gives a pure narrative conclusion in the past, without the typographical separateness of an epilogue; it is the one which contains Milton's apology for the "Dorick" quality of his performance, and promises that the author will yet appear in a serious and mature light as he has scarcely done on this occasion.

Such a breach in the logic of composition would denote, in another work, an amateurism below the level of publication. I do not know whether our failure to notice it is because we have been intoxicated by the wine of the poetry, or dulled by the drum-fire of the scholars' glosses, or intimidated by the sense that the poem is Milton's. Certainly it is

Milton's; therefore it was intended; and what could have been in his mind? I have a suggestion. A feature that obeys the canon of logic is only the mere instance of a universal convention, while the one that violates the canon is an indestructibly private thing. The poor "instance" would like so much to attain to the dignity of a particular. If Milton had respected the rule of composition, he must have appeared as any other author of pastoral elegy, whereas in his disrespect of it he can be the person, the John Milton who is different, and dangerous, and very likely to become famous. (It is ironical that the lapse in question celebrates Fame.) The logical difficulties in the work of an artist capable of perfect logic may be the insignia of an individuality which would otherwise have to be left to the goodness of the imagination; and that is a calculation which lies, I think, under much modern art. There are living poets, and writers of fiction, and critics at the service of both, who have a perfect understanding of the principle. The incoherence or "difficulty" in the work is not necessarily to be attributed to the unresourcefulness of the artist, as if he could not have straightened everything out if he had desired, but sometimes to his choice. Under this head comes that licentious typography in which we may find one of the really magnificent manifestations of our modernity. The author is like some gentleman in the world of fashion who is thoroughly initiated, yet takes great pains to break the rule somewhere in order that nobody will make the mistake of not remarking his personality. If there is any force in this way of reasoning, we may believe that Milton's bold play with the forms of discourse constitutes simply one more item in his general insubordinacy. He does not propose to be buried beneath his own elegy. Now he had done a thing somewhat on the order of the present breach in his *L'Allegro* and *Il Penseroso*. There is a comparative simplicity to these pieces amounting almost to obviousness, but they are saved in several ways. For one thing, they are twin poems, and the parallelism or contrast is very intricate. More to our point, there is a certain lack of definition in the substantive detail; long sentences with difficult grammatical references, and uncertainty as to whether the invocation has passed into the action, and as to just where we are in the action. That trick was like the present one, indicating that the man is getting ahead of the poet, who is not being allowed to assimilate the matter into his formal style.

More accurately, of course, *they would like to indicate it*; the poet being really a party to the illusion. Therefore he lays himself open to the charge of being too cunning, and of overreaching himself; the effect is not heroic but mock-heroic. The excited Milton, breathless, and breaking through the logic of composition, is charming at first; but as soon as we are forced to reflect that he counterfeited the excitement, we are pained and let down. The whole poem is properly an illusion, but a deliberate and honest one, to which we consent, and through which we follow the poet because it enables him to do things not possible if he were presenting actuality. At some moments we may grow excited and tempted to forget that it is illusion, as the untrained spectator may forget and hiss the villain at the theatre. But we are quickly reminded of our proper attitude. If the author tends to forget, all the more if he pretends to forget, we would recall him to the situation too. Such license we do not accord to poets and dramatists, but only to novelists, whose art is young. And even these, or the best of these, seem now determined, for the sake of their artistic integrity, to surrender it.

So *Lycidas*, for the most part a work of great art, is sometimes artful and tricky. We are disturbingly conscious of a man behind the artist. But the critic will always find too many and too perfect beauties in it ever to deal with it very harshly.

THE JUDGING OF
CONTEMPORARY LITERATURE
David Daiches[*]

Daiches believes that the critics' greatest obstacles in assessing the work of their contemporaries are "temporary factors playing unduly on the emotions" and sensibilities. A second obstacle is the reactionary nature of taste that has been educated by the achievement of the preceding age or ages. Conversely, a third obstacle is the tendency to prize any departure from tradition as worthwhile originality. Sound criticism, Daiches concludes, requires an "organic view of literature" and "an insight into the nature and conditions of literary activity which can only come with wide and deep experience."

Perhaps criticism has always appeared to be in a chaotic state to the contemporary observer. Certainly to-day it seems to be in a state of unprecedented confusion. Among the more serious critics there is no agreement at all concerning the nature of literary value, while most critics of the periodical press agree at least in superficiality and ineffectiveness. It is not so much that we lack standards by which to judge as that we differ hopelessly on what it is we are judging. One critic praises a novel because it is written in a flowing English; another condemns it because it portrays a kind of life that can only be found in occasional corners of the worst city slums; a third praises it because it establishes contact with the proletariat; another condemns it because

it belongs to no tradition of writing; yet a fifth praises it for the same reason; a further critic praises it for the insight and detailed observation shown in the description of a lamp-post at midnight. The catalogue might be extended indefinitely. Differences of opinion are natural and to a certain extent desirable, but differences of this kind—differences which show the critics quite unconcerned to isolate those factors in a work of literature which determine its value as literature—indicate a very disturbing state of affairs.

We need to-day a keener sense of literary value. This is not to say that we require a set of rules whose application will reveal the worth of a book. It is a sense of the uniqueness of literary value that is required—its difference from, at least its relation to, other values. We can allow differences concerning the na-

* The essay is reprinted from *New Literary Values*, by David Daiches, Oliver & Boyd Ltd., 1936, by permission of the author.

ture of this value, but we must demand agreement on its existence if criticism is to serve any literary function at all. Criticism at present is serving several functions—psychological, sociological, political, ethical, even metaphysical—and in so far as it serves these functions adequately it is valuable, but when criticism fulfilling any or all of these functions masquerades indiscriminately as "literary" the resulting confusion is overwhelming. The sociologist will find a value in Dickens, the psychologist a value in Shakespeare, the feminist a value in Meredith, and other specialists will find other values in the same writers. But literary worth is distinct—even if, as some hold, it is composite—and to allow this fact to be obscured is ultimately to oust literature from the world of art altogether and to deny any usefulness to writing which cannot be viewed as the handmaid of some scientific or epistemological activity. That the present tendency in criticism is already helping to produce an inferiority complex among imaginative writers and academic critics—especially the latter—can be judged from the increasing habit of stressing the "difficulty" of literature (it requires as painstaking work as science, in fact) and dwelling on the laboratory methods of e.g. Shakespearean criticism as a means of justification.

It may be argued that to seek for a purely literary value is to divorce literature from life, but that is to miss the point: literature has its own relation to life—closer than that of psychology or philosophy—and it is precisely in order that this relation should not be obscured that its uniqueness should be understood and appreciated. It is doing no service to literature to identify the value of poetry with its value for the psychologist or the worth of fiction with its interest to the sociologist. That may be one way of in-creasing the reading public, but it requires little argument to prove that sooner or later the reaction on literature is going to be most harmful.

Perhaps this confusion of values is partly self-induced by the critics as a means of escape from the uncomfortable problem of how to judge contemporary literature. The worst work is always *interesting* from one point of view or another—indeed the worse the work often the more interesting it is. To the psychoanalyst, bad poetry is as helpful as good in investigating the mental processes at work: in the unfinished second-rate product the processes may stand more clearly revealed. So the modern critic can always justify his errors of judgment by appealing to some particular specialist and explaining that it was to *him* the work was interesting and that's what he meant all along. But we cannot allow such specious methods, and the problem of judging our contemporaries must be faced squarely.

And it is a problem. Let anyone who doubts it study the early nineteenth century reviews and make a list of the appalling errors of judgment committed by some really fine minds. Let them consider what some intelligent contemporaries thought of Wordsworth and Coleridge and Keats—political prejudice apart—and remember Scott's opinion of the poetry of Joanna Baillie. It is enough to daunt the most confident. It is not a simple question of one school failing to appreciate another. The situation is much more disconcerting than that; it involves the failure (and its converse) on the part of some trained and even sensitive critics to recognise any literary worth in works which, fundamentally, did actually embody the elements which they held to constitute such worth. The critics were not myopic or squint-eyed, but downright blind. They went astray in applying their own standards, in addition to failing to appreciate new ones. And the reason was just a difference of approach, a difference of method, which came between them and the real object. Examples of this are commonplaces in the history of criticism, and it applies to music and the visual arts as well as to literature. Can we attempt to analyse those factors which tend to vitiate the judging of contemporary literature?

Sensibility differs in different ages more radically than we are sometimes aware, and an awareness of the nature of contemporary sensibility is indispensable in judging modern literature. We must be able to discount the appeal made to an overwrought mind by temporary factors playing unduly on the emotions. Such factors belong to an age as much as to individuals and are perhaps the greatest obstacle to the critic in assessing the work of his own day. An obvious example of this would be the temporary appeal of patriotic poetry at the beginning of a war or of hysterical "horror" poetry at the end. It was not easy to see in 1918 that Wilfred Owen was by far the best of the war poets, but as soon as the special type of sensibility evoked by the war had disappeared his pre-eminence was generally recognised. In Mr. Middleton Murry's autobiography *Between Two Worlds* occurs this illuminating passage:

In the previous number of *Rhythm* I had written a dithyrambic review of Mr. James Stephens' book of poetry, *The Hill of Vision*. A poem in it which had, indeed, moved me deeply, called "The Lonely God," I had forthwith declared to be better than Milton: a dozen lines of it were worth the whole of *Endymion*. What had happened, quite simply, was that the poem *had* moved me, where modern poetry seldom did move me, and that I declared the fact in these ridiculous terms—setting it above *Paradise Lost*, which did not then move

me, and *Endymion*, which I had never really read.

In this case an individual is concerned, but a whole age may make a very similar kind of error. The eighteenth century elevated many a poet of whom to-day few have heard above a poet like Donne, whom the age as a whole had "never really read." For certain temporary causes the critics were unnaturally sensitive to one kind of literature and unnaturally insensitive to another. And this is not a defect of any one age; every age has its weaknesses and its blind spots, and a time when every kind of literature will be equally appreciated is inconceivable, if indeed it is desirable. Skelton is in favour to-day, but two hundred years ago he was execrated. Neither the favour which he enjoys at present nor the disfavour under which he so long laboured was due entirely to intrinsically literary reasons at all. The sensibility of the present age is unnaturally appreciative of Skelton. And almost every reaction and counter-reaction in literary taste points the same moral.

Another point to consider is that the critics of any one age are educated in the taste of the preceding age. When a twentieth century academic critic turns to verse, he generally writes in a nineteenth century idiom. As Wordsworth pointed out, the poet himself creates the taste by which he is to be judged; it generally take a generation or longer for this taste to be formed. So here is another factor which tends to confuse the judging of contemporary literature. And this explains, too, the unnatural impatience of many present-day poets with Victorian literary standards and traditions. They realise that these standards are formed on the basis of a previous age's achievement: they fail to realise that the standards are perfectly adequate when applied to work of a certain kind, with a certain function, although they are irrelevant to work with a different function altogether.

There is also such a thing as a quite irrational change in literary taste, which is apt to influence the critic at all points quite apart from his conscious attitude. How far such changes affect the fundamentals of literature is a debatable question, but that they concern every one of its accidentals cannot be questioned. A certain metre might be deemed "vulgar" by one generation while all other generations might find no fault of that kind with it whatever. Even definitions of such terms as "sentimental," "profound," "poetic," etc., are constantly changing. What is sentimental to a vicious degree to one age might appear restrained and classical to another.

An equally distorting factor is the tendency of any given generation to pride itself on producing work of historical importance and originating a highly significant new tradition. This leads to a judging of literature based entirely on this supposed historical standard and often to a complete abandonment of any adequate literary criterion. This attitude is particularly rife at the present day, when poets are praised for defining new attitudes, for breaking away from a certain tradition, for being in a certain movement, quite irrespective of the poetic value of their work. *The Waste Land*, for example, is frequently praised as poetry for quite irrelevant reasons. This is not to say that *The Waste Land* is not good poetry, but that the reasons often given for its being acclaimed good poetry are quite beside the point. The inability to distinguish between the *good* and the *important* is a frequent critical deficiency. We find it not only in discussion of contemporary work, but also very commonly in academic criticism of past literature—the

type of criticism which puts *Gorboduc* above *Hamlet*, because while the latter was merely an experiment in an already established mode, the former was the first play of its kind. Undoubtedly works which are of historical importance deserve close study and are of considerable interest, but this does not mean that they are necessarily of any intrinsic value as literature. The historical critic is concerned with quite different values from those assessed by the purely literary critic. An attempt to take up a historical point of view in criticising contemporary work often leads to a complete lack of perspective which succeeding ages will at once detect and deride, and may also produce a confusion of values which will add greatly to the difficulty of the contemporary critic's already difficult task.

But can the critic find no anchor to prevent him from drifting on the tide of changing taste and muddled standards? There is the obvious safeguard of a fixed standard firmly adhered to and ruthlessly applied. That was the method of the early eighteenth century, and though it brought the critics a certain peace of mind in their activity (which was satisfactorily counteracted by personal animosity of the Pope *v.* Dennis variety) and a very genuine insight in judging their own kind of work, it narrowed their point of view so lamentably as to make it quite impossible for them to judge adequately anything written even in their own language outside their own age. Today we know better than to apply rules and to speak of "kinds": have we not had over a hundred years of romantic freedom to profit by?

But have we profited? Have we found any more adequate method of judging contemporary literature? We have found out how to judge literature impressionistically, to play the cultured egoist and spin bookfulls of criticism out of our own indulged emotions. Let us be quite clear concerning the value of this type of Romantic criticism. It often results in products which are themselves genuine literature; many of the nineteenth century essayists, working on these lines, have produced pleasing literary work of the kind known as *belles-lettres*, and it would be churlish as well as uncritical to deny value to this type of writing as some of our modern critics are inclined to do. But treated simply as literary criticism their work is valueless. When Hazlitt chats about Orlando Friscobaldo—

I can take mine ease in mine inn with Signor Orlando Friscobaldo as the oldest acquaintance I have. Ben Jonson, learned Chapman, Master Webster and Master Heywood are there—

it is pleasant and readable but certainly not criticism. This is true, also, of such a passage as this from Lamb:

I confess for myself that (with no great delinquencies to answer for) I am glad for a season to take an airing beyond the diocese of the strict conscience—not to live always in the precincts of the law-courts—but now and then, for a dream-while or so, to imagine a world with no meddling restrictions—to get into recesses, whither the hunter cannot follow me—

. . . Secret Shades
Of woody Ida's inmost grove,
While yet there was no fear of Jove.

I come back to my cage and my restraint the fresher and more healthy for it. I wear my shackles more contentedly for having respired the breath of an imaginary freedom. I do not know how it is with others, but I feel the better always for the perusal of one of Congreve's—nay, why should I not add even of Wycherley's—comedies.

It is no critical help to discourse smoothly about a character in a play as though he had an independent existence, or to prefix "Master" to the names of Webster and Heywood, neither does Lamb make a real contribution to criticism when he informs us of some personal facts of the kind quoted. Both these writers did produce some real criticism in addition to their personal essays, but their descendants are writing neither pleasing essays nor criticism of any value. To apply this egoistic method of criticism to contemporary writing, as so many writers are still doing, is the very height of literary folly. It is impossible to achieve by this method any adequate estimate of the work in consideration; it is a simple shirking of the issue and generally implies a complete lack of real critical ability, indeed of any intellectual ability. Far from making any attempt to discount those factors which vitiate contemporary criticism, such a method deliberately surrenders to those factors, deliberately allows the writer to be influenced and prejudiced by those forces which have just been discussed. There are only too many examples of the sad mess such writers make in discussing contemporary poetry. Perhaps no one can be entirely successful in discussing the poetry of his own day, there is always something to blind the critic or distort his vision, but the personal essay type of criticism is the most patently inadequate and by its very nature is unfitted even to begin such a task.

So if eighteenth century rigour cannot provide the anchor, nineteenth century licence is even less successful. Where, then, are we to turn? Can the "touchstone" theory of Matthew Arnold give us any help? That is perhaps the most treacherous theory of all. It implies a view of literature which is fundamentally unsound—a view which regards the total literary achievement of a civilisation as something static, determined, both qualitatively and chronologically, so that we

can take examples of great literature produced during a certain period of time and
apply them as touchstones to literature
of another period. As though there would
be any point in judging a line like Hopkins'

And you were a liar O blue March day

by putting beside it

In la sua volontade è nostra pace,

[In his will is our peace]

or in judging Eliot's lines

Shall I say, I have gone at dusk through
    narrow streets
And watched the smoke that rises from the
    pipes
Of lonely men in shirt-sleeves, leaning out
    of windows? . . .

by setting it alongside

Absent thee from felicity awhile,
And in this harsh world draw thy breath in
    pain,
To tell my story.

Such juxtapositions tell us exactly nothing. Not that there are no highest common factors to all great literature; if the
phrase "great literature" means anything
at all these highest common factors must
exist; but this is not the way to bring
them out. In any case, Arnold's criterion
applies only to single lines and cannot
be applied at all to complete works.

Arnold's touchstone method is due to
an insufficiently organic view of literature, and in noting this we can discover
at least a point of view—if nothing more
precise—that will help the critic to
achieve some sort of objectivity in judging contemporary literature. The critic
must always bear in mind the *flexibility*
of literature, its capability of infinite

variety, its habit of throwing up quite
new achievements which reflect back on
the past and make us see all that has gone
before in a new light at the same time
as the new achievements themselves gain
added significance from being viewed in
relation to the body of previous writing.
We cannot judge a line of Hopkins by
comparing it with a line of Dante any
more than we can judge a line of Dante
by comparing it with a line of Hopkins.
The quality and substance and merit of
Dante's poetry are not fixed for all
time, but change and grow richer as
subsequent literature changes and develops, reflecting back new light on the
past. It is as though a gem were set in an
environment which was continually expanding and growing more brilliant, so
that the gem itself took on new reflections and was seen in an ever-changing
light, responding to its altering environment with a constantly enhanced glory.
So that in judging contemporary literature we cannot, for example, take the
achievement of the previous four hundred years and extract from that a standard or a definition to apply to the ten
years after the four hundredth. We must
extract our standard or definition from
all four hundred and ten years first before we are in a position to give adequate
consideration to contemporary achievements. This is all the more necessary at a
time like the present when many new
forms of literature are bewildering the
critics, who are driven to take a standard
from previous literature to apply to the
present, instead of taking all literature,
including that of their own day, in their
view and deducing criteria accordingly.
This does not mean that the view of
contemporary literature will necessarily
be more favourable; but it will be more
understanding and therefore more just.

Further, the contemporary critic must
be more than ordinarily careful to distinguish between absolute and historical

value. In an age of self-conscious movements, when the clique and manifesto are much in evidence, cool-headedness regarding absolute literary value is rare. The tendency to a multiplicity of "schools" and the assessing of work solely with reference to such schools does not make for criticism which is likely to stand the test of time.

But what is this "absolute literary value" which we have been discussing? This, of course, is the main problem, and it can only be solved by the individual critic. The highest common factor of great literature may be defined quite differently by different critics of equal sensitivity and experience, and others again may prefer not to define it at all. But a knowledge of it is possible and need not necessarily be accompanied by consistent definition. The conditions of such knowledge are difficult and exacting. It demands not only this organic view of literature already mentioned, but an insight into the nature and conditions of literary activity which can only come with wide and deep experience. The critic must know something of the relation of theory to practice throughout the course of literary history, he must be familiar with the manifold changes in taste and point of view which have occurred in the past and be able to correlate them to a view of the scope of literature as a whole. He must be able to view a contemporary work at once in isolation, purely on its own merits, and in its relation—its complex and many-sided relation—to previous literature. And, perhaps most important of all, he must be able to distinguish clearly between the "universal" and the "particular" and note the presence or absence of one in the other. This distinction has reference to the one criterion of literary worth which cannot

change and which is at the basis of all adequate critical theory from Aristotle onwards.

This is vague and shadowy advice for the critic who wishes to free himself from the snares that lie in wait for those who sit in judgment on contemporary literature. Yet what more can be said? Perhaps this, that contemporary assessment can never be entirely adequate, and the greatest critic will leave some mistakes for posterity to laugh at. The best advice can only be negative: avoid rules, avoid egoistic impressionism, avoid treating literature as a matter of personal "purgation" for the writer, avoid seeking a false *justification* for writing which has no objective value. Ultimately there is no justification for literature which is not a literary one—and this fact is not so obvious as it sounds, if we are to judge from the number of critics who ignore it.

At all events, the judging of contemporary literature is not a task for the dilettante or the gossip writer or the armchair critic. Methods which may be profitable or at least interesting in discussing aspects of past literature are neither when employed in discussing the work of the critic's own day. Contemporary criticism is a serious and difficult business. One of the best ways of learning to appreciate its difficulty and at the same time helping oneself to see into the nature of real criticism is to study the bad "misses" of the great critics of the past. That will indicate more clearly than anything the kind of trap that is always awaiting the critic and perhaps gives him a greater sense of responsibility. For most contemporary criticism shows neither responsibility nor humility, and without these two virtues no critical work of any worth can be achieved.

INDEX
OF AUTHORS AND TITLES